Farming and Birds in Europe:

The Common Agricultural Policy and its Implications for Bird Conservation

D0930478

Farming and Birds in Europe:

The Common Agricultural Policy and its Implications for Bird Conservation

*Deborah J. Pain and
Michael W. Pienkowski
(Editors)*

Advisory Panel: James Dixon, Clive Potter, Nigel Robson,
Graham Tucker

ACADEMIC PRESS
San Diego   London   Boston
New York   Sydney
Tokyo   Toronto

This book is printed on acid-free paper.

Copyright © 1997 by ACADEMIC PRESS.

All Rights Reserved.

No part of this publication may be reproduced or transmitted in any form or by any means, electronic or mechanical, including photocopy, recording, or any information storage and retrieval system, without permission in writing from the publisher.

Academic Press, Inc.
525 B Street, Suite 1900, San Diego, California 92101-4495, USA
http://www.apnet.com

Academic Press Limited
24–28 Oval Road, London NW1 7DX, UK
http://www.hbuk.co.uk/ap/

ISBN 0-12-544280-7

Library of Congress Cataloging-in-Publication Data

A catalogue record for this book is available from the British Library

Typeset by Paston Press Ltd, Loddon, Norfolk

Printed in Great Britain by The University Press, Cambridge

97 98 99 00 01 02 EB 9 8 7 6 5 4 3 2 1

Contents

Contributors

Dr Albert J. Beintema, Instituut voor Bos-en Natuuronderzoek (IBN-DLO), Bosrandweg 20, Postbus 23, 6700 AA Wageningen, The Netherlands.

Dr David Campión, Estación Biológica de Doñana, Consejo Superior de Investigaciones Científicas, Avda. de María Luisa s/n, 41013 Sevilla, Spain.

Dr Pablo Campos, Instituto de Economía y Geografía (IEG-CSIC), c/Pinar 25. E-28006 Madrid, Spain.

Professor Eduardo De Juana, Dpto. de Biología Animal 1 (Vertebrados), Facultad de Biología, Universidad Complutense, E-28040 Madrid, Spain.

Dr Mario Díaz, Departamento de Ecologia, Facultad de Biología, Universidad Complutense, E-28040 Madrid, Spain.

Mr James Dixon, Royal Society for the Protection of Birds, The Lodge, Sandy, Bedfordshire SG19 2DL, UK.

Dr José A. Donázar, Estación Biológica de Doñana, Consejo Superior de Investigaciones Científicas, Avda. de María Luisa s/n, 41013 Sevilla, Spain.

Dr Euan Dunn, Royal Society for the Protection of Birds, The Lodge, Sandy, Bedfordshire SG19 2DL, UK.

Dr Andy Evans, Royal Society for the Protection of Birds, The Lodge, Sandy, Bedfordshire SG19 2DL, UK.

Professor Mauro Fasola, Dipartimento Biologia Animale, Università, Piazza Botta 9, 27100 Pavia, Italy.

Dr Norbert Lefranc, Direction Régionale de l'Environnement, Protection de la Nature, 19 Avenue Foch F-57005 Metz, France.

Mr Miguel A. Naveso, SEO-BirdLife, Carretera de Humeda, 63-1, E-28224 Pozuelo, Madrid, Spain.

Dr Deborah J. Pain, Royal Society for the Protection of Birds, The Lodge, Sandy, Bedfordshire SG19 2DL, UK.

Dr Michael W. Pienkowski, Royal Society for the Protection of Birds, The Lodge, Sandy, Bedfordshire SG19 2DL, UK.

Dr Clive Potter, Wye College, University of London, Wye, Ashford, Kent TN25 5AH, UK.

Dr Dick Potts, The Game Conservancy Trust, Fordingbridge, Hampshire, SP6 1EF, UK.

Mr Fernando J. Pulido, Cátedra de Biología y Etología, Facultad de Veterinaria, Universidad de Extremadura, E-10071 Cáceres, Spain.

Dr Xavier Ruíz, Departament Biologia Animal, Universitat, Av. Diagonal 645, 08028 Barcelona, Spain.

Dr Nigel Robson, 43, Ave. St. Hubert, 1970 Wezembeek-Oppem, Belgium.

Dr David Stroud, Joint Nature Conservation Committee, Monkstone House, City Road, Peterborough PE1 1JY, UK.

Dr Francisco Suárez, Dpto. Interuniversitario de Ecología, Facultad de Ciencias, Universidad Autónoma, E-28049 Madrid, Spain.

Dr José L. Tella, Estacíon Biológica de Doñana, Consejo Superior de Investigaciones Científicas, Avda. de María Luisa s/n, 41013 Sevilla, Spain.

Dr Graham Tucker, Ecoscope Applied Ecologists, 9 Bennell Court, Comberton, Cambridge CB3 7DS, UK.

Foreword

by

Franz Fischler

(EU Commissioner for Agriculture and Rural Development)

I welcome the publication of this book because it covers an important and developing area of work for the European Commission and for the EU Member States. It is now widely recognised that, in the past, agriculture policy did not take sufficient account of the important relationships between farming and the environment. Historically, policies aimed at promoting more efficient agriculture have caused over-production and loss of wildlife. Increasingly, however, agricultural policymakers, including the Commission, have sought to change this as part of a re-orientation of policy. The CAP is evolving, some say too slowly and others say too quickly. What is certain, is that the direction of CAP reform supports the role of farmers as managers of rural areas, and not simply as producers for the market.

This book helps guide our understanding of one important aspect of rural land use, namely the management of land for biodiversity and especially for birds. Birds make good indicators of the state of the countryside, they are at the summit of the food chain and they migrate and cross national borders – they are true Europeans. They are also popular: over 1.5 million people are members of bird conservation societies in Europe and many millions more take delight in the beauty of nature. As this book shows, conservation of Europe's birds depends on the proper management of farmland. For birds, and for other wildlife, it is the decisions made by the many millions of European farmers that dictate their future.

The European Commission has done much to try and resolve the conflicts between farming and wildlife. Within the framework of the Vth Action Programme on the Environment and reform to the CAP, there are numerous programmes of research and support to projects in Member States which support integrated farming, organic farming and management of farmed habitats. Central to our policies has been the development of the 'Agri-environment' Regulation which accompanied the 1992 CAP reforms. The many programmes that Member States have prepared under this have had a good start, but there is more to be done to develop environmental policies as more central elements of our agricultural policies.

With the 1992 CAP reform the EU made a step towards a more integrated rural policy which encompasses quality food production, rural development and protection of the countryside.

I welcome this book as an excellent example of collaboration between experts and practitioners from many institutions and organisations located in many countries across the European Union. The detailed case studies illustrate numerous examples of how wildlife and farming could develop harmoniously together. I believe it will be useful to the many people who have to develop practical and cost-effective environmental policies in agriculture.

Preface

Farming and Birds in Europe can be separated into three distinct sections.

Chapters 1–4 provide important background information to the book, describing: the types of farmed landscape and ways that these have developed within the European Union; the influence that the Common Agricultural Policy has had upon this process; the importance of farmed land for biodiversity – focusing upon birds; the impact of agricultural intensification upon birds over the last 40 years.

Chapters 5–12 are case studies detailing the relationships between selected bird species and farmed habitats or farming systems, and the impact that agricultural intensification has had and is having upon birds and farmland biodiversity. These case studies span the European Union and incorporate low and high input farming systems covering the production of a wide range of agricultural commodities. We have allowed limited repetition of essential background information between case study chapters (5–12) to enable an audience with some grounding in agricultural policy and bird conservation to select and read case studies as individual entities.

Chapters 13 and 14 draw conclusions from the preceding chapters and outline the directions that agricultural policy reforms need to take in the future if farmland diversity is to be conserved.

Acknowledgements

We are very grateful to the following people, for their many constructive comments on the whole volume: Sylvia Sullivan for copy-editing; Lennox Campbell, Matthew Rayment, Gwyn Williams, Ian Fisher. Thank you to the following people for their helpful comments on various chapters; Mark Avery, Andy Evans, Mike Everett, Paul José, John Taylor, José Luis Tellería, Jane Sears. We would like to acknowledge the valuable discussions on many aspects of this subject with many participants in the European Forum on Nature Conservation and Pastoralism which have contributed greatly to the development of ideas. In particular, thanks are due to Eric Bignal, Davy McCracken, David Baldock, Heather Corrie, Colin Tubbs and Natacha Yellachich.

The Advisory panel (James Dixon, Clive Potter, Nigel Robson and Graham Tucker) provided essential guidance and help from the early stages of this project through to completion, as well as writing many key chapters.

Spanish to English translation (Chapters 5, 7 and 11) was carried out by Susie Kershaw and French to English (Chapter 9) by Deborah Pain.

For support work throughout, we would like to thank Hannah Bartram, Ian Dawson, Wendy Grant, Anita McClune, Lynn Giddings and Duncan McNiven.

Abbreviations

ADAS	Formerly Agricultural Development Advisory Service (UK)
AWU	Annual Work Unit (1AWU = the agricultural work done by one full time worker in one year)
BBSRC	Biotechnology and Biological Sciences Research Council (UK)
BTO	British Trust for Ornithology
CAP	Common Agricultural Policy
CEECs	Central and eastern European countries
CLA	Country Landowners Association (UK)
CRP	Conservation Reserve Programme (US)
DDT	Dichloro diphenyl trichloroethane (a persistent pesticide)
DNBP	2-sec-butyl-4, 6-dinitrophenol (a pesticide)
EAGGF	European Agricultural Guidance and Guarantee Fund (part of the CAP)
ECU	European Currency Unit
EEA	European Economic Area
EEC/EC*	European Economic Community
ESA	Environmentally Sensitive Area
EU*	European Union
FEOGA	French acronym (and usual abbreviation) for EAGGF
GATT	General Agreement on Tariffs and Trade
GCT	Game Conservancy Trust
GPD	Gross Domestic Product
GIS	Geographic Information System
GLM	Generalized Linear Model
HLCA	Hill Livestock Compensatory Allowances (part of the CAP)
IACS	Integrated Administration and Control System (data collection for the CAP)
IBA	Important Bird Area
IDB	Internal Drainage Board (UK)
IUCN	International Union for the Conservation of Nature
LEADER	Liaisons Entre Actions de Developpement de l'Economie Rural (French acronym for links between actions for development of the rural economy – a part of the EU Regional Development Programme)
LFA	Less Favoured Area (in respect of agricultural productivity)
LU	Livestock Unit
MAFF	Ministry of Agriculture Food and Fisheries (UK)

MEKA	Marktentlastungs- und Kulturlandschaftsausgleich (Programme from Bayern, Germany, for promoting extensive farming)
NCC	Nature Conservancy Council (UK)
NFU	National Farmers Union (UK)
NRA	National Rivers Authority (NRA)
PSD	Pesticide Safety Division (UK)
RSAS	Rotational set-aside
RSPB	Royal Society for the Protection of Birds
SAS	Set-aside
SPA	Special Protection Area (under the EC Directive on the Conservation of Wild Birds)
SPEC	Species of European Conservation Concern
SSSI	Site of Special Scientific Interest (UK)
UAA	Utilized Agricultural Area
VAT	Value Added Tax
WSG	Wader Study Group

*The EEC first included 6 Member States. This increased to 9 in 1973, 10 in 1981, 12 in 1986 and 15 in 1995. In January 1986, the EEC became the EC. In January 1992, the EU came into being, including the same Member States as the EC but embracing wider responsibilities. The terms EU and EC are often used interchangably, although there are differences in technical meaning. In the text, numbers prefixed by EU or EC indicate the number of Member States at that time.

CHAPTER

1

Why farming and birds in Europe?

DEBORAH J. PAIN & JAMES DIXON

INTRODUCTION

Western European society has grown remarkably affluent in the second half of this century. Alongside economic growth, there has also been an increase in popular support for the protection of the environment from the consequences of economic development, such as pollution, over-exploitation of natural resources and threats to human health. Of particular concern has been a reduction in the numbers and the variety of animals and plants, termed biodiversity, and the habitats on which they depend.

Concern for the conservation of species, habitats and landscapes means that the environmental arena is no longer the preserve of a small number of naturalists and scientists, or of the increasingly well-supported voluntary organizations. The public and both regional and national governments are now involved, and conservation is an increasingly international issue which unites Member States of the European Union, with growing recognition of the need for co-ordinated action.

Farmland accounts for nearly half of the total land surface of the EU; it is very diverse and supports a wide range of wildlife. However, until relatively recently, the conservation value of farmland habitats was not recognized. Much of this value has been lost or degraded over the last 40 years owing to the unprecedented rate of change in farmland management. Recently there has been, and continues to be, considerable concern over the effects these changes have upon diversity, from species to landscapes (O'Connor & Shrubb, 1986; Woods *et al.*, 1988; Tucker and Heath, 1994).

That nature should be conserved is rarely disputed. The problem lies in determining who should be responsible, the overall strategy and the cost. As

FARMING AND BIRDS IN EUROPE
ISBN 0-12-544280-7

Copyright © 1997 Academic Press Ltd
All rights of reproduction in any form reserved

farming is the major land-use in the EU, an obvious starting point for co-ordinated international action is the Common Agricultural Policy, one of the EU's few truly 'common' policies. However, this already complex policy and its effects are greatly influenced by others, such as international trade agreements and national fiscal policies.

Scientific organizations, governments and voluntary groups have devised strategies for nature conservation against a background of scarce resources, a lack of political will and outdated land-use policies.

Despite the growing popular support for wildlife, particularly birds, resulting both in a rapid change in the nature of political support and an increase in funding for conservation, the constraints imposed by outdated rural land-use policies are still a major limitation to effective conservation. Since World War II, European land-use policies have been dominated by the imperative of increasing food production to meet the demands and expectations of a largely urban society. Other land-uses such as forestry, leisure and nature conservation have traditionally been relegated to land not needed for food production.

Furthermore, much of the nature conservation legislation was based on thorough analysis in the 1940s. Observations at that time pointed to industrial and urban development, rather than farming, as the main threats to nature. As a consequence, the mechanisms available to conservationists have tended to focus on site protection. Use of these has tended to push conservation into defensive positions, rather than facilitating the use of site protection measures as part of a wider, integrated strategy. We cannot expect to reverse the decline in much of our wildlife unless we act beyond, and add to, these site-based strategies. In doing so we must first understand the many commercial forces at work in the countryside and the policies which affect them, before we can hope to influence them.

Indeed, the fact that nature conservation is considered as just another (minority) land-use illustrates part of the problem. In addition to areas devoted to nature reserves, the concept of conservation of nature, soils, and ecosystems generally should pervade all land-uses. This is at the core of the concept of sustainability. (Sustainable use is defined by the Convention on Biological Diversity as 'the use of components of biological diversity in a way and at a rate that does not lead to the long-term decline of biological diversity, thereby maintaining its potential to meet the needs and aspirations of present and future generations.') This has, at last, been recognized strongly by governments throughout the world in committing themselves to this Convention at Rio de Janeiro. The Convention requires, in Article 6, not only that national strategies will be developed for the conservation and sustainable use of biological diversity, but also that these be incorporated in the strategies, plans and programmes for the other sectors of the economy.

There is a growing need to re-assess the strategies adopted by nature conservation organizations. It is abundantly clear that changing rural land-use policy in Europe requires a much clearer targeting of conservation effort based on rationally determined priorities (Wynne *et al.*, 1995). In this book we illustrate the importance of the farmed landscape for the conservation of both birds and biological diversity. We seek to demonstrate how and to what extent farmland birds of conservation concern depend on farming systems, and that components of agricultural intensification are often responsible for declines in bird populations. We also develop a rationale for determining the priorities for bird conservation action. We have tried to determine whether existing, largely site-based nature conservation strategies are sufficient to address the most urgent problems for the conservation of birds and other wildlife in Europe. Our analysis makes the case for a much broader approach to nature conservation. Through maintaining farmed landscapes, and managing farmland in an environmentally sensitive fashion throughout Europe, the people of Europe will not only contribute to the conservation of birds and biological diversity, but also move some way towards fulfilling a wide range of other social and environmental objectives, including a less polluted environment and a sustainable future for local communities (Taylor & Dixon, 1990).

THE FARMING REVOLUTION

A diversity of farmed landscapes

The farmed landscapes of Europe are very diverse, reflecting an ancient history of human settlement. Human use of the landscape, and consequently the composition and distribution of habitats and wildlife communities, has changed gradually across many centuries. Essentially, north-western Europe is one of the areas of the world where, until recently, humans could almost be considered an integral part of the biodiversity. The development of the varied farming practices was governed by the climatic and physical gradients across the continent. The Atlantic west of Europe has extensive areas of pasture and semi-natural moorland supporting a livestock industry based on grass-fed animals. In central northern Europe arable cultivation dominates, both on the small scale part-time farms and on the large 'industrial' scale where modern technology is widely applied. In southern Europe, the Mediterranean climate extends the range of crops grown, but also imposes considerable constraints through drought and poor soils. In Scandinavia and much of central Europe, farm holdings are often very small and associated with forestry enterprises (Tucker, unpublished data). The range of agricultural land-uses in the European Union is illustrated in Table 1.

Farmland constitutes 41% (128 million ha) of the land area of the European Union (EU15) and 58% (118 million ha) of the land area of the EU prior to

Table 1 Agricultural land-use in the European Union

Country	Total area (×1000 ha)	% Utilized agricultural area (UAA)	% UAA arable and permanent crops		% UAA grass	Area under forest and woodland (×1000 ha)
			Arable	Perm.		
Austria	8 400	41.0	40.0	0.0	56.6	–
Belgium	3 052	44.7	52.2	1.2	45.1	617
Denmark	4 309	65.0	91.9	0.4	1.0	493
Finland	33 700	7.9	95.9	0.0	3.9	–
France	54 909	55.7	58.1	4.0	37.2	14 810
Germany	24 862	44.7	61.3	1.6	36.9	7 401
Greece	13 196	43.5	50.9	20.4	14.2	5 755
Ireland	7 028	81.1	18.1	0.0	81.1	327
Italy	30 131	57.1	51.8	19.3	28.4	6 434
Luxembourg	257	49.0	44.1	1.2	54.6	89
Netherlands	4 148	49.9	44.8	1.8	52.2	330
Portugal	9 207	49.2	64.1	19.1	16.8	2 968
Spain	50 475	53.7	57.4	18.1	24.5	12 511
Sweden	45 000	7.5	82.7	0.0	17.2	–
UK	24 414	75.6	35.7	0.3	58.5	2 297
EU15	313 088	41.0	57.0	7.8	35.0	54 032

Source: Eurostat (1995).

recent enlargement (EU12)[1] (Table 1). The diversity and dynamism of European agriculture makes description or classification difficult (as described by Potter, Chapter 2). However, the influences of many external factors have been common to most forms of farming, particularly changing markets, technologies and policies (see, e.g. Beaufoy *et al.*, 1994; Bignal *et al.*, 1994; Woods *et al.*, 1988). Throughout much of the second half of this century, such factors have been driven by the move to encourage greater production of food from European farms. This has been achieved, largely through increased chemical and energy inputs. The consequences include increased pollution from chemical production industries and agricultural run-off, a loss of habitat quality and quantity and thus farmland biodiversity, and a loss of employment followed by rural depopulation. The costs of increased food production have been great.

Post-war land-use policies

The development after World War II of Europe's economy has involved an increasingly urban population engaging in more and more technologically sophisticated manufacturing and service industries. Rural policy has been aimed largely at increasing levels of food production. In most countries of Europe this has been done by 'guaranteeing' the financial returns of farmers by 'intervening in' and supporting food markets (Taylor & Dixon, 1990; Marsh & Tangermann, 1992).

In the 1950s and '60s, such policies adopted by the German government were adapted to create a free-trade area, initially for France and Germany but later extended to include the original six members of the European Economic Community (Germany, France, Belgium, Italy, the Netherlands and Luxembourg). The Common Agricultural Policy (CAP) of the EEC came into being under the then Commissioner for Agriculture, Sicco Mansholt (Robson, Chapter 3).

The CAP was designed to increase the 'self-sufficiency'[2] of European food production by restructuring farming, and guaranteeing and protecting markets. Farmers were encouraged to invest in land, machinery and new technology. The CAP provided incentives for farmers to adopt new technologies and methods, and so increase the yields of all supported crops, particularly cereals, and of milk and livestock. It also promoted a restructuring of European farming, increasing the average size of farms, encouraging specialization, and providing incentives

---

[1] The European Union of 12 countries (EU12 – Belgium, Denmark, France, Germany, Greece, Ireland, Italy, Luxembourg, the Netherlands, Portugal, Spain, UK) was expanded to include Austria, Finland and Sweden (EU15) in January 1995.

[2] Self-sufficiency has been used here to indicate the production of total food requirements. This has not been used to suggest that Europe was self-sufficient in the energy and chemical inputs necessary to achieve this level of food production. Indeed, this often forgotten element undermines some of the basis of the policy.

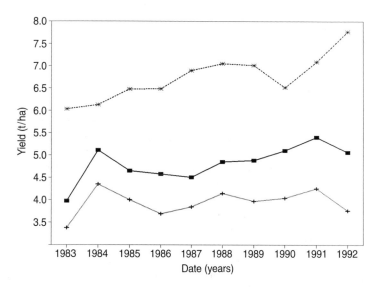

Figure 1 Yields of cereals in the EU12, 1983–92. ■—■: wheat; *- - -*: maize; +····+: barley. (From Eurostat, 1995.)

for investment. This led to a considerable reduction in labour and an increase in farm size, with a remarkable increase in output per farm (Figure 1 – although efficiency, i.e. output per unit input, has been sacrificed, to the extent that it takes more additional energy input to grow the produce than is released through consumption (Johnson, 1993)).

Similar national policies had been adopted in other countries, and the accession of the UK, Ireland, Denmark, Greece and, more recently, Spain and Portugal have continued and accentuated these changes in all 12 countries of the (now) European Union. In January 1995 Austria, Sweden and Finland joined the EU, bringing the Union to one of 15 countries and creating the largest free-trade area in the world. Discussions are beginning which could pave the way for a further 10 or 15 countries from the Mediterranean region and central and eastern Europe to join within 15 years (CEC, 1995).

Have land-use changes resulted only from the CAP?

Although the CAP has often dominated land-use policies, it is of course only one influence on farmers. National economic and land-use planning can also be very significant. For example, in France, policies of inheritance stemming from the Napoleonic era have led to very small, uneconomic farms in many areas. Policies such as *remembrement* and the organization SAFER are designed to restructure whole villages so changing farm size – the opposite effects of those which would result by splitting farms amongst siblings. Taxation policies in many countries have encouraged investment in land and agriculture (Robson, Chapter 3).

In the Bundesland of Bayern, Germany, local agricultural policies have encouraged small part-time farms with excess labour which is available for industry in nearby towns. Similar policies have been adopted in the newly acceded countries of Scandinavia and Austria to provide seasonal labour for forestry. In some areas, national or local policies have accentuated the objectives of the CAP by providing additional aids to make farming more capital-intensive, as has been the case in the Highlands and Islands of Scotland.

In recent years, there have, however, been schemes addressing the need to promote low-intensity systems, the maintenance of agriculturally active people (and maintenance of rural communities). One example is from Scotland where Scottish Natural Heritage has set up demonstration projects to illustrate how sympathetic environmental management could become an integral part of agricultural operations given correctly targeted support (Allen, 1995). Although the establishment of such schemes is encouraging, they are insignificant compared with production-based schemes.

The greatest influence over farming has, undoubtedly, been the philosophical one behind a *de facto* land-use policy, namely the collective desire of Europe to grow two ears of corn where previously there had been one. This has led to distortions elsewhere, particularly in consumer, nutritional and health policies (which are outside the scope of this book) and other aspects of land-use. The dominance of agriculture has meant, for example, that most support for disadvantaged rural areas on ostensibly social grounds is paid via farming, neglecting other parts of rural society. Subsidized agricultural production has raised land values and encouraged the adoption of afforestation policies aimed at 'marginal' agricultural land, so threatening semi-natural habitats (Woods *et al.*, 1988).

Effects on wildlife

The land-use philosophy which marginalized nature conservation was very damaging to wildlife. Radical changes to the way in which we manage our farmed land have occurred since the turn of the century with the advent of mechanization. Since the 1950s, the intensification of farming techniques has taken place at an unprecedented rate, largely driven by the desire for self-sufficiency in food production, an objective that has been not only supported, but positively encouraged, through CAP financial incentives. Farmers, predictably, responded to these incentives, and any that wanted to maintain more sustainable practices were financially disadvantaged through not responding to the same incentives. The CAP, with its universally applicable prices and hydra-like range of aids to investment, has been called the engine of destruction in the countryside – and rightly so (RSPB, 1995). It is also true that many aspects of the CAP continued and developed further destructive national policies already in place, especially in those states such as UK which joined the then EEC after other countries.

Many of us are familiar with, and have observed some of these changes taking place. Farming has become more versatile, with potential to farm new areas and introduce new and different types of crop and pastoral farming. This has been achieved by controlling water levels and providing enough chemical and energy inputs to overcome environmental constraints, thereby producing a standardized environment lacking its regional characteristics.

Increased mechanization, along with land drainage, has resulted in a change in field structure, with a reduction in boundary features and increased field size. More use of chemicals, fertilizers and pesticides has certainly increased yields, but has also changed the botanical composition of pasture and arable land alike, with a net loss in both plant and animal diversity (O'Connor and Shrubb, 1986; Barr, 1990; Bunce, 1993; Wynne *et al.*, 1995). Increased mechanization and holding size resulted in a reduced labour force per unit area.

No part of the great diversity of life illustrates the scale, speed and popular concern of these changes more graphically than birds.

Figure 2 Grassland with mixed flowers in the UK, a rare sight since the widespread use of agro-chemicals. (Photo by C.H. Gomersall/RSPB.)

CANARIES IN THE COAL MINE

Why birds?

Bird conservation is an important point of entry for biodiversity conservation in general, and birds are often used as biological indicators of healthy environments (e.g. Pienkowski, 1991; Moser et al., 1995; Tucker et al., unpublished data). Problems of scale, cost and expertise make detailed information on distributions and population changes in plants and invertebrates more difficult to collect and order even on a local scale, let alone a pan-European one. Birds are almost certainly the best researched and monitored group, and fairly good information exists on bird populations and distribution within the EU, including historical data for describing trends.

Declines in populations or ranges of bird species often result from loss or modification of habitats, with associated impacts upon other wildlife. Birds have been used to indicate the quality of water (Eriksson, 1987; Ormerod & Tyler, 1993), the marine environment (Furness, 1987; Montevecchi, 1993), the condition of forests (Helle & Järvinen, 1986; Angelstam & Mikusinski, 1994), metal pollution (Jenkins, 1975; Ohi et al., 1981) and the impact of pesticides (Hardy et al., 1987).

Although birds are widely considered to be good indicators of the overall health of our environment, they are often, at least locally, less sensitive bioindicators than certain other groups. Population declines in birds often occur with a time lag, following changes in their habitats, such as declines in populations of plants, invertebrates or other animals upon which they depend (as illustrated in Potts, Chapter 6 and Lefranc, Chapter 9). Declines in farmland birds, as described below, are symptomatic of detrimental changes to the farmed environment, and signal a considerable loss of biodiversity throughout European farmland. Given that farmland covers 40% of the land surface of the EU (60% of EU12), this is clearly a serious change. Severe declines in such 'robust' indicator species sound loud warning bells, and make the best possible case for taking immediate action to stem such declines.

Birds are familiar to us all. They are widespread, highly visible, attract considerable public support, and many migratory species cross national and political frontiers. Using bird species that have declined as the warning signs of wider environmental damage – the canaries in the coal-mine – must increase the impetus for change of priorities in agricultural policy. Our farmed habitats have to be managed in a more sustainable fashion, not just for birds but for the conservation of wildlife and biological diversity in general. It is a sobering thought that the environmental damage we are witnessing is happening in the very fields where we grow the food on which we ourselves depend.

Figure 3 Wader flock at the RSPB's Snettisham Reserve, Norfolk, UK, an important staging and wintering site. (Photo by C.H. Gomersall/RSPB.)

Holding the line – bird conservation through site protection

Until the agricultural recession of the 1930s and the revolution in production in the 1940s, farmers were very much viewed as custodians of the countryside. Farming was synonymous with stewardship of the land and management of the countryside. As part of post-World War II reconstruction, wildlife conservation was to a large extent 'site-based' (i.e. based on the protection of specific sites of special importance or uniqueness for one or more species, or through supporting a particularly high wildlife diversity). Such sites were often relics of 'semi-natural' habitats which were frequently marginal to modern farming, forestry and other commercial land-uses and so left unmanaged. In many (now EU member) countries, designation as national or regional parks and nature reserves has primarily involved unmanaged land where human intervention has been minimal.

National conservation organizations, legislation and training rarely made provision for the designation of areas which included anything but very small-scale traditional management. To a certain extent, this remains the philosophy behind much nature conservation and protection today, and this tends to reduce nature conservation to a small-scale sectoral land-use, rather than an approach which should be integrated through other uses. The latter approach would be more in line with ideas of sustainability and integrated planning. It would also mean that people's lives would be enriched by wildlife rather than having this experience restricted to special occasions at special places. An integrated approach would also be less likely to lead to current pollution problems.

Site protection measures have played, and always will play, an important part in European bird conservation. Many bird species concentrate at specific sites at particular stages of their annual cycle (Figure 3) as this may confer advantages such as an abundant food supply, good conditions for breeding, shelter or predator avoidance. The loss of key sites can have adverse effects on total populations (Goss-Custard, 1985). Birds are particularly vulnerable to the loss or degradation of specific sites if they breed colonially, concentrate or 'refuel' there on migration, or are restricted to rare or fragmented habitats. The protection of such critical sites is obviously important. To conserve birds more effectively at different stages in their annual cycles, the concept of protecting a network of sites has been adopted by many national and international agencies over recent years (Ministry of Agriculture, Nature Management and Fisheries, 1990; Natura 2000 and Ramsar sites as described below).

Not surprisingly, the constraints imposed by land-use policies and an emphasis on the importance of site protection have greatly influenced the wide variety of international Conventions and Directives currently in force. These advocate or include provision for site protection measures and include the following: Ramsar Convention on Wetlands of International Importance especially as Waterfowl Habitat; Berne Convention on the Conservation of European Wildlife and Natural Habitats; Bonn Convention on the Conservation of Migratory Species of Wild Animals; Convention Concerning the Protection of the World Cultural and Natural Heritage; Directive of the Council of the European Economic Community on the Conservation of Wild Birds (Birds Directive 79/409/EEC); and the Directive on the Conservation of Natural Habitats and of Wild Fauna and Flora (Habitats Directive 92/43/EEC). The last two Directives are among the most significant as they are legally binding and enforceable.

One of the particular strengths of the Birds Directive is that it indicates requirements including, *but beyond*, site measures. It requires Member States to take appropriate special protection measures to maintain populations of all species of wild birds that occur naturally in their European territories. As part of this requirement, Member States have set up 'Special Protection Areas' (SPAs) — the most suitable areas in numbers and size for the conservation of bird species.

The more recent Habitats Directive (92/43/EEC) is also potentially one of the strongest pieces of Community legislation aimed at wildlife protection. The Directive encourages measures that will '... maintain or restore, at favourable conservation status, natural habitats and species of wild fauna and flora of Community interest'. The Directive incorporates mechanisms for the protection of habitats and associated species, as well as some focused on species. In order to protect habitats, a network of protected sites, 'Natura 2000', including natural or semi-natural habitats of Community importance, will be set up. It is notable that, as has often been the case with other Community Directives and International Conventions concerned with conservation, managed habitats such as agricultural land are excluded and the emphasis is on sites rather than wider areas. However, as noted earlier, this approach is changing, with emphasis on sustainable use in all policies central to the Convention on Biological Diversity, and foreshadowed as 'wise use' in the earlier 'Ramsar' Convention on the Wetlands of International Importance.

The frequent exclusion of managed land from conservation agreements and legislation reflects an old underlying philosophy that conservation value is found only or mainly in 'natural' and semi-natural areas, as well as the unwillingness by EU institutions to intervene in the management of 'private' land. However, the Directive does make several significant advances over previous site protection legislation, in that it recognizes that positive site management is often necessary. To date, much of the management of protected areas throughout the Community has been negative management, which has concentrated upon stopping inappropriate development or use of protected areas. Positive management agreements, where sites have been managed to maintain or enhance their conservation interest, have been few and far between.

Some people object philosophically to the concept of managing nature reserves, but human influence is so pervading that almost no parts of the planet are unaffected. We certainly favour management of a minimal kind to have maximum effect, but also see a strong place for management in those systems in which people and wildlife have developed a stable relationship over hundreds of years (Pienkowski and Bignal, 1993).

In terms of the conservation of bird species within the Community, the intention is for SPAs to be included within the Natura 2000 network. Considerable information documenting sites of particular importance has been collated, primarily by non-governmental organizations, to promote the implementation of the agreements and measures detailed above. Notably, BirdLife International[3] published *Important Bird Areas (IBAs) in Europe* (Grimmett & Jones, 1989), which for the first time used a standardized evaluation to list a continent-wide network of sites that, if protected, would safeguard a proportion of Europe's birds. These sites are important for concentrations of birds at various times of year, or for threatened or vulnerable species. IBAs cover 9.6% of the land surface of the EU (EU12) and all satisfy the criteria set down by the Commission for SPA designation, although they have no official status. Table 2 lists IBAs and SPAs in the European Union.

Although the majority of SPAs are, or incorporate, one or more IBAs, most IBAs do not have SPA designation. Even when they do, the level of protection afforded to SPAs is often very limited, and many have been damaged throughout the EU (McNiven, 1994). This possibly stems, in part, from governments seeing agriculture as having only one purpose, namely food production, regardless of its consequences for the environment. Governments may have been reluctant to introduce changes expanding SPA designation owing to the perception that this

---

[3] BirdLife International was formerly known as the International Council for Bird Preservation.

Table 2 Surface areas classified as important Bird Areas (1989) and Special Protection Areas (1996) in the European Union (EU12)

Country	Country area (km²)	Designated SPAs* No.	Designated SPAs* Area (km²)	IBAs† No.	IBAs† Area (km²)	IBA as a % of land area
Belgium	30 519	36	4313	41	5 440	17.8
Denmark	43 093	111	9601	118	>10 000	> 23.3
France	549 086	99	7069	152	25 800	4.7
Germany	356 949	494	8537	143	13 840	3.9
Greece	131 957	26	1916	113	14 461	11.0
Ireland	70 283	75	1579	110	2 690	3.8
Italy	301 281	80	3164	140	35 100	11.7
Luxembourg	2 586	6	14	3	955	36.9
Netherlands	41 478	23	3276	70	7 964	19.2
Portugal	92 071	36	3323	36	5 320	5.8
Spain	504 765	149	25 338	288	93 740	18.6
UK	244 139	126	4396	261	11 515	4.7
Total (EU12)	2 368 207	1216	72 526	1475	226 825	9.6

*By 01/04/96 (Natura 2000, 1996).
†From Grimmett & Jones (1989).

may restrict the productive capacity of some rural areas and have negative impacts upon economic development, especially in less developed regions of the EU. However, this does not have to be the case, as is illustrated throughout this book.

Site protection is, and always will be, of great importance for the conservation of species, and the conservation potential of site protection measures is expanding under new Directives (such as the Habitats Directive) and given new attitudes. However, even given adequately funded and policed site protection throughout the EU, their ability to conserve many bird species would still be limited by 'natural' reasons (Pienkowski & Bignal, 1993).

Although many birds congregate at sites, this is often only during one or certain stages of their life cycle, and they are dispersed throughout the wider environment at other times (Stroud et al., 1990). Furthermore, even when concentrated at sites, such as when nesting, birds may often widely disperse for feeding. Other species are always very thinly spread across very large areas of suitable habitat, including many birds of prey, game birds, woodpeckers and passerines.

Protected sites may be influenced by the management of natural resources surrounding them. For example, many wetlands of major importance for birds, such as the Coto Doñana in southern Spain and other Mediterranean wetlands, have suffered as a result of pollution or increased water demand owing to inappropriate location of industry, increased tourism, urbanization and other developments in surrounding unprotected areas (e.g. see Finlayson *et al.*, 1992). Many other human activities can also affect the quality of a protected area – such as spray drift from farming operations or the deposition of atmospheric pollutants, for example in 'acid rain' (e.g. see Swedish Ministry of Agriculture, 1983; Dudley, 1987).

The financial commitment and infrastructure dedicated to site protection both in Member States and the EU as a whole illustrate the philosophy that predominated for many years – an environment divided between protected areas and farmed or otherwise managed productive land. The failure of this concept to recognize the importance for wildlife of managed land in the wider environment has been amply demonstrated by the meetings of the European Forum on Nature Conservation and Pastoralism (most recently McCracken *et al.*, 1995) and by a recent project of BirdLife International (described below and by Tucker, Chapter 4). The latter shows that many bird species of international conservation concern are dispersed over a wide area, and simply cannot be protected adequately through a network of sites.

At the beginning of this century, site protection measures alone probably were a viable and appropriate means of conserving birds and other species. At that time, before the advent of widespread intensification, production farming was itself seen as countryside management, and supported rich and diverse wildlife communities. However, with the unprecedented changes to the farmed landscape that have occurred over the last 50 years, site safeguard alone is obviously now wholly inadequate.

More widely directed measures are possible. The EU Directive on the Conservation of Wild Birds 1979 recognized this need in requiring special protection measures for birds including, but not limited to, Special Protection Areas. This has provided the legal basis and policy stimulus for some measures in the countryside as a whole, deploying various mechanisms. Some examples are given by Pienkowski (1993) and Hill *et al.* (1996).

These examples include Regional Indicative Forest Strategies. The UK has a relatively low proportion of land under forest, and current policies favour substantial increase. However, the major increase has been by planting extensive areas of even-age North American coniferous trees in upland areas, rather than by re-establishment of native-species woodlands in upland and lowland areas. This has a negative major impact on the natural and semi-natural populations of characteristic plants and animals and ecosystem processes. There are also considerable impacts on other aspects of the environment and the local communities. Accordingly, Regional Councils in Scotland each prepared an indicative strategy showing areas where there should be a presumption in favour of, or against, afforestation (subject to local considerations), taking account of these various interests and impacts. Initially, there was no mechanism to take account of nature conservation factors alongside other interests. However, conservation scientists noted that these strategies could potentially assist in fulfilling the UK's commitments under the EU Birds Directive. Fortunately, data gathered largely by volunteers in Britain and elsewhere in Europe were available to provide the necessary sound basis on which to provide nature conservation advice (see Galbraith & Pienkowski, 1990; Galbraith & Bates, 1991).

Other examples include the routine use of information on the distribution and vulnerability of seabirds at sea to plan the least potentially damaging locations and seasons for oil exploration and development in the North Sea (Carter *et al.*, 1993; Tasker & Pienkowski, 1987; Tasker *et al.*, 1990). A further example of more relevance to farming situations is the current initiative to phase out the use of lead in gun-shot.

All these developments and others have been at least partly based on the commitment to take special measures to conserve birds as required by the EU Directive. The commitments made under the Convention on Biological Diversity greatly extend these themes, and we look to further developments on these useful bases. Although some of the existing initiatives have relevance to nature conservation on farmland (e.g. the maintenance of low-intensity grazing systems in preference to forestry plantations, and the phasing out of lead shot), it is notable that the central issues of farmland conservation have not yet been addressed by such measures (Pienkowski, 1993). We turn now to bring together some of the needs in this area.

Farming for birds – bird conservation in the wider environment

Since Neolithic times, humans have altered and managed large parts of the European landscape through farming. Changes from natural to semi-natural habitats were gradual, taking place over centuries, and much wildlife adapted to, and sometimes came to depend on, the habitats created by long-established farming systems. However, as discussed above, agricultural intensification this century, and especially over the last 40 years, has radically changed farmed land. As a consequence of these more recent changes much wildlife has suffered, and over the last 20–25 years we have seen spectacular declines in the populations and ranges of many common and widespread farmland birds. In the UK a bird population monitoring scheme has existed since the 1960s, and recent detailed analysis of data showed dramatic declines of many farmland species, such as the skylark *Alauda arvensis* and the song thrush *Turdus philomelus* (Figure 4) (Sharrock, 1976; Marchant *et al.*, 1990; Gibbons *et al.*, 1993).

Elsewhere in Europe, farmland bird populations have been affected in a similar way. A recent initiative by BirdLife International, described by Tucker

Figure 4 Song thrush singing. (Photo by M.W. Richards/RSPB.)

(Chapter 4), has provided the best and most recent Europe-wide analysis of the conservation status of all Europe's birds (Tucker & Heath, 1994). This project aimed to identify those European bird species in urgent need of conservation measures, the priority habitats and landscapes for these species, the extent of these habitats in each European country and the land-use changes or other threats that are adversely affecting these habitats and landscapes. The first objective involved collecting data on populations, ranges and trends of all species in each European country over a 20-year period. The recently published results, *Birds in Europe: their conservation status* (Tucker & Heath, 1994) includes a list of Species of European Conservation Concern (SPECs).

The main message to have come from *Birds in Europe* is that 195 species (38% of Europe's bird species) have an unfavourable conservation status, mostly because of substantial declines. The results of this project have also revealed that virtually all SPECs are dispersed within the wider environment at some stage of their annual cycle, and that farmland contains more species with an unfavourable conservation status than any other habitat. It is also notable that, of the 20 species that regularly occur in Europe but are threatened by global extinction, seven depend upon farmed land at some stage of their life cycle (Collar *et al.*, 1994).

In order to know how to stop or reverse declines in such species, we must have a clear idea of what these species require from their environments. Although it is easy to imagine the ways in which agricultural intensification may have affected birds, there have been relatively few detailed ecological studies that have identified the precise mechanisms resulting in population declines. Fortunately, there are some exceptions, including the long-term population study of the grey partridge (*Perdix perdix*) in Britain, carried out by G. R. Potts of the UK Game Conservancy Trust (Potts, 1986; Chapter 6; Potts & Aebischer, 1995). In addition, the ecology of the corncrake Crex crex has been well studied (Williams *et al.*, 1991; Stowe *et al.*, 1993; Green, 1995), and much work on other species is currently underway.

The results of studies described in Chapters 5–12 strongly support the need for habitat conservation measures in the wider environment, and illustrate the importance that farmed land plays as essential habitat for some birds. Although farmed land covers 60% of the land surface of the EU, there has been little recognition in the past of just how important farmed habitats are for wildlife conservation. This book confirms the need for a new philosophy for nature conservation that accommodates the 'wider countryside' as a priority.

TOWARDS A NEW LAND-USE PHILOSOPHY FOR EUROPE

To bring about a changed vision of land-use and wildlife requires not only a shift towards policies that support the management of land rather than market intervention, but also a change in emphasis in nature conservation policies. Site protection and wider countryside policy approaches must be seen as additional and complementary – with both approaches essential.

New priorities for nature conservation

In this book, we discuss the conservation problems faced by those birds that depend on farmed land in the wider environment. Environmental conservation needs appropriate and sustainable management of the whole of our landscape for the benefit of birds, biological diversity, the sustainability of rural communities and the quality of life of all people that ever venture into the countryside. The way that the countryside is managed is now of primary importance alongside the need to protect sites and species.

Many physical planning laws have for many years protected good quality agricultural land, diverting built development such as housing and roads on to land of lower potential for agricultural productivity, but often of greater landscape and conservation value. During the years of agricultural expansion, the philosophy that sanctified agricultural production marginalized other uses of land and resources in rural areas, clearly demonstrated by the policies which have driven nature conservation in recent years.

Whilst some nature conservationists have long recognized the need to integrate conservation into land-use policies, the legislation and perceptions of the needs of food production have forced the adoption of strategies that tend to limit protection to a 'representative' range of sites and landscape features. However, the out-dated imperatives of food production and the power of the farming and agro-chemical lobbies have meant that even such sites have rarely been protected from damaging intensive farming activity, even if they have been protected from built development. Across Europe, site and habitat protection policies have been compromised by the interests of food production, even when this has led to inefficient energy use and product surpluses. The direction of agricultural activity has been heavily influenced by agricultural policies. Whether or not farmers wished to farm more sensitively, in order to make a living they have been pushed into more capital investment, energy and chemical use and other intensifications.

This has been reinforced by agricultural training emphasizing industrial production rather than multiple use of the countryside. The dominant land-use philosophy has consistently rejected the idea that conservation might have an equal claim on land, whether to protect habitats or to re-create them. Moreover, the management of farmland itself has been considered largely a matter for farmers motivated by the narrow policies focused on production objectives.

A new era for farming

While some parts of the CAP remained true to the original and widely supported objectives of feeding a hungry Europe through technological and structural developments of farming, successive national governments and the European Union have modified the CAP in response to short-term demands and crises. Rarely has the CAP suffered revolutionary changes, but the number, complexity and effects of the evolutionary change have been vast (see Robson, Chapter 3). During the 1980s, however, a number of factors led to pressures to change the mechanisms of the CAP, although the aims of reform have been wider than the original objectives. These pressures relate to internal problems with the CAP, greater public scrutiny, increased expectations of rural areas for society at large, and an increasingly global outlook within trade and political development.

The CAP has generated such large increases in production and structural changes in agriculture that its original mechanisms are now widely considered to be inappropriate. Production levels, particularly of grains, milk and livestock products, that are greater than EU self-sufficiency were probably barely dreamt of by the originators of the CAP, but their reality today has led to a spiralling escalation of costs to tax-payers, reductions in real terms in farm incomes, and conflict with international trading partners who allege unfair subsidization of exported food. These problems and the solutions adopted have led to changes in the objectives of the CAP and are elaborated by Robson (Chapter 3). More importantly, however, the changes that have happened (and will have to continue in the future) will require a new philosophy of land-use in Europe.

Relatively minor reforms were made to the CAP during the late 1980s.

Principal of these were the reduction in guarantees to farmers of supported prices, and the introduction of means of reducing supply, such as quotas on production (e.g. for milk) and on inputs such as land (e.g. for cereals). More recently, a number of concurrent crises, particularly over international trade, forced the European Council of Agriculture Ministers to adopt a package of more substantial reforms to the CAP in May 1992. Further controls on inputs of land were introduced for cereals, with a semi-compulsory set-aside being introduced in concert with a 29% reduction in prices for cereals. A package of measures was introduced accompanying these reforms to promote early retirement, forestry and protection of the environment.

While not so radical as some proposals, these reforms signal changed objectives for farming. The 'MacSharry' reforms were important because they considered the nature of support to farmers and not just its level. This raised important questions about the justification for making large transfers of money overtly from tax-payers to farmers. It is difficult to justify these payments on 'agricultural' grounds, given the reasons for change in the first place, and so the discussions have centred on the need to ensure that the countryside remains managed.

The environmental consequences and opportunities for managing for farmland wildlife, at least in part, were compromised significantly by the production ethic. Until relatively recently, the willingness of governments to impose measures that make the price of food fully reflect the environmental consequences of farming was small indeed. The active management of farmland with wildlife as one of its main objectives was considered by farmers, conservationists and governments as an unlikely possibility except where farmers did this from their own personal interest. However, recent tentative moves to integrate environmental considerations into policy, and an enhanced awareness and understanding by farmers and conservationists of their mutual interests have allowed an accommodation of some wildlife management on farms (see Potts, Chapter 6; Bignal et al., 1994; McCracken et al., 1995). Of much greater significance, however, is a reversal in exclusively production-maximizing trends in farming and a changing philosophy of land-use as a whole.

Current agricultural policy is perverse in that, for historic reasons, public funds are provided predominantly for market support, for which there is an increasing consensus that there is now little justification. Furthermore, the impacts of intensive agricultural activity leading to high costs in other economic sectors (e.g. water supply, public health, transport infrastructure) are not charged to agriculture; neither are the damage to the environment or to future agricultural potential, e.g. through soil erosion. There is, however, a sound economic case for supporting those farming activities which provide public goods and which have no market, e.g. maintaining wildlife and landscape. This has now been recognized, but the balance is still so heavily in favour of production support that farmers operating environmentally sensitive ways are still penalized compared with those undertaking environmentally damaging activities. This could – and should – be changed, with benefits to both the

environment and public expenditure. However, it requires that the consequences of policy changes be thought through, rather than assuming that the
target of the policy will be the only effect. Sadly, this approach is not yet
apparent. Instead, continued support needs to be linked to environmental
performance on farms, by making clear the wildlife and landscape objectives
and monitoring them. We are encouraged by the increasing readiness of policy
makers, at least in the EU, to consult in advance with conservation scientists and
policy specialists (Anon., 1995; Bignal, 1995; Dixon, Chapter 14).

Farming for nature

It is likely that further reforms to agriculture will be introduced within the next
ten years (CEC, 1995). These are likely to implement further the new agenda for
agriculture. Increased production, regardless of social or environmental costs, is
no longer required. Farmers will have to control the costs of inputs and increase
the quality, rather than quantity, of production. Most significantly, food
production need no longer be the dominant use of land in Europe.

Objectives complementing those of food production can be accommodated
on farmed land, and these may become the main objective of agricultural land-
use in certain cases. This may lead in some cases to minor modifications to
farming and sometimes to a clear duality of purpose where farming practices
contribute to wildlife or landscape conservation. In a small number of areas, the
needs of wildlife or environmental protection (or other land-uses such as
recreation, built development or forestry) may mean an end to commercial food
production.

Changes to the Common Agricultural and other EU Policies can bring about a
shift in emphasis by supporting the maintenance or enhancement of
environmentally-friendly land management both within and outside protected
sites. With appropriate incentives, it is possible to bring about wide-scale
changes to our environment that will have not only wildlife benefits, but also
social, cultural and long-term economic benefits (CEC, 1992). However, to do
this we need a fundamental re-assessment of the way we view our landscape. We
must no longer see farming and wildlife conservation as separate entities, and
from a production viewpoint no longer need to. They are integral parts of a
system working in dynamic equilibrium – and we must learn to view them and
treat them as such. The conservation of biological diversity on farmland will not
be possible unless such an approach is adopted. Without this, the ideals and
international agreements forged in Conservation on Biological Diversity will be
undermined.

To a greater or lesser extent the debate on future policies for farming has
defined the environmental objectives of public support to farmers. What is
necessary, however, is the need to articulate and define these objectives more
clearly in the future. An excellent opportunity exists to match this need with the

increasing body of information defining the problems faced by farmland birds. We are now entering a new period for farmland birds, during which there will be opportunities to adjust farming practices, via policy, for the benefit of birds and other wildlife. We need to re-define historical concepts of stewardship towards the land so that increasingly, we should be farming the land for nature as much as for food, and for both in a sustainable fashion.

Making progress

This book considers the agricultural landscapes of Europe in the light of this changing philosophy and examines the policies that are being adapted, adopted or dropped. An understanding of these is vital if we are to integrate the objectives for bird conservation (and to use birds as indicators for biodiversity conservation) on farmland in Europe. It is also vital that we understand the precise ecological relationships on which conservation depends. Our intention in this book is to harness current understanding to the new rural land-use philosophy for Europe. The case studies that form a major part of this book describe the ecological relationships that exist between birds and farming. More importantly, however, they illustrate the feasibility of designing and implementing policy instruments to bring about a new philosophy of land-use – across the whole of Europe.

REFERENCES

ALLEN, S. (1995) Scottish Natural Heritage NW Region; agriculture demonstration projects. In D.I.M. McCracken, E.M. Bignal & S.E. Wenlock (eds), *Farming on the Edge: the nature of traditional farmland in Europe, Proceedings of the Fourth European Forum on Nature Conservation and Pastoralism*, p. 189. Trujillo, Spain, 2–4 November 1994.

ANGELSTAM, P. & MIKUSINSKI, G. (1994) Woodpecker assemblages in natural and managed boreal and hemi-boreal forest – a review. *Annales Zoologici Fennici*, 31: 157–172.

ANON. (1995) Meeting with Agriculture Commissioner Dr Franz Fischler. *La Cañada*, 3: 6.

BARR, C.J. (1990) *Countryside Survey Main Report*. Peterborough: Nature Conservancy Council.

BEAUFOY, G., BALDOCK, D. & CLARK, J. (1994) *The Nature of Farming. Low intensity farming systems in nine European countries*. London: Institute for European Environmental Policy.

BIGNAL, E. (1995) Forum workshop in Brussels – the CAP, environmental policies and environmental practice. *La Cañada*, 4: 6.

BIGNAL, E., McCRACKEN, D., PIENKOWSKI, M. & BRANSON, A. (1994) *The Nature of Farming: traditional low intensity farming and its importance for wildlife*. Brussels: World Wide Fund for Nature.

BUNCE, R.G.H. (1993) *Ecological Consequences of Land Use Change*. London: Department of the Environment Report.

CARTER, I.C., WILLIAMS, J.M., WEBB, A. & TASKER, M.L. (1993) *Seabird Concentrations in the North Sea: an atlas of vulnerability to surface pollutants*. Peterborough: Joint Nature Conservation Committee.

CEC (Commission of the European Communities) (1992) Council Regulation 2078/92. Luxembourg: Official Journal of the EC.

CEC (Commission of the European Communities) (1995) Study on alternative strategies for the development of relations in the field of agriculture between the EU and the associated countries with a view to future accession of these countries Draft for discussion by EU Heads of Government, CEC, Brussels.

COLLAR, N.J., CROSBY, M.J. & STATTERSFIELD, A.J. (1994). *Birds to Watch 2: The world list of threatened birds*. Cambridge: BirdLife International (Conservation Series No. 4).

DUDLEY, N. (1987) *Cause for Concern: an analysis of air pollution damage and natural habitats*. London: Friends of the Earth.

ERIKSSON, M.O.G. (1987). Some effects of freshwater acidification on birds in Sweden. In A.W. Diamond & F.L. Filion (eds) *The Value of birds*, pp. 183–190. Cambridge: International Council for Bird Preservation (Technical Publication 6).

EUROSTAT (1995) *Statistics in Focus*, ISSN 1024-4263, Luxembourg: Commission of the European Communities.

FINLAYSON, M., HOLLIS, T. & DAVIS, T. (1992) Managing Mediterranean Wetlands and their Birds. International Waterfowl and Wetlands Research Bureau Special publication No. 20.

FURNESS, R.W. (1987) Seabirds as monitors of the marine environment. In A.W. Diamond & F.L. Filion (eds) *Bird Census and Atlas Studies (Proc. XIIth Int. Conf. on Bird Census and Atlas World)*, pp. 217–230. Cambridge: International Council for Bird Preservation (Technical Publication 6).

GALBRAITH, C.A. & BATES, M. (1991) Regional forest strategies and bird conservation. In D.A. Stroud & D. Glue (eds) *Britain's Birds in 1989/90: the conservation and monitoring review*, pp. 23–24. Thetford: British Trust for Ornithology/Nature Conservancy Council.

GALBRAITH, C.A. & PIENKOWSKI, M.W. (1990) Bird conservation as a basis for land-use policies in Britain. In K. Stasny & V. Bejcek (eds) *Bird Census and Atlas Studies (Proc. XIIth Int. Conf. on Bird Census and Atlas World)*, pp. 191–201. Prague: Institute of Applied Ecology and Ecotechnology Agriculture Unit.

GIBBONS, D.W., REID, J.B. & CHAPMAN, R.A. (1993) *The New Atlas of Breeding Birds in Britain and Ireland: 1988–1991*. London: T. and A.D. Poyser.

GOSS-CUSTARD, J.D. (1985) Foraging behaviour of wading birds and the carrying capacity of estuaries. In R.M. Sibly & R.H. Smith (eds) *Behavioural Ecology*, pp. 169–188. Oxford: Blackwell.

GREEN, R.E. (1995) The decline of the corncrake *Crex crex* in Britain continues. *Bird Study*, **42**: 66–75.

GRIMMETT, R.F.A. & JONES, T.A. (1989) *Important Bird Areas in Europe*, pp. 1–888. Cambridge: International Council for Bird Preservation Technical Publication No. 9.

HARDY A.R., STANLEY, P.I. & GREIG-SMITH, P.W. (1987) In A.W. Diamond & F.L. Filion (eds) *The Value of Birds*, pp. 119–132. Cambridge: International Council for Bird Preservation Technical Publication 6.

HELLE, P. & JÄRVINEN, O. (1986). Population trends of north Finnish landbirds in relation to their habitat selection and changes in forest structure. *Oikos*, **46**: 107–115.

HILL, D., TREWEEK, J., YATES, T. & PIENKOWSKI, M. (eds). (1996) *Actions for Biodiversity in the UK: approaches in UK to implementing the Convention on Biological Diversity*. Ecological Issues No. 5. British Ecological Society/Field Studies Council.

JENKINS, C. (1975) Utilisation du pigeon biset *Columbia livia* comme temoin de la pollution atmospherique par la plomb. *C. R. Hebd. Seances Acad. Sci. Ser. D*. **281**: 1187.

JOHNSON, N. (1993) *Cleaner Farming*. London: Centre for the Exploitation of Science and Technology.

MARCHANT, J.H., HUDSON, R., CARTER, S.P. & WHITTINGTON, P. (1990) *Population Trends in British Breeding Birds*. Tring: British Trust for Ornithology.

MARSH, J. & TANGERMANN, S. (1992) *The Changing Role of the Common Agricultural Policy*. London: Belhaven Press.

McCRACKEN, D.I.M., BIGNAL, E.M. & WENLOCK, S.E. (1995) Farming on the edge: the nature of traditional farmland in Europe. In *Proceedings of the Fourth European Forum on Nature Conservation and Pastoralism*, pp. 1–215. Trujillo, Spain, 2–4 November 1994.

McNIVEN, D.M. (1994) A review of the effectiveness of the European Council Directive 79/409/EEC on the conservation of wild birds. A perspective from EC bird conservation organizations. Royal Society for the Protection of Birds unpublished report.

MINISTRY OF AGRICULTURE, NATURE MANAGEMENT AND FISHERIES. (1990) *Nature Policy Plan of the Netherlands*. Ministry of Agriculture, Nature Management and Fisheries, The Hague.

MONTEVECCHI, W.A. (1993) Birds as indicators of changes in marine prey stocks. In R.W. Furness & J.D.D. Greenwood (eds) *Birds as Monitors of Environmental Change*, pp. 217–266. London: Chapman & Hall.

MOSER, M., BIBBY, C., NEWTON, I., PIENKOWSKI, M., SUTHERLAND, W.J., ULFSTRAND, S. & WYNNE, G. (1995) Bird conservation: the science and the action: conclusions and recommendations. *Ibis*, **137**: S3–S7.

NATURA 2000 (1996) Natura Barometer p. 6. Natura 2000, DG XI Newsletter, Issue 1, May 1996.

O'CONNOR, R.J. & SHRUBB, M. (1986) *Farming and Birds*. Cambridge: Cambridge University Press.

OHI, G., SEKI, H., MINOWA, K., OSHAWA, M., MIZOGUCHI, I. & SUGIMORI, F. (1981) Lead pollution in Tokyo, Japan: the pigeon (*Columbia livia*) reflects its amelioration. *Environmental Research*, **26**(1): 125.

ORMEROD, S.J. & TYLER, S.J. (1993) Birds as indicators of change in water quality. In R.W. Furness & J.D.D. Greenwood (eds) *Birds as Monitors of Environmental Change*, pp. 179–216. London: Chapman & Hall.

PIENKOWSKI, M.W. (1991) Using long-term ornithological studies in setting targets for conservation in Britain. *Ibis*, **133**(Supplement 1): 62–75.

PIENKOWSKI, M.W. (1993) (ed). *A Contribution to the Development of a System to Assess Nature Conservation Quality and to Set Targets for the National Action Plan Required by the Convention on Biological Diversity*. Joint Nature Conservancy Committee, Report No. 163, Peterborough.

PIENKOWSKI, M. & BIGNAL, E. (1993) Objectives for nature conservation in European Agriculture. In J.B. Dixon, A.J. Stones & I.R. Hepburn (eds) *A Future for Europe's Farmed Countryside: Proceedings of an International Conference*, pp. 21–43. Sandy: The Royal Society for the Protection of Birds (Studies in European Agricultural and Environmental Policy No. 1).

POTTS, G.R. (1986) *The Partridge: pesticides, predation and conservation*. London: Collins.

POTTS, G.R. & AEBISCHER, N.J. (1995) Population dynamics of the Grey Partridge *Perdix perdix* 1793–1993: monitoring, modelling and management. *Ibis*. **137**(Supplement 1): 29–37.

RSPB (1995). *The Future of the Common Agricultural Policy*. Sandy: The Royal Society for the Protection of Birds.

SHARROCK, J.T.R. (1976) *The Atlas of Breeding Birds in Britain and Ireland*. Berkhampstead: T. & A.D. Poyser.

STOWE, T.J., NEWTON, A.V., GREEN, R.E. & MAYES, E. (1993) The decline of the corncrake *Crex crex* in Britain and Ireland in relation to habitat. *Journal of Applied Ecology*, **30**: 53–62.

STROUD, D.A., MUDGE, G.P. & PIENKOWSKI, M.W. (1990). *Protecting Internationally*

Important Bird Sites: a review of the EEC Special Protection Areas in Great Britain. Peterborough: Nature Conservancy Council.

SWEDISH MINISTRY OF AGRICULTURE (1983) *Acidification: a boundless threat to our environment.* Solna, Sweden: National Swedish Environment Protection Board.

TASKER, M.L. & PIENKOWSKI, M.W. (1987) *Vulnerable Concentrations of Birds in the North Sea.* Peterborough: Nature Conservancy Council.

TASKER, M.L., WEBB, A., HARRISON, N.M. & PIENKOWSKI, M.W. (1990) *Vulnerable Concentrations of Marine Birds West of Britain.* Peterborough: Nature Conservancy Council.

TAYLOR, J.P. & DIXON J.B. (1990) *Agriculture and the Environment: towards integration.* Sandy: The Royal Society for the Protection of Birds.

TUCKER, G.M. & HEATH, M.F. (1994) *Birds in Europe: their conservation status.* Conservation Series No.3. Cambridge: BirdLife International.

WILLIAMS, G., STOWE, T. & NEWTON, A. (1991) Action for Corncrakes. *Royal Society for the Protection of Birds Conservation Review,* 5: 47–53.

WOODS, A., TAYLOR, J.P., HOUSDEN, S.D., HARLEY, D.C. & LANCE, A.N. (1988) *The Reform of the Common Agricultural Policy.* Sandy: The Royal Society for the Protection of Birds.

WYNNE, G.R., AVERY, M.I., CAMPBELL, L., GUBBAY, S., HAWKSWELL, S., JUNIPER, A., KING, M., NEWBERY, P., SMART, J., STEEL, C., STONES, A., STUBBS, A., TAYLOR, J.P., TYDEMAN, C. & WYNDE, R. (1995) *Biodiversity Challenge.* Sandy: Biodiversity Challenge Group, c/o The Royal Society for the Protection of Birds.

2

Europe's changing farmed landscapes

CLIVE POTTER

SUMMARY

The damaging environmental impact of modern agriculture is now so well documented that it has become one of the fixed elements of debate about agricultural policy reform. Indeed, the CAP itself is heavily implicated in the often dramatic changes that have swept through the European countryside during the last 30 years. This chapter describes the processes of agricultural intensification, specialization and marginalization that are the root of the problem and assesses the extent to which they can be said to have been fashioned by farm support. It highlights differences in the pace of change between the north and south of the European Union but identifies patterns that are common to both. A conclusion is that while the pressures for further intensification and decline are substantial, the potential for establishing agricultural stewardship through policy reform is very significant indeed.

INTRODUCTION

European Commission officials, casting around for a suitable phrase to describe the farming industry, once coined the title 'Green Europe' to describe all things agricultural. It is a useful, if slightly misleading epithet, still in wide use, which sums up the sector's real and symbolic importance some 30 years after the

FARMING AND BIRDS IN EUROPE
ISBN 0-12-544280-7

Copyright © 1997 Academic Press Ltd
All rights of reproduction in any form reserved

invention of the Common Agricultural Policy. Green Europe occupies a place of importance in the minds of policy-makers out of all proportion to its declining real economic significance – agriculture made up just 2.4% of the total Gross Domestic Product (GDP) of Member States in 1992 (EU12) compared with over 5.6% in 1970 (EC6). However, there were still 12 million or more people depending directly on agriculture for some part of their income in 1994 and in certain Member States the 'primary industries' are very important, in the local rural economy at least. For an explanation of the industry's political prominence one need look no further than the CAP itself, once described as the boldest experiment in the political economy of Europe for decades.

For environmentalists, the significance of agriculture has long been obvious, even without the policy dimension. From the simple fact that over 127 million hectares of the EU's land surface was in agricultural use in 1994, flows recognition of agriculture as both a motor of change and a potentially important agent of conservation in the European countryside. The damaging environmental impact of modern agriculture is now so widely documented that it has become one of the fixed elements of the debate about farm policy reform. Few commentators contemplating the vast literature on agriculture and the environment spawned by natural and social scientists are likely to deny the once controversial claim that contemporary farming practices – capital intensive, specialized and organized on an increasingly large scale – are damaging the rural environment. As Batie (1988) observes, growing public apprehension of this fact has led to a critical shift in views about farming, so that where once a productive agriculture was seen as part of the solution to natural resource degradation, it is now bracketed as part of the problem. A more recent and constructive development, however, has been the search for ways in which agricultural change can be managed, and certain agricultural systems and practices encouraged through policy reform in order to re-establish the principle of agricultural stewardship. It is this latter aspect which is the subject of the present book.

Writing generally about environmental policy change, Weale (1990) has remarked that reform has to start with the recognition of a problem and the emergence of a consensus about what is causing it. Despite what has just been said, these conditions were not satisfied simultaneously in the agriculture and environment field. Indeed, merely recognizing that a problem existed took some time, and there was a noticeable lag between publication in the 1960s of the first scientific studies describing various environmental impacts, and the development of public interest and concern. Nonetheless, the 1970s saw a growing conviction amongst environmentalists and commentators that many of the adverse environmental effects being observed were intrinsic to, or at least strongly associated with, modern agriculture. Westmacott (1983), for instance, describes how the traditional concern with protecting farmland for farmers in Member States like France gradually gave way to a recognition of the need to protect the environment from farming; in the UK, where the debate has always had a strong conservationist slant, Wibberley (1976) thought he recognized as early as 1968 'a widening gap in action and thought between those wanting infertility in land-use and mixtures in those uses (the conservationists) and those wanting maximum fertility and single land uses (the farmers)'.

Though later in arriving, agreement about the causes of the problem – Weale's second condition – is now increasingly well established. According to Cook (1989), by the mid 1980s there was a consensus amongst commentators in many western countries that agriculture's environmental and resource problems derive from the same causes, namely an evolving complex of agricultural technologies and policies that together bring about a more intensively specialized and concentrated pattern of agricultural production. In particular, the CAP is now heavily implicated in the often dramatic changes that have swept (and are still sweeping) through the countryside of EU Member States. As Cheshire (1990) famously put it: 'the problem is not one of ill will and ignorance, but of a system (the CAP) which systematically establishes financial inducements to erode the countryside and offers no rewards (to those) who wish to farm in ways which enrich and enhance the rural environment'. In other words, the issue was not so much the behaviour of individual farmers, as the nature of the policy framework in which they took their decisions and proceeded to act.

This chapter, and the one following, examines the evidence for this last point of view in some detail. We look first at the basic anatomy of farming in Europe today, pointing out in passing the still very significant north/south divide in agricultural structures and practices. A review of the main features of recent agricultural change is followed by an analysis of their environmental effects in different regions and landscapes of the European Union and a discussion of the role of the CAP as the most important protagonist in this story.

CONTRASTING AGRICULTURES

Diversity is still the keynote of rural Europe, at least in agricultural terms. Despite three decades of a process of modernization and restructuring so widespread that it might be expected to have eliminated all national and regional differences, save those dictated by soil and climate alone, important differences remain in terms of the pattern and structure of farming. Various attempts have been made to identify the main agricultural regions of the EU in order to capture these. Table 1 summarizes the main farmed landscapes, based on an analysis of natural and cultural conditions. A basic geographical distinction, implicit in Table 1, to which all analysts eventually return, is between north-west, central and southern Europe. Merlo (1991), for instance, distinguishes between the large scale and highly productive farming linked to arable and livestock products which tends to characterize agriculture in the north-west, and the mixed and rather more fragmented pattern of production characteristic of the Central region, comprising southern Germany and France to north-central Italy. The south, meanwhile, stands apart as a region where the

Table 1 Types and characteristics of farmed landscapes in Europe

Landscape type	Defining characteristics
Open field	Wide undulating fields parcelled into large rectangular areas, interspersed with woodland blocks
Former enclosure	Open arable landscapes broken only by fragmentary hedgerow boundaries and small woods
Polder	Extensive and very flat, intersected by dykes, canals, roadways and rivers
Mediterranean open	Wide treeless fields of grain in the open plains, olives on gentle slopes, some grazing
Huerta	Compartmentalized landscape of orchards and vegetables, quarter terraced and divided by irrigated ditches
Coltura promiscua	Terraced landscape comprising vertical layers of orchards, olives, grapes and fruit
Montado	Extensive 'orchard' pastures of olives or oaks undergrazed by sheep and/or cattle
Bocage	Gently undulating landscape, mainly of pasture and woodland enclosed by stone walls or hedges
Semi-bocage	Less uniform and hillier version of bocage
Kampur	Irregular landscape of enclosed fields, woodland or forest blocks
Montagues	Lower alpine landscape largely of summer pastureland broken by tracts of forest

Source: based on Meeus *et al.* (1990).

later onset of intensification, and pressing natural constraints, have left larger pockets of small and economically marginal farmers engaged in the production of Mediterranean products. As Duchene *et al.* (1985) put it, 'While Community [*sic*] agriculture has largely changed from a peasant to an industrial one, it has travelled only part of the way – especially in the Mediterranean, the south and west of France, and in Ireland'.

Table 2 shows that the pattern of farming follows this rough north/south divide, with crops accounting for a much greater share of gross agricultural output in southern Member States and livestock being very much more important in the north. The fact that demand for fruit, vegetables, olive oil and wine has grown even more sluggishly than for meat or cheese, and enjoys less market protection than cereals, milk, beef and sugar beet, etc. grown in the north, for example, means of course that Mediterranean countries tend to specialize at the

Table 2 The pattern of agricultural production in EC12 1984 (% gross agricultural output)

Country	Livestock products	Mediterranean products	Cereals Potatoes Industrial crops
Luxembourg	84.6	7.6	7.4
Ireland	83.4	3.2	11.5
Denmark	70.9	2.1	17.9
Germany	69.1	11.6	14.8
Belgium	66.3	12.8	12.7
Netherlands	66.0	18.4	8.2
UK	61.3	9.3	25.3
France	51.3	20.1	23.0
Spain	40.1	34.5	23.6
Italy	39.0	40.5	14.6
Portugal	37.6	41.2	10.4
Greece	31.1	47.4	11.8

Source: based on Duchene *et al*. (1985).

vulnerable end of the product range which, until comparatively recently, has received least CAP support.

Table 3 presents data from the latest EU Farm Structures Survey of 1989/90 and shows the distribution of farms by size. It emphasizes the further differences in the farm structures of north and south. In Greece, for instance, 78% of holdings are less than 5 hectares in size, while in the UK just 13% of farms fall into this category. Indeed 16% of farms in the UK are of 100 hectares or more but only 1% of Belgian, Greek, Italian, Portuguese and Dutch ones. Farms of 50 hectares or more nonetheless make up a significant proportion of farms in Denmark (19%), France (16%), Ireland (11%) but particularly in the UK (33%). These large differences in average farm size, coupled with the regional specialization of production noted above, result in very pronounced differences in farm family income. In 1991/92 this ranged from a 3396 ECU average in Portugal to a 37 118 ECU average in the Netherlands, making Dutch farmers on average 11 times better off in terms of agricultural income than their Portuguese colleagues.

One can only agree with Duchene *et al*. (1985), who liken EU agriculture to a large animal with a powerful head and body, provided by the 20% of farms responsible for 80% of output, and a very long tail at the extremity of which are the small, semi-subsistence farms that are scattered across the farmed landscapes of the south and on the agricultural margins in the north.

Table 3 Agricultural holdings in the EU in 1989/90 by size class

	Number of holdings (thousands)					
	<5 ha	5–20 ha	20–50 ha	50–100 ha	≥100 ha	Total
Belgium	32.1	29.4	18.6	4.1	0.8	85.0
Denmark	2.2	32.2	31.3	12.2	3.4	81.3
Germany	216.8	243.1	159.8	38.9	6.7	665.3
Greece	718.5	183.9	18.1	2.5	0.7	923.7
Spain	971.4	410.4	124.9	48.8	38.2	1593.7
France	277.4	279.6	228.1	128.6	43.5	1017.2
Ireland	19.2	72.4	59.4	15.7	3.9	170.6
Italy	2099.1	439.5	87.7	24.7	13.7	2664.7
Luxembourg	1.1	0.8	1.1	1.1	0.1	4.1
Netherlands	40.3	46.9	31.6	5.3	0.7	124.8
Portugal	492.4	83.5	13.6	3.9	5.4	598.8
UK	33.5	67.9	60.7	42.5	38.5	243.1
EU12	4904	1889.6	894.9	328.3	155.6	8172.4

Source: Eurostat (1994).

KEY FEATURES OF RECENT AGRICULTURAL CHANGE

Statistics like these hint at the uneven nature of recent agricultural change, for while natural endowments and the constraints of soil and climate are obviously important determinants of these 'contrasting agricultures', the existing pattern is also the outcome of a process of restructuring that has proceeded faster and more extensively in some regions than others.

In outline, the story of post-World War II agricultural change in Europe runs something like this: from the 1960s onwards, farms throughout north-western Europe and a little later in the south, embarked on an intensification of production which involved applying ever-increasing quantities of mineral fertilizers, pesticides and farm chemicals to each hectare of land in production and/or increasing stocking rates. Since 1950, applications of nitrogen fertilizer in EU countries have increased well over 400-fold. The large scale use of pesticides is similarly a phenomenon of the last 30 years and from a low base, rates of increase have been dramatic. In France, for example, total annual pesticide use increased from 25 000 to 100 000 tonnes between 1971 and 1981. Figure 1, based on data from the Food and Agriculture Organization (FAO) Fertilizer Yearbooks, relates fertilizer use to the area farmed to give an index of use. With a base of 100 for the years 1955–57, the index doubles by 1966 and quadruples by 1979. Figure 2, meanwhile, shows that increases have been greater in some countries than others, with Ireland, France, Italy and Greece

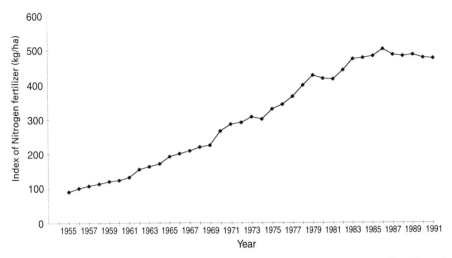

Figure 1 Index of nitrogen fertilizer per hectare, EU10. (Source: Eurostat, various dates.)

seeing fertilizer use grow rapidly from a low base. The mechanization of production which went with this meant a virtual revolution in farming techniques. One mode of production, dependent on horsepower and manpower, has disappeared. It has been replaced by another based on tractors, chemicals and oil.

To be specific, this meant also an increase in the scale of production as technological changes, embodied in new machinery and equipment, led to the substitution of capital for labour, enabling fewer farm workers to manage more hectares and larger livestock units. This second defining feature of contemporary agricultural change is reflected in the 30% reduction in agricultural manpower that took place between 1970 and 1988 and the equally impressive 45% increase in the number of farm machines in use and 46% increase in energy consumption (Rae, 1993). A combination of increasing output, due largely to massive chemical inputs and falling labour input, contributed directly to agriculture's impressive productivity record, with output per worker more than doubling between 1973 and 1992 for the EU10. If one takes gross production value measured in ECUs/hectare as an indicator of the level of intensity and the average number of hectares cultivated per annual work unit (AWU) or the average number of livestock units being managed by each 'worker' as an indicator of the scale of arable and livestock farms respectively, then Figure 4, compiled from Eurostat data, shows clearly just how significant intensity and scale increases have been since the 1960s. Indeed, on this basis Meeus *et al.* (1990) calculate that the intensity of EU farming has increased from an average of 300 ECU/ha in 1964 to well over 700 ECU/ha by the late 1970s, with the scale of arable enterprises on average doubling over the same period.

Perhaps most interesting are regional and inter-country differences in the pace

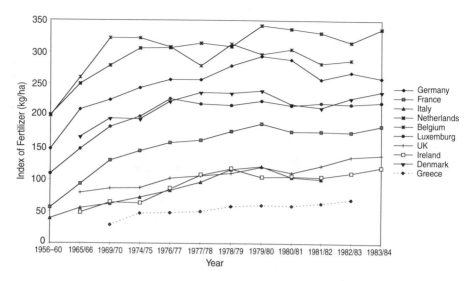

Figure 2 Consumption of commercial fertilizers by Member State. (Source: Eurostat, 1994.)

and extent of these changes. As Meeus *et al.* (1990) point out, the picture is far from one of uniform change along a linear path; some regions, such as Normandy and Picardy in France, and parts of middle England, have experienced huge increases in the scale of production, while in others, such as the Italian regions of Campania and Liguria, both scale and intensity increased over the period 1964–77. In national terms (see Figure 4), it is evident that Dutch agriculture has undergone further massive intensification from an already high base while in France, Germany and some other Benelux countries, the emphasis has been on increasing the scale of farming operations. Britain, with farm structures already appreciably larger than those of most other Member States (see above), has seen further increases in both the intensity and scale of production. As far as can be judged from this analysis, certain Member States like Spain and Portugal have intensified faster than they have restructured, though increases in scale have been far from insignificant. There are two conclusions to be drawn from this broad pattern of change. Firstly, that countries or regions which were the first to modernize and restructure are continuing to do so and that a further concentration of productive power in the farming industry is very likely. Indeed, agricultural 'growth poles' can already be identified, notably in the Paris basin, eastern England and northern Germany, and these will increase their share of total output in the years ahead. Secondly though, it is also clear that an uneven 'catching up' process is under way which will see accelerating change and a duplication of northern 'industrialization' of agriculture on the most productive land in the south. A corollary to this is a

(a)

(b)

Figure 3 Technological advances have increased harvesting capability as illu'
(a) the arable binder harvesting of the early 1970s (photo by RSPB) and (b) the
machinery of today (photo by C.H. Gomersall/RSPB.)

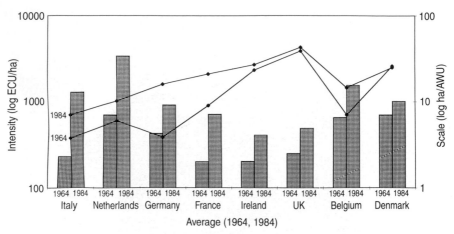

Figure 4 Trends in intensity (bars) and scale (plots) of production for selected EU Member States, 1964–84. AWU: annual work units. (Source: Eurostat, various dates.)

marginalization of farms on the agricultural fringes that are unable to compete in a more open market place.

THE ENVIRONMENTAL CONSEQUENCES

The environmental repercussions of these momentous changes have been generating public concern for some considerable time and, while there are still gaps in knowledge, especially relating to southern Member States, there is no longer any doubt about the scale or severity of the problem. Throughout the EU, agricultural change has operated on a number of levels, fragmenting and simplifying many farmed landscapes through the removal of hedgerows, trees, small woods, ponds and the restoration or 'improvement' of wetland and grassland. This has also seriously reduced the ecological integrity and extent of larger blocks of semi-natural vegetation and habitat mosaics in more marginal areas. In the north, it was the displacement of mixed farming centred on a bocage-type landscape of small enclosures and the accompanying outward expansion of intensive arable production which first triggered concern. In what may be described as the former enclosure landscapes of lowland England, north- Denmark and in the classic bocage of northern France and Belgium, the al of hedgerows from the late 1960s onwards to facilitate larger scale operations was the most visible sign of gathering agricultural change. w loss in the UK is perhaps better documented than almost anywhere wake of the UK Government's comprehensive Countryside Survey. that as recently as the early 1980s, 28 000 km of hedgerow were

Figure 5 Laid hazel hedge in Wales. From the 1960s onwards hedgerows have been removed to facilitate larger scale farming operations. (Photo by C.H. Gomersall/RSPB.)

being removed annually (Barr *et al.*, 1993). Similar changes hold true for large parts of north-western Europe. For example, Baldock (1990) reports a large scale disappearance of hedges, copses and lines of trees from the landscape of Brittany and Normandy since the 1960s. Land consolidation schemes, and the sudden increase in the scale of farming operations that they bring in their wake, have affected as much as a fifth of all agricultural land in Belgium, northern France, Germany and the Netherlands. Fewer hedges, trees, ditches and field boundaries is the usual result.

Meanwhile, the greater use of farm chemicals that is the main instrument of intensification also contributed greatly to a reduction in biodiversity on agricultural land via a number of pathways. The wider use of nitrogen fertilizers, by enabling less fertile marginal land to be brought into production, has also contributed indirectly to the loss of semi-natural vegetation and habitat. Baldock (1990) describes a parallel process in all other Member States, further reporting a widespread decline in the extent of grazing marshes and wet meadows throughout north-western Europe. In Belgium, for instance, over 1000 hectares were being drained annually during the 1960s and 1970s, while in the UK 4% of wetlands were lost over the same period, and 55% were lost in the Netherlands. In France wetland loss has averaged 10 000 hectares each year since the early 1970s. A very similar picture could be presented for other habitat types such as dry grasslands, deciduous woodland and heath.

The cumulative effect of all these changes is a general impoverishment of the lowland farmed landscape. Habitat loss and fragmentation has meant that three species of flowering plants, three or four dragonfly species, and one butterfly species have become extinct in Britain since 1947 (Green, 1990). In Germany, agricultural intensification has been identified as the primary cause of declines in up to 400 species of vascular plants. The 'Red List' of endangered species shows that 30% of flowering plants, 40% of bird species and 50% of mammal species are either extinct or endangered in Germany, overwhelmingly because of agricultural change (Agra-Europe, 1991). As a recent British study concluded, the legacy of decades of intensification and landscape change is a situation in which wildlife interest has been pushed back into small refuges to 'exist as fragments of habitat in the cracks between commercial land uses' (Adams *et al.*, 1992).

Neither has intensification been confined to arable regions. The equivalent intensification of livestock production is reflected in a steady climb in livestock numbers throughout north-west Europe. In Ireland, for example, sheep numbers have tripled in just eight years (Baldock *et al.*, 1994), while in the UK they rose by 79% between 1985 and 1992. The resulting pressure to bring into production and re-seed grassland to support larger flocks and herds is reflected in declining areas of heath, moor and semi-natural grassland. Up to 150 000 hectares of 'rough grazing' were reclaimed between 1978 and 1994 in Britain for example (Barr *et al.*, 1993), while in Ireland 'improved' permanent grass has been advancing at the expense of rough grazing at the rate of 4000 ha per year since the mid 1980s (Clark J., personal communication 1995).

Paradoxically, nature has suffered as much from the abandonment of land and decline in management as from intensification in many marginal areas. In the lowlands, some land which was previously grazed, particularly steep land and heathland, is no longer farmed, especially where mixed farming has declined and a farm has become entirely arable. In the uplands, the rationalization of livestock holdings has often been accompanied by a trend towards ranching the more remote, marginal areas. There has been a shift away from over-wintering stock 'on the hill' in favour of keeping them in the 'in-bye'. This has led to a loss of conservation interest from under-grazing and declining management (Felton & Marsden, 1990). In France, further extensification of production in marginal areas is associated with the abandonment of land, with commensurate changes in vegetation that lead to the loss of characteristic species and open conditions, to such an extent that they are rarely to the conservation good. Certainly the marginalization of traditional low intensity systems of livestock production such as those found in and around the Massif Central is of growing concern (see Baldock *et al.*, 1994).

An almost equivalent process of intensification on the best land, coupled with the marginalization or slow decline of traditional farming practices elsewhere, can now be seen taking place across the farmed landscapes of the south. Accession of Portugal and Spain to the EC in 1986 was the signal for rapid development of the farm sector, with an often dramatic transformation of farming systems and structures (see Etxzarreta & Viladomiu, 1989). According to these authors, it was in the open Mediterranean landscapes of central Spain and Portugal that the spreading irrigation of arable land permitted a general intensification of arable production from the 1970s onwards, a process much accelerated by the CAP. Specifically, irrigation obviates the need for fallowing, with the result that less than 40% of arable land was left fallow in Spain compared with well over 50% in the middle 1970s (Baldock et al., 1994). Dryland production in Spain is significantly more intensive than it once was, and monocultural systems are steadily displacing the traditional rich mosaic of arable crops, vines, olives and other permanent crops that offers such a rich habitat for steppeland birds. As Baldock et al. (1994) point out, although there are still large tracts of countryside where low-intensity arable production prevails, further intensification is inevitable in all but the most unproductive regions. Suarez et al. (see Chapter 11) estimate that between four and nine million hectares were still being managed along traditional dryland production lines in 1992, but that under the National Hydrological Plan up to two million hectares are targeted for irrigation and upgrading, largely in dryland cereal areas. In areas with very arid conditions and poorer soils, meanwhile, land abandonment is a real possibility, with effects that vary with location. Other environmentally valuable permanent crops such as the traditional olive groves which survive in Greece, Italy, Spain and Portugal are increasingly neglected or even abandoned. According to Naveso (1993), traditional olive production in Spain is already economically marginal and liable to be replaced in many areas with a more intensive crop. Portuguese montados and Spanish dehesas, intricate systems of farming which involve grazing within open woodland and between scattered individual trees (usually cork and holm oaks) together with small scale arable production, continue to be major depositories of biodiversity in southern landscapes. However, intensification threatens here as well. Baldock (1990) reports a steady erosion due to neglect, and conversion to more specialized arable use, often facilitated by irrigation. Significant declines in the area of dehesa have been reported in Extremadura and western Andalucía (see Díaz et al., Chapter 7).

Livestock numbers are also increasing in southern Member States, and there has been a very definite concentration of production on the pastureland with highest production potential, at the expense of marginal grassland. Meanwhile, the wider use of bought-in feed is bringing about profound changes in the pattern of grazing, with stock that were once moved between winter and summer grazings now being kept on lowland pasture all the year round. Transhumance, the long-established seasonal movement of stock, is far less widespread than it once was. Its decline has two effects. First, grazing pressure is increased on grassland in the plains and valley bottoms. The grass steppes of central Spain, traditionally grazed at low intensities and of great importance for birds including Montagu's harrier Circus pygargus, the little bustard Tetrax tetrax, and the globally threatened great bustard Otis tarda, are now beginning to exhibit vegetation changes brought about by over-grazing, for instance

(Sears, 1991). There is also evidence that the presence of greater numbers of livestock (cattle and sheep) all the year round is disturbing the agro-ecology of the environmentally very valuable agro-silvo pastoral systems characteristic of the dehesas of western Spain and the montados of central Portugal. According to Díaz *et al.* (Chapter 7), this affects the shrub vegetation and even the tree cover and is already influencing natural regeneration by reducing acorn production and seeding. Second, the decline of transhumance threatens the mountain pastures that are such important repositories of conservation value in the montague-type landscapes of the Pyrenees and the Alps (Pain, 1993). In a pattern that is reminiscent of the linked intensification and decline which affected upland Britain, summer pastures are now undergrazed or even abandoned, with a resultant loss of the existing habitat mosaic.

CAUSES AND PROCESSES

As has been said, describing the problem does not itself make the case for reform unless it is linked to an understanding of underlying causes. While it is clear from the above that agricultural change is heavily implicated in the continuing transformation of Europe's countryside, the key question here is: why has combined intensification and abandonment taken place? Contrary to our earlier assumption, not all commentators would agree that public policy has been one of the driving forces behind agricultural change. Buckwell (1990), for instance, argues against what he sees as a naive 'policy thesis' which attributes specific aspects of environmental change to particular features of the system of farm support. Pointing to the long-term nature of the trend towards greater intensity and scale of agricultural production in Member States, Buckwell is keen to stress the importance of technologically induced changes in farming systems. Moreover, his technological juggernaut has a momentum of its own because 'irrespective of the pressure of demand and the state of the market, the drive to reduce production costs and thereby create short run profit is a powerful incentive for innovation and thus for research. To some extent technology truly appears as '"manna from heaven"' (Buckwell, 1990).

The implication is that even without government intervention, the last 30 years would still have seen the rapid introduction of chemical and mechanical inputs to land – that is so heavily implicated in environmental change. Having said that, even the most agnostic of commentators are unable to ignore the scale of government intervention in agriculture over this period, and most would concede that farm support has exerted an influence over the course of agricultural development, even if they are unspecific about precise causality. Basic economics suggests a positive relationship between product prices and output which chiefly operates in the short-run by encouraging a greater use of inputs, in other words, an intensification of production. Recent research from the Organization of Economic Co-operation and Development (OECD) reported by Rae (1993), based on a comparison of the usage of various environmentally sensitive inputs in OECD countries, found a strong positive and indeed even exponential relationship with rates of assistance measured in producer subsidy equivalents.

Other analyses of long-term trends in input-use support the hypothesis that agricultural intensity is positively related to rates of government farm assistance (including capital subsidies). The entry of Member States into the CAP meant that 'farmers found themselves operating in an economic environment offering price levels previously undreamt of. Given the rapid acceleration in agricultural change observed in the EEC 6 from the 1960s onwards, this is at least consistent with the argument that agricultural support plays a significant role in the process of agricultural change' (Cheshire, 1990). More recently, the progressive extensification of New Zealand agriculture following the dismantling of price supports in 1989 confirms, in reverse as it were, the validity of the intensification hypothesis (Fairweather, 1992).

However, in the long run, it is the interaction of farm support with technical progress which has brought about the changes in the structure, pattern and practice of farming that have had such profound environmental effects. Munton *et al.* (1990) point to the way in which the institutional apparatus of government support established since the 1930s has provided a vital foundation for rapid technological innovation in the industry. Above all it is the climate of security created by the high price guarantees offered to Europe's farmers under the CAP which, by ensuring a rapid adoption and diffusion of new technologies, has brought about widespread changes in farming systems and practices over the long term. It would appear that once the farmers became convinced that price support was likely to continue, they used the short-run profits of higher prices to re-equip their farms and refashion their farming systems, bringing about the restructuring of rural land-use that has already been described. Although our understanding of the relationship between adoption rates and profitability is still incomplete (Whitby & Harvey, 1988), it is generally agreed that it is usually positive rather than negative, and that uptake is most rapid when agriculture is profitable and farmers feel financially secure.

In terms of the agricultural 'treadmill', farmers no longer face falling product prices because state intervention prevents the downward adjustment that would otherwise occur. They do, however, soon face rising land values and rents because, as farming is now more profitable and more people want to become farmers and those already farming want to expand, a rising demand for land meets a fixed supply. The resulting inflation in land values has its own environmental effects, increasing the opportunity cost of uncultivated land, and encouraging farmers to bring more land into production, or intensify on the land already farmed, with the loss of semi-natural vegetation and landscape features which this involves.

Supporters of what might be called the 'strong policy thesis' would go further than this in arguing that the present environmental costs of European agriculture are much more directly a product of the CAP that has been designed and implemented over the last 30 years. Guaranteeing a fair standard of living to the agricultural industry has always been a prime objective and, from the beginning, it was clear that this would be pursued through a protectionist policy of border protection and market intervention aimed at creating a high price regime (Tracy, 1989). Faced with the choice presented in the Mansholt Plan of 1968 between continuing with this approach or opting for a low price policy which aimed to restructure the industry and improve the living standards of a smaller community of competitive farmers, policy-makers chose the former. They attempted to maintain a 'large' agriculture by guaranteeing product prices but linking this to a programme of modernization through a range of fiscal and other measures. The strategy was to minimize the amount of structural change that took place and, in the words of the Treaty of Rome, 'to increase agricultural productivity by promoting technical progress and by ensuring the rational development of agricultural production and the optimum utilization of the factors of production, in particular labour'.

As Fennell (1985) comments, the reality has been that the CAP has been much more concerned with the pursuit of production than productivity. Rather than encouraging improved productivity in the Mansholtian sense – i.e. maintaining or even reducing industry output but lowering the unit costs of production through restructuring – the approach has been to encourage the use of additional capital inputs in the expectation of an even greater rise in output. This has been achieved through a variety of subsidies designed to lower the real user cost of capital and encourage widespread modernization and re-equipment. It has been argued that such structural and fiscal measures may well have been much more important in determining the extent, pace and nature of technical change than the price support measures themselves. Taken together with the effects of minimum wage legislation in agriculture, these policies have certainly played a role in changing the relative costs of capital and labour which subsequently encouraged a substitution of capital for land and labour and the associated technical change which has given rise to many of the agricultural environmental changes previously described. Bowers and Cheshire (1983), well-known advocates of this view in the UK, have pointed to the way in which scientific and technical progress has been applied to production within an existing distribution of farm size, a policy calculated, in their view, to maximize environmental damage because of the resulting greater intensification of production compared with changes in scale. Actually, what has happened has been a faster increase in the scale of farming operations than in farm structures themselves as farmers have striven to realize economies of scale by specializing and hence increasing throughput in a smaller number of enterprises. The result is the landscape change described above.

CONCLUSION

European agriculture has been transformed in the space of thirty years through an unprecedented rapid process of intensification, specialization and increases in scale. The process has been uneven and it is still very much in progress, especially in the south where it started later and had farther to go in terms of modernization and restructuring. It is hard to underestimate the impact on landscapes and wildlife throughout Europe's countryside. Despite important differences in the nature and pace of change between northern and southern regions of the Union, there are broadly parallel pressures at work and a pattern of linked intensification and decline is common to both. Attributing precise cause and effect is rather more difficult, though few any longer question the pivotal role played by the CAP. The driving influence of policy is both depressing and encouraging. The slow pace of progress towards reforming the CAP means that substantial incentives remain in place, encouraging further intensification and advancing the frontiers of agricultural change. But it also underlines the enormous potential for establishing agricultural stewardship through policy reform. It is to the policy debate that we therefore now turn.

REFERENCES

ADAMS, W.M., BOURN, N. & HODGE, I. (1992) Conservation in the wider countryside. *Land Use Policy, October*: 235–248.

AGRA-EUROPE (1991) *Agriculture and the Environment: how will the EC resolve the conflict?* Agra-Europe Special Report 60, London.

BALDOCK, D. (1990) *Agriculture and Habitat Loss in Europe*. Discussion paper No.3, London: World Wide Fund for Nature International.

BALDOCK, D., CLARK, J. & BEAUFOY, G. (1994) *The Nature of Farming: Low intensity farming systems in nine European countries*. London: Institute for European Environmental Policy.

BARR, C., BUNCE, R., CLARK, R., FULLER, R., FURSE, M., GILLLESPIE, M., GROOM, G., HALLAM, C., HORNING, M., HOWARD, D. & NESS, M. (1993) *Countryside Survey 1990: Main Report*. London: Department of the Environment.

BATIE, S. (1988) Agriculture as the Problem: new agendas and new opportunities. *Southern Journal of Agricultural Economics*, 20: 1–12.

BOWERS, J. & CHESHIRE, P. (1983) *Agriculture, the Countryside and Land Use – an economic critique*. London: Methuen.

BUCKWELL, A. (1990) Economic signals, farmers' response and environmental change. *Journal of Rural Studies*, 5(2): 149–160.

CHESHIRE, P. (1990) The environmental implications of European agricultural support policies. In D. Baldock & D. Conder (eds) *Can the Common Agricultural Policy fit the Environment?*, pp. 10–17. London: Institute of European Environmental Policy/Council for the Preservation of Rural England/World Wide Fund for Nature.

COOK, K. (1989) The environmental era of US agricultural policy. *Journal of Soil and Water Conservation*, September-October, 362–366.

DUCHENE, F., SZCZEPANIK, E. & LEGG, W. (1985) *New Limits on European Agriculture: politics and the Common Agricultural Policy*. London: Croom Helm.

EUROSTAT (1994) *Agricultural Statistical Yearbook 1994*, Brussels.

ETXZARRETA, M. & VILADOMIU, L. (1989) The restructuring of Spanish agriculture and Spain's accession to the EEC. In D. Goodman & M. Redclift (eds) *The International Farm Crisis*, pp. 135–155. The International Farm Crisis. Macmillan.

FAIRWEATHER, J. (1992) *Agrarian Restructuring in New Zealand*. Canterbury: Lincoln University.

FELTON, M. & MARSDEN, J. (1990) *Heather Regeneration in England and Wales: a feasibility study*. Peterborough: Nature Conservancy Council.

FENNELL, R. (1985) A reconsideration of the objectives of the Common Agricultural Policy. *Journal of Common Market Studies,* **33**(3): 257–276.

GREEN, B. (1990) Agricultural intensification and the loss of habitat, species and amenity in British grasslands. *Grass and Forage Sciences,* **45**: 365–372.

MARSH, J. (1985) Can budgetary pressures bring CAP reform? In J. Pelkmans (ed.) *Can the Common Agricultural Policy be Reformed?*, pp. 107–121. Maastrict: European Institute of Public Administration.

MEEUS, J., WIJERMANS, M. & VROM, M. (1990) Agricultural landscapes in Europe and their transformation. *Landscape and Urban Planning,* **18**: 189–352.

MERLO, M. (1991) The effects of late economic development on land use. *Journal of Rural Studies,* **7**: 445–457.

MUNTON, R., MARSDEN, T. & WHATMAN , S. (1990) Technological change in a period of agricultural adjustment. In P. Lowe, M. Whatmore & T. Marsden (eds) *Technological Change and the Rural Environment*, pp. 104–124. London: Fulton.

NAVESO, M. (1993) *Estepar, aves y agricultura*. Madrid: La Garcilla, Sociedad Española de Ornitología/Birdlife International.

PAIN, D. (1994) *Case Study of Farming and Birds in Europe:7. Transhumance Pastoralism in Spain*. Sandy: The Royal Society for the Protection of Birds. Unpublished Research Report.

RAE, J. (1994) Agriculture and the environment in the OECD. In C. Williamson (ed.) *Agriculture, the Environment and Trade*, pp. 82–114. Washington D.C.: International Policy Council on Agriculture and Trade.

SEARS, J. (1991) *Case Study of European Farmland Birds:1. Mediterranean Steppelands, Spain, and The Dehesa system, Spain*. Sandy: Unpublished Research Report, The Royal Society for the Protection of Birds.

TRACY, M. (1989) *Government and Agriculture in Western Europe: crisis and response*. London: Harvester-Wheatsheaf.

WEALE, A. (1990) *The New Politics of Pollution*. Manchester: Manchester University Press.

WESTMACOTT, R. (1983) The conservation of farmed landscapes – attitudes and problems in the US and Britain. *Landscape Design,* **8**: 11–14.

WHITBY, M. & HARVEY, D. (1988) Issues and policies. In M. Whitby & J. Ollerenshaw (eds) *Land Use and the European Environment*, pp. 143–177. London: Belhaven Press.

WIBBERLEY, G. (1976) Rural resource development in Britain and environmental concern. *Journal of Agricultural Economics,* **27**: 1.

CHAPTER

3

The evolution of the Common Agricultural Policy and the incorporation of environmental considerations

NIGEL ROBSON

SUMMARY

Farmed land takes up a larger area than any other land-use in the European Union (EU). Agricultural policies are therefore extremely important in relation to how a significant part of the land surface is used and managed. In the 12 earliest Member States of the European Union, the utilized agricultural area is 57% of the total area, and forests cover 25%; the total 'rural' area is thus more than 80% of the territory. The enlargement to 15 Member States in 1995 (EU15) has shifted these proportions, as both Finland and Sweden have very large forest areas (59% and 50% of their territory respectively). In EU15, the utilized agricultural area is 44% of the total and forests are 33%, giving a 'rural' land area of 77%. However, agriculture remains the most important single category, covering 138 million hectares. In the event of further enlargement of the EU to include the 10 central and eastern European countries (CEECs[1]), this agricultural area will increase to nearly 200 million hectares.

The relationship between agriculture and politics has never been easy. Agriculture is one of the oldest industries in human history, and in terms of

[1]CEECs: Poland, Hungary, Czech Republic, Slovak Republic, Slovenia, Romania, Bulgaria, Lithuania, Latvia, Estonia.

FARMING AND BIRDS IN EUROPE
ISBN 0-12-544280-7

Copyright © 1997 Academic Press Ltd
All rights of reproduction in any form reserved

economic development it is extremely important, for it is only when food producers can produce more than their own immediate family needs, that any labour can be released for other activities. It is also an industry in which political intervention is a virtually permanent state of affairs. There are a number of reasons for this. The first is the strategic need to secure the nation's food supply, and the shortages suffered particularly by continental European countries during wars go a long way towards explaining the willingness of the people to pay a certain 'premium' to be sure of having ample food supplies. The second reason relates to the tendency for agricultural producers to be poor because (a) there is a chronic tendency to over-supply the market, (b) consumers spend a lower and lower proportion of each incremental increase in income on food (even the richest people have a physical limit to their capacity to consume food), and (c) industries obtain food and agricultural raw materials at the lowest possible cost in order to be more competitive in the general economic environment.

In Europe, over the last 100 years, there has almost invariably been a degree of political intervention in agriculture, and since the inception of the Common Agricultural Policy (CAP), the industry is virtually controlled by rules and regulations. Increasingly important is the extent to which this intervention harms the environment or to what extent it can be harnessed to improve the environment. This is the subject under discussion in this chapter.

THE ORIGINS OF THE COMMON AGRICULTURAL POLICY

The desire to create a common policy for agriculture was manifested in several attempts, linked to the formation of general economic unions, by Belgium and Luxembourg in 1922, by the Benelux countries (Belgium, the Netherlands and Luxembourg) in 1948, and by the Council of Europe between 1952 and 1954 (Tracy, 1989). However, the successful creation of an agricultural 'common market' eluded the participating governments, although the problems which had to be solved were identified. These factors were influential in the next stages of development.

After centuries of warfare, there was a strong desire in the Europe of the 1950s to create a united political structure with common institutions, and a common market through progressive fusion of national economies. Following a series of initial steps beginning with the European Coal and Steel Community in 1952, the process culminated with Treaties setting up the European Economic Community and the European Atomic Energy Community, which were signed in

Rome by the Six (Germany, France, Italy, Belgium, the Netherlands and Luxembourg) on 25 March 1957 and entered into force on 1 January 1958. One of the principal aims of the Treaty of Rome was the establishment of a common market, with the removal of quantitative restrictions and customs duties between Member States. It also included measures for the free movement of labour, capital and services, and common rules of competition, although Member States continued to control their own economies. Agriculture was included in the common market provisions, and was to be governed by a Common Agricultural Policy. Its objectives are set out in Article 39 of the Treaty establishing the European Economic Community:

1. The objectives of the common agricultural policy shall be:

(a) to increase agricultural productivity by promoting technical progress and by ensuring the rational development of agricultural production and the optimum use of the factors of production, in particular labour;
(b) thus to ensure a fair standard of living for the agricultural community, in particular by increasing individual earnings of persons engaged in agriculture;
(c) to stabilise markets;
(d) to assure the availability of supplies;
(e) to ensure that supplies reach consumers at reasonable prices.

Careful examination of Article 39 (1) (a) and (b), and in particular the word 'thus', '. . . implied that the fair standard of living was to be achieved by means of increased agricultural productivity and by increasing the individual earnings of persons engaged in agriculture. These provisions suggested a preference for structural measures rather than overall price support, but in subsequent practice not much attention was paid to these nuances'(Tracy, 1989). It is important to understand that the politicians, by choosing the route of increasing productivity as the means of increasing earnings, had implicitly adopted the strategy of intensification. The alternative, of restructuring agriculture with a view to increasing the size of farm holdings, and so allowing for more extensive farming, had thus been almost abandoned at the outset of the CAP.

In fact it became apparent rather quickly that there was considerable divergence of view on how the objectives were to be achieved. There followed a long period of heated debate and bargaining by Member States, EC Institutions and groups representing farmers' interests. Agreement was finally reached on a package of regulations on 14 January 1962 (backdated to December 1961).

In the first instance, the main mechanisms were established for cereals, and these consisted of 'target prices' which the internal EC market price was supposed to achieve. From the target price a 'threshold price' or minimum import price was derived, which applied to imports from non-EC countries. The difference between the world price and the threshold price is the 'import levy', designed to protect the EC market from lower prices. Finally an 'intervention price' (below the target price) was fixed, at which level boards operating under EC legislation would buy up products to raise the internal market price towards the target level. In order to be able to export on the world market, export 'refunds' were granted. The main source of finance for the policy was the levies on agricultural imports. Regulations for the common market of other products, which were adopted subsequently, followed these general lines, with some variants for particular cases. The major agricultural markets were, therefore, based on mechanisms of intervention in internal markets and insulation from world markets resulting from the establishment of import levies. These instruments, coupled with what turned out to be high levels of internal price, were to lead to a recurrent series of crises in the ensuing years. In particular, the system of remunerative guaranteed prices and the obligation of the authorities to intervene in the markets and buy up surplus produce meant that farmers could sell as much of the main farm products as they could produce without suffering a reduced price as a result of over-supply.

What is perhaps of greater significance in the creation of the CAP is that the second paragraph of Article 39, which underlines the structural and natural disparities between agricultural regions, and the fact that agriculture 'constitutes a sector closely linked with the economy as a whole', was almost totally ignored. It was not until ten years later that the first structural improvement Directives were adopted (a much weaker legal base than Regulations, as used in the market sector), and for almost the entire history of the CAP, expenditure on structural measures and disadvantaged areas has never exceeded 7.5% of the total EC budget expenditure on agriculture, and in earlier years was normally about 4–5% of such expenditure. The very specific measures adopted to support and influence politically the agricultural industry were such that they had the effect of distinguishing those people whose economic activity was agriculture from people working in other sectors of the economy in the rural regions.

It should be noted that farm structure in Europe is very old and is largely a result of history rather than of any rational allocation of agricultural land. The most productive agricultural land in Europe is also where one finds large farms, whereas in more recently settled countries (USA, Canada, Australia, etc.), the poor land is in very large holdings so that low production per hectare is compensated for by many hectares (ranches in USA, cereal prairies in Canada, for example).

In the middle ages and from the late eighteenth to mid nineteenth centuries 'enclosures' and estate restructuring operations attempted to improve the structure of agricultural holdings, both on the continent and in the UK. However, over much of continental Europe, holdings were being fragmented by the Napoleonic laws on inheritance, whereby on the death of the farm-owner, the holding was divided among the inheriting siblings. After several generations of this process, farms were small and often in a dozen or more pieces spread all over the parish, making efficient operation of the farm very difficult.

These features of farm structure are discussed by Potter (Chapter 2).

THE AGRICULTURAL ECONOMY OF THE EU UNDER THE CAP

The security offered by an agricultural policy with relatively high guaranteed prices, and protection from competition from lower priced products from outside the Community, provided an economic environment which stimulated a great deal of scientific research and development aimed at increasing crop and animal yields, much of it financed by public funds. Figure 1 gives some examples of the results of this investment in terms of yields of crops and animals between 1973 and 1993. The data show that yields of certain crops have doubled, while yields of milk have increased by between 33% and 66%, and beef carcase weights have gone up by between 16% and 33%. In the cases of cereals, milk and beef, part of the increase is by substitution of higher yielding species for those formerly produced. However, selective breeding, more scientific production methods and better management have increased the yield of all agricultural products.

Analysis of long-term developments of any economic sector of the EU is bedevilled by the fact that the Union changes its constituent countries every few years. Beginning as the EEC of 6, it became 9 in 1973, 10 in 1981, 12 in 1986 and 15 in 1995. For the purposes of analysing changes in the parameters of the agricultural sector, two series have been used, a longer term one for EU10 countries from 1973 to 1992, and a shorter term one for EU12 (i.e. the countries which became EU12 in 1986) from 1980 to 1993.

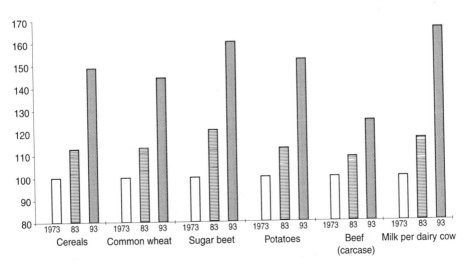

Figure 1 Index of changes in yield of farm products, France (1973 = 100).

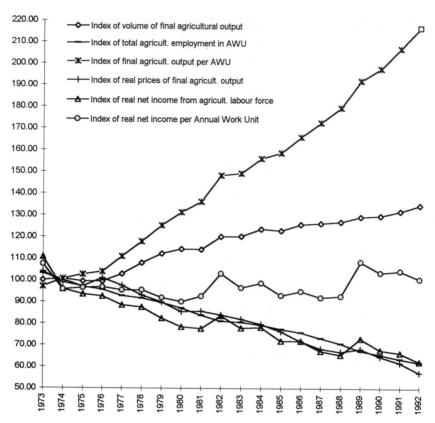

Figure 2 Indices of change in the agricultural economy of the EU10 (1973–1992).

The volume of agricultural production increased by 35% over the longer term, rising at an annual 1.5% (Figure 2): the shorter term increase was slightly less at +1.0%. However, the number of consumers was increasing at only a fraction of these annual rates of change, as the EU population increased at only 0.29% p.a. With production and consumption trends diverging at these rates, it was not surprising that the degree of self-sufficiency of certain products increased rapidly (Table 1), resulting in surpluses requiring disposal policies.

The increase in the volume of agricultural production was accompanied by a rapid decline in the labour force (Figure 2). The equivalent of nearly 4 million full-time workers (Annual Work Units – AWU) left the agriculture of EU10 between 1973 and 1993, over 6 million leaving farming in EU12 over the same period. This outflow produced impressive changes in productivity: the output per worker more than doubled.

Table 1 Degree of self-sufficiency of certain agricultural products in the EU

	Data (%)		
	1973/74, EU10	1983/84, EU10	1991/92, EU12
Total cereals, ex. rice	91	116	120
Wheat	104	134	133
Rye	98	106	122
Barley	105	120	123
Grain maize	55	84	94
Sugar	91	118	128
Fresh vegetables	94	101	106
Fresh fruit, ex. citrus	82	84	85
Wine	103	103	115
Fresh milk products	100	101	102
Whole milk powder	231	342	272
Skimmed milk powder	145	128	152
Cheese	103	107	107
Butter	98	134	121
All meat	96	101	102
Beef	95	108	107
Veal	103	110	113
Pig meat	100	102	104
Poultry meat	102	107	105
Sheep and goat meat	66	76	81

Source: Eurostat.

The increased labour productivity and increased volume of production were accompanied by a fall in real prices for farm products, in spite of the institutional framework and the security of the guaranteed prices. In fact, the real prices of final agricultural production fell by about 3% per annum, and more rapidly in recent years. As a consequence, the increased volume did not compensate for the more rapidly declining real prices. This gave added incentive to maintain returns by further increases in output, through greater intensity of production.

The result of these various developments was that the real income of the agricultural sector suffered a decline of 2.5–2.8% per annum over the last 20 years. Thus the farmers and farm workers realized labour productivity increases of the order of 4% per annum, and their incomes stood more or less still. Over the same period, the overall population income increased annually by 1.5–1.6%.

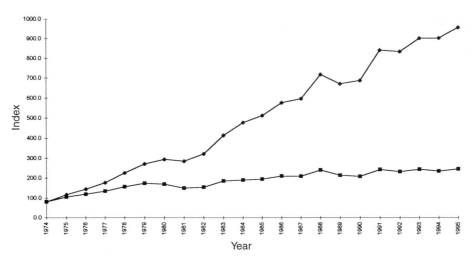

Figure 3 European Agricultural Guarantee Fund expenditure (1974 = 100): ◆, nominal; ■, real.

The expenditure of the Community budget on the CAP increased rapidly from the late 1960s onwards, as a result not only of a substantial increase in the volume of agricultural production, but also of the fact that the Community itself was growing by the accession of new Member States. As it is almost impossible to disentangle the impact of these two components of the budget increase, one can only look at overall development (Figure 3).

In nominal terms, the expenditure of the European Agricultural Guidance and Guarantee Fund (EAGGF, generally known by its French acronym FEOGA) increased by more than 850% from 1973 to 1995, or more than 10% per annum. However, in real terms the change was about 140%, or just over 4% per year. Nevertheless, this rate of increase was considerably faster than the change in agricultural output, as each incremental increase in production placed a disproportionately heavy burden on the price support system. In addition, the guarantee part of the FEOGA is more than 90% of total expenditure. The structural policies, which have increased their importance in recent years, have never utilized more than 9% of total expenditure and for most of the 1970s and 1980s structural expenditure was around 5% of the total. The balance of market to structural expenditure originally envisaged has not so far been realized, the market part consuming the overwhelming majority of EU financing. It should also be mentioned in passing that a high level of national support is also provided to the agricultural sector, as co-financing of EU structural measures and under a vast variety of purely national means of support.

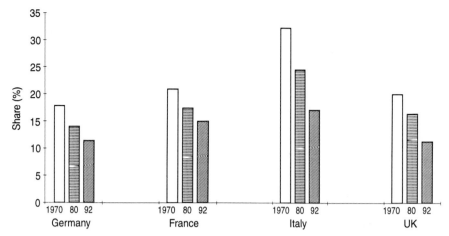

Figure 4 Share of consumer expenditure on food in the final consumption by households.

As one observer noted, 'The situation has deteriorated to such an extent that the overall total of public funds transferred to agriculture through Community and national budgets has reached a level where, even if social security transfers are excluded, it is practically equivalent to the net income of the sector' (Di Carpegna, 1992). In other words, the budgetary transfers to the agricultural sector were almost as great as the net income of the sector, in terms of the absolute sums involved. If the farmers derived little benefit from the economic developments in agriculture, did the consumer? First of all, the basic farm product is a small proportion of what the consumer pays for food, because grading, packing, processing, transport and retail margins represent the greater proportion of the retail price. Secondly, retail price indices for food usually rise less quickly than the general overall price index. Farm prices rise much less rapidly than consumers' food prices. Finally, in all countries, the proportion of total household expenditure on food has declined, sometimes by a significant percentage, as shown in Figure 4.

CAP REFORM – THE BEGINNING OF A VIRTUALLY CONTINUOUS PROCESS

After a series of difficulties and delays, and with the help of some financial compensation for farmers in Germany, Italy and Luxembourg, the 'Common Agricultural Policy' began with an alignment of cereal prices on 1 July 1967. However, even as the CAP was being established, fundamental problems were emerging for European agriculture. The European Commission study of the problems was produced in December 1968 with the title 'Memorandum on the Reform of Agriculture in the European Economic Community' (CEC, 1968), which was more generally known as the 'Mansholt Plan' after the name of the Commissioner for agriculture of the time.

It comes as some surprise to read this document today, for the Mansholt report covers almost every aspect of agricultural and rural policy which has been the subject of political debate from 1968 to the present time, with the exception of environmental questions. The decline in the growth of demand is noted and the increase in supply, with serious surpluses of some products, especially milk. The social aspects of agriculture are analysed at length: farms which are too small, increasing marginalization of farms, lack of alternative jobs in rural areas and the stress of running a farm single-handed. The need to restructure farms is recognized as it is clear that price policy is not able to provide a solution to the income problem. In order to reduce production potential it was proposed that 5 million hectares be removed from the agricultural area of Europe (about 7%), of which 4 million hectares would be turned over to forestry, the rest being for natural parks, green belts and rural holiday homes. This transfer would be of the least productive areas.

The measures proposed were not limited to agriculture, but were to be co-ordinated with other spheres of the economy. In particular, to alleviate the social consequences of an increased transfer of labour out of agriculture, job creation measures were seen as being necessary to provide alternative employment in the areas concerned. Part-time farming was seen as an interim solution. The need was to help about 5 million people to move out of farming and to completely restructure the farming industry by increasing farm-size and creating large and efficient production units of 80–120 hectares of cropland on arable farms, 40–60 cow dairy farms and 150–200 head beef-producing farms. Farms would be modernized, costs reduced and the need for high product prices changed for a policy of prudent prices linked to supply and demand.

Certain principles were spelled out for implementation of the plan: that it was acceptable to farmers; that there was variation in the measures adopted to account for regional diversity; that implementation was largely decentralized; and that the EEC contribution to the cost of implementation was limited to 50% (30% for marketing reforms). Seen from today's perspective, the Mansholt Plan incorporated much which has become the object of a variety of policies and political Acts and Treaties since then. However, at the time, it was almost revolutionary and was sunk by the first principle laid down – that the plan should be acceptable to farmers. In fact, there was violent opposition in the farming world, particularly in relation to the proposal to reduce labour and land, and in France, to the idea of a transition from small family farms to modern commercial units and the consequences of such a change on rural communities.

AGRICULTURE OR ENVIRONMENT?

The proposals for transferring land out of agriculture in the Mansholt plan signify that environmental concerns were to be addressed on land which was not farmed by the modernized agriculture which it aimed to achieve, i.e. that agricultural policy and environment are separate questions to be treated distinctly. The implication was that farmers were not custodians of the country-side, and that farming was not compatible with conservation of flora and fauna. This approach has since been completely abandoned, as will be seen in due course.

Discussions of the Mansholt Plan were lengthy, and it was not until April 1972 that three Council Directives were adopted concerning the modernization of agricultural holdings,[2] the encouragement to cease farming activities and the transfer of utilized agricultural land to improve structures,[3] and socio-economic information and the professional qualification of persons working in agriculture.[4]

Directives are a weaker form of legal instrument than Regulations, because the former must first be transposed into national regulations before they can be applied. In Italy, which had the most severe structural problems, the national measures were not enacted until 1978. It also turned out that the amounts of money on offer (to all countries) were not a sufficient incentive to encourage early retirement, compared with the returns from continuing to farm, and the impact on farm structure was minimal.

However, from then on, there was a gradual realization that farming and the environment are inextricably linked, and that a different type of policy was needed. It was a slow process.

In a Memorandum to the Council in November 1973 (CEC, 1973) entitled 'Improvement of the Common Agricultural Policy', the Commission discussed a very wide range of issues relating to the CAP, among which were: (1) the necessity to develop the CAP in close conjunction with other policies; (2) the designation of 'less favoured areas' which would receive special support measures, and new policies to encourage forestry, especially to help structural change in less favoured areas; and (3) the links between agriculture and protection of the environment, particularly production processes which do not damage the environment and the adoption of Community regulations to protect certain animal species, notably migrating birds. These were important new issues raised in an agricultural policy discussion.

---

[2] Council Directive 72/159/EEC, of 17 April 1972, OJ L96 of 23 April 1972, p. 1.
[3] Council Directive 72/159/EEC, of 17 April 1972, OJ L96 of 23 April 1972, p. 9.
[4] Council Directive 72/159/EEC, of 17 April 1972, OJ L96 of 23 April 1972, p. 15.

THE 'GREENING' OF THE CAP: PRODUCTION, BUDGET, STRUCTURES AND THE ENVIRONMENT

The discussion of agricultural policy so far has indicated that it is a complex mixture of several elements, all evolving as time passes, and each having consequences on the other. In order to try and clarify this evolution, the events are grouped below as those relating mainly to production, to the budget, to farm structure and to environmental questions.

Production

In the context of the United Kingdom's demand to reduce its contribution to the Community budget, the Council of 30 May 1980 mandated the Commission to examine Community policies with a view to avoiding budget situations 'unacceptable' to any Member State. Since agriculture was consuming the majority of the Community budget, it was natural that a particular scrutiny was directed at the CAP. Several documents resulted from this examination (CEC, 1980, 1981a, 1981b). The conclusion of this analysis was that '. . . in the present state of agricultural technology it is neither economically sound nor financially feasible to guarantee price or aid levels for unlimited quantities'. The solution proposed was the introduction of a new basic principle: co-responsibility or producer participation in the financial consequences of surplus production. Consequently, 'guarantee thresholds' were established and co-responsibility levies applied to a whole range of products under common organization of markets regimes, these being introduced in the 1982/83 farm price agreement.

As the cost of the CAP continued to rise, the European Council of June 1983 charged the Commission to examine a series of specific points in relation to the CAP, with the aim '. . . to ensure effective control of agricultural expenditure by making full use of available possibilities and examining all market organizations'. The Commission's report and proposals (published as 'Adjustment of the Common Agricultural Policy', CEC, 1983b), included extending the guarantee threshold system to a series of agricultural products not subject to this arrangement so far, and, perhaps most controversial of all, the establishment of milk quotas. As can be imagined, this series of proposals was not easily accepted by Ministers of agriculture, and it was not until March 1984 that the measures were adopted.

In a consultative document (or 'Green Paper') entitled 'Perspectives for the Common Agricultural Policy', the European Commission (1985a) underlined that the 'real problem' was 'how to ensure the maintenance of a significant number of persons in agriculture by means which do not result in unacceptable waste of economic and financial resources'. Included in a wide-ranging review of the many political and economic aspects impinging on the CAP, the document sets out a number of options in relation to the role of agriculture as a protector of the environment, the better integration of agriculture in regional development, and the question of direct income aid, so as to support incomes while avoiding the need to produce in order to obtain support.

The document posed the problem of a choice between a mixture of restrictive price policy and quantitative limits in order to achieve equilibrium on agricultural markets, or other measures to achieve a degree of social equilibrium between different regions of the Community. In the discussion contained in the document, cereal quotas and 'set-aside' are treated in fairly negative terms, implying that they are not realistic options. However, many other options are considered, including even 'buying out' farmers and the productive capacity that they control.

The Commission's leaning towards a price mechanism to achieve market balance became evident even before consultation on the 'Perspectives' document had terminated, when a 'Commission memorandum on the adjustment of the market organization for cereals' (CEC, 1985b) was presented. This memorandum rejected a drastic price reduction (of around 20%) and production quotas in favour of a co-responsibility levy coupled with stricter quality conditions for acceptance of products for intervention buying, and a change in the hierarchy of prices for different cereals.

The discussion of these documents showed that farmers wanted neither quotas and more bureaucratic control, nor direct income aids, which they distrusted. The conclusion of the Commission was that an appropriate use of price policy, co-responsibility, adjustment of conditions of intervention, diversification of production, improved quality, and structural policy would achieve the equilibrium necessary: in other words, the mixture much as before! However, it was stated that if no adaptation was forthcoming, circumstances would impose the necessary changes.

When these consultations were judged to be ended, the Commission produced a paper entitled 'A future for Community agriculture' (CEC, 1985c), which set out a series of objectives:

(1) gradually to reduce production in sectors which are in surplus and to alleviate the resulting burden on the tax-payer;
(2) to increase diversity and improve the quality of production by reference to the internal and external markets and the desires of consumers;
(3) to deal more effectively and systematically with the income problems of small family farms;
(4) to support agriculture in areas where it is essential for land-use planning, maintenance of the social balance and protection of the environment and the landscape;
(5) to make farmers more aware of environmental issues;
(6) to contribute to the development in the Community of industries which process agricultural produce, and thus involve agriculture in the profound technological changes which are taking place.

It is interesting to note the mention in the fourth objective of 'land-use planning', since there is still not (as yet) a co-ordinated policy on this question.

The policy lines set out in 'A future for Community agriculture' were followed in July 1986 by proposals to modify the structural regulations in line with the conclusions of this document. These included a system of annual premiums for farmers giving certain undertakings with regard to protection of the country-side. The beneficiaries could be farmers who undertook to pursue certain farming practices, through management contracts, for at least five years. The aid in each case was foreseen as being an annual payment per hectare. This proposal led to the adoption of Council Regulation 1760/87 (OJ L167 of 26 June 1987), which modified four structures regulations, to reduce production by promoting more extensive farming, set-aside and measures for environmental and country-side protection, with premium payments to participating farmers. However, the justification behind these measures was clearly not extensification and environmental protection *per se*, but attempts to reduce production of cereals, beef and wine. Thus environmental considerations had become an integral part of the CAP as a result of the problem of surpluses.

The 'Review of action taken to control the agricultural markets and outlook for the Common Agricultural Policy' (CEC, 1987b) comments that the budgetary cost of the CAP continued to rise dramatically ($+40\%$ from 1984 to 1987), even though a number of restrictive measures had been introduced, such as milk quotas and price stabilizer mechanisms, and that substantial savings had been obtained. Much of the cause of this budget increase was due to factors external to the EC – the collapse of world market prices (and consequently higher export refunds) and the devaluation of the US dollar relative to the ECU. However, to avoid exceeding planned budgets, further restrictive measures to control production were deemed necessary.

In September 1987, more draconian proposals were made to limit production and to transfer the consequences of over-production to farm prices and co-responsibility (CEC, 1987c). They consisted of a series of specific attempts to reduce the budget consequences of over-production in a wide range of market sectors: milk – quotas were made permanent and the quantities allowed reduced; cereals – a maximum guaranteed quantity of 155 million tonnes was introduced; oil-seeds – maximum guaranteed quantity of 3.3 million tonnes. This package of proposals was clearly a challenge to the agriculture ministers to get to grips with a market and budgetary situation which was becoming more serious with every passing year. Another element was added in January 1988 when the Commission proposed to allow for set-aside of all arable land, with at least 20% being set aside for five years or more, at the farmers' initiative (CEC, 1988a). The land set aside had to be subject to good husbandry and there would be rules for protecting the environment and natural resources. These proposals became Regulation 1094/88, which greatly enlarged the scope for using set-aside and extensification as one of the important options open to farmers. It also firmly established environmental considerations within the CAP, although outside of the mainstream majority of hectares devoted to modern agricultural production.

Budget

On 1 January 1986, Spain and Portugal joined the EEC and at the same time the EC budget ceiling moved from 1% of VAT to 1.4%, thus in principle providing some relief from the pressure caused by ever-increasing agricultural expenditure. However, in practice expenditure on agricultural markets was increasing at a rate in excess of the guideline laid down by the Summit of Fontainebleau in June 1984, which stated that 'the net expenditure relating to agricultural markets calculated on a three-yearly basis will increase less rapidly than the rate of growth of the own resources base'. (The 'own resource' base of the EC is the revenues from agricultural import levies, and a fixed percentage of the VAT applied to a common schedule of goods and services. The latter is a basis of budget transfers to the EC, whether or not VAT is actually applied to the items by Member States).

The accumulation of problems in the agricultural sector, and the unwillingness or inability of agriculture ministers to deal with them, resulted in the European Council of heads of government discussing these intricate matters in February 1988 in Brussels. A series of linked questions had to be resolved: agricultural surpluses, the budget for agriculture and other policies, the generation of the Community's 'own resources', the introduction of the Single Market. At the end of a marathon meeting which ended in the early hours of 13 February 1988, after two days and two nights, the crisis had been resolved (for details, see Bulletin of the EC, no. 2-1988).

Agreement was reached on the origin and the ceiling of the Community's own resources. This consisted of an application rate of 1.4% of the assessment base for VAT, and a rate in relation to the sum of the other revenues to create a new base representing the sum of gross national product at market prices of the Member States. The annual growth rate of agricultural expenditure could not exceed 74% of the annual growth rate of Community Gross National Product. Special provisions were introduced to deal with depreciating the value of agricultural stocks, which were outside this limitation, and a new monetary reserve was created to resolve the problem of the $US/ECU exchange rate affecting the EC budget. An 'early warning system' was introduced into agricultural budget management (known now as the 'guideline') so that expenditure that began to deviate from established patterns could be detected well in advance, and corrective action taken.

The Council agreed to the introduction of new agricultural stabilizers, as had been proposed, and the set-aside measure, including details of how it should function and the levels of EC contribution to the compensatory premiums. Some changes of detail were made on the new stabilizers, such as a guarantee threshold of 160 million tonnes for cereals (instead of the 155 million proposed), but in broad terms the entire Commission package was agreed.

The reform and co-ordination of the structural funds foreseen in the Single Act was agreed, as well as the doubling of the budget. The priority objectives of the structural funds were agreed, as well as the criteria for determining eligibility for support from these funds, which include rural regions and protection of the environment.

Structures

A communication entitled 'Stocktaking of the Common Agricultural Policy' in February 1975 (CEC, 1975) underlined all of the well-known problems and indicated that, in spite of a series of proposals to tackle fundamental difficulties of the CAP, the Council had not taken decisions of sufficient rigour to deal with the situation. To underline that the market situation in particular was a dynamic one, the Commission undertook to provide short-, medium- and long-term forecasts. Regarding structures, the document complained that the existing Directives had been adopted only partially by Member States and that two Member States had not yet implemented any of the necessary measures.

In February 1974, the Commission submitted a proposal to the Council concerning forestry measures (CEC, 1974), which was to complement the Directive 72/160 on improving agricultural structures and encourage the conversion of land unsuitable for farming to trees. It was never adopted by the Council.

The Council Directive of April 1975 (75/268) on mountain and hill farming, and farming in certain less-favoured areas, allowed Member States to designate such areas as less-favoured and provide the special financial support which has assured the survival of farming in many areas where it may otherwise have disappeared. Since its inception, the areas designated as less-favoured have increased, in some cases substantially, as it is seen as an instrument for providing 'social' support in areas where alternative employment may be scarce. While not an objective of the less-favoured area Directive, assuring the survival of farming in many areas where it might otherwise have been abandoned certainly had environmental benefits. LFAs are usually in 'marginal' farming areas, which, although marginal in terms of agricultural productivity, are usually biologically rich, supporting communities and species that would no longer be sustained if farming became unprofitable and such areas were abandoned. Examples of this are the LFAs in the Highlands and Islands of Scotland, in Ireland, in the Pyrenees, and the transhumance pastoral farming systems of the Iberian peninsula, which support a wide range of raptors and other avian species (see Donazár et al., Chapter 5).

The concept of less-favoured areas was perhaps the first in which the characteristics of the land and its use were taken into account in implementing policy measures. The imbalance of budgetary expenditure in the direction of agricultural price guarantees generated reflections on the efficiency of expenditure of the various structural funds. The outcome was a communication to the Council entitled 'Increasing the effectiveness of the Community's structural funds' (CEC, 1983a). This document proposed to stop financing what were essentially national policies which had no guarantee of contributing to convergence within the EC, to de-compartmentalize the specific structural funds. The aim was to introduce a Community development and structural adjustment policy for priority activities which would be implemented with support from all structural funds in a fully co-ordinated way.

In this general context of re-assessing the relationships between agricultural price guarantees, budget expenditure, and the co-ordination of structural actions, the Commission made proposals for a new Council regulation on improving the efficiency of agricultural structures in October 1983 (CEC, 1983c). The explanatory memorandum that introduces the proposals makes it clear that the structural Directives of 1972 had achieved very little in terms of farm restructuring, land transfer, or farm development, except for increasing intensity and output of products already in surplus. Furthermore, the exploitation of these Directives had been very uneven between Member States, in a way which did not correspond to the relative severity of the problems.

The new proposal removed a condition for eligibility, applied up to that time, which specified a lower limit for development plans. These had to achieve an income comparable to that of non-farm occupations in the region for one to two labour units. This condition has excluded many small farms from benefiting. The new proposal aimed particularly at adapting holdings to improve quality, reduce costs of production, improve living conditions and save energy. It also added a new criterion for support – 'measures for the protection and improvement of the environment'. The proposal also excluded investment aid if numbers of cows or sows were to increase beyond a maximum number per holding with conditions of home-produced feed attached; it debarred all investment aid for eggs and poultry meat; and it disallowed aid where the outcome of the investment aid would produce an income in excess of 120% of the regional reference income.

This proposal was to become the new agricultural structures Regulation 797/85 (OJ L93 of 30 March 1985). However, there were important differences between the original proposal and the final Regulation:

(a) what had been proposed as specific measures in Less-favoured Areas became 'Specific regional measures', and
(b) proposals to improve or maintain the natural landscape became specific measures for 'National aid in environmentally sensitive areas'.

The report 'The future of rural society', which was indicated in the 'Review...' document of August 1987, appeared in 1988 (CEC, 1988c). This report came from a multi-disciplinary group drawn from a number of Commission departments. It covers a range of subject matter much greater than agricultural policy questions, including land-use and environmental pressures, demography, part-time farming and rural unemployment, diversification of the rural economy, energy, infrastructure and industry, tourism and services, and many other aspects. It develops a classification for the problems encountered, stresses the importance of considering these characteristics in integrated planning for rural development, and underlines the importance of the structural funds in the context of finding solutions. From an agricultural policy point of view, this document is an important marker, indicating that politicians are at last beginning to understand that agriculture has close economic links to the locality, and that pursuing a distinct policy for one industry in a rural area to the exclusion of others is not sensible. It is the rural regions themselves which need support, not just some of the people working in them.

Forestry, that other major user of land, was the focus of a communication and specific proposals in November 1988, when the Commission produced a 'Community strategy and action programme for the forestry sector' (CEC, 1988d). As there is no common forestry policy, this document generally proposed modifications to existing structural and forest protection regulations to create a more cohesive pattern of legislation. As forestry covers a land area equivalent to 40% of the agricultural area of the EC, there is no doubt about its economic and environmental importance, and a more rational policy framework was long overdue. In May 1989, this series of proposals was adopted by the Council. In addition to adaptations of structural and protection regulations, the Council modified a regulation on the co-ordination of Structural Funds to allow a financial contribution to develop and optimally utilize woodlands in rural areas in the Community.

The environment

Introduction of environmental considerations into agricultural policy discussions were linked to the first 'Environmental Action Programme'. This was adopted by the Council on 22 November 1973 (OJ C112, 20 December 1973), and included a specific section relating to the ecological consequences of modern production techniques applied in agriculture. The programme stated that it was necessary to carry out a study to establish the effects of such techniques as monoculture, intensive use of fertilizers, excessive use of pesticides, intensive livestock production and the associated risk of organic pollution and microbial contamination, as well as the repercussions of land 'improvements' such as draining marshes, disrupting water flows and removing hedges.

This proposal did not come from the Agriculture department, but from the Environment department of the Commission, signifying that other 'stakeholders' were entering the discussion on the effects of agriculture on the environment of rural areas.

Figure 5 Helicopter spraying pesticides on arable monoculture. The Environmental Action Programme stated the need to establish the environmental effects of such techniques. (Photo by C.H. Gomersall/RSPB.)

The second 'Environmental Action Programme' adopted by the Council on 17 May 1977 reinforced the endeavours of the former programme to establish a better understanding of the environmental impacts of farming and forestry practices, and to collect objective data. It is in the context of this environmental action programme that the idea of 'measures relating to rural land-use' appeared. Was this an embryo land-use policy?

Environmental considerations took on a more concrete form with a proposal for a Council Regulation on action by the Community relating to the environment (CEC, 1982). This was in response to an initiative whereby the European Parliament had inserted a specific line into the EC budget for 'Community operations concerning the environment'. The emphasis was a shift from remedial to preventative actions for environmental protection. The proposed instruments would provide financial support for two types of priority action: the development of new technologies which are 'clean' (causing little or no pollution) and are more economical of natural resources, in particular raw materials; and the protection of the natural environment in certain sensitive areas of the Community.

The latter action was explicitly linked to the conservation of wild birds and Directive 79/409 (OJ L103 of 25 April 1979). Support was to be in the form of direct grant aid to public authorities or recognized bodies for projects, including land acquisition, contributing towards the protection of the natural environment in sensitive areas of Community interest, such as those covered by Directive 79/409/EEC, the Berne Convention on the conservation of European wildlife and natural habitats, the Bonn Convention on the conservation of migratory species of wild animals, and the Protocol to the Barcelona Convention for the protection of the Mediterranean Sea against pollution. Expenditure intended to compensate for restricting economic activities in such areas in order to safeguard habitats was also proposed as being eligible.

Environmental concerns were placed firmly in the centre of political debate by the signing of the Single European Act in 1986 (CEC, 1986), with its stated objective to integrate environmental protection requirements into the Community's other policies. The text of the Single European Act relating to environment states:

1. Action by the Community relating to the environment shall have the following objectives: (i) to preserve, protect and improve the quality of the environment; (ii) to contribute towards protecting human health; (iii) to ensure a prudent and rational utilization of natural resources.
2. Action by the Community relating to the environment shall be based on the principles that preventive action should be taken, that environmental damage should as a priority be rectified at source, and that the polluter should pay. Environmental protection requirements shall be a component of the Community's other policies.

Although the Single European Act virtually does not mention agriculture, a subsequent communication of the Commission ('Making a success of the Single Act: A new frontier for Europe', CEC, 1987a) discusses agriculture at some length. It recognizes that most farms are family run and that farming has a major role in protecting the countryside. It is acknowledged that efforts are needed to help rural development and that forms of income support other than market prices are needed, particularly in view of the great diversity of the agricultural situation across the Community of 12.

An important part of the document is a section on 'The preservation of the European pattern of agriculture and the outlook', which examines the role of farming and farmers in the social, rural development and environmental aspects of the countryside. A second set of measures were introduced by Regulation 1760/87 (OJ L167, 26 June 1987) which amended previous legislation with the following: introduction of financial aids designed to encourage conversion and extensification of production; the removal of the ceiling on strictly national investment aids for the protection and improvement of the environment; the introduction of an annual premium per hectare for farmers applying farming practices compatible with the protection of the environment; and the granting of additional aid for agricultural vocational training where this is geared to reorientation of production, protection of the environment and woodland management.

In June 1988 the doubling of the Structural Funds between 1987 and 1993 was agreed and, in December 1988, the Council adopted a set of four regulations on reform of the structural funds and their operation. Regulation 4256/88 (OJ L374, 31 December 1988) deals with the European Agricultural Guidance and Guarantee Fund expenditure in the Guidance section and the relationship to agricultural structural policy. Among a series of actions for which new finance became available was 'protection of the environment and maintenance of the countryside'.

The environmental aspects of agriculture were given greater prominence when the Commission produced a communication entitled 'Environment and Agriculture' in June 1988 (CEC, 1988b). This makes the link to efforts limiting production, stating 'It follows that the measures which now need to be taken to ensure a better control of production must be such so as to guarantee that all future progress in the sector is achieved in harmony with environmental requirements, and that an environmental equilibrium is eventually re-established in the zones affected from this point of view'. This document identifies problems, specifically the deterioration of terrestrial habitats and extinction of both flora and fauna, water quality and leaching of nitrates from agriculture, and pesticide concentrations. It also cites soil degradation and erosion, ammonia evaporation from intensive livestock rearing, heavy metal accumulation in soils, and undesirable landscape changes through deforestation, hedgerow removal, drainage of wetlands, etc. Existing policy measures are listed and the fact that Member States are slow to come forward with proposals for EC finance is noted. A series of further measures envisaged are described in broad terms, and there are hints that conditions may be imposed for certain instruments. General principles are set out relating to actions on pesticides, on intensive livestock and crop production. Finally, a series of forthcoming proposals is listed. This statement is a welcome admission that there are clear links between production orientated policies and the consequences for the rural environment.

In January 1989, the Commission produced a proposal for a Council Directive aimed specifically at 'the protection of fresh, coastal and marine waters against pollution caused by nitrates from diffuse sources' (OJ C54 of 3 March 1989, p.4). Not surprisingly, one of the sources was nitrate fertilizers used in agriculture. The proposal also contained limits on livestock numbers per hectare by species. However, when the proposal was finally adopted by the Council in December 1991 (Directive 91/676/EEC, OJ L375, 31 December 1991), the title had become much more specific – 'Protection of waters against pollution caused by nitrates from agricultural sources' – and the livestock limits were replaced by 'codes of good agricultural practice'. These were broader ranging and, linked to other measures in Annex III of the Directive, quite specific in limiting the excessive release of animal and mineral nitrates into water.

Environmental aspects of agricultural policy were also part of a proposal in July 1989 (CEC, 1989) to modify the existing structural regulations in order to speed up the adjustment of farm structure to new objectives of policy. Among other measures proposed was a substantial increase in hectare payments for environmentally sensitive areas, which were adopted in March 1990 (Reg. 752/90, OJ L83, 30 March 1990).

Further encouragement to adopt more environmentally friendly farming practices came in August 1990 (CEC, 1990) with a proposal for a Council Regulation for 'the introduction and the maintenance of agricultural production methods compatible with the requirements of the protection of the environment and the maintenance of the countryside'. This proposal aimed at strengthening existing structures policy by offering significant payments per hectare for following specific management practices, notably using less fertilizer and chemicals, but allowing for other wide-ranging schemes for the upkeep of land. Much of the pressure for less intensive farming was coming not only from the environmental lobby, but also from the continuing and worsening situation of over supply on agricultural markets. Stocks of cereals and beef in particular were increasing at an alarming rate, with an obvious consequence on the EC budget. Something more effective had to be done.

A NEW PHILOSOPHY – THE 'MacSHARRY REFORM'

The Commission was already working on drastic reductions in prices coupled with area payments and premiums on animals, which would be governed by strict compliance conditions. Elements of the proposals were leaked to the press and, in January 1991, agriculture Commissioner MacSharry had to make a statement to the Council. The general background and principles of the reform of the CAP were set out in a 'milestone' document released on 1 February 1991 entitled 'The development and future of the Common Agricultural Policy' (CEC, 1991a). The most controversial proposal was to reduce cereal and oil-seed prices by about 35% over three years, to pay compensations per hectare to farmers, and to introduce the compulsory set-aside of land as a condition of receiving the compensatory payments.

Furthermore, the compensations were to be differential – to pay less per hectare to large farms than small farms, and farms of below a certain area of these crops would not have to set land aside. At the same time, the existing instruments of cereal co-responsibilty levies, maximum guaranteed quantities and stabilizer mechanisms, would be abolished. Extension of the voluntary set-aside scheme was proposed, as well as a new long-term set-aside 'with particular objectives of protecting the natural environment and ecologically friendly afforestation of agricultural land'. Other proposals included reduction of EC milk quotas coupled with compensatory allowances for a limited number of cows, and reducing the beef intervention price by 15% with premiums to be paid per beef animal and suckler cow, subject to a maximum stocking rate per hectare and maximum number per farm. For sheep, premiums were also proposed subject to maximum numbers per farm.

As well as proposals to reform the production side of agriculture, a series of

Figure 6 Mixed wild flowers in a traditionally managed cereal field in the Massif Central, central France. Such management can be supported through the Accompanying Measures. (Photo by D.J. Pain.)

'accompanying measures' were introduced to encourage farmers to use environmentally friendly methods. These were to be implemented through annual aids per hectare, paid for extensive farming, for conserving or re-introducing the diversity and quality of the natural environment, and for undertaking the environmental upkeep of land abandoned by farmers or other persons living in rural communes. These measures represented a significant change in agricultural policy.

As expected, these ideas received a hostile reaction from farmers, and from most Ministers of Agriculture. However, the Commission persevered and, in July 1991, produced a follow-up to the 'reflections' paper of February (CEC, 1991b) which contained similar background material but included detailed proposals for the market sectors, for an agri-environmental action programme for the afforestation of agricultural land, and for a reinforced early retirement scheme. The budget implications were also detailed, being an annual 2300 million ECU for the market measures and 4000 million ECU over five years for the accompanying measures. On the market side, the document comments that the amount is 1000 million ECU less than continuation of the policies in force at the time.

While the political debate on these proposals raged on, the earlier proposal to reinforce the voluntary set-aside contained in the structures regulations was adopted by the Council in July 1991 (Regulation 2328/91, OJ L218 of 6 August 1991). A further encouragement to environmentally sound farming came with the adoption of Council Regulation 2092/91 on organic production of agricultural products and their labelling (OJ L198 of 22 July 1991).

In October 1991, the legal texts of the 'MacSharry Reform' (as it was known by then) were published, and the Council got down to serious consideration of reforming the CAP. A proposal for oil-seeds had been delivered in July, following a General Agreement on Tariffs and Trade (GATT) 'panel' on the existing oil-seeds régime (CEC, 1991c, 1991d, 1991e).

After many months of hard bargaining, and the defence of its proposals by the Commission against a bitter campaign by farmers predicting the end of conventional agriculture (they wanted to keep the status quo), the 'MacSharry Reform' was adopted by the Council in June 1992. There were some significant changes from the original proposals, the most noteworthy being that compensatory payments were no longer differentiated according to the area of arable crops on the farm. However, the accompanying measures were modified very little and now offer a real opportunity for farmers to adopt alternative land management practices (OJ L215 of 30 July 1992, pp. 82, 96). Premiums are paid for more extensive farming for a period of at least five years, and there are payments for environmental set-aside, which must be undertaken for at least 20 years.

These regulations marked a major change in thinking on the role of agricultural policy and the place of farming and farmers in land management and rural development. The one weakness seems to be that while the best land for conservation is that which has not already been farmed to a degree of intensity (and where support is most needed but least paid), the policy which was evolving provided support mainly to farmers adopting a change in current land-use practices. The links between agriculture and other activities in the countryside were strengthened further by the structural funds. 'The future of Community initiatives under the structural funds', produced in June 1993 (CEC, 1993b), underlines the need for active organization and local initiative if rural development is to be achieved successfully. This means involving all of the people concerned, not just farmers.

AGRICULTURE AND ENVIRONMENT

Concerns about development and the environment were addressed by the Council in a Resolution on 'a Community programme of policy and action in relation to the environment and sustainable development' (OJ C138 of 17 May 1993). The characteristics of sustainable development are identified as: maintenance of the overall quality of life, continuing access to natural resources, avoidance of lasting environmental damage.

The European Parliament had already called on the Commission to 'make environmental protection a central objective of the CAP'. . . 'and subsidy by unit of surface area in the interests of nature conservancy' (CEC, 1993c). The programme of policy action included these elements, but was less all-embracing, with a target of 15% of agricultural area under management contracts and management plans for all rural areas in danger by the year 2000.

The creation of the cohesion financial instrument in the context of the Treaty on European Union signed in Maastricht in 1992, added further financial resources for environmental projects contributing to the objectives of Article 130r of the Treaties establishing the European Communities (which had been introduced by the Single European Act). Article 130r sets out the objectives of Community action relating to the environment and states that environmental protection requirements shall be a component of the Community's other policies. The cohesion instrument is aimed at Member States with a per capita GNP of less than 90% of the Community average, and this targets Ireland, Greece, Portugal and Spain in particular. As environmental considerations usually come second to economic ones, this funding is important in trying to finance environmental improvements. The full Cohesion Fund, with financial resources from 1993 to 1999 totalling 15 150 million ECU, was established in May 1994 (Regulation 1164/94, OJ L130 of 25 May 1994).

Set-aside of arable land under CAP reform was still a subject of lively debate, and the Commission raised a number of questions in a document entitled 'Possible developments in the Policy of arable land set-aside, particularly relating to non-rotational set-aside, maximum rates of set-aside, the transfer between producers of set-aside and the potential conflicts between short-term and long-term set-aside' (CEC, 1993a). In June 1993, the rate of non-rotational set-aside was fixed at the rotational rate plus 5%, making 20% in total, with certain exceptions. In September of the same year, detailed rules on set-aside were set down in two regulations that specified which actions and uses of set-aside land were authorized, and which were ineligible for compensatory payments (OJ L238 of 23 September 1993, pp. 19, 21).

It must be clearly said that set-aside is not a land-use policy which aims at the most rational exploitation of land characteristics, but a device for reducing supply of certain crops. In addition, its geographic distribution is very uneven, because it depends on the structure of agriculture and the distribution of arable area. In effect, set-aside is predominantly found in northern Europe, where farms are large.

The extent of set-aside and Environmentally Sensitive Areas

Table 2 shows the uptake of the voluntary five-year set-aside by Member States over the period 1988–1993, and the distribution of the obligatory set-aside applied to 'professional' farmers in 1994/95 under the CAP reform regulations. About 1.8 million hectares were involved in the voluntary scheme (2.6% of arable area), which was mainly in Italy (45%), Germany (27%), France (13%) and the UK (9%). However, expressed as a percentage of arable land, the area in France is lower than the other three.

Obligatory set-aside removed 6.0 million hectares from farming in 1994/95, or nearly 9% of the arable area. Because this set-aside is related to individual farm size, the distribution by Member State is quite different from the voluntary set-aside, the greatest area being in France, followed by Germany, Spain and the UK. The arable area set-aside varied from less than 1% in Greece to 12% in Germany.

Environmentally Sensitive Areas constitute nearly 4.6 million hectares, or 3.6% of the Utilized Agricultural Area (UAA) of EU12. At Member State level the ESAs vary from almost nothing to over 20% of the UAA in Germany (Table 3).

The Structural Funds were made more effective by a series of amendments to the original regulations in July 1993, and in April 1994 the list of rural areas able to benefit from 'Objective 5(b)' structural fund finance was published (OJ L96 of 14 April 1994). Objective 5(b) relates to the development of rural areas through

Table 2 Areas of set-aside under different regulations

	Areas in five-year set-aside, 1988–1993*		Areas in annual set-aside, 1994/95†	
	Hectares	As % of arable ha	Hectares (000s)	As % of arable ha
Belgium	814	1	26	3.2
Denmark	8 224	3	269	10.5
France	227 111	1.3	1934	10.9
Germany	483 186	4.2	1386	12.1
Greece	714	0	18	0.6
Ireland	1 752	0.2	37	4.9
Italy	792 944	8.9	249	2.8
Luxembourg	90	0.2	2	3.6
Netherlands	15 738	1.8	14	1.6
Portugal	0	0	67	2.3
Spain	89 578	0.6	1340	8.8
UK	155 255	2.4	662	10
Total	1 775 406	2.6	6004	8.9

*Source: Agricultural Situation in the Community (1993) and The Agricultural Situation in the European Union (1994), European Commission.
†Source: European Commission (1995), internal document.

Figure 7 View of set-aside farmland in the UK, where uptake was fairly high. (Photo by A. Hay/RSPB.)

Table 3 Environmentally Sensitive Areas (ESAs) in the European Union (by area and percentage of Utilized Agricultural Area – UAA)

	ESAs	
	Hectares (000s)	As % of UAA
Denmark	128	4.6
Germany	2560	21.6
France	115	0.4
Italy	944	5.5
Netherlands	76	3.8
UK	741	4.0

Source: European Commission data for 1990.

preservation of the countryside and the environment, rural and tourist infra-structures, development of forestry activities, etc.

That the thinking of leading political figures had evolved to accept the concept of the integration of agriculture and environmental concerns was clearly demonstrated in a landmark speech by the European Commissioner for Agriculture and Rural Development in June 1995 (Fischler, 1995c). In it he acknowledges that the initiative for environmental protection did not come from the mechanisms of the CAP, but from those concerned with the environment. However, the conclusion drawn was that 'Protecting the environment has to be an integral component of a strategy for the agricultural sector: it must flow from the CAP itself'.

EASTERN EUROPE AND THE CAP

The Summit of European Heads of State of Government held in Copenhagen in June 1993 agreed that the associated countries in central and eastern Europe could become members of the European Union if they desired. Accession could take place as soon as an associated country is able to assume the obligations of membership by satisfying the economic and political conditions required. This opening of the European Union to the CEECs[5] immediately raised questions on how the CAP could be extended to these countries, without considerable difficulties resulting. If EU price levels were applied to the CEECs, a great stimulus to production would take place, just as the EU was getting to grips with the surpluses of previous years.

The prospects of enlargement of the EU to the east caused a flurry of activity, resulting in a number of studies and reports on how the CAP could be implemented in the CEECs. Some of these reports concluded that the CAP could not be extended to eastern Europe without first being radically changed, thereby avoiding a huge increase in the cost of the CAP in a Europe of 25 countries. The reforms proposed usually consisted of lowering EU price supports to world price levels, further decoupling of direct payments to farmers and their reduction over time, and the introduction of income support payments linked to environmental services. Others argue that the parlous condition of CEEC agriculture and lack of both investment and available capital for this are such that it will take years before Eastern European agriculture can recover to a condition of reasonable productivity.

The real situation is somewhere between these two. It is clear that a great deal depends on economic and institutional improvements in the CEECs, on reform of the land market, and on the availability of resources for investment and regeneration of a viable farming industry. A series of reports for each of the ten countries, produced by the Commission in July 1995, makes it clear that circumstances vary considerably from one to another. Although there is a

---

[5] CEECs: Poland, Hungary, Czech Republic, Slovak Republic, Slovenia, Romania, Bulgaria, Lithuania, Latvia, Estonia.

significant production potential, it is severely hampered by lack of capital, major farm structure problems, and very inefficient and monopolistic food industries. These problems are being addressed, but it will take at least another five to ten years to achieve significant progress. In conclusion, CEEC agriculture is less in need of a high level of price and income support for farmers, than of targeted assistance for restructuring, investment for modernization and diversification of agriculture and the food industry, and improvement of rural infrastructure.

Over the period of time leading up to eastwards enlargement of the EU, the agricultural policies and industries of both the EU and the CEECs will evolve, and it is the 'evolution rather than revolution' approach which was stressed by Commissioner Fischler in Warsaw (Fischler, 1995a). While the EU progresses towards a policy of decoupled payments, rural development and environmentally considerate agriculture, the CEECs have several basic problems to resolve before they can merge into an enlarged European Union. The results of these changes on land-use and the environment need to be closely monitored, so that the CEECs do not repeat the earlier mistakes of the EU in developing over-intensive, chemically dependent farming systems driven by maximizing profits with little regard for the impacts on native flora and fauna. Western European experience can greatly help the East in this context. The relationship of continuing development of the CAP and the implications for expansion of the EU to the CEECs was examined in some detail in a study on alternative strategies in this context (CEC, 1995). The probable consequences of continuing the status quo in policy, of radical reform, and of further developing the '1992' (or MacSharry) approach are examined. The clear conclusion is that further development of the '1992' policy, implying less reliance on price support, compensation by direct payments where necessary, and greater integration of market policies, rural development and environmental policies is the best approach to the future for both the EU and the CEECs.

WINDS OF CHANGE

Over recent years, more forward-thinking farmers have realized that internal and external pressures will force the CAP to change further. The 'MacSharry Reform' had hardly been implemented before farmers became concerned about even more radical change in the future, caused by pressures from conclusion of the GATT Uruguay Round, enlargement of the Community to include Austria, Sweden and Finland on 1 January 1995, and potential future expansion to central and eastern European countries. The UK National Farmers Union faced the problem squarely in a discussion document entitled 'Real choices' (NFU, 1994), which concludes that future policy is a choice between input quotas and set-aside or a move to decoupling, i.e. the removal of intervention price support and direct income support from the public exchequer. While input quotas would restrict supply and raise prices, import tariffs and export subsidies would be needed to prevent international competition. Decoupling would allow prices to fall to market clearing levels, although the whole cost of income support would fall on public funds, whereas the classic CAP puts much of the burden on the consumer.

Other prominent farmers were realizing that the CAP had to be modified in the direction proposed by environmentalists, and that 'the situation in the countryside is economically and politically unsustainable' as Oliver Walston (1994) put it. Such forward thinking people called for CAP subsidies to be redirected from production support to maintenance of the landscape and wildlife, cutting pollution, and rebuilding rural economies. Even international chemical companies began experimenting with pure organic farming (*Financial Times*, 1994a). The fact that the countryside was suffering continuing damage was highlighted by the Department of the Environment, who reported an annual loss of 16 000 miles of hedgerow in England and Wales between 1990 and 1993 (*The Times*, 1994).

Towards the end of 1994 and during the whole of 1995, an increasingly voluble debate ensued on further reform of the CAP, particularly in the UK and British media. The Royal Institute of International Affairs proposed that agricultural subsidies to farmers should be phased out in favour of a 'safety net' of social and environmental payments in rural areas (*Financial Times*, 1994b). The relationship between compliance with the non-rotational set-aside obligation, environmental set-aside, and the use of set-aside for afforestation purposes was examined by the Commission, and a more clear situation established between the options open to farmers (CEC, 1994).

The fact that farming subsidies had become very visible to the public, and may be subject to limits per farm business at some point in time (as in the USA) was explained to farmers by Walston (1995). He pointed out that if subsidies were paid for environmental reasons, there would be no logical reason to limit payments to individual farms, and that no discrimination between farms or regions could be entertained, since the environment encompasses all land. The NFU president disagreed, saying that it could only lead to more bureaucracy and cost (*Financial Times*, 1995a), but the NFU saw clearly that if support payments were separated from production, then clear reasons would be needed for their justification. Others were already convinced that safeguarding, managing and enhancing the function of rural areas as an environmental reservoir would be the prime justification for support to agriculture in the future (*Financial Times*, 1995b). However, it was admitted that such payments go most easily to farmers who need not change their farming very much to obtain them. The Royal Society for the Protection of Birds (RSPB) joined in the discussion, arguing that farming should become more market orientated by phasing out production subsidies, supply controls and border protection, with subsidies being paid only for achieving wider environmental and social objectives (RSPB, 1995). The Society set out a sequence of possible policy decisions and a timetable by which its proposals could be implemented within a period of 15 years from 1995. The Country Landowners Association (CLA) took the view that such ideas were too confined to the environment, and that not only agriculture had to be maintained in good shape, but also the whole rural economy through job promotion, better transport and adequate health, welfare, education, retail and community services (*Farmers Weekly*, 1995a). The CLA backed this up with a further policy paper later in the year, which aimed to reduce the constraints of supply control and high dependence on subsidies, and to replace them progressively with decoupled payments, which would themselves be phased out in favour of countryside management programmes and alternative rural enterprise (Agra Europe, 1995a). It was suggested that the 1992 agri-environment schemes would never have a significant impact at the current levels of funding.

The dual role of agriculture was clearly understood by the politicians, as evidenced by an informal Council of agriculture ministers in March 1995 (Agence Europe, 1995), but this also showed that the debate would be extremely difficult and was far from over. The Commission rejected calls for drastic cuts in support, but was in favour of a consistent evolution away from targeting agricultural markets and towards a comprehensive rural development policy which embraces protection of the agricultural environment (Fischler, 1995a). A few days later, this approach was put in the context of 'sustainable agriculture and rural development' in which environmental, social and economic factors are part of a comprehensive decision making framework (Fischler, 1995b). To put this in concrete terms, the Commission approved grants for 'LEADER' programmes worth 1.4 billion ECU in six Member States. 'LEADER' is the French acronym for links between actions for development of the rural economy (Liaisons Entre Actions de Développement de l'Economie Rural). These provide global grants or integrated operational programmes to which Member States can apply for financial assistance in the context of rural development (for an explanation of LEADER, see OJ C180 of 1 July 1994).

The NFU 'Real choices' document of March 1994 was followed up in March 1995 by 'Taking real choices forward' (NFU, 1995). This examined in more detail a series of policy questions, including 'decoupling' of payments from production and environmental policy. On decoupling, it concludes that it would be extremely important that agriculture improves its marketing performance and diversifies production – something which is not universally recognized. Decoupling is analysed at some length with regard to environmental policies, as it is recognized that a series of alternative applications exist. For this reason, certain objectives are set out: to match land-use to land capacity, to manage existing wildlife and landscape features, to restore wildlife habitats and landscapes, to reduce the intensity of husbandry, and to increase the diversity of farming systems. It is concluded that these objectives may be achieved through a combination of different means, and that any changes in policy should be assessed in relation to their contribution to these objectives.

A paper published by the European Policy Forum (Josling & Tangermann, 1995) set out a series of steps which could be pursued to 'complete the CAP reform', of which the first suggestion is to expand the option of voluntary set-aside with compensation payments.

The British Minister of Agriculture expressed the view that radical change of the CAP before enlargement to the east is unavoidable (Waldegrave, 1995), which elicited a remark from EuroMP Terry Wynn (1995) that it would be helpful if the Minister were to enlighten everybody on what his proposals were. This correspondence drew a stinging rejoinder from the Swedish Minister of Agriculture:

> The EU is an organization which is based on free trade and free competition within all fields — with the exception of agriculture. With its regulations, quotas and five-year plans, the CAP resembles more the reincarnation of the Soviet system of planned economy than a concept for co-operation in a modern Europe. Sweden considers that Europe must retain some payments related to the agricultural sector, but this must be primarily connected to regional politics and environmental undertakings. The intention cannot be that most of today's payments go to those who need them least: the intensive large-scale farms. This is not survival of the fittest, but rather survival of the fattest. . . (Winberg, 1995).

The preponderance of production-related payments was cited as a reason why they could not be reduced, since farmers would not agree (Richardson, 1995). However, Commissioner Fischler asked German farmers if '. . . we can tell the tax-payer forever that compensation is an agricultural function?'. He concluded that paying farmers to perform their vital environmental role would have to become a priority (Agra Europe, 1995b). In a study of the CAP and its future development for the Swedish government, Astrom (1995) noted that protection of the environment was not one of the objectives for agricultural policy enshrined in the Treaty of Rome, but concluded that

> . . . a politically sustainable agricultural policy must be able to handle both the positive and the negative effects of agriculture on the environment, thus winning the confidence of the public. This is a crucial weakness in current policy, and it must be corrected while adapting CAP to modern needs.

The farming press pointed out that proposals for radical farm policy reform in the USA would certainly have repercussions for the debate going on in Europe (*Farmers Weekly*, 1995b), while farmers in the USA had become so entangled in the support system that they preferred reduced subsidies to some of the more radical alternatives (*Financial Times*, 1995c).

From all of these ideas, there are a number of different 'models' which can be developed (and are developing spontaneously), and which can be envisaged in isolation or in combination with each other.

One option is a form of dual development where large commercial farms continue more or less as before, but possibly with lower levels of inputs, while the smaller farms derive their income from a combination of farming and other gainful activities – the so-called pluriactive households. For these farms to continue, a necessary condition is the availability in the area of other employment or business opportunities. It is often the lack of such alternative earning opportunities which prevents this type of development taking place. In short, investment and development in the non-farm sector of the local economy is needed to provide other opportunities. The way in which farm households adjust to changing agricultural and economic circumstances was the subject of an in-depth study covering 12 European countries and spanning five years, carried out by the Arkleton Trust (1992) for the European Commission. This study shows clearly that the pluriactive, multi-income farm is already a very common model in all parts of Europe, and that the evolution of farm family behaviour can be linked to a number of analytical factors.

Another possible development is a move to sustainable farming systems which have much lower input levels or are even biologically closed systems. This implies lower intensity, with lower costs, although the revenue achieved may still be adequate since both output and costs are reduced. Such farms would qualify for biological labelling of their products, which normally obtains a price premium.

A further potential development is a system of conditional support, within the framework of the classic CAP model, where support is provided under conditions of cross-compliance related to agricultural practices and environmental criteria.

A variant of the above model would be a multi-purpose agriculture which provides 'contract services' of food production, countryside stewardship, nature conservation, biological diversity assurance, etc. in return for payment under contractual terms. Pressures from the 'nature lobby' and the 'countryside lobby' could push agriculture in the direction of this model, since there is little doubt that the non-farmers outnumber the farmers, and debate on such issues is becoming more vociferous.

Ideally, all or several of these alternatives could be combined in the complete integration of rural policy into regional policy. This would involve support for the whole regional economy and all its activities, rather than support for a small percentage of individuals whose economic activity happens to be farming. The consequences of supporting only one group in a region has become evident in rural depopulation of certain areas of France and other European countries. The idea that support for agriculture will 'trickle down' to other sectors is not very convincing, particularly as the number of farmers dwindles steadily.

One consequence of reform of the CAP which has already caused the public to question the policy is the payment of compensation for not using land. This is particularly true now that the payments to a given individual can be calculated. Under the former policy, protection and support were not transparent, as import levies and intervention buying were not linked to individuals.

There are thus a number of national and European factors which will influence the future shape of the CAP. In addition, there are external and international factors such as economic and political developments related to

Eastern Europe, the implementation of the recent GATT agreements and political and commercial developments in both north and south America which influence competitivity and trade. Pressure will undoubtedly continue from more efficient and lower cost producers to limit support to farmers in the European Union, and thus to further modify the CAP.

One thing is absolutely certain, that European Union agricultural policy will be subject to continuing change in the future, as it has been since its inception, but the pace of change in future will be more rapid.

REFERENCES

AGENCE EUROPE (1995) UE/CONSEIL AGRICULTURE: les Ministres ont reconnu le 'double role' de l'agriculture. 16 March, 10.

AGRA EUROPE (1995a) UK landowners launch a 'rural policy for Europe, 28 April.

AGRA EUROPE (1995b) Paradoxes in EU policy development, 21 July.

ARKLETON TRUST (1992) *Farm Household Adjustment in Western Europe 1987–91*. European Commission, 1993.

ASTROM, S. (1995) A possible improvement of Common Agricultural Policy – a report to the Swedish cabinet, 29 September.

BULLETIN OF THE EC (1988) Bulletin of the EC, no. 2 – 1988. European Commission, Office for Official Publications of the European Communities.

CEC (Commission of the European Communities) (1968) Memorandum on the Reform of Agriculture in the European Economic Community.

CEC (Commission of the European Communities) (1973) Improvement of the Common Agricultural Policy, 5 November.

CEC (Commission of the European Communities) (1974) Proposal for a Council Directive concerning forestry measures, 26 February (OJ No. C44 of 19 April 1974, p. 14).

CEC (Commission of the European Communities) (1975) Stocktaking of the Common Agricultural Policy. Supplement to the Bulletin of the European Commission No. 2/75.

CEC (Commission of the European Communities) (1980) Reflections on the Common Agricultural Policy. Supplement to the Bulletin of the European Commission No. 6/80.

CEC (Commission of the European Communities) (1981a) Report from the Commission of the European Communities to the Council pursuant to the mandate of 30 May 1980. Supplement to the Bulletin of the European Commission No. 1/81.

CEC (Commission of the European Communities) (1981b) Guidelines for European Agriculture, COM(81)608, 23 October.

CEC (Commission of the European Communities) (1982) Proposal for a Council Regulation on action by the Community relating to the environment, COM(82)849 final, 11 January.

CEC (Commission of the European Communities) (1983a) Increasing the effectiveness of the Community's Structural Funds. Supplement to the Bulletin of the European Commission No. 3/83.

CEC (Commission of the European Communities) (1983b) Adjustment of the Common Agricultural Policy COM(83)500, 29 July. Supplement to the Bulletin of the European Commission No. 4/83.

CEC (Commission of the European Communities) (1983c) Proposal for a Council Regulation

(European Commission) on improving the efficiency of agricultural structures, COM(83)559, 10 October.

CEC (Commission of the European Communities) (1985a) Perspectives for the Common Agricultural Policy: the Green Paper of the Commission, COM(85)333, 13 July.

CEC (Commission of the European Communities) (1985b) Commission memorandum on the adjustment of the market organization for cereals, COM(85)700, 14 November.

CEC (Commission of the European Communities) (1985c) A future for Community agriculture, COM(85)750, 18 December.

CEC (Commission of the European Communities) (1986) Single European Act. Supplement to the Bulletin of the European Commission No. 2/86.

CEC (Commission of the European Communities) (1987a) Making a success of the Single Act: a new frontier for Europe, COM(87)100, 15 February.

CEC (Commission of the European Communities) (1987b) Review of action taken to control the agricultural markets and outlook for the Common Agricultural Policy, COM(87)410, 3 August.

CEC (Commission of the European Communities) (1987c) The application of agricultural stabilisers, COM(87)452, September.

CEC (Commission of the European Communities) (1988a) Proposal for a Council Regulation amending Regulations (European Commission) No. 797/85 and No. 1760/87 as regards the set-aside of agricultural land and the extensification and conversion of production, COM(88)1, 18 January.

CEC (Commission of the European Communities) (1988b) Environment and Agriculture, COM(88)338, 8 June.

CEC (Commission of the European Communities) (1988c) The future of rural society, COM(88)371, 29 July 1988. Supplement to the Bulletin of the European Commission No. 4/88.

CEC (Commission of the European Communities) (1988d) Community strategy and action programme for the forestry sector, COM(88)255, 11 November.

CEC (Commission of the European Communities) (1989) Adjustment of the agricultural structures policy, COM(89)91, 3 July.

CEC (Commission of the European Communities] (1990) Proposal for a Council Regulation (European Commission) on the introduction and the maintenance of agricultural production methods compatible with the requirements of the protection of the environment and the maintenance of the countryside, COM(90)366, 3 August. (OJ C267 of 23 October).

CEC (Commission of the European Communities) (1991a) The development and future of the Common Agricultural Policy, COM(91)100, 1 February.

CEC (Commission of the European Communities) (1991b) The development and future of the Common Agricultural Policy: follow-up to the Reflections Paper COM(91)100 of 1 February 1991 – Proposals of the Commission, COM(91)258, 22 July 1991.

CEC (Commission of the European Communities) (1991c) Future support for producers of oilseed, COM(91)318, 31 July.

CEC (Commission of the European Communities) (1991d). Reform of the Common Agricultural Policy: legal texts, COM(91)379, 18 October, and COM(91)409, 31 October.

CEC (Commission of the European Communities) (1991e) Reform of the Common Agricultural Policy – legislation. Measures to accompany the reform of the market support mechanisms, Community aid scheme for forestry measures in agriculture, Community early retirement scheme for farmers, COM(91)415, 31 October.

CEC (Commission of the European Communities) (1993a) Possible developments in the policy of arable land set-aside, COM(93)226, 18 May.

CEC (Commission of the European Communities) (1993b) The future of Community Initiatives under the Structural Funds, COM(93)282, 16 June.

CEC (Commission of the European Communities) (1993c) Towards sustainability, Office for Official Publications of the European Communities, 1993, p. 17.

CEC (Commission of the European Communities) (1994) The relationship between compliance with the non-rotational set-aside obligation, environmental set-aside and the use of set-aside land for afforestation purposes, COM(94)2062, 9 December.

CEC (Commission of the European Communities) (1995) Study on alternative strategies for development of relations in the field of agriculture between the EU and the associated countries with a view to future accession of these countries (Agricultural Strategy Paper), CSE(95)607.

DI CARPEGNA, R. (1992) Agriculture in The Community: prospects and constraints. In *Agriculture in Europe: Development, constraints and perspectives*, p. 58. European Commission.

Farmer's Weekly (1995a) CLA sets out rural vision of the future, 17 February.

Farmer's Weekly (1995b) Radical USA proposals for subsidy cuts cast a shadow over Europe, 1 September.

Financial Times (1994a) Chemical group puts organic farming on trial, 6 July.

Financial Times (1994b) Replace Common Agricultural Policy subsidies, says think tank, 29 November.

Financial Times (1995a) Britains NFU sees 'very real danger' of farm policy renationalisation, 20 January.

Financial Times (1995b) Safeguarding an environmental reservoir, 25 Januuary.

Financial Times (1995c). Plan for subsidy cuts finds favour with US farm groups, 14 December.

FISCHLER, F. (1995a) The European Union and Central Europe. In *Second Annual Conference of Agra Europe*, Warsaw, 7 April.

FISCHLER, F. (1995b) Agriculture and the Environment: Experience of the European Union, In *Third Session of the Commission on Sustainable Development*, New York, 12 April.

FISCHLER, F. (1995c) *Common Agricultural Policy Reform and Environmental Protection*, The Commodity Club, Washington D.C., 5 June, p. 12.

JOSLING, T., & TANGERMANN, S. (1995) Toward a Common Agricultural Policy for the next century, *European Policy Forum*, April.

NFU (National Farmers Union), (1994) Real Choices: a discussion document, March.

NFU (National Farmers Union), (1995) Taking Real Choices Forward, 16 March.

RICHARDSON, D. (1995) Britain stands alone on farm policy reform, *Financial Times*, 1 August.

RSPB (Royal Society for the Protection of Birds) (1995) *The Future of the Common Agricultural Policy*, Sandy, Bedfordshire, February.

TRACY, M. (1989) *Government and Agriculture in Western Europe 1880–1988*, Third Edition, Harvester Wheatsheaf.

The Times (1994) 16,000 miles of hedges being lost each year, 22 July.

WALDEGRAVE, W. (1995) Radical change to Common Agricultural Policy vital to a wider EU, *Financial Times*, 28 June.

WALSTON, O. (1994) Reported in 'Farmers join environmentalists in reform call'. *Financial Times*, 5 July.

WALSTON, O. (1995). In 'Talking Point'. *Farmers Weekly*, 13 January.

WINBERG, M. (1995) Greater ambition needed for Common Agricultural Policy. Letters, *Financial Times*, 7 July.

WYNN, T. (1995) Common Agricultural Policy reform memorandum. Letters, *Financial Times*, 6 July.

CHAPTER

4

Priorities for bird conservation in Europe: the importance of the farmed landscape

GRAHAM TUCKER

SUMMARY

This chapter aims to assess the importance of the farmed landscape for birds and to identify conservation priorities for them. To do this, it is first necessary to place farmland in the context of historical effects of agriculture on the landscape (as illustrated by Potter, Chapter 2) and bird populations. The current importance of farmed habitats for birds is then assessed, followed by a review of the major threats to these habitats and their species. Last, on the basis of these assessments, a broad strategy for the conservation of farmland birds is outlined.

The farmed landscape is defined here in its broad sense, as being all habitats that are managed primarily for food production (i.e. crops or animals). Such habitats therefore include arable farmland, grasslands (including steppelands, alpine grasslands, wet grasslands, upland rough grassland), moorland, pastoral woodlands (e.g. Spanish 'dehesas'), orchards and other perennial crops, such as olives. Heathlands and Mediterranean shrublands (i.e. maquis and garrigue) are not included although they are often grazed by livestock.

FARMING AND BIRDS IN EUROPE
ISBN 0-12-544280-7
Copyright © 1997 Academic Press Ltd
All rights of reproduction in any form reserved

THE EFFECTS OF AGRICULTURE ON HABITATS AND BIRDS IN EUROPE

Effects on the landscape

The European landscape has been profoundly affected by human activities over the last 10 000 years. Nowadays, as the natural forest that once covered most of the continent has been replaced, large areas of truly natural habitat can be found only in parts of northern Europe and some mountainous regions. In particular, the spread and development of agriculture has caused the most widespread changes (see the following chapters for more detailed accounts).

Although such changes reduced the extent of primary biotopes and their species, they probably led initially to an increase in large-scale biodiversity in Europe (Hampicke, 1978; Kornas, 1983) through the creation of new semi-natural habitats. These include heath and shrublands, grasslands, and pastoral woodlands, as well as entirely artificial habitats such as annually cultivated and perennial crops. As change was slow, many species were able to adapt and expand into these new habitats where they mimicked natural conditions. For example, the great bustard *Otis tarda* spread from the natural primary steppes, maintained by indigenous herbivores such as saiga *Saiga tatarica*, to secondary steppes, maintained by livestock, and even to extensive cereals (Cramp & Simmons, 1980). With the continued loss of primary habitats, such as natural steppes, many species became dependent on these low-intensity agricultural habitats and the farming practices that maintain them.

Such low-intensity traditional farming landscapes may have a high biological diversity, especially where a variety of crops occur in small fields within a matrix of other habitats such as hedgerows, woodlots, ponds, marshes and fallowland, etc. (Lowe *et al.*, 1986; Rackham, 1986; Fry, 1991). In addition to their importance for certain species and overall biodiversity, these traditional landscapes are also highly valued for their scenic qualities and cultural significance (Birks *et al.*, 1988).

However, particularly rapid technological advances, economic development and political initiatives in the twentieth century have driven further massive agricultural expansion and intensification within the European Union (EU) (Body, 1983; Lee, 1987; IUCN, 1991; Potter, Chapter 2; Robson, Chapter 3) and elsewhere (e.g. Hanski & Tiainen, 1988; IUCN, 1991; Fésüs *et al.*, 1992; Bernes, 1993; Stanners & Bourdeau, 1995). Further major losses of the remaining natural habitats and biologically rich semi-natural habitats resulted (Baldock, 1990).

In recent decades overall farmland area has decreased in most European countries. In the current 15 EU countries, farmland declined by an average of 9.6% over the 30-year period 1960–1990 (CEC, 1995a). Over the same period agricultural area declined in eastern Europe by a similar amount. Subsequently there has been even more widespread agricultural abandonment in the region

(CEC, 1995b). Despite this overall trend, local agricultural expansion has continued at the same time, often at the expense of remaining natural and semi-natural habitats. Wetlands in particular have continued to be drained and converted to agriculture as the resulting farmland is often highly productive and grants for conservation are often available. Baldock (1990) notes that, whilst the scale of conservation is now much reduced, there are still individual sites that are under threat, and documents continued losses in a number of countries.

Impacts of intensification

The intensification of farming systems (i.e. increases in inputs) has led to widespread degradation of non-agricultural habitats elsewhere. In particular, the ploughing of old grasslands, application of high rates of inorganic fertilizer and frequent accidental pollution incidents due to run-off from intensive stockyards, silage stores and manure pits have raised water nutrient levels and caused widespread wetland eutrophication (Irving, 1993). Eutrophication of terrestrial habitats as a result of atmospheric pollution derived from intensive stockyards in western Europe is thought to be a major problem in parts of central Europe (Ellenberg et al., 1989). Other frequent detrimental effects of modern agricultural practices on surrounding habitats include pesticide drift (Moore, 1983), and disturbance from machinery and aerial crop spraying, etc. Water abstraction for agriculture is a problem in parts of Europe, particularly the south. About 18% of agricultural land is irrigated in Italy, 16% in Portugal, 13% in Greece, and 11% in Spain (CEC, 1995a). Such large demands for water can lower water tables and thereby alter or even destroy wetlands, as for example, in the Daimiel National Park (SGOP, 1983).

Agricultural expansion and intensification have also led to increased fragmentation of remaining natural and semi-natural habitats, such as forests, marshes and heathlands, with a variety of potentially detrimental effects (e.g. Wilcove et al., 1986; Merriam, 1988; Bink et al., 1994; Kirby, 1995; Opdam et al., 1995; Wiens, 1995). Fragmentation reduces the size of remnant habitat patches, and thus the proportion of edge habitat increases. Boundaries also tend to become more abrupt and patches more widely separated. The increase in proportion of edge habitat affects vegetation structure and composition, and in turn associated animal communities (Wilcove et al., 1986). Otherwise suitable habitats may become too small for species that have large minimum home ranges (often the case for large animals and top-level predators), whilst populations of remaining species may become so small they are at risk of extinction from chance events (Schaffer, 1981; Gilpin & Soulé, 1986; Soulé, 1987; Simberloff, 1988; Pimm, 1991; Ryan & Siegfried, 1994). If the habitat fragments are highly isolated and the species has a low rate of dispersal, recolonization following extinction may be slow or even impossible. In the event of climatic change, some geographical continuity of potential habitat is required if species with poor dispersal abilities are to be able to shift their ranges, and thereby survive (Pienkowski & Bignal, 1993).

If species are lost as a result of these effects, then community composition is altered and further consequences may occur. For example, the loss of large predators, which are particularly sensitive to area effects of habitat fragmentation (Temple, 1991), may lead to increases in large herbivores which in turn leads to increased browsing, changes in vegetation structure and further community modification (e.g. Angelstam, 1992).

Fragmentation effects are, however, largely based on expectations from theoretical models and empirical evidence for them is actually rather meagre (Opdam, 1991; Wiens, 1995; Opdam *et al.*, 1995; Simberloff, 1995). Much of the evidence that does exist is based on studies carried out in highly intensively farmed landscapes, such as the Netherlands. The generality of these studies to other parts of Europe is questionable as less intensively managed farmland landscapes may be more hospitable to species dispersing through them.

Agriculture-related threats to the remaining natural and other non-farmed habitats have, to some extent, caused conservationists to overlook the importance of farmland habitats themselves and the threats to them (Bignal & McCracken, 1993). In fact, probably the most serious loss of avian biodiversity in Europe this century has occurred through the intensification of agricultural practices on existing farmland, from semi-natural habitats, such as 'dehesas' and steppes, to already fairly intensive arable systems. These farmland habitats have been steadily degraded through agricultural intensification such as drainage, irrigation, increased use of pesticides and fertilizers, over-grazing, crop specialization and loss of important adjoining features such as trees, hedgerows and ponds (e.g. Jenkins, 1984; O'Connor and Shrubb, 1986; Beintema, 1988; Goriup *et al.*, 1991; Díaz *et al.*, 1993; De Juana *et al.*, 1993; Pain, 1994a,b,c; Fuller *et al.*, in press, and the following chapters in this publication). Similar changes in grassland habitats in the United States have also led to farmland bird declines (Askins, 1993; Peterjohn & Sauer, 1993; Warner, 1994). The scale and pace of these recent changes are such that agriculture-dependent species are no longer able to adapt. As a result, we are now in the position where agricultural intensification is the most frequent cause of European bird population declines (Tucker & Heath, 1994). Furthermore, lost species are not being replaced by others as conditions change, as formerly happened when man changed the structure and composition of landscapes. Rather, we now see a general impoverishment of biodiversity in agricultural habitats. As this chapter will demonstrate, farmland habitats are now, quite simply, the foremost bird conservation priority in Europe.

Birds as indicators of impacts on other flora and fauna

Most of the information available on the impacts of agriculture on biodiversity is on birds. This is largely because in some respects birds can be easily used as indicators of broad environmental changes (Peakall & Boyd, 1987; Furness *et al.*, 1993). They are relatively simple to identify and observe, have a well established classification and systematics and are therefore comparatively easy to document with confidence. This, combined with their general popularity, has produced a wealth of information on birds, much of which has been collected by amateurs, to the highest of standards, under the guidance of professional ornithological research bodies. Birds are also common and widespread – and because amateur work can cover a wide geographical area, broad-based monitoring of bird distributions, numbers and even reproductive success can be provided. Numerous ecological studies, such as those of habitat use, population regulation, feeding ecology and behaviour and migration, have also been carried out by amateurs and professionals alike. As a result, bird populations and their ecology are currently better understood than any other taxonomic group.

Birds may not, however, be the most sensitive of environmental indicators as many species appear relatively resilient to change. Although they tend to be high in the food-chain and can therefore indicate disruption to food webs, responses may be slow and difficult to interpret. Bird numbers also tend to be regulated by density-dependent processes, so their population sizes may be buffered against environmental impacts (Furness *et al.*, 1993). Their migration movements may make it difficult to determine the original location where impacts may be occurring. The mobility of birds also facilitates the relocation of populations when conditions change or their recolonization if habitats recover.

Many bird species also appear to be relatively general in their habitat and food requirements. As described above, species such as the great bustard adapted to non-intensive agricultural habitats where these mimicked the broad structure of their original habitats (in this case steppe grasslands). However, some species do have more restricted habitat requirements and are less adaptable. For example, the pallid harrier *Circus macrourus*, sociable plover *Chethusia gregaria* and black lark *Melanocorypha yeltoniensis* appear to be dependent on natural steppe grasslands and are now restricted in Europe to small remnants of these habitats on the Russian–Kazakhstan border (Tucker & Heath, 1994). Further-more, even those species that have adapted to agricultural habitat change have their limits. Consequently, many species are now declining as agricultural intensification leads to habitat changes that exceed these. Thus great bustard populations have become extinct over much of western Europe this century and continue to decline elsewhere (Tucker & Heath, 1994). Similarly, many other species that initially adapted to semi-natural and low-intensity agricultural habitats, such as white stork *Ciconia ciconia*, corncrake *Crex crex* and chough *Pyrrhocorax pyrrhocorax*, have also shown recent declines.

Because birds may be less sensitive to environmental change, declines in their populations arising from agricultural intensification may be less severe than in other taxa. Indeed, wild plant populations have already been devastated in most agricultural landscapes in Europe (e.g. Kornas, 1983; Hodgson, 1987; van Dijk, 1991). We must therefore assume that, although the effects of agriculture on birds also reflect the effects on other taxa, these are likely to be very much underestimated. In other words, the loss of bird diversity is likely to be the 'tip of

Figure 1 The corncrake, a globally threatened species in decline throughout much of Europe. (Photo by C.H. Gomersall/RSPB.)

the iceberg' in terms of overall biodiversity loss in agricultural habitats. Nevertheless, because many of the causes of biodiversity loss are likely to be common to birds and other taxa, recommendations for bird conservation here, and elsewhere, are also likely to contribute to the conservation of biodiversity in general.

THE IMPORTANCE OF AGRICULTURAL HABITATS FOR BIRDS

Data sources

This review of the importance of agricultural habitats focuses on patterns of species richness and conservation status of birds. Assessments of species richness at the European scale are based on habitat use data provided by Habitat Working Groups during the preparation of BirdLife International Habitat Conservation Strategies (Tucker, in press). Data on the conservation status of birds is based on a recent comprehensive assessment of the status of Europe's

Table 1 Species of European Conservation Concern (SPECs)

Category 1	Species of global conservation concern because they are classified as Globally Threatened, Conservation Dependent or Data Deficient according to IUCN criteria (Mace & Stuart, 1994) by Collar *et al.* (1994)
Category 2	Species whose global populations are concentrated in Europe (i.e. more than 50% of their global population or range in Europe) and which have an Unfavourable Conservation Status in Europe
Category 3	Species whose global populations are not concentrated in Europe, but which have an Unfavourable Conservation Status in Europe
Category 4	Species whose global populations are concentrated in Europe but have a Favourable Conservation Status in Europe

Species are considered to have an Unfavourable Conservation Status if their European Threat Status is Localized, Declining, Rare, Vulnerable, Endangered or Insufficiently Known according to the criteria summarized in Table 2.

birds by BirdLife International (Tucker & Heath, 1994). The study covered the whole of Europe, including the Azores, Madeira, the Canary Islands, European Russia (i.e. east to the Ural mountains), Armenia, Azerbaijan and Georgia, as well as the whole of Turkey and Greenland. A network of national data contributors compiled information on breeding population sizes and trends (1970–1990) for every species in every country, and winter population data were collected where available. These data were used to identify Species of European Conservation Concern (SPECs). SPECs are divided into four categories according to their global conservation status, their European Threat Status and the proportion of their world population in Europe (Tables 1 and 2).

Species richness across habitats

This study reveals that at a European scale agricultural habitats have the highest overall species richness of any habitat (Figure 2). This is in part due to the size of the habitat itself as species richness measurements depend on the scale at which they are measured, invariably increasing with the size of the area (Schoener, 1976, 1986; Wiens, 1989). There are three main causes of this species–area relationship (Huston, 1994). First, at small scales it is often a sampling artifact. Within a homogeneous area, samples of increasingly large areas are more likely to include an increasing proportion of the total population and thus detect rarer species.

Table 2 Summary of European Threat Status criteria* and categories. All species other than those with Secure status have an Unfavourable Conservation Status

	Population size/status			
	<250 pairs	<2500 pairs	<10 000 pairs	>10 000 pairs†
Large decline‡	Endangered	Endangered	Endangered	Vulnerable
Moderate decline§	Endangered	Endangered	Vulnerable	Declining
No decline	Endangered	Vulnerable	Rare	Secure

* After appropriate adaptations these criteria were also applied to some winter populations. Full details of the criteria are given in Tucker & Heath (1994).

† In addition, species that have more than 10 000 pairs in Europe are categorized as Localized if more than 90% of the population occurs in ten sites or fewer.

‡ Declined in size or range by at least 20% in at least 66% of the population, or by at least 50% in at least 25% of the population between 1970 and 1990.

§ Declined in size or range by at least 20% in 33–65% of the population or by at least 50% in 12–24% of the population between 1970 and 1990.

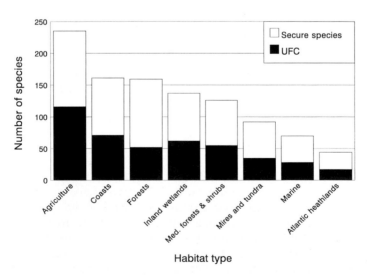

Figure 2 The number of regularly occurring species and species with an Unfavourable Conservation Status (UFC) in each broad habitat type in Europe.

Second, the relationship may result from an equilibrium between extinction rates and immigration rates, as postulated by the theory of island biogeography (MacArthur & Wilson, 1963, 1967).

Last, and of most importance to this study, at large scales of analysis the species–area relationship is the result of environmental heterogeneity. Increasing the sample area will include additional habitat types, or variations within these, depending on how habitats are defined. Thus, at the European scale, a broad definition such as agricultural habitats may include as wide a diversity as dry steppe grasslands, upland rough grazing, rice fields, vineyards, and intensive arable systems. The most intensively farmed habitats may typically hold few species but, as described later, many others are rich in species and a significant number are unique to them. Thus, over the broad range of agricultural habitats in Europe, bird diversity is high. At a national scale, the range of habitats may be more restricted, and even more so at the farm scale where only one agricultural habitat type may occur. However, even individual farms may then contain habitat mosaics of different crops, fallowland, hedgerows, ditches, ponds and copses. Indeed, much of the species richness of farmland is likely to be associated with the non-cropped components. Thus the overall diversity of any given area will be a reflection both of the range of habitats it includes and of the diversity of the component habitats.

To examine the effects of area on this European scale study of habitat-related bird species richness, a comparison of national data was carried out. Figure 3 shows the relationship between the number of species breeding in forest and agricultural habitats in a selection of European countries and their corresponding area. Data are taken from the European Bird Database (BirdLife International/European Bird Census Council, 1995), within which species are recorded as occurring in a habitat if more than 10% of its breeding population occurs within it. Insufficient area data were available to do similar analyses on other habitats. Although the data points are considerably scattered, the relationship shown is a typical species–area curve (see for example Huston, 1994) indicating a rapid increase in species with area which gradually levels off. Also, despite large overlaps, it indicates that at equal areas, forest habitats tend to contain more species than agricultural habitats. This supports the hypothesis that the high species richness for farmland habitats across the whole of Europe (Figure 2) is at least in part due to the large area of the habitat. Agricultural habitats (including arable crops, grasslands and permanent crops) cover 42% of Europe compared with 33% by forests (Van de Velde *et al.*, 1994 in Stanners & Bourdeau, 1995).

The result is also not surprising as forests are a structurally complex habitat and it has been well documented that bird species richness is highly correlated to structural complexity (Wiens, 1989). It is, however, also likely that species richness on agricultural habitats has been underestimated owing to methodological limitations. First, the analysis of national species richness (Figure 3) was possible only for breeding species, whereas the Europe-wide analysis (Figure 2) also includes all regularly occurring non-breeding species. Many species occur on farmland in winter, but breed in other habitats. For example, cranes *Grus grus* breed in forest bogs but winter in dry grasslands and dehesas in Spain. Many geese and waders, e.g. golden plover *Pluvialis apricaria*, breed in tundra regions and winter on grasslands. In comparison few, if any, birds move into forests from other habitats in winter.

Second, species are listed in the European Bird Database as occurring in a habitat only if more than 10% of their national population occurs within it. Scarce species will therefore tend to be under-recorded. This is particularly likely to under-estimate agricultural bird richness as for many species such habitats are marginal. For example, several woodpecker, warbler and tit species frequently occur in farmland rich in hedgerows and trees but, in most countries, these populations are small proportions of those in their natural original forest habitats. In contrast, fewer species are likely to have marginal populations in forests and the majority of their populations in other habitats. Such marginal farmland populations may not, however, be of as high conservation value as those in core habitats. Indeed, some may be unviable 'sink' populations maintained by recruitment from productive 'source' populations in core habi-

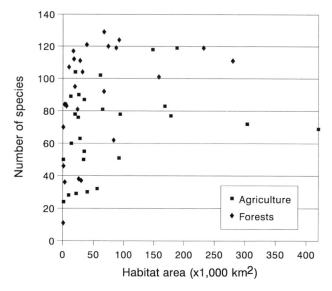

Figure 3 The relationships between the number of breeding bird species in forest and agricultural habitats and habitat area. Individual points represent the total breeding species richness and area of the habitat for the following countries: Austria, Belarus, Belgium, Bulgaria, Cyprus, Denmark, Estonia, Finland, Greece, Hungary, Iceland, Ireland, Italy, Latvia, Lithuania, Luxembourg, Netherlands, Norway, Poland, Portugal, Romania, Spain, Sweden, Switzerland, Ukraine, United Kingdom. Bird data were obtained from the BirdLife International/EBCC European Bird Database and habitat area data are taken from CEC (1995a).

tats. Nevertheless, marginal populations contribute to biodiversity and ecological processes and thus should be conserved.

It is clear from the large-scale European-wide and national analyses that agricultural habitats do have a rich avifauna. This result may seem surprising as casual observation in farmland habitats often gives the impression of an impoverished bird fauna. Whilst this is often true on the most intensive cereal monocultures, which tend to prevail in many parts of Europe, data from bird community surveys suggest otherwise for farmland more generally (e.g. O'Connor & Shrubb, 1986). A selection of breeding bird species richness estimates from a range of terrestrial habitat types and locations in the United Kingdom are summarized in Table 3. Further examples of forest bird community studies are given in Petty & Avery (1990). Direct comparisons of estimates should be treated with caution due to differences in habitat area surveyed and census methods. Nevertheless, although there is wide variation, this reveals that species richness in agricultural habitats is comparable to that of woodland and scrub.

A similar review of species richness in agricultural and other habitats in other parts of Europe is not possible here. However, the following examples suggest that similar patterns may at least be found in parts of Iberia. Tellería *et al.* (1994) found 18 species in spring in farmland in northern Spain, compared with 12 in pine woods and 16 in native forests. In south-western Spain, they found only 12 species on croplands and seven on grasslands compared with 18 in dehesa (pastoral woodland), 15 in woodland and 11 in shrublands. Winter richness, however, was highest on croplands, with 23 species recorded. In Portugal, Pina *et al.* (1990) found 27 species in spring in olive groves, 21 in pine plantations, 31 in holm oak *Quercus ilex* woodland, 25 in Pyrenean oak *Q. pyrenica* woodland, 27 in scrub and 22 in cereals.

Conservation status across habitats

The assessment of species richness is only one of several measures of the importance of a habitat for biodiversity conservation. Its main limitations are that it does not take into account the conservation status of species or their reliance on the habitat in question. Thus a habitat may be more important if it contains a small but unique assemblage of threatened species than one with a rich but less threatened generalist fauna. An analysis of the importance of agricultural habitats in terms of the conservation status of birds using them was therefore carried out. The analysis reveals that nearly half the species of agricultural habitats have an Unfavourable Conservation Status, the highest proportion of any habitat (Figure 2). Furthermore, the fact that many of the birds with an Unfavourable Conservation Status are common and widespread species, such as grey partridge *Perdix perdix*, turtle dove *Streptopelia turtur*, skylark *Alauda arvensis* and swallow *Hirundo rustica*, strongly suggests that the problems facing agricultural habitats are on a massive scale.

Table 3 Breeding bird species richness in woodland, scrub and agricultural habitats in Ireland and the United Kingdom

Habitat	Area (ha)	Number of species recorded in the breeding season	Method*	Reference
Woodland and scrub				
Glen Nant, Argyll				
Mixed deciduous woodland (mostly heavily coppiced):			T	Williamson (1974)
● oak with ash and birch	12	25		
● oak with birch and hazel	7	22		
● oak with birch	7	22		
● birch with oak	7.5	16		
● mature, well spaced, oak	3.25	16		
Porton Down, Wiltshire				
Chalk downland:			T	Morgan (1975)
● grassland	32	13		
● hawthorn scrub	60	33		
● juniper scrub	14	26		
● scots pine	10	16		
Ivinghoe Beacon and Steps Hill, Buckinghamshire				
Chalk grassland and scrub	80	40	T	Williamson (1975)
Wayford, Somerset				
Mixed woodland (71% broadleaves, 29% conifer)	7.7	33–35	T	Parsons (1976)
New Forest				
Even-aged nineteenth century oak plantation	15.2	24–26	T	Irvine (1977)
Ancient beech with oak woodland	8	22–26	T	Irvine (1977)
Dumfries-shire and Spey Valley, Scotland				
Woodlands:			T	Moss (1978)
● spruce plantation	9.2 and 11.1	8 and 9		
● larch plantation	5.8	8		
● pine plantation	11.7 and 12.4	8 and 6		
● birch/pine scrub	12.0	18		
● mixed semi-natural	4.3	18		
● semi-natural pine	8.7	10		

Location	Habitat			Method*	Reference
Leighton Moss, Lancashire	Willow scrub • mature • coppiced	12 7.2	23 26	T	Wilson (1978)
North Wales	Restocked conifer plantations (2–11 years old)	62 × 2–32	31	P	Bibby et al. (1985)
Oxfordshire	Deciduous woodland, predominantly oak and ash	20 × 0.14–18	4–23	T	Ford (1987)
Longbeech Wood, Kent	Sweet chestnut coppice	22.3	26	T	Fuller & Moreton (1987)
Scottish Highlands	Semi-natural birchwoods	36 × 15–100	28	P	Bibby et al. (1989)
Bradfields woods, Suffolk	Ancient, actively coppiced deciduous woodland	62	43	T	Fuller & Henderson (1992)
New Forest	Oak plantation (75–190 years old)	482	33	P	Smith et al. (1992)
	Ancient pasture woodland	641	33	P	Smith et al. (1992)
Farmland Suffolk	Mixed farmland with small woods	89	40–53	T	Benson & Williamson (1972)
Eden Valley, Cumbria	Mostly grassland for hay and pasture; some rough grazing and scrub	88	36–43	T	Robson & Williamson (1972)
Norfolk	Lowland, mixed farmland	100	47–55	T	Bull et al. (1976)
Hilton, Cambridgeshire	Predominantly arable lowland farmland	467	36	T	Wyllie (1976)
Brecon Beacons, Powys	Upland crags and moorland	282	21–27	T	Massey (1978)
Mid-west Ireland	Mostly poor quality grassland with abundant hedges and scrub	5 × c. 5	17–27	T	Lysaght (1989)

*T: territory mapping; P: point counts.

Patterns of species richness, habitat importance and conservation status within agricultural habitats

As described above, agricultural habitats are extremely varied and geographically widely spread. A more detailed analysis of the distribution of species at a European scale among different types of farmland is therefore presented here in order to identify broad patterns of use and particular priority habitats.

Arable and agriculturally improved grasslands hold the highest number of regularly breeding, passage or wintering species on farmland habitats (Table 4, Figure 4). Indeed, species richness in these habitats is considerably larger than in all other agricultural habitat types examined. This is most likely due to the high diversity and large area and geographical range of habitats falling within this group. Such farmland includes the most intensive of cereal monocultures, which by themselves have very low species richness, but will also include, for example, mixed farmland, permanent pastures and hayfields, farmed at varying levels of intensity. Thus species may range from the few that can withstand the most intense arable agriculture, such as carrion crow *Corvus corone* and woodpigeon *Columba palumbus*, to those commonly associated with moderately intensive arable farming, such as grey partridge, skylark, crested lark *Galerida cristata*, rook *C. frugilegus*; yellowhammer *Emberiza citrinella* and corn bunting *Miliaria calandra*, to birds of grassland or mixed farmland at the lower end of the intensification spectrum, e.g. white stork, Montagu's harrier *Circus pygargus*, barn owl *Tyto alba*, quail *Coturnix coturnix*, corncrake, little bustard *Tetrax tetrax* and great bustard. Where small woodlots, hedgerows, ponds and ditches, etc., also occur within the landscape then open field bird communities may be supplemented by species more typically associated with forest, scrub or wetland habitats, tawny owl *Strix aluco*, red-backed shrike *Lanius collurio* and mallard *Anas platyrhynchos* being frequent respective examples.

Richness is also high because of the scale of the analysis and the continent-wide spread of the habitat, which encompasses species as widely separated as black-winged kite *Elanus caeruleus* in Iberia, yellow-breasted bunting *Emberiza aureola* in northern Russia and bimaculated lark *Melanocorypha bimaculata* in Turkey. In contrast, some of the other farmland habitat types described here have smaller geographical distributions and therefore have a comparatively restricted pool of species within the range of the habitat.

Habitat importance differs, however, if one looks at the number of species that have the majority of their European populations in each habitat type (Table 4). On this assessment, steppic habitats are of greatest importance, holding major populations of 28 species, just over one-third of the regularly occurring number of species in the habitat. Thus, compared with most habitats they have a fairly specialized and highly dependent avifauna. Similarly, 29% of alpine grassland species have the majority of their populations in these habitats, although this amounts to only 12 species. Twenty species are concentrated on arable and agriculturally improved grass but this is quite a low proportion of the total number of species, reflecting the more general ecological requirements of

Table 4 The number of bird species regularly occurring in agricultural habitats in Europe. Figures in brackets include percentage of total number of species in the habitat

Habitat*	Total number of species	Number of species with majority of population in habitat	Number with an Unfavourable Conservation Status (UFC)	Number with majority in habitat and UFC
Arable and agriculturally improved grass	122	20 (16)	52 (43)	12 (10)
Steppic	80	28 (35)	53 (66)	24 (30)
Wet grasslands	64	3 (5)	30 (47)	2 (3)
Moorland	27	0 (0)	12 (44)	0 (0)
Alpine grasslands	42	12 (29)	24 (57)	5 (12)
Orchards, olive groves and perennial crops	59	0 (0)	23 (40)	0 (0)
Pastoral woodlands	56	2 (4)	23 (41)	2 (4)
Rice cultivations	36	1 (3)	20 (55)	1 (3)

*Arable farmland is regularly cultivated land that receives significant external inputs, especially fertilizers and other agro-chemicals. Agriculturally improved grasslands include those which have been drained, irrigated or re-seeded, or receive additional inputs of artificial or organic fertilizer, but exclude wet and alpine grasslands.

Steppic habitats include steppes, i.e. dry, treeless, flat or undulating grasslands and pseudo-steppes, i.e. cereal and fodder crops grown in low-intensity rotational-systems in steppe regions. Low-intensity systems are low in their use of external inputs. Quantitative definitions of low use are impractical due to variations in input requirements with soil and climatic conditions. Such low input systems, however, show typical characteristics as defined by Beaufoy *et al.* (1994).

Wet grasslands are periodically flooded grasslands or those with water tables close to ground level.

Moorland is defined as *Calluna* dominated habitats in wet Atlantic climates (typically with >1 m/yr precipitation).

Alpine grasslands are those above the treeline.

Pastoral woodlands are artificially opened semi-natural woodlands of varying tree density that are managed primarily for livestock rearing, including winter grazed woodlands of Britain, the 'dehesas' of Spain and 'montados' of Portugal.

many of these birds. In contrast the remaining habitats have no, or very small proportions of, species with the majority of their populations within them. This is because most of these species are more typical of natural habitats such as tundra, forests and wetlands, of which there still remain substantial areas, albeit reduced and often in modified semi-natural states.

If the number of species with an Unfavourable Conservation Status (Tucker

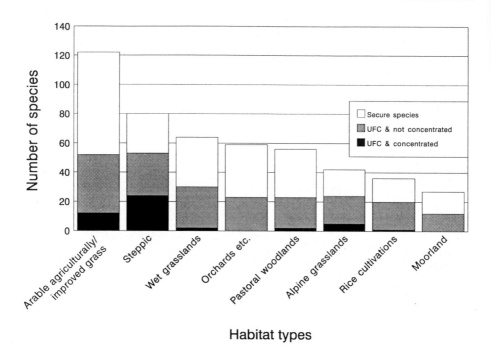

Habitat types

Figure 4 The number of regularly occurring species, species with an Unfavourable Conservation Status (UFC) and species with both an Unfavourable Conservation Status and with the majority of their European population in different types of agricultural habitat in Europe. See Table 4 footnote for habitat definitions.

& Heath, 1994) is taken as an indicator of habitat importance, then again arable and agriculturally improved grasslands are particularly important in terms of the number of species threatened. This probably reflects the widespread changes in habitat quality that have occurred over the last 20–30 years in such farmland, largely owing to intensification (as described above, in the next section and in other chapters of this publication). However, in terms of both numbers and especially the proportion of the bird community with an Unfavourable Conservation Status then steppic habitats are of particular concern. Two-thirds of the species have an Unfavourable Conservation Status, a result that is probably due to both habitat degradation and losses through conversion to intensive irrigated farmland (e.g. Goriup *et al.*, 1991; De Juana *et al.*, 1993; Suárez *et al.*, Chapter 11). The other striking result of this assessment is that all the other habitat types also have a substantial proportion of species with an Unfavourable Conservation Status, the minimum being 40% in orchards, olive groves and perennial crops. Again these high proportions reflect the documented degradation of these habitats (e.g. Beintema & Müskens, 1987; Usher & Thompson, 1988; Hötker, 1991; Thompson & MacDonald, 1995; and chapters in this publication). In

Figure 5 The carrion crow is one of the few species that can withstand highly intensive agriculture. (Photo by A. Hay/RSPB.)

some cases, though, where species have the majority of their populations in other habitats their Unfavourable Conservation Status may be due to factors other than those related to agriculture.

If the above two analyses are combined, then the numbers of species that have both an Unfavourable Conservation Status and their populations concentrated in the habitat can be used as an approximate guide to the most important European species conservation priorities on farmland (Tables 4 and 5, Figure 4). This reveals the particularly high importance of steppic habitats. Thirty per cent of the species in this habitat are concentrated within it and have an Unfavourable Conservation Status. The analysis also reveals that, even on this basis, arable and agriculturally improved grasslands are of high conservation importance; 10% of the species using the habitat have the majority of their populations within it and have an Unfavourable Conservation Status. Alpine grasslands are also of importance in a European continent context, though of the species concerned only lammergeier *Gypaetus barbatus* occurs in the European Union. Other habitats have low proportions and numbers of such high priority species, because, as described above, they hold species that are primarily concentrated in other habitats.

An analysis of habitat importance solely in terms of the occurrence of globally threatened species (Collar *et al.*, 1994) reveals a similar result to the wider

Table 5 Species with an Unfavourable Conservation Status (Tucker & Heath, 1994) and the majority of their European population in particular agricultural habitats (see Tables 1 and 2 for SPEC Categories and Threat Status)

Habitat type and species		SPEC category	Threat status
Steppic			
Lesser white-fronted goose	*Anser erythropus*	1	V
Pallid harrier*	*Circus macrourus*	3	E
Long-legged buzzard	*Buteo rufinus*	3	E
Steppe eagle*	*Aquila rapax*	3	V
Imperial eagle	*Aquila heliaca*	1	E
Lesser kestrel	*Falco naumanni*	1	V
Lanner	*Falco biarmicus*	3	(E)†
Saker	*Falco cherrug*	3	E
Little bustard	*Tetrax tetrax*	2	V
Houbara bustard*	*Chlamydotis undulata*	3	E
Great bustard	*Otis tarda*	1	D
Stone curlew	*Burhinus oedicnemus*	3	V
Cream-coloured courser*	*Cursorius cursor*	3	V
Black-winged pratincole	*Glareola nordmanni*	3	R
Greater sand plover*	*Charadrius leschenaultii*	3	E
Caspian plover*	*Charadrius asiaticus*	3	V
Sociable plover*	*Chettusia gregaria*	1	E
Black-bellied sandgrouse	*Pterocles orientalis*	3	V
Pin-tailed sandgrouse	*Pterocles alchata*	3	E
Dupont's lark	*Chersophilus duponti*	3	V
Black lark*	*Melanocorypha yeltoniensis*	3	V
Short-toed lark	*Calandrella brachydactyla*	3	V
Lesser Short-toed lark	*Calandrella rufescens*	3	V
Trumpeter finch	*Bucanetes githagineus*	3	R
Intensive cultivations and improved grasslands			
Red-breasted goose	*Branta ruficollis*	1	L^w
Red-legged partridge	*Alectoris rufa*	2	V
Grey partridge	*Perdix perdix*	3	V
Quail	*Coturnix coturnix*	3	V
Turtle dove	*Streptopelia turtur*	3	D
Barn owl	*Tyto alba*	3	D
Little owl	*Athene noctua*	3	D
Crested lark	*Galerida cristata*	3	D
Skylark	*Alauda arvensis*	3	V
Swallow	*Hirundo rustica*	3	D
Red-backed shrike	*Lanius collurio*	3	D
Ortolan bunting	*Emberiza hortulana*	2	V

Continued

Table 5 – *Continued*

Habitat type and species		SPEC category	Threat status
Alpine grasslands			
Lammergeier	*Gypaetus barbatus*	3	E
Caucasian black grouse*	*Tetrao mlokosiewiczi*	2	INS
Caspian snowcock*	*Tetraogallus caspius*	3	INS
Radde's accentor*	*Prunella ocularis*	3	V
Great rosefinch	*Carpodacus rubicilla*	3	(E)†
Wet grasslands			
Black-tailed godwit	*Limosa limosa*	2	V
Aquatic warbler	*Acrocephalus paludicola*	1	E
Pastoral woodlands			
Woodchat shrike	*Lanius senator*	2	V
Black-winged kite	*Elanus caerulus*	3	V
Rice cultivations			
Night heron	*Nycticorax nycticorax*	3	D

* Species does not regularly occur on agricultural habitats in the EU.
† Due to poor or insufficient data, the threat status is provisional.
ʷ Habitat is only used for passage or in winter.

assessment described above (Table 6). Ten globally threatened species use agricultural habitats; five of the ten occur in steppic habitats and have the vast majority of their European populations in this particular type of habitat. Three occur in the European Union. Indeed, Spain alone holds about 60% of European lesser kestrels *Falco naumanni* and 50% of great bustards, the latter probably representing a substantial proportion of the world population (Tucker & Heath, 1994).

Arable and agriculturally improved grasslands also hold five globally threatened species, although only one is concentrated in such habitats. The entire world population of the red-breasted goose *Branta ruficollis* is highly dependent on cereals and grasslands as its main winter feeding habitat in Romania and Bulgaria (Vangeluwe & Stassin, 1991; Sutherland & Crockford, 1993). In fact the species may be threatened by possible future agricultural abandonment in their preferred wintering sites (Hunter & Black, 1996). Imperial eagle *Aquila heliaca*, lesser kestrel and great bustard populations will also use some arable and agriculturally improved grassland habitats, but these are typically relatively low intensity and occur within primarily steppic landscapes (Tucker, in press). Densities and productivity in such marginal habitats are also usually low. The corncrake was also formerly widespread in moderately agriculturally improved

Table 6 Globally threatened species (Collar *et al.*, 1994) in Europe that use agricultural habitats (see Table 2 for Threat Status definitions)

Species		Threat status	Habitats			
			Arable and improved grass	Steppic	Wet grass-land	Pastoral wood-land
Lesser white-fronted goose*	*Anser erythropus*	V		†ʷ		
Red-breasted goose*	*Branta ruficollis*	Lʷ	†ʷ			
Spotted eagle	*Aquila clanga*	E			†	
Imperial eagle	*Aquila heliaca*	E	‡	†		
Spanish imperial eagle	*Aquila adalberti*	E				‡
Lesser kestrel	*Falco naumanni*	V	‡	†		
Corncrake	*Crex crex*	V	‡		‡	
Great bustard	*Otis tarda*	D	‡	†		
Sociable plover*	*Chettusia gregaria*	E		†		
Aquatic warbler	*Acrocephalus palu-dicola*	E			†	

* Species does not regularly occur on agricultural habitats in the EU.
†Habitat supports the majority of the population.
‡Species regularly occurs.
ʷHabitat is only used for passage or in winter.

grasslands, chiefly where they were traditionally managed as hay meadows. Consequently, with the decline of traditional management practices, the corncrake has now almost vanished from grasslands in western Europe and is mostly declining elsewhere (Tucker & Heath, 1994; Green & Rayment, in press; Croukford *et al.*, 1996).

Wet grasslands in eastern Europe are of considerable importance for the spotted eagle *Aquila clanga*, aquatic warbler *Acrocephalus paludicola* and they also hold corncrake. Another particularly important farmland habitat for globally threatened species is pastoral woodlands, specifically the 'dehesas' of Spain which hold important populations of the endemic Spanish imperial eagle *Aquila adalberti*.

These analyses of species richness, habitat use and species conservation status confirm the importance of certain agricultural habitats for birds and the urgent need for conservation measures within them. They indicate that some low-intensity agricultural habitat types are of particular importance, especially steppic habitats, though also alpine grasslands. This supports to some extent the farming systems expected by Baldock *et al.* (1993) to be of 'high-natural-value' (HNV). These included steppic habitats and high mountain pastures. However, these results also clearly indicate that a wide category of farming types including some moderately intensive cultivations and agriculturally improved grasslands should also be regarded as conservation priorities. Overall, this wide range of agricultural types has the highest species richness and, more importantly, the highest number of species with an Unfavourable Conservation Status, a significant number of which have the majority of their populations within the habitat. Only the most intensively farmed habitats have an extremely impoverished bird fauna (Table 7) and probably a generally low natural value.

Although it is clearly vital that the remaining semi-natural habitats are conserved, we must not neglect other more intensive agricultural habitats. As Potts (Chapter 6) notes, 'until recently the vast majority of conservationists and policy makers were unconcerned about the ecological state of the cereal ecosystem'. It now appears that we may perpetuate this mistake if we underestimate the remaining wildlife value of our more typical farmland. Only in the most intensive farmland is it justifiable to refer to wildlife value as being pushed back to 'exist as fragments of habitat in the cracks between commercial land uses' (Adams *et al.*, 1992, p. 47 cited by Potter, Chapter 2).

The results of this review show that many arable and agriculturally improved grassland habitats still have high nature conservation value, but this is declining more rapidly than in any other habitat. We therefore need to identify ways of conserving the remaining fauna and flora on such farmland, as well as improving the quality of farmland where possible.

MAJOR THREATS TO PRIORITY SPECIES OF AGRICULTURAL HABITATS

To conserve agricultural birds it is necessary to identify the most frequent threats to them. An analysis of threats to declining agricultural species has therefore been carried out using the information provided by experts in their accounts of individual species in Tucker & Heath (1994). Unfortunately, it is not possible from such accounts to judge the importance of threats in terms of effects on population dynamics. Nevertheless, the proportion of species that are thought to have declined as a result of each threat can be estimated, and this gives an indication of the greatest threats to agricultural birds at a European scale. A similar analysis is presented in Tucker & Heath (1994), which indicates that agricultural intensification (excluding pesticide effects) affects 42% of species (more than any other threat), indirect effects of pesticides (e.g. reduced food resources) 24%, agricultural abandonment 22%, agricultural expansion 13%, over-grazing 13% and direct effects of pesticides (e.g. poisoning) 7%. The analysis presented here, however, is restricted to agricultural species and direct

Table 7 Stages of agricultural improvement and some characteristic birds

State	Natural ecosystem→	Semi-natural→ Secondary habitat through forest clearance and maintained by grazing, burning or cutting	Agriculturally improved grasslands and mixed farmland→ Secondary grassland, improved through (e.g.) drainage, fertilizer use or re-seeding with indigenous species, with or without arable crops. Some non-farmed habitats (e.g. hedgerows, ponds, etc.) remaining	Highly intensive arable systems Temporary non-indigenous grasslands (e.g. for silage) and arable monocultures dependent on continuous high inputs (e.g. fertilizer, pesticides and irrigation). Non- farmed marginal habitats absent
Example habitats and some characteristic species*	Tundra (grazed by reindeer): numerous waders and waterfowl	Moorland: **Hen harrier**, merlin, red grouse, **black grouse, curlew,** meadow pipit, raven	Kestrel, **grey partridge, lapwing, little owl, crested lark, skylark,** swallow, rook, starling	Woodpigeon, carrion crow
	Peatlands: golden plover, **dunlin,** greenshank	Dry grasslands: **long-legged buzzard, saker, little bustard, black-billed sandgrouse, pin-tailed sandgrouse, lesser short-toed lark**		
	Primary steppes in Russia with extremely extensive grazing by livestock: **steppe eagle, pallid harrier,** demoiselle crane, **sociable plover,** white-winged lark, **black lark**	Wet grasslands: **white stork, snipe, great snipe, black-tailed godwit, redshank,** yellow wagtail		
	Alpine grasslands (above natural treeline) with natural herbivores (e.g. chamois) or extensive grazing by livestock: **caucasian black grouse, lammergeier,** alpine chough, snow finch	Traditional hay meadows: **corncrake, quail, barn owl,** whinchat		

*Species in bold have an Unfavourable Conservation Status in Europe.

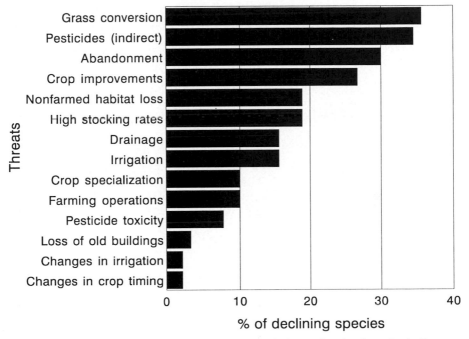

Figure 6 The frequency of agricultural threats to declining farmland species in Europe (Tucker & Heath, 1994).

agricultural threats, and further separates agricultural intensification into a number of subdivisions (Figure 6). Declining species are those that have declined in size or range by at least 20% in 33–65% of their European population, or by at least 50% in 12–24% of their European population between 1970 and 1990 (Tucker & Heath, 1994).

Intensification

The results from the study of bird declines clearly reflect the broad patterns of change in farming practices seen as a result of the general intensification of agricultural systems across Europe (e.g. Potter, Chapter 2; Robson, Chapter 3). The conversion of grasslands to cultivated fields is the most frequent threat, affecting 37% (i.e. 33) of the 90 declining agricultural species. In part this is due to the conversion of semi-natural grasslands to arable agriculture. This has been a particular problem in the steppe regions of eastern Europe over the last 20 years, and has been the primary cause of many declines in steppe species such as steppe eagle *Aquila nipalensis*, pallid harrier, sociable plover and black lark

Figure 7 Woodlarks have been lost in many areas where grassland habitats have been lost. (Photo by C.H. Gomersall/RSPB.)

(Belik, 1991; Tucker & Heath, 1994). Most of the steppes suitable for arable agriculture have, however, now been ploughed up and further significant losses are unlikely. Similarly, in western Europe, and particularly the EU, losses of remaining semi-natural grasslands to arable agriculture are now low as, due to current cereal surpluses, economic incentives are generally unavailable. Local exceptions to this do occur, however, an important example being in Spain where dry shrub steppes are being ploughed for the cultivation of hard wheat, to the detriment of species such as Dupont's lark *Chersophilus duponti* (Suárez & Oñate, 1994).

The most widespread losses of grassland result from the conversion of agriculturally improved grasslands (e.g. drained and fertilized) to arable crops. Such losses are due to the increasing tendency towards farm specialization and the replacement of traditional mixed rotational farming systems, with monocultures dependent on high inputs of artificial fertilizer. Many species were able to withstand the conversion of semi-natural grasslands to arable farmland where this was within mixed systems, because grasslands were retained within the farming landscape. The conversion of these last grass habitats often results therefore in the loss of a wide variety of species (e.g. great bustard, black-bellied sandgrouse *Pterocles orientalis*, barn owl, roller *Coracias garrulus* and woodlark *Lullula arborea*).

Driven by technological developments and the general process of intensification, a massive growth in pesticide use has occurred across most of Europe over the last 20–30 years (Potts, 1986; Potter, Chapter 2). The direct toxic effects of pesticides, notably the organochlorines, have been well studied and documented (e.g. Newton, 1979; Potts, 1986; Ratcliffe, 1993) and to a large extent alleviated by bans on the most toxic substances. Now a major problem appears to be the indirect effects of pesticides through the loss of food resources such as insects and weed seeds. This analysis reveals that 34% of agricultural bird species that are declining on a European scale are believed to be threatened by these indirect effects (Figure 6). However, with the exception of the grey partridge (Potts, 1986; 1990), causal links between population declines in these species and the effects of pesticide applications on food resources are unproven. Unfortunately, most of the implied threats from pesticides are based on associations between declines and pesticide use and inferences from species' biological requirements. This is mainly because the effects of pesticides are superimposed on an already complex and rapidly changing system and the large-scale and long-term studies that are necessary to unravel and prove such effects are very rare.

Studies comparing conventional with organic farming systems (with no pesticide applications) in Denmark (Braae et al., 1988; Petersen, 1994) and the United Kingdom (Wilson, 1993; Wilson & Browne, 1993; Chamberlain et al., 1995) have found organic farms to support higher densities of many farmland species and higher breeding success of yellowhammer and skylark. However, in these studies factors other than pesticides may be involved. Nevertheless the wealth of circumstantial evidence, and the detrimental effects of pesticides documented by the detailed research studies on the grey partridge, clearly indicate that the issue is of major conservation concern. To date action to investigate and alleviate this problem has been wholly inadequate. Further urgent research is obviously needed but, according to the precautionary principle, it is meanwhile prudent to take measures (such as those proposed by Potts, Chapter 6) to reduce the expected impact of pesticides.

Many of the other threats relating to farming practices are associated with each other and form part of a general process of intensification. Developments in cereal crops production, in the form of high rates of fertilizer application, use of new fast-growing and disease-resistant varieties, combined with autumn sowing, lead to dense tall crops in the spring, unsuitable for many ground-nesting species such as the stone curlew Burhinus oedicnemus (Green, 1988) and skylark (Schläpfer, 1988). Similarly, agricultural improvement of rough grass through drainage, re-seeding and fertilizer applications is thought to be responsible for declines in curlew Numenius arquata (Baines, 1988), black-tailed godwit Limosa limosa and redshank Tringa totanus (Batten et al., 1990; Beintema, 1991; Beintema et al., Chapter 10). Such grassland improvements then often lead to higher stocking levels, to the detriment of any remaining breeding waders as the trampling of nests becomes a frequent cause of breeding failure (O'Connor & Shrubb, 1986; Beintema & Müskens, 1987). Agriculturally improved grasslands are often used for silage production, and species such as the corncrake and curlew then suffer extremely high egg and chick mortality

Figure 8 Redshank wading in shallow water. Grassland intensification is thought to be responsible for the decline of this species. (Photo by C.H. Gomersall/RSPB.)

during harvesting (Hölzinger, 1987; Stowe *et al.*, 1993). Other ground-nesting species (e.g. stone curlew) suffer similar losses from other farming operations, such as the rolling of grass, harrowing and applications of agro-chemicals (Batten *et al.*, 1990). These operations require large machinery, which is most efficient when working in large fields. Field enlargement has therefore been widespread and has resulted in massive losses of marginal habitats such as hedges, woodlots, marshes, ponds, ditches and patches of rough grass. Hedgerow loss has been particularly excessive, for example: in Britain 22% (175 000 km) were destroyed between 1947 and 1985 (Fuller *et al.*, 1991) and in the 1980s losses continued at a rate of 28 000 km per year (see Potter, Chapter 2). Similar losses have occurred elsewhere in north-west Europe and have probably contributed to declines in such species as kestrel *Falco tinnunculus*, turtle dove, red-backed shrike, and ortolan bunting *Emberiza hortulana* (Tucker & Heath, 1994).

The enlargement of fields has reduced landscape diversity as the sizes of habitat patches increase. This has been further exacerbated by the tendency to specialize in the most economically viable crop types (in the prevailing climate of subsidies). Such crop specialization has led to a polarization of farming systems, which are increasingly either purely arable or purely livestock-based (O'Connor & Shrubb, 1986; Potter, Chapter 2). This, together with the decreased crop rotations (such as grass leys described above), has considerably reduced the diversity of crops, and therefore habitats, in the farmland landscape. Many farmland birds rely on crop mosaics to meet differences and seasonal shifts in nesting and feeding requirements. The effects of reduced crop diversity are difficult to study but declines in the great bustard (Kollar, 1996), stone curlew (Batten *et al.*, 1990), skylark (O'Connor & Shrubb, 1986; Schläpfer, 1988) and chough (Bignal *et al.*, 1989; in press) have been attributed to them.

Drainage of grasslands reduces the likelihood of winter flooding and therefore feeding opportunities for a variety of wildfowl. Breeding sites such as marshes and ponds, formerly of considerable importance for garganey *Anas querquedula* and pintail *A. acuta* (Rutschke, 1989), have also been lost. Drainage also reduces the accessibility of soil invertebrates to waders and can lead to more rapid vegetation growth in spring, making grasslands unsuitable for nesting (Green & Cadbury, 1987; O'Brien & Self, 1994; Beintema *et al.*, Chapter 10).

Irrigation leads to considerable disturbance which alone causes desertion of habitats by shy species such as the great bustard. Electricity lines are also needed to supply pumping stations, and the high density of overhead lines that result can cause significant levels of mortality from collisions at night or in fog, in great bustards, large raptors and storks (MOPT, 1992; Martín-Novella *et al.*, 1993; MOPTMA, 1994). It is, however, the further agricultural intensification that drainage and irrigation allow that often is the main problem. Grassland drainage often leads to the agricultural changes described above, or conversion to cereals. Similarly, irrigation schemes lead to conversion to cereals and rapid intensification with high applications of fertilizer, modern fast-growing crops, loss of marginal habitats and frequent applications of pesticide. Such drainage, particularly of upland grasslands, is now much reduced (Tucker, in press), but, in contrast, irrigation schemes in southern Europe are commonplace and continue to be proposed, often with EU funding. In Spain alone, 10 000 km^2 of land were brought under new irrigation between 1970 and 1989 (Egdell, 1993) and a further 6000 km^2 are to be irrigated according to the National Hydrological Plan (Suárez *et al.*, Chapter 11).

Agricultural abandonment

Paradoxically agricultural abandonment is no less a threat to farmland birds than many of the processes of intensification. It is a particular threat to semi-natural agricultural habitats, as these are most likely to be financially unviable, although abandonment through the failure of intensification programmes is not unusual (Lee, 1987; Egdell, 1993). Such habitats are often important for birds (as described in the previous section) and other fauna and flora (Baldock *et al.*, 1993; Bignal & McCracken, 1993; Beaufoy *et al.*, 1994). Large areas of such semi-natural pastoral grassland habitat are currently being abandoned in eastern Europe following the collapse of communism in the region (CEC,

1995b). Abandonment is detrimental because, in the absence of the former natural herbivores, scrub encroachment normally results and the open habitat that is essential for most farmland species is lost. Another variant of abandonment is intensification of some previously low-intensity land funded by the sale of other land for afforestation, the result being a decrease in natural value in both zones (Bignal *et al.*, 1988; Pienkowski, 1989). Although some scrub and forest birds may benefit from these changes, few of them have an Unfavourable Conservation Status as these habitats are generally increasing in Europe (Lee, 1987). Most scrub and heath species with an Unfavourable Conservation Status require open habitats such as those maintained by extensive grazing. In contrast, most forest species with an Unfavourable Conservation Status require ancient climax forest, which would require centuries to develop. Furthermore, in many areas, such forests may not be able to recover because soil has eroded since the clearance of the original forest cover. Thus, in terms of bird conservation objectives, large-scale abandonment of semi-natural and other farmland habitats of high conservation importance and their replacement with scrub, or even forest, is usually likely to be detrimental.

Differences between western and central and eastern Europe

Threat analysis confirms the widely held view that most declining agricultural species in Europe are threatened by the continued process of intensification on existing farmland and by the loss of the remaining semi-natural agricultural habitats through either intensification or abandonment. These threats have been particularly prevalent in western Europe where agriculture has been most intense (Stanners & Bourdeau, 1995). As a result, farmland species have been found to be predominantly declining in western Europe but not in central and eastern European countries (CEEC), a pattern well illustrated by the national population trends of the skylark (Figure 9). Other farmland birds with an Unfavourable Conservation Status in Europe that have substantially declined (i.e. by at least 20% in more than 33% of their populations), between 1970 and 1990, in western Europe but not in the CEEC are turtle dove, little owl *Athene noctua*, crested lark, tawny pipit *Anthus campestris* and ortolan bunting (Tucker & Heath, 1994). In addition, 33 other species that do not currently have an Unfavourable Conservation Status in Europe, including lapwing *Vanellus vanellus*, snipe *Gallinago gallinago*, cuckoo *Cuculus canorus* and whinchat *Saxicola rubetra*, declined in western Europe but not in the CEEC. Although such species are not currently at risk on a European scale they, and probably many more species, may become so in the future if similar agricultural practices are followed in the CEEC as in the west. Despite the current trend towards abandonment in the CEEC region described above (with its own different problems), agricultural intensification is likely in the long-term (CEC, 1995b).

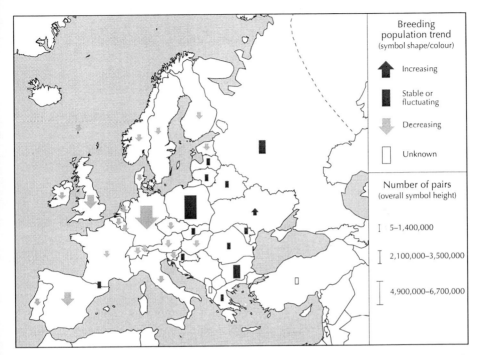

Figure 9 Population trends in the skylark *Alauda arvensis* in Europe between 1970 and 1990.

A STRATEGY FOR FARMLAND BIRD CONSERVATION

It is clear from this and other reviews (e.g. Baldock, 1990; Hötker, 1991; Baldock *et al.*, 1993; Tucker & Heath, 1994) that conservation actions to date have been largely ineffective in maintaining farmland bird populations in Europe and particularly in the EU. This is in part due to the rapid and enormous scale of change that has occurred in farming systems in the region over the last 20–30 years. However, a major reason must be that, until recently, the conservation measures available were limited essentially to site-based approaches such as the designation of protected areas and establishment of nature reserves. The approach limited to site-based measures has made major contributions to saving the last refuges of much wildlife but has not conserved agricultural species for three main reasons.

(1) As mentioned above, most agricultural species are widely dispersed (at least at some stage in their annual cycle) and therefore cannot be conserved by

protected areas alone. Even on our most optimistic forecast these areas would cover only a small fraction of the farmed landscape.

(2) Conservation efforts have mainly concentrated on natural habitats and very few protected areas for agricultural species have been designated even for those species that might benefit from a site-based approach (e.g. great bustard). For example, in Spain 2.5 million ha have been listed as Important Bird Areas for steppe species (de Juana, 1988; Grimmett & Jones, 1989), but up to now almost none of this is protected (Suárez et al., Chapter 11). Again this is partly due to the mistaken, but widespread, view that agricultural habitats and species are of low conservation importance. It is also in part due to the difficulty conservationists have had in influencing economically important land-uses.

(3) Statutory protection of sites does not ensure the maintenance of the farming practices that many of the important bird species rely on, such as extensive grazing, rotational cropping systems with fallow and an absence of pesticides. The EU Environmentally Sensitive Areas (ESA) scheme goes some way to addressing this by offering payments to farmers who voluntarily farm in a prescribed environmentally beneficial way. The scheme undoubtedly provides some excellent opportunities to implement conservation measures for some birds such as the great bustard (e.g. Naveso, 1992; Naveso & Groves-Reines, 1992; Naveso & Fernández, 1993). However, initially ESAs were essentially site-based and therefore unable to deal with the wider problem of declining agricultural species. The recent implementation of the Agri-Environment Regulation (EC Reg. 2078/92) has widened the ESA concept by developing zonal programmes which may include measures applied to whole regions. However, funding for this is limited and adequate for only a fraction of the proposed schemes (BirdLife International, 1994).

It is therefore clear that wide-scale measures that integrate conservation objectives into all aspects of agricultural policy are essential (Pienkowski & Bignal, 1993; Tucker et al., 1993; Tucker, in press). To address European bird conservation priorities these objectives must include:

(1) The avoidance of further losses of natural and semi-natural non-agricultural habitats to agriculture.

(2) The maintenance of existing low-intensity farming systems on remaining semi-natural habitats.

(3) The avoidance of further intensification, and the restoration of habitats of high nature conservation value.

(4) The reduction of inputs in highly intensified systems and appropriate restoration of important habitat features, such as hedgerows and ditches.

Although agricultural policy is always likely to be primarily driven by economic, social and political needs, opportunities to incorporate these conservation objectives do exist, and are increasing as a result of the case made by conservationists (as described by Robson, Chapter 3 and Dixon, Chapter 14).

The biological importance of semi-natural and low-intensity farming systems and the need to take urgent measures to conserve them is now being widely accepted, for example through the High-Natural-Value concept (Baldock *et al.*, 1993; Beaufoy *et al.*, 1994) and to some extent addressed through measures such as the Agri-environment Regulation. However, the desirability of adopting less intensive farming methods is only slowly gaining wide recognition, and is still subject to resistance. Indeed, it has been proposed that intensification should be encouraged so that less land can be used for agriculture and more land released for nature conservation (Agra Europe, 1996). The results of this review, echoed in several specific case studies described in this publication (e.g. Potts, Chapter 6; Suárez *et al.*, Chapter 11), clearly indicate that such an approach would be deleterious for bird conservation. The consequences would be an increase in scrub and eventually some forest habitats, but as described above these would be of low habitat quality and consequently low conservation value. It is also doubtful that a substantial amount of land would be made available for nature conservation, as much land would probably continue to be used for economic purposes, for example, forestry or the production of crops that are not in surplus.

The restoration of specific habitats, such as some types of wetlands, moorlands and heathlands that have been lost to agriculture, could provide some important conservation benefits. However, the restoration of such habitats is time-consuming, technically difficult and very expensive, if possible at all (e.g. Putwain & Rae, 1988; Sutherland & Hill, 1995). Only a small proportion of released land could conceivably be converted to habitats of high conservation value.

Of course the conversion of some intensive agricultural land to forests and other more natural habitats may provide bird and other wildlife conservation benefits, especially in the long-term. However, the re-creation of such habitats in the landscape should not be seen as a substitute for more environmentally sustainable land-use over wide areas. Overall, arable farmland and agriculturally improved grasslands have a particularly high number of birds with an Unfavourable Conservation Status. Further intensification of these habitats would assuredly lead to the continuation of the declines in these species and a significant deterioration in the conservation status of many more species, such as lapwing, linnet *Carduelis cannabina*, yellowhammer and corn bunting, which are already declining in much of the EU (Hudson *et al.*, 1994; Donald *et al.*, 1994; Tucker & Heath, 1994). Furthermore, intensification would exacerbate the abandonment of marginal non-intensive agriculture on semi-natural habitats. As described above, the maintenance of such farming practices on these habitats is of considerable importance for the conservation of birds and other wildlife. Thus the net result of further intensification would undoubtedly be the continued massive loss of biodiversity on a scale unparalleled in any other European habitat.

ACKNOWLEDGEMENTS

I am extremely grateful to Colin Bibby, Nigel Collar, Jim Dixon, Rob Fuller, Debbie Pain, Mike Pienkowski, Clive Potter and Nigel Robson, all of whom provided valuable comments and advice during the preparation of the manuscript. I am also indebted to Melanie Heath who co-authored *Birds in Europe: their conservation status*, upon which much of this paper is based. Hugo Rainey provided assistance with data collection and the manuscript was ably typed by Regina Pfaff.

REFERENCES

ADAMS, W.M., BOURN, N. & HODGE, I. (1992) Conservation in the wider countryside. *Land Use Policy*, October: 235–248.

AGRA EUROPE (1996) High-yield farming 'key to increased food demand'. 16 February: 4.

ANGELSTAM, P. (1992) Conservation of communities – the importance of edges, surroundings and landscape mosaic structure. In L. Hannson (ed.) *Ecological Principles of Nature Conservation*, pp. 9–70. London: Elsevier.

ASKINS, R.A. (1993) Population trends in grassland, shrublands and forest birds in Eastern North America. In D. M. Power (ed.) *Current Ornithology 11*, pp. 1–34. New York: Plenum Press

BAINES, D. (1988) The effects of improvement of upland grassland on the distribution and density of breeding wading birds (*Charadriiformes*) in northern England. *Biological Conservation*, 45: 221–236.

BALDOCK, D. (1990) *Agriculture and Habitat Loss in Europe*. Gland, Switzerland: World Wide Fund for Nature International (Common Agricultural Policy Discussion Paper 3).

BALDOCK, D., BEAUFOY, G., BENNETT, G. & CLARK, J. (1993) *Nature Conservation and New Directions in the European Communities Common Agricultural Policy*. London: Institute for European Environmental Policy.

BATTEN, L.A., BIBBY, C.J., CLEMENT, P., ELLIOTT, G.D. & PORTER, R.F. (eds) (1990) *Red Data Birds in Britain: action for rare, threatened and important species*. London: T. and A.D. Poyser.

BEAUFOY, G., BALDOCK, D. & CLARK, J. (1994) *The Nature of Farming*. Peterborough: Joint Nature Conservation Committee.

BEINTEMA, A.J. (1988) Conservation of grassland bird communities in The Netherlands. In P. D. Goriup (ed.) *Ecology and Conservation of Grassland Birds*, pp. 105–111. (Technical Publication 7), Cambridge.

BEINTEMA, A.J. (1991) Status and conservation of meadow birds in the Netherlands. *Wader Study Group Bulletin*, 61(Suppl.): 12–13.

BEINTEMA, A.J. & MÜSKENS, G.J.D.M. (1987). Nesting success of birds breeding in Dutch agricultural grasslands. *Journal of Applied Ecology*. 24: 743–758.

BELIK, V.P. (1991) In A. N. Khokhlov (ed.) *Recent Data on Bird Species, Distribution and Ecology in the Northern Caucasus*, pp. 109–111. Stavropol: Savropol Pedagogical Insitute.

BENSON, G.B.G. & WILLIAMSON, K. (1972) Breeding birds of a mixed farm in Suffolk. *Bird Study*, 19: 34–50.

BERNES, C. (1993) *The Nordic Environment: present state, trends and threats*. Copenhagen: Nordic Council of Ministers.

BIBBY, C.J., PHILLIPS, B.N. & SEDDON, A.J.E. (1985) Birds of restocked conifer plantations in Wales. *Journal of Applied Ecology*, **22**: 619–633.

BIBBY, C.J., BAIN, C.G. & BURGESS, D.J. (1989) Bird communities of highland birchwoods. *Bird Study*, **36**: 123–133.

BIGNAL, E.M., CURTIS, D.J. & MATTHEWS, J.L. (1988) *Islay: land-types, bird habitats and nature conservation. Part 1: land use and birds on Islay.* Peterborough: Chief Scientist Directorate Report No. 809, Nature Conservancy Council.

BIGNAL, E., BIGNAL, S. & CURTIS, D.J. (1989) In E. Bignal & D.J. Curtis (eds) *Choughs and Land-use in Europe*, pp. 102–109. Clachan· Scottish Chough Study Group.

BIGNAL, E. & McCRACKEN, D. (1993) Nature conservation and pastoral farming in the British uplands. *British Wildlife*, **4**: 367–376.

BIGNAL, E.M., McCRACKEN, D.I., STILLMAN, R.A. & OVENDEN, G.Y. (in press). Feeding behaviour of nesting choughs in the Scottish Hebrides. *Journal of Field Ornithology*.

BINK, R.J., BAL, D., VAN DEN BERK, V.M. & DRAAIJER, L.J. (1994) *Toestand van de natuur 2.* Wageningen, The Netherlands: IKC-NBLF.

BIRDLIFE INTERNATIONAL (1994) The implementation of the agri-environment regulation (European Commission 2078/92). Cambridge: BirdLife International.

BIRKS, H.H., BIRKS, H.J., KALAND, P.E. & MOE, D., eds. (1988). *The Cultural Landscape: past, present and future.* Cambridge: Cambridge University Press.

BODY, R. (1983) *Agriculture: the triumph and the shame.* London: Maurice Temple Smith.

BRAAE, L., NOHR, H. & PETERSEN, B.S. (1988) [*The Bird Fauna of Conventional and Organic Farmland*]. Copenhagen: Miljoministeriet, Miljostyrelsen (Miljoprojekt 12). (In Dutch.)

BULL, A.L., MEAD, C.J. & WILLIAMSON, K. (1976) Bird-life on a Norfolk farm in relation to agricultural changes. *Bird Study*, **23**: 163–182.

CEC (Commission of the European Communities) (1995a) Europe's environment: statistical compendium for the Dobris assessment. Luxembourg: European Commission,

CEC (Commission of the European Communities) (1995b) Agricultural situation and prospects in the Central and Eastern European Countries. Summary Report, Brussels: European Commission.

CHAMBERLAIN, D., EVANS, J., FULLER, R. & LANGSTON, R. (1995) Where there's muck, there's birds. *British Trust for Ornithology News*, **200**: 15–17.

COLLAR, N.J., CROSBY, M.J. & STATTERSFIELD, A.J. (1994) *Birds to Watch 2: the world list of threatened birds.* Cambridge: BirdLife International (BirdLife Conservation Series no. 4).

CRAMP, S. & SIMMONS, K.E.L., eds. (1980) *The Birds of the Western Palearctic*, 2. Oxford: Oxford University Press.

CROCKFORD, N., GREEN, R., ROCAMORA, G., SCHÄFFER, N., STOWE, T. & WILLIAMS, G. (1996) Corncrake. In B. Heredia, L. Rose & M. Painter (eds) *Action plans for globally-threatened birds in Europe.* Strasbourg: Council of Europe.

DE JUANA, E. (1988) Areas importantes para las aves esteparias. *La Garcilla*, **71–72**: 18–19.

DE JUANA, E., MARTÍN-NOVELLA, C., NAVESO, M.A., PAIN, D. & SEARS, J. (1993) Farming and birds in Spain: threats and opportunities for conservation. *Royal Society for the Protection of Birds Conservation Review*, **7**: 67–73.

DÍAZ, M., NAVESO, M.A. & REBOLLO, E. (1993) Respuestas de las comunidades nidificantes de aves a la intensificación agrícola en cultivos cerealistas de la Meseta Norte (Valladolid-Palencia, España). *Aegypius*, **11**: 1–6.

DONALD, P.F., WILSON, J.D. & SHEPHERD, M. (1994) The decline of the corn bunting. *British Birds*, **87**: 106–132.

EGDELL, J.M. (1993) *Impact of Agricultural Policy on Spain and Its Steppe Regions.* Sandy: Royal Society for the Protection of Birds.

ELLENBERG, H., RÜGER, A. & VAUK, G. (1989) [*Eutrophication: the most serious threat in nature conservation*]. Norddeutsche Naturschutzakademie (Berichte 2). (In German.)

FÉSÜS, I., MÁRKUS, F., SZABÓ, G., TÖLGYESI, I., VARGA, Z. & VERMES, L. (1992) *Interaction Between Agriculture and Environment in Hungary.* Gland, Switzerland: International Union for Conservation of Nature and Natural Resources (Environmental Research Series No. 5).

FORD, H.A. (1987) Bird communities on habitat islands in England. *Bird Study,* **34**: 205–218.

FRY, G.L.A. (1991) In F.B Goldsmith & M.G. Morris (eds) *The Scientific Management of Temperate Communities for Conservation: the 31st symposium of the British Ecological Society, Southampton, 1989,* pp. 415–443. Oxford: Blackwell Scientific Publications.

FULLER, R.J. & HENDERSON, A.C.B. (1992) Distribution of breeding songbirds in Bradfield Woods, Suffolk, in relation to vegetation and coppice management. *Bird Study,* **39**: 73–88.

FULLER, R.J. & MORETON, B.D. (1987) Breeding bird populations of Kentish sweet chestnut (*Castanea sativa*) coppice in relation to age and structure of the coppice). *Journal of Applied Ecology,* **24**: 13–28.

FULLER, R., HILL, D. & TUCKER, G. (1991) Feeding the birds down on the farm: perspectives from Britain. *Ambio,* **20**: 232–237.

FULLER, R.J., GREGORY, R.D., GIBBONS, D.W., MARCHANT, J.H., WILSON, J.D., BAILLIE, S.R. & CARTER, N. (in press). Population declines and range contractions among lowland farmland birds in Britain. *Biological Conservation.*

FURNESS, R.W., GREENWOOD, J.J.D. & JARVIS, P.J. (1993) Can birds be used to monitor the environment? In R.W. Furness & J.J.D. Greenwood (eds) *Birds as Monitors of Environmental Change,* pp. 1–41. London: Chapman & Hall.

GILPIN, M.E. & SOULÉ, M.E. (1986) Minimum viable populations: processes of species extinction. In M. E. Soulé (ed.) *Conservation Biology: the science of scarcity and diversity,* pp. 19–34. Suderland: Sinauer Associates Inc.

GORIUP, P.D., BATTEN, L.A. & NORTON, J.A., eds. (1991) *The Conservation of Lowland Dry Grassland Birds in Europe.* Proceedings of an international seminar held at the University of Reading 20–22 March 1991. Peterborough: Joint Nature Conservation Committee.

GREEN, R.E. (1988) Stone-curlew conservation. *Royal Society for the Protection of Birds Conservation Review,* **2**: 30–33.

GREEN, R.E. & CADBURY, C.J. (1987) Breeding waders of lowland wet grassland. *Royal Society for the Protection of Birds Conservation Review,* **1**: 10–13.

GREEN, R.E. & RAYMENT, M.D. (in press). Geographical variation in the abundance of the corncrake *Crex crex* in Europe in relation to the intensity of agriculture. *Bird Conservation International.*

GRIMMETT, R.F.A. & JONES, T.A. (1989) *Important Bird Areas in Europe.* Cambridge: International Council for Bird Preservation (Technical Publication 9).

HAMPICKE, U. (1978) Agriculture and conservation – ecological and social aspects. *Agriculture and the Environment,* **4**: 25–42.

HANSKI, I. & TIAINEN, J. (1988) Populations and communities in changing agro-ecosystems in Finland. *Ecological Bulletins (Copenhagen),* **39**: 159–168.

HODGSON, J.G. (1987) Growing rare in Britain. *New Scientist,* **1547**: 38–39.

HÖLZINGER, J., ed. (1987) *Avifauna Baden-Württemberg. 1: Gefährdung und Schutz.* [*Birds of Baden-Württemberg. 1: Threats and conservation*]. Karlsruhe: E. Ulmer Verlag. (In German.)

HÖTKER, H., ed. (1991) *Waders Breeding on Wet Grasslands.* Tring: Wader Study Group.

HUDSON, R., TUCKER, G.M. & FULLER, R.J. (1994) Lapwing *Vanellus vanellus* populations in relation to agricultural changes: a review. In G.M. Tucker., S.M. Davies & R.J. Fuller (eds) *The Ecology and Conservation of Lapwings* Vanellus vanellus, pp. 1-33. Peterborough: Joint Nature Conservation Committee (UK Nature Conservation Series 9).

HUNTER, J.M. & BLACK, J.M. (1996) Red-breasted Goose. In B. Heredia, L. Rose & M. Painter (eds) Action plans for globally-threatened birds in Europe. Strasbourg: Council of Europe.

HUSTON, M.A. (1994) *Biological Diversity: the coexistence of species on changing landscapes.* Cambridge: Cambridge University Press.

IRVINE, J. (1977) Breeding birds in New Forest broad-leaved woodland. *Bird Study*, **24**: 105–110.

IRVING, R. (1993) *Too Much of a Good Thing: nutrient enrichment in the U.K.'s inland and coastal waters*. Godalming: World Wide Fund for Nature.

IUCN (1991) *The Environment in Eastern Europe: 1990*. Cambridge: International Union for Nature Conservation and Natural Resources (Environmental Research Series 3).

JENKINS, D. (1984) *Agriculture and the Environment*. Cambridge: Natural Environment Research Council (Proceedings of Institute of Terrestrial Ecology symposium No. 13).

KIRBY, K. (1995) *Rebuilding the English Countryside: habitat fragmentation and wildlife corridors as issues in practical conservation*. Peterborough: English Nature (Science Series no. 10).

KOLLAR, H-P. (1996) Great Bustard. In B. Heredia, L. Rose & M. Painter (eds) Action plans for globally-threatened birds in Europe. Strasbourg: Council of Europe.

KORNAS, J. (1983) Man's impact on flora and vegetation in Central Europe. *Geobotany*, **5**: 277–286.

LEE, J. (1987). European land use and resources: an analysis of future European Commission demands. *Land Use Policy*, **4**: 179–199.

LOWE, P., COX, G., MacEWAN, M., O'RIORDAN, T. & WINTER, M. (1986) *Countryside Conflicts: the politics of farming, forestry and conservation*. Aldershot: Gower Publishing Company.

LYSAGHT, L.S. (1989) Breeding bird populations of mid-west Ireland in 1987. *Bird Study*, **36**: 91–98.

MacARTHUR, R.H. & WILSON, E.O. (1963) An equilibrium theory of insular zoogeography. *Evolution*, **17**: 373–387.

MacARTHUR, R.H. & WILSON, E.O. (1967) *The Theory of Island Biogeography*. Princeton: Princeton University Press.

MACE, G. & STUART, S. (1994) Draft IUCN Red List categories. *Species*, **21–22**: 13–24.

MARTÍN-NOVELLA, C., CRIADO, J. & NAVESO, M.A. (1993) [The mark of the new Common Agricultural Policy: nature conservation and water management]. *Ecosistemas*, **5**: 24–27. (In Spanish.)

MASSEY, M.E. (1978) The breeding bird community of an upland nature reserve in Powys 1970-1977. *Bird Study*, **25**: 167–174.

MERRIAM, G. (1988). Landscape dynamics in farmland. *Tree*, **3**: 16–20.

MOPT (Ministerio de Obras Públicas y Transportes) (1992) [*Project guidelines of Hydrological Catchment Plans*]. Madrid: Ministerio de Obras Públicas y Transportes. (In Spanish).

MOPTMA (Ministerio de Obras Públicas, Transportes y Medio Ambiente) (1994) [*Natural Hydrological Plan: analysis of scenarios*]. Dirección General de Obras Hidráulicas, Ministerio de Obras Públicas, Madrid: Transportes y Medio Ambiente. (In Spanish.)

MOORE, N.W. (1983). Ecological effects of pesticides. In A. Warren & F.B. Goldsmith (eds) *Conservation in Perspective*, pp. 159-179. Chichester: John Wiley and Sons Limited.

MORGAN, R. (1975) Breeding bird communities on chalk downland in Wiltshire. *Bird Study*, **22**: 71–83.

MOSS, D. (1978) Diversity of woodland song-bird populations. *Journal of Animal Ecology*. **47**: 521–527.

NAVESO, M.A. (1992) *Propuesta de declaración de la zona de Madrigal-Peñaranda como Area Ambientalmente Sensible*. Madrid: Sociedad Española de Ornitología (unpublished).

NAVESO, M.A. & FERNÁNDEZ, J. (1993) Propuesta de programla de zona para el área de La Serena en aplicación del reglamento CEE 2078/92. Madrid: Sociedad Española de Ornitología (unpublished).

NAVESO, M.A. & GROVES-REINES, S. (1992) Propuesta de declaración de la zona de Tierra de Campos como Area Ambientalmente Sensible. Madrid: Sociedad Española de Ornitología (unpublished).

NEWTON, I. (1979) *Population Ecology of Raptors*. Berkhamsted: T. and A. D. Poyser.

O'BRIEN, M. & SELF, M. (1994) Changes in the numbers of breeding waders on lowland wet grasslands in the UK. *Royal Society for the Protection of Birds Conservation Review*, 8: 38–44.

O'CONNOR, R.J. & SHRUBB, M. (1986) *Farming and Birds*. Cambridge: Cambridge University Press.

OPDAM, P. (1991) Metapopulation theory and habitat fragmentation: a review of Holarctic breeding bird studies. *Landscape Ecology*, 5: 93–106.

OPDAM, P., FOPPEN, R., REIJEN, R. & SCOTMAN, A. (1995) The landscape ecological approach in bird conservation: integrating the metapopulation concept into spatial planning. *Ibis*, 137(1): 139–146.

PAIN, D. J. (1994a) Case studies of farming and birds in Europe: Olive farming in Portugal. Sandy: Royal Society for the Protection of Birds Unpublished Research Report.

PAIN, D.J. (1994b) Case studies of farming and birds in Europe: Rice farming in Italy. Sandy: Royal Society for the Protection of Birds Unpublished Research Report.

PAIN, D. J. (1994c) Case studies of farming and birds in Europe: Transhumance pastoralism in Spain. Sandy: Royal Society for the Protection of Birds Unpublished Research Report.

PARSONS, A.J. (1976) Birds of a Somerset wood. *Bird Study*, 23: 287–293.

PEAKALL, D.B. & BOYD, H. (1987). Birds as bio-indicators of environmental conditions. In A.W. Diamond & F.L. Filion (eds) *The Value of Birds*, pp. 113–118. Cambridge: International Council for Bird Preservation (Technical Publication 6).

PETERJOHN, B.G. & SAUER, J.R. (1993) North American breeding bird survey annual summary 1990–1991. *Bird Populations*, 1: 1–15.

PETERSEN, B. (1994) Interactions between birds and agriculture in Denmark: from simple counts to detailed studies of breeding success and foraging behaviour. In E.J.M. Hagemeijer & T.J. Verstrael (eds) *Bird Numbers 1992, Distribution, monitoring and ecological aspects: proceedings of the 12th International Conference of IBCC and EOAC*, Noordwijkerhout, Netherlands, September 14–18 1992. Beek-Ubbergen: Statistics Netherlands, Voorburg/Heerlen and SOVON.

PETTY, S.J. & AVERY, M.I. (1990) Edinburgh: Forest bird communities. Forestry Commission (Occasional paper 26).

PIENKOWSKI, M.W. (1989) Introduction, overview and discussion. In E.M. Bignal & D. J. Curtis (eds) *Choughs and Land-Use in Europe*, pp. 1-3. Argyll: Scottish Chough Study Group.

PIENKOWSKI, M. & BIGNAL, E. (1993) Objectives for nature conservation in European agriculture. In J.B. Dixon., A.J. Stones & I.R. Hepburn (eds) *A Future for Europe's Farmed Countryside*, Proceedings of an international conference, No.1, pp. 21–43. Sandy: Royal Society for the Protection of Birds (Studies in European Agricultural and Environmental Policy No. 1).

PIMM, S. L. (1991) *The Balance of Nature?* Chicago: University of Chicago Press.

PINA, J.P., RUFINO, R., ARAÚJO, A. & NEVES, R. (1990) Breeding and wintering passerine densities in Portugal. In K. Stasny & V. Bejcek (eds) *Bird Census and Atlas Studies*. Proceedings of the XIth International Conference on bird census and atlas work, Prague, pp. 273–276. Institute of Applied Ecology and Ecotechnology, Agriculture University, Prague

POTTS, G.R. (1986) *The Partridge: pesticides, predation and conservation*. London: Collins.

POTTS, G.R. (1990) Causes of the decline in partridge population and effects of the insecticide dimethoate on chick mortality. In J.T. Lumeij & Y.R. Hoogeveen (eds) *The Future of Wild Galliformes in The Netherlands*, pp. 62–71. The Hague: Gegevens Koninklijke Bibliotheek.

PUTWAIN, P.D. & RAE, P.A.S. (1988) *Heathland Restorations: a handbook of techniques*. British Gas plc (Southern), Liverpool and University of Liverpool Environmental Advisory Unit.

RACKHAM, O. (1986) *The History of the Countryside*. London: J.M. Dent and Sons.

RATCLIFFE, D. (1993) *The Peregrine Falcon*, 2nd edition. London: T. and A. D. Poyser.

ROBSON, R.W. & WILLIAMSON, K. (1972) Breeding birds of a Westmoorland farm. *Bird Study*, 19: 203–214.

RUTSCHKE, E. (1989) *Die wildenten Europas [Ducks of Europe]*. Berlin: VEB Deutscher Landwirtschaftsverlag.

RYAN, P.G. & SIEGFRIED, W.R. (1994) The viability of small populations of birds: an empirical investigation of vulnerability. In H. Remmert (ed.) *Minimum Animal Populations*, pp. 3–22. Berlin: Springer-Verlag (Ecological Studies Vol. 106).

SCHAFFER, M.I., (1981) Minimum population sizes for species conservation. *BioScience*, 31: 131–134.

SCHLÄPFER, A. (1988) [Population studies of the skylark *Alauda arvensis* in an are of intensive agriculture]. *Ornithologische Beobachter*, 85: 309–371. (In German).

SCHOENER, T.W. (1976) The species-area relation within archipelagos: models and evidence from island land birds. In H.J. Frith & J.H. Calaby (eds) *Proceedings 16th International Ornithological Conference*, pp. 629–642. Canberra: Australian Academy of Sciences.

SCHOENER, T.W. (1986) Patterns in terrestrial vertebrates versus arthropod communities: do systematic differences in regularity exist? In J. Diamond & T.J. Case (eds) *Community Ecology*, pp. 556–586. New York: Harper and Row.

SGOP (1983). Estudio de la explotación de aquas subterráneas en las proximidades del Parque Nacional de las Tablas de Damiel y su influencia sobre el suporte hidrico del ecosistema. Madrid: Ministerio de Obras Públicas y Urbanismo (Report 12/83).

SIMBERLOFF, D. (1988) The contribution of population and community biology to conservation science. *Annual Review Ecology Systematics*, 19: 473–511.

SIMBERLOFF, D. (1995) Habitat fragmentation and population extinction of birds. *Ibis*, 137(1): 105–111.

SMITH, K.W., BURGES, D.J. & PARKS, R.A. (1992) Breeding bird communities of broadleaved plantation and ancient pasture woodlands of the New Forest. *Bird Study*, 39: 132–141.

SOULÉ, M.E., ed. (1987) *Viable populations for conservation*. Cambridge: Cambridge University Press.

STANNERS, D. & BOURDEAU, P., ed. (1995) *Europe's Environment: the Dobris Assessment*. Copenhagen: European Environment Agency.

STOWE, T.J., NEWTON, A.V., GREEN, R.E. & MAYES, E. (1993) The decline of the Corncrake *Crex crex* in Britain and Ireland in relation to habitat. *Journal Applied Ecology*, 30: 53–62.

SUÁREZ, F. & OÑATE, J. (1994) Dupont's Lark. In G.M. Tucker & M.F. Heath (eds) *Birds in Europe: their conservation status*, pp. 350–351. Cambridge: BirdLife International (BirdLife Conservation Series no. 3).

SUTHERLAND, W.J. & CROCKFORD, N.J. (1993) Factors affecting the feeding distribution of Red-breasted Geese *Branta ruficollis* wintering in Romania. *Biological Conservation*, 63: 61–65.

SUTHERLAND, W.J. & HILL, D.A. (1995) *Managing Habitats for Conservation*. Cambridge: Cambridge University Press.

TELLERÍA, J.L., SANTOS, T. & DIÁZ, M. (1994) Effects of agricultural practices on bird populations in the Mediterranean region: the case of Spain. In E.J.M. Hagemeijer & T.J. Verstrael (eds) *Bird Numbers 1992. Distribution, monitoring and ecological aspects*, pp. 57–74. Proceedings of the 12th International Conference of IBCC and EOAC, Noordwijkherhout. Beek-Ubbergen: Statistics Netherlands, Voorburg/Heerlen and SOVON.

TEMPLE, S.A. (1991) The role of dispersal in the maintenance of bird populations in a fragmented landscape. *Acta XX Congressus Internationalis Ornithologici Basel*, 20: 2298–2305.

THOMPSON, D.B.A. & MACDONALD, A.J. (1995) Upland heather moorland in Great Britain: a review of international importance, vegetation change and some objectives for nature conservation. *Biological Conservation*, 71: 163–178.

TUCKER, G.M. (in press) Habitat conservation for birds in Europe: a conservation strategy for the wider environment. Cambridge: Birdlife International (Conservation Series No. 6).

TUCKER, G.M. & HEATH, M.F. (1994) *Birds in Europe: their conservation status*. Cambridge: BirdLife International (BirdLife Conservation Series no. 3).

TUCKER, G.M., HEATH, M. & GRIMMETT, R.A. (1993) Towards a strategy for the conservation of dispersed species in Europe. *Royal Society for the Protection of Birds Conservation Review*, 7: 74–79.

USHER, M.B. & THOMPSON, D.B.A., eds. (1988) *Ecological Changes in the Uplands*. Oxford: Blackwell Scientific Publications (Special Publication of the British Ecological Society 7).

VAN DE VELDE, R.J., FABER, W., VAN KATWIJK, V., SCHOLTEN, H.J., THEWESSEN, T., VERSPUY, M. & ZEVENBERGEN, M. (1994) *The Preparation of a European Land Use Database*. RIVM (Report no. 712401001), Bilthoven, Netherlands.

VAN DIJK, G. (1991) The status of semi-natural grasslands in Europe. In P.D. Goriup., L.A. Batten & J.A. Norton (eds) *The Conservation of Lowland Dry Grassland Birds in Europe*, pp. 15–36. Peterborough: Joint Nature Conservation Committee.

VANGELUWE, D. & STASSIN, P. (1991) Hivernage de la Bernache à cou roux *Branta ruficollis* en Dobroudja septentrionale, Roumanie et revue du statut hivernal de l'espèce [Wintering of the Red-breasted Goose *Branta ruficollis* in northern Dobrogea, Romania, and a review of the species' wintering status] (In French). *Gerfaut*, 81: 65–99.

WARNER, R.E. (1994) Agricultural land use and grassland habitat in Illinois: future shock for midwestern birds? *Conservation Biology*, 8: 147–156.

WIENS, J.A. (1989) *The Ecology of Bird Communities: Foundations and patterns, 1*. Cambridge: Cambridge University Press.

WIENS, J.A. (1995) Habitat fragmentation: island v landscape perspectives on bird conservation. *Ibis*, 137(1): 97–104.

WILCOVE, D.S., CHARLES, H., McLELLAN & DOBSON, A.P. (1986) Habitat fragmentation in the temperate zone. In M.E. Soulé (ed.) *Conservation Biology*, pp. 237–256. Sunderland, USA: Sinauer Associates, Inc.

WILLIAMSON, K. (1974) Breeding birds in the deciduous woodlands of mid-Argyll, Scotland. *Bird Study*, 21: 29–44.

WILLIAMSON, K. (1975) The breeding bird communities of chalk grassland scrub in the Chiltern Hills. *Bird Study*, 22: 59–70.

WILSON, J. (1978) The breeding bird community of willow scrub at Leighton Moss, Lancashire. *Bird Study*, 25: 239–244.

WILSON, J.D. (1993) The British Trust for Ornithology birds and organic farming project – one year on. *British Trust Ornithology News*, 185: 10–12.

WILSON, J.D. & BROWNE, J.J. (1993) Habitat selection and breeding success of Skylarks *Alauda arvensis* on organic and conventional farmland. British Trust for Ornithology Research Report. No. 129), Thetford.

WYLLIE, I. (1976) The bird community of an English parish. *Bird Study*, 23: 39–50.

5

Extensive grazing and raptors in Spain

JOSÉ A. DONÁZAR, MIGUEL A. NAVESO,
JOSÉ L. TELLA & DAVID CAMPIÓN

SUMMARY

Extensive farming systems are widely distributed throughout Spain. Many of these low-input systems have been in place for centuries, and much wildlife, some of which is globally endangered, depends upon their continued existence. In mountain areas, mosaic habitats, e.g. a mix of grassland, scrub and scattered forest, fulfil the requirements of raptors. In steppe areas, winter stubbles and short to medium-term fallow are important for many raptor species, as these areas support abundant prey. In all areas, under low-input grazing systems, the carcases of livestock provide a regular food supply for vultures.

However, low-input grazing systems are unlikely to remain economically viable far into the future. Headage payment subsidies for livestock under the Common Agricultural Policy (CAP) have resulted in intensification of grazing systems in many areas, although they have not stopped the abandonment of livestock farming in isolated rural areas. Although the 1992 CAP reform was a step towards integrating environmental considerations into agricultural policy, no clear integration has yet been achieved.

In this chapter, we describe extensive grazing systems in Spain, and the importance of these for a range of raptors. We then examine policy options for the maintenance of traditional grazing systems, and recommend a combination of mechanisms. These include a strengthening of the Agri-environment Regulation (2078/92), and a shift from headage to area payments, together with the application of incentives that enable rural economies to be sustainable.

FARMING AND BIRDS IN EUROPE
ISBN 0-12-544280-7
Copyright © 1997 Academic Press Ltd
All rights of reproduction in any form reserved

INTRODUCTION

Distribution and relative importance of extensive grazing systems in Spain

In general, extensive grazing systems may be defined as those semi-natural habitats which are used to a greater or lesser extent by livestock, and in which stocking densities are low enough to allow some of the natural ecological processes to continue to operate. In the dehesas, for example, the presence of tree and shrub vegetation is a clear indicator of the original vegetation. In the moorlands, the existing vegetation is halophitic scrub with scattered *Juniperus* trees.

The main management features of extensive (low-input) grazing systems are:

(1) Little or no use of inputs such as pesticides, fertilizers, water.
(2) Low stocking densities (this term is relative, depending upon the carrying capacity of the land and thus natural or local conditions). Stocking densities of extensive grassland are discussed later.
(3) Un-stabled livestock. In the extensive grazing systems of the dehesas, the average farm size is approximately 500 ha (Campos, 1993a). Although only 6% of farm properties in Spain are larger than this, they represent 55% of all agricultural land (Egdell, 1993). The stock graze freely, with access restricted on only a small percentage of dehesa, which is usually used for the production of fodder crops. In extensive grazing in pseudosteppes, the shepherd moves the sheep flock every day from the village where it is kept at night to various grasslands, winter stubble or traditional short to medium-term fallows. These traditional fallows are different from those set-aside as a requirement of the 1992 Common Agricultural Policy (CAP) reforms (CEC, 1992a).
(4) Even in grasslands, it is unusual for land to be grazed for long periods without interruption. Rotation is usually practised in these areas, but on long cycles of 5–10 years (see Campos, 1993b; Naveso & Fernández, 1993; Díaz *et al.*, 1996). This prevents excessive invasion of the halophitic scrub. The grazing areas which have been ploughed are usually given over to crops for a single year. Grasslands, therefore, are not uniform but a mosaic of short to medium-term fallows (3–5 years) interspersed with low-input cereal crops, grassland and scrubland with occasional cropping.

On the basis of the characteristics described above, almost 30 million hectares, 60% of the land area of Spain, can be defined as extensive grazing systems (Table 1).

Table 1 Surface areas used for agriculture and forestry in Spain

Land use	Dry land	Irrigated	Total
Cultivated arable	8 925 248	2 253 068	11 178 316
Fallow arable*	4 131 930	201 935	4 333 865
Open woodland and cultivation or fallow†	1 109 163	—	1 109 163
Grazed woodland*	3 593 444	—	3 593 444
Pastures and meadows*	1 228 308	201 363	1 429 671
Dry grasslands*	5 135 628	—	5 135 628
Scrubland†	4 918 150	—	4 918 150
Timber forest	7 184 828	—	7 184 828
Permanent crops	4 098 343	714 218	4 812 561
Abandoned land (pastures and open scrubland)‡	3 535 031	388 590	3 923 621
Subtotal agriculture and forestry land in Spain	43 860 073	3 759 174	47 619 247
Rivers and lakes			550 047
Others			2 301 961
Total Spanish land surface			50 471 255

Source: elaborated from MAPA (1989).
*†Extensively grazed: *usually; †often.
‡Rarely grazed.

Origin and types of extensive grazing systems

The various types of extensive grazing systems, all of which are important for raptors and other wildlife, cover wide areas (Figure 1).

The present landscape began to appear from about the twelfth century (although its origin is much earlier even than this), when the powerful stock-farmer's association (La Mesta) was formed. A redistribution of land occurred at that time to give the farmers the best grazing areas. A century later, when the number of stock-farmers increased, new pastures were needed and, in response to pressure from La Mesta, the majority of land remained, and remains, unfenced to allow movement of stock between different regions (Cabo & Manero, 1987).

The different kinds of extensive grazing habitats can be defined as follows:

Pseudosteppes

The term pseudosteppes includes a diversity of ecosystems in flat or slightly undulating areas with scant or no tree vegetation, an average rainfall of below 700 mm per annum, and with a long period of extremely low water levels in

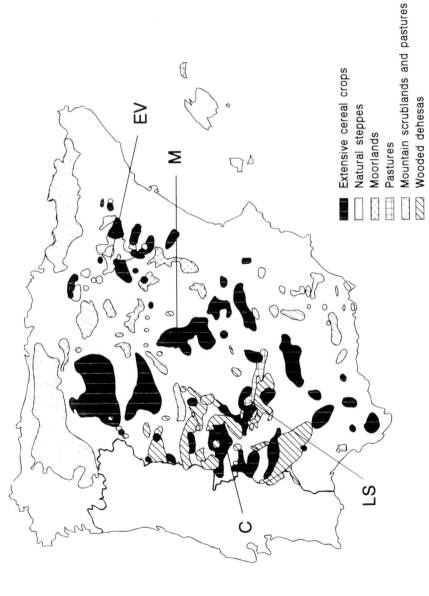

Figure 1. Major extensive grazing areas in Spain. C, Cáceres; LS, La Serena; M, Madrid; EV, Ebor Valley. Source: Ellaborated from Suárez y Garza, 1980; Alonso y Alonso, 1990; Alonso y Alonso, 1990; Garza y Surárez, 1990; MAPA (1983–88).

which rainfall is far lower than evapotranspiration (de Juana *et al.*, 1988; Suárez, 1988; Suárez *et al.*, 1991; Urmeneta & Naveso, 1993). This system is described in detail by Suarez *et al.* (Chapter 11).

Pseudosteppe covers the following types of habitats:

(i) Dry cereal crops. Land is used for annual dry cropping, principally of cereals (wheat and barley), legumes and sunflowers. Every year a percentage of the land is left fallow in rotation; this percentage varies significantly. The most productive areas are mainly used for arable production and have the lowest percentage of land under fallow. Less fertile land has a much higher proportion (15–40%) of fallow (Majoral, 1987).

In south-western Spain, less than 25% of dry arable land is cultivated annually. The remainder is used as 'rotational medium-term fallows', mainly for extensive beef, lamb and mutton production, although in some areas this extends to dairy production for cheese (Peco & Suárez, 1993; Púlido *et al.* 1994). The livestock feed mainly on medium-term fallow and traditionally extra feed is given only to fatten lambs for meat (Naveso & Fernández, 1993; Fernández & Naveso, 1993a). This fallow receives no pesticide treatment, except if there are outbreaks of locust. Then, pesticide treatment occurs when the grass is dry due to low water levels in spring (Barros, 1994).

In south-western Spain, dry cereal cropping is found in a mosaic landscape with areas of grazed dehesa, cultivated and shrubby dehesa (see below).

The province of Castilla y León, despite significant reduction of fallow in recent decades, remains the most important extensive sheep rearing region (Egdell, 1993). Here, the sheep feed on the winter stubble and legume crops which are leased to the shepherds. These legume crops are not treated with any pesticides (Naveso, 1992; Naveso *et al.*, in press.).

(ii) Moorlands. These are pseudosteppes with a very continental climate. Rainfall is over 700 mm per annum, and minimum temperatures (around 15°C) are well below those of all other types of pseudosteppes. The characteristic vegetation is dominated by various chamaephytes (low growing perennials with buds at or close to the ground, e.g. *Thymus* spp, *Salvia lavandulifolia*, *Genista scorpius*).

Stock rearing is the main farming activity in the moorland areas. The average farm has about 325 sheep, for meat and wool production, and approximately 20% of the property is used for the cultivation of cereals and legumes. The stock usually graze on common land leased on a yearly basis by stock-farmers from the municipal authority (Peco & Suárez, 1993). The abundance of scrub areas reflects sparse stocking levels, which fall during winter as part of the stock is moved in autumn or winter to more temperate areas of the south-west.

(iii) Dry grasslands. These are the warmest steppes with minimum temperatures in winter of around 0°C, and are located in pockets in the Ebro Valley, the south-east and parts of the south-west. They also cover a significant proportion of the

Canary Islands, although these areas are not discussed here as they are of little significance for raptors. Annual rainfall is less than 350 mm. The vegetation is sparse scrub, although species vary between areas. In the Ebro Valley, these include *Ononis tridentata, Helianthemum lavandulifolium*, and in the southeast, *Anabis articulata* and *Helianthemum almeriense* (Suárez, 1994). In these areas, land-use has traditionally been cereal cultivation in mosaics with dry grassland, or with scrub at higher altitudes (Manrique & De Juana, 1991).

Dehesas

The dehesas are unique to the west Mediterranean region. Using the strict definition of wooded dehesas, these cover an area of 3 million hectares (Díaz *et al.*, Chapter 7). Iberian wooded dehesas are a kind of wood-pasture composed of grasslands, cereal croplands and Mediterranean scrub, densely interspersed with oak trees in a savannah landscape (Díaz *et al.*, 1996). The tree species include mainly holm oak *Quercus ilex rotundifolia* and, more sparsely, cork oak *Quercus suber* (Campos, 1995) and rarely oak *Q. pyrenaica*. The dehesas are farmed by selective clearing of the trees to encourage growth of grass and ensure regular production and high quality of acorns (Rupérez, 1957). Because of the low stock numbers, part of the farm is ploughed every 7–10 years to eliminate scrub and retain the quality of grazing land. More than 10% of dehesa areas are used for cereal cultivation, to produce feed for livestock in the dry season if they are not moved to nearby mountain areas. The climate is sub-humid Mediterranean with warm summers (maximum temperatures of around 35–40°C) and rainfall of up to 1000 mm annually, each autumn–winter (MAPA, 1981). The livestock, which is not stabled, is mainly beef cattle (Pulido *et al.*, 1994).

Mountain grasslands

Livestock rearing has been practised for hundreds of years in the mountains of Spain. Particularly in central and northern areas, the rural communities are located in the valleys. Livestock farming involves the use of available grass and scrubland areas located in valleys and on the upper slopes of the mountains, over varying areas and periods of time. In part, these grass and scrub areas developed over the centuries as a result of forest clearance to obtain wood and rear cattle (Fillat *et al.*, 1995; Abellá, 1995).

Transhumance

Transhumance has been practised for more than eight centuries and is an example of the close relationship between habitats such as steppes, dehesas and high mountain grasslands (De Juana *et al.*, 1993).

Transhumance involves the seasonal movement of livestock between moun-

Figure 2 Las Bardenas, Navarra and Aragon, north-east Spain is an arid steppe area in the Ebro Valley. A transhumance system of sheep husbandry has existed there for centuries, with sheep spending the summer in the Pyrenees and wintering on the Las Bardenas steppes. (Photo by D.J. Pain.)

tain grasslands used in summer and more temperate areas in winter. The movement of animals is motivated by the natural vegetation produced by the Mediterranean climate and the great variations in physical relief throughout the Iberian Peninsula. This movement of livestock was made possible by the creation of the 'cañadas reales' (drovers' roads) in the thirteenth century. The movements take place along two main routes: from the Ebro Valley to the Pyrenees, and from the south-west to the central mountains and the north-west of the Peninsula (Ruíz & Ruíz, 1986).

Today this practice is declining and, most of the remaining practitioners, most do not use the traditional methods. In the eighteenth century, 3.5 million animals were moved along the 'cañadas reales' on foot. Now, most of the livestock are moved by train and lorry, but where distances between summer and winter pasture are small, they are still moved on foot. For example, every year 80 000–100 000 sheep are driven by shepherds between the northern steppes of the Ebro Valley and summer pastures in the Pyrenees (Pain & Dunn, 1995).

HISTORICAL TRENDS IN EXTENSIVE LIVESTOCK FARMING IN SPAIN: ECONOMIC VIABILITY AND THE IMPACT OF THE COMMON AGRICULTURAL POLICY (CAP)

Historical trends in livestock numbers

We have not presented figures detailing livestock numbers because, certainly before the 1970s and even during the 1980s, the majority of statistics were extremely unreliable. Instead, we discuss trends as they provide a broad picture of changes in livestock numbers during the period 1930 to 1990.

In general the pattern observed is common to all species (cattle, sheep, goats and pigs). A decline in extensive livestock farming began at the end of the 1930s, coinciding with the Spanish civil war. This continued throughout the 1950s and 1960s, with the mechanization of farming and migration of the human population from rural areas to towns. These factors led to an increase in cultivated land to the detriment of grassland areas, along with less clearance activity and farming of dehesa scrubland. At the end of the 1970s, livestock levels began to increase, except for pigs which did not recover until the 1980s when the fight against swine fever began to show results (García, 1995; MAPA, 1993; Pulido *et al.*, 1994).

A consequence of this large reduction in livestock farming was a profound change in land-use, with a reduction in unproductive and grassland areas which were ploughed up during the 1950s and 1960s, and a subsequent reduction in fallow, remaining grassland and rough grazing areas, which were mainly converted to cereal production in pseudosteppe and dehesa areas (see for example Garrabou *et al.*, 1986; Majoral, 1987). Over this period, the dehesas were also subjected to thinning, the clearance of scrub was reduced, and the dehesa pasture areas were taken over by crops (Campos, 1984; Díaz *et al.*, Chapter 7).

After Spain joined the European Community in 1986, there was a significant increase in sheep and goat numbers. However, part of this increase simply resulted from better record keeping. With the Community reform, in 1989 statistics on the sheep sector improved as livestock subsidies for sheep and goats required farmers to declare all of their stock (Egdell, 1993; Pulido *et al.*, 1994).

From an economic viewpoint, sheep and goat meat production is much more profitable than that of cattle or Iberian pig. At the beginning of the 1990s, Spain was producing almost a quarter (23.0%) of the total sheep meat and a third (31.9%) of the total goat meat produced in the EU. On the other hand, beef represented only 6% of EU production (CEC, 1991). Production of Iberian pig meat suffered a drastic reduction with the arrival of swine fever in the 1960s (Viñuela, 1992). It took more than 20 years for anti-swine fever programmes to take effect and for Salamanca and the whole of Extremadura to be declared 'free from swine fever' (CEC, 1991, 1993, 1994a, 1994b; Sánchez, 1994).

Economic viability of extensive livestock systems in Spain

The sheep sector in Spain is mainly for meat production. Production of dairy derivatives such as cheese is relatively important in the pseudosteppe areas of the two Castillas and La Serena in Extremadura. The extensive livestock systems are barely viable economically and are highly dependent on subsidies (Table 2 – although the economic viability of all European agricultural systems is distorted by policy – see Dixon, Chapter 14). Economic analyses of the livestock farms show that approximately one third of gross earnings come from CAP sheep subsidies (Naveso & Fernández, 1993; Urmeneta & Naveso, 1993; Fernández & Naveso, 1993b; Peco & Suárez, 1993). The other crucial element in the viability calculation is the number of sheep on the property and the limited availability of labour, because it is assumed that on average one person can adequately manage some 400–450 sheep. Such farms are still largely family-run, as reflected by the fact that the salaried labour costs represent only 6% of total costs (Table 2).

For the economics of extensive livestock farming in the dehesas, see Díaz *et al.* (Chapter 7).

The impact of the CAP on extensive livestock systems: changes in stocking densities and livestock management

Livestock farming began to intensify from the mid-1970s. During the period 1974–90, in Extremadura, beef production rose by 145%, whilst sheep production rose by 66%, 55% of this increase occurring between 1986 and 1990, mainly as a result of subsidies (Pulido *et al.*, 1994). In general, extensive livestock production was significantly affected after Spain joined the European Community in 1986. As regards sheep, the import of lambs from other countries led to a general fall in prices, and the price of wool also fell. However, the cost of renting grassland and of labour increased (Peco & Suárez, 1993). As a result, livestock farms became less competitive and this has been compensated by subsidies to sheep and goat farmers only in Less Favoured Areas (areas with special disadvantages for farming activities compared with conditions that produce average EU food production levels. In Spain, 75% of agricultural land is classified as LFA). These livestock subsidies represent between 25% and 35% of gross income. If they were withdrawn, the net earnings of livestock farmers would be close to zero, and the majority of extensive livestock farms would not be economically viable (Table 3).

The importance of subsidies as a secure source of income has led to significant changes in stock management. The main changes have been as follows.

Changes in stocking densities in Less Favoured Area (LFA) and non-LFA pseudosteppes

In La Serena, south-western Spain, the number of sheep increased by almost

Table 2 Fixed and variable costs and income per head of sheep on a stock farm in Bardena (14 properties). Costs are included for weaning of 1.51 lambs per ewe

Adults (including 14.64% replacement)	Pesetas/sheep
Trough food:	
Bought in hay (alfalfa, etc.)	856
Concentrate (feed + grain)	821
Other food by-products	284
Straw	352
Subtotal	2 313
Grassland fodder:	
Lease of grassland	1 598
Own forage production	729
Subtotal	2 327
Cost of feeding 1.51 lambs/ewe	1 578
Subtotal feeding costs	6 218
Fixed costs:	
Structural charges (repayment costs)	1 248
Wages	217
Social Security and taxes	533
Machine-shearing	125
Health	432
Various	150
Subtotal	2 705
Total fixed and feeding costs	8 923
Income:	
12.3% sheep annual replacement costs	186
Sale of 1.22 lamb/ewe	8 839
Sale of manure	165
Wool	25
Sheep premium	3 221
Total income	12 436
Profit	3 513

25% between 1982 and 1989. Livestock densities increased from an average of 1.4 to 1.9 head of sheep per hectare (Naveso & Fernández, 1993). On some farms the livestock density reached 3 head per hectare. Although livestock densities have generally increased in Spain since accession to the EC (see above),

Table 3 Cost and revenue per head of sheep without including CAP subsidies

	La Serena	Cáceres	Jarama Steppes	Ebro Valley
Cost	9325	7875	9190	8923
Revenue	9050	9075	13630	9215

These figures illustrate the importance of CAP subsidies for the economic viability of extensive livestock farms.

there have been reductions in some areas. For example, in pseudosteppe areas of the Madrid region (which are not defined as Less Favoured Areas) in recent years, sheep have not been replaced rapidly enough to maintain numbers (Fernández & Naveso, 1993c). This reflects a growing lack of interest in livestock farming. However, in these areas, reduced numbers of livestock have not necessarily resulted in reduced earnings, largely because production is also focused upon cheese, which has higher profit margins than meat and thus has a buffering effect. The reduction in livestock numbers appears to be related to social factors, including a lack of interest in rural areas by young people.

Changes in the livestock production system: reduction in female sheep breeding and replacement rates in pseudosteppes and LFA dehesas

Because headage payments are so attractive (providing up to a third of gross incomes), shepherds now tend to keep ewes until they are older, even though they are less productive (fewer lambs and less cheese) than younger ewes. Delay in the average age at which breeding female sheep are replaced has changed from seven or eight years to 11 or 12 years (Pulido *et al.*, 1994), and the annual replacement rate has fallen from between 12% and 15%, to between 8% and 9%. Although the older ewes are less productive, and the cost of breeding is reduced, this has been offset by a fall in lamb prices.

These increased livestock densities resulting from headage payments could, from an ecological viewpoint, have positive repercussions for vultures, through increasing the amount of carrion on the land. However, preliminary studies show that increased livestock densities lead to a reduction in green pastures or even an increase in the area of bare land, with the consequent loss of grassland quality and reduction in density and diversity of steppe bird communities (Naveso & Fernández, 1993).

Changes in livestock management and stocking densities in mountain pasture and scrublands

There is a dearth of information reviewing the full impact of the CAP and livestock policies in mountain pasture areas.

In the Cordillera Cantábrica for example, the extensive dairy livestock

systems have suffered significantly owing to the introduction of a milk production quota well below milk production levels in these areas before Spain
joined the EU. However, in some remote mountain areas, the abandonment of
livestock activities has reduced previous over-grazing (Baldock & Beaufoy,
1993).

Since Spain joined the European Community, livestock numbers have
increased markedly across some mountain areas of Asturias and León, probably
as a result of subsidies available for livestock in LFAs. These varying changes,
which have proven very damaging both to wildlife and to human communities,
demonstrate the importance of ensuring that policies allow conservation objectives to be taken into account at a regional level if overall objectives for
European conservation and regional policy are to be met.

In some corners of the Pyrenees, a 'scrub invasion' process is occurring with
the gradual decline of transhumance from the Ebro Valley to the Pyrenees
(Baldock & Beaufoy, 1993; Fillat et al., 1995). However, this effect seems to be
relatively local. Given that the regions located to the south of the Pyrenees are
not Less Favoured Areas, the availability of LFA payments for sheep spending
90 days in LFAs is an incentive for shepherds in the Ebro Valley to practise
transhumance.

In some mountain areas of southern Spain, the existence of sheep and goat
payments has led to a marked increase, particularly in the number of goats, and
there seems to be heavy over-grazing of certain pasture and scrubland (Baldock
& Beaufoy, 1993).

Although information about trends in livestock numbers in mountain areas is
incomplete, two trends can be identified: over-grazing as a result of the
concentration of livestock in easily accessible areas; and a trend towards
abandonment and invasion of scrub, owing to the absence of livestock in less
accessible mountain areas.

ECOLOGICAL AND CONSERVATION VALUE FOR BIRDS OF PREY

Patterns of species' dependence on grazing habitats

In Europe, grasslands and other open areas with a grassland component support
a large number of bird species, many of which are threatened (see Goriup et al.,
1991; Tucker, 1991). Spain supports the largest numbers of threatened bird
species in Europe (de Juana et al., 1988; Alonso & Alonso, 1990, 1995). These
include: birds of prey, both diurnal and nocturnal, the common crane Grus grus,
great and little bustards Otis tarda, Tetrax tetrax, black-bellied and pin-tailed
sandgrouse Pterocles alchata and P. orientalis, and many passerines, mainly
larks such as Dupont's lark Chersophilus duponti, and the lesser short-toed lark

Calandrella rufescens (Manrique & De Juana, 1991). Many of these species have high population densities in extensive cereal farming areas, especially where land is cultivated every other year, such that half of the land every year is left as fallow dry arable land, used for grazing livestock.

Birds of prey are one of the groups which depend most heavily on extensive grazing and the grassland habitats which this activity provides. This dependency arises in two different ways.

(i) Dependence on grassland areas with high levels of available prey (predatory raptors). Unlike the grasslands of central Europe, Mediterranean grasslands do not have a great diversity or abundance of small mammal species. However, they do have large numbers of intermediately sized herbivorous mammals, mainly rabbits *Oryctolagus cuniculus.* The close association between grasslands and rabbits is extremely important. Areas of particular rabbit abundance are grassland shrub mosaics, which provide a certain amount of cover for the rabbits (Soriguer, 1988). The rabbit is the main prey for 17 species of Mediterranean birds of prey. For five of these, the rabbit represents 30% of their diet: black vulture *Aegypius monachus*, golden eagle *Aquila chrysaetos*, Spanish imperial eagle *Aquila adalberti*, Bonelli's eagle *Hieraaetus fasciatus* and eagle owl *Bubo bubo*. A further 11 species of mammals and reptiles regularly feed on rabbits (Jacksic & Soriguer, 1981).

Natural dry-grassland or steppe-like habitat may shelter sizeable populations of grasshoppers Orthoptera and other invertebrates that are potential prey for several species of raptor, but birds of prey are not particularly abundant in these habitats, since they provide scant nesting sites and/or perches, although lesser kestrels *Falco naumanni* appear regularly where human settlements are available for nesting.

Cereal steppes (pseudosteppes, according to Tucker, 1991), have replaced natural dry grasslands and also support significant numbers of potential prey, mainly grasshoppers (Hellmich, 1991; Naveso *et al.*, in press). Montagu's harriers *Circus pygargus* frequently nest in cereal crops. However, the number of arthropods in pseudosteppes is significantly depressed by the intensity of biocide treatments (Tucker, 1991). When cereal crops are interspersed with other land-uses, forming mosaic agricultural systems with marginal habitats and short to medium terms fallows, there is an increase in diversity and biomass of arthropods, small mammals and game species (Beintema, 1991; Thomas *et al.*, 1992; Boatman, 1994; Martínez, 1994), which encourages the presence of larger numbers of raptor species.

(ii) Dependence on livestock corpses (scavenging raptors). The diet of the four species of Iberian vultures, griffon vulture *Gyps fulvus*, black vulture, Egyptian vulture *Neophron percnopterus* and bearded vulture *Gypaetus barbatus* includes a high percentage of livestock carrion (Donázar, 1993). The amount of livestock in the diet varies according to the density and availability of extensively farmed livestock (Donázar, 1993). In other Mediterranean areas of Europe a

Figure 3 The golden eagle is one of the 17 species of Mediterranean birds of prey for which the rabbit is a major prey item. (Photo by C.H. Gomersall/RSPB.)

similar pattern has been noted, e.g. for the bearded vulture on the island of Corsica (Thibault *et al.*, 1993). Medium-sized facultative scavengers such as red and black kites *Milvus milvus* and *M. migrans*, golden and Spanish imperial eagles, will also occasionally feed on domestic ungulate carrion (Hiraldo *et al.*, 1991), but with less dependence.

To conclude, at least 17 species of diurnal raptors, some of which are globally threatened, depend on prey and habitats related to grazing activities in Spain (Table 4; Tucker & Heath, 1994; Tucker, Chapter 4).

Distribution and habitat selection of raptors in relation to grassland availability

The majority of information about the level of dependency of raptors upon grazing habitats is circumstantial, often based on observational feeding studies in relation to ungulate carrion resulting from extensive farming systems. There

Figure 4 The diet of the Egyptian vulture and the three other vulture species found in Iberia includes a high percentage of carrion. (Photo by W.S. Paton/RSPB.)

are very few detailed assessments of the real extent and availability of grassland habitats and livestock, and how these relate to the distribution and abundance of raptors in Mediterranean ecosystems. The information available is discussed below.

Landscape parameters (macrohabitat scale)

The distribution and abundance of birds of prey has been related to the availability of habitats and/or food (Cody, 1985). For example, the presence and density of black vultures and griffon vultures in Spain has been connected with the existence of high levels of extensive livestock farming (sheep, goats, cows and horses – De Juana & De Juana, 1984). Similarly, the wider distribution and higher densities of griffon, Egyptian and bearded vultures in the western than in the eastern Pyrenees is linked to the wide development of extensive sheep farming in the west (Dendaletche, 1982). More specifically, certain behavioural traits of the scavengers, such as the withdrawal of the griffon vulture to higher altitudes in the mountains of southern Europe, have been interpreted as being governed by seasonal movements of transhumance livestock between grazing areas (Donázar, 1993). There are no such clear interpretations of the relationship between the distribution and abundance of predatory raptors (at least on a

Table 4 Species of European Conservation Concern (SPEC) categories, present status and populational trends of raptor species, the conservation of which is related to grazing activities in Spain

Species	SPEC category*	European threat status†	Spanish population trend
Black-winged kite *Elanus caeruleus*	3	Vulnerable	Increasing
Black kite *Milvus migrans*	3	Vulnerable	Stable
Red kite *Milvus milvus*	4		Decreasing
Bearded vulture *Gypaetus barbatus*	3	Endangered	Increasing
Egyptian vulture *Neophron percnopterus*	3	Endangered	Decreasing
Griffon vulture *Gyps fulvus*	3	Rare	Increasing
Black vulture *Aegypius monachus*	3	Vulnerable	Increasing
Short-toed eagle *Circaetus gallicus*	3	Rare	Stable
Hen harrier *Circus cyaneus*	3	Vulnerable	Decreasing
Montagu's harrier *Circus pygargus*	4		Decreasing
Spanish imperial eagle *Aquila adalberti*	1	Endangered	Increasing
Golden eagle *Aquila chrysaetos*	3	Rare	Decreasing
Booted eagle *Hieraaetus pennatus*	3	Rare	Stable
Bonelli's eagle *Hieraaetus fasciatus*	3	Endangered	Decreasing
Lesser kestrel *Falco naumanni*	1	Vulnerable	Decreasing
Kestrel *Falco tinnunculus*	3	Declining	Decreasing
Peregrine *Falco peregrinus*	3	Rare	Decreasing

Source: Tucker & Heath (1994) and unpublished data.

*1: species of global conservation concern; 2: concentrated in Europe and with an unfavourable conservation status; 3: not concentrated in Europe but with an unfavourable conservation status; 4: concentrated in Europe and with a favourable conservation status.

†Defined as follows. *Secure*: population more than 10 000 breeding pairs and in neither moderate nor large decline, not localized.

Declining: population in moderate decline and population more than 10 000 breeding pairs.

Rare: population in neither moderate nor major decline but consisting of fewer than 10 000 breeding pairs.

Vulnerable: population in major decline and consisting of more than 10 000 breeding birds, or in moderate decline and consisting of fewer than 10 000 pairs, or population in neither moderate nor in large decline but consisting of fewer than 2500 pairs.

Endangered: population in major decline and consisting of fewer than 10 000 pairs, or in moderate decline and consisting of fewer than 2500 pairs, or in neither moderate nor major decline but consisting of fewer than 250 pairs large scale) and the availability of grazing habitats. However, in Scotland it has been suggested that the range of the golden eagle may have expanded (at least locally) where pastoralism is the key land-use (Watson, 1991).

Macrohabitat analyses require accurate measurements of landscape features, including habitat availability, and the use of models to forecast the probability of a species being present, according to a series of environmental variables. Geographic Information Systems (GIS) are being increasingly employed to help in the task of assessing available habitat. The distribution and abundance of a range of species which are potentially dependent on grazing systems in Spain have been analysed and are described below.

Bearded vulture. This species currently nests only in the mountains of the Pyrenees. It feeds mainly on bones obtained from ungulate corpses, primarily sheep, domestic goats and chamois *Rupicapra rupicapra* (see reviews in Heredia & Heredia, 1991). The distribution of this species would thus be expected to depend upon the availability of livestock and of open areas in which they graze. Using Generalized Linear Models (GLMs) based on 30 independent variables to evaluate the physiography, climate, human utilization, livestock and land-use, it was shown that the population density of bearded vultures increased with altitude and snow days (Donázar *et al.*, 1993a). A positive relationship was also found between the proportion of an area suitable for grazing and the density of the bearded vulture population. However, the availability (according to de Juana & de Juana, 1984) of livestock had no apparent effect on population density, although this may be because of the difficulty of obtaining accurate measurements of livestock availability.

Spanish imperial eagle. Since the last century, the imperial eagle has shown a significant decline in western Europe, owing to a range of factors, including the destruction of preferred hunting habitat (Mediterranean scrub with an abundance of rabbits – González, 1991). To try to determine which factors control the presence of eagles, González *et al.* (1990) assessed grid areas with and without eagles according to 32 variables including physiography, climate, degree of landscape development and management, and type of land-use. The analyses showed that eagles appeared in areas with a typically Mediterranean climate providing both nesting habitats (woods) and hunting habitats (Mediterranean scrub with rabbits). They completely avoided areas converted into irrigated land. Intensive radio-tracking of young eagles throughout the whole of Andalucia showed that the individuals concentrated their activities in well-defined areas, all characterized by large expanses of grassland and Mediterranean scrub and, consequently, high rabbit densities (Ferrer, 1993).

Lesser kestrel. The lesser kestrel population fell from being very abundant in Spain (more than 100 000 pairs in the 1960s) to some 5000 pairs in 1989 (González & Merino, 1990). The causes of decline have been the subject of much discussion, and include the destruction of favourable hunting habitats

Figure 5 Male lesser kestrel perched on the roof of a farm building. The lesser kestrel population in Spain has declined dramatically over the last 30 years. (Photo by C.H. Gomersall/RSPB.)

where the lesser kestrels catch arthropods (mainly grasshoppers). In 1993/94 there was an accurate population census of part of the Andalucian population, and the factors determining the presence and abundance (size of colonies) of lesser kestrels were analysed. The results of the study (Donázar *et al.*, 1993b) showed the presence of lesser kestrels to be positively related to areas of non-intensive dry-farming of herbaceous crops, and negatively related to areas with abundant scrub and trees. The sizes of breeding colonies were similarly correlated with these factors.

Case study: Mediterranean mountains in Navarra. In 1993/94, a study was carried out in an area of 3500 km² of Mediterranean mountains in Navarra, northern Spain (D. Campion, unpublished data). As is the case throughout the whole of southern Europe, human activities have transformed the habitats in this area in a variety of ways. Pasture and scrubland areas have been formed by modification of the original *Quercus* forests for agri-grazing systems, and there is significant variation across the area, with other land-uses (intensive farming, charcoal-making) predominant in some places, creating a mosaic landscape.

All foraging raptors were recorded at 300 representative selected points. Each point-count was characterized by 22 variables measured using a digital system (GIS). Multiple regression analyses were performed to determine the significance of main habitat features for each species. The analyses showed that the

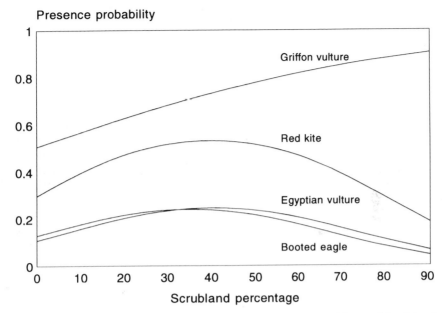

Figure 6 Presence probability versus percentage of area occupied by scrubland for four raptor species.

percentage of area occupied by scrubland is important for some raptors as foraging habitats. Booted eagle *Hieraaetus pennatus*, red kite, Egyptian vulture and griffon vulture benefit from this kind of land-use. After taking into account other variables in the models, these species positively select ($P < 0.001$) scrubland pastures, as can be seen in Figure 6.

In the study area, all raptor species (except the griffon vulture) are medium-sized predators and/or scavengers and they seek their prey (mainly rabbits, red-legged partridges *Alectoris rufa*, lizards, voles and small carrion) in scrubland pastures. These 'generalist' raptors are more readily found in mosaic habitats; when habitat diversity decreases, these species begin to avoid such areas. In this habitat, griffon vultures almost exclusively seek sheep corpses, which are very common as a result of the extensive traditional farming system. In fact, scrubland pastures originate from sheep farming.

Structural parameters (microhabitat scale)

The way in which individual birds select their foraging habitat is determined by the structure, extent and diversity of available habitats, and the abundance of potential prey in each (Cody, 1985). In order to reach valid conclusions, habitat selection studies must provide detailed descriptions of habitats, and comprehensive monitoring of animal movements and activities (see reviews in Giron *et al.*, 1987).

Few studies have investigated the selection of hunting habitat by raptors in Mediterranean ecosystems. Information currently available is given below.

Egyptian vulture. The Egyptian vulture is the European vulture which is least dependent on livestock for its food since it is able to include a significant number of corpses of rabbits and smaller animals (Donázar, 1993). However, across wide areas, especially in the mountains, it appears to be closely linked to extensive grazing (Dendaletche, 1982; Donázar & Ceballos, 1988). In 1987 in the Ebro valley in Navarra, one breeding and three non-breeding Egyptian vultures were radio-tracked (Donázar & Ceballos, 1987; Ceballos & Donázar, 1988). Analyses of their habitat selection showed that the Egyptian vultures focused their search for food in predictable places (carrion tips, rubbish dumps). Their relationship with extensive stock-farming was not strong, and was limited to regular visits to farmyards where they fed on carcases of sheep left by shepherds beside the pens. There appeared to be a stronger relationship with sheep farming in mountain areas, as shown by dietary analyses (Ceballos & Donázar, 1988).

Lesser kestrel. In 1989/90 the habitat selection of this species was studied in the lower Guadalquivir valley, in order to determine the habitats preferred for hunting, and whether this depended on the yield obtained (Donázar *et al.*, 1993b). Through radio-tracking 13 birds, it was shown that natural grassland isolated between plots of land or in river valleys was the preferred habitat of lesser kestrels, with more than 50% of hunting activity focused in these areas although they represented less than 1% of territory available. The second most preferred habitat was cereal fields. Sunflower fields were avoided almost completely. The habitat preferences were related to the yield from hunting activity: habitats selected were those where it was most economical to catch prey.

During 1994, a similar study was undertaken in the Monegros of Aragón, using 28 radio-tagged birds (Tella *et al.*, unpublished data). Provisional results show that extensive cereal crops (used by livestock in alternate years) were positively selected, whilst irrigated crops and areas of scrub were avoided. Positive selection was also noted in the margins and on the edges of fields. Studies in the cereal pseudosteppes of north-western Spain and central Turkey found a strong correlation between the availability of extensive habitats, without agro-chemical treatments (grassland, edge habitats and grazed legume crops), high prey density (grasshoppers and lizards), and number of lesser kestrel pairs in colonies located within a radius of less than 3 km (Naveso *et al.*, in press; Parr *et al.*, in press.).

Case studies: Doñana National Park. Extensive stock-farming has shaped the landscape of Doñana and other wetland areas for centuries, and has resulted in large areas remaining free of aquatic and woody vegetation (Lazo, 1995; Mayol & Sargatal, 1995). In Doñana la Marisma, extensive lagoons and wet grazing areas created by winter floods were used by livestock (cattle and horses) in summer. In addition, the shepherds burnt areas of scrubland (Moreno & Villafuerte, 1995), to create grazing areas for livestock.

The Marisma area is the winter habitat of numerous species of aquatic birds which include up to 80 000 greylag geese *Anser anser* (Aguilar, 1986). The highest density of birds of prey in Doñana occurs on the edge of the Marisma, where high densities of rabbits and aquatic birds can be found (Palomares *et al.*, 1991). The Spanish imperial eagle reaches its maximum world density and obtains highest productivity in this area (Ferrer & Donázar, 1996), and black kites are also abundant and productive here (Viñuela, 1991). Highest densities of other threatened predators such as the Iberian lynx *Lynx pardina* are also found in the border areas between Mediterranean scrub and the marisma (Palomares *et al.*, 1991).

Radio-tracking studies on wintering red kites showed considerable use of the marisma in dry years, when it was not flooded. In wet years, the kites used open areas within the Mediterranean scrub. The latter habitat is also the main one used by the sedentary red kite population throughout the year (Heredia *et al.*, 1991). The marisma is the main habitat used by the summer population of black kites, with the majority of prey obtained there both in dry and wet years (Veiga & Hiraldo, 1990).

Population trends in raptors in relation to changes in grazing activities

Populations of most European birds of prey have declined significantly during the last century (Bijleveld, 1974). The causes of this decline are extremely varied, but one of the most frequently cited is habitat loss. Either direct loss of, or changes to the management of extensive grazing areas (pseudosteppes, dehesas and mountain pastures), has been related to observed reductions in populations of both scavengers (Donázar, 1993), and species that depend on prey existing in such areas (lesser kestrel; González & Merino, 1990). The evidence which exists to support this hypothesis is summarized below.

Scavenging raptors. During this century up to the 1970s, the distributions and populations of the four species of Iberian vulture experienced sizeable reductions. More recently there has been a slow recovery, very slight for the Egyptian and bearded vultures, and quite marked in the case of the griffon and black vultures (see review in Donázar, 1993).

Reliable data on population fluctuations have existed in the Pyrenees of Navarra since 1969 (Donázar & Fernández, 1990). These population changes do not appear to be related to livestock density, as the amount of dead livestock

Figure 7 Griffon vulture soaring. In Navarra, 'muladares' or carcase tips, and extensive livestock farming provide for most of the diet of the griffon vulture. (Photo by D.J. Pain.)

(sheep and goats) available for vultures has always exceeded their require-ments (Donázar & Fernández, 1990). The decline and recovery of the griffon vulture seems to be more related to human persecution and its cessation after the 1970s (Donázar & Fernández, 1990; Donázar *et al.*, 1993a). Persecution would also appear to explain the reductions in populations of other scavengers (Donázar, 1993). It is generally agreed that nowadays the availability of food for vultures is very high (Arroyo *et al.*, 1990; Donázar & Fernández, 1990). Indeed, in Navarra it has been calculated that extensive livestock farming provides 75% of the food requirements of the griffon vulture population; the rest being provided by rubbish dumps or 'muladares' where dead animals are discarded from farms and slaughterhouses (Fernández, 1988). Today, the non-breeding populations of Egyptian vultures and both red and black kites depend almost exclusively on food obtained from muladares and rubbish bins (Sunyer, 1988; Blanco, 1995; Blanco, unpublished data; Donázar *et al.*, in press), making such places important tools for the conservation and manage-ment of these species. However, current EU health regulations are seeking to close down the traditional muladares and replace them with septic tanks, which are not accessible to scavengers. As septic tanks are relatively costly, in many places livestock carcases are now left to rot in deep open pits, and this 'half way house', still illegal, has considerably worsened the hygiene conditions at carcase dumps. It is anticipated that the reduction in food that would result from septic tanks, along with the bad reputation that scavengers could acquire due to their association with the current disease ridden open carcase pits could potentially jeopardize the populations of certain scavenging raptors (Sunyer, 1988; Fernández, 1988; Tella, 1993). If this food source were to disappear, scavengers would be almost entirely dependent upon the continuation of extensive livestock farming.

Lesser kestrels and extensive farming. Thousands of years ago, the lower Guadalquivir valley was transformed into an area where the principal crops cultivated were cereals and olive trees. Livestock used to be extremely important, but pasture was scarce, and thus the fallow land that followed the cereal harvest was used for grazing by sheep and goats. Sowing crops one year in two, or one year in three, meant that large areas remained available every year for extensive grazing. In the 1950s, the situation changed: mechanization and the arrival of fertilizers made annual cultivation possible, leading to the disappearance both of fallows and of extensive livestock farming (Montaner et al., 1986). This process has occurred throughout many valleys in southern Spain. As described above, lesser kestrels select natural grasslands and fields under rotating cereal crops. Without doubt, the virtual disappearance of grazing land in many areas has led to a significant reduction in the amount of food available for this and other bird species (Donázar et al., 1993b). Today, in the lower Guadalquivir valley, chick starvation occurs in lesser kestrel colonies, reducing breeding success to levels which will not sustain the population (Hiraldo et al., in press).

ANALYSIS OF POLICY OPTIONS, CONCLUSIONS AND RECOMMENDATIONS

Analysis of policy options

The economics, and both social and environmental aspects of extensive grazing systems could be significantly influenced through a number of different agricultural policy options. The main ones are: changes in market prices, cross-compliance or eco-compatibility, livestock quotas, area payments, stocking density limits, and agri-environmental schemes.

The last three options are discussed below, and some of the others briefly mentioned. They could have beneficial effects, from a socio-economic and environmental point of view, considering the vulnerability of extensive livestock farming systems and their extremely high environmental value. For more detailed descriptions of the influence that the former three options can have upon extensive agricultural management see Díaz *et al.* (Chapter 7) and Suárez *et al.* (Chapter 11).

The replacement of headage payments by area payments

A precedent for this was established by the CAP reform of 1992, which introduced payments per hectare in the arable sector. Similarly, in the beef sector, the 1992 reforms introduced an extensification premium for stocking levels of less than 1.4 livestock units (LUs) per hectare, and stocking density limits for eligible cattle. These measures represent a first step towards integration of the environment into the CAP livestock regime. The sensitivity and vulnerability of extensive livestock systems to changes in subsidies and, to a lesser extent, to market changes was illustrated earlier in this chapter. In some sectors, such as sheep, approximately 80% of the increase in livestock densities over the period 1980–1990 occurred after Spain joined the European Community in 1986, and gained access to subsidies per head of livestock. Rigorous studies analysing the effects of policy upon extensive farming systems, and their consequences for raptors and other wildlife, are desirable. However, with the evidence currently available, we can conclude that the increase of local livestock densities in LFA pseudosteppes, and the associated over-grazing, could seriously affect globally threatened species such as the lesser kestrel. This is because a loss of both amount and quality of herbaceous cover would occur in pastures, with consequently reduced prey densities (Parr *et al.*, in press).

The introduction of payments per hectare instead of per head of livestock would clearly reduce the likelihood of trends towards increased stocking levels. However, to ensure economic viability of extensive grazing farms, hectarage payments should be applied on the basis of property size, and not of average regional production levels, which was the way CAP reform arable payments operated. It is likely that in the foreseeable future there will be a dramatic increase in the 'economic marginalization' of agricultural land in Spain, in response to the low productivity of cereal crops and extensive livestock. Those areas not likely to be transformed into more intensive systems risk abandonment (Sumpsi, 1995). Economically marginal areas of cereal production, if abandoned, may be used for afforestation schemes within the framework of Regulation 2080/92. The inadequate implementation of this regulation threatens to destroy large areas of habitat with considerable natural value, maintained until now by extensive farming (Baldock & Beaufoy, 1993).

Stocking densities

The CAP has led to a general intensification of stocking levels in the dehesas (and in the Portuguese equivalent, montados). This is because, even when supposedly incorporating environmental elements, the CAP tends to overlook the way in which its component measures affect extensive systems. One of the management features of extensive livestock farms is that stocking densities are adjusted to maximize their exploitation of the grasslands and to minimize their dependence on external food sources. In the past, stocking densities in the dehesas were well below one livestock unit per hectare. The reduction in meat intervention prices has led to an increase in stocking levels to obtain maximum beef premiums, even though maximum stocking densities for subsidy were set. This is partly because these densities were set too high (at 3.5 livestock units per hectare, falling to 2.0 livestock units per hectare in 1996), and these are not reached in the dehesas even after the above-mentioned intensification. Constraints on increasing livestock levels as a result of grassland productivity were offset by increasing the purchase of fodder (Pulido et al., 1994).

The maintenance and encouragement of extensive livestock systems throughout the EU requires an approach that is both regionalized and takes into account the wide variety of different natural conditions that exist. This is essential for the conservation of Mediterranean extensive livestock systems. Both the recent and the future enlargement of the EU, planned for the year 2005 with the countries of central and eastern Europe, require much greater regionalization in order to obtain real environmental benefits.

Agri-environmental schemes

The introduction of accompanying measures and, particularly EEC Regulation 2078/92 (CEC, 1992b), was considered by the Member States to be one of the most flexible ways of integrating the environment into agricultural policy. In the case of livestock farming, some Member States have included programmes to encourage its extensification, especially in mountainous and Less Favoured Areas. These programmes had some specific environmental objectives, with reductions in stocking densities determined by and adapted to the habitats for which the area programmes were designed (BirdLife International, unpublished data). However, there has been virtually no uptake by farmers owing to the fact that maximum premiums under community regulations are similar to the per head premium for sheep in Less Favoured Areas. Therefore, farmers maximized profits through rearing more livestock per hectare than are compatible with environmental considerations, and claiming headage payments. Assuming that this problem is resolved, the application of EEC regulation 2078/92 and the introduction of area programmes for extensive livestock systems has been shown to be one of the most flexible CAP measures which may help to ensure viability of livestock farms and the achievement of clear environmental objectives (see for example Baldock & Beaufoy, 1993; Urmeneta & Naveso, 1993; Naveso & Fernández, 1993).

The Community's main objective in introducing quotas was to prevent any further increases in the total number of ewes in each Member State, and consequently put a finite limit on the cost of headage payments. However, the quotas are not attached to land area, thus their impact on land management in any particular area is very limited (Egdell & Dixon, 1993).

Obviously, the beef premium introduced did not take into account the low stocking densities found under extensive beef production in the dehesas. To achieve nature conservation objectives, we suggest a mixture of policy options such as eco-compatibility, and making livestock subsidies conditional on farmers opting into agri-environmental schemes. Farmers not complying with environmental requirements would receive only market returns. The agri-environment schemes should incorporate premiums fixed according to ecological requirements and natural conditions in different regions. This, together with a shift towards area payments, could fulfil clear conservation objectives and should compensate for price cuts in future World Trade Organization agreements.

Conclusions and future scenarios

Extensive livestock farming is one of the main factors influencing land-use and landscape in Spain. Livestock are moved to exploit a mosaic of available habitats, thus extensive livestock farming provides a link between, and influences the ecology of, a wide range of habitats and ecosystems (pseudosteppes, dehesas, mountain grasslands and scrublands).

As discussed earlier in this chapter, for the majority of extensive farming systems, direct subsidies have more influence than certain market changes.

The maintenance of grazing areas within Mediterranean ecosystems favours the presence of numerous threatened species, including birds of prey. The survival and abundance of many predatory raptors are highest where the grazing areas form varied mosaics with Mediterranean scrub, which support high rabbit populations (the main prey of many raptors in Mediterranean ecosystems). The cereal areas of the pseudosteppes are important for various threatened species, for which these contain important sources of food (mainly grasshoppers), especially when they are cultivated with alternating fallow and grasslands.

Those raptors which are exclusively scavengers depend largely on extensive livestock farming for their food. At present, however, there appears to be an abundant food supply available for these birds. Their requirements are largely met by feeding on 'muladares' (where carcases of livestock from intensive farming are discarded) and refuse dumps, although the future of this food supply is uncertain.

Owing to scant economic returns for extensive farming, direct subsidies per head of livestock (rather than by area), the gradual abandonment of rural areas, and payments for afforestation of arable land (EEC regulation 2080/92 – CEC 1992c), the dual trends of abandonment of more economically marginal areas, and the intensification of livestock farming in areas of higher production potential is likely to continue. On a landscape scale, these changes may lead to a homogenization of the landscape with the loss of mosaic areas incorporating extensive farming and grazing systems.

The most likely scenarios for the future of these extensive livestock farming areas are: afforestation, abandonment of crops in some areas and intensification in others, mainly through regrouping of plots (i.e. farm restructuring) and/or irrigation. According to Mahlau (1991), the working population in the agricultural sector fell by c. 4.4% per annum between 1965 and 1980. This average rate of decline has accelerated since Spain joined the EC12 (MAPA, 1993). Afforestation leads to habitat loss, while abandonment and intensification result in loss of habitat quality in the short term, and possibly total habitat loss in the long term. The existence of approved afforestation plans, and the National Irrigation Plan (MAPA, 1995b) make these changes likely. The solution lies in a more integrated approach to rural land-use policy, to ensure that farming activities are not lost because rural life is unattractive relative to urban life.

Recommendations

The future of extensive farming systems depends upon a range of factors. Future policy options should consider the following:

(1) A shift to area payments should help to reduce over-grazing in certain areas, and abandonment in others. In economically marginal areas at risk from abandonment, area payments could increase farmer's returns sufficiently to allow for an increased investment in stock.

(2) The establishment of maximum livestock payments should be flexible and take into account regional environmental conditions. The Agri-Environment regulation is probably the best tool that currently exists to achieve the necessary degree of CAP regionalization. However, the fact that reimbursement to Member States under the Guarantee Fund is up to only 75% is a clear limitation for the implementation of this regulation in the poorest regions throughout Europe.

(3) Area payments should ensure the future economic viability of extensive farms. This may require higher payments in places where natural conditions limit stocking densities.

(4) Policy should be integrated. In particular, greater co-ordination between the 1992 accompanying measures is required, along with careful planning in the implementation of measures. Payments for the extensification or maintenance of appropriate stocking densities under the Agri-environmental Regulation, to achieve specific environmental objectives, should be set at a level that provides at least as high an economic incentive as other available schemes (such as afforestation) that may be in conflict with the said environmental objectives.

(5) Policy options should be flexible to the needs of local farming systems. Policies which are suitable for other parts of Europe may not deliver in certain parts of Spain.

(6) Ideas should be developed and implemented on the use of structural funds to benefit extensive livestock systems, e.g. through training, and the development of marketing initiatives for traditional products.

At a more general level, the objectives defined in the CAP should be reconsidered. They were formulated in 1957 and now no longer reflect the problems of the agricultural and livestock sectors, or the priorities of the citizens of the EU. We suggest that Article 39 of the EU Treaty should consider and ensure the conservation of the environment and landscape diversity. We also suggest that the same article should also cover the sustainable development of rural areas to strengthen the economic and social cohesion of the EU. Today, rural development and agriculture policies are not sufficiently well integrated to fulfil the new role of farmers in Europe, as defined under the 1992 CAP reform, i.e. that of producers of food, managers of landscapes and protectors of the environment.

REFERENCES

ABELLÁ, M.A. (1995) Extensive farming and/or tourism in the Covadonga National Park, Asturias-Léon, Spain? In D.I. McCracken, E.M. Bignal & S.E. Wenlock (eds) *Farming on the Edge: the nature of traditional farmland in Europe*, pp. 74–81. Peterborough: Joint Nature for Conservation Committee.

AGUILAR, J. (1986) Numerical trends, habitat use and activity of Greylag Geese wintering in southwestern Spain. *Wildfowl*, 37: 35–45.

ALONSO, J.A. & ALONSO, J.C. (1990) *Distribución y demografiá de la Grulla Comun (*Grus grus*) en España*. Colección Técnica. Madrid: ICONA.

ALONSO, J.C. & ALONSO, J.A. (1990) Parámetros demográficos, selección de hábitat y distribución de la *Avutarda* (Otis tarda) en tres regiones españolas. Colección Técnica: Madrid: ICONA.

ALONSO, J.C. & ALONSO, J.A. (1995) The Great Bustard *Otis tarda* in Spain: Present status, recent trends and an evaluation of earlier censuses. *Biological Conservation* (in press).

ARROYO, B., FERREIRO, E & GARZA, V. (1990) *Segundo censo nacional de buitre leonado (*Gyps fulvus*): Población, demografiá y conservación*. Serie Técnica. Madrid: ICONA.

BALDOCK, D. & BEAUFOY, G. (1993) *Nature Conservation and New Directions in the European Commission Common Agricultural Policy*. London: Institute for European Environmental Policy.

BARROS, C. (1994) Contribución el estudio de la biología del alcaraván *Burhinus oedicnemus* en España. Memoria presentada como tesis Doctoral. Madrid: Universidad Autonóma de Madrid.

BEINTEMA, A.J. (1991) In D.J. Curtis, E.M. Bignal & M.A. Curtis (eds) *Birds and Pastoral Agriculture in Europe*, pp. 97–101.

BIJLEVELD, M. (1974) *Birds of Prey in Europe*. London: Macmillan Press Limited.

BLANCO, G. (1995) Seasonal abundance of black kites associated with the rubbish dump of Madrid, Spain. *Journal of Raptor Research*, 28: 242–235.

BOATMAN, N. (1994) *Field Margins: integrating agriculture and conservation*. British Crop Protection Council Monograph No. 58. British Crop Protection Council.

CABO, A. & MANERO, F. (eds) (1987) *Geografiá de Castilla y León*. Tomo 4. Valladolid: Ambito Ediciones S.A.

CAMPOS, P. (1993a) Valores comerciales y ambientales de las dehesas españolas. *Agricultura y Sociedad*, 66: 9–41.

CAMPOS, P. (1993b) *Economiá y energiá en la dehesa extremeña*. Madrid: Instituto de Estudios Agrarios, Pesqueros y Alimentarios.

CAMPOS, P. (1995) Dehesa economy and conservation in the Iberian Peninsula. In *Proceedings of the Fourth European Forum on Nature Conservation and Pastoralism* (Trujillo, Spain) pp. 112–117.

CEBALLOS, O. & DONÁZAR, J.A. (1988) Actividad, use del espacio y cuidado parental en una pareja de alimoches (*Neophron percnopterus*) durante el periodo de dependencia de los pollos. *Ecologia*, 2: 275–291.

CEC (Commission of the European Communities) (1991) Decisión 91/112/CEE de 12 Febrero por la que se modifica la decisión 89/21/CEE de Consejo, relativa a inaplicación excepcional las prohibiciones por causa de la peste porcina Africana para determinadas partes del territorio de España. Luxemburg: Commission of the European Communities.

CEC (Commission of the European Communities) (1992a) Council Regulation 1765/92. Luxemburg: Official Journal of the EC.

CEC (Commission of the European Communities) (1992b) Council Regulation 2078/92. Luxembourg: Official Journal of the EC.

CEC (Commission of the European Communities) (1992c) Council Regulation instituting a Community aid scheme for forestry measures in agriculture. EE EEC 2080/92. Luxemburg: Commission of the European Communities.

CEC (Commission of the European Communities) (1993) Decisión 93/443/CEE por la que se modifica por segunda vez la decisión 89/21/CEE del Consejo, relativa a inaplicación excepcional las prohibiciones por causa de la peste porcina Africana para determinadas partes del territorio de España. Luxembourg: Commission of the European Communities.

CEC (Commission of the European Communities) (1994a) Decisión de la Comisión 94/788/CE por la que se modifica la decision 89/21/CEE del Consejo relativa a la inaplicación excepcional de las prohibiciones por causa de la P.P.A. para determinadas partes del territorio de España.

CEC (Commission of the European Communities) (1994b) Decisión de la Comisión por la que se establece excepciones a las prohibiciones relativa a la P.P.A. en determinadas regiones españolas y se deroga la Decisión 89/21/CE.

CODY, M.L. (1985) *Habitat Selection in Birds*. Orlando: Academic Press, Inc.

DE JUANA, E. & DE JUANA, F. (1984) Cabaña ganadera y distribución y abundancia de los buitres común *Gyps fulvus* y negro *Aegypius monachus* en España. *Rapinyaires Mediterranis*, 2: 32–45.

DE JUANA, E., SANTOS, T., SUÁREZ, F. & TELLERÍA, J.L. (1988) Status and Conservation of steppe birds and their habitats in Spain. In P. Goriup (ed.) *Birds of Savannas, Steppes and Similar Habitats*, pp. 113–123. Cambridge: International Council for Bird Preservation Technical Publication no. 7.

DE JUANA, E., MARTIN-NOVELLA, C., NAVESO, M.A., PAIN, D. & SEARS, J. (1993) Farming and Birds in Spain: Threats and Opportunities for Conservation. *Royal Society for the Protection of Birds, Conservation Review*, 7: 67–73.

DENDALETCHE, C. (1982) Ondes trophiques et strategies animales d'utilisation de l'espace. *Acta Biologica Montana*, 1: 15–29.

DÍAZ, M., GONZÁLEZ, E., MUÑOZ-PULIDO, R. & NAVESO, M.A. (1996) Habitat selection patterns of common cranes *Grus grus* wintering in holm oak *Quercus ilex* dehesas of central Spain: effects of human management. *Biological Conservation*, 75: 119–123.

DONÁZAR, J.A. (1993) *Los buitres ibéricos*. Madrid: Reyero ed.

DONÁZAR, J.A. & CEBALLOS, O. (1987) *Uso del espacio y tasas reproductoras en el alimoche* (Neophron percnopterus). Madrid: Informe inédito. ICONA.

DONÁZAR, J.A. & CEBALLOS, O. (1988) Alimentación y tasas reproductoras del alimoche (*Neophron percnopterus*) en Navarra. *Ardeola*, 35: 3–14.

DONÁZAR, J.A. & FERNÁNDEZ, C. (1990) Population trends of the griffon vulture *Gyps fulvus* in northern Spain between 1969 and 1989 in relation to conservation measures. *Biological Conservation*, 53: 86–91.

DONÁZAR, J.A., HIRALDO, F. & BUSTAMANTE, J. (1993a) Factors influencing nest site selection, breeding density and breeding success in the Bearded Vulture (*Gypaetus barbatus*). *Journal of Applied Ecology*, 30: 500–514.

DONÁZAR, J.A., NEGRO, J.J. & HIRALDO, F. (1993b) Foraging habitat selection, land-use changes and population decline in the Lesser Kestral *Falco naumanni. Journal of Applied Ecology*, 30: 515–522.

DONÁZAR, J.A., BUSTAMANTE, J., NEGRO, J.J. & HIRALDO, F. (1994) Estudio del ceznícalo primilla en España. Factores determinantes de la distribucíon y densidad de problacíon. SEO/ Birdlife & CSIC.

DONÁZAR, J.A., CEBALLOS, O. & TELLA, J.L. (in press). Communal roosts of Egyptian vultures (*Neophron percnopterus*): population dynamics and conservation.

EGDELL, J. (1993) *Impact of Agriculture Policy on Spain and its Steppe Regions*. Studies in European Agriculture and Environment Policy No. 2. Sandy: Royal Society for the Protection of Birds.

EGDELL, J. & DIXON, J. (1993) Proposal for Changes to EC Livestock Policies. A Discussion Paper. Sandy: Royal Society for the Protection of Birds.

FERNÁNDEZ, C. (1988) Inventariación y valoración de los muladares para las aves carroñeras. Unpublished report. Pamplona: Gobierno de Navarra.

FERNÁNDEZ, J. & NAVESO, M.A. (1993a) Zonal Programme proposal in accordance with the (European Commission) 2078/92 Regulation for the steppeland area of La Serena (unpublished report). Madrid: Sociedad Española de Ornitología/BirdLife.

FERNÁNDEZ, J. & NAVESO, M.A. (1993b) Programa de Zona del área esteparia de las terrazas de los rios Jarama y en Henares en aplicación del reglamento CEE/2078/92 (unpublished report). Madrid: Sociedad Española de Ornitología/BirdLife-Agencia de Medio Ambiente.

FERNÁNDEZ, J. & NAVESO, M.A. (1993c) Zonal Programme proposal for the implementation of the Flats of Southern Cáceres in accordance with the European Commission regulation 2078/ 92 (unpublished report). Madrid: Sociedad Española de Ornitología/BirdLife.

FERRER, M. (1993) Reduction in hunting success and settlement strategies in young Spanish imperial eagles. *Animal Behaviour*, 45: 406–408.

FERRER, M. & DONÁZAR, J.A. (1996) Density-dependent fecundity by habitat heterogeneity in an increasing population of Spanish Imperial eagles. *Ecology*, 77: 69–74.

FILLAT, F., CHOCARRO, C., GODED, L., FANLO, R., CANTERO, C., REINÉ, R., PARDO, F., GARCÍA, A., ALONSO, L., FERNÁNDEZ–BERMÚDEZ, F. & LÓPEZ, A. (1995) Extensive management of grasslands. Impact of conservation of biological resources and farm output. DGXI AIR3-CT Commission of Europe, Brussels. *Quercus*, 107: 24–26.

GARCÍA, M.A. (1995). Evolución reciente de la ganadería en España. *Quercus*, 107: 6–9.

GARRABOU, R., BARCIELLA, C. & JIMÉNEZ, J.I. (eds) (1986) *Historia agraria de la España contemporánea. 3. El fin de la agricultura tradicional (1990–1960)*. Barcelona: Editorial critica.

GARZA, V. & SUAREZ, F. (1990) Distribución, población y selección de hábitat de la *Alondra de Dupont* (Chersophilus duponti) en la Pennínsula Ibérica. *Ardeola*, 37: 3–12.

GIRON, B.A., MILLSAP, B.A., CLINE, K.W. & BIRD, D.M. (1987) *Raptor Management Techniques Manual*. Washington: National Wildlife Federation.

GONZÁLEZ, L.M. (1991) *Historia natural del águila imperial ibérica* (Aquila adalberti Brehm 1861). Madrid: Serie Técnica. ICONA.

GONZÁLEZ, J.L. & MERINO, M. (1990) *El cernicalo primilla* (Falco naumanni) *en la Peninsula ibérica*. Madrid: Serie Técnica. ICONA.

GONZÁLEZ, L.M., BUSTAMANTE, J. & HIRALDO, F. (1990) Factors influencing the present distribution of the Spanish Imperial Eagle. *Biological Conservation*, 59: 45–50.

GORIUP, P.D., BATTEN, L.A. & NORTON, J.A. (1991) *The Conservation of Lowland Dry Grassland Birds in Europe*. Peterborough: Joint Nature Conservation Committee.

HELLMICH, J. (1991) *La avutarda en Extremadura*. Alytes, Monografía 2.

HEREDIA, B., ALONSO, J.C. & HIRALDO, F. (1991) Space and habitat use by Red Kites *Milvus milvus* during winter in the Guadalquivir marshes: a comparison between resident and wintering populations. *Ibis*, 133: 374–381.

HEREDIA, R. & HEREDIA, B. (1991) *El quebrantahuesos (Gypaetus barbatus) en los Pirineos*. Serie Técnica. Madrid: ICONA.

HIRALDO, F., BLANCO, J.C. & BUSTAMANTE, J. (1991) Unspecialized exploitation of small carcases by birds. *Bird Study*. 38: 200–207.

HIRALDO, F., NEGRO, J.J., DONÁZAR, J.A. & GAONA, P. (in press). A demographic model for a population of the endangered lesser kestrel in southern Spain. *Journal of Applied Ecology*.

JAKSIC, F.M. & SORIGUER, R.C. (1981) Predation upon the European rabbit (*Oryctolagus cuniculus* L.) in Mediterranean habitats of Chile and Spain: a comparative analysis. *Journal of Animal Ecology*, 50: 269–281.

LAZO, A. (1995) El ganado bovino asilvestrado de Doñana. *Quercus*, 107: 21–23.

MAHLAU, M. (1991) *Production, Marketing and Consumption of Animal Products in Spain. Economics of Animal Production in Mediterranean European Commission countries*. Kiel: Wissenschaftsverlag Vauk Kiel KG.

LUCIO, A.J., PURROY, F.J. & SAENZ DE BURUAGA, M. (1992) La *Perdiz Pardilla* (Perdix perdix) en España. Colección Tecnica. Madrid: ICONA.

MAJORAL, R. (1987) La utilización del suelo agricola en España. Aspectos evolutivos y locacionales. *El Campo*, 104, 13–26. Vizcaya.

MANRIQUE, J. & DE JUANA, E. (1991) Land use changes and the conservation of dry grasslands birds in Spain: a case study of the Almeria province. In Goriup, P.D., Batten, L.A. & Norton, J.A. (eds) *The Conservation of Lowland Dry Grassland Birds in Europe*, pp. 49–58. Peterborough: Joint Nature Conservation Committee.

MAPA (Mapa de cultivos y aprovechamientos) (1981) *Mapa de cultivos y aprovechamientos de Villanueva de la Vera*. Madrid: Ministerio de Agricultura, Pesca y Alimentación.

MAPA (Mapa de cultivos y aprovechamientos) (1983–88) Mapas de Cultivos y aprovechamientos provinciales. Madrid: Ministerio de Agricultura, Pesca y Alimentación.

MAPA (Ministerio de Agricultura, Pesca y Alimentación) (1993) *Anuario de Estadistica Agraria de 1990*. Madrid: Ministerio de Agricultura, Pesca y Alimentación.

MAPA (Ministerio de Agricultura, Pesca y Alimentación) (1995a) *El futuro del Mundo Rural*. Madrid: Secretaria General de Desarrollo Rural y Conservación.

MAPA (Ministerio de Agricultura, Pesca y Alimentación) (1995b) *Avance del Plan Nacional de Regadios* Secretaria General de Desarrollo Rural y Conservación de la Naturaleza. Ministerio de Agricultura, Pesca y Alimentación.

MARTÍNEZ, C. (1994) Habitat selection by the Little Bustard *Tetrax tetrax* in cultivated areas of Central Spain. *Biological Conservation*, 67: 125–128.

MAYOL, J. & SARGATAL, J. (1995) El ganado como instrumento de conservación en los humedales. *Quercus*. 107: 16–20.

MONTANER, J., FOURNEAU, F., LLEO, J., PAREDES, J., ACOSTA, G. & CEBALLOS, R. (1986) *Evolución de los paisajes y ordenación del territorio en Andalucia Occidental*. Madrid: Instituto del Territorio y Urbanismo.

MORENO, S. & VILLAFUERTE, R. (1995) Traditional management of scrubland for the conservation of rabbits *Oryctolagus cuniculus* and their predators in Doñana National Park, Spain. *Biological Conservation*, 73: 81–85.

NAVESO, M.A. (1992) Proposal to declare the area of Villafáfila as Environmental Sensitive Area. Junta de Castilla y León – Sociedad Española de Ornitología/BirdLife, Madrid (unpublished report).

NAVESO, M.A. & FERNÁNDEZ, J. (1993) Proposal of Zonal Programme for La Serena steppeland area according to the implementation of the 2078/92/E European Commission regulation. Sociedad Española de Ornitología/BirdLife, Madrid (unpublished report).

NAVESO, M.A., PARR, S. & YARAR, M. (in press). Differences between lesser kestrel *Falco naumanni*, great bustard *Otis tarda* and little bustard *Tetrax tetrax* population size and structure, prey availability and agricultural land use in Spain and Turkey. In *International Symposium on Conservation of Steppe Birds and their Habitats*, Valladolid, 12–15 October 1995.

PAIN, D. & DUNN, E. (1995) The effects of agricultural intensification upon pastoral birds: lowland wet grasslands (The Netherlands) on transhumance farming (Spain) pp. 90-98. In D.I. McCracken, E.M. Bignal & S. Wenlock (eds). *Farming on the Edge: the nature of traditional farmland in Europe*. Proceedings of the fourth European Forum on Nature Conservation and Pastoralism, Trujillo, Spain.

PALOMARES, F., RODRIGUEZ, A., LAFFITTE, R. & DELIBES, M. (1991) The status and distribution of the Iberian Lynx *Felis pardina* (Temminck) in Coto Doñana Area, SW Spain. *Biological Conservation*, 57: 159–169.

PARR, S., NAVESO, M.A. & YARAR, M. (in press). Habitat and food surrounding lesser kestrel *Falco naumanni* colonies in Central Turkey. *Biological Conservation*.

PECO, B. & SUÁREZ, F. (1993) Recomendaciones para la gestión y conservación del medio natural frente a los cambios relacionados con la Política Agraria Comunitaria (PAC). Madrid: Universidad Autónoma de Madrid-ICONA. (unpublished report).

PULIDO, F., ESCRIBANO, E. & RODRIGUEZ, A. (1994) El ecosistema español actual e incidencia de la reforma de la PAC. A.Y.M.A., 34(4–5): 123–133.

RUÍZ, M. & RUÍZ, J.P. (1986) Ecological history of transhumance in Spain. *Biological Conservation*, 37: 73–86.

RUPÉREZ, A. (1957) *La encina y sus tratamientos*. Madrid: Ediciones selvicolas.

SÁNCHEZ, C. (1994) *La última batalla contra la peste procina. El boletin*. Madrid: Ministerio de Agricultura, Pesca y Alimentación.

SORIGUER, R.C. (1981) Biologia y dinámica de una población de conejos (*Oryctolagus cuniculus* L) de Andalucia occidental. *Doñana, Acta Vertebrata* 8(3) (special issue).

SORIGUER, R.C. (1988) *Diversidad y abundancia de los micromamiferos ibéricos*. I Congreso Mundial sobre el bosque y matorral mediterráneo. Cáceres.

SUÁREZ, F. (1988) *La Garcilla*, 71–72: 12–17.

SUÁREZ, F. (1994) Mediterranean steppe Conservation: A background for the development of a future strategy. Brussels: DGXI/153/94, Commission of Europe.

SUÁREZ, F., SAINZ, H. SANTOS, T. & GONZÁLEZ-BERNÁLDEZ, F. (1991). *Las estepas ibéricas*. Unidades Temáticas Ambientales de la Secretaria de Estado para las Politicas del Agua y del Medio Ambiente. Madrid: MOPT.

SUMPSI, J.M., VARELA-ORTEGA, C., IGLESIAS, E. (1995) *The CAP and the Environment*. Brussels: DGVI, Commission of Europe.

SUNYER, C. (1988) *Importancia y manejo de basureros y muladares para la conservación de las poblaciones de aves rapaces y el control de la rabia selvática*. Dirección General de Medio Ambiente. Madrid: MOPU.

TELLA, J.L. (1993) *Inventariado de los muladares y su importancia para el alimoche en el valle medio del Ebro*. Diputación General de Aragón. Zaragoza.

THIBAULT, J.-C., VIGNE, J-D. & TORRE, J. (1993) The diet of young Lammergeiers *Gypaetus barbatus* in Corsica: its dependence on extensive grazing. *Ibis*, 135: 42–48.

THOMAS, M.B., WRATTEN, S.D. & SOTHERTON, N.W. (1992) Creation of "island" habitats in farmland to manipulate populations of beneficial arthropods: predator densities and species composition. *Journal of Applied Ecology*, 29: 524–531.

TUCKER, G.M. (1991) The status of lowland dry grassland birds in Europe. In P.D. Goriup, L.A.

Batten & J.A. Norton (eds) *The Conservation of Lowland Dry Grassland Birds in Europe*, pp. 37–48. Peterborough: Joint Nature Conservation Committee.

TUCKER, G.M. & HEATH, M.F. (1994) *Birds in Europe: their conservation status*. Cambridge: BirdLife International Series No. 3.

URMENETA, A. & NAVESO, M.A. (1993) Propuesta de Programa de Zona en aplicación del Reglamento 2078/92/CEE del área esteparia de Bardenas Reales y el Vedado de Guara. Madrid: Sociedad Española de Ornitología/BirdLife (unpublished report).

VEIGA, P. & HIRALDO, F. (1990) Food habits and the survival and growth of nestlings in two sympatric kites (*Milvus milvus* and *Milvus migrans*). *Holarctic Ecology*. **13**: 62–71.

VIÑUELA, J. (1991) Ecologia reproductiva del milano negro *Milvus migrans* en el Parque Nacional de Doñana. Tesis Doctoral (inédita). Madrid: Universidad Complutense de Madrid.

VIÑUELA, E. (1992) El virus de la peste porcina Africana. In Ministerio de Agricultura, Pesca y Alimentación (eds) *El Cerdo Ibérico, la Naturaleza, la Dehesa*, pp. 79–92. Madrid.

WATSON, J. (1991) The Golden Eagle and pastoralism across Europe. In Curtis, D.J., Bignal, E.M., & Curtis, M.A. (eds) *Birds and Pastoral Agriculture in Europe. Proceedings of the Second European Forum on Birds and Pastoralism*, pp. 56–67. Port Erin, Isle of Man, 26–30 October 1990. Scottish Chough Study Group/Joint Nature Conservation Committee.

CHAPTER

6

Cereal farming, pesticides and grey partridges

DICK POTTS

SUMMARY

The decline of the grey partridge *Perdix perdix* parallels that of a suite of bird species currently declining on farmland. Unlike the other species, however, the status, ecology and population dynamics of the grey partridge have been the subject of research, both intensive and extensive, stretching back to the early 1930s. As a result, the science base is strong and the causes of the partridge decline are known: a collapse of biodiversity on farmland particularly in cereal crops, which involved hundreds of species of plants and insects as well as the birds.

Four successive developments are singled out as particularly important, all aspects of intensification in the cereal ecosystem: the use of herbicides; the abandonment of undersowing as the technique for establishing grass/legume leys; the polarization of grassland and cereal ecosystems including the abandonment of arable farming in hill regions; and the summer use of foliar insecticides. The impact on partridges of this intensification has been through the increased mortality of chicks starved of insect food.

The 28-year study of grey partridges on the Sussex Downs is used to quantify the effect of these developments in cereal husbandry and to judge the repercussions of the CAP Reforms of 1992. Contrary to what was intended in those Reforms, intensification has continued with, simultaneously, adverse effects of set-aside, increased use of insecticides and, locally, the arable reversion option as one of the agri-environment measures.

The partridge decline could readily be reversed by more effective policies. A

FARMING AND BIRDS IN EUROPE
ISBN 0-12-544280-7
Copyright © 1997 Academic Press Ltd
All rights of reproduction in any form reserved

biodiversity initiative grant-aided scheme for conservation headlands and undersowing together with more widespread use of the wild bird cover option on flexible set-aside and buffer zones for broad spectrum insecticides could restore partridge populations with concomitant benefits for farmland wildlife in general. Six proposals are given, see page 173.

More than any other bird species, the grey partridge could be said to be a barometer of the biodiversity in cereal-based farmland ecosystems (Potts, 1986). It lives mainly in cereal crops, feeds on a wide variety of insects and plants, benefits from mixed farming and is perhaps the most thoroughly monitored species amongst an assemblage of about 8000 (excluding micro-organisms) which live, or lived, in the arable crops of Europe. The species is also highly sensitive to changes in its environment. What is more, despite much lip-service and small-scale attempts to make agriculture more conservation-sensitive, many farming policies still further *reduce* the numbers of this bird.

THE IMPORTANCE OF THE CEREAL ECOSYSTEM

Supplying 60% of all food, cereals are by far the most important crop globally. They cover more than 14% of the entire surface area of the first 12 countries of the European Union (EU): an area greater than the British Isles. Include the crops that rotate with cereal crops, and it becomes obvious that the cereal ecosystem is a most important part of the European countryside. In the UK the area given over to cereals occupies 17% of the total surface area; 16 times the combined area given over to all local and national nature reserves (Potts, 1991). Yet, until recently, the vast majority of conservationists and environment policy-makers were unconcerned about cereal ecosystems. This had to do partly with the perceived (and recent) lack of biodiversity in cereal crops. Partly too it stemmed from the fact that so few policy-makers understood farmland ecology. Their lack of concern may also have had something to do with the 'barometer' itself being a quarry species. Efforts to restore partridge numbers were thus often thought – wrongly – to be efforts simply to restore shooting bags.

Whatever the cause, through the 1970s and early 1980s conservationists focused their concerns almost entirely on rare or localised species and on the loss of species-rich woodlands, heathlands, wetlands and coastal areas. This was not entirely surprising in that such areas, including agricultural wetlands, were still being lost rapidly. The rate of loss of these habitats has markedly decreased recently and, through the declines of such species as the bustards, shrikes, larks, buntings, the rare arable flowers and some butterflies and other insects, it is increasingly realized that the threat from modern arable systems is of a world-wide nature and that ecological deterioration in the wider countryside is by far the most important cause of species decline amongst birds (Gibbons *et al.*, 1993; Tucker & Heath, 1994). No species reflects changes like these better than the grey partridge (Potts, 1986; Aebischer & Potts, 1990). In North America, much attention has been given to the decline of migrant songbirds that winter in neotropical forests. However, grassland nesting birds, which include those of cereal crops, have over the period 1966–91 shown steeper, more consistent and more geographically widespread declines than any other bird species in North America, including neotropical migrants (Knopf, 1994). In passing, it is more than noteworthy that most of these declines have continued in the USA despite the 15 million hectares of temporary grassland created since 1987 in the Conservation Reserve Programme (CRP) (Reynolds et al., 1994).

THE PARTRIDGE DECLINE

How many partridges were present before the decline, how many remain, and what is their future? Judging from national estimates of partridge harvest (bags) available from most countries (Potts, 1986; Birkan & Jacob, 1988), supplemented by studies of the relationship of shooting to spring stocks (Aebischer, 1991a) and several long-term studies including direct population density measurements (Potts, 1986), I estimate the stock of grey partridge in Europe in the 1930s at more than 20 million pairs. From the estimates of Tucker & Heath (1994) it is reasonable to put the present total at less than 3.5 million pairs, equivalent to an overall decline in breeding stocks of at least 83%. This has been a huge loss of a valuable natural resource, costing providers of sport (I estimate) £50 million annually in additional stocking expenses.

Annual falls in partridge numbers have averaged 4–7% in most countries since the 1950s, though there are signs in the Game Conservancy Trust's (GTC's) long-term study of partridges on the Sussex Downs (Potts & Vickerman, 1974) and in the British Trust for Ornithology's (BTO's) Common Bird Census that the rate of decline has slowed, probably in response to the recent string of warm summers, which, other things being equal, improve chick survival (Potts, 1986). The grey partridge is on the Nature Conservancy Council/Royal Society for the Protection of Birds (NCC/RSPB) Red Data List. Under the International Union for the Conservation of Nature (IUCN) Red List, because numbers are still relatively high globally, the species is not considered 'vulnerable' i.e. defined as 'qualitative analysis showing the probability of extinction in the wild (globally) is at least 10% within the next 100 years'. However, it is considered 'vulnerable' in Europe in Appendix 1 of Tucker & Heath (1994). When compared with the undoubtedly globally endangered corncrake Crex crex it is, however, increasing in fewer countries (0 compared with 1), stable in fewer (2 compared with 3) and declining in more (31 compared to 27). No other species amongst those covered by Tucker & Heath is declining so much in terms of numbers or in so many countries. What is more, a suite of up to 40 species dependent on arable land, ranging from the great bustard Otis

Figure 1 In Europe, the grey partridge is estimated to have declined by at least 83% since the 1930s. (Photo by R. Revels/RSPB.)

tarda to the skylark *Alauda arvensis* and corn bunting *Miliaria calandra*, show signs of declining in a strikingly similar way.

The grey partridge has a greater potential for recovery than many other species, because it breeds in its first year (unlike, for example, the great bustard) and has the largest clutch size of any bird species in the world. So, if we could change its ecological status this species could recover faster than other birds, in less than seven years, given the chance (Potts, 1986). In addition, a large number of people, at first only hunters (*sensu lato*) but now joined by some conservationists, are putting their weight behind such a restoration of numbers. So far, however, this has been with little effective support from farming policies.

CHANGES IN THE CEREAL ECOSYSTEM

As in other countries, many dramatic changes have occurred in cereal crops since the beginning of World War II. These changes have vastly increased yields (threefold in the UK) so that, despite an increased world population, famines are now the result of wars rather than shortages of food. Not only that but much greater quantities of food are produced from virtually the same area of land,

Figure 2 Intensively managed wheat monoculture in Sussex, UK, in June, showing tramlines. Supports low biodiversity. (Photo by G. R. Potts.)

thus avoiding the need to convert even more natural habitats to agriculture (Adams, 1990; Avery, 1995).

Many changes have occurred in sequence and in parallel to bring this about, for the most part founded on the use of inorganic fertilizers and pesticides and the breeding of varieties able to exploit the availability of these chemicals. The main system change is described as intensification, i.e. increased outputs per unit area of crop. Of course, other changes have occurred, such as the change from scythes to mowers, and from horses to tractors.

The simple definition of intensification used above is important because it means it can be brought about by two different processes, namely confining cropping to more productive land or by increasing outputs from a given area of land. We will return to these separate effects later, when dealing with set-aside.

Intensification in the cereal ecosystem has taken many forms, but all of them have since the 1940s taken the system towards monoculture. Hedges and other boundary cover have been removed so that fields have become bigger; rotations have become less complex or even disappeared (e.g. continuous cereals); mixed farms have given way to specialized farms, and mixed farming regions have given way to specialized regions. The effects of intensification in cereal production have not been confined to the cereal area, because they have enabled farmers to escape the need for grass/cereal rotations. Thus cereals have given way to grass in the west of Britain and grass has given way to cereals in the east.

Farm livestock has become separated from the crops needed to feed them. Farmyard manure, a mixture of dung and straw, has given way to slurry, a mixture of dung and water in the west, and to surplus straw and burning (or now incorporation) in the east. All these changes have brought about a massive decline in biodiversity in the countryside (Potts, 1986, 1991). The key sequences in the intensification of cereal cropping are shown in Figure 3.

The UK cereal-field flora and fauna are basically a mixture of remnants of preceding natural habitats, vestiges of the communities of steppe ecosystems,

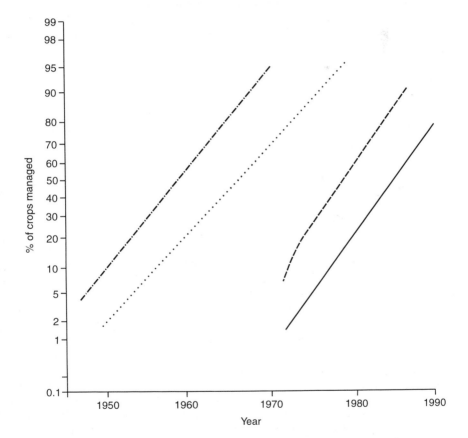

Figure 3 Key sequences in the intensification of cereal cropping in the UK over the period 1945–1990: · — · — ·, herbicides (50% coverage 1958); · · · · ·, not undersowing (50% abandonment 1966); – – –, foliar fungicides (50% coverage 1978); ——, summer insecticides in wheat (50% coverage 1985). The data for 'first herbicides' are from Potts (1986) after Woodford (1964); not undersowing from Potts (1970a); foliar fungicides from Potts (1986), Sussex Study Area, and foliar insecticides from Potts (1993). Plots are least squares regressions through accumulating arithmetic probabilities.

and ruderal and Mediterranean species, each symbiotic with the cereal ecosystem. Although the cereal ecosystem is not stable, because without human management it would disappear, a distinct and diverse cereal flora and fauna has been present for thousands of years. The cereal ecosystem pre-dates heather moorland (Stevenson & Birks, 1995), coppice woodland (Rackham, 1986), and even chalk grassland (Tittensor, 1991). It contains up to 700 species of plants in Europe and some 2000 species of insects and spiders are found in it in the UK alone (Potts, 1991). Although the flora and fauna in cereal fields are today much poorer than in nature reserves, they involve more individuals because of the much greater size of area covered. What is more, whereas many bird species in nature reserves and some other habitats now have relatively stable populations, the vast majority of bird species in areas occupied by cereal crops are declining (Gibbons *et al.*, 1993; Tucker & Heath, 1994). Widening the species affected to include the insects justifies the belief that the partridge acts as a barometer for wildlife in the cereal ecosystem (see Figure 4).

CAUSES OF THE DECLINE OF THE GREY PARTRIDGE: THE SCIENCE

The population dynamics of the grey partridge are uniquely well studied among farmland birds, through conservation research involving an integrated approach by monitoring and modelling, backed up by large-scale temporal and spatial experiments and widespread practical management.

Breeding densities averaged over many years vary up to 40-fold from locality to locality, with the levels determined by density-dependent mortality, mostly predation at the nest and to a lesser extent by density-dependent dispersal, in response to the availability of nesting cover during the time in spring when pairs settle (Potts, 1986; Potts & Aebischer, 1989, 1991). The population dynamics of the partridge have been explored in detail. It has been shown that any increase in the sum total of the combined density-dependent mortalities (because they each increase with density and thereby reduce subsequent density, they are interdependent), plus the density-independent mortality (principally starvation of chicks) will cause mean population densities to fall. The way in which this happens can best be illustrated by calculating the term K which is the sum of all losses of eggs, chicks and adults through a breeding cycle starting with a typical clutch (15 eggs) and ending with recruitment to the breeding stock. Prior to the decline of the species, the total annual log mortality (K) of stable populations averaged 1.0, whereas after the period 1952–62 in the UK, later elsewhere, K rose to 1.18. A total K of 1 is equivalent to an overall survival from egg to breeding adult of 10%: 1.18 is equivalent to 6.6%. Thus there was a fall of 34% in overall survival (6.6/10). This resulted in considerable declines and has brought mortality almost to the point that, if sustained, ensures inevitable extinction within 50 years (Potts & Aebischer, 1995).

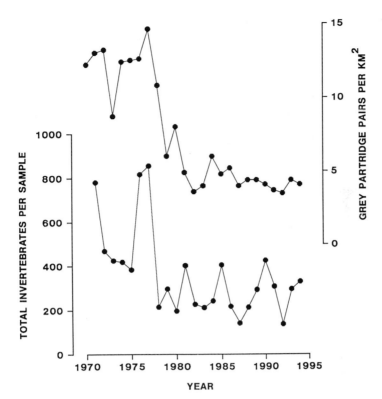

Figure 4 *Upper*: grey partridge spring stocks as pairs per km² in the West Sussex Study Area from 1969–1994 (from Potts & Aebischer, 1995). *Lower*: total invertebrates per Dietrick vacuum insect net sample, of approximately 0.5 m², from cereal crops in the third week of June 1970–1994 (from Aebischer, 1991b, updated). The invertebrate means are shifted one year to the right to correspond to resultant changes in pair density.

Almost all the extra mortality derives from chick starvation, shown by experiments to be due to shortages of the insect foods of chicks brought about by the use of herbicides (Rands, 1985, 1986; Potts & Aebischer, 1991). As a consequence of the decline of the partridge, gamekeepers switched their attention from protecting nests from predation to other activities or they were made redundant. Usually overall mortality did not increase because, as populations crashed, shooting became insignificant (Potts, 1980) and densities were too low to invoke much predation (see Potts & Aebischer, 1995).

All this may appear straightforward, or at least plausible, but it must be stressed that these explanations arose out of work by many people extending over a century through many countries. No doubt the work involved could nowadays be telescoped dramatically, but it would still be impossible to unravel the above causation chains without an integration of intensive field studies (involving such techniques as radio tracking broods with simultaneous monitoring of chick food and survival), general long-term monitoring of survival, simulation modelling, and field experimentation. In particular, a thorough understanding of the role of predation on partridges was necessary before the impact of insect shortages could be quantified. This explained, for example, how populations existing at very different densities could decline in the same way and, indeed, why one population did not decline at all (Potts & Aebischer, 1995). While similar data are not yet available for other farmland species, it probably errs on the right side of caution to conclude that the other species which are declining in the same way, in the same habitats, may well be affected by similar processes.

Particularly important insect prey for the grey partridge chicks are, in descending order of importance: (1) small diurnal ground beetles (Carabidae); (2) sawfly and other caterpillars (Symphyta and Lepidoptera); (3) leaf beetles (Chrysomelidae) and weevils (Curculionidae); (4) plant bugs (Heteroptera) and leaf hoppers (Cicadellidae); and (5) aphids (Aphididae) (Potts & Aebischer, 1991). Around half of the annual and spatial variation in chick survival rates in the Sussex study area was attributable to variations in abundance of their insect food. To restore partridge numbers it is therefore first necessary to restore the abundance of the rather specialized insects on which the chicks feed (Potts, 1986). One possible reason why other groups of invertebrates are not preferred is that they are often secondary hosts of dangerous partridge parasites such as nematodes and cestodes (Potts, 1986 and unpublished).

A complex of farming activities has been shown to affect the abundance and availability of the foods partridge chicks prefer, of which three are paramount:

(1) *Insecticides.* All of the five groups suffer great mortality, sometimes effectively 100%, through the application in spring and summer of insecticides (such as dimethoate) to control cereal aphids (Vickerman & Sunderland, 1977; Sotherton *et al.*, 1987; Sotherton, 1990; Duffield & Aebischer, 1994). These effects have been repeated in recent attempts to control the orange wheat blossom midge *Contarinia tritici* using the officially recommended broad-spectrum compounds chlorpyrifos and triazophos.

(2) *Herbicides.* The four most important of the five insect groups are dependent on broad-leaved weeds (Chiverton & Sotherton, 1991; Sotherton, 1991; Sotherton & Moreby, 1992) and, in the case of sawfly caterpillars, grass weeds (Vickerman, 1974). They are therefore adversely affected by herbicides.

(3) *Undersowing.* The sawflies, and to a lesser extent leaf beetles and weevils, are dependent on undersowing, i.e. the use of cereals as a nurse for grass. This was at one time the universal way of establishing ley grassland (Potts, 1986). The use of this technique declined rapidly through the late 1960s and 1970s (Potts, 1970a; Aebischer, 1990) until today it plays a tiny fraction of its former role (Figure 3).

CURRENT AGRICULTURAL POLICIES

The whole basis of the Common Agricultural Policy (CAP) and its reforms rests on a political desire for a more equitable distribution of incomes in rural areas. This has been achieved by artificially supporting the prices of major commodities, and by protecting European farmers from international markets. This distortion of market forces has led to surplus production of food, resulting in the introduction of additional distortions in the form of supply control measures such as milk and livestock quotas and arable set-aside. The 1992 CAP reforms introduced cuts in support prices for beef and arable crops, compensating farmers by means of direct repayments. Support to farmers' incomes under the CAP has therefore been secured through economic inefficiency, high consumer prices and growing budgetary costs (see Robson, Chapter 3).

The CAP nonetheless has brought considerable social benefits, and although there are adverse consequences for natural resources and other so-called 'negative externalities', there would almost certainly be even greater problems for the environment if the CAP were suddenly abolished – larger farms, larger fields, more polarized systems, even fewer people on the land. For a time, crops and stock would be managed in ways that were most economic. The more entrepreneurial farmers who reject the mediocrity imposed by the CAP would be delighted. Some years later, however, biological processes could begin to catch up and restore a balance. These include, for example, more parasites (e.g. nematodes currently controlled by anthelmintics), 'new' diseases (e.g. rhizomania in sugar beet) and aquifer pollution (e.g. atrazine and IPU herbicides) as a result of geographical concentration and lack of rotation, or genetic resistance to pesticides. In the interim, the costs to farm wildlife could be spectacular. But this is not to say all is well with the CAP, even now that it has been reformed, for as this chapter shows, that would be absurd. All is far from well, as the position of the partridge shows.

The CAP reforms of 1992 may eventually help to bring about some of their intended extensification (of crops and livestock), but I agree with the reviewers who, from a different perspective to mine, also found the reforms not capable of addressing the complexity, variety and time scales of the issues involved (ECDGEFA, 1994). The story of the grey partridge helps us to understand how, for one species dependent on the most important of the CAP crops, further reform is necessary and indeed how it could be most effective. There is startling scope for reform given that only 1% of the CAP budget is spent on environmental schemes, and given the frequently expressed view that quotas, set-aside and other supply controls cannot be realistic options for the twenty-first century (e.g. Waldegrave, 1995). This chapter ends with new proposals designed to solve some of the problems.

FIRST REFORMS OF THE CAP – THE MacSHARRY REFORMS

For any policies for bird conservation on farmland in the European Union to be effective they must be compatible with, or ideally part of, the CAP itself. Prior to 1984, when milk quotas were introduced, the CAP had been a system entirely geared to encourage production. However, pressure was building up from two directions for the reform of the CAP. Both arose from intensification – the need to reduce surpluses and, to an increasing extent, the need to deal with the environmental problems. Such were the difficulties of getting agreement on the market measures that the first measures introduced were those enabling the Environmentally Sensitive Areas. Over the next seven years a series of policies came and went, culminating in the full 1992 reform package with its three-pronged approach to cereals – the most important part of which was the Arable Area Payment Scheme set out in Regulation 1765/92. This was an ingenious method of disconnecting aid from production by making direct payments to farmers on the basis of areas in production rather than yield, but it was always too fine a balance as to whether farmers would still aim for maximum possible yields, and therefore high inputs. In any case, the costs of the most damaging insecticides are so low that they can be ignored by cereal growers. Finally, because the system was phased in over three years, and because market prices have firmed, the system has not operated in the way intended, i.e. to encourage extensification. Not only that, but scientific advances, such as genetically engineered resistance to broad-spectrum herbicides, threaten to bring about yet more intensification and, for the first time, true monocultures. This is worrying.

The second part of the Reforms in Regulation 1765/92, set-aside, certainly succeeded in controlling surpluses (e.g. see statement by EU Agriculture Commissioner, Franz Fischler, on the benefits of CAP Reform, 1 July 1995 and Weekly Digest of The Home-Grown Cereals Authority, 22 April 1995). However, it did not, at least in its early years, help the environment. In its first year in particular, it undoubtedly caused considerable harm to ground-nesting birds (Poulsen & Sotherton, 1992; Mañosa, 1994). New schemes are in place that allow environmentally friendly use of set-aside, but they do not encourage it – as we shall see when we return to this subject. Meanwhile, set-aside tends to drive intensification because it increases market prices, an effect exacerbated because it also occupies a disproportionately high proportion of fields in marginal production where it displaces wildlife, such as rare arable flowers.

The most enlightened part of the 1992 Reforms was the Agri-environment Regulation 2078/92. Unfortunately, this part of the Reform has been subject to delays both in formulation and in implementation ever since it was first considered. In the UK, the government at first claimed that the objectives of the Regulation were being achieved through the ESAs, but these are geographically limited, exclude arable land (in contrast with the situation in Spain) and moreover, in some areas, reward the conversion of arable to grass, with consequent adverse effects on arable wildlife (Wakeham-Dawson, 1994). The

Game Conservancy Trust's long-term monitoring in the Sussex Downs ESA reveals a decline of 28% *per annum* of partridges in the ESA arable reversion areas from designation to 1994, *14 times as great as in areas not taking this ESA option* (Aebischer & Potts, in press).

Thus, all three of the measures embodied in the 1992 reform are thoroughly unsatisfactory and in urgent need of further reform to save the hitherto common, and now rapidly declining, farmland birds.

CONSERVATION OF SPECIES UPON WHICH PARTRIDGE CHICKS FEED

Insecticides

Among birds, the partridge has a unique history of documentation regarding the direct adverse effects of insecticides, mostly arsenic, in incidents going back almost to the seventeenth century (Young, 1804; Hawker, 1844; Carson, 1962); denocate and DNBP in a series of incidents in the 1940s and early 1950s; and most widely known, the effects of dieldrin seed dressings beginning in 1955 (Potts, 1986). All of these chemicals have now been phased out in the UK.

The background of the phasing out of these chemicals is important because the experience with DDT and other chlorinated hydrocarbons created a belief, still met with today, that the ecological threats posed by insecticides have been dealt with. They have not. Insecticide use has continued to increase with concomitant effects on non-target insects and the species that feed on them like the grey partridge. These chemicals are now used on a scale unthought of when the regulatory systems were established for pesticide toxicity. Just as regulatory systems avoided the arrival of Rachel Carson's 'silent spring', so new ones are needed to prevent a 'silent summer'.

Our present concern at The Game Conservancy Trust has its origins in the outbreak of cereal aphids in wheat on the South Downs in the summer of 1968. The summer use of insecticides gradually escalated through the 1970s and 1980s. In the Trust's Sussex study area, at least, this even continued through a period when the trend in cereal aphid numbers was downwards (Aebischer, 1991b). This escalation has damaged populations of the grey partridge and, presumably, other farmland species with similar requirements. The problem could be tackled on two fronts: chemical specificity and integrated pest management. Much research has since been undertaken on the biological control of pests (e.g. that summarized in Cavalloro & Sunderland, 1988; Wratten & Powell, 1991; Glen *et al.*, 1995).

Chemical specificity

The first need is to restrict the spring or summer use in cereals of the broadest spectrum insecticides, classically represented by dimethoate. Even by the mid-

1970s it was obvious that the adverse effects of this chemical on insect communities in cereal crops were severe and prolonged when used in summer (Vickerman & Sunderland, 1977). However, it was (and remains) cheap and, despite an educational campaign including many scientific papers, questions by politicians in both Houses of Parliament, direct representations to the manufacturers and an official Review by the Pesticide Safety Division (PSD) of MAFF, it is still one of the most popular and widely used compounds.

An equally broad-spectrum insecticidal compound, pyrazophos, was introduced in 1984 as a barley fungicide for control of mildew *Erysiphe graminis* and net blotch *Rhynchosporium secalis*. The manufacturers were eventually persuaded by the PSD, using data produced by Sotherton and colleagues (Sotherton & Moreby, 1984; Sotherton *et al.*, 1987) to apply a label to their product which pointed out that it 'may have insecticidal properties'. However, the fact that the compound was very little used was, I suggest, due to its alleged ineffectiveness against foliar diseases rather than to any concern for the environment. It has now been removed from the UK cereal pesticide market. Suppose, however, that it had been a market leader covering an annual area of cereals of, say, 1.5 million hectares – the area sprayed with a successor, fenpropimorph (Davis *et al.*, 1991). What then would have been the ecological damage? Would its use have been prevented? On present form -- very probably not.

In some cases, where an insecticide cannot be banned, farmers could be encouraged to use the more target-specific alternatives, of which the best example is pirimicarb (Sotherton, 1990). Farmers trying to protect gamebird food species certainly did begin to switch to this chemical (Vickerman *et al.*, 1976) even though it was up to five times more expensive than dimethoate, and did so at least until the arrival of the synthetic pyrethroids. These were originally for use on cereals in the autumn, and there was at first a moratorium on summer use, lifted in 1990 for deltamethrin and alpha-cypermethrin. These pyrethroids are safer for tractor-drivers who operate the sprayers; they are used in much smaller quantities, and have lower levels of toxicity to mammals, birds and bees. They are clearly more environment-friendly than many other insecticides. Nevertheless, they adversely affect a broad spectrum of insects and other invertebrates compared with, say, pirimicarb.

Insecticide impacts rose again when the ecologically preferable pirimicarb and the synthetic pyrethroids were found to be ineffective against the orange wheat blossom midge in the outbreaks of this pest in 1993, 1994 and 1995. Because of the phenomenal scale of use (e.g. >300 000 ha in June 1994) and the fact that broad-spectrum insecticides were used (chlorpyrifos and triazophos) there can be little doubt that the adverse effects of insecticides on cereal crop non-target insects, and thus on the birds that eat them, were greater in both 1993 and 1994 than in any previous year. Judging from an event a decade earlier amongst finches there may even have been direct mortality due to chlorpyrifos (Simpson, 1984). These compounds were widely used again in 1995 when aphicides, including dimethoate, were also applied on a large scale.

Partridge chick survival rates monitored in The Game Conservancy Trust's study area on the South Downs continually from 1968 to 1995 show an adverse effect of insecticides, almost exactly that predicted (Potts, 1977) before any insecticide was used (Table 1). The population consequences are serious for a species already in decline.

The effects of insecticide treatments may persist for up to six years (Aebischer, 1990), although they may be alleviated in the first year of spraying by excluding headlands (the margins of the fields used for turning farm machinery round) of 12 m width, as is advised by The Game Conservancy Trust (6 m are stipulated by PSD for synthetic pyrethroids and dimethoate). An Agricultural Development Advisory Service (ADAS) survey in 1994 found that 28% of fields sprayed against the midge had not been sprayed to the field edge, and it was clear that many farmers using the approved compounds had been trying to reduce the ecological damage as a result of GCT advice. Excepting Heteroptera which dwell mostly in headlands, the beneficial effects of this safeguard will unfortunately be diluted where there is repeat spraying in subsequent years because the saved insects will disperse into the – much larger – sprayed areas.

It is probably not feasible to compensate farmers in the UK for insect damage to their grain on the grounds that the damage weakens the marketing of grain *vis-à-vis* competitors, especially non-European Union competitors who, it is said, would not be willing to be so constrained. Farmers may not want to use insecticides in summer but they clearly will use them so long as their competitors use them.

The cereal growing regime that produced the highest gross margins in a large number of trials in 1994 included four treatments with insecticides, including dimethoate (Norman, 1994). A spokesman for the company concerned, Velcourt, was reported as saying 'There is nothing to make us change strategy. Making the most profit out of a cereal crop is still about producing tonnes' (*Farmers Weekly*, 3 February 1995).

Table 1 Grey partridge chick survival rates and insecticide use on the Sussex Downs

	Insecticide use		
	Slight/none	Slight/none but intensive from 1989	
1968–1988 (n = 21)	27 ± 2%	30 ± 3%	1.22 n.s.
1989–1995 (n = 7)	34 ± 3%	23 ± 4%	3.52 $P < 0.02$

The reduction in survival to 0.68 of the control (23%/34% = 0.68) compares with 0.71 predicted in the equation of Potts (1977), which related densities of various insects eaten by chicks to chick survival through a multiple regression model.

Summer insecticide use has become routine on winter wheat and the controls on insecticides suggested at the end of this chapter would make an ideal condition for farmers to comply with in return for receiving Arable Area Payments.

Integrated pest management

The grassy raised strips known as 'Beetle Banks' grew out of initial research by Nick Sotherton and later collaborative research at the University of Southampton, which began as long ago as 1976. Beetle Banks are well researched, well costed, practical and have been trialled on many farms for several years (Thomas et al., 1991). The benefits are currently being documented by Dr Nigel Boatman of The Game Conservancy Trust. They are used to divide large fields, and their purpose is to encourage quality in situ overwintering sites for the important predators of cereal aphids, such as the carabid beetles Demetrias atricapillus, Agonum dorsale and rove beetles of the genus Tachyporus. Conserving these predators could contribute to a reduction in the need for insecticides.

Found at present in strips that add up to at least 96 km on 20 farms (approximately 288 ha), Beetle Banks are increasing in number, but they have not yet reached anywhere near their potential for there is as yet no mechanism in farming policy to foster them. Measures were however introduced in April 1996 as part of the MAFF's new Countryside Stewardship Scheme. Although useful to as many species as hedgerows, the banks are not hedgerows – which rules them out for the many hedgerow protection management incentives. Neither the Ministry of Agriculture Fisheries and Food (MAFF), who commissioned the original research, nor the EU Commission have been able to clarify whether, or in what circumstances, Beetle Banks and other non-permanent strips and narrow borders could be included in the 'actual area' of cultivated land declared under the Integrated Administration and Control System (IACS). IACS is a fraud control system and the penalties for over-declaration of cultivatable area can be severe. For this reason no-one, least of all a farmer, seems able to risk defining whether or not Beetle Banks take up the 'significant area of the field' mentioned in the IACS guide. Therefore they are not to be counted as arable land; so, for the present, the only way to incorporate Beetle Banks on an arable farm is within 20 m-wide strips of non-rotational set-aside (one of the options in the system now known as 'Flexible set-aside'). Until 1995/96 this kind of set-aside was not an economic option on arable farms, especially those where soils are all of similar production potential. More land had to be taken into set-aside (e.g. in 1995 15%, not 12%) and, because it would be in the form of strips across the middle of fields, it would be inconvenient. The amount of set-aside needed for the Beetle Bank itself was a tiny fraction of the extra 3% needed for the flexible set-aside (even less of the 5% required in other EU countries). Removal of the differential in September 1995 was a major step forward towards achieving more generally the considerable environmental benefits of flexible set-aside.

Conservation Headlands

There were a few attempts in the 1970s to avoid the use of herbicides in strips of cereals, and at the end of that decade and the beginning of the next several schemes to protect endangered arable flowers were introduced in Germany (e.g. Schumacher, 1987). Against this background, and with knowledge gained from radio-tracking of partridge broods, the first serious attempt to restore partridge chick food began in 1982 as a series of GCT trials on the Manydown Estate, Hampshire. These trials were motivated by the objective of improving the game shooting.

The outer 6 m margin of cereal fields was grown as the rest of the field, except that no herbicides were used to control broad-leaved weeds and no insecticides were used. Trials over the next few years, which at first excluded all herbicides (and later only those that remove plants beneficial to insects eaten by chicks), showed that chick food insect densities doubled and chick survival rates likewise (Rands, 1986), with many other benefits to butterflies and other wildlife (Sotherton, 1991). The scheme spread through the arable areas of the UK until in 1994 there were about 1920 km of Conservation Headlands (see Table 2) albeit out of a possible 640 000 km of suitable field edges. Although a tiny proportion of what is possible, the value of the technique to grey partridge populations is proportionately much greater because the Conservation Headlands are used almost entirely to help conserve partridges. Some spectacular successes with Conservation Headlands, particularly towards the north of the UK and in Sweden (Chiverton & Sotherton, 1991, 1992), will mean that on a few partridge-orientated estates the technique will probably continue to spread, but not without difficulty.

Set-aside has slowed the growth in uptake of Conservation Headlands because farmers, having reduced their acreage through set-aside, need to recover as much as possible of their fixed costs (or overheads) on the rest of the land.

Grants are available for Conservation Headlands only in some Environmen-

Table 2 Kilometres of Conservation Headlands in the UK

	Before mandatory set-aside				After set-aside	
	1989	1990	1991	1992	1993	1994
Inside ESAs	203	235	181	187	114	354
Outside ESAs	533	1602	1406	1610	1595	1565
Total	736	1837	1587	1797	1709	1919

tally Sensitive Areas and in a few Countryside Stewardship Schemes[1], but the cash payments are low and even in these uptake faltered until 1994 when new targets were set (Table 1). Only one ESA, Breckland, has significant areas of cereal crops in Conservation Headlands, 184 km in 1994, followed by South Downs and Wessex with 74 km each.

Nearly all ESAs in the UK are in the uplands or in river valleys, outside the habitat of arable ecosystem species such as the grey partridge. Although some ESAs do incorporate arable areas (e.g. Breckland and South Downs ESAs), the difficulties of defining suitable arable ESAs have not been surmounted – this is a serious problem for the scheme. In The GCT's Sussex study area there was in 1994 and 1995 only about 1 km of Conservation Headlands out of an ideal total of 144 km, mainly because they are supportable only if other measures are also applied. Any benefits of Conservation Headlands so far have been more than wiped out by loss of the cereal habitats through inappropriate arable reversion; a case of one step forward and several back! As mentioned earlier, the South Downs ESA measures have adversely affected partridge numbers, already reducing them overall by more than 10%, with hares *Lepus europaeus*, skylarks, corn buntings and the flora all adversely affected (Wakeham-Dawson, 1994). A case has been made that the South Downs ESA pays its way through benefits to the environment, but it was based on estimates of willingness to pay in relation to the objectives of the ESA scheme, not on its actual achievements (Garrod & Willis, 1995). Even today the benefits, or otherwise, of ESAs are not being adequately monitored. Fortunately, in Spain arable areas are included in the ESA scheme, and ESA approval is proving crucial to steppe and cereal birds (e.g. Naveso, 1992). In Germany rare arable flowers have been saved by the Conservation Headland programme (Helfrich, 1989).

Mixed farming

Partridges are not tied to cereals like fish to water, but on modern lowland farms it is effectively like that, for there is no other suitable habitat for brood rearing. Obviously it would be better that the cereals be spaced throughout the area available for production, not concentrated in the zones of highest yield with maximum inputs. For centuries, whenever cereal prices rose, the area devoted to them expanded further towards the geographical margins of cereal production, but with the decline of mixed farming in the 1950s, cereals retreated to the profitable areas despite higher prices and higher yields. This produced a pattern of cropping in the UK more polarized than at any time during the agricultural depression of the 1930s: an eastern grain belt and a western monoculture of grass (Boag & Tapper, 1992). The retreat of the arable ecosystem from huge areas in the west was associated with a commensurate decrease in biodiversity in

---

[1] Support was greatly extended in April 1996 as part of the MAFF's new Countryside Stewardship Scheme.

arable crops of the east. Against this undesirable background for partridges, several recent policies have exacerbated the downward trends.

Arable reversion in largely upland/pastoral ESAs; voluntary set-aside; non-rotational (i.e. fixed) set-aside (without special management); the so-called transfer of set-aside between producers; the nitrate sensitive areas; restrictions in the use of clover within them and on sct aside; and the planting of trees on set-aside, have to a certain extent been steps in the wrong direction, increasing the polarization effect. However, it is true that some of these measures can help to create 'mixed' systems in arable areas, e.g. arable reversion. The compulsory element in set-aside has also helped.

Although Arable Area Payments have helped to reverse the loss of arable land, they have also prevented a return to mixed systems as they are restricted to arable land as at 1991. In conjunction with livestock and milk quotas, they reinforce the existing, polarized distribution of farmland. The combined results of such policies are undoubtedly complex.

Undersown leys

Once covering about a quarter of the entire European arable area, undersown leys are now almost gone, yet on the traditional mixed farms where they are found, they remain a great boon to biodiversity, to the caterpillar larvae of sawflies and in turn to grey partridge (Potts, 1970a), pheasant *Phasianus colchicus* (Hill, 1985), corn bunting (Ward & Aebischer, 1994), skylark (Schläpfer, 1988; Jenny, 1990; Poulsen, 1993) and no doubt many other species, even such as the reed bunting *Emberiza schoeniclus* (Potts, 1986). With this system, spring-sown cereals are used as a nurse for grasses and clovers so that after the cereal harvest a ley is established without further cultivation. As well as helping those species dependent on the grasses (e.g. sawflies) and clovers (e.g. leaf weevils), it preserves those which overwinter in the soil and are adversely affected by post-harvest cultivations. Ironically, subsidies to encourage undersowing were dropped in 1969, the year that its ecological value was first discovered (Potts, 1970a).

Today the opportunity to restore undersowing is not substantial, given that it would be practical only on mixed arable farms with grazing. However, it *is* sorely needed – otherwise what will happen to the wildlife still thriving on the few traditional ley farms? Although such farming now occupies under 9% of The Game Conservancy Trust's Sussex study area, it supports 25% of the partridges and 21% of the corn buntings found in the study area, i.e. nearly three times the number expected.

Because undersowing helped partridges, The Game Conservancy Trust recommended more undersowing as an alternative to direct re-seeded grassland as long ago as 1979 (GCT, 1979). This was without effect because undersowing reduces cereal yields, although because it reduces yields, the net cost of government supporting such a proposal would have been minimal, and it could have been done by re-arranging existing policies (Potts, 1993). An emergency package of incentives is now needed to save some remaining undersowing, and thus some real oases of biodiversity on farmland.

In Denmark a scheme was introduced in 1994 as part of their programme under Regulation 2078/92 which went some way to helping to restore undersowing in that country. Known as the 'rye grass catch crop', payments are up to 200 ECU/ha. The scheme would be ideal for sawfly conservation if the condition 'should be tilled not before 15 February' was extended to 1 June. Most farmers would probably prefer to do that anyway to gain a hay crop.

SET-ASIDE

Set-aside has become a major feature of the countryside. For example, in England in 1993/94 there were 553 000 ha of set-aside compared with 2 480 000 ha of cereals. Most set-aside is of the rotational kind (RSAS). Where it follows cereals and where the natural regeneration option is followed, without mowing or cultivation until the end of May, it could be argued that the effect would be similar to undersowing, i.e. no cultivation between harvest and the emergence of sawflies. However, such a benefit could only be realized if there were no summer use of insecticide in the cereal preceding the SAS and if there were sufficient grasses in the cereal crop to encourage those species of sawflies dependent on them (Barker & Maczka, 1995). Considering these caveats and given the extremely widespread cultivation of RSAS from May 1993, RSAS was no help in its first year. In fact, it was harmful because birds were attracted out of cereal crops into the RSAS to nest, into an area where their nests would be destroyed (Sotherton *et al.*, 1994). Numbers of pheasants hatching and fledging were thus significantly reduced by RSAS (Mañosa, 1994).

Natural regeneration RSAS may help seed-eating birds in the autumn and winter – they certainly congregate there. However, there is no evidence that winter food limits the populations of any of the declining species such as skylark and corn bunting. The grey partridge is attracted to natural regeneration RSAS, particularly to *Polygonum* weeds, but it is not in any way limited by such food supplies if they are absent (Potts, 1970b; Potts, 1986). For another *Polygonum* seed-eating species, the cirl bunting *Emberiza cirlus*, natural regeneration set-aside has been beneficial (see Evans, Chapter 12).

Non-rotational set-aside (usually blocks of mown grassland) has even more disadvantages for partridges than RSAS and the cereal ecosystem *unless* it is in 20 m wide strips planted with some unharvestable, unsprayed cereals (surrogate Conservation Headlands) as is allowed in the Flexible set-aside option known as Wild Bird Cover. There is, however, no incentive or encouragement for such an excellent technique and there are extra costs: establishment and management £1600 (£4.86 per ha over the whole farm) for the Game Conservancy Trust

Figure 5 Wild Bird Cover, Loddington, Leicestershire, UK, June. Unharvestable cereals sown on flexible set-aside; this provides excellent brood rearing cover and supports high biodiversity. (Photo by G. R. Potts.)

managed experimental farm at Loddington. Its value for gamebirds is such that its use will spread. Care will be needed to retain the best options should set-aside be phased out.

On some farms set-aside could be used to produce much the same benefits as arose from undersowing in the past. These benefits could be achieved by allowing spring and summer grazing on natural regeneration set-aside, perhaps in some cases using sheep transferred (under quota) from areas where heather is being overgrazed (still a very serious problem in the uplands). However, there would be several policy hurdles to cross, and it would mean a radical change from previous farming policies — nothing less than an integration of arable and stock farming objectives. There is no sign of such integration although it is urgently needed.

TOWARDS A BETTER FARMING POLICY: ARABLE EXTENSIFICATION

It is inescapable that the basic cause of all of the problems considered in this paper — insecticides, herbicides and absence of undersowing — is the effect of *intensification* of farming on food chains and on habitats. The opposite of intensification (more from a given area of land) is *extensification* (less from a given area of land). Extensification offers an alternative to set-aside as a means of limiting food production. Consequently, there is a case for preserving existing extensive farmland systems (which are generally of high conservation value – Dixon *et al.*, 1993) and introducing schemes to restore extensive farming in place of set-aside.

Although long practised by many traditional farmers, indeed at one time by all farmers, extensive farming was not properly defined in policy until 1989 (Article 4 of EC Regulation 4115). It could have been reintroduced into arable ecosystems from about 1985 under EC R797, article 19, but instead this measure in the UK was confined to pastoral systems. Some years later, extensification was incorporated into arable land under this very article in Spain. In the UK, where it was not, the adverse effect on the grey partridge, brown hare, pheasant, corn bunting, skylark and the rest of the cereal ecosystem was exactly what the GCT had predicted. Mixed farming was and remains best for all these species. Since ESA designation, the trend away from mixed farming has been exacerbated, as we have seen through the arable reversion prescription. An extreme form of this is the abandonment of arable in the high valleys of southern Europe.

There were several attempts to bring extensification onto the EC Agenda in the late 1980s but they were overtaken by the dash for set-aside. Proposed Regulation 366 of 1990 revised in 1991 and finally appearing as the Agri-environment Regulation R2078 in June 1992, offered a prospect of salvation (Potts, 1993). For the first time European legislation was turning to reducing inputs per unit area rather than reducing the area cropped. Tucker & Heath (1994) concluded that at least 46 bird Species of European Conservation Concern (SPECs – see Tucker, Chapter 4) would benefit from proper implementation of this Regulation, but the total could be between 60 and 70, to say nothing of the non-bird species. Few, if any, will benefit in the UK whilst the government confines its main agri-environment obligation to ESAs with inappropriate mechanisms, and to hills and wetlands outside the cereal ecosystem.

A scheme to foster some arable extensification *should be the urgent objective of farming policy-makers throughout Europe*. Prerequisites are:

(1) recognition that the intensification problem relates to *crops* and that it can be solved only by extensification of crops, not by creating or managing other habitats.
(2) rebuttal of the arguments that – notwithstanding set-aside – intensification is generally good for conservation because it confines the adverse effect of intensive farming in ever more intensified crops, thus releasing a greater area for wildlife.
(3) further reform of the CAP to switch enough money from market support mechanisms to specific arable extensification and other conservation measures. Such a package depends on new objectives set in a context of desired sustainability and biodiversity; a rebalanced CAP.

Because they are funded through the market support mechanism, the main part of the CAP funding, the agri-environment measures are an ideal vehicle for supporting such a package. Member States, such as the UK, need to implement agri-environment measures targeted at arable farmland (see Robson, Chapter 3 for details of the Agri-environment Regulation).

It will not be easy, however, and many opportunities have been missed already. Many powerful forces are allied to further intensification. Their main argument is that repeatedly put forward by Lord Barber beginning with his 1989 Massey Ferguson Award lecture entitled 'Anatomy of a "green" Agriculture' and by some leading farmers and farm management companies. The national and international competitiveness of agriculture, they say, depends on high input/high output systems that guarantee production efficient businesses. It is easy to make the case: science, competition and commerce are tangible, wildlife is not, and many leading farmers resent restraints on economic production.

At present farming policies produce external costs to the environment, ultimately to be borne by non-farmers. An example is the annual cost of modern farming to gamebird conservation mentioned earlier: £50 million per annum, valued as the extra game that is bought from game farms to make up for lost production (Potts, 1986). Such 'externalities' lead to the view that farming is so hostile to wildlife that any land taken out of farming must help the environment. Such views are well articulated (e.g. Moore, 1987) and found many echoes during 1988 when set-aside policies were being formulated, to the point where the advice of environmentalists was confusing (Selborne, 1995). In some quarters the dogma persists and the idea that further intensification is good for the environment (because it means less land is employed in agriculture) gains ground (Agra Europe, 1996). This, as we have seen, became one of the arguments against organic farming (Adams, 1990; Avery, 1995). Counter-arguments are becoming popular but they are gaining support mainly in relation to the relatively unchanged arable and pastoral systems of parts of Spain or Poland (e.g. Baldock et al., 1994).

Future progress depends most of all on identifying solutions which enable farmers who wish to restore wildlife to remain internationally competitive without the need to intensify, and hence damage farmland ecosystems. To address this problem, subsidies must be even more thoroughly decoupled from production and geared internationally to environmental objectives, certainly throughout Europe and if possible North America. As we have seen, the effects of intensive farming recognize no frontiers. Moreover, the General Agreement on Tariffs and Trade (GATT), now World Trade Agreement, is not yet able to address these problems.

The failure to implement the results of cereal ecosystem research outlined here begin to parallel those in continental shelf fisheries; the biology has been researched but the political will is not there. As we have seen, R2078 could have been the answer. It was not to be. What a lost opportunity. There is time, just, to put things right (and 2078 still offers some opportunities if suitable programmes are introduced at national level). If we fail, how will we explain failure to future generations, given that so little needs to be done that can achieve so much?

SUMMARY OF PROPOSALS AND PROSPECTUS

(1) Using the new regulatory mechanisms of the Pesticide Safety Directorate, ban the use of broad spectrum insecticides during the period 15 March – 1 September from the outer 12 m of all UK cereal fields. Discourage the use of organophosphates in any part of the cereal fields after 1 May and, if an aphicide is necessary, use compliance mechanisms or incentives to encourage the use of pirimicarb. For the purposes of this proposal the definition of field boundaries – still being removed in 1995 – should be fixed, also via compliance mechanisms. Only valuable and old hedgerows are protected under the 1995 Environment Act.

   This measure will conserve insects that are the food of birds, important pollinators like wild bees, beneficial insects such as spiders and beetles that keep down the numbers of cereal aphids and other crop pests, and species intrinsically of conservation or aesthetic interest, like butterflies.

(2) Under R2078, with urgency, grant aid Conservation Headlands as a stand-alone option in the Countryside Stewardship Scheme. In the ESAs, extend and improve the Conservation Headland incentives and allow these even when the farmers adopt no other ESA options. A proposal has been accepted under the key habitats plan part of the UK biodiversity initiative with costings rising from £1.05 million in 1996 to £2.11 million in the year 2000, but more needs to be spent.

   In addition to the benefits mentioned in (1), this measure would save rare and endangered arable flowers and conserve insects which live on crop-tolerable, broad-leaved plants, and thus in turn provide food for species such as partridges, pheasants and other birds. In time, the game species will respond and recover to the point where their value perpetuates the system after grants are withdrawn. So in areas where game is important, this measure would be temporary, and could be discontinued after a minimum of five years.

(3) Under R2078, give the highest possible grant aid for traditional undersowing in spring sown cereals with mixtures of forage legumes and grasses. This would be a modification of the scheme already available in Denmark. Alternatively, remove the obligation of set-aside (or some of it) on growers who undersow.

   This measure would specifically benefit sawflies and their caterpillars and thus benefit species such as partridge, corn bunting and skylark and, because it involves spring cropping, species such as the lapwing *Vanellus vanellus*.

(4) In ESAs allow arable reversion schemes to continue only when it is clear that no rare arable flora are present, and phase out the policy altogether for new applicants.

This measure will avoid grant-aided destruction of rare arable flora, especially of hilly ground in light soil areas, e.g. the South Downs.

(5) On set-aside, by grant aid and in other ways, encourage the flexible option and, within that option, the cropping with unharvestable, untreated cereals as currently allowed in Wild Bird Cover.

This measure will be of particular benefit on farms where for one reason or another conservation headlands are not a practical proposition. Although this measure is beneficial to the farming interest in that it does not involve any interference with cereal crops, unlike conservation headlands, it is a measure which is presently too costly for all but a handful of cereal growers. Should set-aside disappear, the Wild Bird Cover option should be added to the Countryside Stewardship menu.

(6) Under R2078, allow grazing on set-aside in the case where there is no increase in the stock on the farm. This will extensify grazing under R2078, without any extra expense, and will reduce use of nitrogen. Grazing or haying has been allowed in seven out of the past eight years in the USA (Gerard, 1995), so it should be permitted here.

This measure, as well as benefiting livestock by giving them more ground, would also avoid the use of herbicides to control grass weeds. Non-grass weeds such as thistles could be controlled by measures currently allowed in ESAs, e.g. weed-wipe. Because it increases the grazing area whilst keeping stocking levels the same, less nitrogen would be needed on the presently grazed area. If sheep transferred from the Less Favoured Areas (LFA) could also be transferred on to the set-aside, it would relieve severe grazing pressure in the uplands, currently of serious conservation concern.

None of these proposals are radical. They fit into the objective of the EU of achieving a 'cheaper, more environmentally friendly way of looking after the countryside' that is now EU policy (Jacques Santer, EU President, reported in the *Daily Telegraph*, 20 May 1995).

Nonetheless, these changes collectively require pressures for change hitherto mustered only through GATT. Is environmental awareness able to exert similar pressure? I hope so.

ACKNOWLEDGEMENTS

I would like to thank my colleagues, especially Nick Sotherton, Nicholas Aebischer, Nigel Boatman and Peter Thompson for their help in sections of this paper, and Wendy Smith for preparing it.

REFERENCES

ADAMS, N. (1990) The case against organic farming. *New Scientist*, 15 September: 68.

AEBISCHER, N.J. (1990) Assessing pesticide effects on non-target invertebrates using long-term monitoring and time-series modelling. *Journal of Functional Ecology*, 4: 369–373.

AEBISCHER, N.J. (1991a) Sustainable yields: gamebirds as a harvestable resource. *Gibier Faune Sauvage*, 8: 335–351.

AEBISCHER, N.J. (1991b) In L.G. Firbank, N. Carter, J.F. Darbyshire & G.R. Potts (eds) *The Ecology of Temperate Cereal Fields*, pp. 305–331. Oxford: Blackwell Scientific Publications.

AEBISCHER, N.J. & POTTS, G.R. (1990) In L. Somerville & C.H. Walker (eds) *Pesticide Effects on Terrestrial Wildlife*, pp. 257–270. London: Taylor & Francis.

AEBISCHER, N.J. & POTTS, G.R. (in press). Spatial changes in grey partridge distribution in relation to 25 years of changing agriculture in Sussex. *Gibier Faune Sauvage*.

AGRA EUROPE (1996) High yield farming 'key to increased food demand'. Agra Europe, 16 February, p. 4.

AVERY, D. (1995) Preserving wildlife habitat – with agrochemicals. *The Agronomist*, Spring: 10–12.

BALDOCK, D., BEAUFOY, G. & CLARK, J. (1994) *The Nature of Farming: Low Intensity Farming Systems in Nine European Countries*. London: Institute for European Environmental Policy.

BARKER, A. & MACZKA, C. (1995) How different grasses and cereals perform as hosts for sawfly larvae. *Annual Review of The Game Conservancy*, 26: 73–74.

BIRKAN, M. & JACOB, M. (1988) *La Perdrix Grise*. Faune Sauvage, Hatier.

BOAG, B. & TAPPER, S.C. (1992) The history of some British gamebirds and mammals in relation to agricultural change. *Agricultural Zoology Reviews*, 5: 273–311.

CARSON, R. (1962) *Silent Spring*. London: Hamish Hamilton.

CAVALLORO, R. & SUNDERLAND, K.D. (1988) *Integrated Crop Protection in Cereals*. Proceedings of a Meeting of the EC Experts' Group, Littlehampton 25–27 November 1986. Rotterdam: Balkema.

CHIVERTON, P.A. & SOTHERTON, N.W. (1991) The effects on beneficial arthropods of the exclusion of herbicides from cereal crop edges. *Journal of Applied Ecology*, 28: 1027–1040.

CHIVERTON, P. & SOTHERTON, N.W. (1992) Conservation Headlands in Sweden 1991. *Annual Review of The Game Conservancy*, 23: 47–48.

DAVIS, R.P., GARTHWAITE, D.G. & THOMAS, M.R. (1991) *Arable Farm Crops in England & Wales*. Pesticide Usage Survey Report 85. London: MAFF Publications.

DIXON, J.B., STONES, A.J. & HEPBURN, I.R. (1993) *A Future for Europe's Farmed Countryside*. Proceedings of an international conference (Studies in European Agriculture and Environmental Policy No. 1, Royal Society for the Protection of Birds, Sandy, UK).

DUFFIELD, S. & AEBISCHER, N.J. (1994) The effect of spatial scale treatment with dimethoate on invertebrate population recovery in winter wheat. *Journal of Applied Ecology*, 31: 263–281.

ECDGEFA (1994) EC Directorate General for Economic and Financial Affairs, Report Number 4.

GCT (Game Conservancy Trust) (1979) *Game and Shooting Crops*. Green Booklet 2. Fordingbridge.

GARROD, G.D. & WILLIS, K.G. (1995) Valuing the Benefits of the South Downs Environmentally Sensitive Area. *Journal of Agricultural Economics*, 46: 160–173.

GERARD, P.W. (1995) *Agricultural Practices, Farm Policy and the Conservation of Biological Diversity*. USDI National Biological Service, Biological Science Report 4. Washington DC.

GIBBONS, D.W., REID, J.B. & CHAPMAN, R.A. (1993) *The New Atlas of Breeding Birds in Britain and Ireland 1988-1991*. London: T. and A.D. Poyser.

GLEN, D.M., GREAVES, M.P. & ANDERSON, H.M. (eds) (1995) *Ecology and Integrated Farming Systems*. Chichester: Wiley.

HAWKER, P. (1844) *Instructions to Young Sportsmen in All That Relates to Guns and Shooting*, 1922 edn. London: Herbert Jenkins Limited.

HELFRICH, R. (1989) Das 'Acker-und Wiesenrandstreifenprogramm' in Bayern – ein Programm zur Verbesserung der gesamtökologischen Situation in der Feldflur. Schriftenreihe Bayer. *Landesamt für Umweltschutz*, 89: 155–160.

HILL, D.A. (1985). The feeding ecology and survival of pheasant chicks on arable farmland. *Journal of Applied Ecology*, 22: 645–654.

JENNY, M. (1990) Nahrungsökologie der Feldlerche (*Alauda arvensis*) in einer intensiv genutzten Agrarlandschaft des schweizerischen Mittellandes. *Der Ornithologische Beobachter*, 87: 31–53.

KNOPF, F. (1994) Avian assemblages on altered grasslands. Studies in Avian Biology 15. pp. 247–257. A Century of avifaunal change in western North America.

MAÑOSA, S. (1994) The impact of rotational set-aside on pheasants. *The Game Conservancy Review of 1993*, 25: 83–84.

MOORE, N.W. (1987) New life for old farmland. *New Scientist*, 3 September: 50–52.

NAVESO, M.A. (1992) *Propuesta de declaracion de la zona de Villafáfila como area ambientalmente sensible*. Sociedad Española de Ornitologia y Juanta de Castilla y León.

NORMAN, K.R. (1994) *Arable Farming for Profit: 1994 results*. Dorchester: Velcourt Group Plc.

POTTS, G.R. (1970a) Recent changes in the farmland fauna with special reference to the decline of the Grey Partridge (*Perdix perdix*). *Bird Study*, 17: 145–166.

POTTS, G.R. (1970b) Studies on the changing role of weeds of the genus *Polygonum* in the diet of partridge (*Perdix perdix*). *Journal of Animal Ecology*, 7: 567–576.

POTTS, G.R. (1977) Some effects of increasing the monoculture of cereals. In J.M. Cherrett, & G.R. Sagar (eds) *Origins of Pest, Parasite, Disease and Weed Problems*, pp. 183–202. Oxford: Blackwell Scientific Publications.

POTTS, G.R. (1980) The effects of modern agriculture, nest predation and game management on the population ecology of partridges (*Perdix perdix* and *Alectoris rufa*). *Advances in Ecological Research*, 11: 1–82.

POTTS, G.R. (1986) *The Partridge: Pesticides, Predation and Conservation*. London: Collins.

POTTS, G.R. (1991) The environmental and ecological importance of cereal fields. In L.G. Firbank, N. Carter, J. F. Darbyshire & G.R. Potts (eds) *The Ecology of Temperate Cereal Fields*, pp. 3–21. Oxford: Blackwell Scientific Publications.

POTTS, G.R. (1993) *Agriculture Fit for the Countryside. Massey Ferguson National Agricultural Award Lecture*. House of Lords: Environmental aspects of the Reform of the Common Agricultural Policy 14, pp. 86–104. London: HMSO.

POTTS, G.R. & VICKERMAN, G.P. (1974) Studies on the cereal ecosystem. *Advances in Ecological Research*, 8: 107–197.

POTTS, G.R. & AEBISCHER, N.J. (1989) Control of population size in birds: The grey partridge as a case study. In P.J. Grubb & J.B. Whittaker (eds) *Toward a More Exact Ecology*, pp. 141–161. Oxford: Blackwell Scientific Publications.

POTTS, G.R. & AEBISCHER, N.J. (1991) Modelling the population dynamics of the Grey Partridge: conservation and management. In C.M. Perrins, J.-D. Lebreton & G.J.M. Hirons (eds) *Bird Population Studies: Their Relevance to Conservation Management*, pp. 373–390. Oxford: Oxford University Press.

POTTS, G.R. & AEBISHCER, N.J. (1995) Population dynamics of the Grey Partridge *Perdix perdix* 1793–1993: monitoring, modelling and management. *Ibis*, 137(1): 29–37.

POULSEN, J.G. (1993) Comparative ecology of skylarks (*Alauda arvensis*) on arable land. Unpublished MSc. Thesis, University of Aarhus.

POULSEN, J.G. & SOTHERTON, N.W. (1992) Crow predation in recently cut set-aside land. *British Birds*, 85: 674–675.

RACKHAM, O. (1986) *The History of the Countryside*. London: J.M. Dent & Sons.

RANDS, M.R.W. (1985) Pesticide use on cereals and the survival of partridge chicks: A field experiment. *Journal of Applied Ecology*, **22**: 49–54.

RANDS, M.R.W. (1986) The survival of gamebird chicks in relation to pesticide use on cereals. *Ibis*, **128**: 57–64.

REYNOLDS, R.E., SHAFFER, T.L., SAUER, J.R. & PETERJOHN, B.G. (1994) Conservation Reserve Program: Benefit for grassland birds in the Northern Plains. *Transactions of the 59th North America Wildlife and Natural Resources Conference*, pp. 328–336.

SCHLÄPFER, A. (1988) Population studies of the Skylark (*Alauda arvensis*) in an area of intensive agriculture. *Ornithologische Beobachter*, **85**: 309–371 (in German).

SCHUMACHER, W. (1987). Measures taken to preserve arable weeds and their associated communities in central Europe. In J.M. Way and P.W. Greig-Smith (eds) *Field Margins*, BCPC Monograph No. 35, pp. 109–112.

SELBORNE, THE EARL OF (1995) The role of nature conservation organizations in implementing Agenda 21. *Journal of Applied Ecology*, **32**: 255–262.

SIMPSON, V.R. (1984) Chlorpyrifos and wildlife. *Veterinary Record*, **114**: 101–102.

SOTHERTON, N.W. (1990) The effects of six insecticides used in UK cereal fields on sawfly larvae (*Hymenoptera:Tenthredinidae*). In *1990 Brighton Crop Protection Conference – Pests & Diseases*, pp. 999–1005.

SOTHERTON, N.W. (1991) Conservation headlands: a practical combination of intensive cereal farming and conservation. In L.G. Firbank, N. Carter, J.F. Darbyshire & G.R. Potts (eds) *The Ecology of Temperate Cereal Fields* , pp. 373–397. Oxford: Blackwell Scientific Publications.

SOTHERTON, N.W. & MOREBY, S.J. (1984) Contact toxicity of some foliar fungicide sprays to three species of polyphagous predators found in cereal fields. Tests of Agrochemicals and Cultivators No. 5. *Annals of Applied Biology Supplement*, **104**: 16–17.

SOTHERTON, N.W. & MOREBY, S.J. (1992) Beneficial arthropods other than natural enemies in cereals. In *Interpretation of Pesticide Effects on Beneficial Arthropods. Aspects of Applied Biology*, **31**: 11–19.

SOTHERTON, N.W., MOREBY, S.J. & LANGLEY, M.G. (1987) The effects of the foliar fungicide pyrazophos on beneficial arthropods in barley fields. *Annals of Applied Biology*, **111**: 75–87.

SOTHERTON, N.W., BOATMAN, N.D., MAÑOSA, S. & ROBERTSON, P.A. (1994) In *Arable Farming Under CAP Reform. Aspects of Applied Biology*, **40**: 497–505.

STEVENSON, A.C. & BIRKS, H.J.B. (1995) Heaths and moorland: long-term ecological changes, and interactions with climate and people. In D.B.A. Thompson, Alison J. Hester & Michael B. Usher (eds) *Heaths and Moorland: Cultural Landscapes*, pp. 224–239. Edinburgh: Scottish Natural Heritage.

THOMAS, M.B., WRATTEN, S.D. & SOTHERTON, N.W. (1991) Creation of 'island' habitats in farmland to manipulate populations of beneficial arthropods: predator densities and emigration. *Journal of Applied Ecology*, **28**: 906–918.

TITTENSOR, R.M. (1991) *West Dean: A history of conservation on a Sussex estate*. Bognor Regis: Felpham Press.

TUCKER, G.M. & HEATH, M.F. (1994) *Birds in Europe: their conservation status*. (Birdlife Conservation Series no. 3), pp. 366–367. Cambridge: BirdLife International.

VICKERMAN, G.P. (1974) Some effects of grass weed control on the arthropod fauna of cereals. In *Proceedings of the 12th British Weed Control Conference, 1974*, pp. 929–939. Farnham: B.C.P.C.

VICKERMAN, G.P., POTTS, G.R. & SUNDERLAND, K.D. (1976) The cereal aphid outbreak, 1975. *Annual Review Game Conservancy*, **7**: 28–34.

VICKERMAN, G.P. & SUNDERLAND, K.D. (1977) Some effects of dimethoate on arthropods in winter wheat. *Journal of Applied Ecology*, **14**: 767–777.

WAKEHAM-DAWSON, A. (1994) Hares and skylarks as indicators of environmentally sensitive farming on the South Downs. Unpublished PhD Thesis, The Open University.

WALDEGRAVE MP, THE RT. HON. WILLIAM (1995) Pressures on the CAP. In B.J. Marshall & F.A. Miller (eds) *Priorities for a New Century – agriculture, food and rural policies in the European Union*, CAS Paper 31. Reading: Centre for Agricultural Strategy.

WARD, R.S. & AEBISCHER, N.J (1994) *Changes in Corn Bunting Distribution on the South Downs in Relation to Agricultural Land Use and Cereal Invertbrates*. English Nature Research Reports No. 129. Peterborough: English Nature.

WRATTEN, S.D. & POWELL, W. (1991) Cereal aphids and their natural enemies. In L.G. Firbank, N. Carter, J.F. Darbyshire & G.R. Potts (eds) *The Ecology of Temperate Cereal Fields*, pp. 233–257. Oxford: Blackwell Scientific Publications.

WOODFORD, E.K. (1964) Weed control in arable crops. Proceedings of the VII British Weed control Conference III, pp. 944–962. Farnham.

YOUNG, A. (1804) *A General Review of the Agriculture of Norfolk*. London: Board of Agriculture.

CHAPTER

7

The Spanish dehesas: a diversity in land-use and wildlife

MARIO DIÁZ, PABLO CAMPOS &
FERNANDO J. PULIDO

SUMMARY

This chapter is devoted to the analysis of wooded dehesas (hereafter dehesas), which are pasturelands populated by holm (*Quercus ilex*) and/or cork (*Quercus suber*) oaks, with an understorey of open grassland, cereal crops or Mediterranean scrub – most commonly with a typical savannah appearance. This kind of ancient agro-silvo-pastoral system is exclusive to the western Mediterranean Basin, and supports a high number of endangered bird species both in spring and winter.

After a brief introduction on the historical development, definition, location and current extent of dehesas, we review current knowledge on the relationships between bird populations and the features of the dehesa that affect them, and that are in turn affected by land-use. The aim of this is to encourage the development of predictive models relating changes in bird populations to land-use changes through their effect on habitat features (land-use distribution at a landscape scale, and food abundance and habitat structure at a within-habitat scale). A major problem with the sustainability of the dehesas, i.e. the lack of tree regeneration in relation to land-use, is addressed.

Dehesas are shaped and maintained by human use, which largely depends upon socio-economic conditions. We review the historical changes in socio-economic conditions, their relationship with the creation of dehesas from natural Mediterranean forests, the causes of the crisis in traditional dehesa management, and the current economic output of dehesa systems. From this

FARMING AND BIRDS IN EUROPE
ISBN 0-12-544280-7
Copyright © 1997 Academic Press Ltd
All rights of reproduction in any form reserved

background, we outline the most likely future economic trends of dehesa farming.

Using the above biological and socio-economic information, we try to predict broad patterns of change in dehesa bird populations, and make recommendations on conservation policy and applied research aimed at preserving and enhancing the role of dehesas for the long-term maintenance of European bird diversity.

INTRODUCTION

The term 'dehesa' appears to come from the old-Castillian word 'defesa', which means defence, in this case against open grazing: the Mesta, a very powerful Castillian organization of transhumant livestock raisers (Klein, 1920), pushed successfully to maintain large tracts of grassland open to transhumant sheep herds during the Middle Ages (see Donázar *et al.*, Chapter 5). To counteract these rights, the sedentary livestock raisers gradually achieved, from the late Middle Ages onwards, the privilege to close their lands against roaming livestock, especially in south-western Iberia where Castillian sheep spent the winter. These lands *defended* against transhumant herds would then have been the first dehesas.

The ploughing and clearing of the original Mediterranean forests and scrublands to provide defended grazing areas increased slowly between the sixteenth and the nineteenth centuries, paralleling the rate of human population growth. This transformation was accelerated during the second half of the nineteenth century and the first half of the twentieth, in such a way that the process of colonization of the original Mediterranean forests to give the dehesas, which started in the early Middle Ages with the development of extensive sheep raising, can be considered to have been completed by the middle of this century.

In recent years, the term 'dehesa' (and its Portuguese counterpart 'montado') has been used, especially in an academic context, by conservationists mainly to refer to wooded pastures located in south-western Iberia. However, the term also refers to treeless grassland (provided it is defended against open grazing) both historically and currently: in fact, the first dehesas of the Llanos de Cáceres (Cáceres province), La Serena (Badajoz) and Valle de Alcudia (Ciudad Real) were completely deforested (just as they are now), and both landowners and land-managers of the Spanish administrations do not distinguish between wooded and treeless grasslands that are privately owned and exploited.

This chapter is devoted exclusively to the wooded dehesas because main features of their wildlife are very different from those of treeless dehesas (see Suárez *et al.*, Chapter 11). Hence, we shall use the term 'dehesa' meaning 'wooded dehesa' unless otherwise stated. Bearing this in mind, the Spanish

Figure 1 Dehesa landscape in the Parque Natural de los Alcornocales (Finca La Jarda, Cádiz province, southern Spain). Cork, cattle and big game are the main commercial products in this region. (Photo by J.L. Miñón.)

dehesas and Portuguese montados can be defined as pasturelands populated by holm oak *Quercus ilex* and, to a lesser extent, cork oak *Quercus suber*, with an understorey of open grassland, cereal crops or Mediterranean scrub, most commonly with a typical savannah appearance. The most typical dehesas represent a broad transition between the Mediterranean scrub and forest areas with low livestock densities still found in the Iberian Peninsula, and the open arable croplands and grasslands (treeless dehesas), created by the complete removal of tree cover (see Table 1 for a description of the types of forest land in Spain).

The traditional use of dehesas was maintained until the end of the 1950s (Campos, 1984). This includes tree management (thinning, selection of the highest quality and most productive trees, and pruning: Rupérez, 1957; Bauer, 1980; San Miguel, 1994) for the production of acorns, charcoal, firewood and cork; tillage for cereal cultivation; and scrub clearance. These last practices, together with tree thinning, are designed to encourage the development of a grass ground cover. This, together with acorns, provides food for indigenous

Figure 2 Dehesa landscape in the buffer zone of the Parque Natural de Monfragüe (Finca Valero, Cáceres province, western Spain). Sheep and Iberian pig farming are the main commercial products in this area. (Photo by F.J. Pulido.)

breeds of sheep and cattle and, to a lesser extent, also indigenous pigs and goats. The agricultural and forestry practices involve long (4–20 years) crop rotations, as well as slow woodland turnover, owing to the poor quality of the soils (Gascó, 1987; Montero, 1988). These rotations create a land-use mosaic within each dehesa area, with mixed plots differing in the structure and composition of their understorey vegetation and in their productivity (Díaz et al., 1993). Dehesa farms are generally private estates, employing salaried staff, and most of them are around 500 ha in size (Campos, 1993).

The dehesas and montados are located mainly in the west and south-west of the Iberian Peninsula, mainly on flat or gently sloping areas at 400–800 m above sea level with poor, acidic soils and a dry Mediterranean climate (Campos & Martín, 1987). Estimates of the extent of dehesas vary according to the criteria used to define them, and official statistics are lacking.[1] However, it is widely agreed that they cover more than 3 million ha in Spain (Campos, 1992, 1993; San Miguel, 1994). Assuming that practically all the land covered with holm oak and cork oak trees in the west and south-west of the Iberian Peninsula (Extremadura, Western Andalucía, Salamanca, Ciudad Real, Jaén, Zamora and

---

[1] Extremadura is the exception, providing a special register of dehesa areas of more than 100 ha. In December 1988 these included nearly 2 million ha of wooded and treeless dehesas.

Table 1 Area of forest land* in Spain in 1992 (in thousands of hectares)

Category	Wooded forest land†					Treeless forest land‡					Forest land $k = e + j$	UAL¶
	Open forest land			Timber forest land d	Total $e = c + d$	Scrubland f	Pastureland			Total $j = f + i$		
	Ploughed a	Unploughed b	Total $c = a + b$				Meadow g	Rough grassland‖ h	Total $i = g + h$			
Badajoz	34	393	427	95	522	116		596	596	712	1234	2036
Cáceres	69	400	469	182	651	191	59	567	626	817	1468	1840
Extremadura	**103**	**793**	**896**	**277**	**1173**	**307**	**59**	**1163**	**1222**	**1529**	**2702**	**3876**
Cádiz	1	123	124	28	152	73	3	120	123	196	348	676
Córdoba	37	288	325	87	412	76		122	122	198	610	1318
Huelva		215	215	334	549	96		94	94	190	739	950
Sevilla	28	119	147	51	198	100		110	110	210	408	1308
Western Andalucía	**66**	**745**	**811**	**500**	**1311**	**345**	**3**	**446**	**449**	**794**	**2105**	**4252**
Ciudad Real	49	132	181	89	270	256		342	342	598	868	1889
Jaén		74	74	210	284	126		168	168	294	578	1300
Salamanca	18	238	256	39	295	59	56	396	452	511	806	1170
Zamora		30	30	55	85	65	57	232	289	354	439	973
Remaining dehesa	67	474	541	393	934	506	113	1138	1251	1757	2691	5332
Total dehesa§	**236**	**2012**	**2248**	**1170**	**3418**	**1158**	**175**	**2747**	**2922**	**4080**	**7498**	**13460**
Rest of Spain	17	1684	1701	6085	7786	3807	1146	6687	7833	11 640	19 426	33 156
Spain	**253**	**3696**	**3949**	**7255**	**11 204**	**4965**	**1321**	**9434**	**10 755**	**15 720**	**26 924**	**46 616**

*Land covered with trees, scrub and treeless grassland. Its extent is 26 924 000 ha, equivalent to 58% of the useful agricultural area (the remaining useful agricultural areas are arable croplands). †Forest lands covered with open woodland or tree plantations for timber. In the ten provinces included in the dehesa area, wooded forest lands, considered by some authors as equivalents to wooded dehesas, cover around 3 418 000 ha, but nearly a third of them, 1 170 000 ha, are pine and eucalyptus tree plantations (timber forest land) devoted to timber production and only lightly grazed. Open woodlands (open forest land), either ploughed or not, cover the remaining 2 248 000 ha. ‡Forest lands covered with scrub or pasturelands, either meadow or rough grassland (this later including esparto-grass fields). Large-scale, long-rotation arable cropping which includes dry grassland and scrubland is not included. In the dehesa area, treeless forest lands extends over 4 080 000 ha. §It is assumed that all the forest land in west and south-west Spain has some private agroforestry use, although pastoral activities usually are marginal or nil in the timber forest lands. On this basis, dehesa systems occupy more than 6 million ha in the west and south-west of Spain. This splits into 35% wooded dehesa (wooded forest lands excluding those used for timber) and 65% treeless dehesas (treeless forest land). Dehesa exploitations thus form 47% of the useful agricultural land within the dehesa area. Other provinces bordering those ten shown in the table such as Avila, Madrid, Toledo and Málaga also hold relatively smaller proportions of dehesa exploitations. ¶Useful agricultural land, i.e. land where vegetation is grown for agricultural purposes. The UAL is the sum of cultivated land and forest land. ‖Includes rough grazing and esparto-grass fields. Source: own calculations and MAPA (1994).

Figure 3 Herd of red cows (*Vaca retinta andaluza*), an indigenous breed from southern Spain. (Photo by J.L. Miñón.)

Alentejo) is managed as dehesa, it can be considered to cover an estimated 2 248 000 ha in Spain (Table 1), and 869 000 ha in Portugal (Coelho, 1989; Campos, 1991). Thus, dehesas in the west and south-west of the Iberian Peninsula cover more than 3 117 000 ha.

Despite the lack of systematically collected data, a notable decrease in the area of dehesa has been detected in Extremadura (Elena *et al.*, 1987) and in western Andalucía (Fernández-Alés *et al.*, 1992). This reduction may be attributed to changes in land-use (removal of oaks, increased cultivation, irrigation, and afforestation with pines and eucalyptus). In recent years, tree-density has also been reduced locally due to the death of holm and cork oaks throughout the dehesa area (Brasier, 1992; Fernández & Montero, 1993). There are believed to be many causes of this phenomenon, known as 'seca', although its significance is at present unknown; causes noted to date include drought, incorrect pruning, fungal proliferation, ageing of the woodland, ploughing too close to the trees and a range of factors related to soil structure and composition, field orientation and slope.

BIOLOGICAL ANALYSIS OF THE DEHESA

Dehesas and montados represent the remaining major wood-pasture systems of Europe and are particularly important due to the diverse wildlife that they support (e.g. Baldock *et al.*, 1994; Bignal *et al.*, 1994). Management of dehesas has traditionally been low-intensity crop and livestock farming, largely resulting in an open landscape with wooded grassland. Today, this land-use mosaic supports a wide diversity of plant and animal species associated with the trees, the grasslands, or both. Up to 60 plant species per m^2 have been recorded for the grasslands (Marañón, 1991), and dehesas have been shown to support more diverse communities of butterflies (Viejo *et al.*, 1989) and passerines (Tellería *et al.*, 1994) than neighbouring denser woodland, grasslands, or arable areas.

In addition, the importance of the dehesas in preserving biological diversity on a continental scale is reflected by the high number of endangered bird species that they support (Table 2; Tucker & Heath, 1994; AMGHWK, 1994). Some of these species depend on the conservation of the dehesas for the maintenance of viable populations. One such case is Spanish imperial eagle *Aquila adalberti*, whose world population comprises some 130 pairs, the majority of which are found in the Spanish dehesas (González, 1991). Other threatened species such as black vulture *Aegypius monachus*, black stork *Ciconia nigra* and Iberian lynx *Lynx pardina* reproduce in the wildest and most remote stretches of Mediterranean forest, whereas the neighbouring dehesas are their main feeding areas (González & Merino, 1988; Rodríguez & Delibes, 1990; Donázar, 1993).

Finally, the dehesas provide the main habitat for large numbers of wintering birds coming from more northerly European latitudes. Most of the 60 000–70 000 common cranes *Grus grus* wintering in Iberia use the dehesas between November and February (Alonso & Alonso, 1990). Furthermore, between 6 and 7 million wood pigeons *Columba palumbus* (Purroy, 1988) and a larger number of passerines (mainly robins *Erithacus rubecula*, chaffinches *Fringilla coelebs*, meadow pipits *Anthus pratensis*, black redstarts *Phoenicurus ochruros*,

---

Table 2. Notes

*1: species of global conservation concern; 2: species concentrated in Europe with an unfavourable conservation status in Europe; 3: species not concentrated in Europe and with an unfavourable conservation status in Europe; 4: species concentrated in Europe and with a favourable conservation status in Europe (Tucker & Heath, 1994).

†E: endangered; V: vulnerable; R: rare; D: declining; S: secure.

‡1: important (more than 75% of the European population depends on the dehesas); 2: moderately important (10–75% of the European population); 3: marginal (less than 10% of the population); w = important for wintering populations (AMGHWK, 1994). Parentheses indicates provisional status.
Source: AMGHWK, 1994.

Table 2 Species of European Conservation Concern (SPECs) whose populations depend completely or partially on the dehesas

	SPEC*	Threat status†	Importance‡
Black stork *Ciconia nigra*	3	R	2
White stork *Ciconia ciconia*	2	V	3
Black-shouldered kite *Elanus caeruleus*	3	V	1
Black kite *Milvus migrans*	3	V	2
Red kite *Milvus milvus*	4	S	3
Black vulture *Aegypius monachus*	3	V	2
Short-toed eagle *Circaetus gallicus*	3	R	2
Spanish imperial eagle *Aquila adalberti*	1	E	2
Booted eagle *Hieraaetus pennatus*	3	R	2
Kestrel *Falco tinnunculus*	3	D	3
Common crane *Grus grus*	3	V	1w
Stock dove *Columba oenas*	4	S	2w
Woodpigeon *Columba palumbus*	4	S	1w
Turtle dove *Streptopelia turtur*	3	D	2
Barn owl *Tyto alba*	3	D	3
Scops owl *Otus scops*	2	(D)	3
Little owl *Athene noctua*	3	D	3
Tawny owl *Strix aluco*	4	S	3
Bee-eater *Merops apiaster*	3	D	3
Roller *Coracias garrulus*	2	(D)	3
Green woodpecker *Picus viridis*	2	D	3
Thekla lark *Galerida theklae*	3	V	2
Woodlark *Lullula arborea*	2	V	3
Robin *Erithacus rubecula*	4	S	2w
Blackbird *Turdus merula*	4	S	2
Song thrush *Turdus philomelos*	4	S	3w
Mistle thrush *Turdus viscivorus*	4	S	2
Subalpine warbler *Sylvia cantillans*	4	S	2
Sardinian warbler *Sylvia melanocephala*	4	S	2
Orphean warbler *Sylvia hortensis*	3	V	2
Blackcap *Sylvia atricapilla*	4	S	2w
Spotted flycatcher *Muscicapa striata*	3	D	2
Crested tit *Parus cristatus*	4	S	3
Blue tit *Parus caeruleus*	4	S	1
Short-toed treecreeper *Certhia brachydactyla*	4	S	3
Great grey shrike *Lanius excubitor*	3	D	2
Woodchat shrike *Lanius senator*	2	V	1
Jackdaw *Corvus monedula*	4	(S)	2
Spotless starling *Sturnus unicolor*	4	S	2
Chaffinch *Fringilla coelebs*	4	S	2
Serin *Serinus serinus*	4	S	2
Greenfinch *Carduelis chloris*	4	S	3

and song thrushes *Turdus philomelos*) winter in the dehesas (Herrera & Soriguer, 1977; Herrera, 1980; Tellería, 1988; Tellería *et al.*, 1988; Díaz & Pulido, unpublished observations).

The effects of land-use on birdlife

Habitat changes resulting from human activity have been identified as primary factors in the decline of many vertebrate species (see Primack, 1993; Caughley, 1994, and references therein). Although conservation action to stem population declines does not always require complete knowledge of the factor(s) responsible for the declines (see Pain & Pienkowski, Chapter 13), a good understanding of species' habitat requirements is one of the best tools when designing programmes to prevent or reverse such declines. In order to determine a species' habitat requirements in a quantitative way, multivariate models addressing the relationships between the species and the habitat variables are constructed. The use of such models enables us to:

(1) present in an explicit and quantitative form the relevant variables for each species or group of species (for example, Morrison *et al.*, 1992);
(2) make precise forecasts of the effects of any habitat alterations on the populations studied (Schamberger & O'Neil, 1986);
(3) provide a basis for habitat management, designed to promote its suitability for the threatened species (Verner *et al.*, 1986) and foster its stability in the medium and long term (Paul & Robertson, 1989; Lubchenco *et al.*, 1991).

The dehesas, as managed systems, are subject to the influence of economic factors, which are reflected in changes in farming practices. Ideally, we should be able to predict the effects upon wildlife of any changes to cultivation and stock-rearing practices that could potentially result from changing economic dynamics. Such knowledge would also enable the development of agricultural policies with objectives that incorporate the conservation of biological diversity. To achieve this goal, predictive models must use as independent variables those habitat features which are most sensitive to the influence of the farming practices (Figure 4; Díaz & Pulido, 1995). This approach is used below, illustrating the importance of basing the interpretation of wildlife–habitat relationships upon those habitat features which may be altered by human use.

Patterns of animal distribution in relation to habitat use and management are analysed on (1) a landscape scale and (2) a within-habitat scale. In the first case, species distribution is analysed over all or a major part of its geographical range. In the second case, the effect of patchiness in vegetation structure and production caused by the heterogenous distribution of dehesa management practices is investigated.

Landscape scale. To analyse species distribution patterns on a biogeographical scale, preferences are explored by type, size and distribution of large landscape units (Wiens *et al.*, 1987). For this, the climate, topography and land-use are

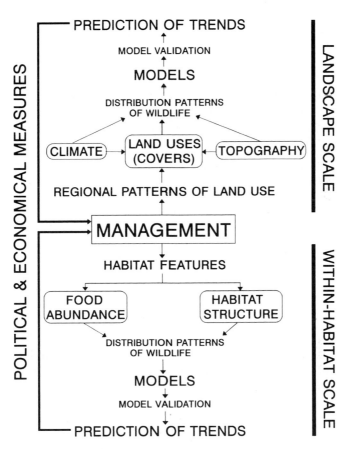

Figure 4 Diagram showing the influence of human management on the distribution patterns of wildlife at both landscape and within-habitat scale (as well as the modelling of these patterns that is required to predict the effects of management on wildlife).

measured, and used in empirical models relating them to the presence/absence or abundance of the species studied (Figure 4). This procedure has been used by González *et al.* (1990) to determine the environmental features characterizing habitat occupation for the Spanish imperial eagle, in 500 km² grid cells throughout its whole distribution area. These authors assessed 32 variables describing the climate, land-use and socio-economic characteristics in a sample of occupied and unoccupied grid cells. They developed a discriminant model, correctly classifying more than 80% of the grid cells with or without eagles. The analysis revealed a preference for areas with continental Mediterranean climate, with dehesa and scrub vegetation, and with a high percentage of land managed for hunting wild rabbits *Oryctolagus cuniculus*. Spanish imperial eagles tend to avoid open treeless landscapes. Using this model, it is possible to estimate the probability that this species will disappear in specific areas in response to changes such as deforestation or a reduction in rabbit numbers (González, 1991).

Within-habitat scale. Dehesa management creates a patchwork of sectors within each dehesa estate that differ in their productivity, structure, and composition of understorey vegetation (Díaz *et al.*, 1993). According to these habitat features, dehesa plots can be classified into effectively three broad types:

(1) grazed plots that occupy the majority of the total area, and are characterized by a low percentage cover of shrubs, and a high percentage cover of short herbaceous plants at ground level;

(2) shrubby plots that have high percentage of shrub cover (mainly gum cistus *Cistus ladanifer*, several *Halimium* species, lavenders such as *Lavandula stoechas*, and leguminous species such as brooms *Lygos* sp. and *Genista* spp.), and are the result of secondary succession due to abandonment or very light grazing;

(3) cultivated plots that generally occupy around 10% of the farmed area (Campos, 1992), and are characterized by low cover of vegetation at ground level, but a cereal crop (wheat, barley, oats or rye) which is well developed between March and June (Pulido & Díaz, 1992; Díaz *et al.*, 1993).

Long cereal rotations and shrub thinning result in variation in the location of grazed, shrubby and cultivated plots in time and space both within one estate and in adjacent properties.

To understand how the vertebrate fauna responds to structural vegetation gradients, we can construct models where the dependent variable is the abundance or behaviour of the study species, and the independent variables describe the habitat structure and/or food availability (Figure 4). Using this approach, researchers have identified to date the environmental factors determining habitat selection by various birds, including breeding and wintering species, and those using tree and understorey cover.

Effects of winter food availability

Holm oak acorns are abundant (Díaz *et al.*, 1993) and have a high fat and low tannin content (Herrera, 1977; Almeida *et al.*, 1992). These characteristics may explain their importance as food resources for the majority of birds wintering in the dehesas. The ground availability of acorns increases from October to December in the three dehesa types, and subsequently decreases towards the end of winter as they are consumed by wild animals and livestock (Figure 5; Díaz *et al.*, 1993, 1996). Acorn abundance is similar in shrubby and grazed plots within dehesas, with few acorns remaining at the end of winter, whilst availability is

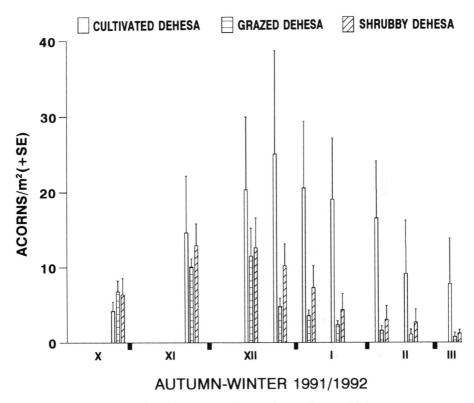

Figure 5 Average acorn abundances according to date and type of dehesa management. $N = 4$ plots per management type and date. Acorns were counted in two permanent squares of sides 0.5 m, in random locations under the canopies of 20 trees in each plot. See Díaz *et al.* (1993, 1996) for a more detailed description and analysis.

significantly greater and relatively high in cultivated dehesas towards the end of the season. Numbers of common cranes present during winter in the Valle del Tiétar dehesas (Toledo, Central Spain) were positively correlated with numbers of acorns on the ground, and this acorn abundance was negatively correlated with livestock numbers (Tellería *et al.*, 1994; Díaz *et al.*, 1996). These patterns suggest that the consumption of acorns by livestock in grazed and shrubby dehesas may have determined the distribution of cranes, as they exploit a common food resource (Díaz *et al.*, 1996).

The importance of acorns as a winter food resource has also been shown in a study of body condition of wintering birds (Herrera, 1977; Jordano, 1989). In the oak woods of Sierra Morena (southern Spain), the robin is one of the most abundant wintering species because of the arrival of migrants coming from the rest of Europe. From December, the high consumption of pieces of acorns broken open by other species of birds and mammals enables robins to increase their weight rapidly by accumulating fat reserves. In fact, birds including acorns in their diet show significantly better body condition than birds consuming mainly insects and/or fleshy fruits (Herrera, 1977). This presumably allows them to withstand low night temperatures in winter, as well as the journey to their breeding grounds, with less risk of starvation.

Effects of habitat structure on breeding birds

In spring there is the annual peak in numbers and biomass of arthropods (Herrera, 1980), and consequently the bird communities include many insectivorous species. Blue tit *Parus caeruleus* is the dominant species (up to 20 birds per 10 ha; Pulido & Díaz, 1992), feeding exclusively on arthropods of holm oak foliage (Ceballos, 1972; Pulido & Díaz, 1994). However, in spring the density of blue tits is not related to food availability. In fact, the quantity of suitable arthropods (measured in units of energy) is an order of magnitude greater than the energy requirement of the tits, suggesting a clear excess of available food for this and other species with similar requirements (Díaz & Pulido, 1993). Despite this lack of relationship within the normal range of variation of insect abundance, fumigation with various types of insecticides to control the caterpillars of defoliating lepidoptera (Robredo & Sánchez, 1983) may cause a reduction in the abundance and breeding success of the dominant insectivorous passerines, as suggested by some preliminary results for blue tits (Pascual *et al.*, 1991) and great tits *Parus major* (Cabello de Alba, 1992). The effects of insecticides may be either direct (i.e. poisoning) or indirect, by reducing drastically the birds' food supply. Direct and indirect effects may be expected from the use of chemical insecticides, whilst biological insecticides (e.g. *Bacillus thuringiensis* toxins) in principle are likely to have only indirect effects (Sánchez-Herrera & Soria, 1987; Fernández & Cabezuelo, 1993).

When food is not limiting, the main factor determining bird distribution patterns tends to be habitat structure (Wiens, 1989). Thus, in dehesas, significant associations have been found between groups of species and the vegetation structure resulting from the different types of dehesa management (Pulido & Díaz, 1992). In the Monfragüe dehesas (central-western Spain), *Sylvia* warblers and blackbird *Turdus merula* are associated with areas of high shrub cover, whilst crested lark *Galerida cristata* and corn bunting *Miliaria calandra* are found only in cultivated plots. Tree-nesting but ground-feeding species are more associated with grazed dehesas, whilst there is no relationship between tree-dependent species and gradients of understorey vegetation. Overall, the diversity of the bird community is greater in the grazed plots, whilst the highest densities are found in the shrubby plots (Pulido & Díaz, 1992).

Dehesa management also produces considerable variations in tree density and age (but not tree size), which appear to have important effects on birds (Díaz & Pulido, 1995). For bird species that feed mainly or exclusively in the tree canopies, different tree densities involve different flying costs, such that a direct relationship between tree density and bird abundance would be expected. In fact, a study of the factors affecting blue tit density within dehesas shows that tree density, as well as the availability of natural holes for nesting, successfully explained 50% of the variance of blue tit abundance (Díaz & Pulido, 1995; Pulido, 1996).

From the studies reviewed, we can conclude that the species which depend on the dehesas respond both to factors acting at a landscape scale, and to trophic and structural factors within dehesas. All of these factors are significantly influenced by dehesa management, which affects the extent and fragmentation of this environment (Fernández-Alés et al., 1992) as well as the food abundance, structure of understorey vegetation, and tree density. Through these common variables, the studies reviewed show a connection between the bird abundance patterns in the dehesa and the effects of management.

Traditional use and long-term stability of the dehesa

The conservation of the wildlife linked to managed habitats depends on the continuation of management practices, which have a primarily commercial function for the local population. The long-term maintenance of traditionally-managed systems is likely to depend upon recognition of their environmental as well as their commercial value, whose sum gives the total economic value of such managed systems (Pearce & Turner, 1990; Campos, 1992; Pearce, 1993). The output of the dehesas includes both marketable products (food, cork, charcoal and firewood) and environmental goods. Despite the scarcity of environmental research into the dehesa systems, it is generally considered that some types of traditional dehesa management confer certain environmental benefits, which can be maintained only through the continuation of such management. These environmental benefits have not been assessed to date for dehesa systems, so it is important to evaluate the commercial viability of individual farms. If a dehesa farm is not commercially viable, but it is considered to maintain some (non-evaluated) environmental value, the latter can be calculated as the minimum external monetary payment for environmental benefits to be given to the owner in order to maintain both commercial viability and the management practices needed to preserve the environmental value.

This approach requires that the management practices whose negative commercial value are to be compensated will ensure the ecological stability of the farming system (long-term persistence; Larsen, 1994). There are, however, biological problems that could potentially undermine stability. In the dehesas, the main such problem is the lack of woodland regeneration (Montero, 1988). This appears to result from the negative impact of cultivation and livestock rearing practices on the production of acorns and the survival of seedlings and young trees. For instance, in a study carried out on dehesas in the Valle del Tiétar (Central Spain; Díaz, unpublished data) in June 1993, a total of 255 seedlings and 21 ramets (new plants produced vegetatively – i.e. clones) produced in that year were found over a total area of 2250 m^2 (0.1 and 0.009 seedlings and ramets per m^2, respectively). The majority of the seedlings (89%) were found in only one of the 9 plots studied (Figure 6), and there were no seedlings nor ramets older than one year. These results, although very preliminary, support the idea of nil recruitment of new plants, probably due to the consumption of acorns by livestock. Indeed, the pattern of seedling density among types of dehesa plots (grazed, shrubby, and cultivated) was directly related to patterns of acorn abundance (Figure 5), which was in turn negatively related to the pattern of grazing pressure (see above and Díaz et al., 1996). The density of ramets, however, did not differ between types of dehesa plots (Figure 6). There is currently insufficient supporting information to allow us to draw generaliz-

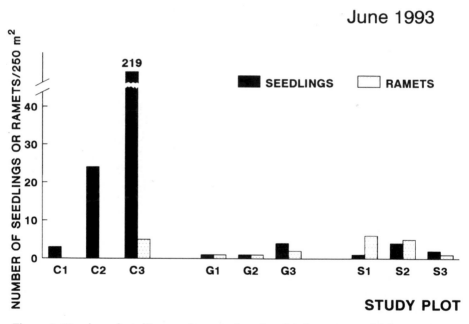

Figure 6 Number of seedlings and ramets found under three types of dehesa management in the Valle del Tiétar (Central Spain). Number of seedlings and ramets found in nine plots (three for each type of use of dehesa plots; C1–3: cultivated dehesas; G1–3: grazed dehesas; S1–3: shrubby dehesas) located in the Valle del Tiétar (Central Spain), and sampled in June 1993 (five random transects of 50 × 1 m per plot). No seedlings or ramets older than one year were found (Díaz, unpublished data). The results of the analyses of the variance for the number of seedlings and ramets per transect according to plot and type of use showed significant effects of both factors ($F_{2,36} = 6.48$, $P = 0.004$ and $F_{2,36} = 4.94$, $P = 0.013$ respectively, for type of use and plot) and their interaction ($F_{4,36} = 4.75$, $P = 0.004$) in the case of the seedlings, and no significant effects ($P > 0.2$) in the case of the ramets.

ations from these results, in spite of the importance of the apparent lack of natural regeneration of dehesa woodland with respect to its long-term maintenance. However, there is plenty of indirect evidence of this problem, and most authors indicate that the main problem facing the dehesas is the ageing of the woodland (Rupérez, 1957; Montero, 1988). This presumably results in loss of productivity, greater susceptibility to disease, and, in the long term, a reduction in the number of trees. The fact that this problem has long been recognized (before the recent changes in use of the dehesas described later; Rupérez, 1957) suggests that the lack of regeneration may be a problem inherent to traditional farming methods used in dehesas. Most dehesas appear to be as old as their trees, with little tree regeneration over the last two centuries, although presumably, dehesa management has included some long periods of abandonment during which some tree regeneration could occur. According to this, simply restoring traditional management will not necessarily suffice to ensure the long-term maintenance of this farming system.

SOCIO-ECONOMIC ANALYSIS OF THE DEHESA

The creation and destruction of the dehesa

The distribution, structure and configuration of the dehesa woodland is the result of human intervention, through clearance, thinning and pruning of the once natural vegetation (Campos, 1995c). The commercial value of the byproducts (firewood, charcoal and, marginally, leaves to feed livestock) generally compensated for the costs of management. Landowners also benefited from general woodland management through future financial returns (for example, increased production of acorns and other foods; Campos, 1995c). Thus, under the economic and social conditions existing prior to the 1950s, dehesa woodland was formed and managed in a commercially viable way.

Livestock farming in the dehesa favoured the maintenance of open wooded grasslands, enabling the preservation of various breeds of indigenous livestock adapted to the grazing resources of the dehesa in what were, until recently, favourable commercial conditions. In particular, economic interest in the Iberian pig encouraged conservation of holm oak woods, since acorns were the main food for autumn fattening of this species (Diéguez, 1992). Nevertheless, the tendency to over-exploit this resource makes regeneration of the woodland difficult or impossible, leading to progressive ageing and reduced density of trees, as discussed. Thus, the loss of woodland quality stems mainly from the owners' desire for immediate gain even at the cost of reducing future returns from the dehesa (Campos, 1992).

The rotation of cereal crops with natural pastures is customary practice in the dehesas. In 1992, 10.5% of the open forest land in the dehesa area was ploughed (Table 1). Until the early 1960s, wheat for human consumption was the main cereal together with fodder grain (barley, oats and rye). Today, however, both

Figure 7 Making picón, a kind of charcoal made by partial burning of holm oak branches after pruning. (Photo by J.L. Miñón.)

cereal and the less common hay crops are grown solely for animal feed (Table 1). Until the mid-1970s, the Spanish government also encouraged the mechanization of arable farming by giving subsidies for cutting holm oaks. This has increased thinning and even the complete removal of trees in some areas of dehesa. Mechanization also hinders the natural regeneration of trees by destroying seedlings more effectively than traditional ploughing.

In summary, the transformation of original Mediterranean forests, which in the past was a commercially viable activity, has involved (1) the creation of dehesas, maintained for the commercial interest of crop, livestock and forestry production and (2) more recently, the removal of woodlands and the formation of open grazing areas and arable croplands. The ratio of treeless dehesa to wooded dehesa is currently 1.8:1 (Table 1).

The dehesa systems are completely dependent on continuous management to maintain their productive capacity. An increase in the intensity of livestock and arable uses described above is likely to accelerate the loss of trees. Conversely, very low livestock densities could result in scrub invasion and lead to a reduction in grazing area, as could the absence of ploughing and periodic cropping (Diario Oficial de Extremadura, 1986).

The crisis of traditional dehesa management

The current crisis in production of crops, wood products and indigenous livestock in the dehesa has four economic causes which began to appear at the end of the 1950s.

(1) *Emigration to the north of Spain and elsewhere in Europe*. The high rate of unemployment in dehesa areas depressed wage levels and stimulated emigration to the north of Spain and elsewhere in Europe. At the beginning of the 1960s, for the first time, the owners of dehesa properties found it difficult to obtain specialized labour (for example stockmen). Wages began to rise in real terms, and continue to do so.

(2) *African Swine fever*. Of all livestock feeding on acorns in the dehesa, the Iberian pig was the most profitable. The appearance of African Swine fever in Spain in 1960 (Viñuela, 1992) resulted in significant monetary losses for the dehesa landowners. By the mid-1980s only 4000–6000 pure Iberian pigs remained in Spain, compared with 567 000 in 1955 (Dobao *et al.*, 1987).

(3) *The fall in price of Iberian pig fatty products*. The Iberian pig is very efficient at converting plant material (acorns, etc.) to protein and fat. Pig products

Figure 8 Iberian pigs eating holm oak acorns in a Spanish dehesa. The recovery of Iberian pig farming will increase the interest of dehesa owners in preserving holm oak trees. (Photo by F.J. Pulido.)

commanded a high price until the beginning of the 1960s, when new dietary trends led to a substantial drop in demand for bacon and other traditional pig raw materials. This, together with the effect of African Swine fever, had a very negative impact on the hitherto healthy commercial economy of the dehesas (Campos, 1984).

(4) *The replacement of firewood and charcoal by gas and electric power.* As the use of gas and electricity became more widespread in homes, there was a dramatic reduction in the demand for charcoal and firewood (Elena *et al.*, 1987). Consequently, prices fell, as did capital investment in the dehesa (Campos, 1995c), and shrub clearance and pruning activities ceased to be profitable. By the end of the 1960s, those inhabiting dehesa regions used mainly electricity and gas for cooking.

To summarize, the commercial crisis in the dehesas, which began at the end of the 1950s, resulted from the simultaneous occurrence of diverse phenomena, including those described above. These circumstances have continued with varying intensity until recent times, with the exception of African Swine fever, which is currently under control (Viñuela, 1992).

Current economic output of the dehesa

For more than two decades there has not been a positive market for capital investment in the dehesa. The net commercial margin (NCM) most frequently ranges around ± 2% of capital (Table 3). However, capital gains (CG) in the medium-term have been running slightly above the rate of inflation (Campos, 1993). Table 3 shows that the dehesa offers a moderate commercial profitability rate (p_c) in the absence of public aid.

How can we explain the continuation of slightly favourable medium-term real capital gains, together with moderate operating profitability rates?[2] The

---

[2] The total private profitability rate (p_{tp}) can be calculated by the sum of the profitability rate arising from commercial private surplus (p_{cp}) and the private environmental profitability rate (p_{ep}):

$$p_{tp} = p_{cp} + p_{ep}$$

The commercial private profitability rate (p_{cp}) is the sum of the operating profitability (p_o) and capital gains (c_g) rates

$$p_{cp} = NOS/C + CG/C = p_o + c_g$$

The operating profitability rate is the quotient between the net operating surplus (NOS) and the immobilized capital (C). The capital gains rate is the quotient between capital gains (CG) and the immobilized capital.

The private environmental profitability rate (p_{ep}) is the monetary value of consumption of environmental services by the owners' family and the public authorized by the owner, net of cost involved in the offer of environmental services (net private environmental margin: NEM_p) with relation to the monetary value of immobilized capital (C):

$$p_{ep} = NEM_p/C$$

Table 3 Resources managed, income and returns from a sample of wooded dehesas in south-west Spain (from Campos, 1994, 1995b)

Category	Estate (zone*)					
	MP (CA)	AL (BA)	NA (BA)	ME (CC)	SO (CC)	CB (SA)
Resources†						
Holm oak		×	×	×	×	×
Cork oak	×	×		×		
Cattle	×	×				×
Sheep			×		×	
Pigs		×	×		×	
Deer	×			×		
Crops	×	×	×	×	×	
Income and returns‡						
NCM (pta ha^{-1})	−5 908	3 354	−1 158	2 265	3 468	2 400
NOSb (pta ha^{-1})	2 399	1 643	11 577	−2 417	4 356	3 200
NOS (pta ha^{-1})	−3 509	4 997	10 419	−152	7 824	5 600
CG (pta ha^{-1})	−18 280	−2 580	−9 806	−8 682	−13 676	−54 377
C (pta ha^{-1})	408 660	482 845	435 774	216 220	345 498	330 600
p_c (%)	−1.4	0.7	−0.3	1.0	1.0	0.7
p_o (%)	−0.9	1.0	2.4	−0.1	2.3	1.7
p_{cp} (%)	−5.3	0.5	0.1	−4.1	−1.7	−14.8

*CA: Cádiz; BA: Badajoz; CC: Cáceres; SA: Salamanca.

†×: attribute present.

‡pta: peseta.

NCM: net commercial margin. Market return derived from commercial activities. Obtained by the difference between the gross production and total costs, without taxes or subsidies.

NOSb: net operating subsidies after deduction of indirect taxes. Direct financial aid received by the owners of the management of specific farm activities, net of production-related taxes.

NOS: net operating surplus. Income received by the owner. Calculated by adding the net commercial margin and the operating subsidies net of indirect taxes (NOS = NCM + NOS).

CG: capital gains. Estimated income from the property derived from the variations in price of the capital, net of capital losses (Campos, 1995b).

C: immobilized capital. Average estimated value of the commercial resources used during the season to obtain the gross product. It is calculated as

$$C = FC^i + \tfrac{1}{2}(GIFC_o) + \tfrac{1}{2}(CC - IP),$$

where FC^i: initial fixed capital; $GIFC_o$: gross investment in fixed capital coming from outside the farm; CC: current cost; IP: intermediate production. p_c: commercial profitability rate; p_o: operating profitability rate; p_{cp}: commercial private profitability rate.

answer could lie in the owners' increasing awareness of the environmental value of dehesas. In many cases, the dehesas are considered to be unique, special possessions. The owners increasingly behave as self-sufficient units, exploiting the environmental features and products of their own dehesas, in such a way that their family and guests benefit. We can therefore hypothesize that one of the main causes of the capital gains lies in these environmental benefits generated by the dehesa. The private profitability (p_{tp}) of the dehesa arises from both its commercial (Campos, 1993) and its environmental values (Campos, 1994, 1995c). The environmental captured value (i.e. the economic benefit to the owner derived from environmental values) is both pure (i.e. the use cannot be controlled by the owner) and quasi-public/private (i.e. the use can be controlled by the owner – Kopp & Smith, 1993). In some cases, the latter may be exclusively consumed by people authorized by the owner,[3] so that owners can profit from it. Thus, some quasi-public/private environmental resources of the dehesa may be captured so that an environmental component may be included in the private profitability of the dehesa. This internalization of part of the environmental profits of the dehesas is shown in the price of the land. The price variations between areas with similar operating profitabilities (p_{cp}) arise to a large extent from their different environmental capital incomes and, conversely, the similarity in land prices with unequal operating profitabilities can be explained by the disparities in their environmental profitabilities (p_{ep}).

The rate of social profitability (p_s) of the dehesa depends on the commercial and environmental income net of capital losses (C^l).[4] The variations in environmental income and capital caused by the land-use are important in the dehesa. The lack of research into environmental valuation of the dehesa makes it impossible to give precise figures on which to estimate their monetary value,[5] on the basis of variations in value of environmental property and services, by use. It is interesting to note that appropriate human intervention can guarantee maximum absolute values in the long term for the sum of commercial and

---

[3] Dehesa estates are generally privately owned, so that movements within dehesa areas are constrained to the public paths and roads. The density of such public networks is generally low because of the low population density and the large size of dehesa estates. Dehesa owners can control access to their land for people who wish to enjoy the wildlife or landscape of the dehesa. These public environmental values then become quasi-public/private environmental values which can directly benefit the owner.

[4] The social profitability rate (p_s) can be measured by the sum of the profitability rate arising from the commercial income net of subsidies (p_c) and the environmental profitability rate (p_e). The rate of capital loss through destruction or death is deducted from the sum of commercial and environmental profitability rates. The rate of capital loss (c_l) can be estimated using the quotient between the capital loss (C_l) and the immobilized capital (C):

$$p_s = NCM/C + NEM/C - C^l/C = p_c + p_e - c_l$$

[5] A study is currently being carried out into the recreational use value of the dehesa in the Monfragüe natural park under the framework of the European Union Environmental Research projects (DG XII EP-CT94-0367), co-ordinated by David Pearce – The Measurement and Achievement of Sustainable Development.

environmental income. Also, they can minimize losses of natural and improved capital (the latter owing to the abandonment of silvicultural practices). To achieve this, the positive externalities (i.e. wildlife conservation, soil protection) derived from land-uses must be paid for when there is a negative net present value for the commercial margin resulting from such use. This payment can compensate commercial losses thus encouraging the maintenance of use (Campos, 1992, 1995a). The abandonment of production activities producing a negative net surplus in the dehesa reduces long-term absolute returns and could in some cases increase the rate of capital loss in the short and medium term. For conservation of the dehesa to be sustainable, productive use must continue. This could be compatible with maximizing both commercial and environmental incomes in the long term, and increasing employment.

Future economic trends of the dehesa

The conservation and economy of the dehesa are linked to market development and public intervention. The market tends to increase the price of raw material inputs purchased. Labour costs will possibly form an increasing part of the future total costs. It is harder to anticipate the evolution of commercial production prices as this is more uncertain than the trend in input prices. The prices of standard dehesa goods (for example, cattle and sheep) will tend to fall if the market becomes more competitive. It is the typical or unique dehesa products (for example, Iberian pig and cork) which could benefit from a local and global 'quality' market if it is possible to increase demand. This growth potential will require a major development of the currently inadequate marketing mechanisms for dehesa products. In conclusion, in the short and medium term, the market tends to discourage some traditional dehesa commercial activities, while others may be developed by promoting local production, transformation and general consumption of their unique and emerging products (for example hunting or agri-tourism).

The current decline in trading of dehesa products will result in the abandonment of traditional management practices, a reduction in grazing land and wooded area and consequently a deterioration in the environmental value of the dehesas (see below). This trend could be partially arrested via public subsidies and/or a broadening of the market to include certain goods and services currently defined as environmental. The public subsidy would be based on direct and indirect payments to owners for use in conservation-oriented management of natural resources, whilst certain environmental goods and services would tend to be partially internalized by the market. This is the case, for example, with the profit that both dehesa owners and people living in dehesa areas can obtain from environmentally driven activities such as agri-tourism, nature tourism and second homes.

Current public subsidies in the dehesas comprise mainly direct community aid

Figure 9 Cork extraction in southern Spain, one of the most profitable uses of Mediterranean forests. Ensuring the regeneration of cork oaks will be essential to the dehesa economy. (Photo by P. Campos.)

to livestock production,[6] aimed at maintaining the income of the owners, regardless of the environmental effects of the farming practices. In the dehesa, maintaining working practices may be beneficial for the conservation of environmental resources. However, if current forms of financial support for stock rearing (direct subsidies per head of cattle, sheep and goats) are maintained in the dehesa, this could jeopardize conservation of the woodland. Current support encourages increased stock densities, which often result in over-grazing, and the maintenance of high stocking densities through supplementary feeding (Pulido & Escribano, 1995).

[6] Muñoz & Serrano (1993) estimate the amount of direct community aid received by Extremadura for cattle, sheep, and goat farming at a little over 13 866 million pesetas in 1992. Almost all of these stock graze on the dehesas. The value of their meat in 1992 was 30 525 million pesetas (Abellán, 1993), i.e. the European Community provided an additional subsidy of 45 pesetas for every 100 pesetas paid by the the market for the meat produced in the dehesa. The Iberian pig does not receive direct community subsidies.

The environmental resources of the dehesa also offer a solid basis for the creation of new markets for environmental goods and services in the spheres of residential or nature tourism. This relies upon developing a market intensity that is compatible with maintenance of the environmental values exploited. How far these new markets can arrest the decline in the non-unique, traditional commercial goods of the dehesa it is impossible to say, given the high level of uncertainty surrounding the process of internalization of environmental production in the dehesa.

CONCLUSIONS

The changes in land-use which have taken place in the dehesas since the 1950s may have caused a significant fall in populations of the most vulnerable bird species, and this may continue if farming trends, resulting from the economic and political trends described (Campos, 1992, 1994, 1995c), develop as predicted. These trends and their possible effects on the birds may be summarized as follows.

Changes in land-use, owing to low short-term profitability of the dehesas in comparison with irrigated land and forest crops. These trends have been particularly dramatic in the areas with the largest original cover dehesas (Extremadura, Elena *et al.*, 1987, and western Andalucía, Fernández-Alés *et al.*, 1992). This may have changed or reduced the distributions of species associated with dehesa, like the Spanish imperial eagle or the crane. At present, this process of land-use change seems to have largely stopped, although the loss of woodland continues to occur owing to an apparent increase in death rate of the trees.

Local increases in livestock density, resulting from subsidies. Such increases could significantly reduce acorn availability during the winter, which could affect those species exploiting this resource (e.g. crane, wood pigeon, crows, small passerines). Similarly, increased livestock pressure and over-grazing would affect the shrub vegetation, grassland and even tree cover, and consequently the bird species that depend on them.

Abandonment of tree management (pruning, thinning and replanting). This has resulted from the fall in market value of dehesa forestry products, high management costs, and long turnover in the event of replanting (in general, maturation periods of more than 50 years; Campos, 1992).

The main effects of abandonment are a loss in tree quality, which in turn causes lower leaf and acorn production (Rupérez, 1957), and an apparent increase in tree mortality (Brasier, 1992) and absence of regeneration, which consequently reduces tree density. These effects could have obvious consequences on the bird populations associated with trees (e.g. tits, goldcrests, shrikes and raptors), both during the breeding season and in winter. Ultimately, this could lead to an accelerated reduction in tree density with consequent effects on flora, fauna and soil quality.

Abandonment of ploughing for crop cultivation and maintenance of grassland, owing to the relatively cheaper price of feed brought in from other areas; substitution of domestic livestock by game for hunting (Campos, 1992). This would result in increased shrub cover at the expense of open grassland. This could benefit species that depend on shrubs as a source of food or refuge such as warblers (*Sylvia* spp.) and blackbirds, and be detrimental to those requiring open areas for foraging (e.g. raptors, shrikes, finches).

It must be noted that these trends are only tentative estimates made using preliminary information. On the one hand, trends in the market and public intervention are too uncertain to be used as a basis for detailed predictions of their effects on a local scale. On the other hand, the available information regarding habitat requirements of species occupying the dehesas requires more detailed analysis. In particular, it is essential to validate their general applicability through checking predictions across a wide geographical area (Morrison *et al.*, 1992). Such analysis is necessary to provide detailed guidance for recommendations regarding political regulatory measures, and monetary incentives, which include the maintenance and improvement of the natural and cultural assets of the dehesas amongst their objectives. Some start in this has been made by the classification, across nine European countries, of low-intensity farming systems and their importance to wildlife (Baldock *et al.*, 1994). This work emphasizes the role of maintaining dehesa farming for the preservation of European biological diversity.

RECOMMENDATIONS

Conservation policy

The value of the dehesa to society must be acknowledged to be a total economic value, i.e. incorporating commercial and environmental returns (Pearce, 1993; Campos, 1994, 1995a). Although the returns from traditional commercial activities have decreased (because of rising costs of inputs and wages, and falling prices of some dehesa forestry products such as charcoal and firewood), growing internalization of environmental values owing to their increasing appreciation (both by landowners and society in general) has improved incentives to engage in traditional land management practices. The type of environmental management that enhances land values might not necessarily be the same as that which best sustains biodiversity. Thus the internalization of the environmental benefits might not necessarily lead to a desirable outcome in terms of the broader social environmental benefits (or even traditional practices). It is consequently very difficult to predict the outcome of this dual trend, but it is to be hoped that this increase in appreciation of environmental values will reverse the current reduction in agricultural and forestry farming practices.

To date, public intervention has not encouraged directly the conservation of the natural resources of the dehesa, because subsidies have not been specifically assigned to commercial and environmental activities with positive conservation benefits. Since 1994 there have been some tentative steps towards public intervention through financing the reafforestation of abandoned agricultural land.[7] The environmental effects of reafforestation would however depend upon location, type of farmland and management.

At present, there is insufficient information about commercial margins and environmental benefits to calculate appropriate levels of incentives for retention and restoration of traditional land management practices. The Commission of the European Communities is aware of this deficit, and has recommended the creation of a system of economic accounting for forestry and agroforestry systems in Europe, although this has not yet been established (COM, 1988).

Any change in the system of direct aid to farm estates must take into account the sustainability of the cultural and environmental contributions of the dehesa to the well-being of society. One way of establishing the monetary value of a grant would be to set it at a level which ensures land-managers receive an amount higher than the absolute value of the negative net commercial margin (NCM). In this way, land-use practices that are environmentally valuable but commercially unprofitable can be maintained by compensating their commercial losses. A variation on this application would be to estimate the monetary value of the environmental benefits of land management, and set the level of incentive accordingly (Campos, 1995c).

Applied research

To evaluate the information both available and lacking, we have carried out a literature review covering the technical, biological and economic factors that influence the functioning of dehesas (Campos & Naredo, 1989; Díaz & Pulido, 1995).

Economic factors

Although the natural resources of the dehesa are shaped by management, there remains a poor understanding of dehesa economics. Only one group of Spanish and Portuguese researchers is currently investigating this (Campos, 1995b).

---

[7] EEC Regulation 2.080/92 of 30 June 1992, established a community regime for aid to forestry measures in agriculture (Official Diary of the European Communities, 30 July 1992).

This situation is compounded by the lack of statistical information on dehesa systems (COM, 1988; Campos, 1995c), and the difficulties associated with organizing a multidisciplinary study.

To investigate dehesa economics, information must be collected systematically at an operational scale (i.e. at the scale of a farm), since the accounts of agricultural holdings do not incorporate comprehensive appropriate information. The production of techno-economic information at farm level is an extremely ambitious task. Access to economic accounts of forestry and agroforestry properties is a necessary prerequisite to any significant advance in knowledge of the private and social profitability of the dehesa.

Given the multiple uses of the dehesa, it is more relevant to study the economy of the whole system rather than its individual components (Campos, 1992, 1993, 1994, 1995a, 1995b). A knowledge of the economics of individual components (cork, livestock, etc.) is obviously necessary for applied research, but it cannot be carried out in isolation from an analysis of the whole system as an economic entity.

Such an analysis requires information on the ecological stability of the dehesa system, to ensure its conservation. Consequently, a multidisciplinary approach is necessary, incorporating environmental values, although this obviously increases the difficulties of conducting an economic analysis. Applied research projects carried out within the dehesa have been based on discrete plots, and natural scientists have not previously incorporated information on the socio-economic factors influencing dehesa management (Campos & Naredo, 1989). There is an active interest among specialists in the creation of a Dehesa Institute which would enable promotion of interdisciplinary research into Mediterranean agroforestry systems. However, the Iberian administration has not responded to this interest, in spite of requests made long ago by specialists (Campos & Martín, 1987).

Technical and biological factors

Most research has considered those technical and biological components of the dehesa that have the greatest commercial interest, the most important of these being pastures. So far, little basic biological research, or research applied to biodiversity conservation, has been conducted, and integrated research is certainly required if the dehesas are to survive.

Management practices should be established to achieve a proper age-structure of the woodland. To date, essentially forestry-based approaches have been proposed, comprising planting and felling on very long rotations by sectors within each property (Rupérez, 1957) with uncertain or negative current commercial profitability. Research is required to investigate both natural and management factors that affect the development of new trees (consumption of acorns and seedlings by wild and domestic herbivores, effects of grazing on germination and development of seedlings, etc.). The monetary costs of management to encourage natural regeneration (e.g. temporary exclusion of grazing and crop cultivation) also requires investigation. Such information will allow for the development of management regimes that encourage woodland regeneration, while maintaining environmental benefits and ensuring commercial profitability in the long-term.

It is also of utmost importance to gather information on, and model, wildlife–habitat relationships in animal groups for which information is currently lacking (carnivores, ungulates, reptiles, amphibians, and various bird species amongst the vertebrates). The combined use of such models would facilitate the development of management strategies designed to maintain the biological diversity of the dehesas, hence avoiding activities which would otherwise be centred excessively on a few emblematic species. Studies to adequate depth on a large number of species is impracticable but management based on studies of a range of ecologically representative species would be both feasible and advisable.

Finally, it is important to assess the effect of wildlife on the commercial production of the dehesas. This will allow estimation in monetary terms of at least part of the commercial costs implied in maintaining its environmental value.

REFERENCES

ABELLÁN, J. (1993) La producción agraria en 1992. In Facultad de Ciencias Económicas y Empresariales de la Universidad de Extremadura (ed.) *La Agricultura y la Ganadería Extremeña en 1992*, pp. 22–45. Badajoz: Caja de Badajoz.

ALMEIDA, J.A.A., MARINHO, A.A.M. & BAPTISTA, M.E.S. (1992) Valor nutritiro da bolota e da lande. In Servicio de Investigación Agraria de la Junta de Extremadura (ed.) *II Coloquios sobre el Cerdo Mediterráneo*, pp. 9–10. Badajoz: Junta de Extremadura.

AMGHWK (ARABLE AND MESOPHILE GRASSLAND HABITAT WORKING GROUP) (1994) Habitat action plan for arable and mesophile grassland habitats. Draft working paper, mimeo. Kécskemet, Hungary: Birdlife International.

ALONSO, J.A. & ALONSO, J.C. (eds) (1990) *Distribución y Demografía de la Grulla Común (Grus grus) en España*. Madrid: ICONA.

BALDOCK, D., BEAUFOY, G. & CLARK, J. (1994) *The Nature of Farming – low intensity farming systems in nine European countries*. London: Institute for European Environmental Policy.

BAUER, E. (1980) *Los Montes de España en la Historia*. Madrid: Ministerio de Agricultura.

BIGNAL, E., McCRACKEN, D., PIENKOWSI, M. & BRANSON, A. (1994) *The Nature of Farming – traditional low intensity farming and its importance for wildlife*. Brussels: World Wildlife Fund for Nature.

BRASIER, C.M. (1992) Oak tree mortality in Iberia. *Nature*, 360: 539.

CABELLO DE ALBA, F. (1992) Efectos de un tratamiento aéreo masivo con Malathion contra lepidópteros defoliadores de la encina sobre las comunidades de aves de un encinar adehesado. *Ecología*, 6: 199–206.

CAMPOS, P. (1984) *Economía y Energía en la Dehesa Extremeña*. Madrid: Instituto de Estudios Agrarios, Pesqueros y Alimentarios.

CAMPOS, P. (1991) Presente y futuro del alcornocal. In M.G. Guerreiro (ed.) *O Ambiente na Península Iberica. Perspectivas a Montante*, pp. 205–223. Lisboa: Universidade de Trás-os-Montes e Alto Douro, Universidade Internacional.

CAMPOS, P. (1992) Spain. In S. Wibe & T. Jones (eds) *Forests: Market and Intervention Failures. Five Case Studies*, pp. 165–200. London: Earthscan.

CAMPOS, P. (1993) Valores comerciales y ambientales de las dehesas españolas. *Agricultura y Sociedad*, 66: 9–41.

CAMPOS, P. (1994) The total economic value of agroforestry systems. In N.E. Koch (ed.) *The Scientific Basis for Sustainable Multiple-Use Forestry in the European Community*, pp. 33–47. Brussels: European Commission (ref. F.II.3-SJ/0012).

CAMPOS, P. (1995a) Conserving commercial and environmental benefits in the western Mediterranean forest. In L.M. Albisu & C. Romero (eds) *Environmental and Land Use Issues: an Economic Perspective*, pp. 301–310. Kiel: Wissenschaftsverlag Vauk Kiel KG.

CAMPOS, P. (1995b) Análisis Técnico y Económico de Sistemas de Dehesas y de Montados. Informe Final. Projecto UE DGVI CAMAR CT-90-28. Madrid: IEG (CSIS).

CAMPOS, P. (1995c) Dehesa forest economy and conservation in the Iberian Peninsula. In D.I. McCracken, E. Bignal & S.E. Wenlock (eds) *Farming on the Edge: The Nature of Traditional Farmland in Europe*, pp. 112–117. Peterborough: Joint Nature Conservation Committee.

CAMPOS, P. & MARTÍN, M. (eds.) (1987) *Conservación y Desarrollo de las Dehesas Portuguesa y Española*. Madrid: Ministerio de Agricultura, Pesca y Alimentación.

CAMPOS, P. & NAREDO, J.M. (1989) Aspectos conceptuales y metodológicos en la gestión racional del sistema agrario adehesado. In MaB España-UNESCO (ed.) *Seminario sobre dehesas y sistemas agrosilvopastorales similares*, pp. 19–39. Madrid: MaB España-UNESCO.

CAUGHLEY, G. (1994) Directions in conservation biology. *Journal of Animal Ecology*, 63: 215–244.

CEBALLOS, P. (1972) Protección de las aves insectívoras. Alimentación natural de *Parus major* y *Parus caeruleus*. *Memoria de la Real Academia de Ciencias Exactas, Físicas y Naturales de Madrid, Serie Ciencias Naturales*, 25: 1–61.

COELHO, I.S. (1989) *O Sistema Productivo Montado*. Lisboa: INIA.

COM (1988) Estrategia y Acción de la Comunidad en el Sector Forestal, 255 final. In A. Novas (ed.) *El Sector Forestal en la CEE*, pp. 143–164. Madrid: ICONA.

DIARIO OFICIAL DE EXTREMADURA (1986) *Ley 1/1986, de 2 de mayo, sobre la Dehesa en Extremadura*. Department of the Environment, 40: 503–528.

DÍAZ, M. & PULIDO, F.J.P. (1993) Relaciones entre la abundancia de artrópodos y la densidad del Herrerillo Común *Parus caeruleus* en dehesas durante el periodo prerreproductor. *Ardeola*, 40: 33–38.

DÍAZ, M. & PULIDO, F.J.P. (1995) Wildlife-habitat relationships in the Spanish dehesa. In D.I. McCracken, E. Bignal & S.E. Wenlock (eds) *Farming on the Edge: The Nature of Traditional Farmland in Europe*, pp. 103–111. Peterborough: Joint Nature Conservation Committee.

DÍAZ, M., GONZÁLEZ, E., MUÑOZ-PULIDO, R. & NAVESO, M.A. (1993) Effects of food abundance and habitat structure on seed-eating rodents in Spain wintering in man-made habitats. *Zeitschrift für Säugetierkunde*, 58: 302–311.

DÍAZ, M., GONZÁLEZ, E., MUÑOZ-PULIDO, R. & NAVESO, M.A. (1996) Habitat selection patterns of common cranes *Grus grus* wintering in holm oak *Quercus ilex* dehesas of central Spain: effects of human management. *Biological Conservation*, 75: 119–123.

DIÉGUEZ, E. (1992) Historia, evolución y situación actual del cerdo ibérico. In Ministerio de Agricultura, Pesca y Alimentación (ed.) *El Cerdo Ibérico, la Naturaleza, la Dehesa*, pp. 111–135. Madrid: MAPA.

DOBAO, M.T., RODRIGÁÑEZ, J., SILIÓ, L. & TORO, M.A. (1987) Implicaciones del cambio de estructura de población en la conservación del cerdo ibérico. In P. Campos & M. Martín (eds)

Conservación y Desarrollo de las Dehesas Portuguesa y Española, pp. 179–188. Madrid: Ministerio de Agricultura.

DONÁZAR, J.A. (1993) *Los Buitres Ibéricos. Biología y Conservación.* Madrid: J.M. Reyero.

ELENA, M., LÓPEZ, J.A., CASAS, M. & SÁNCHEZ DEL CORRAL, A. (1987) *El Carbón de Encina y la Dehesa.* Madrid: Ministerio de Agricultura, Pesca y Alimentación.

FERNÁNDEZ, J. & CABEZUELO, P. (1993) Efectos de varios plaguicidas utilizados en la encina sobre la fauna avícola terrestre. *Boletín de Sanidad Vegetal, Plagas,* **19**: 687–705.

FERNÁNDEZ, J.A. & MONTERO, G. (1993) Prospección de secas en *Quercus* de Extremadura y La Mancha. *Montes,* **32**: 32–36.

FERNÁNDEZ-ALÉS, R., MARTÍN, A., ORTEGA, F. & ALÉS, E.E. (1992) Recent changes in landscape structure and function in a Mediterranean region of SW Spain (1950–1984). *Landscape Ecology,* **7**: 3–18.

GASCÓ, J.M. (1987) Condicionamientos del medio natural de las dehesas extremeñas desde las perspectivas de su desarrollo compatible con el mantenimiento de su capacidad productiva. In P. Campos & M. Martín (eds) *Conservación y Desarrollo de las Dehesas Portuguesa y Española*, pp. 19–35. Madrid: Ministerio de Agricultura.

GONZÁLEZ, J.L. & MERINO, M. (1988) Censo de la población española de Cigüeña negra. *Quercus,* **30**: 12–17.

GONZÁLEZ, L.M. (1991) *Historia natural del Aguila Imperial Ibérica* (Aquila adalberti *Brehm, 1861).* Madrid: ICONA.

GONZÁLEZ, L.M., BUSTAMENTE, J. & HIRALDO, F. (1990) Factors influencing the present distribution of the Spanish Imperial Eagle *Aquila adalberti. Biological Conservation,* **51**: 311–319.

HERRERA, C.M. (1977) Ecología alimenticia del Petirrojo (*Erithacus rubecula*) durante su invernada en encinares del Sur de España. *Doñana, Acta Vertebrata,* **4**: 35–59.

HERRERA, C.M. (1980) Composición y estructura de dos comunidades mediterráneas de passeriformes. *Doñana, Acta Vertebrata,* **7**: 1–340.

HERRERA, C.M. & SORIGUER, R. (1977) Composición de las comunidades de passeriformes en dos biotopos de Sierra Morena Occidental. *Doñana, Acta Vertebrata,* **4**: 127–138.

JORDANO, P. (1989) Variación de la dieta frugívora otoño-invernal del petirrojo (*Erithacus rubecula*): efectos sobre la condición corporal. *Ardeola,* **36**: 161–183.

KLEIN, J. (1920) *The Mesta. A Study in Spanish Economic History, 1273-1836.* Cambridge, Massachusetts: Cambridge University Press.

KOPP, R.J. & SMITH, V.K. (1993) Understanding damages to nature assets. In R.J. Kopp & V.K. Smith (eds) *Valuing Natural Assests. The Economics of Natural Resource Damage Assessment,* pp. 6–20. Washington D.C.: Resources for the Future.

LARSEN, J.B (1994) Ecological stability of forest ecosystems. In N.E. Koch (ed.) *The Scientific Basis for Sustainable Multiple-use Forestry in the European Community,* pp. 23–31. Brussels: Working document for the European Commission. Ref. F.II.3-SJ/0012.

LUBCHENCO, J., OLSON, A.M., BRUBAKER, L.B., CARPENTER, S.R., HOLLAND, M.M., HUBBELL, S.P., LEVIN, S.A., MacMAHON, J.A., MATSON, P.A., MELILLO, J.M., MOONEY, H.A., PETERSON, C.H., PULLIAM, H.R., REAL, L.A., REGAL, P.J. & RISSER, P.G. (1991) The sustainable biosphere initiative: an ecological research agenda. *Ecology,* **72**: 371–412.

MARAÑÓN, T. (1991) Diversidad en comunidades de pasto mediterráneo: modelos y mecanismos de coexistencia. *Ecología,* **5**: 149–157.

MAPA (Ministerio de Agricultura, Pesca y Alimentación) (1994) *Anuario de Estadística Agraria 1992.* Madrid: MAPA.

MONTERO, G. (1988) *Modelos para Cuantificar la Producción de Corcho en Alcornocales* (Quercus suber *L.) en Función de la Calidad de Estación y de los Tratamientos Selvícolas.* Madrid: INIA.

MORRISON, M.L., MARCOT, B.G. & MANNAN, R.W. (1992) *Wildlife-habitat Relationships. Concepts and Applications.* Madison: University of Wisconsin Press.

MUÑOZ, A. & SERRANO, R. (1993) Las ayudas directas comminitarias al subsector garadero. In Facultad de Ciencias Económicas y Empresariales de la Universidad de Extremadura (ed.) *La Agricultura y la Ganadería Extremeña en 1992*, pp. 199–216. Badajoz: Caja de Badajoz.

PASCUAL, J.A., PERIS, S. & ROBREDO, F. (1991) Efectos de tratamientos forestales con cipermetrina y malatión sobre el éxito de cría del Herrerillo Común (*Parus caeruleus*). *Ecología*, **5**: 359–374.

PAUL, E.A. & ROBERTSON, G.P. (1989) Ecology and the agricultural sciences: a false dichotomy? *Ecology*, **70**: 1594–1597.

PEARCE, D.W. (1993) *Economic Values and the Natural World.* London: Earthscan.

PEARCE, D.W. & TURNER, R.K. (1990) *Economics of Natural Resources and the Environment.* London: Harvester Wheatsheaf.

PRIMACK, R.B. (1993) *Essentials of Conservation Biology.* Sunderland, Massachusetts: Sinauer.

PULIDO, F.J. (1996) Comportamiento de alimentación distribución especial: ejemp á con el herrerillo común (*Parus caeruleus*) en un ambiente natural parcheado. MSc Thesis, Universidad Complutense de Madrid.

PULIDO, F.J.P. & DÍAZ, M. (1992) Relaciones entre estructura de la vegetación y comunidades nidificantes de aves en las dehesas: influencia del manejo humano. *Ardeola*, **39**: 63–72.

PULIDO, F.J.P. & DÍAZ, M. (1994) Diet and prey type selection of adult and young blue tits (*Parus caeruleus*): the effect of correcting for prey digestibility. *Ardeola*, **41**: 153–161.

PULIDO, F. & ESCRIBANO, M. (1995) The dehesa system: economy and environment. Analysis of typical dehesas of south west of Badajoz province (Spain). In L.M. Albisu & C. Romero (eds) *Environmental and Land Use Issues: an Economic Perspective*, pp. 463–474. Kiel: Wissenschaftsverlag Vauk Kiel KG.

PURROY, F.J. (1988) Sobre la invernada de la Pabma Torcaz (Columba palumbus) en Iberia. In J.L. Tellería (ed.) *Invernada de Aves en la Península Ibérica*, pp. 137–151. Madrid: Sociedad Española de Ornitología.

ROBREDO, F. & SÁNCHEZ, A. (1983) Lucha química contra la lagarta verde de la encina, *Tortrix viridana* L. (Lep.: Tortricidae). Evolución de las técnicas de aplicación desde los primeros ensayos y trabajos realizados hasta el momento actual. *Boletín del Servicio de Sanidad Vegetal, Plagas*, **9**: 253–272.

RODRÍGUEZ, A. & DELIBES, M. (1990) *El lince ibérico (Lynx pardina) en España. Distribución y problemas de conservación.* Madrid: ICONA.

RUPÉREZ, A. (1957) *La Encina y sus Tratamientos.* Madrid: Ediciones Selvícolas.

SÁNCHEZ-HERRERA, F. & SORIA, S. (1987) La problemática fitosanitaria del encinar – especial referencia a las dehesas. In MaB España-UNESCO (ed.) *Seminario sobre dehesas y sistemas agrosilvopastorales similares*, pp. 50–62. Madrid: MaB España- UNESCO.

SAN MIGUEL, A. (1994) *La Dehesa Española. Origen, Tipología, Características y Gestión.* Madrid: Escuela Técnica Superior de Ingenieros de Montes.

SCHAMBERGER, M.L. & O'NEIL, L.J. (1986) Concepts and constraints of habitat-model testing. In J. Verner, M.L. Morrison & C.J. Ralph (eds) *Wildlife 2000. Modeling Habitat Relationships of Terrestrial Vertebrates*, pp. 5–10. Madison: University of Wisconsin Press.

TELLERÍA, J.L. (1988) Caracteres generales de la invernada de las aves en la Península Ibérica. In J.L. Tellería (ed.) *Invernada de Aves en la Península Ibérica*, pp. 13–22. Madrid: Sociedad Española de Ornitología.

TELLERÍA, J.L., SANTOS, T. & CARRASCAL, L.M. (1988) La invernada de los paseriformes (O. Passeri formes) en la Peninsula Ibérica. In J.L. Tellería (ed.) *Invernada de Aves en la Península Ibérica*, pp. 153–166. Madrid: Sociedad Española de Ornitología.

TELLERÍA, J.L., SANTOS, T. & DÍAZ, M. (1994) Effects of agricultural practices on bird populations in the Mediterranean region: the case of Spain. In E.J.M. Hagemeijer & T.J.

Verstrael (eds) *Bird Numbers 1992. Distribution, monitoring and ecological aspects*, pp. 57–75. Beek-Ubbergen: Statistics Netherlands and SOVON.

TUCKER, G.M. & HEATH, M.F. (1994) *Birds in Europe: their Conservation Status*. Cambridge: BirdLife International.

VERNER, J., MORRISON, M.L. & RALPH, C.J. (eds) (1986). *Wildlife 2000. Modelling Habitat Relationships of Terrestrial Vertebrates*. Madison: University of Wisconsin Press.

VIEJO, J.L., VIEDMA, M.G. & MARTÍNEZ E. (1989) The importance of woodlands in the conservation of butterflies (Lep: Papilionoidea and Hesperioidea) in the centre of the Iberian Peninsula. *Biological Conservation*, 48: 101–114.

VIÑUELA, E. (1992) El virus de la peste porcina africana. In Ministerio de Agricultura, Pesca y Alimentación (ed.) *El Cerdo Ibérico, la Naturaleza, la Dehesa*, pp. 79–92. Madrid: MAPA.

WIENS, J.A. (1989) *The Ecology of Bird Communities,* 2 vols. Cambridge: Cambridge University Press.

WIENS, J.A., ROTENBERRY, J.T. & VAN HORNE, B. (1987) Habitat occupancy patterns of North American shrubsteppe birds: the effects of spatial scale. *Oikos*, 48: 132–147.

8

Rice farming and waterbirds: integrated management in an artificial landscape

MAURO FASOLA & XAVIER RUÍZ

SUMMARY

During the last one hundred years, the area of natural wetlands in western Europe has been greatly reduced. This has been largely due to population growth, with associated urbanization and increased demand for water, and through conversion of land to agriculture. However, the cultivation of rice has increased over this period in Mediterranean Europe, and rice fields may serve as partial but valuable replacements for the lost natural wetlands. Rice fields are especially important as feeding habitats for herons during the breeding season, and for waders and ducks during migration and overwintering. However, there is considerable variation in the quality and suitability of rice fields as feeding habitats between Mediterranean regions. This chapter considers the factors influencing the importance of rice fields for birds, and how these have been and can be influenced by agricultural policy.

THE RICE CULTIVATION SYSTEM

Rice occupies a larger area than any other crop in the world; 40% of the human population depends on it as a primary food resource (Swaminathan, 1984; Forés & Comín, 1992). It is grown on 1 500 000 km², 11% of the world's arable

Copyright © 1997 Academic Press Ltd
All rights of reproduction in any form reserved

land, and over 90% of the crop is grown in Asia. Rice cultivation is confined to latitudes from 53°N to 40°S by minimum temperature requirements during germination (18–25°C). Rice is very adaptable, growing under a range of conditions from dry to completely submerged, aided by its efficient system of respiratory canals. About half of the total rice production is on dry land, the rest in shallow, flooded fields with a water depth usually of 15–25 cm, but as much as 3–5 m (Vergara, 1985; De Datta, 1986).

In southern Europe, rice fields are temporary aquatic ecosystems, with periods of flooding during the summer and of drying during winter, the reverse of the natural water cycle of Mediterranean wetlands. Because of this, rice fields may play an important role as substitute wetlands especially during spring, when Mediterranean regions experience periods of drought. Some rice fields are flooded also during the winter to attract birds for hunting, creating suitable habitats for ducks, waders and gulls, particularly in the Ebro Delta and the Albufera de Valencia in Spain, and in the Camargue in southern France (Pirot *et al.*, 1984; Ferrer & Martínez-Vilalta, 1987). Rice field ecosystems are highly dynamic; their physical and chemical parameters and water levels change very quickly, and their biological communities develop rapidly (Rossi *et al.*, 1974; Pont, 1977). However, pesticide use, water level changes and mechanical operations may be detrimental to the productivity of some rice field biota and to their use by waterbirds (Ruíz *et al.*, 1979, 1984, 1992).

DISTRIBUTION OF RICE CULTIVATION IN EUROPE

Rice cultivation in the European Union (EU) occurs only in Mediterranean countries and is concentrated mainly in particular regions of Italy, Spain, France, Portugal and Greece (Figure 1). European rice fields account for only 0.3% of the surface area of world rice production. In Italy, rice has been grown since the fifteenth century, but spread mainly during the second half of the nineteenth century, following the construction of new irrigation canals. Until the 1930s, rice cultivation was widespread throughout the lowest parts of the river Po plain, but afterwards retreated to a 5000 km² north-western sector where it is very intensive in terms of capital and energy input; and occupies between 5% and 95% of the total land area in the provinces of Vercelli, Novara and Pavia. Rice is also grown in some parts of the Po Delta area. Small areas of rice farming occur in Sardinia and in Apulia. In Spain, rice was introduced with Islamic invasions in the eighth century, and it is presently grown mainly in the Ebro Delta, the Albufera de Valencia and the Marismas del Guadalquivir. Rice is grown in coastal areas of central and southern Portugal; in northern Greece in the Axiós Delta area; and in southern France in the Rhone Delta area.

Rice cultivation is restricted to some of the main wetland regions, since the alluvial plains of the great rivers are best suited to meet the high irrigation

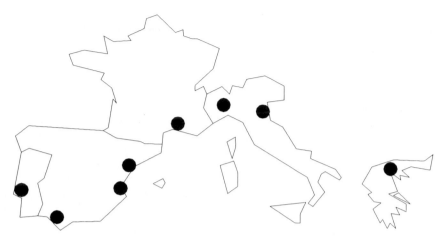

Figure 1 Main regions of rice cultivation in the EU. Small areas of rice cultivation occur in other regions, for example Sardinia and Apulia in Italy.

demands (Forés & Comín, 1992). The area used for rice production has slightly increased during the last decade in each country (Table 1). Production methods have become highly mechanized and capital intensive, resulting in increased yields which, in Italy and certain other parts of the Mediterranean, are currently among the highest in the world.

FARMING TECHNIQUES

In southern Europe, rice needs 130–180 days to mature. Agricultural operations, which vary between regions, include:

(1) Land preparation and fertilization (March). The soil is levelled, and each field is surrounded by low dykes to retain the water. Shallow ditches are excavated on the soil surface to improve water flow, especially where the surface is not completely levelled. In areas with a very high water table, for example in the Po Delta, ditches as deep as 2 m are excavated to facilitate drying for various management practices.

(2) Flooding and sowing (April). Flooding dates vary between regions from early March to early May. Fields may be flooded early and then dried just before the rice season; early flooding allows for the germination of weed seeds which are killed by the subsequent drainage. However, this method of weed control reduces the need for herbicides only to a limited extent; it is

Table 1 Areas of rice fields (× 1000 ha) in Europe

Country	Area (1000 ha)							Yield (t ha^{-1}) 1990
	1980	1985	1986	1987	1988	1989	1990	
Italy	176	187	193	190	199	206	215	6.7
Spain	68	75	79	80	80	59	89	6.4
Portugal	–	–	30	32	33	33	33	4.5
Greece	18	16	16	18	21	16	16	6.4
France	7	11	11	12	14	17	19	6.5

Source: European Commission, Agricultural Situation in the Community, various years.

practised locally where there is a specific problem, and cannot be used to control a broad spectrum of weed species.

(3) Germination, growth and application of algicides and herbicides (May–June) and insecticides (July–August). In north-western Italy, rice fields are usually under water between April and August, with short drying periods intended to encourage deep rooting by the young rice plants (early May) and to maximize the effect of pesticides (June).

(4) Flowering (July) and maturation (August–September). Usually, the water level is gradually lowered from July.

(5) Harvesting (October).

In most regions, rice fields are allowed to dry out during the winter, owing to the limited availability and high cost of water. However, throughout the Ebro Delta and the Camargue, and in very small areas in north-western Italy, flooding is maintained by hunting organizations to attract waterfowl. The landscape in the area of intensive rice cultivation is often uniform and monotonous, with little or no natural vegetation.

Rice farming methods have changed considerably over the last few decades. Traditionally, rice fields were smaller; field corners were inaccessible to machinery and consequently remained uncultivated; water-levels were relatively high; and when the fields were temporarily drained some water remained in a series of small dykes, allowing some invertebrates and amphibians to survive.

Since the late 1970s, the surfaces of a large proportion of fields have been accurately levelled, using tractors equipped with laser sensors; water is shallower; and the fields are completely dry for long periods. In Italy since 1992, increasing areas of rice have been grown with irrigation delayed until June, and even using dry cultivation methods. These methods employ less temperature-sensitive varieties of rice that require only temporary irrigation, and new modes of herbicide application. The advantage is that less water is used. The quality of the rice grown in 'dry' fields is good, although the yield does not match that of flooded fields. From 1992 to 1995, dry or partially dry cultivation has spread over a considerable portion of the rice fields in north-western Italy. However, in those regions (Po Delta, Ebro Delta, Camargue) where water supply is not limited cultivation techniques are less likely to change. The timing of flooding and other management techniques, and the intensity of management obviously have a profound effect upon invertebrate and vertebrate fauna and their predators, the most notable of which are birds.

RICE FIELD AVIFAUNA[1]

Rice fields in the EU are used by a variety of birds, mainly as feeding habitats and to a lesser extent as breeding sites. Waterbirds do not appear to cause any damage to the rice cultivation, except when large numbers of flamingos trample young plants (e.g. in Camargue and recently in the Ebro Delta (J.-P. Taris, pers. comm.)), and they may even be useful as a natural control for American crayfish *Procambarus clarkii* and *Triops cancriformis*, two crustaceans that are harmful pests of rice crops. Some passerines, crows, ducks, geese and waders including black-tailed godwits, may feed on rice seeds, especially those left after harvest-

Figure 2 Aerial view of recently flooded rice fields, April, north-west Italy. (Photo by M. Fasola.)

[1] For scientific names of birds please refer to Table 2.

ing. Birds are not thought to cause a great deal of direct damage (through consumption) to the rice crop in Europe, although such damage is claimed to occur elsewhere (Mugica Valdes, 1993).

The following account is based upon Fasola & Ruíz (1996). Rice fields are the most important feeding habitat of herons and egrets in southern Europe, although their use varies regionally, as will be illustrated.

Rice fields as foraging habitat

Rice fields are heavily used by waterbirds as foraging habitats, during both the breeding and the wintering seasons. Quantitative information on the use of rice fields is available only for breeding herons (Fasola et al., 1996), and for ducks and waders during autumn and winter (Ferrer, 1982; Martínez-Vilalta, 1985). Further information on the use of rice fields has been provided through dietary analyses (Ruíz, 1985; Llorente et al., 1986, 1987; González-Martín & González-Solís, 1990; Martínez et al., 1992) and local ornithological atlases.

Prey availability varies seasonally, and is related to the flooding regimes carried out in each region. Where, as in Italy, rice fields are flooded only between April and June, the prey mass peaks during June, after which numbers drop off and few prey remain after July. By September, the fields are completely drained. However, where fields are flooded throughout the winter, as in the Ebro Delta, large amounts of prey are available to waterbirds until December (Figure 3).

Rice fields and other aquatic habitats used for foraging by birds throughout the year in north-west Italy are illustrated in Table 2. Many of the species using rice fields in Italy (and elsewhere in the Mediterranean) are Species of European Conservation Concern (SPECs – Table 2; see Tucker, Chapter 4) and thus of high conservation importance.

Breeding season

During the breeding season, the rice fields of southern Europe are used by many waterbirds for breeding or feeding (Table 2).

Yellow-legged and Audouin's gulls use rice fields in the Ebro Delta as alternative foraging areas when their main food, discarded fish from trawling fisheries, is less available (Oro et al., 1995). During periods when there was a trawling moratorium, the percentage of prey obtained from rice fields increased from 13% to 17% for yellow-legged gulls, and from 0 to 20% for Audouin's gulls, which take mainly leeches (class: Hirudinea), crustaceans (mainly American crayfish) and eels Anguilla anguilla from the rice fields. The importance of rice fields as 'buffering' foraging areas for Audouin's gulls becomes evident when chick survival in the Ebro Delta during a trawling moratorium is compared with that in the Columbretes Islands, where there are no rice fields. In the Ebro Delta the moratorium induced food shortage, chick starvation and

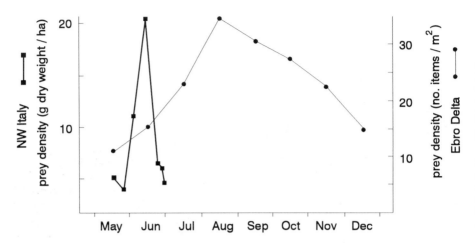

Figure 3 Density of prey seasonally available to herons in the rice fields of north-western Italy, and density of prey for all waterbirds in the rice fields of the Ebro Delta (vertebrates and macroinvertebrates). The two units of measurement differ, and the densities in the two regions cannot be compared. (Source: Fasola & Ghidini, 1983; González-Solís *et al.*, 1996.)

reduced fledging success (0.7 chicks per nest), but in the Columbretes the colonies were partially or totally deserted when discarded fish were not available, and fledging success was reduced to 0.09 chicks per nest (Jiménez & Martnez-Vilalata, in press).

In the Coto Doñana, purple herons use rice fields and canals occasionally, when the natural marshes dry seasonally or during droughts. In the Camargue, greater flamingos foraging in the rice fields in some years cause considerable damage to the rice.

In Portugal, towards the south-west of the Tagus estuary, are areas of reedbed and extensive rice cultivation. White storks breed in this area, and numbers have increased from 23 pairs in 1986 to 74 pairs in 1992. The Barroca rice fields in Alochete county appear to be especially important, with 51 pairs of white storks in 1991 (Pain, 1993). The distribution of breeding white storks appears to be related to the rice field distribution and the availability of electricity pylons as nest sites.

In north-western Italy, small colonies of black-headed gulls, black-tailed godwits, black and white-winged black terns nest sporadically within the fields, while mallards and moorhens frequently nest along the irrigation canals (Table 2; Pulcher, 1981; Fasola, 1986a). In the Ebro Delta 56% of nests of black-winged stilts and 1% of those of avocets *Recurvirostra avosetta* were found in rice fields (Martínez-Vilalta, 1989). Moorhens and coots build floating nests in the fields, and sometimes ducks nest on field margins. Little bitterns nest in loose

Figure 4 Black-winged stilt foraging in a rice field, May, north-west Italy. (Photo by E. Vigo.)

colonies at the margins of the irrigation canals. However, rice fields host few nests in comparison with natural marshes, presumably because management activities during the early phases of cultivation disturb breeding attempts.

Non-breeding season

During the non-breeding season, many waterbirds forage on rice fields, especially during migration (Table 2). Waders use rice fields as stopover foraging habitats during pre- and post-breeding migration, and for resting and feeding in the winter. In Italy and Greece, rice fields are dry from September to March, and consequently are used by migrants only in April during spring migration.

In the Ebro Delta and in the Camargue, some fields are flooded to attract waterfowl for hunting, and they become foraging habitats for ducks, rails, egrets, gulls and waders. As many as 40 small wader species are present in the Ebro Delta during winter, with a total population of between 12 000 and 20 000 birds, the actual number depending upon the area of flooded rice fields (Martínez-Vilalta, 1985). Between 25% and 50% of the waders exploit rice fields with a water depth of less than 8 cm, especially when marine mudflats are inundated by tides. The main species feeding in rice fields are dunlin, little stint, snipe, black-tailed godwit and lapwing. In general, marine intertidal mudflats

Table 2 Waterbirds regularly using four aquatic habitats for foraging during breeding (B), wintering (W) or migration (M), in the inland zones of north-west Italy. Numbers indicate total number of species.

Species	SPEC	Rice fields			Canals			Temporary ponds			Permanent ponds		
		W 15	B 20	M 43	W 13	B 10	M 13	W 11	B 6	M 13	W 21	B 18	M 40
Little grebe *Tachybaptus ruficollis*											+	+	+
Bittern *Botaurus stellaris*	×										+	+	+
Little bittern *Ixobrychus minutus*	×		+	+	+		+					+	+
Night heron *N. nycticorax*	×		+	+	+	+	+				+	+	+
Squacco heron *Ardeola ralloides*	×		+	+		+	+					+	+
Cattle egret *Bubulcus ibis*				+					+	+			
Little egret *Egretta garzetta*		+	+	+	+							+	+
Great white egret *E. alba*		+		+	+								+
Grey heron *Ardea cinerea*		+	+	+	+		+	+				+	+
Purple heron *A. purpurea*	×		+	+		+	+	+		+	+	+	+
White stork *Ciconia ciconia*	×		+	+		+			+	+			+
Glossy ibis *Plegadis falcinellus*	×		+	+					+	+			+
Spoonbill *Platalea leucorodia*	×		+	+									+
Greylag goose *Anser anser*		+		+									
Wigeon *A. penelope*											+		+
Gadwall *A. strepera*	×										+		+
Teal *A. crecca*											+		+
Mallard *A. platyrhynchos*			+	+	+	+	+	+			+	+	+
Pintail *A. acuta*	×										+	+	+
Garganey *A. querquedula*	×										+		+
Shoveler *A. clypeata*									+		+		+
Water rail *Rallus aquaticus*		+		+	+	+	+			+		+	+
Moorhen *Gallinula chloropus*		+	+	+	+	+	+					+	+
Coot *Fulica atra*					+						+	+	+
Black-winged stilt *H. himantopus*			+	+								+	+

Species								
Golden plover *Pluvialis apricaria*	×		+			+		+
Grey plover *P. squatarola*			+		+	+		
Lapwing *Vanellus vanellus*		+	+	+	+	+		+
Knot *Calidris canutus*	×		+			+		+
Curlew sandpiper *C. ferruginea*			+					+
Little stint *C. minuta*			+					+
Dunlin *C. alpina*	×		+			+		+
Broad-billed sandpiper *Limicola falcinellus*	×		+					+
Ruff *Philomachus pugnax*	×		+					+
Jack snipe *Lymnocryptes minimus*	×		+					+
Snipe *Gallinago gallinago*		+	+			+	+	+
Woodcock *Scolopax rusticola*	×		+					
Bar-tailed godwit *Limosa lapponica*	×		+				+	+
Black-tailed godwit *Limosa limosa*	×	+	+		+			+
Whimbrel *Numenius phaeopus*	×		+					
Curlew *N. arquata*	×	+	+		+	+		
Spotted redshank *Tringa erythropus*	×		+					
Redshank *Tringa totanus*	×		+					
Greenshank *T. nebularia*			+					
Green sandpiper *T. ochropus*			+			+	+	+
Wood sandpiper *T. glareola*	×	+	+			+		+
Common sandpiper *Actitis hypoleucos*		+	+	+	+	+	+	+
Turnstone *Arenaria interpres*						+		+
Black-headed gull *Larus ridibundus*	×	+	+	+	+	+	+	+
Common gull *L. canus*	×	+	+	+	+	+	+	+
Yellow-legged gull *L. cachinnans*		+	+	+	+	+	+	+
Common tern *Sterna hirundo*		+	+	+			+	+
Little tern *S. albifrons*	×	+	+				+	+
Whiskered tern *Chlidonias hybridus*	×	+	+					+
Black tern *C. niger*	×	+	+				+	+
White-winged black tern *C. leucopterus*		+	+				+	

Note: Only the waterbirds (Podicipedidae, Ardeidae, Ciconiidae, Threskiornithidae, Anatidae, Rallidae, Recurvirostridae, Charadriidae, Scolopacidae, Laridae, Sternidae) were considered. Data from Brichetti & Fasola (1990), Fornasari *et al.* (1992) and personal unpublished information.

Figure 5 Black tern nesting in a rice field, June, north-west Italy. (Photo by E. Vigo.)

offer larger amounts of prey than rice fields, but the latter provide alternative high-tide feeding habitats.

Moorhens and rails also forage extensively in rice fields during autumn and winter. Black-headed and yellow-legged gulls, the most numerous gulls in the Ebro Delta during winter, feed by following machines working in rice fields, usually forming mixed flocks with other waterbirds, mainly herons. In Spain, rice fields are a key feeding habitat for wintering shoveler, teal, mallard, red-crested pochard, coot, pintail and gadwall. In the Ebro Delta, rice fields are managed very differently by each farmer, creating a mosaic of fields with various degrees of flooding. While no quantitative data are available on heron foraging during the post-breeding season, rice fields are the preferred feeding grounds for all the herons wintering in the Ebro Delta, mainly grey herons, little and cattle egrets. They are especially important while they are still flooded and rich in animal prey from October to December, allowing birds to build up fat reserves before winter (Ruíz, 1985).

From January to March, evaporation reduces the availability of foraging habitats in rice fields and irrigation canals and, even though lowered water levels allow herons to catch prey easily, birds tend to lose weight during this period. In March, in the Ebro Delta there is less suitable habitat to exploit, and cattle egrets adopt an opportunistic feeding strategy. Some little egrets tolerate these adverse conditions by using brackish marshes (González-Martín & González-Solís,

1990). Grey herons, which do not breed in the Ebro Delta, disappear almost completely.

Less rice farming takes place in Portugal than in Italy or Spain, and yields are lower (Table 1). However, certain sites are very important for birds, such as the Tagus estuary in the central part of the Portuguese coast (Pain, 1993). A range of habitats occur within and around the estuary, including mudflats, salt marshes, rice fields and reedbeds. Internationally important numbers (>1% of the biogeographic population) of several wader and waterfowl species occur in winter. For example, the average number of wintering black-tailed godwit in 1988–91 was 15 871, representing >20% of the north-west European population. The Barroca rice fields in Alochete county provide the most important feeding habitat for wintering black-tailed godwit in the Tagus estuary, with approximately 10 000 birds, which feed on rice grains left over from the harvest (Blomert, 1992). These rice fields are also important for overwintering white stork, spoonbill and little egrets.

As rice cultivation in Portugal is the least productive in the EU (Table 1), its future is uncertain. There is insufficient knowledge of the importance of the Tagus rice fields, or the reasons behind the increase in godwit numbers, to estimate the potential impact of any reduction in rice production. However, it is possible that a significant number of birds could be affected – numbers of black-tailed godwits wintering in the Senegal Delta greatly declined from the 1950s to the early 1980s, mirroring a decline in rice cultivation (rice fields were replaced by sugar cane and areas were drained to enable hydrological construction). Cultivated rice constituted >75% of the diet of black-tailed godwits in this area (Treca, 1984).

In summary, a wide range of birds regularly use rice fields. In Italy and Spain, at least 25 bird species of European conservation concern regularly use the rice fields during wintering or migration, and 16 species use them during the breeding season (mainly as feeding habitat).

Rice fields appear to be as important as feeding sites for herons and other waterbirds as the combined total of all other aquatic habitats in southern Europe. In north-western Italy, rice fields host more species than temporary habitats (irregularly flooded irrigation canals and temporary ponds), and approximately the same number of species as permanent ponds (Table 2). In the main deltas of southern Europe, rice fields seem to be used as frequently, and by as many species, as fresh and brackish standing waters, and perhaps more so than the sea, irrigation canals and dry areas. Table 3 presents a qualitative assessment of the use of available foraging habitats by waterbirds in the Mediterranean deltas.

Not many data exist for regions outside the Mediterranean and these relate mainly to the use of rice fields by egrets, herons and ibises in Japan (McClure, 1958; Narusue, 1992; Narusue & Uchida, 1993), in Cuba (Acosta Cruz et al., 1990) and in India (Perennou, 1990); by bitterns in Malaysia (Landsdown & Rajanathan, 1993); and by 70 bird species in Cuba throughout the year (Mugica Valdes, 1993).

Table 3 Qualitative assessment of the use of available foraging habitats by waterbirds in the Mediterranean deltas (Ebro, Rhone, Po, Axiòs)

Species	Relative importance					
	Sea	Brackish	Freshwater	Rice fields	Irrigation canals	Dry land
Breeding season						
Grebes	−	**	***	−	*	−
Bitterns	−	*	***	***	***	−
Herons	−	**	***	***	***	*
Flamingo	−	***	−	−	−	−
Ducks	−	**	***	***	***	*
Rails	−	−	***	***	*	*
Waders	*	***	**	***	*	**
Gulls	***	***	***	**	*	**
Terns	***	***	***	**	***	*
Winter season						
Grebes	***	***	***	−	*	−
Herons	−	**	***	***	***	*
Flamingo	−	***	**	−	−	−
Ducks	*	***	***	***	−	*
Rails	−	−	***	***	*	−
Waders	***	**	**	***	***	*
Gulls	***	***	**	***	*	**
Terns	***	***	**	**	**	−

***: most important; −: not used.
Based on personal communications (respectively by X. Ruíz, H. Hafner, M. Fasola, V. Goutner).

The dependence of herons on rice fields

Like other colonial waterbirds, herons require abundant foraging habitats within commuting distance from a suitable colony site during the breeding season. Heronries with 100+ pairs can exist in the Mediterranean region only when at least 500 ha of good foraging habitat is available within 5 km of the colony (Hafner & Fasola, 1992). In areas lacking natural wetlands, heronries may flourish where large areas of rice field are available. The distribution of heronries in north-western Italy, their number and size, is related to the distribution of the rice fields in the surrounding areas (Fasola & Barbieri, 1978). In the Ebro Delta, the rice fields are a key foraging habitat for herons during breeding and post-breeding dispersal (Ruíz, 1985) when they achieve international importance as stop-over sites (Pineau, 1992).

Figure 6 Night heron feeding in a rice field, May, north-west Italy. The bird has captured a newt *Triturus cristatus*, an unusual prey item in rice fields, where frogs are the most common amphibian. (Photo by E. Vigo.)

The feeding ecology of all breeding herons – squacco heron, cattle egret, little egret, night heron, purple heron and grey heron – has been studied comparatively in all of the five major regions of rice cultivation in Mediterranean Europe: north-western Italy near Pavia, north-eastern Italy near Ferrara, the Camargue (Rhone Delta) in southern France, the Axiós Delta in north-eastern Greece, and the Ebro Delta in north-eastern Spain (Fasola, 1986b, 1994). In four of the five study regions, rice fields covered larger areas than natural foraging habitats within the presumed foraging ranges (10 km) around the heronries. In the Rhone Delta, they were the second-largest habitat.

The prey fed to the chicks was studied at 1–5 colonies in each area, and the use of rice fields and natural habitats was recorded within 10 km of the colonies, together with the foraging success of adults, their prey, and prey availability in the rice fields. Both prey type and biomass differed markedly between regions (Table 4). The main prey items were amphibians in north-western Italy and the Axiós Delta, fish (very abundant although not quantified) in north-western Italy, fish and insects in the Ebro Delta, and insects in the Rhone Delta. Prey biomass was significantly higher (Mann–Whitney U test), by one or two orders of magnitude, in north-western and north-eastern Italy than in the other regions (prey biomass in north-eastern Italy was under-estimated as fish were extremely

Table 4 Estimate of heron prey biomass in the rice fields of southern Europe (average values, in g dry mass per 100 m^2 for all samples)

Prey	NW Italy	NE Italy	Rhone Delta	Axiós Delta	Ebro Delta
Anura (metamorphosed)	2.6	9.3	1	0.8	0.1
Urodela	*	0	0	0	0
Anura (tadpoles)	118.2	16	0.6	6.4	0.7
Reptilia	*	0	0	0	0
Pisces	*	**	0	0	4.8
Crustacea	0.4	0	0	0.4	0
Insecta (imago)	6.2	0.5	1.6	0	4.1
Insecta (larvae >2 cm)	2.9	0	1.5	2.7	3.3
Insecta (larvae <2 cm)	*	0.4	1.5	0.2	0.1
Annelida	1.1	0	0	0.2	0
All prey ('*' not included)	131.4	26.2	6.2	10.7	13.1
Standard deviation (all prey)	183.7	20.8	9.8	11.4	14.1
No. samples	51	13	31	27	12

Organisms not included in the herons' diet were not considered.
*: scarce, not quantifiable; **: abundant, but not quantifiable.
From Fasola *et al.* (in press).

numerous and not quantified there). Other than for Italy, prey biomass did not differ significantly between regions. Prey biomass was lower (although not significantly so) in the Rhone Delta than elsewhere, possibly because only insects were available to herons.

From the feeding ecology data it was possible to attempt two independent estimates of the proportion of food that breeding herons obtain from agricultural habitats (Table 5). A first estimate was based on the number of adults foraging in agricultural habitats as a proportion of the potential number of adults foraging within 10 km of the colonies. A second estimate was based on the proportion of prey that came from rice fields in food regurgitated by chicks. The two estimates were usually fairly similar, with some exceptions (e.g. for purple herons in north-western Italy, where the proportion of birds foraging in rice fields was probably under-estimated). For most heron species and regions, the agricultural habitats supply between 50–100% of the heron's food during the peak breeding period. Only in the Rhone Delta are the rice fields used less than in the other regions. Possible reasons for this are outlined in the following section on 'Threats to Wildlife'.

Little quantitative information exists on the use of rice fields by herons in regions other than the Mediterranean, but they are probably widely used, with varying intensity, throughout the world. Egret species feed in rice fields in Japan (McClure, 1958; Narusue, 1992; Narusue & Uchida, 1993), and rice fields are

Table 5 Proportion of food resources obtained by breeding herons from agricultural habitats

	Squacco heron	Cattle egret	Little egret	Night heron	Purple heron	Grey heron
NW Italy	100/86		97/78	97/63	0/52	96/50
NE Italy	79/88		100/93	100/94		
Rhone Delta	0/?	21/?	10/20	0/46	3/?	0/9
Axiós Delta	48/?		38/67	15/69	0/?	
Ebro Delta	100?	97/?	76/?	53/?	67/?	

The first value for each entry corresponds to the estimate based on the proportion of adults foraging in agricultural habitats (rice fields and irrigation canals), and the second is the estimate based on chick diet obtained from these habitats. From Fasola et al. (1996).

used by five of the nine species of herons in south-east India (Perennou, 1990). Herons, five species of egrets, and two ibis species forage in Cuban rice fields (Acosta Cruz et al., 1990).

In summary, rice fields are the main foraging habitat for the six heron species breeding in north-western Italy and in the deltas throughout Mediterranean Europe, except the Rhone Delta where agricultural habitats offer less prey. Rice fields offer better foraging conditions for herons than natural habitats in north-western and north-eastern Italy, where the number of feeding herons, food intake rates, and prey abundance in rice fields are higher than elsewhere. There is no obvious explanation for the large regional differences in prey type and abundance in the rice fields, and more research into factors that may be influencing habitat use is required.

Rice cultivation regions are strongholds for breeding herons in southern Europe. Particularly important are the heron populations of northern Italy (Table 6, see 'Nature reserves and heronry conservation' below). Night herons and little egrets breeding in this region constitute 41% and 13% respectively of the total European populations. During the 1970s and the 1980s, populations of night, purple and squacco herons fluctuated without a clear trend and remained basically stable, while little egrets and grey heron populations increased (Fasola & Alieri, 1992).

Figure 7 Grey heron-numbers increased in northern Italy during the 1970s and 1980s. (Photo by C.H. Gomersall/RSPB.)

THREATS TO WILDLIFE FROM CHANGING FARMING PRACTICES

Rice cultivation involves periodic flooding over large areas and the creation of a mosaic of environments suitable for different waterbird species. All of the main regions of rice cultivation in the EU (north-west Italy and the deltas) are internationally important areas for birds, particularly in respect of their heron populations. However, the high level of dependence of waterbirds on rice fields may have adverse consequences – the cultivation of rice, like most other crops, is subject to rapidly changing agricultural practices.

In Europe, abandonment of rice cultivation, and use of land for urbanization or for other crops not exploitable by waterbirds, are not immediate threats. In fact, the area of rice cultivation is presently increasing, stimulated by high support prices under the Common Agricultural Policy (CAP) rice regime.

However, over the past 25 years, a number of changes in rice field management have been introduced with the intention of reducing the costs of labour, water use and maintenance, and these do pose potential threats to waterbirds. During the 1970s, rice-sowing practices changed from direct planting of seedlings to grain dissemination, in order to facilitate cultivation, and the quantities of fertilizers and pesticides used in rice farming were increased. The average water depth in rice fields was lowered in the 1980s, largely because of mechanical flattening of the soil in order to reduce water costs. It is possible that lower water levels reduce the availability of fish and tadpoles.

As we have discussed, large regional variations exist in the importance of rice fields for birds, probably owing to differences in prey abundance (Table 4). However, these differences remain largely unexplained. The major factors likely to affect the natural components of the rice field ecosystem are water composition, water level, pesticide use and biogeography. The physical, chemical and biological characteristics of each region may determine the prey composition, abundance and availability in the rice fields. The manipulation of these through agricultural management may, in part, help to explain the variation in intensity of rice field use by herons throughout the Mediterranean.

Water level and composition

Water composition is influenced by the method of irrigation. In some areas, the fields are flooded by a network of extended canals which, through gravity, distribute river water to each field (as in north-west Italy and the Ebro Delta). In other areas, such as the Rhone Delta, water must be pumped into the fields from lower river levels. Pumps filter larger biota and may reduce biodiversity in the rice fields. Water is temporarily lowered for some agricultural practices, for example in order to allow the rice seedlings to root deeply (May), and during the spraying of pesticides (June). Rice fields become gradually dryer from August. Variations in water level impose stresses on the rice field biota. It has been suggested that the improved irrigation schemes of recent years in the Camargue, resulting in a slower throughput of irrigation water, may result in reduced oxygenation and poorer conditions for faunal development (A. Crivelli, pers. comm.).

Toxicological risks

The various types of pesticides used to control algae, infesting dicotyledons, crustaceans and insects within rice fields may have both direct (though generally sublethal) and indirect (by lowering food availability) effects on waterbirds.

Although very rare, mortality as a direct result of agro-chemical poisoning has occurred, and has been associated with declines in waterbird populations, such as purple herons in the Ebro Delta (Ferrer, 1977). Direct poisoning has also been reported in southern Spain. American crayfish are now found in many rice fields of southern Europe (and they are thought to be one important food source in the Tagus area for white storks – A. Beintema, pers. comm.), although they appear to be almost absent from northern Italy. Crayfish are considered an agricultural pest as they burrow into the mud, damaging dykes, and they can also topple rice plants. In 1986, in the rice fields surrounding Doñana National Park, farmers used methyl parathion in an attempt to control the crayfish, despite the use of this chemical being illegal in Spain. As a result, in the region of 30 000 waterbirds are reported to have died (MacKenzie, 1986).

However, there are now more stringent controls on the use of agricultural chemicals and, at least in developed countries, severe poisoning of waterbirds is now very rare.

More difficult to assess are the sublethal effects of bioaccumulation of numerous pesticide residues in birds. However, these risks are decreasing, at least in the developed countries, since most pesticides are now short-lived and more specific. However, organochlorines like PCBs, mainly of industrial origin, are a potential hazard as their cumulative toxicity may be very high (even higher than that of dioxins – Pastor *et al.*, 1995). The release of such chemicals into the environment, and their uptake and distribution in food chains need to be carefully monitored.

Perhaps the greatest potential problem, and also the most difficult to quantify, concerns the indirect effects of pesticides on birds through a reduction in prey. Intensification of agricultural practices is often associated with increases in pesticide use, and the use of new types of pesticide; these could severely reduce the prey biomass available to birds.

In the Camargue, it has been suggested (Hafner *et al.*, 1986) that a reduction in use of rice fields by little egrets over the previous decade may have been related to increased treatment of rice fields (since the early 1980s) with parathion and lindane to control *Triops cancriformis* and chironomid larvae, and possibly reduced prey availability.

A move to 'dry' rice cultivation

Ongoing changes in agricultural practices could potentially have major effects upon the populations of herons breeding in Italy and elsewhere in Mediterranean Europe. For example, in the 1990s, the cultivation of rice on completely dry soils began. Although the yield is lower than in flooded fields, this practice allows capital savings through reduced water use. In 1995, about one-third of the rice fields in some parts of north-west Italy were cultivated on dry soils, and another one-third with irrigation delayed until June. If dry cultivation methods spread fully, the food supply of breeding herons could potentially decline by 50–100%, the amount of prey that is supplied by rice fields (Fasola *et al.*, in press, and Table 5). Although heron populations are affected mainly by winter survival (Den Held, 1981; Hafner *et al.*, 1994), it seems reasonable to suppose that such a reduction in food supply during the breeding season could have a dramatic impact on the heron population.

Delayed irrigation may postpone the peak of food availability to later in the season, but it may not diminish food supply, if the flooding period in June and July proves sufficient for the development of the aquatic prey.

Large-scale hydrological changes

In some areas, hydrological changes as a result of the construction of new reservoirs (and of the diversion of significant amounts of water to other places) are threatening rice cultivation. Increasing demand for water for other uses may cause its price to rise, while diminished river flows may result in salt water intrusion and the regression of delta plains.

NATURE RESERVES AND HERONRY CONSERVATION IN THE RICE FIELDS OF NORTH-WEST ITALY

The 5000 km^2 region of intensive rice cultivation (where rice covers 40% of the land) in northern Italy hosts 39 heronries (Figure 8). This area is also densely populated, ranging from about 200 inhabitants per km^2 in the provinces of Pavia, Novara and Vercelli to 1500 inhabitants per km^2 in the province of Milano. Other than those currently in use, very few potential heronry sites are available in the area (Fasola & Alieri, 1992). Consequently, it is possible that the heron population is limited by nesting sites, or at least is vulnerable to further site destruction.

Site destruction for land reclamation has been the main cause of heronry loss in this area, with 17 heronries lost between 1972 and 1993. These have been partially replaced by only nine new heronries (Fasola & Alieri, 1992).

Many heronries in the rice field area of north-western Italy are now protected by a network of 16 special nature reserves, set up between 1980 and 1985 by the regional governments of Lombardia and Piemonte (Figure 8). These nature reserves aim to conserve small patches of natural wetlands (from 3–10 ha each), and they are being managed in order to maintain the most suitable vegetation structure for the herons. Active management is required to prevent the successional development of wetlands towards unsuitable nesting habitats. This reserve network provides a good example of how the conservation of small natural patches of vegetation may greatly increase the natural value of an intensively cultivated landscape.

Twenty-three of these heronries are internationally important under Ramsar Convention criteria, and some usually hold more than 1000 nests. The largest heronry had 2920 nests of night heron and little egret in 1989. Table 6 indicates the number of nests supported by the 16 Reserves, another 14 heronries with non-specific protection within larger regional parks, and the nine heronries remaining unprotected in this area.

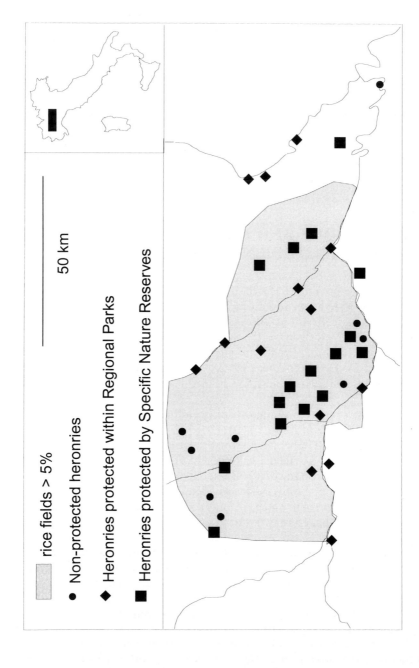

Figure 8 Heronries and their protection status in north-western Italy (the main region of rice cultivation of the EU).

Table 6 The total numbers of heron nests supported on average, between 1981 and 1993, by the 16 special nature reserves, 14 heronries within larger regional parks, and nine unprotected heronries in the rice cultivation provinces of Lombardia and Piemonte (northern Italy)

Species	Nature reserves	Regional parks	Unprotected	Total	% of European population*
Squacco heron	160	70	20	250	2
Little egret	5 100	1300	1100	7 500	13
Night heron	13 500	4400	2800	20 700	41
Purple heron	160	60	40	260	1
Grey heron	200	1200	640	440	3

*Based on the population estimates by Tucker & Heath (1994) and by Rose & Scott (1994).

The network of nature reserves and regional parks provides effective protection for these internationally important wetlands and the herons that breed within the rice field area of north-western Italy. The costs of protecting these areas are low, as their sizes are very small, and they are located on wet sites of little agricultural value.

THE COMMON AGRICULTURAL POLICY AND WATERBIRD CONSERVATION

The Common Agricultural Policy (CAP) has traditionally been associated with agricultural intensification, specialization, and over-production of food. The rice sector, in which growers receive high guaranteed prices and are therefore encouraged to seek high yields, is no exception. In rice field areas, intensification has been reflected by increased use of specialized farm machinery, increases in field size and consequent reduction of field margins, reduction of landscape diversity, increased use of pesticides and fertilizers, and increased irrigation schemes.

These changes have been driven by strong economic pressures, often at least partly resulting from agricultural policies. Waterbird conservation issues will be considered only if environmental concerns are truly incorporated into the Common Agricultural Policy. The importance of rice fields for the conservation of Mediterranean waterbirds should be recognized, and production and bird conservation issues should be addressed in a holistic fashion.

In 1995, the Commission announced proposals to reform the CAP price regime. The proposed reforms, which mirror those introduced for cereals in 1992, involve cuts in the intervention price, compensated for by direct payments based on area cultivated. The move away from price support should help to discourage the further intensification of rice farming in the EU. However, it should be noted that the discouragement of further intensification, or at least the production of high yields, could hypothetically encourage dry rice cultivation, which at present is being kept in check because of the lower yields it produces. The introduction of direct payments does, however, represent an opportunity to attach environmental conditions to the subsidies given to rice farmers. In addition, measures could be introduced under Regulation 2078/92 to maintain and improve the conservation value of rice fields. Possible options include:

(1) To favour extensification in areas of intensive rice production. This should include controls on the use of fertilizer and pesticide, and a reduction in the number of drying periods especially during spring and in areas where rice fields support internationally important populations of waterbirds, such as in north-western Italy. However, it is unrealistic to expect farmers to revert to previous cultivation techniques particularly with respect to water management.

(2) To encourage traditional rice cultivation in flooded fields over the largest possible areas, especially where the recent tendency towards dry cultivation, as in north-western Italy, may endanger internationally important populations of waterbirds.

(3) To support particular rice farming systems that are not yet highly intensive, for example in the Tagus estuary area, and include management criteria that will maintain rice farming in its present form where it is environmentally beneficial.

(4) To create greater landscape diversity among the rice fields, by supporting the maintenance and the recreation of woodlands and wetland patches in rice farming areas, especially in the regions where colonial waterbirds need these habitats as breeding sites (deltas, north-western Italy).

(5) To benefit waterbirds through long-term habitat creation (perhaps by set-aside) where land is diverted into wetlands appropriate for foraging or breeding.

CONCLUSIONS

In many parts of the Mediterranean, natural wetlands have been lost through urbanization and agriculture. Today, rice fields provide essential 'substitute' habitats for a wide range of waterbirds, and support many species that are of conservation concern in Europe. The importance of rice fields for the conservation of Mediterranean waterbirds must be recognized, as must the impact that changing farming practices, especially the increase in dry cultivation techniques, could have upon their populations. Mediterranean rice fields and their bird communities provide a classic example of how wider environmental measures (agricultural management) and site protection (of small copses and woodlands) are necessary in tandem in order to preserve the ecological integrity of an area.

ACKNOWLEDGEMENTS

We are indebted to V. Goutner, H. Hafner, S. Kazantzidis, R. Lansdown, D. Pain, C. Perennou and L. Mugica Valdes for providing information. We wish to thank the many friends who helped with the studies of herons and rice fields: L. Canova and N. Saino through all southern Europe, R. Alieri in Italy, H. Hafner in the Rhone Delta, M. Pyrovetsi in the Axiós Delta, and X. Ferrer in the Ebro Delta. The data for the Ebro Delta were collected thanks to grants PB86-0171 and PB91-0271 from the Spanish Government. The Station Biologique de la Tour du Valat supported our work in France. Research work in Italy was in part supported by the Regione Lombardia and the Provincia di Pavia as applied research for heronry conservation.

REFERENCES

ACOSTA CRUZ, M., MUGICA VALDES, L. & MARTINEZ, P. (1990) Segregacion del subnicho trofico en seis especies de Ciconiiformes cubanas. *Ciencia Biologica*, **23**: 68–81.

BLOMERT, A.-M. (1992) Feeding ecology of black-tailed godwits feeding on rice. In *Abstracts from the 9th International Waterfowl Ecology Symposium*, Hajduszoboszilo, Hungary.

BRICHETTI, P. & FASOLA, M. (1990) *Atlante degli uccelli nidificante in Lombardia*. Brescia: Ramperto.

DE DATTA, S.K. (1986) *Producción de arroz. Fundamentos y practicas*. Mexico: Limusa Ed.

DEN HELD, J.J. (1981) Population changes in the purple heron in relation to drought in the wintering area. *Ardea*, **69**: 185–191.

FASOLA, M. (ed.) (1986a) *Distribuzione e popolazione dei Laridi e Sternidi nidificanti in Italia*. Ricerche Biologia Selvaggina, Suplementi, no. 9.

FASOLA, M. (1986b) Resource use of foraging herons in agricultural and nonagricultural habitats in Italy. *Colonial Waterbirds*, **9**: 139–148.

FASOLA, M. (1994) Opportunistic use of foraging resources by heron communities in Southern Europe. *Ecography*, **17**: 113–123.

FASOLA, M. & ALIERI, R. (1992) Conservation of heronry sites in North Italian agricultural landscapes. *Biological Conservation*, **62**: 219–228.

FASOLA, M. & BARBIERI, F. (1978) Factors affecting the distribution of heronries in Northern Italy. *Ibis*, **120**: 337–340.

FASOLA, M. & GHIDINI, M. (1983) Use of feeding habitat by breeding Night heron and Little Egret. *Avocetta*, **7**: 29–36.

FASOLA, M & RUÍZ, X. (1996) The value of rice fields as substitutes of natural wetlands for waterbirds in the Mediterranean Region. *Colonial Waterbirds*, **19** (Special publication 1): 122–128.

FASOLA, M., CANOVA, L. & SAINO, N. (1996) Rice fields support a large portion of herons breeding in the Mediterranean Region. *Colonial Waterbirds*, **19** (Special publication 1): 129–134.

FERRER, X. (1977) Introducció ornitològica al delta de l'Ebre. *Treballs Institució Catalana Història Natural*, **8**: 227–302.

FERRER, X. (1982) Anátidas invernantes en el delta del Ebro. PhD Thesis. Barcelona University.

FERRER, X. & MARTÍNEZ-VILALTA, A. (1987) Le delta de l'Ebre: un milieu aquatique réglé par la culture du riz. *Oiseau*, **57**: 13–22.

FORÉS, E. & COMÍN, F. (1992) Rice fields, a limnological perspective. *Limnetica*, **8**: 101–109.

FORNASARI, L., BOTTONI, L., MASSA, R., FASOLA, M., BRICHETTI, P. & VIGORITA, V. (1992) *Atlante degli uccelli svernanti in Lombardia*. Milano: Regione Lombardia.

GONZÁLEZ-MARTÍN, M. & GONZÁLEZ-SOLÍS, J. (1990). Datos sobre la alimentación de Ardeidos en el delta del Ebro. *Miscellanea Zoologica*, **14**: 240–244.

GONZÁLEZ-SOLÍS, J., BERNADÌ, X. & RUÍZ, X. (1996) Seasonal variation of waterbird prey in the Ebro delta rice fields. *Colonial Waterbirds*, **19** (Special publication 1): 135–142.

HAFNER, H. & FASOLA, M. (1992) *The relationship between feeding habitat and colonially nesting Ardeidae*. International Wildfowl Research Bureau Special Publication No. 20, pp. 194–201.

HAFNER, H., DUGAN, P.J. & BOY, V. (1986) Use of artificial and natural wetlands as feeding sites by Little Egrets (*Egretta garzetta* L.) in the Camargue Southern France. *Colonial Waterbirds*, **9**: 149–154.

HAFNER, H., PINEAU, O. & KAYSER, Y. (1994) Ecological determinants of annual fluctuations in numbers of breeding little egrets (*Egretta garzetta*) in the Camargue, S. France. *Revue Ecologie (Terre Vie)*, **49**: 53–62.

JIMÉNEZ, J. & MARTÌNEZ-VILALTA, A. (in press) Effects of fishing moratorium on the clutch size and breeding success in two Audouin's Gull (*Larus audouinii*) colonies in Eastern Spain. *Proceedings VI Medmaravis Symposium*, Hammamet 1995.

LANDSDOWN, R. & RAJANATHAN, R. (1993) Some aspects of the ecology of *Ixobrychus* bitterns nesting in Malaysia rice fields. *Colonial Waterbirds*, **16**: 98–101.

LLORENTE, G.A., RUÍZ, X. & SERRA-COBO, J. (1986) Alimentation autumnale de la Nette rousse (*Netta rufina*, Aves Anatidae) dans le delta de l'Ebre, Espagne. *Vie Milieu*, **36**: 97–107.

LLORENTE, G.A., RUÍZ, X. & SERRA-COBO, J. (1987) Alimentación otoñal de la Cerceta común (*Anas crecca*) en el delta del Ebro. *Miscellanea Zoologica*, **11**: 319–330.

MacKENZIE, D. (1986) Crayfish pesticide decimates Spanish birds. *New Scientist*, 16 Oct 1986, **24**.

MARTÍNEZ, C., RUÍZ, X. & JOVER, L. (1992) Alimentación de los pollos de Martinete (*Nycticorax nycticorax*) en el delta del Ebro. *Ardeola*, **39**: 25–34.

MARTÍNEZ-VILALTA, A. (1985) Wintering waders in the Ebro Delta. *Wader Study Group Bulletin*, **43**: 25–28.

MARTÍNEZ-VILALTA, A. (1989) Cens de limicoles colonials del delta de l'Ebre. *Bulletí Parc Natural Delta de l'Ebre*, **4**: 37–40.

McCLURE, E. (1958) Dispersal of egrets on the Kanto Plain, Japan. *Wilson Bulletin*, **70**: 359–371.

MUGICA VALDES, L. (1993) The rice agroecosystem, Cuban fulvous whistling ducks and avian conservation. Thesis, Department of Biological Sciences. Simon Fraser University, Burnaby, Canada.

NARUSUE, M. (1992) Changes in the distribution and extent of breeding colonies of egrets in Saitama Prefecture. *Strix*, **11**: 189–209.

NARUSUE, M & UCHIDA, H. (1993) The effect of structural changes of paddy fields on foraging egrets. *Strix*, **12**: 121–130.

ORO, D., BOSCH, M. & RUÍZ, X. (1995) Effects of a trawling moratorium on the breeding success of the yellow-legged gull (*Larus cachinnans*). *Ibis*, **137**: 547–549.

PAIN, D. (1993) Farming and birds in the European Commission. Case study: Rice farming in Italy. Sandy: Royal Society for the Protection of Birds. Unpublished Research Report.

PASTOR, D., RUÍZ, X., BARCELÒ, D. & ALBAIGÉS, J. (1995) Dioxins, Furans and AHH-active PCB congeners in eggs of two gull species from the Western Mediterranean. *Chemosphere* **31**: 3397–3411.

PERENNOU, C. (1990) Peuplements d'oiseaux aquatiques en milicu anthropisé, un example. Les plaines de la Côte de Coromandel (Inde du Sud-est). Thése, Université Claude Bernard, Lyon.

PINEAU, O. (1992) *Key Wetlands for the Conservation of Little Egrets Breeding in the Camargue*. Slimbridge: International Wildfowl Research Bureau. Special Publication No. 20, 210–214.

PIROT, J.Y., CHESSEL, D. & TAMISIER, A. (1984) Exploitation alimentaire des zones humides de Camargue par cinq éspèces de canards de surface en hivernage et en transit. Modélisation spatio-temporelle. *Revue Ecologia (Terre Vie)*, **39**: 167–192.

PONT, D. (1977) Structure et évolution saissonière des populations de copépodes, cladocères et ostracodes des rizières de Camargue. *Annals Limnology*, **13**: 15–28.

PULCHER, C. (1981) *Uccelli di risaia*. Torino: Word Wildlife Fund, Sezione Piemonte.

ROSE, P.M. & SCOTT, D.A. (1994) *Waterfowl Population Estimates*. Slimbridge: International Wildfowl Reserach Bureau Publication 29. IWRB.

ROSSI, O., A. MORONI, P. BARONI & P. CARAVELLO. (1974) Annual evolution of the zooplankton diversity in twelve Italian rice fields. *Bollettino Zoologia*, **41**: 3.

RUÍZ, X. (1985) An analysis of the diet of cattle egrets in the Ebro Delta, Spain. *Ardea*, **73**: 49–60.

RUÍZ, X., LLORENTE, G.A. & NADAL, J. (1979) Residuos de plaguicidas organoclorados en avifauna del delta del Ebro. Boletin Estación Central *Ecologia*, **8**: 17–24.

RUÍZ, X., LLORENTE, G.A. & NADAL, J. (1984) Distribution pattern of organochlorine compounds in five tissues of Bubulcus ibis nestlings (*Aves, Ardeidae*) from the Ebro Delta, Northeast Spain. *Vie Milieu*, **34**: 21–26.

RUÍZ, X., PETRIZ, J. & JOVER, L. (1992) *PCB and DDT Contamination of Heron Eggs in the Ebro Delta, Spain*. International Wildfowl Research Bureau. Special Publication No. 20, pp. 115–117.

SWAMINATHAN, M.S. (1984) Arroz. *Investigación y Ciencia*, **90**: 52–62.

TRECA, B. (1984). La Barge à queue noire (*Limosa limosa*) dans le delta du Sénégal, régime alimentaire, données biométriques, importance économique. *Oiseau*, **54**: 247–262.

TUCKER, G.M. & HEATH, M.F. (1994). Birds in Europe: Their conservation status. Cambridge: Birdlife International (Birdlife Conservation Series no. 3).

VERGARA, B. S. (1985). *Growth and Development of the Deep Water Rice Plant*. International Rice Research Institute Res. Pap. Ser. 103. Los Baños, Laguna, Philippines, p. 38.

CHAPTER

9

Shrikes and the farmed landscape in France

NORBERT LEFRANC

SUMMARY

This chapter follows a somewhat different format from most other case study chapters (chapters 5–12) in this volume. They deal largely with farming systems which have evolved to produce specific commodities or groups of commodities, and the birds that depend, at least partly, upon the habitats created and maintained by the particular management techniques of these systems. This chapter takes a family of birds, the shrikes, and assesses the role that agricultural intensification has played in the sometimes spectacular population declines of shrike species in the EU, concentrating on the situation in France. This approach has been taken because, in general terms, shrikes do not depend upon any single habitat associated with the production of a specific commodity. Rather, they (in common with much other wildlife) require an 'untidy' open landscape associated with low-intensity farming, be it pastoral, arable or mixed, that incorporates somewhat overgrown (at least by today's standards) field edges, spinneys, roadside verges and other features. As has been illustrated in the initial chapters of this book, such landscapes have long since disappeared throughout much of the EU.

The chapter starts by describing the biology and requirements of different shrike species, and goes on to illustrate the importance of low-intensity agricultural management for maintaining suitable habitats. Options for shrike conservation, both in terms of site-specific measures and agricultural policy, are then considered.

FARMING AND BIRDS IN EUROPE
ISBN 0-12-544280-7
Copyright © 1997 Academic Press Ltd
All rights of reproduction in any form reserved

DISTRIBUTION AND REQUIREMENTS OF SHRIKES IN EUROPE

Distribution

Five, or debatably six, species of shrike nest in the European Union (EU): red-backed shrike *Lanius collurio*; lesser grey shrike *L. minor*; great grey shrike *L. excubitor*; woodchat shrike *L. senator* and masked shrike *L. nubicus*. The sixth species, southern grey shrike *L. excubitor meridionalis*, has traditionally been considered a sub-species of great grey shrike, although it is sometimes treated as a full species, *L. meridionalis* (Isenmann & Bouchet, 1993; Isenmann & Lefranc, 1994). The nominate race of *L. meridionalis* nesting in the EU (i.e. the south of France and the Iberian peninsula) is quite different from *L. excubitor*, and easily identified in the field. Its lead-grey upperparts are much darker; it also shows a well defined white supercilium, a white throat and typical pinkish underparts (Lefranc, 1995).

As a group, the European shrikes are found across a wide range of latitudes and altitudes, although some species are more thermophilic than others; thus distributions vary accordingly (Figures 1(a)–1(e)).

The great grey shrike is the least thermophilic and has a wide distribution in mid and northern latitudes, whilst the southern grey shrike (*meridionalis*) occupies almost exclusively areas with a Mediterranean type climate (to a maximum altitude of almost 1000 m on very sunny slopes – Desaulnay, 1982).

The red-backed shrike is by far the most common shrike in Europe, but has all but disappeared from Britain, for reasons that will be discussed. In France, during the breeding season, this species is almost completely absent from both cold and rainy areas (like Brittany and Normandy, with pronounced maritime climates). It also tends to avoid extremely dry areas (like the Mediterranean plains) and in Spain is even regarded as a mainly 'mountainous' bird.

In France the woodchat shrike is mainly found in Mediterranean areas, and its distribution does not extend as far north as the 18°C July isotherm. This species is found at altitudes of up to 700 m and even higher in certain of the warmer regions of the Massif Central in central/southern France.

The lesser grey shrike is even less cold tolerant, requiring warm dry summers, such as those provided by continental or Mediterranean climates. At least in western Europe it is a bird confined to lowlands or low hilly country.

Finally, the masked shrike also requires very hot dry summers, and within the EU is found only in some parts of Greece. It usually occurs on plains and hills, but can reach an altitude of 1000 m on well exposed slopes.

(a)

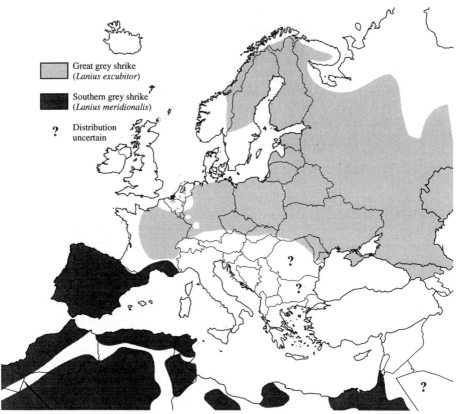

Figure 1 Breeding distributions of the European shrikes (*Lanius* spp.) in north-west Europe: (a) great grey shrike *Lanius excubitor* and the southern grey shrike *Lanius meridionalis*; (b) red-backed shrike *Lanius collurio*; (c) woodchat shrike *Lanius senator*; (d) lesser grey shrike *Lanius minor*; (e) masked shrike *Lanius nubicus*. Redrawn from Lefranc (1993).

(b)

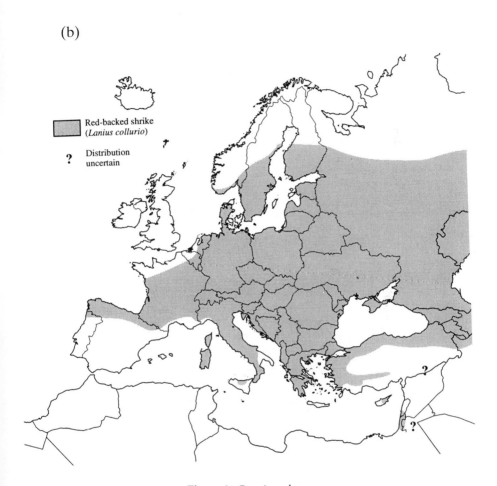

Figure 1 *Continued.*

(c)

Figure 1 *Continued.*

(d)

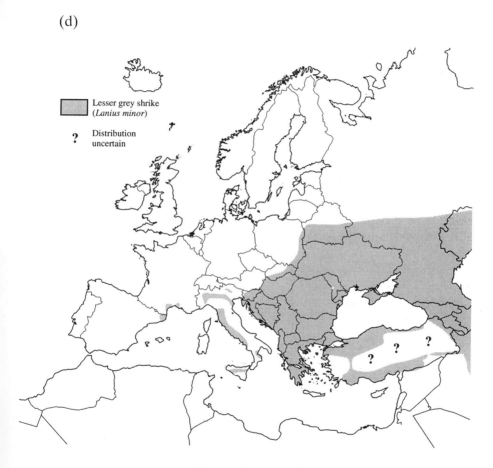

Figure 1 *Continued.*

(e)

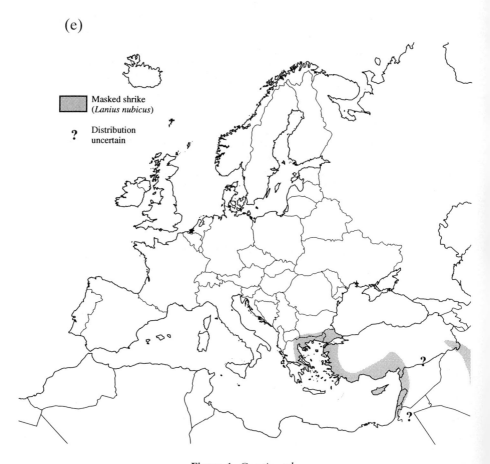

Figure 1 *Continued.*

Requirements

Of the six species listed above, the most detailed research has been carried out on the first four.

All of the habitats occupied by *Lanius* species are more or less open, with scattered trees or bushes. Generally, food comprises large insects, particularly Coleoptera (beetles) and Orthoptera (grasshoppers). Small vertebrates are also eaten, more or less frequently, by *Lanius* species.

Shrikes use a variety of perches to locate their prey. They are 'sit and wait' predators – once prey have been located they are chased and usually caught on the ground. Prey items are often impaled on spines, with larger prey being jammed in between small forked branches. This unusual habit allows shrikes to 'work' their prey using, for example, a spine, the end of a small branch, or barbed wire as a tool. Shrikes will often keep a larder of stored food, to be used in periods of bad weather when insects are fairly inactive and so difficult to locate.

A knowledge of the requirements of shrikes (Table 1) is a prerequisite to writing management prescriptions for species conservation, as will become evident later in this chapter. This is true at the scales of both sites and the wider countryside.

SHRIKES AND THE LANDSCAPE: AN HISTORICAL PERSPECTIVE

Historically, much of Europe was covered by forests, which gradually colonized, or more correctly, recolonized, large tracts of land after the retreat of the glaciers, approximately 10 000 years ago. The four immense and distinct vegetation belts (i.e. Mediterranean forest and scrub, deciduous forest, coniferous forest, and tundra) which now run across Europe between latitudes of 35 and 70°N, have been present for only about the last 4000–5000 years.

It is worth considering the niche that shrikes may have occupied in this primitive forest landscape – so different from the largely managed countryside found today. Strictly dependent upon fairly open land, shrikes would have avoided large densely forested areas. During favourable climatic periods (and climate has fluctuated considerably, even within human timescales), shrikes may have been widely dispersed, occupying natural grasslands and clearings. Clearings in the forest would have been created by a range of events including lightning-induced fires, storms (with flattened stands of trees), or the meandering route changes of rivers and river beds. Forest structure would not have been uniform, with numerous 'edge' effects and scattered open areas, maintained through the activity of insects (xylophagous and defoliating invertebrates) and large herds of ungulates. These forests would also have passed through the

Table 1 Requirements of shrikes during the breeding season

Species	Typical breeding habitat characteristics	Territory size (ha)	Typical nest location and height (m)	Prey taken	Larders	References
Red-backed shrike	Semi-open habitat. Meadows, bushes and perches (c. 1–3 m height) indispensable. Ideally a perch every 20 m	1.0–3.5 average = 1.5	Usually thorny bushes 1–2	Invertebrates and occasionally small vertebrates	Frequent in north of distribution rarer in south	Ullrich (1971) Lefranc (1993) Glutz von Blotzheim (1993)
Lesser grey shrike	Semi-open or very open habitat. High trees and high percentage of bare ground and/or very low (<10 cm) herb layer. Relatively few perches necessary	Tendency to nest in loose colonies 2–6 average = 3.5	High trees (often in top) (2) 6–10 (25)*	Beetles, grasshoppers etc. Rarely small vertebrates	Exceptional	Lefranc (1993) Kristin (1995)
Great grey shrike	Semi-open habitat with variable structures and rich in grassy areas. Alternation of denser and more open parts, perches 6–8 m high and present on average every 30 m (Average c. 5 per ha)	30–50 (100) depending on food-supply effectively available	Trees, sometimes large thorny bushes (2) 7–12 (25)*	Insects, generally large. Small vertebrates, esp. Microtus sp.	Frequent	Ullrich (1971) Lefranc (1993) Glutz von Blotzheim (1993) Schön (1994)

Southern grey shrike	Semi-open habitat dotted with trees and especially thorny bushes and fallow land. High percentage of bare ground and/or low herb layer	10–20	Bushes or small trees 1–2 (3)	Insects and small vertebrates, esp. lizards	Regular	Dohmann (1985) Hernandez (1994) Lefranc (1993)
Woodchat shrike	Open habitats with more trees and perches than in *collurio* habitats. Traditional orchards grazed by cattle or sheep typical in northern part of range. Areas of low herb layer important	2–8 (generally smaller in south of range)	Bushes (particularly in south of range) or lateral branches of trees (2) 4–8	Invertebrates. Occasionally small vertebrates	Irregular. Very variable	Ullrich (1971) Lefranc (1993) Glutz von Blotzheim (1993) Hernandez (1994)
Masked shrike	Open forests (especially *Pinus* and *Quercus*) or cultivated areas well dotted with trees and bushes	2.5 (few data)	Trees, more rarely bushes 2–9	Invertebrates, sometimes small birds	Apparently regular (few data)	Lefranc (1993)

* Extremes in parenthesis.

stages of natural regeneration. Regenerating areas would almost certainly have been occupied by shrikes, especially the red-backed shrike, which probably nested in brambles *Rubus* sp. and blackthorn *Prunus spinosa* – thorny plants avoided by deer. As suggested by Ellenberg (1986), the red-backed shrike was in some ways 'pre-adapted' for subsequent exploitation of extensively managed meadows and pastureland which still contained areas of scrub and thorny bushes.

Like other species of open landscapes, shrikes are almost certain to have benefited from the rapid development of Neolithic society, and the lifestyle based around cultivation and stock rearing. Much of the area covered by forest gave way to the cultivated land, pastures and meadows that today provide important hunting grounds for shrikes. Previously wooded areas have been cleared and managed for centuries, using either scythes or domestic stock, or both. This 'golden age' for shrikes in Europe, precipitated by agricultural development, lasted for a considerable time and depended upon extensive farming systems.

However, this period came to an abrupt end in the 1950s. A symbolic date is 1 January 1958, when the Treaty of Rome came into force within the European Community. Article 39 of this Treaty outlined the foundations of the Common Agricultural Policy (CAP). National and Community-wide objectives within the CAP were to strengthen efforts further to intensify, and so increase, agricultural production. This intention was due to concerns over food shortage which had already been expressed by many countries during and immediately after World War II (Teulon, 1993).

POPULATION AND RANGE TRENDS OF SHRIKES IN EUROPE

Since the early part of the last century, ornithologists from many countries have noticed fluctuations in shrike populations. However, from about 30 years ago most species have declined substantially in the majority of countries. Declines have included decreases in breeding ranges, fragmentation of populations, and density reductions at sites still occupied. The recent review of the conservation status of birds in Europe (Tucker & Heath, 1994; see also Tucker, Chapter 4) shows that all *Lanius* species in Europe are of Conservation Concern as a result of declines in population and/or range. Estimated breeding populations and rates of decline are illustrated in Table 2. Populations of all shrike species declined by more than 20% in France between 1970 and 1990 (Tucker & Heath, 1994).

Declines in shrike populations have generally been ascribed to two main causes: climatic fluctuations, and habitat deterioration within the breeding range (see reviews in: Lefranc, 1993; Glutz von Blotzheim, 1993). Additional

Table 2 Population status of shrikes in Europe

Species	Breeding population size (thousand pairs)	SPEC category*	Status†	Criteria‡	Countries with a large large decline between 1970 and 1990	
					Population	Range
Red-backed shrike	2300–5900	3	(Declining)	Moderate decline	Sweden United Kingdom	The Netherlands United Kingdom
Lesser grey shrike	77–320	2	(Declining)	Moderate decline	Austria France Poland Slovakia Slovenia	Belarus France Poland Slovakia Slovenia
Great grey shrike	330–1400	3	Declining	Moderate decline	Austria Germany Romania	Austria
Woodchat shrike	450–1200	2	Vulnerable	Large decline	Czech Republic Germany Poland Slovakia Switzerland Ukraine	Czech Republic Poland Slovakia Switzerland Ukraine
Masked shrike	7–56	2	(Vulnerable)	Large decline		

Source: Tucker & Heath (1994) (see Chapter 4).

*Species with an unfavourable conservation status whose populations are concentrated in Europe = SPEC 2; whose populations are not concentrated in Europe = SPEC 3.

†*Secure*: population more than 10 000 breeding pairs and in neither moderate nor large decline, not localized. *Declining*: population in moderate decline and population more than 10 000 breeding pairs. *Vulnerable*: population in major decline and consisting of more than 10 000 breeding birds, or in moderate decline and consisting of fewer than 10 000 pairs, or population in neither moderate nor in large decline but consisting of fewer than 2500 pairs. Parentheses indicate provisional status.

‡Trend data were defined as:

Moderate decline: applied to a breeding or wintering population which has declined in size or range by at least 20% in at least 33–65% of the population or by at least 50% in 12–24% of the population between 1970 and 1990, and where the total size of populations that declined is greater than the total size of populations that increased.

Large decline: applied to a breeding or wintering population which has declined in size or range by at least 20% in at least 66% of the population or by at least 50% in at least 25% of the population between 1970 and 1990, and where the total size of populations that declined is greater than the total size of populations that increased.

Figure 2 Male red-backed shrike feeding chicks at the nest. (Photo by M.W. Richards/ RSPB.)

possible factors include periodic droughts in wintering areas, an increase in trapping or hunting during migration, and loss of habitat through urbanization and other factors.

Two species appear to be particularly sensitive both to climatic and habitat changes: the woodchat shrike and the lesser grey shrike. Over the last 150 years, these species have shown periods of marked increase and decline more or less in parallel. However, the lesser grey shrike, a very thermophilic species with very precise habitat requirements, has shown the more dramatic population changes in population and range (Figure 3 – Niehuis, 1968; Lefranc, 1978).

Between 1800 and 1850, and again towards the end of the nineteenth century, the lesser grey shrike was widespread, and even very common in many regions of France, Germany, Luxembourg and Belgium, with a distribution reaching the North Sea. At the turn of the century, there was a very marked decrease, followed by two periods of relative abundance during the 1930s and towards the middle of the 1950s. Following this period, a new decline commenced, and the lesser grey shrike, which had not nested in Luxembourg since 1900 nor Belgium since 1930, disappeared from Switzerland in 1972, the north-east and centre of France in 1975 and Germany in 1978.

In western Europe today, the species is confined to the Mediterranean, with its stable and favourable climate. However, as a result of habitat changes, the species has even become rare there. Approximately 70 pairs of lesser grey shrikes

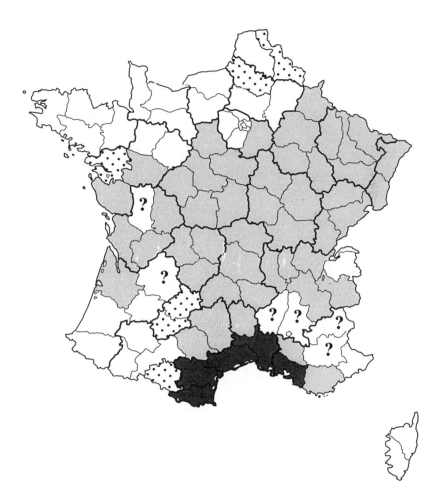

Figure 3 Changes in the breeding distribution of the lesser grey shrike *Lanius minor* in France. Between 1803 and 1991, the lesser grey shrike occasionally bred in the areas indicated by stippled dots. The species has, at various times during this period, bred regularly in the light grey and black shaded areas, but between 1980 and 1991, only bred in the areas shaded black. Question marks indicate areas where little is known of the distribution. Redrawn from Lefranc (1993).

exist in two colonies in north-eastern Spain (Catalonia). In France, only about 50 pairs are known of, primarily in two colonies in the Hérault and Aude Departments (see Figure 4 for administrative regions and towns mentioned in the text). The species has also undergone a rapid decline in Italy, where it is recognized as 'very vulnerable' and included in the Red Data List (Frugis & Schenk, 1981). Over the last few years, lesser grey shrikes have again appeared sporadically in small numbers in some places (including Switzerland). However,

Figure 4 Map of France illustrating the administrative regions, 'départements' and towns of France mentioned in the text.

one question that merits consideration is whether, given the general habitat deterioration that has occurred, the species could regain some lost ground were climatic conditions to improve again?

The woodchat shrike's distribution has also retracted towards the south. At the beginning of the nineteenth century, birds bred as far north as Grodno in Belarus and Kiev in the Ukraine. Like that of the lesser grey shrike, its decline started at about the beginning of the 1850s. It was interspersed with periods of increase that were clearly related to climatic fluctuations (see reviews in: Glutz von Blotzheim, 1993; Lefranc, 1993).

Anecdotally, it is interesting to note that in 1856, the species appears to have nested on the Isle of Wight in the United Kingdom (Ferguson-Lees, 1965), and

Figure 5 Male woodchat shrike with lizard, Spain. Although the woodchat shrike is still widespread in Spain and Italy, local declines have been reported over the last 30 years. (Photo by D. Kjaer/RSPB.)

that in the 1870s, birds regularly bred in the 'Père Lachaise', a famous cemetery in the centre of Paris (Quépat, 1874). Towards the end of the nineteenth century 'hundreds of birds' (Quépat, 1899) could still be seen together near Metz, in the north-east of France. The situation today is very different. The last phase of the decline, which was extremely rapid, started at the beginning of the 1960s. From about that date on, it is assumed that large-scale habitat degradation also began to play a major role, e.g. field regrouping, use of pesticides, disappearance of traditional orchards (see reviews in: Glutz von Blotzheim, 1993; Lefranc, 1993). Today, the woodchat shrike has practically disappeared from Luxembourg and Belgium, and become very rare in Germany and Switzerland (about 30 pairs in each country in 1995 – Kowalski, 1993; Schaub, 1995). In France, the total population probably does not exceed 10 000 pairs (estimated at 6000–10 500 pairs in 1994 – Lefranc, unpublished data), with about half of these birds occurring in the Mediterranean Departments of Languedoc and Roussillon. These last strongholds are threatened by changes in farming methods and particularly by the decline of sheep-rearing (Dayde, 1995). Although the woodchat shrike is still widespread in Spain and Italy, local declines have been reported over the last 30 years (see reviews in: Glutz von Blotzheim, 1993; Lefranc, 1993 and unpublished data).

The distribution of the red-backed shrike has also contracted over the last two centuries. The most spectacular decline, which has taken place in the UK, was described by Peakall (1962) and brought up to date by Bibby (1973, 1993).

Before 1850, this species was widely distributed throughout England and Wales, with the northernmost limit almost reaching Scotland. At the beginning of the twentieth century, the breeding distribution was already restricted to Wales and southern England. In 1960, the population was estimated (perhaps over-estimated) at 253 pairs (Peakall, 1962; Bibby, 1973). By 1971 only 81 pairs remained, with just 40 pairs (mainly in East Anglia) by 1976 (Sharrock, 1976). Today the species is considered to be extinct as a regular British breeding species.

The dramatic decline in Britain has by some (e.g. Bibby, 1973) been partly attributed to the effect of climatic change on food supply. Egg-collecting and habitat changes might also been implicated in the decline, although to a lesser extent. However, views as to the impact of climate are conflicting, and other authors consider agricultural intensification to have been responsible for the decline in Britain (Evans, 1995).

Certainly, throughout continental Europe, habitat degradation is considered to be the major cause of decline (Tucker & Heath, 1994). This species is more cold tolerant than the lesser grey or woodchat shrikes, and remains by far the most widely distributed throughout the EU, although over the last 30 years it has become rare or even extinct in low altitude areas subject to intensive agricultural practices. However, it is reassuring to note that over the last few years measurable increases have been recorded in densities and even, but to a much lesser extent, in distribution in some areas where habitat conditions have remained fairly stable in France, Germany and Belgium. This could possibly have been due to recent hot summers that may have benefited insect populations, and therefore shrike reproductive success (Van Nieuwenhuyse & Vandekerkhove 1989; Kowalski, 1993; Lefranc, unpublished data).

Overall, climatic fluctuations appear to have had little effect upon the great grey shrike, although they could perhaps be used to explain certain distributional changes in the Finno-Scandinavian region. Small numbers of birds colonized Denmark from the end of the 1920s, and there was a southerly expansion of the breeding range in Finland between 1950 and 1975. A similar spread south was noted in Sweden over the same period, and Olsson (1980) attributed this to the creation of suitable open habitat through large-scale deforestation.

In Central Europe, the great grey shrike has undergone a significant decline since the end of the 1950s. Agricultural intensification appears to have had a substantial impact upon this species, which requires a large territory with many perches and a large grassland component (see Table 1). It has adapted well to extensive types of farming systems producing landscapes similar in structure to its primeval habitats, but cannot survive in areas where secondary succession of completely open land results in closed forests (Glutz von Blotzheim, 1993; Lefranc, 1993; Schön, 1994). Locally, populations fluctuate significantly because of the effects of harsh winters (for example 1978/79), irregular fluctuations in prey populations (e.g. *Microtus arvalis*), and increased populations of certain predators, especially corvids (see reviews in Glutz von Blotzheim, 1993; Lefranc, 1993). The great grey shrike has not nested in Switzerland since 1986. At the beginning of the 1960s, this species still maintained a widespread distribution at low and medium altitudes. In Germany today, there are only approximately 1200–1500 pairs, with highest densities in Bavaria (the northern part). In Luxembourg and Belgium, populations of 100 pairs (600 at the beginning of the 1960s) and around 200 pairs respectively remain (J.P. Jacob & G. Bechet, pers. comm.).

In France, the several thousand great grey shrikes are mainly distributed in a large band from Limousin (Auvergne) to Champagne-Ardenne (Lorraine). The contraction of this species' distribution is evident from a comparison of the 'French Atlases of Breeding Birds' that were produced respectively for the period 1970–75 (Yeatman, 1976) and for the period 1985–89 (Yeatman-Berthelot & Jarry, 1994). Between these two periods, the distribution contracted significantly in the west and south-west, although considerable ground was lost elsewhere, for example in Bourgogne and Alsace.

No reliable data exist on population fluctuations of the southern grey shrike in the south of France and the Iberian peninsula. In France, it is estimated that about 1500 pairs exist (Lefranc, unpublished data). The northern part of the Languedoc-Rousillon region is still well populated, but current habitat changes may threaten the species, for example, the decline in sheep-rearing and extensive farming in general, and afforestation (Dayde, 1995; Lefranc, unpublished data).

Equally dissatisfying is the lack of information on the past and present population status of the masked shrike in Greece. However, limited data suggest that this species was more widely distributed during the last century, when it could still be seen close to Athens (see review in Lefranc, 1993).

It is evident from the above discussion that shrike populations have suffered considerably over recent decades as a result of habitat degradation. The following sections give examples of some of the ways in which shrike habitats, especially agricultural habitats have been degraded.

HABITAT CHANGES AND SHRIKES

The widespread effects of agricultural intensification

Within the countries of the EU, large-scale agricultural production techniques have involved a high level of mechanization, an increase in field size, drainage and irrigation, and the widespread use of pesticides and fertilizers. The rapid transformation of agriculture to a 'heavy industry' has been reflected in France, for example, by the increase in tractor numbers. Practically non-existent in 1945, more than a million tractors were in use in the 1960s, and a million and a half today (Teulon, 1993). Field regrouping, or *remembrement* to create larger working units in order to facilitate agricultural operations, is an integral part of agricultural policy. Such restructuring became important in France from 1950. More than 13 million of a potential 18 million hectares have already been regrouped (Le Roy, 1994). Approximately 300 000 hectares are regrouped each year, although in some years considerably larger areas are involved (maximum of 530 000 ha regrouped in 1970). Until 1975, the possible effects of these activities upon landscape quality or flora and fauna were not even acknowledged officially. There has been a little progress since then, as will be discussed.

The German term *Flurbereinigung* (cleaning the countryside) is a realistic translation of what has also happened to the French landscape: the disappearance of enormous areas of 'non-productive' habitats including copses, hedges, marshes, ponds, banks, ditches and even paths. For example, between 1950 and the beginning of the 1980s, 2 million kilometres of hedgerows disappeared in France (Office National de la Chasse, 1984).

The industrialization of agriculture has taken place primarily on the plains and low altitude plateaux. It is also, not surprisingly, in these areas that shrike populations have shown large declines even though climatic conditions in the lowlands are particularly favourable for them. Ornithological publications are teeming with examples of local declines in shrike numbers (see reviews in Glutz von Blotzheim, 1993 and Lefranc, 1993). Through the destruction of millions of kilometres of hedges, avenues of trees, copses and orchards, modern agriculture has removed a considerable amount of potential nesting habitat for shrikes, as well as indispensable hunting perches. Many important feeding areas with high densities of large insects have also disappeared. Such areas, often meadows or areas of mixed cultivation, have largely given way to vast monocultures. In 1970, grasslands still occupied 43.3% of the total area devoted to agriculture. In 1989, their extent was already reduced to 37%, arable fields having gained much ground in lowlands (Ministère de l'Agriculture, 1990).

For France, maize cultivation provides a good example of the types of changes that have taken place. Until the beginning of the 1950s, very little maize was grown in Europe. For a long time production was limited to specific areas (south-west, mainly Aquitaine), but has now spread into many others. Production has increased from 400 000 t in 1950 to 12.8 Mt in 1991, not including the 1.4 Mt of maize-ensilage produced as domestic stock feed (Roudié, 1993). Maize production and meadows (for stock feed) are in direct competition. This has resulted in loss of some meadows, and intensification of others, and has encouraged intensive stock-rearing. These processes have had a very detrimental effect upon shrike populations. More intensive management of meadows, with substantial additions of fertilizers, results in an impoverishment of flora and fauna (especially invertebrates) (Delpech, 1975; Meyer, 1995). Fertilized grass grows very quickly and soon becomes too dense for numerous invertebrates that live at the soil surface. Consequently, shrikes find little food, as invertebrates are both less abundant and less available than in the original extensively managed meadows (Ellenberg, 1986; Schaub, 1995). This, and the absence of bushes, can result in adults having difficulty feeding their young owing to the increased energy expended when foraging far from the nest (Diehl, 1971).

In addition to deliberate fertilizer additions, atmospheric pollution carries nitrous oxides emitted by industry, transport and energy production industries (Blab *et al.*, 1988). The large quantities of pesticides used also contribute to the reduction in potential shrike food.

Figure 6 Agricultural intensification has resulted in the removal of many hedges and other nesting habitats of shrikes, and a reduction in the numbers of unsprayed meadows and roadside verges that support high invertebrate densities and provide good feeding habitat for several species. (Photo by RSPB.)

It has also been suggested (although not proven) that certain pesticides may be responsible for some direct mortality in the lesser grey shrike, as a high number of eggs have been found unhatched, and young have been found dead in the nest (Lefranc, 1970; Bara, 1995).

Agricultural intensification has resulted in a large reduction in the number of farm workers (see Chapter 3), and the abandonment of agriculture in areas where farming is considered as an uneconomic activity. Between 1982 and 1989 the total area used for agricultural activities was reduced by 60 000 ha per year (Ministère de l'Environnement, 1990). This has mainly resulted from the abandonment of farming activities in medium-altitude mountainous areas, where milk and meat have traditionally been the main products. In France, many large plateaux have also been affected, including the famous 'Causses' in the south of the Massif Central. Although still holding good populations of shrikes, these areas are increasingly being abandoned following a decline in sheep farming. Once abandoned, the areas are either planted with conifers, or

Figure 7 View of a forestry plantation. Abandoned farmland may be used for afforestation, often aided by European Union funding. (Photo by C.H. Gomersall/ RSPB.)

allowed to regenerate into forest naturally. This transforms the landscape, and results in the loss of many plants and animals associated with pastureland. It is notable that financial aid provided under a European Union Regulation (Regulation 2328/91, Article 26, of 15 July 1991) has encouraged afforestation by farmers (see Chapter 3).

Shrikes, along with many other species, are subject to the dual threats of intensification and abandonment of agriculture.

Refuges in 'degraded' forest habitats

Shrikes will still today exploit clearings in forested areas, either planned (within forestry management programmes) or accidental. Such areas probably re-create fairly similar conditions to those in the original habitats occupied. Red-backed shrikes readily use open sunny clearings and this species is also well adapted to regularly felled plantation forestry, which encourages scrubby growth. With this type of management, widespread throughout France, the forest passes through several stages from small trees (either resulting from natural regeneration or planted when necessary) to mature stands. The red-backed shrike is regularly present only when the trees are small. Equally, some birds will nest during the regenerative stage after preparatory cutting, which considerably opens the old stands prior to the final growth and felling.

In the Vosges, at an altitude of 300 m, Lefranc (1979) recorded a high density of this species (up to eight pairs per 10 ha) in an open fir-tree *Abies alba* forest covering about 10 ha. Several large trees remained in the area, but the shrikes were attracted to patches of natural regeneration, and it was here that nests were built. The area looked rather 'untidy' and was scattered with piles of dead branches, stumps and uprooted root systems, as well as pioneer species like willows *Salix* sp. and broom *Sarothamnus*, all of which may act as perches. In this ideal habitat (which would rapidly become unsuitable as succession progressed) the average territory size was little more than 1 ha. In addition, the reproductive success was remarkably high. The nests, difficult to locate, were discovered mainly during the incubation stage and even, for a few of them, when they contained small young. Of 21 nests found, 19 (90.5%) fledged young. Breeding success was much lower overall in a study area mainly composed of young spruce *Picea abies* plantations and open country (pastures, meadows) with bushes. Of 88 nests found during the egg-laying stage, only 37 (42%) produced fledged young. Most failures were due to predators and bad weather. This difference may be due to better concealed and protected nests in the 'untidy' forest habitat.

Locally, red-backed shrikes also benefited from afforestation that occurred after an agricultural depression. Again, it is possible to cite the example of the Vosges (Lefranc, 1979) where, as in many other areas, red-backed shrikes occupied spruce plantations. These plantations provide suitable nest sites and hunting territories although, of course, only for a few years. As soon as the vegetation has reached approximately 3.5 m high, the habitat becomes too enclosed across the foraging area, and red-backed shrikes disappear. The average height of nests in spruce plantations was 1.3 m (range of 0.25–5 m).

Great grey shrikes will also exploit forest clearings if they are sufficiently large (a minimum of several tens of hectares), and in a relatively flat area giving the bird a commanding view of the whole territory (see reviews in: Glutz von Blotzheim, 1993; Lefranc, 1993). The use of newly cut areas in Sweden has already been mentioned above (Olsson, 1980), but locally this species may also occupy areas devastated by violent storms. Fischer (1994) has reported this in the Westerwald in Rheinland-Pfalz (Germany). Of 25 pairs of great grey shrikes present in 1994 in a study area covering 131 km², 14 or 15 nested in forest clearings, created in winter 1990 by strong winds or deliberate clearing (spruce plantations) at an average altitude of 400 m. All of the other pairs continued to nest in the neighbouring valley still dominated by extensive cultivated grassy areas.

An investigation of the status of shrike populations in France 1993/94 (Lefranc, unpublished data) illustrates how they (especially the southern grey shrike) can benefit from fires in Mediterranean forest. Such events are usually considered to be complete catastrophes, and for many species, such as Hermann's tortoise *Testudo hermanni*, this is certainly true. However, Prodon (1987) stressed the importance of such events for maintaining regional biodivsersity. He draws attention to the fact that Mediterranean ecosystems support an original 'historic' avifauna only in non-climax vegetation stages, in other words the most open or 'degraded' habitats.

Fairly open forestry is often found in military areas. Continual movements of tanks and artillery usually inhibit the development of completely closed environments. Such areas (provided that they have not been subject to chemical treatments) can be sanctuaries for a wide range of flora and fauna, including shrikes. A good example is the military encampment at Marche-en-Famenne (Belgium) where, according to Van der Elst (1990), the highest density of great grey shrikes in the country is found, i.e. up to 10 pairs on 12 km^2 of suitable habitat (forests and built-up areas excluded).

However, it is notable that in spite of the ability of the red-backed shrike and other species to exploit such habitats, populations are still declining.

Shrikes in rural areas: the importance of stock rearing and pastoralism

Not surprisingly, in most low altitude areas shrikes have disappeared from intensively managed arable areas where trees, hedges and areas of long grass have been removed in order to maximize production. However, even given the extent and rapidity of intensification, red-backed shrikes, with their modest requirements (such as 1.5 ha average territory size), may sometimes be found when small 'islands' of less intensively managed land exist. Particularly important in such areas is habitat 'microstructure', for example, unsurfaced rural paths and roads bordered by bushes and small fallow areas. These areas can play an important, even essential role for shrikes, as insect-rich hunting grounds (Lefranc, 1993).

Small natural enclaves within a landscape dominated by arable monocultures are not, however, sufficient to retain the great grey shrike, with its more exacting territory requirements (see Table 1). For example, this species has now completely disappeared from the Alsace plain in the north-east of France. At the beginning of the 1960s, a couple of hundred pairs still occupied this area, but the inexorable increase in maize production has fragmented the great grey shrike's habitat, and the small areas of mesophilic or humid meadow that remain are insufficient to support the species (CEOA, 1989).

Some features are indispensable if shrikes are to be retained in the rural countryside. Firstly, an adequate number of well distributed vertical structures are required both for nesting and as hunting perches, such as copses, hedges, trees or isolated bushes. Also essential are hunting sites rich in potential prey items – invertebrates and small mammals. All recent studies have pointed to the importance of meadows and pasture within shrike territories (reviews in Glutz von Blotzheim, 1993; Lefranc, 1993). A good example is given by the great grey shrike in Luxembourg. This state of 2586 km^2 still held about 600 pairs of great grey shrikes at the end of the 1950s (Hulten & Wassenich, 1960). Today only 50–100 pairs remain and Béchet (in press) has analysed the habitat characteristics of 50 territories. They were generally 50–100 ha in size and 90% of them contained a wide range of well distributed vertical perches. The territory area was mainly composed of meadows and pasture, each such habitat covering 30–40%. Cultivated areas were also present, covering from 10 to (exceptionally) 40% of the total area. They were, however, occupied by shrikes only if they (still) contained micro-habitat structures: overgrown paths, isolated trees or bushes, banks, small fallow areas, etc. In addition, 70% of territories contained small areas of other habitats, such as orchards and marshes, dotted sporadically within them.

There is a strong association between shrikes and meadow-pastures. The structural diversity found in extensively managed pastures is especially important. Bushes are sometimes maintained by farmers as markers around fields used by cattle. Trees and bushes (especially hawthorn *Crataegus* sp.) are sometimes allowed to become well developed, as they provide shelter for the cattle both during hot spells and cold wet spells. Numerous hunting perches (fence posts) are present. All shrikes will use such perches, but fence post height (*c.* 1.4 m) is particularly suitable for the red-backed shrike which takes most of its prey from the ground within a 10 m radius of the hunting perch (Solari & Schudel, 1988; Moes, 1993). Prey items in this habitat are generally abundant throughout the shrike's breeding season. Wagner (1993) illustrated that the red-backed shrike, a fairly generalist feeder, is well adapted to exploit seasonally abundant invertebrates from different taxonomic groups. This species will also exploit coprophilic insects (*Aphodius, Geotrupes* and *Onthophagus* sp. etc.) attracted to cattle dung, especially from mid-May to mid-July. In extensively managed pastures, these insects are not only abundant, but also easy to detect as the grass is short owing to grazing activity. The trampling and grazing of cattle creates a field surface with a very irregular microstructure. The studies by Brandl *et al.* (1986) in Hessen (Germany) not only illustrate the strong selection of red-backed shrikes for pasture, but also show that they achieve their highest reproductive success in such habitats. On average, successful pairs raise significantly more young (*c.* five) than pairs breeding in meadows or fallow land (*c.* four). According to the German authors quoted above, this could be because of a high abundance and, above all, a better availability of food items in pastures.

This 'association' between domestic stock and shrikes holds both in the mountains and plains. In the most northern part of its distribution, north-east France, Germany and Switzerland, the woodchat shrike is present only at low altitudes where weather conditions are favourable. In these areas, this species is found almost exclusively in standard orchards, and prefers low tree densities (40–100 trees per ha) with an understorey grazed by cattle and sheep (Ullrich, 1971). These excellent 'lawn-mowers' maintain a very close-cropped sward. Hair and wool that is lost, for example on barbed wire fencing, is used locally as nesting material by woodchat shrikes. The same orchards may be used year after year by the same male. It is remarkable that in Alsace, birds returning to their traditional territories will abandon them very rapidly if cattle or sheep are not present (Bersuder & Koenig, pers. comm.). The same birds, recognizable thanks to colour rings, can subsequently be found in grazed orchards, often several kilometres away from their traditional sites.

The red-backed shrike and, more seldom, the great grey shrike, can also be found in orchards associated with villages at low altitude (on the plain). Less thermophilic than the woodchat shrike, these two species are also able to exploit the persistence of traditional agricultural practices at higher altitudes (Lefranc, unpublished data). Because of the effects of intensification, highest densities of these species are now found at medium altitude mountainous sites – in effect refuge zones. Red-backed shrikes are therefore present in all open sunny areas of French mountainsides, including the slopes of the Alps, where they may occasionally nest as high as 2050 m in the Savoie (Isenmann in Lefranc, 1993). Particularly high breeding densities are found in the Massif Central (the Auvergne). Approximately 60 000 pairs nest in this region, within four Departments covering 25 950 km^2 (Duboc, 1995; Lefranc, unpublished data).

The Auvergne also supports the highest populations of great grey shrikes: approximately 1450 pairs. Although this species is rare in the valleys, good populations still exist on the vast grazed plateaux above 600 m. The highest population density of this species is found on the Planèzes plateau at an average altitude of 1000 m – several pairs nest at almost 1300 m. In all cases, the large territories of this species are found in areas that are both fairly open and fairly flat, with plateaux certainly preferred to mountain slopes. This species is totally absent from the Alps, but fairly good densities can be found on the open grazed plateaux of the Jura mountains in Franche-Comté, where several hundred pairs remain, usually below 800 m (Montadert, pers comm.; Lefranc, unpublished data).

Case study: the lesser grey shrike

As discussed, this species has become extremely rare in Western Europe. Although climate has very probably played an important part (continuous reduction of breeding success in series of wet summers and so progressive disappearances of whole populations: Niehuis, 1968; Lefranc, 1978, and reviews in Lefranc, 1993; Glutz von Blotzheim, 1993), agricultural intensification has certainly also played a very significant role in the decline. Approximately 25 years ago, this species still nested at middle latitudes, for example in the Kochersberg in the Alsace plain near Strasbourg at c. 48.35 N, one of the regions of France famous for its accentuated continental climate – warm dry summers and low rainfall (Escourrou, 1982).

This species was very well adapted to cultivated steppe areas, with scattered small areas of mixed cultivation, incorporating large areas of bare soil such as tobacco fields, beetroot, vines etc. Alfalfa fields were also used by lesser grey shrikes. These insect-rich habitats also provided nest building material, for instance in the form of alfalfa blades and various fragrant flowers. Generally, nests were built in fruit trees (apple, pear, and, less frequently, cherry trees) which grew at the sides of the many small roads that crisscrossed the region. Sometimes there was only one tree in a territory (Lefranc, 1978, 1993).

Today, many of the areas historically occupied by lesser grey shrike are still flat and open, and superficially appear to be suitable for the species. Many traditional nest sites still exist, but field sizes are much larger. The small areas of meadow have disappeared, and along with them, populations of large or medium sized insects. In the 1960s, the Kochersberg still supported four species of shrikes. Today, the only species found there is the red-backed shrike, and even this has become very rare (Lefranc, 1993).

In France today (1996), the lesser grey shrike is regularly found only in two areas, 60 km from each other, in the Hérault and Aude Departments (south of France). The total population is c. 50 pairs. In 1875, this species was 'very very [sic] common' in this region according to Lacroix (in Lefranc, 1978). The Mediterranean area of France has apparently not undergone any significant climatic fluctuations over the last 150 years, although they have affected northern and central Europe (Salomonsen, 1948; Kalela, 1949; for a general review see also Williamson, 1975; Le Roy Ladurie, 1983). The environment, however, has been significantly transformed, notably through the progressive planting of the largest vineyard in the world, in the Languedoc-Roussillon region. It is in this gigantic wine producing region (3570 km^2) that the two 'oases' supporting the last lesser grey shrike populations survive. These areas cover approximately 20 and 100 km^2. They have also been considerably affected by agricultural intensification, but are still fairly structurally diverse. There are still tall trees (for nest sites); plane trees *Platanus hybrida* along the roadsides at one site, and white poplars *Populus alba*, black poplars *Populus nigra* and ash *Fraxinus oxyphylla* at the other site. There are also open ground crops, such as vines and fields of melons. Finally, there is the indispensable fallow land, some of which comprises dry meadows, occasionally slightly humid meadows, sometimes grazed by sheep. Meadows and vines are still harmoniously interwoven giving rise to a mosaic landscape. Lesser grey shrikes take large numbers of prey from the meadows and along the various field margins between fallow land and vines (Lefranc, 1993; Bara, 1995). They also regularly feed upon insects associated with overgrown paths, banks and ditches. This is particularly true for those birds whose territories comprise almost 90% bare earth (pers. obs.). This shrike is, obviously, absent from the large areas of vine monoculture. It would be impossible for birds to breed in such areas even were they rich in prey items, owing to the absence of trees. However, vines are completely absent from the territories of only a few pairs. In these rare cases, the meadows have areas of very short cropped vegetation, maintained so by sheep grazing, showing that large herbivores can even be of benefit to this species of shrike (Lefranc, 1993; Bara, 1995; Bechet *et al.*, 1995).

WHAT FUTURE FOR SHRIKES IN THE EUROPEAN UNION?

The sensitivity of different shrike species

The previous sections of this chapter have illustrated that the four species upon which detailed studies have been carried out are all undergoing dramatic declines in Europe. This may also be the case for the southern grey shrike (in the south of France and the Iberian peninsula) and the masked shrike (in Greece) (Lefranc, 1993).

Amongst the well studied species, the least threatened is undoubtedly the red-backed shrike. It is the least thermophilic species, thus adapts readily to a wider altitudinal range, requires only a small territory, and has remained common, especially at medium altitudes. Even so, it is declining.

The great grey shrike is considerably more vulnerable. In medium-latitudinal Europe, from the Massif Central of France to the Netherlands, this species has largely disappeared from low altitudes (far more dramatically than the red-backed shrike). It requires large territories (cf. reviews in Glutz von Blotzheim, 1993; Lefranc, 1993), and cannot survive where monocultures cover the plains. Today, the refuges of this species show very limited distribution, being alluvial valleys still bordered by meadows, undulating plateaux, etc. The situation for this species appears to be somewhat better in Nordic countries where it is to be found in open taiga forests, reminiscent of primitive habitats and mainly composed of pines and birches and dotted with marshes and raised bogs. It also exploits areas of large-scale deforestation.

The future of the woodchat shrike is equally precarious. At mid-latitudes in Europe, this thermophilic species cannot find refuge in medium-altitudinal mountainous areas. The future of this species now largely depends upon what happens to the grazed orchards that still remain around certain villages. More to the south, in areas influenced by the Mediterranean climate, this species could potentially colonize slopes and plateaux, like the Causses in the south of France. However, this habitat is particularly threatened by agricultural abandonment and subsequent forest regeneration.

This is also a problem, in the same regions, for the red-backed and southern grey shrikes. The latter species, whether considered to be a sub-species of the great grey shrike or a full species, is very typical of this area and merits special attention within its restricted distributional range.

Finally, the most threatened species in western Europe is clearly the lesser grey shrike. Because of its climatic requirements (hot dry summers), this species is present almost only at low altitudes in the EU (or in well exposed sunny areas). It is particularly attracted by agricultural landscapes with large areas of very short vegetation or bare soil, and has more than likely suffered from a reduction in available prey in the many areas subject to pesticide use. This is probably also the species most likely to suffer direct effects of pesticides as it picks up its prey in cultivated fields or vineyards.

Current levels of protection for shrike conservation

All species of shrike are legally protected in the different countries of the EU, and so deliberate persecution is illegal. Little direct persecution exists in most EU countries except Greece, where numerous passerine species are still trapped or shot during migration. This situation is particularly worrying for the red-backed and lesser grey shrikes, as large numbers of these species gather in the Balkans during autumn migration. On the island of Chios alone, 400 000 red-backed shrike are reputedly shot each autumn (Choremi & Spinthakis in Bayle, 1994).

The Birds Directive (79/409) requires that the habitat of threatened species be conserved. Article 4 of the Directive requires that Member States take special measures, including the designation of Special Protection Areas (SPAs), in order to preserve or restore adequate areas of habitat for bird species listed in Annex I (including red-backed and lesser grey shrikes) of the Directive and other migratory species (effectively including the other shrike species).

Traditionally, national protection measures, both before and after ratification of the Birds Directive in 1979, mainly involved the designation of reserves. In France today, approximately 130 'national' reserves exist. These usually include 'exceptional' habitats, such as estuaries, strips of primary forest, lakes important for water birds, high mountain areas, and small islands. Shrikes are mainly absent from these areas.

There is, however, one notable exception: the stony steppeland (or 'coussous') of La Crau (Bouches du Rhône). This unique desert-like area was historically the delta of the Durance river. It is the only nesting site in France of pin-tailed sandgrouse *Pterocles alchata* and lesser kestrel *Falco naumanni*. La Crau also supports good populations of little bustard *Tetrax tetrax* and stone curlew *Burhinus oedicnemus*. It is also one of the strongholds of the southern grey shrike. In 1994, 66 territories were reported in an 11 500 ha area (Lefranc & Lepley, 1995) including completely unsuitable areas (total absence of bushes). This represents about half of the entire population estimated to nest in the whole Bouches du Rhône Department (Lefranc, unpublished data). Most of that part of the Crau that has not already been destroyed has now been classified as an SPA, but the area has still not been designated as a national reserve. The remaining intact semi-natural areas of the Crau are maintained through low-intensity sheep grazing (approximately 35 000 sheep in 1985, or three sheep per ha). However, such methods are increasingly subject to the pressures of intensification. Proposals have been made to replace the coussous with industrial-scale peach farms. Hundreds of hectares have already disappeared in this way (Cheylan *et al.*, 1990).

Site protection is undoubtedly important, especially locally and where species are rare and/or have restricted distributions. However, such measures are almost totally inadequate for shrike conservation, except occasionally for the red-backed shrike and, exceptionally, for the southern grey shrike.

Hopes for the future?

The conservation of small high quality sites will never adequately conserve shrikes (or other species) that occupy the 'wider environment', which is mainly farmland. The CAP, based solely upon an increased production ethic, has resulted in significant environmental mismanagement of farmland.

However, in May 1992 the CAP was reformed (see Robson, Chapter 3). Although the main aim of these reforms is to reduce production levels, and so agricultural surpluses, a second objective is to encourage production methods that are less environmentally damaging. Measures originating from Article 19 of EEC Regulation 797/85 and Articles 21–24 of EEC Regulation 2328/91, have recently been pulled together in the Agri-environment Regulation (2078/92), and should benefit flora, fauna and meadow ecosystems in general. However, benefits for shrikes, and other farmland species, will depend upon the adoption of suitable schemes by Member States.

In France in 1994, 54 of 62 projects (87%) covered by the Articles 21–24 of EEC Regulation 2328/91 involved meadows. However, the conservation of such sensitive habitats will do nothing to help shrikes regain lost ground in zones that have become very intensively managed. The current subsidies proposed to farmers are too low to encourage them to adopt more extensive farming methods. However, the provision of better targeted subsidies could support traditional farming methods, or even improve them by imposing strict environmental conditions upon the techniques used.

In France, it is anticipated by the government and by local authorities that such measures (amongst others) will be applied to areas where farming is an economically marginal activity. This should help both to maintain the wider countryside and to keep farmers employed. This is beneficial where abandonment is a problem, and should help to maintain traditional 'shrike-friendly' farming methods (mainly in mid-mountainous areas).

European Regulations, such as the 'LIFE Programme', which funds priority research projects, may also help if suitable shrike related projects are proposed and accepted.

A LIFE project directly involving shrikes has been carried out in the south of France on the Causse du Larzac (Dayde, 1995). Small flocks of sheep (mainly used for milk production) once grazed the Causse, and large herds of domestic stock were seasonally present as part of a transhumance system. The presence of shrikes in this area is still associated with areas of (current or recent) farming activity, especially stock grazing. In addition to shrikes, the survival of other species such as the Ortolan bunting *Emberiza hortulana* in this area can be ensured only as long as extensive pastoralism is maintained. The LIFE programme suggested the initiation of an 'ex Article 19' type programme on the Causse. The aim would be to maintain agricultural activities thanks to an agri-environment programme. This type of initiative would also contribute to the maintenance of a traditional landscape which is typical of the Causse, and likely to attract nature tourism. For the time being this initiative is just a proposal.

The application of agri-environment measures is also necessary to ensure the future of a population of lesser grey shrikes occupying a real 'island reserve' in the lower part of the Aude valley. In this area support is necessary for the conservation of a mosaic landscape of vines, large trees, fallow land and, if possible, meadows. The area must be a minimum of 20 km^2. Pesticide use should also be limited. To date, schemes incorporating favourable management techniques have been proposed to the grape farmers, and initial reactions appear encouraging. One aspect of such a scheme is already underway (started on 29 June 1996) whereby a cuvée (vintage) of wine named 'lesser grey shrike' is being sold with a contribution of 2 francs a bottle towards the enhancement and sensitive management of lesser grey shrike habitat. The scheme is managed by the regional government, Mediterranean Environment Agency and regional wine producers. A similar approach is being considered for the grazed meadows of Lorraine, which still house populations of the woodchat shrike, wryneck *Jynx torquilla* and little owl *Athene noctua*.

Such actions still need to be developed, but they are dependent on Member States devising suitable programmes and targeting the right areas, and even then they tend to remain very localized. As discussed above, very intensively managed areas will hardly be included in such programmes. However, it is hoped that one day, areas left fallow under set-aside schemes will be subject to adequately funded regulations, officially aimed at protecting wildlife, not only game species. Shrikes could play a leading role as bio-indicator species.

The limits of intensive production must almost have been reached. The populations of species like the shrikes, grey partridge *Perdix perdix* and corncrake *Crex crex* have shrunk dramatically. The impoverishment of biological diversity is not the only negative consequence of intensification. Soil and water quality have also been affected, and landscapes robbed of their originality. It is difficult to believe that we have so far missed the opportunity to develop a reasoned and realistically sustainable agricultural system, one in which food production and environmental protection both play important parts. To date, environmental considerations still play but a small part, restricted to the 'accompanying measures'.

Within the framework of sustainable development, it would be adequate to develop an agricultural environment that moves away from the intensive and specialized systems of today, and incorporates not only economic, but also social and ecological considerations.

REFERENCES

BARA, T.H. (1995) La population de Pies-grièches à poitrine rose (*Lanius minor*) de la basse plaine de l'Aude en 1994. *Alauda*, 63: 191–198.
BAYLE, P. (1994) Massacre de migrateurs à Chios. *L'Oiseau Magazine*, 35: 22–24.

BÉCHET, A., ISENMANN, P. & MAUFFREY, J.F. (1995) Un deuxième site de nidification de la Pie-grièche à poitrine rose en Languedoc. *Alauda*, 63: 243–244.

BÉCHET, H.G. (in press) Status and habitat structures of the Great Grey Shrike (*Lanius excubitor*) in Luxembourg. In *International Shrike Symposium*. Florida 1993.

BIBBY, C. (1973) The red-backed shrike : a vanishing British species. *Bird Study*, 20: 103–110.

BIBBY, C. (1993) The red-backed shrike. In D.W. Gibbons, J.B. Reid & R.A. Chapman (eds) *The New Atlas of Breeding Birds in Britain and Ireland in 1998–1991*, pp. 282–283. London: T. and A.D. Poyser.

BLAB, J., RUCKSTUHL, T.H., ESCHE, T.H. & HOLZBERGER, R. (1988) *Sauvons les papillons*. Paris Gembloux: Duculot.

BRANDL, R., LUBCKE, W. & MANN. W. (1986) Habitatwahl beim Neuntöter *Lanius collurio*. *Journal für Ornithologie*, 127: 69–78.

CEOA (Centre d'Etudes Ornithologiques d'Alsace) (1989) *Livre rouge des oiseaux nicheurs d'Alsace*. Ciconia: Numéro Spécial.

CHEYLAN, G., MEGERLE, A., RESCH, J. (1990) *La Crau, steppe vivante*. Ed. Jürgen Resch. Radolfzell.

DAYDE, S. (1995) *L'avenir des pies-grièches et du Bruant ortolan sur le Causse du Larzac méridional*. BTSA Legta Olivier de Serres.

DELPECH, R. (1975) Contribution à l'étude expérimentale de la dynamique de la végétation prairiale. Thèse Université Paris XI.

DIEHL, B. (1971) Productivity investigation of two types of meadows in the Vistula valley: XII Energy requirements in nestling and fledging red-backed shrikes (*Lanius collurio* L.). *Ekologia Polska*, 19: 235–248.

DESAULNAY, P.H. (1982) Statut et répartition de la Pie-grièche grise dans les régions Sud-Ouest, Midi-Pyrénées et Languedoc-Roussillon. *Bulletin de L'Association Regionale Ornithologique du Midi et des Pyrénées*, 6: 2–4.

DOHMANN, M. (1985) Morphologische Unterschiede und Verhaltensdifferenzierungen bei verschiedenen Raubwürgerrassen. Dissertation. Universität Tübingen.

DUBOC, P. (1995) Les Pies-grièches en Auvergne: approche du suivi de leur densité. *Le Grand Duc*, 46: 2–8.

ELLENBERG, H. (1986) Warum gehen die Neuntöter (*Lanius collurio*) in Mitteleuropa im Bestand zurück? *Corax*, 12: 34–46.

ESCOURROU, G. (1982) *Le climat de la France*. P.U.F. Paris.

EVANS, A. (1995) Forgotten farmland birds. *BTO News*, 199: 10–11.

FERGUSON-LEES, J.J. (1965) Studies of less familiar birds. 137. Woodchat Shrike. *British Birds*, 58: 461–464.

FISCHER, K. (1994) Bestandsentwicklung und Habitatnutzung des Raubwürgers (*Lanius excubitor*) im Raum Westerburg (Westerwald). *Fauna Flora Rheinland-Pfalz*, 7: 277–290.

FRUGIS, S. & SCHENK, H. (1981) Red List of Italian birds. *Avocetta*, 5: 133–142.

GLUTZ VON BLOTZHEIM, U. (1993) *Handbuch der Vögel-Mitteleuropas* Bd 13 III, *Sittidae-Laniidae*. Wiesbaden: Aula.

HERNANDEZ, A. (1994) Seleccion de habitat en tres especies simpatricas de alcaudones (Real, *Lanius excubitor*, Dorsirrojo *Lanius collurio* y Comun, *Lanius senator*) : segregacion interespecifica. *Ecologia*, 8: 395–413.

HULTEN, M. & WASSENICH, V. (1960) *Die Vogelfauna Luxemburgs*, I Teil. Luxembourg: Societé des Naturalistes Luxembourgeois.

ISENMANN, P. & BOUCHET, M.A. (1993) L'aire de distribution française et le statut taxinomique de la Pie-grièche méridionale (*Lanius elegans meridionalis*). *Alauda*, 61: 223–227.

ISENMANN, P. & LEFRANC, N. (1994) Le statut taxinomique de la Pie-grièche méridionale (*Lanius meridionalis*) TEMMINCK 1820. *Alauda*, 62: 138.

KALELA, O. (1949) Changes in geographic ranges in the avifauna of northern and central Europe in relation to recent changes in climate. *Bird Banding*, **20**: 77–103.

KOWALSKI, H. (1993) Bestandssituation der Würger *Laniidae* in Deutschland zu Anfang der 1990 er Jahre. *Limicola*, 7: 130–139.

KRISTIN, A. (1995) Why the lesser grey shrike (*Lanius minor*) survives in Slovakia : food and habitat preferences, breeding biology. *Folia Zoologica*, **44**: 325–334.

LEFRANC, N. (1970) La Pie-grièche à poitrine rose (*Lanius minor*) dans le Nord-Est de la France. Fluctuations, statut actuel, notes sur la reproduction. *ORFO*, **40**: 89–103.

LEFRANC, N. (1978) La Pie-grièche à poitrine rose (*Lanius minor*) en France. *Alauda*, **46**: 193–208.

LEFRANC, N. (1979) Contribution à l'écologie de la Pie-grièche écorcheur *Lanius collurio* dans les Vosges moyennes. *ORFO*, **49**: 245–298.

LEFRANC, N. (1993) *Les pies-grièches d'Europe, d'Afrique du Nord et du Moyen-Orient.* Lausanne, Paris: Delachaux et Niestlé.

LEFRANC, N. (1995) Identification des pies-grièches "grises" de France et du Paléarctique occidental. *Ornithos*, 2: 110–123.

LEFRANC, N. & LEPLEY, M. (1995) Recensement de la Pie-grièche méridionale *Lanius meridionalis* en Crau sèche. *Faune de Provence C.E.E.P.*, **16**: 87–88.

LE ROY, P. (1994) *L'avenir des agricultures françaises.* Paris: PUF.

LE ROY LADURIE, E. (1983) *Histoire du climat depuis l'an Mil.* Paris: Flammarion.

MINISTÈRE DE L'AGRICULTURE (1990) *Graph agri 90.* Agreste Annuaire des graphiques agricoles.

MINISTÈRE DE L'ENVIRONNEMENT (1990) *Etat de l'Environnement.* Ministère de l'Environnement, edition 1990. Paris.

MEYER, M. (1995) Ecosystèmes prairiaux et entomofaune: présentation de cas spéciaux concernant les espèces menacées (lépidoptères, orthoptères). *Colloque int. biodiversité et gestion des écosystèmes prairiaux (résumé)*, Metz 8–10 juin 1995.

MOES, M. (1993) Habitatnutzung beim Neuntöter (*Lanius collurio*). *Regulus Wissenschaftliche Berichte*, **12**: 1–26.

NIEHUIS, M. (1968) Die Bestandsentwicklung des Schwarzstirnwürgers *Lanius minor* in Deutschland unter besonderer Berücksichtigung des Nahetals und Rheinhessen. *Mainzer Naturwissenschaftlichés Archiv*, 7: 185–224.

OFFICE NATIONAL DE LA CHASSE (1984) *Remembrement agricole et faune sauvage.* Paris.

OLSSON, V. (1980) Recent changes in the distribution of the great grey shrike (*Lanius excubitor*) in Sweden. *Fauna och Flora*, **75**: 247–255.

OZENDA, P. (1994) *Végétation du continent européen.* Lausanne, Paris: Delachaux et Niestlé.

PEAKALL, D.B. (1962) The past and present status of the Red-backed Shrike in Great-Britain. *Bird Study*, 9: 198–216.

PRODON, R. (1987) Incendies et protection des oiseaux en France méditerranéenne. *ORFO*, **57**: 1–12.

QUÉPAT, N. (1874) *Ornithologie parisienne.* Paris: Lib. Baillière and Fils.

QUÉPAT, N. (1899) *Ornithologie du Val de Metz.* Paris.

ROUDIÉ, P.H. (1993) *La France. Agriculture, forêt, pêche depuis 1945.* Paris: Dalloz.

SALOMONSEN, F. (1948) The distribution of birds and the recent climatic change in the north-Atlantic area. Dansk. *Ornithologisk Forenings Tidsskrift*, **42**: 85–99.

SCHAUB, M. (1995) Lebensraumansprüche des Rotkopfwürgers in der Nordwestschweiz. Diplomarbeit. Un. Basel.

SCHÖN, M. (1994) Kennzeichen des Raubwürger-Lebensraumes (*L. e. excubitor*) im Gebiet der südwestlichen Schwäbischen Alb: Jahreszeitliche Nutzung und Revier-Grösse, Struktur-Merkmale und Veränderungen, Kleinstrukturen und Bewirtschaftung. *Ökologie der Vögel*, **16**: 253–495.

SHARROCK, J.T.R. (1976) *The Atlas of Breeding Birds in Britain and Ireland*. Berkhamstead: Poyser.

SOLARI, C.H. & SCHUDEL, H. (1988) Nahrungserwerb des Neuntöters (*Lanius collurio*) während der Fortpflanzungszeit. *Der Ornithologische Beobachter*, 85: 81–90.

TEULON, F. (1993) *La politique agricole commune*. Paris: PUF.

TUCKER, G.M. & HEATH, M.F. (1994) *Birds in Europe: their conservation status*. Cambridge: Conservation Series No. 3. BirdLife International

ULLRICH, B. (1971) Untersuchungen zur Ethologie und Ökologie des Rotkopfwürgers (*Lanius senator*) in Südwestdeutschland im Vergleich zu Raubwürger (*Lanius excubitor*), Schwarzstirnwürger (*Lanius minor*) und Neuntöter (*Lanius collurio*). *Vogelwarte*, 26, 1–77.

VAN DER ELST, D. (1990) Avifaune des milieux non forestiers du camp militaire de Marche-en-Famenne. *Aves*, 27: 209–244.

VAN NIEUWENHUYSE, D. & VANDEKERKHOVE, K. (1989) Populatiestijging van de Grauwe Klauwier (*Lanius collurio*) in het zuiden van de Gaume (België) in de periode 1979—1988. *Oriolus*, 55: 60–65.

WAGNER, T.H. (1993) Saisonale Veränderungen in der Zusammensetzung der Nahrung beim Neuntöter (*Lanius collurio*). *Journal für Ornithologie*, 134: 1–11.

WILLIAMSON, K. (1975) Birds and climatic change. *Bird Study*, 22: 143–164.

YEATMAN, L. (1976) *Atlas des oiseaux nicheurs de France*. Paris: Société Ornithologique de France.

YEATMAN-BERTHELOT, D. & JARRY, G. (1994) *Nouvel Atlas des oiseaux nicheurs de France 1985–1989*. Paris: Société Ornithologique de France.

CHAPTER

10

Birds and wet grasslands

ALBERT J. BEINTEMA, EUAN DUNN
& DAVID A. STROUD

SUMMARY

Many species of birds, particularly waterfowl and waders, are associated with
lowland wet grasslands in Europe. Most of the breeding species have declined in
numbers and range in the last 40 years as a consequence of increasing intensity
of the agricultural management of these grasslands and especially in response to
increases in fertilizer inputs and drainage regimes. The rate and extent of these
declines have varied between species, as a consequence of their differing
ecological requirements, and between countries, reflecting differing degrees of
agricultural development. The ecological causes of the declines are generally
well understood, and sympathetic grassland management on nature reserves
and elsewhere has demonstrated that declines in numbers of breeding wet
grassland birds can be not only halted but also reversed. In EU countries, the
response to these declines has been both to acquire and manage protected areas
as well as to encourage appropriate wider countryside measures, principally
through agricultural incentive mechanisms. The site-based approach is important in order to maintain key concentrations, but will never alone be sufficient to
conserve viable national and international populations throughout their ranges.
Wider countryside measures have met with variable success. There is an urgent
need to improve the focus of these measures, using existing ecological knowledge of the requirements of grassland birds, so as to halt declines at a European
level. Such measures should also address the restoration of formerly wet
grassland areas that have now been degraded through agricultural intensification and drainage. The creation of wide-scale demonstration projects in different countries would be a useful first step.

FARMING AND BIRDS IN EUROPE
ISBN 0-12-544280-7
Copyright © 1997 Academic Press Ltd
All rights of reproduction in any form reserved

The ecological understanding exists to formulate such a programme of habitat restoration: what is lacking is the political will to undertake it on a wide enough scale, although recent European Community initiatives on wetland conservation have resulted in the issues gaining a significantly higher political profile. The time is right for further and deeper policy reform at national and European levels. These issues are the subject of this chapter, which is based on detailed studies in the Netherlands, but includes also material from the UK and elsewhere for comparison.

INTRODUCTION

Wet grasslands – a bird's eye view

Agricultural grasslands and their bird faunas in Europe bear some resemblance to the vast natural grasslands of the Siberian steppe and the North American prairie. Before considering the occurrence of birds in agricultural, specifically wet, grasslands, we consider their distribution in steppe and prairie, because the natural patterns observed there help us to understand the difficulties encountered in seemingly simple matters such as defining the birds of lowland wet grasslands in Europe.

Wet grassland birds in steppe and prairie prefer wet conditions in early spring, resulting naturally from heavy rainfall, inundation (e.g. in river floodplains), or snow melt. Less obvious, but equally important, is the need for moist conditions later in the season (Green, 1988). The rate of soil drying is a factor limiting the occurrence of many species of waders and ducks, and is affected not only by precipitation but also by evapo-transpiration and hence temperature. Therefore, wet grassland birds in the Siberian steppe are most widely distributed in the moist, cool, northern transition zones where steppe grades into forest-steppe and taiga. Farther south, the birds become increasingly restricted to the vicinity of ponds, lakes or streams. Bird zones in the steppe region more or less reflect the differing vegetation zones (Knystautas, 1987).

In North America, the vast north–south mountain range barriers of the Rockies cause the vegetation zones in the prairie region also to run from north to south (instead of east–west as they do in Asia), with tall-grass prairie in the eastern half of the Great Plains, and short-grass prairie farther west. Yet, the birds do not follow these zones. Most wet grassland birds are found in a rather narrow belt through the northern states of the US and southern Canada, running from east to west through tall-grass and short-grass prairie alike. However, towards the west the birds become more restricted to those vicinities with standing surface water. Farther south, late spring conditions are too dry for most wet grassland bird species (Beintema, 1986).

Similar gradients are found in Europe. Between the cold limit in the north and the dry hot limit in the south, dairy farming extends in a belt from the west to the east. However, the strength of the association between dairy farming and wet grassland birds changes also from west to east.

In the very humid oceanic climate of western Britain and Ireland, 'lowland wet grassland birds' are not necessarily restricted to lowlands as a consequence of very high levels of precipitation. Wet grasslands and their birds are not exclusively found in the lowlands, and may be independent of groundwater (e.g. Baines, 1988). Lapwing *Vanellus vanellus* and snipe *Gallinago gallinago* occur in areas of high precipitation as upland birds, nesting on sloping ground (Baines, 1988; Calladine *et al.* 1990). In the very extreme north and west of Britain and Ireland, a particular type of wet grassland occurs in the form of machair, coastal grasslands associated with low coastal landforms where calcareous shell sand is washed and blown ashore. Machair is frequently associated with systems of low-intensity agriculture and its topography results in extensive winter flooding, with some areas remaining wet throughout the year, thus providing a wide range of breeding and feeding opportunities for waterfowl. Extremely high breeding densities of lapwing, snipe, dunlin *Calidris alpina*, oystercatcher *Haematopus ostralegus*, ringed plover *Charadrius hiaticula* and curlew *Numenius arquata*, as well as other waterfowl, can occur in these areas (Fuller *et al.*, 1986; Shepherd & Stroud, 1991; Nairn & Sheppard, 1985).

In south and east England, however, the occurrence and habitat selection of these waders are more characteristic of the Netherlands, north-western Germany, and Denmark. Lowland wet grassland birds in this region are restricted to lowlands, where the water table is permanently near ground level, although not necessarily dependent on the presence of standing surface water. Farther east in Europe, such as in Poland, wet grassland birds become very much restricted to river valleys and lakesides (Tomialojc, 1987).

Along this west–east gradient in Europe, we also see great variations in land-use, linked with the size of different countries, their accessibility, human population density, and economic status. Both in the west (Britain and Ireland) and the east (Poland) there is much regional as well as local variation in land-use intensity. In the central part (notably in the Netherlands), however, this variation is almost absent, with every square metre of grassland farmed as intensively as conditions permit.

At the eastern end of the gradient it is fairly simple to identify lowland wet grassland of importance to birds, the river valleys obviously qualifying while the higher, drier, meadows poor in birds do not. In the spectrum of habitats attractive to wet grassland birds, the extremes are readily identifiable. Even though at the western end (in the British Isles) these include a range of upland areas, it is relatively easy to identify the optimum (lowest and wettest) parts, and in these it is even possible to speak of natural or semi-natural conditions.

The real problem in this spectrum of identifying habitats suitable for wet grassland birds lies in the middle of the gradient. Two-thirds of the Netherlands consist of agricultural grassland, and (apart from nature reserves) none of it can be classified as natural or even semi-natural (Beintema, 1988). With few

Table 1 Birds of farmed wet grasslands (meadow birds) of primary importance (i.e. Dutch population is largely dependent on grassland) in the Netherlands

Species	Dutch population (pairs)	%EU*
Mallard *Anas platyrhynchos*	200 000–400 000	23
Shoveler *Anas clypeata*	10 000–14 000	40
Garganey *Anas querquedula*	1000–1900	14
Tufted duck *Aythya fuligula*	7500–11 000	5
Oystercatcher *Haematopus ostralegus*	80 000–100 000	50
Lapwing *Vanellus vanellus*	200 000–275 000	27
Curlew *Numenius arquata*	6500–8000	6
Black-tailed godwit *Limosa limosa*	85 000–100 000	86
Redshank *Tringa totanus*	24 000–36 000	24
Snipe *Gallinago gallinago*	2400–3100	1
Ruff *Philomachus pugnax*	400–800	1
Skylark *Alauda arvensis*	150 000–175 000	1
Meadow pipit *Anthus pratensis*	70 000–100 000	2
Yellow wagtail *Motacilla flava*	40 000–70 000	4

*Percentage of EU population (including Sweden and Finland) in the Netherlands (includes data from Hustings, 1992; Groot & van der Jeugd, 1994).

exceptions, Dutch grasslands are no longer subject to any form of inundation, they have highly manipulated ground water tables, and completely artificial plant communities which result from heavy fertilizer addition. 'Rough grazing' does not exist and even terms like 'permanent pasture' and 'hayfields' are no longer applicable. All fields are alike, whether they are being grazed or mown. Grazing and mowing may alternate between, or even within, seasons. When compared with grasslands in other countries, no-one would ever consider classifying a Dutch dairy farm as lowland wet grassland, if it were not for the presence of lowland wet grassland birds in quantities unknown elsewhere (Beintema, 1986, 1988; Beintema *et al.*, 1995; Table 1).

Because of these differences between countries, lowland wet grasslands are, for the purpose of this chapter, simply defined as grasslands rich in lowland wet grassland birds – selected from the bird's point of view.

Birds in lowland wet grasslands of the Netherlands

With few exceptions (such as coastal meadows and machair), grazed or mown grassland in Europe is of secondary origin, having been created long ago by human transformation of natural wetlands (e.g. freshwater marshes, swamps, peatbogs, riverine forests and salt marshes) into agricultural pastures and meadows (Rackham, 1986; Tomialojc, 1987; Ward, 1994). Wet grasslands thus generally occur on either peat or clay/silt soils.

The bird faunas of wet grasslands are also of secondary origin and no species is found exclusively in agricultural grassland (Beintema, 1983, 1986, 1991a). Throughout the European Union, however, wet grasslands support an estimated 600 000 pairs of various wader species, amounting to more than half of the total numbers of waders breeding in the EU (Hötker, 1991a). Their conservation through appropriate measures is thus a high priority in a European context (Pienkowski, 1991; Stanners & Bourdeau, 1995).

Species vary in their degree of dependence upon grassland, and this may vary regionally within species. This explains why there is no consensus concerning the definition or classification of grassland birds, not even within a country as small as the Netherlands. For instance, tufted duck *Aythya fuligula* is considered a typical grassland bird in the Dutch province of Noord-Holland, but not so in Drenthe, where it remains a species of lakesides, ponds and streams. By contrast, curlew is increasingly found in grasslands in the Province of Drenthe, but not so in Noord-Holland, where it is restricted to dune valleys.

Species composition in grasslands changes with time. In the Netherlands a hundred years ago, curlew and oystercatcher were not found on dairy farms, but ruff *Philomachus pugnax* and corncrake *Crex crex* were common. In the Eem valley in the Dutch province of Utrecht (roughly 1500 ha) ruff used to be the most abundant wader species, with more than 1500 females nesting at the turn of the century. Lapwing and redshank *Tringa totanus* were less common, and black-tailed godwit *Limosa limosa* much less common, with only a few hundred pairs nesting. The ruffs have all gone, redshank have been reduced to a few hundred, and lapwing and black-tailed godwit populations rose to 1000–1500 pairs in the 1950s before they started to decline again. In Britain, Holloway (1996) has demonstrated similar changes over the last century.

The change in species composition follows a pattern, in response to the continuous increase in fertilizer input, and the accompanying intensification of agricultural use. First, a certain fertilizer input is needed to make it 'profitable' for a bird to become a meadow bird, probably simply through an increase of food availability. Further increases in fertilizer input should enable some species to occur at even higher densities. At the same time, however, earlier mowing dates and increased stocking rates will reduce the probability of successfully producing offspring. Eventually a level of intensive grassland management is reached above which the species is no longer able to produce enough offspring to compensate for its normal adult mortality. The species will reach its maximum density just below this critical level, above which collapse and extinction follow (Beintema, 1983, 1986, 1991a).

Lower and upper critical levels of grassland management intensity, between which grasslands are viable breeding habitats, differ between species. There is a tendency for small species to move in and drop out at lower levels of intensification than large species. Species that passed their upper critical level decades ago are considered 'vulnerable' (ruff, redshank, snipe), while species that fairly recently passed their lower critical level and are still expanding are considered 'not vulnerable' (curlew, oystercatcher). Opinions on lapwing and black-tailed

Figure 1 One hundred years ago, oystercatchers were not found on dairy farms in the Netherlands. Today, one-third of the European population nests in the Netherlands. (Photo by C.H. Gomersall/RSPB.)

godwit are divided, the latter increasingly being considered vulnerable nowadays, although it was still on the increase in the Netherlands as recently as the 1950s (Beintema, 1983, 1986, 1991a). Hypothetical vulnerability ranges for seven wader species are given in Figure 2.

Evaluation of lowland wet grassland birds: an example from the Netherlands

There are many ways to list, classify, and evaluate wet grassland birds. In the Netherlands, 28 species are listed as characteristic of wet grasslands, 14 of which (see Table 1) are considered of primary importance, such that their Dutch population is largely dependent on grassland, a situation which prevails over a large part of the country. The remainder nest in grassland less regularly, or only locally.

Alternatively, species can be listed according to abundance, the rarer species being considered more valuable. Of course, rarity may vary on an international, national, or even local scale. One can also look at vulnerability or indicator value, whereby the most vulnerable species (ruff, snipe) serve as measures of successful nature management in wet grasslands. Finally, one can list species

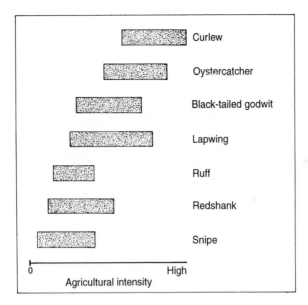

Figure 2 Hypothetical range of tolerance of meadow birds to agricultural intensity. (Source: Beintema, 1986.)

according to international importance, in terms of international responsibility for populations. The classic example is the black-tailed godwit, of which over 80% of the EU (and European) population are concentrated in the Netherlands (see Table 1).

Different outcomes resulting from use of different criteria are illustrated by ruff and oystercatcher. In terms of vulnerability and good indicator value, the ruff is the most valuable meadow bird in the Netherlands, and oystercatcher the least (Beintema, 1983). In terms of international importance, this is just the opposite, with one-third of the entire European oystercatcher population nesting in the Netherlands, compared with only a negligible proportion of the European ruff population. Obviously, international importance depends on political boundaries. Before Sweden and Finland joined the EU, the Dutch population of ruffs was numerically important within the EU (33%), but with the inclusion of these countries the Dutch proportion has dropped to below 1%.

In the national and international evaluation of priorities for grassland birds, both range and population trends are widely used as determining criteria. In this book we conform to Species of European Conservation Concern or SPECs (Tucker & Heath, 1994), as defined and identified in the Wet Grasslands Habitat Action Plan, drawn up by BirdLife International and RSPB. Lowland wet grassland SPECS occurring in the EU are listed in Table 2. At a national level (e.g. Osieck & Hustings, 1994; Avery *et al.*, 1995) the unfavourable conser-

Figure 3 Over 80% of the European population of black-tailed godwits nest in the Netherlands. (Photo by G. McCarthy/RSPB.)

vation status of wet grassland birds is increasingly seen as a priority for action (e.g. DoE, 1995).

THE PROBLEM

Historical development of dairy farming in the Netherlands

Traditionally, dairy farming developed in places too wet for crop farming, often on peaty soils or wet, weak clays. Large areas of grassland in the wet peat areas of the western Netherlands thus developed from moorland, which was cultivated for buckwheat in the Middle Ages. Drainage led to oxidation and shrinkage of the peat, which resulted in a progressive lowering of the soil surface. This ended when the surface became too low to allow further drainage by gravity. The fields, now lying almost on groundwater level, became too wet for crop farming and turned into wet grassland (Beintema, 1986). With improved drainage methods in the seventeenth century (windmills) the process of sinking continued, but the fields remained wet grassland. A very similar pattern of progressive drainage and land shrinkage has occurred widely in other

Table 2 Species of European Conservation Concern (SPECs) with significant breeding populations on European wet grasslands

Species	SPEC*	Status†	Criteria	Trend in the Netherlands‡
Curlew *Numenius arquata*	3 (w)	Declining	Moderate decline	Fluctuating
Black-tailed godwit *Limosa limosa*	2	Vulnerable	Large decline	Small decrease
Redshank *Tringa totanus*	2	Declining	Moderate decline	Small decrease
Ruff *Philomachus pugnax*	4			Large decrease

Source: Tucker & Heath (1994).

*SPEC category: 1: species of global conservation concern; 2: concentrated in Europe and with an unfavourable conservation status; 3: not concentrated in Europe but with an unfavourable conservation status; 4: concentrated in Europe and with a favourable conservation status. (w): refers to wintering population.

†The European threat status was defined as follows: *Secure*: population more than 10 000 breeding pairs and in neither moderate nor large decline, not localized. *Declining*: population in moderate decline and population more than 10 000 breeding pairs. *Vulnerable*: population in major decline and consisting of more than 10 000 breeding birds, or in moderate decline and consisting of fewer than 10 000 pairs, or population in neither moderate nor in large decline but consisting of fewer than 2500 pairs.

‡Trend data was defined as: *Moderate decline*: applied to a breeding or wintering population which has declined in size or range by at least 20% in at least 33–65% of the population or by at least 50% in 12–24% of the population between 1970 and 1990, and where the total size of populations that declined is greater than the total size of populations that increased. *Large decline*: applied to a breeding or wintering population which has declined in size or range by at least 20% in at least 66% of the population or by at least 50% in at least 25% of the population between 1970 and 1990, and where the total size of populations that declined is greater than the total size of populations that increased.

areas also, e.g. the East Anglian fens (Darby, 1956) and the Somerset Levels and Moors (Green & Robins, 1993; Williams and Bowers, 1987 – Table 3). However, in other areas, notably those on alluvial soils, this pattern may differ considerably.

Dairy farming also developed on old peat deposits at sea level that had been covered with a thin layer of marine clay during transgression periods. These areas, found mostly in the Dutch provinces of Noord-Holland and Friesland, but also in adjacent northern Germany (notably in Schleswig-Holstein), presently form the prime Dutch habitat for meadow birds, thanks to the combi-

Table 3 Loss of coastal grazing marshes in four areas of east and south England since the 1930s

Site	Period	Former area (ha)	Area remaining (ha)	Loss (%)	Source
Broadland marshes (Norfolk)	1930–1984	19 992	12 646	37	Broadland FoE (1985)
East Essex	1938–1981	11 749	2 083	82	Williams & Hall (1987)
North Kent	1935–1982	14 750	7 675	48	Williams et al. (1983)
Romney Marsh (Kent)	1931–1980	c. 16 000	7 200	55	Sheail & Mountford (1984)

Source: after Williams & Bowers (1987).

nation of natural fertility of the clay topsoil and permanent sogginess owing to the underlying soaked peat. These wet conditions cause slow annual development of the sward, and thus prevent early mowing or grazing, in spite of the inherent soil fertility. By contrast, the use of artificial fertilizers (along with increased drainage) has facilitated early mowing and grazing, which may inhibit successful nesting of many bird species (Beintema, 1986, 1988; Green, 1988). To summarize, the main factor that distinguishes Dutch grasslands from those of most other European ones, and renders them attractive to meadow birds, is the high water table which causes slow spring growth of the vegetation and retards accessibility for livestock and machinery, in spite of fertile soils (Beintema & Müskens, 1987).

Dairy farming also developed on coastal meadows, especially along the Waddensea in the northern part of the Netherlands (notably Friesland), Germany and Denmark. These areas have been considerably extended by land-claim in the upper tidal zone, a process which had already started in the Middle Ages. In these areas, permanent pastures are more common than hayfields. By contrast, grasslands developing in the river valleys were more often used for hay, as a result of sometimes prolonged inundation.

Traditionally, there was a distinction between grassland used as pasture, where cattle could feed during summer, and hayfields, where hay was cut to feed them in winter. Hayfields were usually the wetter parts, being often inundated during winter and spring, the farthest away from the farms, and the least fertilized. As a result, a distinction developed between plant and animal communities in pastures and hayfields. This distinction has gradually disappeared with the progressive intensification of land-use. Drainage, heavy use of fertilizer, re-seeding, and uniform land-use have led to strong levelling and uniformity in grassland areas. The number of plant species has been dramatically reduced, in favour of a few highly productive grass species (notably *Lolium perenne*), followed by a similar impoverishment of fauna.

The greatest leap in agricultural intensification has taken place during the twentieth century, characterized by fertilizer inputs increasing from less than 40 kg nitrogen per hectare per year around the turn of the century to currently 400 kg ha^{-1} (Beintema *et al.*, 1985; van der Meer, 1982). Consequently, overall cattle densities have increased to an average of 3.5 head per hectare in the Netherlands (Beintema, 1986).

The most dramatic changes in the Netherlands have taken place since the 1950s, when farmers not only intensified the use of their land but the government started to implement large-scale reallocation programmes. These reassigned ownership of historically highly fragmented land holdings to provide larger, contiguous units under single ownerships. These programmes proved very destructive to natural assets because they were accompanied by large-scale infrastructural changes (e.g. enhanced drainage, and new road and bridge building) as well as facilitating aspects of grassland intensification. In some other countries, such as the UK, conversion to arable also had major impacts. In France, loss of wet grasslands to maize continues.

Since the 1980s, counter-measures have begun to emerge through enhanced national nature conservation policies, as well as through changes in EU legislation consequent upon needs to control the over-production of dairy products.

Impact of agricultural change on grassland birds

The effects of increased drainage (and in some cases subsequent conversion to arable), which stopped natural regular flooding of wet grasslands, are obvious, and represent direct habitat destruction for many birds (Green & Robins, 1993; Ward, 1994). These changes affect also those wet grassland birds which could also be classified as marsh birds, such as various rail species.

Less obvious, but equally severe in its long-term impact on breeding birds, has been the gradual agricultural intensification of grasslands. This intensification may not result in great visible change in appearance – this has even led some to deny that intensification has been a major cause of disappearance of birds, and to argue instead that their decline must result from hunting in southern countries, proliferation of predators (as a result of nature conservation!), or drought in Sahelian Africa.

Research in the Netherlands has shown that high losses occur during the chick stage of the life cycle of grassland waders. A range of factors influence chick survival, and it is believed that increasing levels of fertilizer application may be to the detriment of wader chicks through changing invertebrate prey composition (Siepel, 1990; Beintema, 1991b). However, although high losses occur at the chick stage, the main cause of decline is increased egg loss. Early

Figure 4 Increased water management has reduced the regular flooding of many areas like this flood meadow (Upware, UK) and destroyed the habitats of many wet grassland birds. (Photo by C.H. Gomersall/RSPB.)

mowing and increased stocking rates reduce the probability of safe hatching, so much that recruitment becomes insufficient to compensate for natural adult mortality, irrespective of the fledging success of those that hatch. This phenomenon, combined with the variation in the capacity of different species to replace lost clutches, and the timing of breeding, explains the differences in upper critical levels of tolerance shown in Figure 2 (Beintema, 1983, 1986; Beintema & Müskens, 1987; Ward, 1994).

Duck species nesting in grassland differ in vulnerability, such that the population response of mallard *Anas platyrhynchos* is comparable to that of oystercatcher and lapwing; shoveler *Anas clypeata* has a similar vulnerability rating (medium) to black-tailed godwit; whilst garganey *Anas querquedula* is as vulnerable as ruff.

In the Netherlands, more grassland birds breed than in any other European country (Hötker, 1991a; Table 1), yet the decline of the most vulnerable species (ruff, snipe, garganey) started as early as the first half of this century, and greatly accelerated in the 1950s. Less vulnerable species (black-tailed godwit, shoveler) started to decline rapidly in the 1970s. During the 1980s, species like ruff and snipe survived mostly in reserves, but had practically disappeared from normally managed farmland. During this period the decline of the populations of black-tailed godwit, lapwing and shoveler stabilized or even started to show slight recovery (albeit to much lower levels than 20 years before), as various nature conservation measures, aimed at grassland management, started to have an effect (Groot & van der Jeugd, 1994).

Intensification of farming practice is not the only threat in wet grasslands, and is coupled with the threat of abandonment. Abandonment takes place where natural handicaps inhibit agricultural intensification, and no young farmers are found willing to farm under difficult conditions where only a low income can be generated. Where farmers stop farming (as a result of retirement etc.), fields become overgrown, and in the case of wet grasslands, eventually change into carr or marsh woodland.

Abandonment is not a serious problem in densely populated and heavily used areas such as the Netherlands, northern Germany, and Denmark. It is, however, a problem in some remoter parts of Britain and Ireland (e.g. Bignal & McCracken, 1996), and especially in rural France (e.g. Bruneel, 1994), although in the latter case it rarely concerns wet grasslands.

Although not part of the EU, Poland provides a very clear example of what happens to wet grasslands at both ends of the intensity scale. In the Biebrza Marshes, in the north-east of the country, the Biebrza River annually inundates large tracts of wet grasslands until late in spring creating a landscape exceptionally rich in breeding waterfowl (Dyrcz & Witowski, 1987; Klosowscy et al., 1991). Even in late July, farmers often had to wade out to their plots, to mow by hand, and to leave the hay to dry in stacks above the water. Stacks could be brought in by late August, or in winter when the marshes froze over. In rapidly modernizing Poland there is no place for such labour-intensive management of wet grasslands. They are either drained and intensified, or abandoned. Although a large part of the Biebrza Valley was declared a National Park in 1994, the future of the wet grassland component of the marshes is very uncertain as it seems unlikely at present that financially adequate structures can be found to continue the park's traditional management methods on a large enough scale.

SOLUTIONS

Wet grassland bird policies in the Netherlands

In the first half of the century, nature conservation mainly took two forms: the establishment of nature reserves, and legislative restrictions of hunting and egg collecting.

The first law relating to bird conservation in the Netherlands came into effect in 1912, but it was renewed and greatly expanded in 1936. The law protected most wet grassland species during the breeding season, and also their eggs (except those of the lapwing during the early part of the season).

However, neither the bird protection law nor reserves could stop the decline of grassland birds, because nature conservation measures did not include grassland management at all, and the prohibition of egg destruction did not apply either to cattle or to mowing machines. The need to include grasslands in the national network of nature reserves became evident in the 1950s, and the number of grassland reserves started to increase very rapidly in the 1960s.

In the 1970s, however, it became clear that even the establishment of reserves could not maintain the large and important populations of wet grassland birds in the Netherlands. In 1975, the 'Relatienota' came into effect with the aim of achieving a sustainable relationship between agriculture and the environment. The Relatienota enabled farmers outside reserves to be compensated financially for loss of income if they agreed to later mowing, reduced drainage, and lower levels of fertilizer application and stocking rates.

To implement the Relatienota, special areas have been designated. Within the boundaries of these areas, part of the land has to be acquired by the government or by private organizations as nature reserves, and part of the land must be brought under management agreements. These are concluded on a voluntary basis, for a period of five years, beyond which continuation is also voluntary.

The goal set in the Relatienota was to bring 100 000 ha of farmland under management agreements in a first phase, and part of this would eventually be set aside as reserves. Although this would also include some areas in the higher altitude parts of the country, some traditionally used arable land, and some areas primarily of botanical value, by far the greatest extent would be wet grassland, where the conservation of meadow birds was the principal objective. After completion of the planning stage of this first phase, and depending on the results, another 100 000 ha would be brought under management agreement in a second phase.

After publication of the Relatienota document in 1975, it took many years before the system started to work and the early years of the scheme were devoted mostly to discussion. Eventually in 1979, after an inventory of priority areas had been completed, the first 85 000 ha were delineated and by 1982 the number of management agreements had started to increase. The first phase has now been completed, and designation of areas for the second phase started in 1994. Table 4 gives the situation in the Netherlands on 31 December 1994.

Management agreements vary in the level of restriction on farming practices, mostly by differences in the earliest allowable mowing date. Agreements are thus classified, in ascending order of restrictiveness, as respectively 'passive', 'light', and 'heavy'. The passive package was designed to compensate farmers for retaining natural handicaps (such as unfavourable water tables), but requires no active management, in favour of birds or other wildlife. Light packages do require other active management, but differ from heavy ones in not requiring delayed mowing and grazing. The level of financial compensation similarly varies according to the stringency of the package. There are various additional measures, such as restrictions on drainage, the use of chemicals, and fertilizer inputs.

Generally, only farmers with natural handicaps on their land (high water table) choose heavy agreements. In recent years, there has been a tendency

Table 4 Uptake of Dutch grassland management incentives for meadow birds under the 'Relatienota' scheme as at 31 December 1994

Province	Area for which management plans have been made (ha)	Total area of reserves completed in Relatienota areas (ha)	Total area of management agreements (ha)	Number of participating farmers
Groningen	5 006	1 192	1 596	254
Friesland	13 105	3 194	5 251	510
Drenthe	10 270	2 585	2 953	417
Overijssel	11 780	1 996	4 034	679
Gelderland	15 572	1 924	5 955	863
Utrecht	6 027	1 031	2 127	246
Noord-Holland	11 524	2 735	5 313	515
Zuid-Holland	10 749	1 380	2 772	297
Zeeland	4 856	838	1 360	376
Noord-Brabant	9 587	1 482	2 327	490
Limburg	10 234	997	2 777	571
Flevoland	110	0	0	0
Total	108 820	19 354	36 465	5218

Source: Beintema *et al.* (1995).

amongst farmers to prefer the less restrictive agreements since they regard the 'heaviest' agreements as preventing them from doing anything at all with their land, and providing inadequate compensation. These less restrictive agreements, however, have turned out to be ineffective for bird conservation, so much so that in the new agreement packages they have been excluded (from 1994 onwards) and thus will be phased out by the year 2000.

At the outset, there was much scepticism over the cost and effectiveness of the Relatienota, but after 15 years of practical experience it appears that at present, outside the reserves network, it is the most powerful policy in the Netherlands for conserving large populations of wet grassland birds (Dunn, 1994). Some have criticized the whole basis of the voluntary approach on the grounds that it will never deliver effective conservation for meadow birds, especially for black-tailed godwits, and have called for compulsory measures. Until such a programme emerges, however, there is no alternative to ensuring that the gradual increase in uptake of (beneficial) 'heavy' management incentives continues, whilst also seeking better packages for farmers and birds alike (Dunn, 1994).

The Dutch province of Friesland has a long tradition of individual protection of wader nests in grassland, by either leaving a narrow strip of grass around the nest during mowing, or by placing an iron framework over the nests to prevent

Table 5 Area (ha) covered by schemes giving voluntary protection to meadow bird nests since 1980 (this scheme is separate from Relatienota)

	Friesland	Zuid-Holland	Noord-Holland	Overijssel	Groningen
1980	40 000				
1981	41 557	250			
1982	46 521	760			
1983	48 810	1415			
1984	50 974	2414			
1985	54 464	2507	1250		
1986	62 000	2642	1050		
1987	64 000	2558	1100		
1988	65 676	2970	1200		
1989	69 500	2933	1800		
1990	70 171	2755	2900		
1991	74 402	2924	3850	8 901	
1992	78 000	3738	4330	11 498	
1993	77 819	5064	5242	14 800	
1994	85 880	7042	7609	19 388	2378

Source: Beintema *et al.* (1995).

them from being trampled by cattle (Guldemond *et al.*, 1993). This activity, which mostly benefits those waders with easily visible nests, in particular lapwing, has been traditionally linked to the habit of collecting lapwing eggs in the early part of the season. Nest protection is now stimulated by the government through the appointment of a national co-ordinator, and it is gaining popularity in other provinces (Table 5).

The concept that farmers might produce not only dairy products but also specified environmental benefits (and be paid by society so to do) is a relatively new one in the Netherlands (e.g. that a farmer can claim to have a certain number of nests on his land, and be paid for each that successfully hatches). How this may be implemented, and how a controlling structure might be set up, is still under study. Experiments on nature production payment, on a local scale, are already under way.

Wet grassland bird policies in the UK

In the UK, the increase in arterial drainage systems since the 1920s and the provision of state grant-aid for the installation of field and arterial drainage since the 1940s have led to a substantial reduction in the area of lowland wet grassland (Williams & Bowers, 1987; Table 3) and populations of breeding waders (Smith, 1983; O'Brien & Smith, 1992). This has occurred not only

Figure 5 Lapwing nest of eggs. Nest protection, originally to prevent egg collecting and more recently cattle trampling, has been stimulated by the Netherlands government and is gaining popularity. (Photo by S.C. Porter/RSPB.)

through major floodplain drainage schemes affecting wide areas, but also through the cumulative effects of the loss of many small wetlands (e.g. loss of single wet fields with naturally little drainage, ponds and simplification of watercourses) at the scale of the farm. Although inland populations of species such as snipe and redshank were widely distributed in Britain in the late 1960s (Sharrock, 1976), by 1982, these species had become highly restricted in lowland England and Wales to a few areas with core protected sites (Smith, 1983). This trend was accentuated even more by 1989, when 40% of all lowland snipe in England and Wales were estimated to occur on reserves (O'Brien & Smith, 1992). By 1993, the entire (but small) British breeding population of black-tailed godwit was restricted solely to managed nature reserves (Ogilvie, 1996).

Policy responses to the decline of populations of meadow birds in the UK have been varied. As in the Netherlands, the establishment of protected areas and their management has long been seen as of fundamental importance (Massingham, 1924; Stroud *et al.*, 1990). There are two main categories of protected area in the UK. Sites of Special Scientific Interest (SSSIs – Areas of Special Scientific Interest (ASSIs) in Northern Ireland) are notified for their features of special importance, with land ownership remaining unaffected. Appropriate nature conservation management is encouraged through a system which,

Figure 6 Widely distributed at inland sites in Britain in the 1960s, redshank had become highly restricted to a few core areas by the early 1980s. (Photo by C.H. Gomersall/RSPB.)

broadly, forbids certain specified 'Potentially Damaging Operations', while encouraging sympathetic management through positive management agreements with owners and occupiers. Nature reserves are the other type of protected area, and these are usually owned (or leased) and managed by either statutory or non-governmental nature conservation organizations. In nature reserves, a much finer degree of control over conservation management is possible (e.g. Everett, 1987; Self *et al.*, 1994), and there are numerous examples to show that numbers of breeding and wintering waterfowl may relatively easily be enhanced using simple management techniques (Andrews & Rebane, 1994; Figures 7(a), (b)).

Comparison of national surveys of breeding waders in 1982 and 1989 showed that, whereas for lapwing different levels of site protection were not associated with any differences in trends of numbers, there was such a relationship for snipe and redshank. There had been large declines in snipe on more than

Figure 7 (a) Numbers of breeding ducks and waders at Pulborough Brooks RSPB nature reserve (West Sussex) before and after the retention of high ditch-water levels and the construction of permanent pools. (b) Numbers of breeding waders at the Loch Gruinart RSPB nature reserve (Islay, Scotland) before and after hydrological management specifically for waders which began in 1989/90. (Redrawn from Self *et al.*, 1994.)

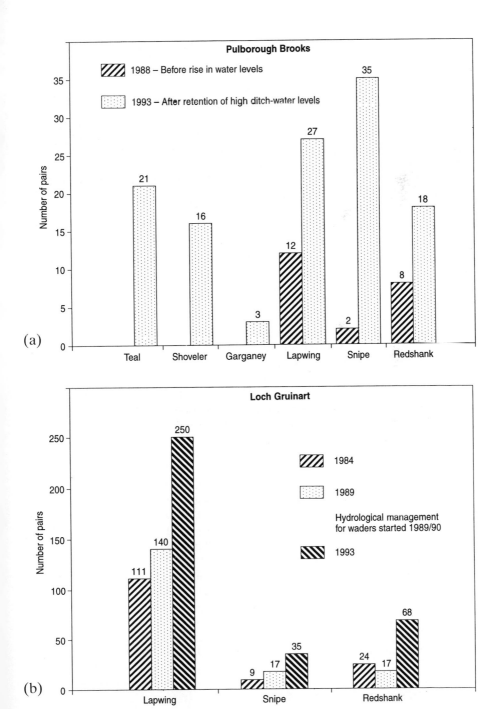

(a)

(b)

40% of unprotected sites, but only on 15% of reserves. For redshank, more than half of unprotected sites showed a decline in numbers compared with less than 25% on reserves (O'Brien & Smith, 1992).

Of course, even protected areas are rarely isolated from surrounding hydrological influences. On the Somerset Levels and Moors, declines of breeding and wintering waterfowl through the 1970s and 1980s have been closely related to the extent and scale of pump drainage in the catchment (Green & Robins, 1993). This has highlighted the need for wider hydrological measures in the catchments of important wetlands as a necessary complement to formal site protection and management measures.

In response to these needs, and especially to fulfil international obligations, a Watertable Management Scheme was established in England and Wales in 1994 by a range of statutory and regulatory bodies (MAFF et al., 1994). The aim of these plans is to define the optimal water level management regime for each site which reflects a balance of all needs, although giving particular emphasis to national and international nature conservation obligations. Highest priority in drafting and plan implementation is being afforded to internationally important wetlands such as Ramsar sites and Special Protection Areas (MAFF et al., 1994), although plans will also be prepared for other important wetlands such as those in ESAs (e.g. the Somerset Levels and Kent Marshes), National Parks, and eventually all SSSIs. The plans will be drawn up by the relevant flood defence operating authority following agreement with interested parties, including organizations representing conservation, agriculture and flood defence interests. It is intended that all grazing marsh SSSIs in the UK will have operational plans by the year 2000 (DoE, 1995). The guidance document (MAFF et al., 1994) highlights the scope for restoration and enhancement measures where past drainage activities have resulted in damage. The effectiveness of this scheme remains to be assessed, but has high potential.

In September 1994, a new Land Drainage Act came into force in England and Wales. This Act consolidates the duties of local authorities when acting as drainage bodies, to further conservation of wildlife when making decisions relating to land drainage and flood defence. It brings the environmental duties of local authorities in line with those of the other statutory regulatory bodies (such as the National Rivers Authority (NRA)[1] and Internal Drainage Boards (IDBs)) who also operate in England and Wales. The Act also empowers Ministers to intervene to prevent drainage activities proposed by IDBs where they are likely to damage nature conservation interests of national and international importance.

The first ESA in the UK (although initially a pre-ESA measure), and indeed the political impetus for the establishment of this policy measure at an EC level (Article 19 of Regulation No. 797/85), came through conservation conflicts in the Halvergate Marshes of the Norfolk Broads, where there was a need to create

---

[1] Now included within the Environment Agency.

an agricultural incentives mechanism that would encourage the maintenance of traditionally farmed wet grassland and prevent conversion of traditionally grazing marsh to arable (the detailed background to this case is presented by Lowe *et al.*, 1986). The effectiveness of ESAs in maintaining healthy lowland wet grassland bird assemblages in the UK has been variable. First, the schemes cover only certain areas (although nature conservation organizations in the UK have long argued that ESA-type incentive payments should be available for all farmers, thus allowing much wider-scale benefits). Even within ESAs, however, the scheme is voluntary and uptake has been variable within different areas. In part, this may be because incentive levels in some ESAs have been perceived by some farmers to be insufficiently high. Finally, management prescriptions within some ESAs have not been targeted especially at lowland wet grasslands and their birds – rather being aimed instead at more general nature or landscape conservation benefits.

Recently established 'wider-countryside' farmland management schemes with implications for wet grassland conservation include Tir Cymen in Wales and Countryside Stewardship in England. Both these schemes offer conservation payments to farmers for an agreed programme of sympathetic farmland management, and both are applicable to, although not exclusive to, wet grasslands. The schemes have been well received by the farming community, although are capable of further enhancement in conservation application (as detailed by Wynne *et al.*, 1995). A full review of their efficacy with regard to aspects of wet grassland conservation has yet to be undertaken.

There is short-term further potential for the re-creation of wet grassland through the use of non-rotational set-aside options (Firbank *et al.*, 1993), although this has limitations in application (Wynne *et al.*, 1995), especially as grazing is not allowed on such land.

In recent years a number of advisory publications have set out to encourage better nature conservation practice on farmland. *Conservation and Land Drainage Guidelines* (Water Space Amenity Commission, 1983) was addressed specifically at the question of best conservation practice in the design and execution of land drainage schemes. The *Rivers and Wildlife Handbook* (Lewis & Williams, 1984) and a series of other publications took the theme of better nature conservation practice on rivers, in wetlands and on farmland forwards (e.g. see Andrews & Williams, 1988; Williams *et al.*; 1988). More recent publications (Lack, 1992; Firbank *et al.*, 1993; RSPB *et al.*, 1994; Charter, 1995) provide a wealth of information on appropriate management and restoration techniques. Although information aimed at already sympathetically minded farmers seeking technical information is valuable, of longer-term importance in influencing thinking is 'training the advisers'. Thus, *Farming and Wildlife: a practical management handbook* (Andrews & Rebane, 1994) was targeted primarily at agricultural colleges and agricultural/land-use advisers, whereas *The New Rivers and Wildlife Handbook* (RSPB *et al.*, 1994) was aimed at river engineers and managers, especially in the statutory agencies (NRA and River Purification Boards) as well as in the private water companies.

Table 6 UK Biodiversity Action Plan objectives and targets for coastal and floodplain grazing marsh in UK

Maintain the existing habitat extent (300 000 ha) and quality

Rehabilitate 10 000 ha of grazing marsh habitat which has become too dry, or is intensively managed, by the year 2000. This would comprise 5000 ha already targeted in ESAs, with an additional 5000 ha

Begin creating 2500 ha of grazing marsh from arable land in targeted areas, in addition to that which will be achieved by existing ESA schemes, with the aim of creating as much as possible by the year 2000

Grazing marsh is an important habitat for a range of birds, invertebrates and plant communities. There is considerable potential for the enhancement of this biological interest and a target of 5000 ha is considered achievable providing this is carefully targeted at core areas and where reversing fragmentation is feasible. In some cases this may be in areas where there is potential to recreate this habitat from land currently under arable cultivation. The figure of 2500 ha could produce significant benefits if targeted carefully

---

Source: DoE (1995).

In the longer term, however, wide-scale restoration of lowland wet grasslands in the UK can only come about through strategic policy decisions at a national level (e.g. Thomas *et al.*, 1995), integrated into the catchment management planning process. The UK Government's response to the Convention on Biological Diversity has led to the recent publication of the UK Biodiversity Steering Group's proposals (DoE, 1995) for species and habitat action plans (the implementation of which has been costed). This is an important step forward in this regard with great potential to integrate the currently disparate actions of many regulatory agencies and other organizations. The Action Plan for coastal and floodplain grazing marshes sets a number of detailed targets (Table 6), as well as outlining potential costs and identifying lead agencies for specific actions.

Although a number of new initiatives have commenced in the UK, there is no evidence yet that population indices for breeding snipe and redshank have yet started to recover to former levels. This will be the real test of success.

Wet grassland bird policies in the EU

The first policy steps undertaken in the EU took place at the lower end of the intensity scale, in subsidizing those farmers in Less Favourable Areas to prevent abandonment – although LFA support has been applied in markedly different ways between countries (Lowe *et al.*, 1986). Although the primary goal was to help the farmers, this also led to the safeguarding of management in areas with high natural values. The system was first set up to help farmers in mountain areas (notably in France), especially above the timberline, but it also became applicable in lowland wet grassland, in places where it was impossible or too expensive to improve drainage. In the area of Waterland, in the central part of the Dutch province of Noord-Holland, where many fields could only be reached by boat, farmers had been receiving EU money under the Less Favoured Areas Act before the Relatienota came into effect. This sort of compensation has since been fully integrated into the Relatienota, so that management agreements are now being partly financed by EU funds.

If the tide of wet grassland habitat loss and degradation in Europe could be turned, there can be no doubt that the conservation benefits would be enormous. What is needed now is governmental and EU commitment to wide-scale habitat restoration and creation through the appropriate reform of national and European agricultural policies and development of suitable incentive packages. Broadly, the ecological understanding exists to formulate such a programme of habitat restoration: what is lacking is generally the political will to undertake it on a wide enough scale. The recent attention being given specifically to wetlands by the European Commission can only be helpful in this regard; indeed emphasis is given to the conservation of wet meadows and floodplain grasslands throughout the Commission's recent Communication to the Council and European Parliament (CEC, 1995).

On some coasts, such as those of much of the UK, current changes give rise to both major threats and opportunities in respect of wet grasslands and related habitats. Sea level rise, combined with fixed sea defences, are resulting in the 'coastal squeeze' of wetlands. However, increasing recognition that working with nature is a cost-effective approach to sea defences is giving rise to possibilities of 'managed retreat' and the re-creation of wetlands to protect the coast. There are some similar potential ideas for inland river-bund systems.

RECOMMENDATIONS

The Wader Study Group's (WSG) recommendations (Pienkowski, 1991) concerning the conservation of wet grasslands and their waders remain valid and should be given priority:

(1) All remaining semi-natural wet grassland should be safeguarded as nature reserves or other protected areas in which management for nature conservation has priority. In some areas, effective management may be possible only through site-ownership by conservation bodies.

(2) Also outside protected areas, traditional low-intensity farming should be encouraged. This should include financial support for pastoral and mixed farming and the related rural communities, to prevent both intensification of agriculture and abandonment of farming.

(3) Financial support should be provided also to encourage the return of intensive arable areas to low-intensity pastoral or mixed systems. Policies encouraging shifts from cereal-growing to other land-uses should allow the use of grazing animals in areas of actual or potential nature conservation importance.

(4) No financial support should be given in wet grassland areas of nature conservation importance for the intensification of agriculture nor for new arterial drainage works or installation or replacement of field drains. The implementation of EEC policies for rural areas should give priority to nature conservation rather than agricultural production.

(5) Water abstraction from water courses and aquifers which would lower the water levels in grasslands that hold breeding waders should not be permitted.

(6) The 'wise-use' of lowland peatlands for low-intensity grazing systems should be encouraged in preference to short-term, high-intensity systems leading to soil-loss.

(7) Wet grassland areas should be managed consistently, as short-term changes in management prevent wader density and productivity reaching adequate levels.

(8) In all areas (protected areas and outside) in which support for nature conservation is provided, there should be agreed aims and management. These aims, whether related to birds or other nature conservation aspects, should be specified. This management should be monitored (and provision for monitoring included in the budget). The monitoring should be planned both to check on effective use of resources and to allow refinement of management prescriptions.

(9) In all wet grassland areas managed for breeding waders, prescriptions should stress water management, and should take account of the seven issues listed by Pienkowski (1991).

(10) Support should be provided for studies monitoring the condition of wet grasslands and their bird populations; for research on ways of conserving them; and for disseminating knowledge widely.

There is a great need to develop a European population monitoring programme for breeding waders. International overviews such as those of Piersma (1986) and Hötker (1991b) are crucial to place national conservation initiatives in a wider European context as well as to disseminate national information internationally. In particular, there is an urgent need to implement the proposed WSG project to re-assess European breeding wader populations, and the initiative (outlined by Bignal & Pienkowski, 1994) to develop closer links between related programmes to maintain traditional forms of pastoral agriculture.

REFERENCES

ANDREWS, J. & REBANE, M. (1994) *Farming and Wildlife: a Practical Management Handbook.* Sandy: Royal Society for the Protection of Birds.

ANDREWS, J. & WILLIAMS, G. (1988) The development of wildlife conservation on rivers. *RSPB Conservation Review, number* **2**: 78–80.

AVERY, M.I., GIBBONS, D.W., PORTER, R., TEW, T.E., TUCKER, G. & WILLIAMS, G. (1995) Revising the British Red Data List for birds: the biological basis of UK conservation priorities. *Ibis,* **137**: S232–239.

BAINES, D. (1988) The effects of improvement of upland, marginal grasslands on the distribution and density of breeding waders (Charadriformes) in northern England. *Biological Conservation,* **45**: 221–236.

BEINTEMA, A.J. (1983) Meadow birds as indicators. *Environmental Monitoring and Assessment,* **3**: 391–398.

BEINTEMA, A.J. (1986) Man-man polders in The Netherlands: a traditional habitat for shorebirds. *Colonial Waterbirds,* **9**: 196–202.

BEINTEMA, A.J. (1988) *Conservation of Grassland Bird Communities in The Netherlands.* International Council for Bird Protection. Technical Publication 7. Cambridge: International Council for Bird Protection.

BEINTEMA, A.J. (1991a). What makes a meadow bird a meadow bird? *Wader Study Group Bulletin,* **61**(Supplement): 3–5.

BEINTEMA, A. (1991b) Insect fauna and grassland birds. In D.J. Curtis, E.M. Bignal & M.A. Curtis (eds) *Birds and pastoral agriculture in Europe,* Proceedings of the second European Forum on Birds and Pastoralism. Port Erin, Isle of Man, 26–30 October 1990, pp. 97–101.

BEINTEMA, A.J. & MÜSKENS, G.J.D.M. (1987) Nesting success of birds breeding in Dutch agricultural grasslands. *Journal of Applied Ecology,* **24**: 743–758.

BEINTEMA, A.J., BEINTEMA-HIETBRINK, R.J. & MÜSKENS, G.J.D.M. (1985) A shift in the timing of breeding of meadow birds. *Ardea,* **73**(1): 83–89.

BEINTEMA, A.J., MOEDT, O. & ELLINGER, D. (1995) *Ecologische Atlas van der Nederlandse Weidevogels.* Haarlem, the Netherlands: Schuyt and Co.

BIGNAL, E.M. & McCRACKEN, D.I. (1996) Low-intensity farming systems in the conservation of the countryside. *Journal of Applied Ecology* (in press).

BIGNAL, E.M., & PIENKOWSKI, M.W. (1994) International group on nature conservation and cultural landscapes. *Wader Study Group Bulletin,* **75**: 9–10.

BROADLAND FRIENDS OF THE EARTH (1985) Memorandum submitted by Broadland FoE in First Report from House of Commons Environment Committee on the operation and effectiveness of Part II of the Wildlife and Countryside Act. Vol. II. London: HMSO.

BRUNEEL, C. (1994) Abandonment and rural change: le case du Parc Naturel Regional du Haut-Jura (France). In D.I. McCracken, E.M. Bignal & E. Wenlock (eds) *Farming on the Edge: the nature of traditional farmland,* pp. 182–186. Peterborough: Joint Nature Conservation Committee.

CALLADINE, J., DOUGILL, S., HARDING, N. & STROUD, D.A. (1990) Moorland birds of the Campsie Fells, Touch Hills and west Ochil Hills, Stirling: habitats, distribution and numbers. *Forth Naturalist and Historian,* **13**: 53–69.

CHARTER, E. (1995). *Farming with Wildlife in Mind: a handbook for farmers in Orkney.* Kirkwall: Orkney Farming and Wildlife Advisory Group.

CEC (Commission of the European Communities) (1995) Wise use and the conservation of wetlands. Com (95) 189 final. Luxembourg.

DARBY, H.C. (1956) *The Draining of the Fens.* Cambridge: Cambridge University Press.

DoE (Department of Environment) (1995) *Biodiversity: the UK Steering Group Report.* Two volumes. London: HMSO

DUNN, E. (1994) Case studies of farming and birds in Europe: lowland wet grasslands in The Netherlands and Germany. Studies in European Agriculture and Environmental Policy 10. Unpublished Report. Sandy: Royal Society for the Protection of Birds.

DYRCZ, A. & WITOWSKI, J. (1987) Numbers, distribution and interspecific relations of breeding waders in natural Biebrza fen and adjacent reclaimed marsh. *Wader Study Group Bulletin*, 51: 42–44.

EVERETT, M.J. (1987) The Elmley experiment. Royal Society for the Protection of Birds. *Conservation Review*, 1: 31–33.

FIRBANK, L.G., ARNOLD, H.R., EVERSHAM, B.C., MOUNTFORD, J.O., RADFORD, G.L., TELFER, M.G., TREWEEK, J.R., WEBB, N.R.C. & WELLS, T.C.E. (1993) *Managing Set-aside Land for Wildlife.* Insitute for Terrestrial Ecology Research Publication 7. London: HMSO.

FULLER, R.J., REED, T.M., BUXTON, N.E., WEBB, A., WILLIAMS, T.D. & PIENKOWSKI, M.W. (1986) Populations of breeding waders Charadrii and their habitats on the crofting lands of the Outer Hebrides, Scotland. *Biological Conservation*, 37: 333–361.

GREEN, R.E. (1988) Effects of environmental factors on the timing and success of breeding Common Snipe *Gallinago gallinago* (Aves: Scolopacidae). *Journal of Applied Ecology*, 25: 79–93.

GREEN, R.E. & ROBINS, M. (1993) The decline of the ornithological importance of the Somerset Levels and Moors, England and changes in the management of water levels. *Biological Conservation*, 66: 95–106.

GROOT, H. & VAN DER JEUGD, H. (1994) Weidevogels in de graslandgebieden van Nederland; trends en huidige dichtheden. Rep. for Informatie- en Kennicentrum van de directie Natuur, Bos, Landschap en Fauna (IKC-NBLF), Ministerie van Landbouw, Natuurbeheer en Visserij.

GULDEMOND, J.A., PARMEBTIER, F. & VISBEEN, F. (1993) Meadow birds, field management and nest protection in a Dutch peat soil area. *Wader Study Group Bulletin*, 70: 42–48.

HOLLOWAY, S. (1996) *The Historical Atlas of Breeding Birds in Britain and Ireland: 1875–1900.* London: T. and A.D. Poyser.

HÖTKER, H. (ed.) (1991a) Waders breeding on wet grasslands in the countries of the European Community – a brief summary of current knowledge on population sizes and population trends. *Wader Study Group Bulletin*, 61(Supplement): 50–55.

HÖTKER, H. (ed.) (1991b) Waders breeding on wet grasslands. *Wader Study Group Bulletin*, 61(Supplement).

HUSTINGS, M.F.H. (1992) Aantallen en trends van Nederlandse broedvogels in (1960–91). Documentatie ten behoeve van de herziening Rode Lijst. Interne rapportage SOVON aan Vogelbescherming.

KLOSOWSCY, G., KLOSOWSCY, S. & KLOSOWSCY, T. (1991) Ptaki biebrzanskich bagien. [*The Birds of Biebrza Marshes*]. Warsaw: KSAT.

KNYSTAUTAS, A. (1987) *The Natural History of the USSR.* London: Century Hutchinson.

LACK, P. (1992) *Birds on Lowland Farms.* London: HMSO.

LEWIS, G. & WILLIAMS, G. (1984) *Rivers and Wildlife Handbook.* Royal Society for the Protection of Birds (Sandy) and Royal Society for Nature Conservation (Nettlesham).

LOWE, P., COX, G., MacEWEN, M., O'RIORDAN, T. & WINTER, M. (1986) *Countryside Conflicts. The politics of farming, forestry and conservation.* Aldershot: Gower.

MAFF (Ministry of Agriculture, Fisheries and Food) WO, ADA, English Nature and National Rivers Authority (1994). *Waterlevel Management Plans: a procedural guide for operating authorities.* Ministry of Agriculture, Fisheries and Food.

MASSINGHAM, H.J. (1924). *Sanctuaries for Birds and How to Make Them.* London: Bell and Sons.

NAIRN, R.G.W. & SHEPPARD, J.R. (1985) Breeding waders of sand dune machair in north-west Ireland. *Irish Birds*, **3**: 53–70.

O'BRIEN, M., & SMITH, K.W. (1992) Changes in the status of waders breeding on wet lowland grasslands in England and Wales between 1982 and 1989. *Bird Study*, **39**: 165–176.

OGILVIE, M.A. & THE RARE BREEDING BIRDS PANEL. (1996) Rare breeding birds in the United Kingdom in 1993. *British Birds* (in press).

OSIECK, E.R. & HUSTINGS, F. (1994) Rode lijst van bedreigde en blauwe lijst van belangrijke soorten in Nederland. Technical Rapport Vogelbescherming Nederland 12. Zeist: Vogelbescherming Nederland.

PIENKOWSKI, M.W. (1991) Discussion and recommendations. *Wader Study Group Bulletin*, **61**(Supplement): 86–88.

PIERSMA, T. (1986) Breeding waders in Europe. *Wader Study Group Bulletin*, **48**(Supplement): 1–16.

RACKHAM, O. (1986) *The History of the Countryside*. Dent, London.

RSPB (Royal Society for the Protection of Birds), National Rivers Authority and Royal Society Nature Conservation (1994) *The New Rivers and Wildlife Handbook*. Sandy: Royal Society for the Protection of Birds.

SELF, M., O'BRIEN, M. & HIRONS, G. (1994) Hydrological management for waterfowl on Royal Society for the Protection of Birds lowland wet grassland reserves. *RSPB Conservation Review*, **8**: 45–56.

SHARROCK, J.T.R. ed. (1976) *The Atlas of Breeding Birds in Britain and Ireland*. Tring: British Trust for Ornithology/Monkstown, County Dublin: Irish Wildbird Conservancy.

SHEAIL, J. & MOUNTFORD, J.O. (1984) Changes in the perception and impact of agricultural land improvement: the post-war trends in the Romney Marsh. *Journal of the Royal Agricultural Society*, **145**: 43–55.

SHEPHERD, K.B. & STROUD, D.A. (1991) Breeding waders and their conservation on the wetlands of Tiree and Coll, Inner Hebrides. *Wildfowl*, **42**: 108–117.

SIEPEL, H. (1990) The influence of management on food size in the menu of insectiverous animals. In M.J. Someijer & J. van der Blom (eds) *Experimental and Applied Entomology*. Amsterdam: Nederlandse Entomologische Vereniging.

SMITH, K.W. (1983) The status and distribution of waders breeding on wet lowland grassland in England and Wales. *Bird Study*, **30**: 177–192.

STANNERS, D. & BOURDEAU, P. (eds) (1995) *Europe's Environment: the Dobrís Assessment*. Copenhagen: European Environment Agency..

STROUD, D.A., MUDGE, G.P. & PIENKOWSKI, M.W. (1990) *Protecting Internationally Important Bird Sites: a review of the European Economic Committee Special Protection Area network in Great Britain*. Peterborough: Nature Conservancy Council.

THOMAS, G., JOSÉ, P. & HIRONS, G. (1995) Wet grassland in the millennium. *Enact: Managing Land for Wildlife*, **3**(1): 4–6.

TOMIALOJC, L. (1987) Breeding waders in Poland – their past and present status. *Wader Study Group Bulletin*, **51**: 38–41.

TUCKER, G.M. & HEATH, H.F. (1994) *Birds in Europe: their conservation status*. BirdLife Conservation Series 3. Cambridge: BirdLife International.

VAN DER MEER, H.G. (1982) In A.J. Corrall (ed.) *Efficient Grassland Farming*, Occasional Symposium. 14, pp. 61–68. Hurley, Berkshire: British Grassland Society.

WARD, D. (1994) Management of lowland wet grassland for breeding waders. *British Wildlife*, **6**: 89–98.

WATER SPACE AMENITY COMMISSION (1983) *Conservation and Land Drainage Guidelines*. London: WSAC.

WILLIAMS, G. & BOWERS, J.K. (1987) Land drainage and birds in England and Wales. *RSPB Conservation Review*, **1**: 25–30.

WILLIAMS, G. & HALL, M. (1987) The loss of coastal grazing marshes in south and east England, with special reference to east Essex, England. *Biological Conservation*, **39**: 243–253.

WILLIAMS, G., HENDERSON, A., GOLDSMITH, L. & SPREADBOROUGH, A. (1983) The effects on birds of land drainage improvements in the North Kent Marshes. *Wildfowl*, **34**: 33–47.

WILLIAMS, G., NEWSON, M. & BROWNE, D. (1988) Land drainage and birds in Northern Ireland. *RSPB Conservation Review*, **2**: 72–77.

WYNNE, G., AVERY, M., CAMPBELL, L., GUBBAY, S., HAWKSWELL, S., JUNIPER, T., KING, M., NEWBERY, P., SMART, J., STEEL, C., STONES, T., STUBBS, A., TAYLOR, J., TYDE-MAN, C. & WYNDE, R. (1995). *Biodiversity Challenge*, second edition. Sandy: Royal Society for the Protection of Birds.

CHAPTER

11

Farming in the drylands of Spain: birds of the pseudosteppes

FRANCISCO SUÁREZ, MIGUEL A. NAVESO & EDUARDO DE JUANA

SUMMARY

Pseudosteppes are characterized by a mosaic of habitats including cereal crops, dry legumes and winter and 3–5 year fallows, which are always grazed. However, the pseudosteppe mosaic differs considerably between regions, mainly because of different soil and weather conditions. Wetter and more productive areas are mainly used for cereal production, and have only a small fallow component, while drier areas have more fallow land, grassland and scrubland, and are used mainly for livestock production. These different land-use mosaics support many bird species that are declining throughout Europe, including globally threatened species, like the great bustard *Otis tarda*. Areas of extensive cereal production are also important wintering grounds for a wide range of species that breed at more northerly latitudes. However, only a small percentage of the pseudosteppes have any formal protection.

Pseudosteppes are economically marginal farming systems, with cereal yields of less than half the average European Union yields, and have been subject to intensification in recent years. If current trends towards cutting the prices of agricultural goods continue, two things seem likely to happen to the pseudos-teppes. These are: intensification of the land with higher production potential, mainly through irrigation and farm re-structuring, accompanied by abandon-ment, and sometimes afforestation of the least productive land. In both cases, habitat diversity would be reduced – and consequently the biological diversity of the pseudosteppe would be affected.

FARMING AND BIRDS IN EUROPE
ISBN 0-12-544280-7
Copyright © 1997 Academic Press Ltd
All rights of reproduction in any form reserved

In this chapter we discuss the importance of the pseudosteppes for birds, recent agricultural changes, and possible future trends. The impact of these trends is evaluated, and policy suggestions are made for the conservation of biodiversity.

PSEUDOSTEPPES – PAST AND PRESENT

What are pseudosteppes?

The terms 'pseudosteppe', 'dry grassland' and 'extensive cereal crops' have been subject to numerous interpretations and definitions within the Mediterranean region. Steppes were mentioned in an ornithological context almost 40 years ago by Valverde (1957, 1958), who considered them to extend across a wide geographical area including North Africa and the Iberian Peninsula. His definition included landscapes predominantly comprising short chamaephytic shrubs (low growing perennials, with buds at or close to the ground), dry grassland dominated by annual therophytes (plants completing their life cycle rapidly under favourable conditions, and surviving as seeds under hostile conditions) and several dry crops. Other authors define Mediterranean steppes as comprising only arid or semi-arid areas (e.g. Margalef, 1947; Braun Blanquet & Bolós, 1957), whereas some consider only zones of natural vegetation, excluding crops (e.g. Suárez, 1981, 1983; Tellería et al., 1988a). However, most authors agree that 'pseudosteppes' are characterized by the presence of certain species of birds, linked with open spaces, scant vegetation, a flat or slightly undulating topography and Mediterranean climate, with average annual rainfall of less than 600–700 mm (De Juana et al., 1988; Suárez, 1988, 1994; De Juana, 1989).

There are three fundamental reasons for these varying definitions. First, the physical environment and vegetation of these landscapes differ considerably at local and regional levels: the lithology, type of soil and composition of vegetation are extremely variable, although it is generally accepted that the vegetation communities are dominated by low chamaephytes or annuals, with a high proportion of bare ground and almost complete absence of developed shrubs and trees.

Second, there is debate over the origin of these landscapes. The majority of authors believe they developed as a result of various human activities (fires, felling woodland and scrub, ploughing, grazing, etc.), most of which date back to the Roman period (Villar, 1925; Suárez et al., 1992). However, in the more arid zones in the south-east of the Peninsula and in areas with soils that do not favour vegetation development (e.g. certain chalky areas of the Ebro Valley), it is believed that, to a greater or lesser extent, these areas would have existed without human intervention (Braun Blanquet & Bolós, 1957; Saínz Ollero,

1988; Suárez et al., 1992). This hypothesis is supported by the presence of a suite of birds with marked adaptations to the steppe environment in Iberian archaeological deposits dating back to the Pleistocene age (great bustard Otis tarda and crested lark Galerida cristata in the Middle Pleistocene, great bustard, little bustard Tetrax tetrax, Thekla lark Galerida theklae and calandra lark Melanocorypha calandra in the Upper; Hernández, 1993, 1994).

Finally, there is no clear, specific separation between natural vegetation and agricultural areas. There is considerable regional variation, with large differences in both the proportion of agricultural land, grassland and shrub-steppes, and the way in which such areas are managed for livestock. Thus, periods between ploughing a particular field can vary between one and 7–8 years and livestock stocking levels between virtually nil and 2–3 head of sheep per hectare (0.3–0.4 livestock units (LUs) ha^{-1}). Hence, vegetation structure and field composition are very diverse in Iberian extensive cereal farming areas, owing to variations in the number of years of natural succession after ploughing, and variation in the spatial distribution of the various agricultural uses and crops (cultivated, stubble, fallow, Figure 1).

Because of this diversity, in this chapter we consider dry grasslands and extensive cereal crops in their broadest sense and describe them as 'pseudosteppes' (see González Bernáldez, 1988, for a discussion on this topic). This definition includes both the restricted range chamaephyte scrub and semi-arid grasslands as well as crops, i.e. the definition accepted by Valverde (1957), De Juana et al. (1988), De Juana (1989) and Goriup & Batten (1990). Similarly, owing to variation in the agricultural terms used regionally in Spain and elsewhere in Europe, for the purposes of this chapter we use the following terms: cultivated, arable and stubble (which have widely accepted meanings), winter fallow (fields left fallow over winter and ploughed and cultivated in February–April) and short–medium-term fallow (to describe arable fields left unploughed for a varying number of years, then ploughed in January–February prior to sowing; these fields are kept as grassland for livestock).

Pseudosteppe distribution

The distribution of pseudosteppes in Spain is vast (Figure 2). The areas where winter fallow is traditional practice now cover 4 million hectares (MAPA, 1994a), constituting approximately 20% of all cultivated land in Spain, or 50% of the total cereal growing area. In addition, there are approximately half a million hectares of dry grassland and more or less permanent chamaephyte shrub-steppes (Suárez, 1994). This figure (4.5 million hectares) is extremely high when compared with other EU countries, where similar landscapes exist, i.e. Portugal, France and Italy (see e.g. Petretti, 1988; Cheylan et al., 1990; Suárez, 1994). For reference purposes, the important bird areas (IBAs) on steppe-land cover approximately 2 057 000 ha in Spain, while they cover 59 000 ha in Portugal and France and 33 000 ha in Italy.

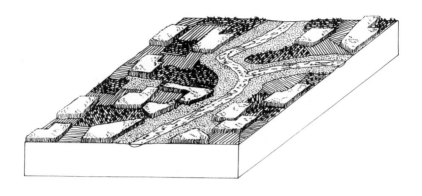

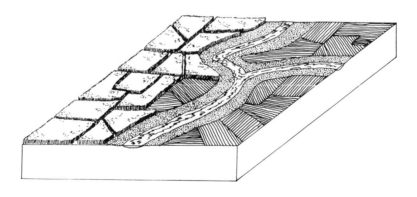

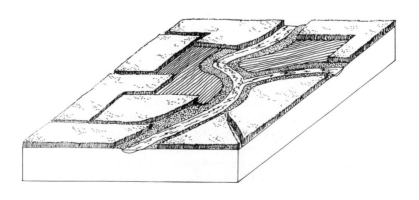

Figure 2 Distribution of main steppe areas in mainland Spain showing the location of the main provinces referred to in the text. (a) León; (b) Soria; (c) Zaragoza; (d) Cáceres; (e) Albacete; (f) Almería. Source: De Juana *et al.* (1993).

Figure 1 (*Opposite*) Block diagram of spatial distribution of agricultural land-use in three Iberian pseudosteppes with different levels of intensification. *Top* (La Serena, Extremadura): area where landholding concentration has not been introduced and where the short–medium-term fallow system is practised. *Middle* (Cobeña, Madrid): area where strip farming is practised and landholding concentration has not been introduced. *Bottom* (Tierra de Campos, Castilla y León): area where landholding concentration has been introduced and the area of fallow land has been considerably reduced.

In winter, sheep use short-medium term fallow and pastures, stubble, and cultivated land; in spring short-medium term fallow and pastures are used; in summer stubble is used; in autumn practically all areas (except those already ploughed) are used.

Fallow

Stubble

Cultivated

Short-medium term fallow and pastures

This chapter refers mainly to Spain, where there are the largest numbers and the highest populations of steppe bird species in the EU (De Juana *et al.*, 1988; Tucker, 1991).

The evolution of land-use

In the pseudosteppes, climate and soil types limit land-use to cereal cultivation together with winter and short–medium-term fallow and sheep farming. Land-use varies in different areas from a high proportion of cereal cultivation on the most productive land to a high proportion of extensive (low input) livestock rearing on the least productive land, with animals feeding on the short–medium-term and winter fallow (Majoral, 1987). The most widely grown crops are various dry cereals and pulse crops in a one, two- or three-year rotation system (Figure 3).

At present, this system is maintained only in some areas, the majority of which have been identified as IBAs (Grimmet & Jones, 1989; De Juana, 1990). Nevertheless, in a large proportion of these, especially in parts with the highest rainfall and/or best soils, there has been substantial intensification, and it is now common to find annual crops. The relative surface areas dedicated to each crop type have also changed: today in many areas, barley is the most widely grown crop, followed by wheat, with a few pulses grown for grain or fodder. As a result of EU subsidies, since Spain's entry into the EU and its progressive integration into the CAP, there has been a considerable increase in the area of sunflowers (2 ha, 668 ha, and 1 456 000 ha in Spain in 1945, 1980 and 1992 respectively; MAPA, 1994a) and, in regions of traditional cultivation (e.g. Aragón), in hard wheat (109 000 ha and 630 000 ha in Spain in 1988 and 1992 respectively; MAPA, 1994a).

The main types of livestock reared have been sheep, followed by goats, for the production of meat and occasionally milk. These animals used a variety of cultivated areas and pasture lands on a seasonal basis (Figure 1), although traditionally in many of these areas a proportion of the flocks were managed by local or long-distance transhumance (droving from summer to winter pastures, see e.g. Ruíz & Ruíz, 1986; Donázar *et al.*, Chapter 5). Other uses (apiculture, small game hunting, aromatic plant and mushroom gathering, etc.) had, and may still have, some local importance.

Consequently, the present landscape and use of the Iberian pseudosteppes is significantly different from that existing in former times (see a summary in Garrabou *et al.*, 1986; Majoral, 1987). The process of change started long before the application of the CAP in Spain, but the policy has certainly contributed. In addition to important socio-economic changes, since the 1960s, these modifications have been characterized by:

(1) substantial regional variation in total cultivated area;
(2) large changes in the relative areas of each crop;

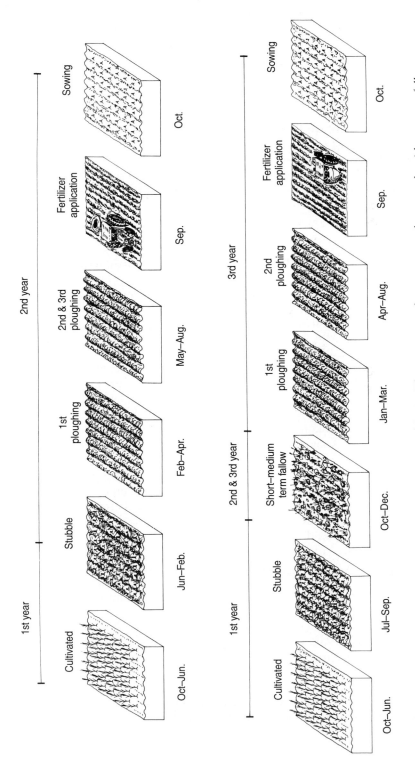

Figure 3 Approximate farming calendar for crop zones of Spain. The upper part shows an annual crop cycle with one year fallow, whilst the lower represents a short–medium-term two year fallow.

(3) a reduction in areas of winter and short–medium-term fallow;
(4) an increase in irrigation and crops grown under plastic.

As will be explained later, many changes in land-use are of significance to birds, mainly those relating to:

(1) concentration of landholdings;
(2) increased use of pesticides and inorganic fertilizers;
(3) cultivation of earlier growing crop varieties.

The last two factors influence the agricultural calendar by bringing forward the harvest date and reducing inter-cropping periods.

Effects of agricultural intensification upon pseudosteppe landscapes

The statistics relating to changes in land-use and management are very revealing, albeit only as broad indicators, since the majority of statistics are regional – and the municipal and district figures tend to have a considerable margin of error. Trends have differed in the major cereal producing regions. In Castilla y León and Castilla–La Mancha, cultivated areas have increased by 11.1 and 7.0% by 1992, taking the crop surface in 1975 as a reference point, i.e. the first year for which reliable data are available (MAPA, 1975, 1994a). In Andalucía, the area under cultivation has remained relatively stable (+ 0.2%), whilst in Extremadura and Aragón there have been reductions (28.7 and 8.0% respectively), although in Aragón there seems to have been some increase over the last couple of years.

The relative percentages of crops grown have also changed considerably: dry pulse crops for grain or green fodder, which were still important crops in the 1960s, have been largely replaced by cereals and oil-seed crops. This change is well illustrated by the relative differences in percentages of pulse crops grown in some of the typical pseudosteppe provinces. Between 1975 and 1992 there were significant decreases in percentages in four of the six provinces investigated (Almería: the percentage of pulses grown in 1992 was 58% of that in 1975; in León this figure was 50%; in Zaragoza, 35%; and in Cáceres, 41%). In the remaining two provinces, the area has either decreased slightly (Albacete, 78%) or remained fairly stable (Soria, 99%).

There has also been a reduction in the area of fallow land in all regions (Figure 4). Although in the 1950s half the total 'dry cultivation' area was fallow, in 1973 this figure had fallen to 38% and in 1992 to 29%. In the most prominent cereal areas of Castilla y León, fallow lands now cover only 15% of the cultivated area (Cabo & Manero, 1987). Simultaneously, cultivation has become more intensive in many areas. The area of irrigated land was 3 208 000 ha in 1992, representing a 161% increase since 1900, and a 77% increase since 1960.

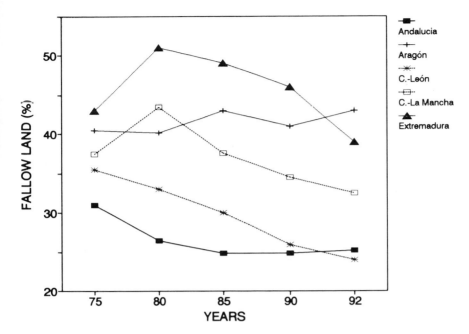

Figure 4 Development of fallow areas on a regional basis in the Spanish pseudosteppes. For geographical location of the provinces see Figure 2. Source: MAPA (1994a).

A similar trend took place for cultivation under plastic: in the province of Almería, areas doubled between 1960 and 1988, affecting numerous pseudosteppe areas (Manrique & De Juana, 1991).

A considerable increase in the use of inorganic fertilizers has been recorded, although in recent years this seems to have fallen back owing to the rise in prices. Thus, the use of inorganic fertilizers in Spain rose from virtually nil in the 1950s, to 620 000 million tonnes of nitrogen in 1970 and 1 080 000 million tonnes in 1990 (Díaz et al., 1994). However, the use of inorganic fertilizers in Spain is falling, and is still very low compared with countries with more intensive agriculture (e.g. average application rates of 39, 124, 185 and 552 kg N ha^{-1} in Spain, France, Germany and Holland respectively (Díaz et al., 1994); application rates in Spanish dry cereal farming areas are about 75 kg N ha^{-1} (MAPA, 1994b)).

Finally, the amalgamation of small landholdings is estimated to have affected 5.5 million hectares between 1956 and 1984, resulting in a twofold increase in the average plot size over the period 1962–89 (Barceló et al., 1995).

Trends in livestock numbers are difficult to establish owing to the lack of reliable statistics. Although in the 1970s sheep stocking levels in the majority of pseudosteppe areas fell to what were possibly their lowest numbers since the 1940s, there seems to have been a subsequent recovery or even increase in many areas. In addition, livestock management systems have become more intensive.

There have been increases in stocking levels and supplementary feeding, and landholdings have been fenced off, resulting in partial-inhousing of flocks (see for example in La Serena, Extremadura; Peco & Suárez, 1993).

On a landscape scale, these changes have resulted in a reduction in habitat diversity, and this is believed to have had negative consequences for the populations and conservation status of pseudosteppe birds, as discussed below.

UNIQUE BIRD SPECIES IN DECLINE

The composition of bird communities within the Iberian pseudosteppes varies considerably, both within and between regions. It has been postulated (Suárez *et al.*, 1992) that the breeding bird communities of the Iberian Peninsula can be considered to occupy one of two vegetation/climatic gradients: herbaceous–shrub-steppe and continental–rainy. In the former gradient, the bird communities in crops and chamaephyte shrub-steppes mark the extremes, characterized respectively by the appearance of species such as the calandra and thekla larks. The communities of arid shrub-steppes in south-eastern Iberia, and chamaephyte shrubs on the high plateaux ('páramos') in the centre of the Peninsula, mark extremes in the latter gradient, with skylark *Alauda arvensis* and lesser short-toed lark *Calandrella rufescens* as typical bird species. These communities can be typified and sub-divided into four broad groups: semi-arid shrub-steppes, 'páramo' shrub-steppes, semi-arid pasture lands and, interspersed and related to all these, cereal and dry crop farming (Suárez, 1981, 1994; Tellería *et al.*, 1988a).

Breeding birdlife comprises both birds that nest on the ground, or on very low shrubs, i.e. truly 'pseudosteppe' species, and others that nest in buildings, on ledges and gullies or in woodland and groves, but feed mainly in dry crop areas. It is obviously more difficult to define the latter group precisely. Table 1 shows the most characteristic species in both groups in the Iberian Peninsula (De Juana, 1989).

The pseudosteppe supports not only large numbers of birds, but also many bird species of high conservation value (De Juana *et al.*, 1988, 1993; Goriup, 1988; Tucker, 1991). Within Europe, certain of these species are found only in the Iberian Peninsula (black-bellied sandgrouse *Pterocles orientalis*, Dupont's lark *Chersophilus duponti*, lesser short-toed lark, trumpeter finch *Bucanetes githagineus*). Numbers of most other pseudosteppe species found in Spain are higher than elsewhere in Europe. This is clearly reflected in the recent BirdLife International review of the conservation status of the birds of Europe (Tucker & Heath, 1994; Tucker, Chapter 4). Of a total of 52 species found in this habitat throughout Europe, Spain has the largest populations of 33 (64%) of these. Only Turkey and Russia have comparable or larger populations of some species, but these occur mainly outside Europe.

Table 1 Birds of Iberian steppe environments including typical steppe birds (ground nesters) and other species that use steppes during the breeding season

(a) Species for which largest European populations are found in Spain

Ground nesters	Others
Red-legged partridge *Alectoris rufa*	Griffon vulture *Gyps fulvus*
Quail *Coturnix coturnix*	Egyptian vulture *Neophron percnopterus*
Little bustard *Tetrax tetrax*	Lesser kestrel *Falco naumanni*
Great bustard *Otis tarda*	Peregrine falcon *Falco peregrinus*
Stone curlew *Burhinus oedicnemus*	Barn owl *Tyto alba*
Collared pratincole *Glareola pratincola*	Little owl *Athene noctua*
Black-bellied sandgrouse *Pterocles orientalis*	European bee-eater *Merops apiaster*
Pin-tailed sandgrouse *Pterocles alchata*	European roller *Coracias garrulus*
Dupont's lark *Chersophilus duponti*	Wood lark *Lullula arborea*
Calandra lark *Melanocorypha calandra*	Black wheatear *Oenanthe leucura*
Short-toed lark *Calandrella brachydactyla*	Great grey shrike *Lanius excubitor*
Lesser short-toed lark *Calandrella rufescens*	Chough *Pyrrhocorax pyrrhocorax*
Crested lark *Galerida cristata*	Jackdaw *Corvus monedula*
Thekla lark *Galerida theklae*	Spotless starling *Sturnus unicolor*
Tawny pipit *Anthus campestris*	Serin *Serinus serinus*
Black-eared wheatear *Oenanthe hispanica*	Linnet *Cardeulis cannabina*
Corn bunting *Miliaria calandra*	
Trumpeter finch *Bucanetes githagineus*	

(b) Other species

Ground nesters	Others
Hen harrier *Circus cyaneus*	White stork *Ciconia ciconia*
Montagu's harrier *Circus pygargus*	Kestrel *Falco tinnunculus*
Skylark *Alauda arvensis*	Rock dove *Columba livia*
Northern wheatear *Oenanthe oenanthe*	Stock dove *Columba oenas*
Fan-tailed warbler *Cisticola juncidis*	Hoopoe *Upupa epops*
Spectacled warbler *Sylvia conspicillata*	Swallow *Hirundo rustica*
	Lesser grey shrike *Lanius minor*
	Raven *Corvus corax*
	House sparrow *Passer domesticus*
	Tree sparrow *Passer monyanus*
	Rock sparrow *Petronia petronia*
	Goldfinch *Carduelis carduelis*

Population data from Tucker & Heath (1994).

Population trends

Tucker & Heath (1994), state that 38% of total European birds are Species of European Conservation Concern (SPECs). For pseudosteppe species this figure reaches almost 81% (Table 2, and see Tucker, Chapter 4). Without doubt, this is one of the habitat types within which the greatest proportion of regularly occurring species are SPECs. The proportion of SPECs is greater for ground-nesting species (85.7% vs 66.7% for the other species). Seventy-six per cent of the 21 ground-nesting SPECs, and 38% of the 21 SPECs nesting elsewhere, are classified as Endangered, Vulnerable or Rare. Thus, in total, pseudosteppe habitats support four Endangered, 17 Vulnerable, three Rare and 11 Declining species, with only seven which are considered SPECs with Secure populations and ten species which do not achieve SPEC classification.

Two of the SPECs associated with pseudosteppes, the great bustard and the lesser kestrel *Falco naumanni*, are globally threatened species (Collar *et al.*, 1994), with one near-threatened, the little bustard.

The population trends between 1970 and 1990 for the 42 SPECs associated

---

Table 2. *Notes*

Source: Tucker & Heath (1994).

*Species of European Conservation Concern (SPECs) have their category indicated in brackets: (1) species of global conservation concern; (2) concentrated in Europe and with an unfavourable conservation status; (3) not concentrated in Europe but with an unfavourable conservation status, and (4) concentrated in Europe and with a favourable conservation status.

The European threat status was defined as follows (see Tucker & Heath (1994)). *Secure*: population more than 10 000 breeding pairs and in neither moderate nor large decline, not localized. *Declining*: population in moderate decline and population more than 10 000 breeding pairs. *Rare*: population in neither moderate nor major decline but consisting of fewer than 10 000 breeding pairs. *Vulnerable*: population in major decline and consisting of more than 10 000 breeding pairs, or in moderate decline and consisting of fewer than 10 000 pairs, or population in neither moderate nor in large decline but consisting of fewer than 2500 pairs. *Endangered*: population in major decline and consisting of fewer than 10 000 pairs, or in moderate decline and consisting of fewer than 2500 pairs, or in neither moderate nor major decline but consisting of fewer than 250 pairs.

Trend data was defined as: *Moderate decline*: applied to a breeding or wintering population which has declined in size or range by at least 20% in at least 33–65% of the population or by at least 50% in 12–24% of the population between 1970 and 1990, and where the total size of populations that declined is greater than the total size of populations that increased. *Large decline*: applied to a breeding or wintering population which has declined in size or range by at least 20% in at least 66% of the population or by at least 50% in at least 25% of the population between 1970 and 1990, and where the total size of populations that declined is greater than the total size of populations that increased.

For moderate and large increases similar criteria have been used, i.e. replace decline with increase in the previous definitions.

Table 2 Conservation status of Iberian pseudosteppe birds*

Ground nesters	Others
Non-SPECs	
Northern wheatear	Rock dove
Fan-tailed warbler	Hoopoe
Spectacled warbler	Raven
	House sparrow
	Tree sparrow
	Rock sparrow
	Goldfinch
Secure	
Montagu's harrier (4)	Stock dove (4)
Corn bunting (4)	Jackdaw (4)
	Spotless starling (4)
	Serin (4)
	Linnet (4)
Declining	
Great bustard (1)	Kestrel (3)
Calandra lark (3)	Barn owl (3)
Crested lark (3)	Little owl (3)
	European bee-eater (3)
	European roller (3)
	Swallow (3)
	Lesser grey shrike (3)
	Great grey shrike (3)
Rare	
Trumpeter finch (3)	Griffon vulture (3)
	Peregrine falcon (3)
Vulnerable	
Hen harrier (3)	White stork (2)
Red-legged partridge (2)	Lesser kestrel (1)
Quail (3)	Woodlark (2)
Little bustard (2)	Chough (3)
Stone curlew (3)	
Black-bellied sandgrouse (3)	
Dupont's lark (3)	
Thekla lark (3)	
Short-toed lark (3)	
Lesser short-toed lark (3)	
Skylark (3)	
Tawny pipit (3)	
Black-eared wheatear (2)	
Endangered	
Collared pratincole (3)	Egyptian vulture (3)
Pin-tailed sandgrouse (3)	Black wheatear (3)

Table 3 Population trends between 1970 and 1990 in Europe and Spain for the 42 Species of European Conservation Concern (SPECs) associated with the Iberian pseudos-teppes

	Number and percentage of species		
	Ground nesters	Others	Total
Europe			
Large decline	15 (71.4%)	6 (28.6%)	21 (50.0%)
Moderate decline	3 (14.3%)	8 (38.1%)	11 (26.2%)
Population < 10 000 pairs	1 (4.8%)	2 (9.5%)	3 (7.1%)
Others	2 (9.5%)	5 (23.8%)	7 (16.7%)
Spain			
Large decline	3 (14.3%)	1 (4.8%)	4 (9.6%)
Moderate decline	14 (66.7%)	12 (57.1%)	26 (61.9%)
Stable or fluctuating	2 (9.5%)	1 (4.8%)	3 (7.1%)
Moderate increase	2 (9.5%)	6 (28.6%)	8 (19.0%)
Large increase	0	1 (4.8%)	1 (2.4%)

Source: Tucker & Heath (1994).

with the Iberian pseudosteppe areas are disturbing (Table 3). In Europe, three-quarters of these have undergone appreciable declines (86% of ground-nesting species). In Spain, 72% of the 33 SPECs appear to be in decline (81% of the ground-nesting species). In many cases, accurate figures concerning population trends are lacking due to the absence of large-scale, long-term population monitoring programmes. However, the information that does exist agrees with the broadly held view that populations of steppe birds are decreasing rapidly, both in Europe as a whole and in Spain (e.g. Goriup, 1988; Martínez & Purroy, 1993; De Juana *et al.*, 1993).

Population trends of globally threatened species are better documented, and show significant declines. In the 1950s, the Spanish population of the great bustard was estimated at around 25 000 birds, compared with only 10 000 in 1981/82 (Ena & Martínez, 1988 – although the latter census may have been deficient and under-estimated the current population which is considered to be between 13 500 and 14 000 birds – Alonso & Alonso, 1990a). The distribution of the little bustard also seems to have undergone a significant reduction in Iberia and, although it is still very common in Castilla–La Mancha, Extrema-dura and the Alentejo, it is already scarce and very localized throughout the whole of the northern half of the Peninsula and in Andalucía (De Juana & Martínez, unpublished data). Similarly, the lesser kestrel population is believed to have fallen from more than 100 000 pairs in Spain at the beginning of the 1960s (Bijleveld, 1974), to 20 000–50 000 during the 1970s (Garzón, 1977) and a mere 4000–5000 in 1989 (González & Merino, 1990).

Figure 5 Male great bustard in spring plumage in fallow land, Spain. The population of globally threatened great bustards has declined from an estimated 25 000 birds in the 1950s to an estimated 13 500–14 000 birds (1990). (Photo by C.H. Gomersall/RSPB.)

Amongst the Endangered species in Europe, the collared pratincole *Glareola pratincola* has decreased in Doñana (Andalucía), where perhaps one half of the European population is located and where a large number of the birds nest in or feed on crops (Calvo, 1994). The pin-tailed sandgrouse *Pterocles alchata* has decreased significantly in various areas (Estrada & Curcó, 1991; Pleguezuelos, 1991), whereas the Egyptian vulture *Neophron percnopterus* is generally considered to be stable (Perea *et al.*, 1990). Finally, the black wheatear *Oenanthe leucura* may be decreasing, although there is little quantitative information (Soler, 1994) and its occupation of cultivated habitats is only marginal.

Wintering birds

The Iberian pseudosteppes are of even greater significance when one considers their role as wintering grounds for birds from other European countries (Tellería, 1988). Although the overall species composition within a region does

Figure 6 Red kite in flight. The majority of western European red kites winter in Spain, and many occupy cereal areas. (Photo by M. Wilding/RSPB.)

not generally change substantially between summer and winter (Suárez *et al.*, 1992), there may be considerable regional differences in relative species densities. The majority of birds migrate from regions with more extreme winter climates; milder climes shelter a high number of pre-Saharan wintering species (Suárez & Saez-Royuela, 1983; Arroyo & Tellería, 1984; Curcó & Estrada, 1987; De Juana, 1988a; Tellería *et al.*, 1988a,b; see also Tellería *et al.*, 1988c). Regional changes in relative species densities between summer and winter, and overall changes in winter densities, are temperature-linked (Tellería *et al.*, 1988a). Several species of particular conservation interest occupy the Iberian pseudosteppes during winter. The majority of western European red kites *Milvus milvus* and cranes *Grus grus* winter in Spain (approximately 60 000 and 50 000–60 000 birds respectively), with many red kites and most of the cranes occupying cereal areas (SEO/BirdLife, unpublished data; Alonso & Alonso, 1990b).

Habitat selection

An understanding of the habitat selection and requirements of pseudosteppe birds is prerequisite to their conservation. The majority of species require a certain diversity of land-uses and agricultural substrates, and requirements vary between species. There are also specific differences at the level of micro-habitat selection. Such detailed knowledge is currently available only for some species (Table 4), but is required to form the basis for forecasting the possible consequences of current and future agricultural policies (but see Rotenberry, 1981).

Table 4 Agrarian substrata selected by steppe birds during the breeding season and winter. Only species with habitat selection sufficiently well-known are included

Species	Breeding season	Winter season	References
Red-legged partridge	Pastures, cultivated land	Pastures, cultivated land	Tellería et al. (1988b)
Quail	Cultivated, pastures	–	Tellería et al. (1988b)
Little bustard	Short–medium fallow land, pulse crops	–	Martínez (1994)
Great bustard	Cultivated, sown, pastures, fallow land, pulse crops	Stubble, pulse crops	Martínez (1991a,b)
Stone curlew	Pastures and short–medium fallow	Pastures with broom	Barros (1995)
Black-bellied sandgrouse	Pastures, short–medium fallow	Pastures, short–medium fallow	De Borbón (1995)
Pin-tailed sandgrouse	Short–medium fallow land, pulse crops	Stubble, cultivated and fallow land	Guadalfajara & Tutor (1987)
Dupont's lark	Shrub-steppes	Shrub-steppes, agricultural land	Garza & Suárez (1990); Suárez & Garza (1989)
Calandra lark	Pastures, fallow, cultivated land	Sown, stubble, fallow	Hernández et al. (1995); Tellería et al. (1988b)
Short-toed lark	Fallow and short–medium fallow	–	Tellería et al. (1988b)
Lesser short-toed lark	Shrubs, halophytic shrubs	Sown, fallow, halophytic shrubs	Hernández et al. (1995); Suárez & Sáez-Royuela (1983)
Crested lark	Fallow, pastures	Ploughed land, stubble	Tellería et al. (1988b)
Thekla lark	Shrubs	Shrubs	Tellería et al. (1988b)
Tawny pipit	Shrubs, pastures	–	Tellería et al. (1988b)
Black-eared wheatear	Shrubs	–	Tellería et al. (1988b)
Corn bunting	Pastures	Stubble	Tellería et al. (1988b)
Skylark	Pastures, fallow	Arable, fallow	Tellería et al. (1988b)
Northern wheatear	Pastures	–	Tellería et al. (1988b)
Spectacled warbler	Shrubs, halophytic shrubs	Shrubs, halophytic shrubs	Hernández et al. (1995)

Possibly, more information is available for the great bustard than other species (Alonso & Alonso, 1990a; Martínez, 1991a,b). The great bustard shows a preference for flat areas with high visibility and absence of human infra-structure (roads, villages, etc.). Within such areas, a seasonal habitat selection has been recorded: cultivated and sown areas are preferred during the spring, as nesting habitat; pastures and short–medium-term fallow areas are used during the chicks' growth period; in winter, stubble is selected, and leguminous crops are preferred throughout the year. Great bustards avoid the most intensively managed sectors, such as irrigated areas, orchards and sunflower fields.

Although the structural landscape requirements of the little bustard are similar to those of the great bustard, little bustards appear to be less sensitive to human activities, and prefer a somewhat different range of land-uses. During the breeding season there is a positive selection for short–medium-term fallow land and leguminous crops, with an avoidance of cereal crops, arable and shrubby areas (Martínez, 1994).

These preferences are similar to those of the pin-tailed sandgrouse during the breeding season. The height and structure of crops appear to influence this habitat selection (Guadalfajara & Tutor, 1987). Throughout the rest of the year, the pin-tailed sandgrouse uses a variety of agricultural areas, moving from stubble at the end of the breeding season, to cultivated areas as crops begin to develop, and on to fallow land when the former have grown (Guadalfajara & Tutor, 1987).

The stone curlew *Burhinus oedicnemus* uses pastures and short–medium-term fallow land during the breeding season, and it tends to avoid pastures with Spanish broom *Retama sphaerocarpa* (Barros, 1995). This situation is partly reversed during the post-breeding period, when they actively seek broom areas, avoiding sown, arable and fallow areas (Barros, 1995).

In the Iberian south-west, the lesser kestrel selects grassland, cereal crops and melon fields, and avoids tree crops and sunflower fields. The declining popu-lation of this species (see earlier) has been linked with the loss of low-intensity crop farming and pasture land (Donázar *et al.*, 1993).

Dupont's lark is typically associated with shrub-steppes, and selects areas with shrub cover of approximately 20–40 cm average height and 30% ground cover during the breeding season (Garza & Suárez, 1990), avoiding sparse crops and pasture lands. Similar areas are occupied in winter (Suárez & Garza, 1989).

Other species of sedentary passerines in central Peninsular pseudosteppes appear to have a more complex behaviour throughout the year (Table 4). Whilst the majority are found in the chamaephyte shrub-steppe areas and pasture lands during the breeding season, in the post-reproductive period and during the winter they favour stubble and fallow lands, avoiding arable areas. This is the case with the skylark and corn bunting *Miliaria calandra* (Tellería *et al.*, 1988b).

What we know of the seasonal changes in species densities and habitat selection leads us to two basic conclusions for bird conservation. First, regional variations in species composition and density suggest that pseudosteppes must be preserved in a variety of different regions. Second, the localized, seasonal variations in preferences for different pseudosteppe habitats, crops and substrates necessitates the maintenance of this diversity. Any reduction in diversity could result in the loss of seasonally important resources for many species. Nonetheless, the populations of some species could benefit from the expansion of certain habitats, e.g. shrub expansion may favour Dupont's lark (Garza & Suárez, 1990). However, intensification, with its accompanying reduced land-use diversity and the presence of irrigated land, would benefit only species linked to human activities, generally of low conservation value (Díaz et al., 1993).

Factors which are considered to have had a negative impact upon bird populations in the pseudosteppes (Table 5) have been recorded by Yanes (1994) and other authors (Tucker & Heath, 1994). The most significant factor, affecting the greatest number of species (62%) is irrigation, followed by afforestation or scrub regeneration (57%), the increase of cultivated areas (52%), the use of pesticides (38%) and changes in stocking densities (38%). However, factors affecting these species vary between areas and are largely unknown. For instance, the disappearance of pin-tailed sandgrouse from Almeria (south-eastern Andalucia) has been associated with the loss of cultivated areas (Manrique & De Juana, 1991), while its decline in the Ebro Valley seems linked to intensification (Estrada & Curcó, 1991). Black-bellied sandgrouse has almost disappeared from Layna Paramos (Soria, Aragón) owing to unknown factors. Shrub encroachment may have been a factor, but it has also been claimed that nest predation and changes in agrarian management have detrimentally affected black-bellied sandgrouse (J. Herranz, pers. comm.). A good example of the relationship between steppe birds and traditional management is given by the lesser kestrel. Lesser kestrel reproductive success has been found to be positively related to the proportion of the area surrounding the nesting colony that is occupied by its selected feeding habitats, i.e. traditional crops, long-term fallow land and pastures (Donázar et al., 1993; Hiraldo et al., 1993).

The actual impacts of specific agricultural changes on most species remain little known. In general, authors have dealt with effects under very broad headings (e.g. intensification of crop farming), and there are few detailed studies on the impacts of specific actions (e.g. reduction of short–medium-term fallow land or area of leguminous crops). Consequently, it is essential that specific habitat selection studies be undertaken in order to develop models for use in forecasting the future prospects for bird species in the Iberian pseudosteppes.

Protection status of pseudosteppe areas

Despite the obvious significance of pseudosteppes for bird conservation, very few of these areas receive any type of legal protection, either national or regional. Table 6 shows the extent of statutory protected areas from the latest

Table 5 Main causes of population declines in pseudosteppes species

Species	Increase in cultivated areas	Reduction in cultivated areas	Crop changes	Reduced fallow	Irrigation or drainage	Cultivation under plastic	Use of early varieties	Pesticides and fertilizers	Change in stocking densities	Electricity cables	Persecution, hunting, disturbance	Afforestation, regrowth of scrub	Predators
Hen harrier	x*				x*				x*		x*	x*	
Montagu's harrier													
Lesser kestrel		x*	x*					x*	x*		x*		
Red-legged partridge		x*		x*			x†				x*	x*	
Quail	x*							x*			x*		
Little bustard	x*†				x*		x*	x*†			x*	x†	x*
Great bustard	x*				x*†		x*†	x*†		x*†	x*		
Stone curlew	x*				x*†		x*†	x*†			x*	x*	x†
Collared pratincole					x*†								
Black-bellied sandgrouse	x*				x*†			x*	x*				
Pin-tailed sandgrouse	x†				x*	x†						x*	
Dupont's lark	x*			x*	x*				x†			x*†	
Calandra lark					x*						x*	x*	
Short-toed lark					x*							x*	x†
Lesser short-toed lark	x*				x*†	x*			x*				
Crested lark			x*		x*			x*	x*			x*	x*†
Thekla lark					x*				x*			x*	x†
Skylark			x*	x*			x*	x*				x*	
Tawny pipit	x*												
Black-eared wheatear											x*		
Trumpeter finch													x*

See Table 1 for scientific names.
*Tucker & Heath (1994).
†Yanes (1994).

Table 6 Pseudosteppe areas in the inventory of Spanish Special Protection Areas (SPAs)

Andalucía	
Cabo de Gata Níjar	Natural Park (1987) 26 000 ha
Punta Entinas-Sabinar	Natural Space (1989) 1960 ha
	Nature Reserve (1989) 785 ha
Desierto de Tabernas	Natural Space (1989) 11 625 ha
Cataluña	
Mas de Melons	Partial Nature Reserve (1987) 1140 ha
Timoneda d'Alfès	Wildlife Nature Reserve (1990) 107 ha
Navarra	
Rincón del Bu	Nature Reserve (1988) 460 ha
Murcia	
Saladares del Guadalentín	Protected Natural Space (1992) with no defined borders

Differences in legally protected areas depend upon regional legislation. Protection status may vary and is controlled by regional regulations.
Source: Centro de Investigación Fernando González Bernáldez (1995).

inventory available (Centro de Investigación Fernando González Bernáldez, 1995). In some, such as the Parque Natural de Cabo de Gata-Níjar, a large part of their area comprises biotopes which are not strictly pseudosteppes, e.g. wetlands, gullies and scrub. However, there are other protected areas which are not included in Table 6 but do have significant pseudosteppe areas, such as the Parque Natural de las Hoces del Río Duratón (Castilla y León), the Parque Regional del Sureste (Madrid) or the Parque Natural del Entorno de Doñana (Andalucía). Consequently, it is difficult to determine the precise extent of protected pseudosteppe land. The seven sites in Table 6 have an overall area of less than 50 000 ha, out of almost 3 million hectares of protected land in Spain. It is evident that there is relatively little interest in conservation of this type of habitat. The Spanish inventory of Important Bird Areas contains no fewer than 60 pseudosteppe areas, with a total land surface of more than 2.5 million hectares (De Juana, 1988b), almost none of which is protected.

A few other important pseudosteppe areas may be considered to be partially protected under other designations, such as the National Hunting Reserves (Reserva Nacional de Caza – Lagunas de Villafáfila, 32 682 ha), National Hunting Refuges (Refugio Nacional de Caza – La Lomaza de Belchite, 961 ha; Laguna de Gallocanta) or Controlled Hunting Zones (Zona de Caza Controlada – Sierra de Fuentes). Finally, two ornithological reserves, 'El Planerón' in Belchite (some 600 ha) and 'Las Amoladeras' in Cabo de Gata (some 900 ha) are managed by a non-governmental organization (Spanish Ornithological Society (SEO)/BirdLife International).

Overall, the proportion of pseudosteppes that have legal protection is far from sufficient at present, especially as their importance for biodiversity, and the need to conserve them, have been recognized since the 1960s (Viedma *et al.*, 1976). This lack of protection emphasizes the need for measures to encourage environmentally sustainable uses of pseudosteppes across wider areas.

THE SOCIO-ECONOMICS OF PSEUDOSTEPPE FARMING SYSTEMS

Agriculture and fishing represented 3.4% of Spain's total Gross Domestic Product (GDP) at market prices in 1993 (MAPA, 1994a), and in 1994 some 9.8% of the active population were working in the sector (Banco de España, 1995). This is a relatively high percentage compared with the rest of the EU (6.2% average in the EU in 1991; Eurostat, 1994). In representative Iberian pseudosteppe regions, 20% of the active population work in farming.

From a historical perspective, there has been a dramatic reduction in the percentage of the active population working in agriculture. In the 1950s, in many regions, this sector employed more than 50% of the active population, and this gradually declined over the next 30 years. After Spain joined the EEC in 1986, this process accelerated, with a reduction to 24% by 1991 (MAPA, 1985, 1994a). Also, it is notable that the farming population is ageing: in the primary sector (agriculture and mining), 45% of the population is aged over 50, whereas amongst farmers only 25% are under the age of 30 (MAPA, 1990).

Owing to the soil and climatic conditions, the farming activities of the Iberian pseudosteppes are characterized by low productivity. In the dry cereal areas, gross yields do not exceed 4 t ha^{-1}, with an average production of below 2.5 t ha^{-1} (MAPA, 1994a). In contrast, the average cereal production in the remaining EU Member Countries is around 6 t ha^{-1} (Tió, 1991).

Net returns to these farms are also very low. Taking into consideration intervention prices, it has been calculated that profits for typical farms are in the order of 125 ECUs ha^{-1} (Naveso, 1992; Naveso & Groves-Reines, 1992; Naveso & Fernández, 1993, see Table 7 for an area of Castilla y León). These low yields and net returns largely determine the viability of such farms, and explain the two main trends which have developed here in recent decades: (1) the increase in average farm size, and/or (2) irrigation to increase production.

The average farm size is growing both through concentration of landholdings and a reduction in the active farming population. The main consequence for bird conservation has been a reduction in diversity of land-use (Díaz *et al.*, 1993).

Irrigation generally results in significantly increased production. With cereals, harvests double, while for sugarbeet, for example, they triple (MAPA, 1990). Nonetheless, the increase in revenue and profits is in many cases not obvious. One consequence of the investments made by farmers in order to increase production has been the increase in debt, which grew by almost 50% during the

Table 7 Profitability of farms growing barley by dry farming and irrigation methods in the Tierra de Campos (Castilla y León)

	Production of barley	
	Dry	Irrigated
Fixed costs (ptas ha^{-1})		
Machinery*	6 500	6 500
Taxes	1 300	2 800
Agricultural insurance	1 800	1 800
Social security†	3 410	3 410
Storage (1 pta kg^{-1})	2 400	4 300
Land rental‡	1 900	6 900
Irrigation (spray-well)	–	9 000
Variable costs		
Seed	5 250	5 625
Seed fertilizer	7 000	11 000
Cover fertilizer	5 500	8 800
Herbicides	2 000	2 000
Pesticides	900	900
Harvesting	5 000	6 000
Total costs	42 960	69 035
Income (1991/92 price)	60 000	100 800
Profit	17 040	31 765

*This includes depreciation, insurance and repairs.
†According to the Social Security System for a self-employed farmer.
‡Calculated using the average value of the farms (47 ha), together with the weighted average of leased land, considering the frequency distribution of the various farm sizes. Values expressed in 1992 pesetas.
Source: Naveso & Groves-Reines (1992).

period 1987–91, reaching approximately 11 million ECUs (Egdell, 1993). In some cases this has led to a situation where once publicly funded investment has been made, the farmer cannot pay for the costs of the distribution network of the irrigation system, and/or questions its economic profitability. In such cases the irrigation infrastructure may remain unused (San Agustín, 1993).

The other important use of the Iberian pseudosteppes, low-intensity sheep rearing, represents an important element in the pseudosteppe economy in areas where the climate or soil conditions are more limiting. Geographically, the regions in which this use plays a major role are located in the centre ('páramos' of the Iberian system), north-east (semi-arid areas in the Ebro Valley) and the south-east and some areas in the south-west (Extremadura). In the first of these

Figure 7 Flock of sheep in pseudosteppe area in Vilafafilla, Spain. Low-intensity sheep rearing is an important use of the Iberian pseudosteppes, especially in areas with lower production potential. (Photo by J. Dixon.)

areas, studied by Peco & Suárez (1993), there is usually mixed arable and livestock farming, with extensive sheep rearing for meat complemented by extensive dry crop farming. In recent decades, intensification has been brought about mainly through an increase in the average flock size, which rose from 50–100 sheep in the 1960s to 300–350, an increase in the average number of pregnancies per ewe, and the average number of lambs per pregnancy. In parallel, there has been a decrease in the zones under crops, leading to a simplification of the landscape and reduction in land-use diversity. The livestock are fed partially on forage obtained from the cultivation of cereals and leguminous crops within the farm, supplemented with bought-in feed. Economic analysis of these mixed farms, and of the cereal farms in other pseudosteppe areas, shows very low economic profitability. Thus, annual returns in the agricultural sector are around 80 ECUs ha^{-1}, whilst in the livestock sector they are of the order of 34 ECUs ha^{-1} (Peco & Suárez, 1993). These results are similar to those encountered in economic studies in the livestock sector in pseudosteppe areas of the Valle del Ebro (Naveso & Fernández, 1993).

It must be noted that approximately one-third of gross earnings from livestock farming in these areas comes from CAP subsidies granted to the sheep sector. The existence of these subsidies, which form a significant and predictable source of income, has on occasions led to an increase in stocking levels in less favourable areas. In La Serena (Extremadura) stocking densities increased from

1.5 to 2–3 head of sheep per hectare between 1986 and 1991, resulting in over-grazing and a local deterioration in the quality of pasture and stock (Naveso & Fernández, 1993, although see also Malo et al., 1994). Sheep farming also appears to have spread since the 1980s in the Sistema Ibérico 'páramos', although densities are still low (0.8 head ha^{-1}). This has been aggravated by the disappearance of transhumance and the declining use of stubble as pasture land. However, even with such increases, these stocking levels, less than 0.3 LU ha^{-1}, are much lower than the usual levels in the majority of semi-natural European habitats.

In summary, from an economic perspective, the pseudosteppes are fairly marginal. The fact that dry cereal farms, low-intensity livestock farms and mixed farms all have low profit margins means that traditional and current agricultural uses depend on income obtained through subsidies. This obviously results in a high degree of uncertainty regarding their stability and future.

FUTURE SCENARIOS

The 1992 CAP reform, which particularly affected the cereal sector, had a major impact on the economy of pseudosteppe farms. With the reduction in inter-vention prices in sectors such as cereals and oil-seed crops, their economic viability became dependent to a large extent on the compensation payments agreed per hectare based on regional production levels. These compensation payments, fixed at the current favourable ECU exchange rates for farmers, together with the instability of farms referred to earlier, largely explain the extraordinary increase in the area of sunflower cultivation during the 1992/93 season at the expense of cereal farming in marginal areas.

At present it is difficult to predict the future of farming in the pseudosteppes (see e.g. Gutiérrez et al., 1993; Suárez, 1994). However, two contrasting trends appear to be developing. These are the abandonment of farming in the economically more marginal areas and greater intensification in more productive areas. In addition there is a more recent trend towards the replacement of pasture land and low-intensity cereal cropping with tree crops, mainly olives and almonds.

The abandonment of agricultural activity is taking place within a disintegrat-ing social fabric, where the population is old, and farms show low profitability. Under these conditions, and assuming no further reforms by the EU in the cereal sector, the afforestation of agricultural land promoted by EC Reg. 2080/92, especially with conifers, could displace cereal cultivation and extensive livestock farming. Other factors, such as the existence of an increasing proportion of aged farmers working part-time in agriculture, and the high proportion of tenant farmers, may increase the impact of afforestation in the pseudosteppes. This is due to the lower labour and annual investment requirements of tree plantations. As a result, many areas in the Sistema Ibérico 'páramos' or the semi-arid south-east could easily find themselves in this situation in the not too distant future. However, from a production perspective, if the subsidies are eliminated, the majority of such replanting is of doubtful economic viability as trees grow slowly under such arid conditions.

The second trend is that of intensification in areas with climate and soil conditions less marginal for agriculture. This can take place via three different mechanisms:

(1) increased use of agro-chemicals;
(2) concentration of landholdings;
(3) transformation from dry to irrigated crop production.

The future impact of trends in agricultural chemical use are difficult to predict in dryland farming. On the one hand, even assuming the hypothetical stabiliz-ation of cereal prices, with the small economic margin, and high agro-chemical prices (see Table 7), it is possible that in many pseudosteppe areas agro-chemical use may not increase. In fact, the growth in the use of fertilizers slowed down for the first time in the 1980s (MAPA, 1990). However, it is likely that in certain areas, where there are still high percentages of fallow and short–medium-term fallow land (more than 50% of the area), many farmers are trying to increase the land under cultivation by using agro-chemicals.

Concentration of landholdings is another factor which may significantly influence intensification. In both the Community Support Frameworks and the Single Programming Documents approved by the EU for regional development covered by Objective 1 (development and structural adjustment of the poorest regions) and Objective 5b (promoting the development of rural areas) in Spain during the period 1994–1999, one of the main types of development considered for European Agricultural Guidance and Guarantee Fund-guidance (FEOGA) financing is the concentration of landholdings. In Objective 1 regions alone, which include a large part of the pseudosteppe regions of Spain, it is anticipated that the concentration of landholdings will affect some 300 000 ha (CEC, 1994). Furthermore, the level of employment in the agricultural sector in Spain is falling at a greater rate than in other EU countries, and a corresponding increase in the size of properties is expected. If the previous hypotheses are correct, many areas characterized by the highly diverse traditional pseudosteppe landscape, could be transformed into a homogeneous landscape with only one or two land-use types and agricultural substrates, and where the hedges will have practically disappeared.

The irrigation of dry crops is another of the key mechanisms of intensifica-tion. According to forecasts in the National Hydrological Plan, there are plans to irrigate 600 000 ha over the next 20 years. The pseudosteppes and dehesas will be most affected. However, the low potential of these agrosystems for the production of any crops other than those causing EU surpluses, along with the requisite maximum base area for receipt of EU funds through FEOGA-guarantee payments, restrict the viability of irrigation projects in the pseudos-teppes. Furthermore, most of the irrigation projects that might be financially viable for farmers would add to existing surpluses, and may not, therefore, be viable from an EU perspective.

The water-use policy aimed at improving agricultural efficiency has recently resulted in significant deterioration of the inner wetlands associated with the Spanish pseudosteppes. The agricultural area irrigated from the water table increased from 431 459 ha to 812 000 ha between 1962 and 1983. An example is the Tablas de Daimiel, where the area irrigated with public and private funds rose from 30 000 to 125 000 hectares between 1974 and 1987 (Bifani et al., 1992), affecting quite significant pseudosteppe areas.

Finally, in areas where the climate is suitable for olive and almond production, there has been a significant increase in plantations (Pastor & Humanes, 1991), many of which have taken place in pseudosteppe areas. This has led to the disappearance of birds typical of pseudosteppe areas and their replacement by species of Mediterranean open scrubs (e.g. melodious warbler *Hippolais polyglotta*, serin *Serinus serinus*, goldfinch *Carduelis carduelis*) in young plantations, and by forest species (great tit *Parus major* and short-toed treecreeper *Certhia brachydactyla*) in the mature ones (Muñoz-Cobo, 1992). However, the future extent of these tree plantations is difficult to evaluate.

With the combination of factors outlined above, and given the maintenance of current prices and subsidies for cereals, olive and almond plantations, a significant loss of pseudosteppe is expected over the next few decades. The viability of pseudosteppes in the medium term depends upon the implementation of an aid system that fully incorporates and supports agricultural practices which contribute to different aspects of production, such as the conservation of natural values or the landscape. The measures proposed under the Agri-environment Regulation (EC Reg. 2078/92) might be an appropriate instrument for this purpose. However, in the pseudosteppes of Castilla y León, where one project has been carried out, they have not been as effective as anticipated, because there has been very little uptake by farmers.

In some extensive grazing zones, the stocking rate has risen sharply, producing local problems as a result of over-grazing. The number of subsidized animals per farm is limited by the CAP, however, and these subsidies now make up one-third of the gross income of extensive sheep farms. Thus, provided that market prices and subsidies do not vary, it seems unlikely that stocking rates will rise significantly, although it is possible that the most deeply rooted grazing regions will undergo a process of intensification. However, we can expect a process of abandonment of grazing areas in the poorest areas, where the human population is aged.

FINAL CONSIDERATIONS

If these trends materialize, there is no doubt that numbers and/or populations of pseudosteppe birds will continue to decline. However, the extent to which this will occur is difficult to predict for individual species as knowledge of their

Figure 8 Sedentary species like the pin-tailed sandgrouse depend upon habitat mosaics and are likely to suffer if agricultural intensification reduces the diversity of land use. (Photo by C. Sanchez/RSPB.)

population dynamics and habitat requirements is currently limited. It is very possible, though, that the population declines observed for many species over recent decades will continue in the coming years, since similar factors are still influencing pseudosteppe management. The only species likely to benefit (in the short term) are those not requiring a diversity of agricultural land-use and substrates in their seasonal changes of habitat selection (e.g. corn bunting).

This general perspective needs to be considered in more detail at a regional level. On the one hand, in some areas significant agricultural intensification is anticipated, through the introduction of irrigation or the concentration of landholdings. This will undoubtedly have the effect of reducing the diversity of agricultural land-use. Many sedentary species (e.g. the great bustard, little bustard, pin-tailed sandgrouse and black-bellied sandgrouse) depend upon these mosaics, and their populations will definitely dwindle. Two additional factors must be taken into account when assessing the potential magnitude of this problem: (1) that the scale on which intensification might be expected to occur is large (10–20% of the total area of the Iberian pseudosteppes) and (2) that different intensities and extents of change may be involved in irrigation and concentration of landholdings.

On the other hand, even without intensive afforestation there could be a significant increase in vegetation height and cover in the most economically marginal areas due to human depopulation and a local decline in extensive livestock raising. This could significantly change the composition of bird communities, encouraging those species which depend more on shrub-steppes (e.g. black-eared wheatear *Oenanthe hispanica*, spectacled warbler *Sylvia conspicillata*). However, certain defined stocking densities could limit this vegetation growth, encouraging low growth chamaephytes or pasture species (Malo *et al.*, 1994). In the short and medium term this would benefit certain passerines associated with pasture lands (e.g. northern wheatear *Oenanthe oenanthe* or tawny pipit *Anthus campestris* in the 'páramos' of Central Spain). Even so, the majority of species need a variety of agricultural land-uses and substrates throughout their annual cycle, and loss of these would almost certainly be detrimental in the medium and long term. Effects upon bird populations would be accelerated by afforestation or the abandonment of livestock grazing which would result in shrub-steppe regeneration.

The majority of pseudosteppe areas lack any kind of national and/or regional legal protection, although certain areas have been declared SPAs (Suárez *et al.*, 1992 – see also Pain & Dixon, Chapter 1). The lack of protection probably stems from three things:

(1) the widely held and uninformed public opinion that as they are either fallow or totally managed landscapes, they must lack any conservation interest;
(2) the high financial cost of conserving agricultural zones in their traditional state (and supporting the human population associated with these farms);
(3) the potential social conflict which could develop due to the farmers' resistance to any additional land regulation standards.

The need to protect a substantial proportion of the Iberian pseudosteppes is both vital and logical, and had in fact already been identified in the 1970s (Viedma *et al.*, 1976). However, only very small areas are likely to benefit from sufficient legal protection over the next few decades. Actions must therefore centre on the conservation of existing areas through agricultural policies using payments to encourage traditional land management practices. In this context, protected areas, or at least part of them, may act as a buffer, acting as reservoirs of populations which could recolonize nearby areas.

An additional problem for the conservation of pseudosteppes and their associated flora and fauna is that previous management experience is limited. In most cases, designation of a protected area involves changes in management (e.g. control of hunting, greater numbers of visitors, etc.), which can result in indirect effects that are difficult to predict (see e.g. Suárez *et al.*, 1993; Yanes & Suárez, 1996). Moreover, the management of reserves may also be affected by two additional factors: (1) the activities carried out outside the reserve, especially if the protected area is small, and (2) lack of historical knowledge of traditional management. In relation to the latter point, it should be remembered that pseudosteppe species are very sensitive to vegetation structure, and that small changes (e.g. determined by ploughing frequency, stocking densities, etc.) may encourage certain species, to the detriment of others (Bignal *et al.*, in press).

For the above stated reasons, two applied research programmes are absolutely vital for the conservation of the Iberian pseudosteppes: one monitoring the development of populations at a regional level, and one investigating, in a detailed way, the effects of the various farming management practices upon bird species and communities.

Human activities, over centuries, have given rise to the Iberian pseudosteppes that exist today. Some pseudosteppes have lost a considerable amount of their natural value. The current economic instability of pseudosteppe farms may result in sudden changes, and their current conservation value may be rapidly lost. It is therefore becoming urgent that rational measures be taken if, as is indicated in Community legislation, it is agreed that these landscapes must be preserved.

REFERENCES

ALONSO, J.C. & ALONSO, J.A. (eds) (1990a) *Parámetros demográficos, selección de hábitat y distribución de la Avutarda (*Otis tarda*) en tres regiones españolas*. Colección Técnica. Madrid: ICONA.

ALONSO, J.A. & ALONSO, J.C. (1990b) *Distribución y demografía de la Grulla Común (*Grus grus*) en España*. Colección Técnica. Madrid: ICONA.

ARROYO, B. & TELLERÍA, J.L. (1984) La invernada de aves en el área de Gibraltar (Cadiz, España). *Ardeola*, 30: 23–31.

BANCO DE ESPAÑA (1995) *Boletín Estadístico, Febrero*. Madrid: Banco de España.

BARCELÓ, L.V., COMPÉS, R., GARCIA, J.M. & TIÓ, C. (1995) *Organización económica de la agricultura española. Adaptación de la agricultura española a la normativa de la UE*. Madrid: Fundación Alfonso Martín Escudero, ed. Mundi-Prensa.

BARROS, C. (1995) Contribución al estudio de la biología y ecología del alcaraván (*Burhinus oedicnemus*) en España. Doctoral Thesis, Universidad Autónoma de Madrid, Madrid (unpublished).

BIFANI, P., MONTES, C. & SANTOS, C. (1992) Economic pressure and wetland loss and degradation in Spain. In M. Fynlaison, T. Hollis & T. Davis (eds) *Managing Mediterranean Wetlands and Their Birds*, pp. 118–121. Slimbridge: IWRP Special Publication No. 20.

BIGNAL, E.M., McCRACKEN, D.I., STILLMAN, R.A. & OVENDEN, G.N. (in press) Feeding behaviour of nesting choughs in the Scottish Hebrides. *Journal of Field Ornithology*.

BIJLEVELD, M. (1974) *Birds of prey in Europe*. London: Macmillan Press.

BRAUN BLANQUET, J. & BOLÓS, O. DE (1957) Les groupements vegetaux du Bassin Moyen de L'Ebre et leur dynamisme. *Anales de la Estación Experimental de Aula Dei*, 5: 1–4. Zaragoza.

CABO, A. & MANERO, F. (eds) (1987) *Geografía de Castilla y León*. Tomo 4: Valladolid. Ambito Ediciones S.A.

CALVO, B. (1994) Medidas para conservar el hábitat de reproducción de la Canastera. *Quercus*. 106: 10–14.

CEC (Commission of the European Communities) (1994) *Marco comunitario de apoyo para las regiones objetivo 1 de España*. European Commission, Brussels.

CENTRO DE INVESTIGACIÓN FERNANDO GONZÁLEZ BERNÁLDEZ (1995) *Espacios Naturales Protegidos del Estado Español*. Madrid: Agencia de Medio Ambiente, Comunidad Autónoma de Madrid.

CHEYLAN, G., MEGERLE, A. & RESCH, J. (1990) *La Crau: steppe vivante*. Radolfzell: Ed. Juergen Resch.

COLLAR, N.J., CROSBY, M.J. & STATTERSFIELD, A.J. (1994) *Birds to Watch 2. The world list of threatened birds*. Cambridge: BirdLife International.

CURCÓ, A. & ESTRADA, J. (1987) Estudio comparativo de la avifuana invernante en las principales comunidades vegetales. *Actas del I Congreso Internacional de Aves Esteparias*, León, pp. 406–419.

DE BORBÓN, M. (1995) Contribución al estudio de la biología y ecología de la ganga (*Pterocles alchata*) y de la ortega (*Pterocles orientalis*) en España. Doctoral Thesis, Universidad Autónoma de Madrid, Madrid (unpublished).

DE JUANA, E. (1988a) La Serena, una comarca esteparia extremeña de singular importancia. *La Garcilla*, **71–72**: 26–27.

DE JUANA, E. (1988b) Áreas importantes para las aves esteparias. *La Garcilla*, **71–72**: 18–19.

DE JUANA, E. (1989) Las aves esteparias en España. *Seminario sobre zonas áridas en España*, pp. 199-221. Madrid: Real Academia de Ciencias Físicas, Exactas y Naturales.

DE JUANA, E. (ed.) (1990) *Áreas importantes para las aves en España*. Madrid: Monografías de la Sociedad Española de Ornitologia 3, Sociedad Española de Ornitologia.

DE JUANA, E., SANTOS, T., SUÁREZ, F. & TELLERÍA, J.L. (1988) Status and conservation of steppe birds and their habitats in Spain. In P. Goriup (ed.) *Birds of Savannas, Steppes and Similar Habitats*, pp. 113–123. Cambridge: International Council for Bird Preservation Technical Publication no 7.

DE JUANA, E., MARTÍN-NOVELLA, C., NAVESO, M.A., PAIN, D. & SEARS, J. (1993) Farming and birds in Spain: Threats and opportunities for conservation. *Royal Society for the Protection of Birds, Conservation Review*, 7: 67–73.

DÍAZ, M., NAVESO, M.A. & REBOLLO, E. (1993) Respuesta de las comunidades nidificantes de aves a la intensificación agrícola en cultivos cerealistas de la Meseta Norte (Valladolid-Palencia, España). *Aegypius*, **11**: 1–6.

DÍAZ, M.C., GARRIDO, S. & GARCÍA, R.A. (1994) Contaminación agraria difusa. *El Campo*, **131**: 93–107.

DONÁZAR, J.A., NEGRO, J.J. & HIRALDO, F. (1993) Foraging habitat selection, land-use changes and population decline in the lesser kestrel *Falco naumanni*. *Journal of Applied Ecology*, **30**: 515–522.

EGDELL, J. (1993) *Impact of the CAP on the Spanish Steppes*. Sandy: Royal Society for the Protection of Birds.

ENA, V. & MARTÍNEZ, A. (1988) Distribución y comportamiento social de la Avutarda. *Quercus*, **31**: 12–20.

ESTRADA, J. & CURCÓ, A. (1991) La Xurra *Pterocles orientalis* i la Ganga *Pterocles alchata* a Catalunya: evolució i situació actual. *Butll. Grup Català d'Anellament*, **8**: 1–8.

EUROSTAT (1994) *Agriculture Statisical Yearbook*. Brussels: ECSC-EC-EAEC.

GARRABOU, R., BARCIELLA, C. & JIMÉNEZ, J.I. (eds) (1986) *Historia agraria de la España contemporánea. 3. El fin de la agricultura tradicional (1900–1960)*. Barcelona: Editorial Crítica.

GARZA, V. & SUÁREZ, F. (1990) Distribución, población y selección de habitat de la Alondra de Dupont, *Chersophilus duponti*, en la Península Ibérica. *Ardeola*, 37: 3–12.

GARZÓN, J. (1977) Birds of prey in Spain, the present situation. In *Proc. World Conference, Birds of Prey*, Vienna, 1975.

GONZÁLEZ, J.L. & MERINO, M. (eds) (1990) *El cernícalo primilla (*Falco naumanni*) en la Península Ibérica. Situación, problemática y aspectos biológicos*. Madrid: Colección Técnica, ICONA.

GONZÁLEZ BERNÁLDEZ, F. (1988) Estepas y pseudoestepas. *La Garcilla*, **71–72**: 4–6.

GORIUP, P.D. (1988). The avifauna and conservation of steppic habitats in Western Europe, North Africa and the Middle East. In P.D. Goriup (ed.) *Ecology and Conservation of Grassland Birds*, pp. 145–157. Cambridge: International Council for Bird Preservation Technical Publication no. 7.

GORIUP, P.D. & BATTEN, L. (1990) The conservation of steppic birds – a European perspective. *Oryx*, **24**: 215–223.

GRIMMET, R.F.A. & JONES, T.A. (1989) *Important Bird Areas in Europe*. Cambridge: International Council for Bird Preservation Technical Publication 9.

GUADALFAJARA, R. & TUTOR, E. (1987) Estudio del uso del hábitat por las gangas en un área esteparia de la Depresión media del Ebro (España). *Actas del I Congreso Internacional de Aves Esteparias*, León, pp. 241—254.

GUTIÉRREZ, A., JIMÉNEZ, B., LEVASSOR, C., MALO, J.E., PECO, B. & SUÁREZ, F. (1993) Los cambios en el paisaje: enseñanzas para un futuro. *Quercus*, **88**: 14–17

HERNÁNDEZ, F. (1993) Catálogo provisional de los yacimientos de aves del Cuaternario de la Península Ibérica. *Archeofauna*, **2**: 231–275.

HERNÁNDEZ, F. (1994) Addenda al catálogo provisional de los yacimientos de aves del Cuaternario de la Península Ibérica. *Archeofauna*, **3**: 77–92.

HERNÁNDEZ, V., ESTEVE, M.A. & RAMÍREZ, L. (1995) *Ecología de las estepas de la región de Murcia. Estructura y dinámica de sus comunidades orníticas*. Murcia: Secretariado de publicaciones e intercambio científico, Universidad de Murcia.

HIRALDO, F., DONÁZAR, J.A., NEGRO, J.J. & GAONA, P. (1993) *Causas de mortalidad, dinámica de poblaciones y modelo demográfico de los cernícalos primillas* Falco naumanni *en el Valle del Guadalquivir*. Sevilla: Junta de Andalucía.

MAJORAL, R. (1987) La utilización del suelo agrícola en España. Aspectos evolutivos y locacionales. *El Campo*, **104**: 13–26.

MALO, J.E., LEVASSOR, C., JIMÉNEZ, B., SUÁREZ, F. & PECO, B. (1994) La sucesión en cultivos abandonados en zonas agropastorales: Semejanzas y diferencias entre tres localidades peninsulares. *Actas de la XXXIV Reunión Científica de la Sociedad Española para el estudio de los Pastos*, pp. 131—136. Santander.

MANRIQUE, J. & DE JUANA, E. (1991) Land-use changes and the conservation of dry grassland birds in Spain: a case study of Almería province. In P.D. Goriup, L.A. Batten & J.A. Norton (eds) *The Conservation of Lowland Dry Grassland Birds in Europe*, pp. 49–58. Peterborough: Joint Nature Conservation Committee.

MAPA (Ministerio de Agricultura, Pesca y Alimentación) (1975, 1985, 1990, 1994a). *Anuario de Estadística Agraria*, Años 1975, 1985, 1990, 1992. Madrid: MAPA.

MAPA (Ministerio de Agricultura, Pesca y Alimentación) (1994b) *Programas de ayudas para fomentar métodos de producción agraria compatibles con las exigencias de protección y la conservación del espacio natural*. Madrid: MAPA.

MARGALEF, R. (1947) Estudios sobre la vida en las aguas continentales de la región endorreica manchega. *Publicaciones Instituto Biología Aplicada*, **4**: 5–51.

MARTÍNEZ, C. (1991a) Patterns of distribution and habitat selection of a great bustard *Otis tarda* population in north-western Spain. *Ardeola*, **38**: 137–147.

MARTÍNEZ, C. (1991b) Selección de microhábitat en una población de avutarda (*Otis tarda*) de un medio agrícola. *Doñana Acta Vertebrata*, **18**: 173–185.

MARTÍNEZ, C. (1994) Habitat selection of the little bustard *Tetrax tetrax* in cultivated areas of Central Spain. *Biological Conservation*, **67**: 125–128.

MARTÍNEZ, F.J. & PURROY, F. (1993) Avifauna reproductora en los sistemas esteparizados ibéricos. *Ecología*, **7**: 391–401.

MUNÕZ-COBO, J. (1992) Breeding bird communities in the olive tree plantations of Southern Spain. *Alauda*, **60**: 118–122.

NAVESO, M.A. (1992) Propuesta de declaración de la zona de Madrigal-Peñaranda como Área Ambientalmente Sensible. Sociedad Española de Ornitologia-BirdLife, Madrid (unpublished).

NAVESO, M.A. & GROVES-REINES, S. (1992) Propuesta de declaración de la zona de Tierra de

Campos como Área Ambientalmente Sensible. Sociedad Española de Ornitologia-BirdLife, Madrid (unpublished).

NAVESO, M.A. & FERNÁNDEZ, J. (1993) Propuesta de programa de zona para el área de La Serena en aplicación del reglamento CEE 2078/92. Sociedad Española de Ornitologia-BirdLife, Madrid (unpublished).

PASTOR, M. & HUMANES, J. (1991) La reforma de la PAC y el olivar. El Campo, 122: 32–35.

PECO, B. & SUÁREZ, F. (coord.). (1993) Recomendaciones para la gestión y conservación del medio natural frente a los cambios relacionados con la Política Agraria Comunitaria (PAC). Universidad Autónoma de Madrid-ICONA, Madrid (unpublished).

PEREA, J.L., MORALES, M. & VELASCO, J.(1990). El alimoche (Neophron percnopterus) en España. Población, distribución, problemática y conservación. Colección Técnica. Madrid: ICONA.

PETRETTI, F. (1988) An inventory of steppe habitats in Southern Italy. In P.D. Goriup (ed.) Ecology and Conservation of Grassland Birds in Europe, pp. 125–143. Cambridge: International Council for Bird Preservation Technical Publication 7.

PLEGUEZUELOS, J.M. (1991) Evolución histórica de la avifauna nidificante en el SE de la Península Ibérica (1850–1985). Sevilla: Consejería de Cultura y Medio Ambiente, Junta de Andalucía.

ROTENBERRY, J.T. (1981) Why measure bird habitat? In E.D. Capen (ed.) The Use of Multivariate Statistics Studies of Wildlife Habitat, pp. 29–32. Vermont: USDA Forest Service.

RUÍZ, M. & RUÍZ, J.P. (1986) Ecological history of trashumance in Spain. Biological Conservation, 37: 73–76.

SAINZ OLLERO, H. (1988) Las estepas ibéricas: su importancia fitogeográfica. La Garcilla, 71–72: 8–11.

SAN AGUSTÍN, M. (1993) Los planes de regadío: su encaje en la nueva Política Agraria Común. El Boletín, pp. 33–39. Madrid: MAPA.

SOLER, M. (1994) Black Wheatear Oenanthe leucura. In G.M. Tucker & M.F. Heath (eds) Birds in Europe, p. 388. Cambridge: BirdLife Conservation Series 3.

SUÁREZ, F. (1981) Introducción al estudio de las comunidades de aves de dos áreas esteparicas peninsulares, la estepa ibérica y las zonas semiáridas del valle del Ebro. Boletín de la Estación Central de Ecología, 17: 53–62.

SUÁREZ, F. (1983) Ornitocenosis estepáricas mediterráneas y eurosiberianas. Memorias del 1er Coloquio de Ecología y Biogeografía, pp. 300–305. Guadalajara, 1981.

SUÁREZ, F. (1988) Las aves esteparias. La Garcilla, 71–72: 12–17.

SUÁREZ, F. (1994). Mediterranean steppe conservation: a background for the development of a future strategy. Brussels: Doc. XI/153/94, Commission of Europe.

SUÁREZ, F. & GARZA, V. (1989) La invernada de la Alondra de Dupont, Chersophilus duponti, en la Península Ibérica. Ardeola, 36: 107–110.

SUÁREZ, F. & SAEZ-ROYUELA, C. (1983) Evolución invernal de las comunidades de aves de dos medios "estepáricos" del Valle del Ebro. Boletín de la Estación Central de Ecología, 24: 67–73.

SUÁREZ, F., SAINZ-OLLERO, H., SANTOS, T. & GONZÁLEZ BERNÁLDEZ, F. (1992) Las estepas ibéricas. Madrid: M.O.P.T., Unidades Temáticas de la Secretaría de Estado para las Políticas del Agua y el Medio Ambiente.

SUÁREZ, F., YANES, M., HERRANZ, J. & MANRIQUE, J. (1993) Nature reserves and the conservation of Iberian shrubsteppe passerines: the paradox of nest predation. Biological Conservation, 64: 77–81.

TELLERÍA, J.L. (ed.) (1988) Invernada de aves en la Península Ibérica. Madrid: Monografías de la Sociedad Española de Ornitologia 1, Sociedad Española de Ornitologia.

TELLERÍA, J.L., SUÁREZ, F. & SANTOS, T. (1988a) Bird communities of the Iberian shrub-steppes: seasonality and structure along a climatic gradient. Holarctic Ecology, 11: 171–177.

TELLERÍA, J.L., SANTOS, T., ÁLVAREZ, G. & SAÉZ-ROYUELA, C. (1988b) Avifauna de los campos de cereales del interior de España. In F. Bernis (ed.) *Aves de los medios urbano y agrícola en las mesetas españolas*, pp. 173–317. Madrid: Monografías de la Sociedad Española de Ornitologia 2, Sociedad Española de Ornitologia.

TELLERÍA, J.L., SANTOS, T. & CARRASCAL, L.M. (1988c) La invernada de los paseriformes (O. Passeriformes) en la Península Ibérica. In J.L. Tellería (ed.) *Invernada de aves en la Península Ibérica*, pp. 153–166. Madrid: Monografías de la Sociedad Española de Ornitoloia 1, Sociedad Española de Ornitologia.

TIÓ, C. (1991) Reforma de la PAC y su impacto a nivel sectorial en España. *ICE*, 700: 79–90.

TUCKER, G.M. (1991) The status of lowland dry grassland birds in Europe. In P.D. Goriup, L.A. Batten & J.A. Norton (eds) *The Conservation of Lowland Dry Grassland Birds in Europe*, pp. 49–58. Peterborough: Joint Nature Conservation Committee.

TUCKER, G.M. & HEATH, M.F. (eds) (1994) *Birds in Europe. Their Conservation Status*. Cambridge: BirdLife Conservation Series 3.

VALVERDE, A. (1957) *Aves del Sahara Español*. Madrid: I.D.A.E.

VALVERDE, A. (1958) Aves esteparias de la Península Ibérica. *Publicaciones Instituto Biología Aplicada*, 27: 41–58.

VIEDMA, M.G., LEÓN, F. & CORONADO, R. (1976) Nature conservation in Spain: a brief account. *Biological Conservation*, 9: 181–190.

VILLAR, E.H. DEL (1925) Avance geobotánico sobre la pretendida "estepa" central de España. *Ibérica*. 23, no 570, 381–393. no 577, 293–505, no 579, 328–333. no 580, 347–350.

YANES, M. (1994) The importance of land management in the conservation of birds associated with the Spanish steppes. In E.M. Bignal, D.I. McCracken and D.J. Curtis (eds) *Nature Conservation and Pastoralism in Europe*, pp. 34–40. Peterborough: Joint Nature Conservation Committee.

YANES, M. & SUÁREZ, F. (1996) Incidental nest predation and lark conservation in an Iberian semiarid shrubsteppes. *Conservation Biology*, 10.

CHAPTER

12

The importance of mixed farming for seed-eating birds in the UK

ANDY EVANS

SUMMARY

Agriculture in the UK has always been in a state of flux, with huge swings occurring in the balance of land in arable and pastoral production. Hitherto, farming techniques involved an intimate mix of both arable and pastoral systems. Changes in farming practice in this country over the past 50 years have led to a geographical polarization of the two systems and a consequent and continuing loss of mixed farm holdings. Moreover, there have been enormous changes within each of the systems as financial pressures have led to a drive towards ever more intensive practices. Both grassland and cereal systems have been driven towards monocultures and therefore are likely to have declined in quality as a wildlife habitat.

Over the past 20 years there have been dramatic and consistent reductions in populations of the majority of farmland seed-eating bird species. This chapter reviews these changes and examines evidence from recent studies that indicates that the impoverishment of the lowland farmland avifauna in the UK could have been the result of the loss and degradation of mixed farming systems.

HISTORY OF MIXED FARMING SYSTEMS IN THE UK

The history of mixed farming systems in the UK is essentially the history of lowland farmland itself. Originally, much of lowland UK was covered in deciduous woodland. As the human population grew, so did the need for

FARMING AND BIRDS IN EUROPE
ISBN 0-12-544280-7
Copyright © 1997 Academic Press Ltd
All rights of reproduction in any form reserved

Figure 1 Hedge laying in Bedfordshire, UK. During the eighteenth and nineteenth centuries, thousands of kilometres of hedgerow were created in the UK. (Photo by C.H. Gomersall/RSPB.)

cultivated land and this was acquired mostly through encroachment into the woodland. Until the sixteenth century agricultural development was slow, culminating throughout much of lowland England in the 'open-field' system in medieval times. Under this system, arable land around clustered farmsteads was shared by villagers and divided into either two or three equal areas.

Under the two-field system an annual rotation of corn and fallow was strictly followed, whereas in the three-field system a year of wheat or rye would be followed by barley, oats or beans and finally, a year of fallow (Briggs & Courtney, 1985). Under both regimes cattle were grazed on the pasture which developed on the fallow, their droppings being an important source of manure. Further pasture and rough grazing was also normally available. Thus both arable and pasture were found together.

During the sixteenth century two things happened to change the nature of farming across the country. Firstly, the Black Death caused severe population reductions in both rural and urban areas and consequently lowered the demand for arable products. Secondly, wool prices started to increase, leading to increased sheep husbandry and the need for enclosure – a process which continued through the eighteenth and nineteenth centuries with the agricultural revolution. This had a profound effect on the landscape, and thousands of kilometres of hedgerow were created (Figure 1) (O'Connor & Shrubb, 1986).

Table 1 The Norfolk four-course rotation

Year	Crop	Use
1	Turnips or swedes	Folded with sheep in winter
2	Spring barley	Cash crop
3	Red clover	Grazed in spring and summer
4	Winter wheat	Cash crop

Source: Briggs & Courtney (1985).

The eighteenth and nineteenth centuries marked a period of slow change, although there were a number of important developments. These included the invention of new implements such as the seed-drill, and introduction of new crops such as the turnip, potato and clover. Clover was particularly important as its nitrogen-fixing qualities enhanced soil fertility and led to the development of the Norfolk four-course rotation (Table 1). Under this system a spring-sown barley crop was often undersown with a clover/grass mixture. After harvest a weedy stubble was left over winter; this developed into a ley pasture, often grazed by sheep. It is claimed that the widespread adoption of this system resulted in a huge (c. 50%) increase in the area of tillage.

From about 1875, international trade became a major force in shaping the industry. Improved communications led to a flood of high quality imported American wheat on to the UK market. This heralded the start of a long period of decline in UK agriculture, culminating in the depression of the 1920s and 1930s, when the price for wheat fell to half that of 50 years earlier. During this period, the area in arable production crashed, especially the cereal area which more than halved. This was compensated by a switch to pasture. Over 1 million hectares of land previously in cereal production were simply abandoned and became 'rough grass' (O'Connor & Shrubb, 1986).

After 1945, Government intervention stabilized the economic situation. Being an island had brought mixed blessings during World War II; in 1940 the German Blitzkrieg was brought to a halt by the English Channel, which saved Britain from being overrun. However, for much of the rest of the War the islands were under a blockade. Britain was dependent on imported food and relied on merchant convoys from across the Atlantic beating the cordons of German 'U' boats, pocket battleships and cruisers. These convoys suffered extremely heavy losses and Britain was in danger of being starved into submission. Because of this, the Government set about ensuring that in future the country would be self-sufficient in terms of food production. In the post-war years they set about this goal with a single-mindedness which shaped farming as it is today.

The principle of guaranteed wheat prices had been established by the Wheat Act of 1932. The Agricultural Act of 1947 delivered a system of guaranteed prices for produce by acreage payments. These measures made it profitable to produce cereals again, once more altering the arable/pasture balance so that today it is much the same as it was in the mid-nineteenth century.

The 'recovery' of the arable/pasture balance has been described as a renaissance of UK agriculture. However, this perspective hides a revolution in farming practices in both systems, which has led to profound changes in the farming landscape. This revolution was driven by an extraordinarily rapid development of technology. Mechanization was perhaps the most obvious change, with the appearance of tractors and, in the 1950s, the first self-propelled combines. Today there is a plethora of different specialist machinery available to speed tillage and harvest of every conceivable crop and to assist with livestock husbandry. Just how radical the effects on the landscape have been is easy to forget:

(1) horses have disappeared from farms and with them oats as a fodder crop;
(2) the farm work force has been drastically reduced;
(3) with effective machines (which require large capital input) come economies of scale. This means that hedgerows have been increasingly removed to give larger fields, and that farming has become more specialized, with farms becoming devoted either to cereals or livestock. This move has been associated with a polarization of agriculture; arable in the east of the UK and pastoral farming in the west (O'Connor & Shrubb, 1986). Furthermore, the operational requirements of heavy machinery have dictated widespread drainage of fields, resulting in soil compaction.

Technological developments have also led to the introduction of ever more effective fertilizers and pesticides. Universal applications of these chemicals to increase yields have resulted in much of the landscape tending towards monocultures. Plant breeding has introduced new varieties; in the 1950s the majority of cereals were spring sown; now over 90% of cereals are sown in autumn or winter. This switch in timing of tillage has been associated with the loss of livestock from arable regions and redundancy of undersown leys with the arrival of inorganic fertilizers. These changes have meant that over-winter stubble fields have largely disappeared from the farmland landscape.

This brief history illustrates that, although there has always been fluctuation in the balance of arable and pasture, recently individual holdings have become increasingly specialized and thus there has been a loss of habitat diversity at the farm level over the past 30 years. Technological developments have led to far fewer farm-workers and more intensive farming operations but at the expense of habitat variety and so, probably, biodiversity.

POPULATION TRENDS OF SEED-EATING BIRDS IN THE UK

Populations of common birds in the UK have been monitored over the past 30 years by the Common Birds Census, run by the British Trust for Ornithology

(BTO)[1] (Marchant *et al.*, 1990). There also exist comparative data on bird distributions across Great Britain between 1968–72 and 1988–91 as a result of atlas work by volunteers co-ordinated by the BTO (Gibbons *et al.*, 1993). Recent analyses suggest that farmland birds are generally in decline (Fuller *et al.*, 1995) and many species of seed-eater have been particularly hard hit (Table 2). Estimates of current trends throughout Europe suggest that the story is similar in many countries (particularly in the north-west – Table 2; Tucker & Heath, 1994). The degree of declines which have occurred in populations means that many species are believed to be of 'unfavourable conservation status' (Tucker, Chapter 4). Tucker also explains how many of the declining seed-eaters are vulnerable because they are confined to agricultural habitats.

That the declines in all of these species were contemporaneous with some of the recent major changes in agricultural practice described above is highly suggestive. However, there have been few ecological studies on farmland seed-eaters and causality cannot be ascribed. Two species have been studied in detail: the grey partridge *Perdix perdix* (see Potts, Chapter 6) and the cirl bunting *Emberiza cirlus*. The latter was the subject of a research project started in 1988 by the RSPB with the aim of designing a recovery programme for the UK population. The findings of this project make a useful case study which sheds some light on the possible reasons for the declines of other passerines. More recent studies on skylark *Alauda arvensis* and corn bunting *Miliaria calandra* verify some of the hypotheses that arose from the cirl bunting project.

ECOLOGY OF CIRL BUNTINGS

Cirl buntings were first discovered in the UK in 1800 in south Devon. Throughout the nineteenth and the first quarter of the twentieth century they colonized much of southern England, pushing northwards until by the mid-1930s they were common and widespread south of a line between the Thames and Severn estuaries (Figure 2). Between then and the late 1960s, the population slowly declined and gaps began to appear in the range. In the 1970s the population collapsed and, by 1982, had been reduced to 167 pairs, most of which were in Devon (Sitters, 1982, 1985). By 1989 numbers had further been reduced to between 118 and 132 pairs (Evans, 1992). The RSPB's study was designed to try to establish the causes of this decline.

In any declining population of a resident bird where there is no emigration, it is self-evident that mortality of fully grown birds is exceeding production of recruits. Cirl buntings were thought to be fairly sedentary, so it was assumed

---

[1] Commissioned by the former Nature Conservancy Council (now funded by the Joint Nature Conservation Committee).

Table 2 Declines in populations of seed-eating birds in the UK and the rest of Europe

Species	Estimated UK population*	Decline in UK numbers (%)†	Decline in UK range (%)*	Countries occupied‡	Decline (%)§
Grey partridge *Perdix perdix*	150 000	82	19	34	91
Turtle dove *Streptopelia turtur*	75 000	77	25	39	51
Skylark *Alauda arvensis*	1 500 000	58	2	40	58
Bullfinch *Pyrrhula pyrrhula*	190 000	76	7	nd	nd
Linnet *Acanthis cannabina*	520 000	52	54	nd	(12)
Tree sparrow *Passer montanus*	110 000	89	20	nd	nd
Reed bunting *Emberiza schoeniclus*	220 000	61	12	nd	nd
Yellowhammer *Emberiza citrinella*	1 200 000	17	7	nd	(9)
Cirl bunting *Emberiza cirlus*	375¶	nd	83	nd	nd
Corn bunting *Miliaria calandra*	30 000	80	32	nd	(22)

nd: no data or data incomplete.
*Declines between 1968–72 and 1988–91 (from Gibbons *et al.*, 1993).
†Declines between 1969 and 1994 (from BTO Press release, 1 August 1995).
‡From Tucker & Heath (1994).
§Percentage of European countries occupied where declines recorded. Brackets indicate number of countries where population known to be in decline (given where data are insufficient to calculate percentage). From Tucker & Heath (1994).
¶RSPB data.

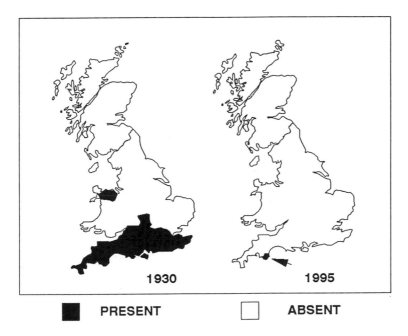

Figure 2 Change in distribution of cirl buntings in the UK between 1930 and 1995. Source: Evans (1992).

that emigration and immigration were low. So little was known about the ecology of cirl buntings prior to this study that it was not clear whether the problem might be one of high mortality or low production (or both). It was important, therefore, to address both aspects of the species' ecology and we designed the study both to measure how birds used the habitat available to them in summer and winter and to measure breeding success. We colour-ringed a sample of birds individually in order to measure dispersal.

Winter ecology

On examining the habitat selected during winter at two study sites, we found that birds fed almost exclusively on stubble fields (Evans & Smith, 1994). At one site the birds used the same field (a barley stubble which had been sold for building development) for all of the three winters of the study. This was the only area of stubble/fallow at this study site. At the other site birds followed the stubble as it moved around the farm with the agricultural rotation (Evans & Smith, 1994). At both sites birds tended to forage in small flocks in the margins of the fields and rarely more than 30 m from the cover of a hedgerow.

During the winter of 1990/91, a wide-scale survey of stubble fields within the

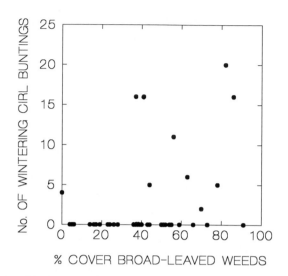

Figure 3 Relationship between broad-leaved weed cover on a stubble field and the number of wintering cirl buntings using it. Spearman rank correlation: $R_s = 0.370$, $n = 41, p < 0.01^{**}$. Source: Evans & Smith (1992).

cirl bunting's range found that fields with a higher incidence of dicotyledonous weeds held higher numbers of cirl buntings (Figure 3; Evans & Smith, 1992). Analysis of faecal samples indicated that birds were taking a range of weed seeds.

Summer ecology

During four summers (1990–93) we investigated breeding success and nestling diet at six sites (Evans *et al.*, unpublished data). Nests were found by following adults returning with nest material or food, or after a break in incubation. Most nests were located in thorny hedgerow bushes such as hawthorn, rose and bramble, or in gorse scrub. The contents of nests were monitored every three days. All chicks were individually measured, weighed and colour-marked. Diet of chicks was assessed by faecal analysis, direct observation and by video-filming returning adults.

Nest survival (the probability of a nest producing fledglings) varied significantly between years from 27% to 47%. Significant seasonal variation was also found; if the first egg was laid before 1 July, any chicks hatched had only a 37% chance of fledging. After this date the probability of survival rose to 90%. The most severe losses occurred at the chick stage early in the season in wet weather. Most chicks died either from starvation or predation, although it is thought that

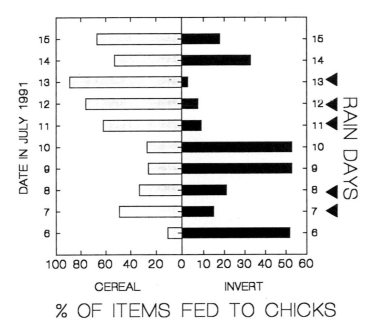

Figure 4 Switch in diet of cirl bunting chicks between invertebrate items on fine days and cereal grain on rainy days. Source: Sitters (1991).

the two causes are linked; hungry chicks beg much more loudly and are more detectable. Growth rates of chicks that were depredated were significantly lower than those which fledged, but similar to those which starved (Evans *et al.*, in press).

Diet was shown to change both in rainy conditions and as the season progressed. On fine days chicks were fed almost exclusively on invertebrate material, but on rainy days the adults switched to feeding them increasing amounts of cereal grain, presumably because insects became inactive or inaccessible in wet weather (Figure 4; Sitters, 1991). Rainfall reduced chick growth rates (Evans *et al.*, in press) and, under conditions of prolonged rain, chick deaths from starvation and predation were common.

Early in the season, when survival was low, chick diet comprised mainly caterpillars, spiders, beetles, and leaf material from dicotyledonous plants. These dietary components were found less frequently in faecal samples as the season progressed but the remains of grasshoppers and crickets (Orthoptera) became increasingly common. In May less than half the faecal samples contained Orthoptera whilst in July and August virtually every sample did (Evans *et al.*, in press). Adults tended to forage in areas of rough or semi-intensified grassland for invertebrates and avoided highly intensified pastures which had been prepared using inorganic nitrogen fertilizers to carry high stock densities.

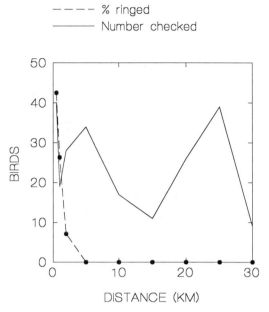

Figure 5 Graph showing percentage of cirl buntings that were colour-ringed as a function of distance from the ringing site.

Dispersal

Each summer a full survey of pairs was carried out. An attempt was made to check the legs of as many individual birds as possible for colour-rings. Figure 5 shows the percentage of birds checked that were colour-ringed, as a function of distance from the main wintering and ringing site. Although many birds were checked at considerable distances, the percentage that was marked declined very rapidly; indeed few birds moved more than 2 km between their wintering area and breeding territory.

Conclusions

These results suggest that the major changes in agricultural practice which have occurred may have had a detrimental effect on the UK cirl bunting population. There is evidence that there has been a decline in both the quantity of over-winter stubble fields and their quality as a food source for seed-eating birds. Although there are no historical data on the extent of winter stubble fields, it is probable that the area of stubble left over winter is correlated positively with the area of spring sown cereals. Even though data on the extent of spring sown

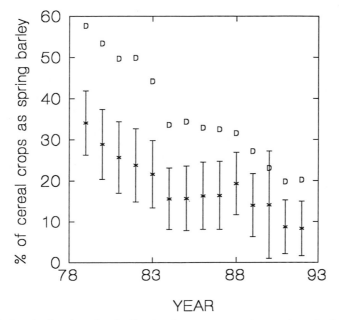

Figure 6 Graph showing the decline in the percentage (mean ± s.e.) of cereal crops grown that were spring barley in the counties formerly occupied by cirl buntings and in Devon (D). Source: Evans & Smith (1994).

cereals have been collected by the UK Government only since 1979, we know that the proportion of cereals sown in the spring has fallen dramatically since the introduction of hardy winter varieties in the late 1960s. Increasingly, stubbles were burnt, ploughed and then sown with the next year's crop in autumn. This trend continued throughout the 1980s, although Devon retained more spring barley than other counties formerly occupied by cirl buntings (Figure 6).

Other changes may have affected the quality of the remaining stubbles. The invention, proliferation and evolution of combine harvesters since the 1930s has led to more rapid and effective harvests, with less spilt grain. Agro-chemical inputs have increased yields by 25–50% since 1970 and the use of herbicides has probably reduced the diversity and abundance of the annual weeds which attract cirl buntings.

Recently there has been an interesting increase in reports of cirl buntings feeding from bird tables. The traditional name for the cirl bunting in the UK was 'the village bunting' because it was often found around rural buildings, particularly farmsteads, stock yards and threshing yards. Today threshing machines have disappeared and improvements in stock husbandry and hygiene standards have vastly reduced such foraging opportunities. In the last few years, however, there has been an explosion of interest amongst the UK public in garden birds,

Figure 7 Male cirl bunting perched. There have been major changes in agricultural practice which may have had a detrimental effect on the UK cirl bunting population. (Photo by C.H. Gomersall/RSPB.)

and several specialist firms now market feeders and foodstuffs specifically for passerines. These new products include grain-based feeds for finches – a far cry from the traditional peanut feeder. It seems that these are being exploited by cirl buntings.

In the summer it appears that breeding success is very variable. This is mainly due to heavy losses of chicks through starvation and predation in wet weather and early in the season. Chicks do much better later in the season when they are fed predominantly on grasshoppers. The preferred habitat of many species of grasshopper is a mosaic of long and short grass with patches of bare earth for oviposition. Although there are no quantitative data on historical trends in grasshopper populations on farmland, it is known that application of nitrogen-based fertilizers has led to uniform, species-poor swards which are poor habitat for orthopterans (van Wingerden *et al.*, 1992). The high stocking densities associated with such intensified pasture cause further reductions in grasshopper populations (van Wingerden *et al.*, 1991). Cirl buntings need areas of 'unintensified' or 'semi-intensified' pasture, grazed at low densities and carrying high populations of grasshoppers.

Cirl buntings make considerable use of hedgerows, both as nesting sites and as cover while foraging in winter. Recent Government figures show that the huge losses of hedgerow in arable and pastoral land in the 1970s continued throughout the 1980s; over 48 000 km (23%) of existing hedgerow were lost between

1984 and 1990 (Barr *et al.*, 1992). There is no evidence, however, that hedgerows are in any way limiting the population within the current UK range of the cirl bunting. Indeed, many areas exist in south Devon which have ample hedgerows but from which the birds have disappeared. Despite this, it is possible that hedgerow loss may have contributed to the decline in more northern and eastern parts of the former range.

Cirl buntings have suffered from large-scale changes both in their wintering and breeding habitat, so perhaps it is not surprising that their UK population should have crashed so dramatically. Ringing studies have demonstrated a very low level of dispersal for cirl buntings: a very important finding as it means that the species needs pasture that has received little or no artificial fertilizer and is grazed at low densities in close proximity to arable land managed to produce weedy over-winter stubble fields. In other words, cirl buntings need a mixed farming system. As we have seen, farming systems in the UK were indeed mainly a mixture of arable and livestock, but over the past half century individual farms have specialized in one or other system, leading to acute polarization.

MIXED FARMING AND OTHER SEED-EATING SPECIES

It appears that loss of mixed farming and degradation of both pastoral and arable elements have contributed to the decline in the UK cirl bunting population. Have other declining seed-eating bird species been similarly affected?

Grey partridge

More is known about the ecology of this species than any other farmland bird as the result of a 25-year study by the Game Conservancy Trust (see Potts, Chapter 6). The severe and widespread decline is a result of intensification (defined as increased output per unit area achieved by increasing inputs) within cereal farming. This has obviated the need for traditional rotations and been accompanied by the polarization of agriculture. The most important elements been reductions in the densities of the insects which form the diet of partridge chicks, with subsequent increased mortality rates of chicks through starvation. Loss of the under-sown leys associated with mixed farming is one contributory factor to this decline in insects.

Skylark

There has been a recent proliferation of studies aimed at elucidating the reasons behind the decline of the skylark on farmland. In winter, the species is concentrated on stubble fields (Wilson *et al.*, 1995, Evans, unpublished data)

Figure 8 Skylark perched on post singing. Skylark numbers declined by 58% on farmland in the UK between 1969 and 1994 (Table 2). (Photo by C.H. Gomersall/RSPB.)

whether these are part of a traditional rotation or created under the rotational set-aside scheme under the 1992 reform of the Common Agricultural Policy (CAP) (Rayment, 1995). Set-aside is discussed in more detail later. Many skylarks that breed in northern European countries are thought to winter in Britain; in fact the UK may support up to 25% of the European population in winter. The loss of over-winter stubble fields in the 1970s and 1980s described earlier may have been particularly important.

Skylarks nest on the ground in tussocks of grass or other low vegetation, from salt marsh to moorland, but they avoid tall, dense vegetation. They can rear up to four broods from April to July (Delius, 1965). Breeding densities and chick production on lowland farmland are particularly low on winter cereals but higher on spring sown cereals and grassland (Table 3; Wilson *et al.*, 1995). During the four months of the breeding season, the vegetation structure within a territory will change markedly as crops grow. It would be advantageous, therefore, to have an intimate mixture of spring and winter cereals, grass leys and root-crops or legumes so that at any stage in the season one crop may be the right height for the skylark's breeding requirements.

In a recent study by the BTO (Evans *et al.*, 1995) chick growth rates were compared on organic and conventional farms. Organic farmers do not apply any pesticides to their crops and instead use traditional methods of weed-control

Table 3 Skylark breeding densities and productivity on lowland farmland

Crop	Territories per 100 ha	Nests per 100 ha	Chicks per 100 ha
Winter wheat	5	2	1.3*
Winter barley	10	9	2.9*
Winter cereals	1.8–3.5	0	?†
Set-aside	33	35	41.3*
(sown grass, cut)	17–44	18.5	?†
Set-aside	36	25	60.1*
(natural regeneration, cut or sprayed)			

*BTO/BBSRC figures.
†GCT figures.
Source: Wilson *et al.* (1995).

and fertilizing. This normally means arable/grass rotations and mixing livestock with cereal production. Chick growth rates were higher on the organic farms, perhaps reflecting the indirect effects of heavy pesticide use on the conventional farms. Moreover, although many birds nested in cereals on the organic farm, the adults often flew to grass strips to forage for food for their young, highlighting the importance of an intimate mix of cereals and grass.

Corn bunting

The status of the corn bunting in the UK lies somewhere between that of the skylark and the cirl bunting in that it has suffered severe losses in numbers and a moderate reduction in range. Most of the abandoned areas have been in the north and west. There have been several studies of corn bunting but most have concentrated on behavioural aspects such as the bizarre and variable mating strategy (Hartley *et al.*, 1993) and the development of song dialects in stable populations (McGregor & Thompson, 1988). A recent BTO national winter survey discovered that the preferred winter habitat was, as for cirl buntings, weedy stubble fields (Donald & Evans, 1994). Thus changes in arable practice in the north and west as a result of specialization and polarization may have contributed to their decline in these regions. In 1993, the BTO conducted a national breeding survey of corn buntings (Donald & Evans, 1995). Volunteers were asked to search randomly selected squares for corn buntings and to record selected habitat details. A comparison could then be made between the habitat in 10 km squares that had lost breeding corn buntings between the 1968–72 Breeding Atlas (Sharrock, 1976) and 1993 and in those which had retained them. This analysis confirmed that most losses occurred in squares where

Figure 9 Corn bunting perched on wooden post. Corn buntings appear to do best under mixed farming regimes. (Photo by M.W. Richards/RSPB.)

pasture dominated over arable. This may suggest that the losses experienced could be due to intensification of pastoral systems. Changes in grassland management could have affected corn buntings in a similar manner to that described for cirl buntings. Alternatively, the cutting of silage fields much earlier than traditional hay meadows could have resulted in the systematic destruction of nests. On the other hand, changes in arable practice may have a much greater effect where there is proportionately little arable land rather than when the majority of land is under this farming system.

In a separate study, the Game Conservancy Trust looked at corn bunting populations on three farms on which they had been studying grey partridges for 25 years (Ward & Aebischer, 1994). On two intensively managed arable farms corn bunting populations had declined considerably but on the third farm (which was managed on a traditional rotation, including grass leys) the population was doing very much better. Studies of the diet of nestling birds showed that, like the grey partridge, sawfly larva were frequently eaten by chicks. Numbers of these insects have been drastically reduced as a result of application of herbicides, which kill the larva's food plant, and as a result of loss of fallow (especially under-sown stubbles).

It is entirely possible that this species has declined in different areas for different reasons but the information available would seem to suggest that corn buntings do best under mixed farming regimes.

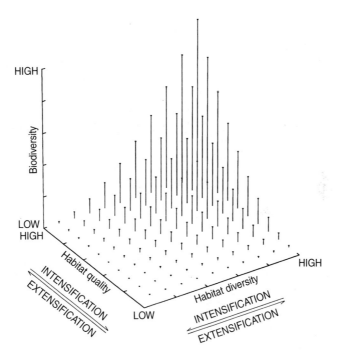

Figure 10 Model showing the increase in biodiversity as a function of increase in habitat diversity and quality. The effects of farming intensification and extensification as defined in the text are illustrated.

WHAT FUTURE FOR FARMLAND SEED-EATERS?

Essentially there have been dramatic declines over the past 30 years, both in the diversity of farmland habitat available to birds and in the quality of the remaining habitat elements. These changes have been brought about by the process generally understood as intensification; i.e. striving for greater output per unit area, often by increasing inputs. This process was initiated by a perceived need for the UK to be self-sufficient in food production (an outdated wartime concept) and has been maintained through substantial financial incentives and massive chemical applications.

Weeds and insect infestations can reduce yields; thus the highest yielding crop is likely to be a monoculture. By definition this is the antithesis of biodiversity. At first sight, the goals of conservationists (to conserve biodiversity), and those of the modern intensive farmer are diametrically opposed (Figure 10).

However, conservation and food production are not necessarily mutually exclusive. Indeed, the evidence presented in this book suggests that most farmland bird species depend on land that is managed by farmers for food.

Conservation goals can be integrated with food production but, if this objective is to be achieved, individual farmers will be required to reduce production and may suffer financially. In order for conservation objectives to succeed, individual farmers will require incentives to adopt different farming practices.

Incentives could include payments, designed either as compensation for reduced productivity or as a reward for production of wildlife habitat. These payments could be made conditional on the adoption of specific management prescriptions or achievement of wildlife targets. The latter may be more popular with the government as it would be hard to verify implementation of prescriptions which involve a reduction in inputs.

A system such as this, designed to produce both food and wildlife, should find acceptance with the tax-payer (compared with the current system of artificial price support for the production of a commodity already in surplus) and also with the farmer who would be managing land for positive goals.

An alternative would be simply to remove price support and let farmers compete on the open market. This would eventually regulate grain production but those farmers who lost out in open competition would tend to be those with smaller, more diverse farms operating without large capital resources or the economies of scale. The larger, specialist 'intensive' cereal farms would win through. The result could make the situation for biodiversity even worse.

However, an ideal, at least from a conservation viewpoint, may be a combination of the two. Free market prices would reduce the incentive to produce surpluses, while environmental payments could be used to encourage the production of wildlife and landscape features, without having to compete with inflated prices.

Over the past decade a host of schemes have become available under the agri-environment regulation of the reformed CAP. In addition, there have been sweeping changes to the farmland landscape as a result of set-aside, a production-control scheme designed under the CAP to reduce the European Union (EU) surplus in grain production. After publication of evidence of the huge reductions in farmland seed-eating and other birds (Marchant et al., 1990; Gibbons et al., 1993; Fuller et al., 1995), there has also been a huge effort to increase the amount of advice available to farmers on how to minimize the effects of modern farming techniques on bird populations.

To what degree can all these changes benefit seed-eating birds? Once again, the cirl bunting provides a good example of how a bird species can respond to changes in agricultural practices.

CONSERVATION OF CIRL BUNTINGS

In 1989, the known population of cirl buntings was just 118 pairs and had been declining for some 50 years; the probability of the species becoming extinct in the UK was regarded as high and the need for conservation action urgent. In 1991, the RSPB prepared a 'Species Action Plan' for the cirl bunting (RSPB, 1991, 1994). Species action plans aim to identify and assess the relative importance of threats to a species, convert research into action to counter these threats, determine areas of responsibility and set targets and establish how success can be measured (see Porter et al., 1990). A series of actions were proposed for the conservation of the cirl bunting, including research and advisory work and monitoring.

As soon as the need for weedy winter stubble fields was discovered (Evans & Smith, 1992, 1994), the RSPB began paying farmers to undertake trial management in six selected locations to leave at least one field as stubble and to sow spring, instead of winter, varieties of cereal. These fields were used to a great extent by wintering cirl buntings.

Another non-governmental organization, the National Trust, contributed financially to further agreements. An agreement was reached and funded by English Nature (the statutory body with responsibility for nature conservation in England) at one of the most important sites, which had already been designated as a Site of Special Scientific Interest (SSSI) because of other factors.

Attempts were made to secure further public funding for the conservation of cirl buntings by proposing a defined area of south Devon (which held over 90% of the UK population) as an Environmentally Sensitive Area (ESA). Attempts were also made to get further sites designated as SSSIs on the basis of cirl bunting presence. Both of these initiatives failed.

Government funding was, however, to play a crucial role in the conservation plan, but from unexpected sources. First, in 1988, set-aside was introduced as a voluntary scheme. Under the scheme farmers were paid to leave land fallow, rather than producing grain on it. This created winter stubbles on a fairly wide scale and, after 1992 when price support was made conditional on participation in the scheme (essentially making entry compulsory), up to 15% of the winter arable farmland landscape was under stubbles.

In 1992, more funding became available for habitat improvement in England through the 'Countryside Stewardship Scheme'. This scheme comes under the Agri-environment Regulation of the CAP and was administered by a government body, the Countryside Commission, until 1996 when it was taken over by the Ministry of Agriculture, Fisheries and Food. Initially, in Devon, the scheme was targeted at farmers on the coastal strip and offered payments to turn arable back to pasture: this was potentially highly damaging as the majority of the remaining cirl bunting sites were on the coast and the birds need a mixed system with at least some arable. When approached, the Commission were quick to change the scheme and get farmers to enter into agreements, not only to create weedy stubble annually but to manage pastures and hedgerows in an appropriate manner. There are now over 13 farms in Countryside Stewardship agreements, together holding over 25 pairs of cirl buntings.

With the advent of appropriate incentive schemes, and good information on

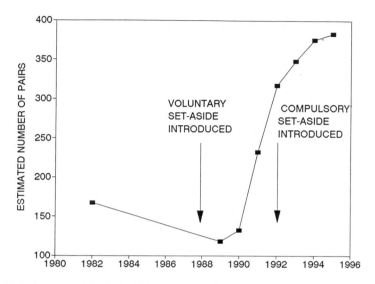

Figure 11 Recovery of the UK cirl bunting population after 1989.

the requirements of the cirl bunting from the RSPB's research programme, the RSPB employed a project officer to promote incentive schemes targetted at key sites, and monitor the population.

Has this action had any effect on the cirl bunting population? In the five years after 1989 the number of known pairs trebled to more than 370 (Figure 11).

CONSERVATION OF OTHER SEED-EATING SPECIES

Although the recovery programme for cirl buntings has so far been successful, it is not an ideal model for other species. Because the cirl bunting had become so rare, it was well suited to individual management agreements with farmers and the whole process could be overseen by a dedicated Project Officer. With the more common and widespread species, however, individual management agreements and site protection measures become less practical.

Recovery programmes for species such as the skylark and corn bunting will have to involve the following steps (Evans *et al.*, 1996).

(1) Research in order to develop and refine prescriptions for management practices to benefit each species.
(2) Effective dissemination of advice to farmers. This advice should embrace not only the best management practices based on current knowledge but also information on what schemes are available under the agri-environment

package and any other EU or national schemes which provide financial incentives to carry out that management.

(3) Adoption of more appropriate recovery schemes. Current schemes under the agri-environment regulation (e.g. ESAs, Countryside Stewardship) were not generally designed to encourage farming practices beneficial to seed-eating birds, although there are opportunities for beneficial management within these schemes (as with the cirl bunting). However, the conservation problem we are facing is so severe that the RSPB is encouraging the UK Government to adopt a package designed specifically to benefit farmland birds (RSPB, 1995). This scheme would promote: reduction of chemical inputs on cropped areas, changing crop rotations to include spring cereals and winter stubbles and conservation of boundaries and small features. Ideally the scheme should also aim to put grassland back into rotations.

The trouble with any scheme under the agri-environment regulation is that lack of resources will ultimately limit its effectiveness, either by restricting the geographical scale over which it operates, or by limiting the degree of sympathetic management that can be undertaken at a specific site. There are two ways in which benefits may accrue to seed-eating birds over a wide scale: extensification (basically a reversal of the process of intensification described earlier) and set-aside. The relative merits of each are described below.

EXTENSIFICATION AND SET-ASIDE

The process of intensification was described earlier as striving for ever increasing yields from a given area. This is generally achieved by increasing artificial inputs either to provide nutrients for the crop or to control competitive plants or damaging fungi or invertebrates. Figure 10 illustrates how this process leads both to reduced habitat diversity (habitat loss in real terms) and reduced quality of remaining habitats. Extensification is the reverse of this process and essentially involves reducing artificial inputs. Farming *is* possible under these conditions. Nutrients can be added to the soil by introducing clover leys as part of a rotation (see Table 1). Insects can be controlled by encouraging natural predators (often killed by non-specific insecticides under conventional regimes). Weed control using grass leys and rotovation can be extremely effective. The logical extension of this process is to farm with no inputs, i.e. organically. Organic farmers can farm extremely successfully; the danger here is that efficient weed control, however achieved, is bad for birds which depend on weed seeds for their winter food supply. A weed is, by definition, a plant growing where it is not wanted; if the process of extensification were to embrace environmental objectives and the broad-leaved 'weeds' preferred by declining bird species were re-defined as 'bird-seed plants' then the farming system might be able not only to tolerate certain non-crop plants, but even encourage them on some fields. Extensification would increase both the diversity and quality of available habitat and thus benefit wildlife. It would also reverse the process of polarization and lead to an increase in mixed farms.

The beauty of extensification as a solution to the conservation crisis currently faced in the UK, and indeed across much of NW Europe, is that extensive systems can be (indeed were for many centuries) sustainable. This means farming within the natural environmental constraints rather than finding artificial means of supporting systems operating outside these constraints. The concept of sustainability has received widespread recognition and support when applied to more immediately tangible examples of unsustainable systems, such as the destruction of rainforest to create temporary beef grazing. Farming in a sustainable manner means conserving natural resources, including biodiversity.

In 1992, receipt of Arable Area Payments by individual farmers in the UK was made conditional on entering the set-aside scheme. For the first time set-aside appeared on a large scale (approximately 15% of arable land). At this time the scheme was almost universally unpopular. Tax-payers did not like it because it was painted by the Press as payment for 'doing nothing'. Farmers did not like it because leaving land 'idle' went against the education of two generations to maximize production. Conservationists did not like it, partly because they were slow to realize the potential of the scheme, partly because the scheme was designed with the sole aim of reducing production surplus and did not address wildlife benefits explicitly, and partly because initial rules for the management of set-aside fields were almost certainly highly detrimental to wildlife. This particularly applied to the first summer when many farmers were under a misconception that they had to cut the green cover on set-aside fields (or indeed cultivate) during May, resulting in many nests of ground-nesting birds, particularly skylark, being destroyed.

Set-aside was, however, perhaps one of the single largest changes in farming practice witnessed in a single season. In fact the potential benefits of set-aside should not be under-estimated. It can increase habitat diversity and habitat quality. The scheme put back one of the most important elements of mixed farming, fallow, into the arable farming system in one season. Set-aside essentially takes a proportion of arable fields out of production for one or more years. Farmers must establish a green cover to prevent leaching and erosion, either by sowing a grass mixture or through natural regeneration. Under the one year (rotational) scheme with natural regeneration this process has produced weedy stubble fields which persist over winter, on a huge scale. Theoretically, this should benefit those seed-eating species which have suffered as a result of the loss of this habitat over the past 20 years. Recent research by the RSPB (Wilson *et al.*, 1995) has indeed shown strong selection for naturally regenerated rotational set-aside over all other field types by a range of over-wintering birds, including skylark, linnet *Carduelis cannabina*, reed bunting *Emberiza schoeniclus* and cirl bunting.

Fallow in the spring can also provide nesting sites for a range of ground-nesting birds. Work by the Game Conservancy Trust (GCT) has shown that

Figure 12 View of set-aside farmland in the UK. (Photo by C.H. Gomersall/RSPB.)

introduction of set-aside can increase survival rates and breeding success of both grey partridge and pheasant *Phasianus colchicus* but that these benefits are lost if green cover is cut or ploughed at the wrong time. Work by the BTO and the Biotechnology and Biological Sciences Research Council (BBSRC) has shown that skylarks not only nest at much higher densities on set-aside fields than cropped fields but also are far more productive on set-aside (Wilson *et al.*, 1995, Table 3).

The third way in which set-aside can benefit birds is by reintroducing grassland to arable prairies. Research is currently underway to determine whether set-aside with a sown grass cover can provide foraging opportunities for breeding birds (particularly under the non-rotational scheme where the same field is left fallow for a number of years).

It seems clear that set-aside has enormous potential to provide conservation benefits, partly because of what it can deliver and partly because of the scale on which the scheme operates. Some of these benefits have been realized but many have not because of a variety of problems. For instance, the rules for management of individual fields have been drawn up explicitly to prevent farmers from benefiting financially. Grazing of a sown green cover at low stock densities may be beneficial in trying to create a sward structure suitable for a particular group of invertebrates, but it has not generally been permitted. Similarly, the administrators have repeatedly insisted on summer cutting of green cover to avoid farmers benefiting from either a hay crop or indeed a grain crop from volunteer (self-sown) cereals. The UK government finally reacted to advice from conservationists and from 1997 cutting or cultivation of set-aside before 15 July will be prohibited. Furthermore, set-aside is a very broad term covering a multitude of different habitat types and has changed rapidly since its introduction. Many farmers have been attracted by the opportunity to grow industrial (non-food) oil crops, leading, in some areas, to a proliferation of rape and linseed rather than the naturally regenerated stubbles so sorely needed by many bird species.

Set-aside has probably provided some respite for the UK's beleaguered populations of seed-eating birds. However, the biggest problem with the scheme is that it is unsustainable. The scheme was designed with only one objective in mind: to reduce cereal surpluses. When this need changes, so will the policy. The world economy is so fickle that it is very difficult to predict what level of cereal production will be required in north-west Europe ten years from now. Policy experts have put forward different scenarios resulting in variation in the level of arable crops to be set aside from 0 to 20%. Funded as it is by public money, set-aside is unlikely to be an acceptable long-term option compared with alternative policies designed to achieve specific social and/or environmental objectives.

To be successful, the set-aside scheme needs to be reframed completely to include explicit conservation measures as one of its primary objectives. This would allow for specific and targeted management options, ensuring that potential benefits were delivered on the ground. Renamed and relaunched as 'conservation farmland', the scheme should be far more palatable to both the paying public and the farmers who would perceive both a purpose and a product.

Of course, such a scheme would also reduce production levels and paradoxically, it is for this very reason that it is probably not a politically acceptable long-term solution. Whilst both the EU and the UK Government have thus far gratefully received any reports highlighting the conservation benefits of the scheme in order to divert criticism, it is unlikely that they will reframe it explicitly to include conservation objectives. This is because if set-aside were to be reframed in the UK to incorporate conservation objectives, and subsequently had to be withdrawn for whatever reason, the Government would be left vulnerable to suggestions of having contravened their declared intention to conserve UK biodiversity. Because of the unpopularity of set-aside among farmers and economists, much attention has focused on abolishing or reducing it and this is seen by many as a greater priority than changes in the set-aside rules themselves. The role of set-aside as a conservation measure is therefore limited by uncertainty about its long-term future, with several recent studies advocating its abolition in conjunction with a cut in cereal prices to world levels (e.g. Josling & Tangermann, 1995). While this is also the view of the UK Government and the recent report by its 'Think-Tank' on the CAP (MAFF, 1995), the European Commission and most Member States are opposed to radical reform (*Financial Times*, 1995). Although there is resistance to reform, international developments such as the General Agreement on Tariffs and Trade (GATT), European expansion and world market demand all raise questions about the long-term future of set-aside.

CONCLUSIONS

The rapid decline of farmland birds in the UK and across north-west Europe illustrates several important points.

(1) If we have a serious undertaking to conserve biodiversity, monitoring is absolutely essential. If we do not know what the trends in our wildlife populations are, we cannot take corrective action.
(2) With the speed of modern technological development, wide-scale conservation problems can develop rapidly.
(3) The kind of habitat degradation described in this chapter can pass unnoticed; few people predicted the impact that loss of mixed farming systems would have on common farmland birds.

The solutions are, generally speaking, relatively simple to correct from a practical point of view. The major obstacle is one of economics. Farming is an enormous industry, currently supported by public money. Action needs to be taken on a wide scale; small-scale schemes will have little impact. It is essential that we move away from the current system of unsustainable production maintained by artificial price support. There are two ways of doing this.

(1) Farming systems could be extensified by reducing inputs (this could be done through disincentives such as a pesticide tax or conditionality). Under this option farmers would still strive to produce food as economically as possible under the existing legislation. The conservation benefits accruing from this course of action would be spin-offs.
(2) Alternatively, conservation benefits could be recognized as legitimate products of farming alongside food production. Targets could be achieved through implementation of prescriptions (or achievement of wildlife targets) which may involve land diversion on a small scale or even some form of extensification on part or all of the farm. Conservation benefits would be paid for through a specifically designed environmental support system operating through incentive schemes.

REFERENCES

BARR, C., BUNCE, R., CUMMINS, R.P., FRENCH, D.D. & HOWARD, D.C. (1992) Hedgerow Change in Great Britain. *Institute of Terrestrial Ecology Annual Report 1991–92*, **21**: 21–24.
BRIGGS, D.J. & COURTNEY, F.M. (1985) *Agriculture and the Environment*. London and New York: Longman.
DELIUS, J.D. (1965) A population study of skylarks *Alauda arvensis*. *Ibis*, **107**: 466–492.
DONALD, P.F. & EVANS, A.D. (1994) Habitat selection by corn buntings *Miliaria calandra* in winter. *Bird Study*, **41**(3): 199–210.

DONALD, P.F. & EVANS, A.D. (1995) Population size and habitat selection of corn buntings *Miliaria calandra* breeding in Britain. *Bird Study*, **42**: 190–204.

EVANS, A.D. (1992) The numbers and distribution of cirl buntings *Emberiza cirlus* breeding in Britain in 1989. *Bird Study*, **39**: 17–22.

EVANS, A.D. & SMITH, K.W. (1992) Bird Numbers: Distribution, Modelling and Ecological Aspects (Poster Appendix). In E.J.M Hagemeijer & T.J. Verstrael (eds) *Proceedings XIIth International Conference IBCC and EOAC*, pp. 23–28.

EVANS, A.D. & SMITH, K.W. (1994). Habitat selection of cirl buntings *Emberiza cirlus* wintering in Britain. *Bird Study*, **41**(2): 81–87.

EVANS, A.D., APPLEBY, M., DIXON, J., NEWBERY, P. & SWALES, V. (1996) What future for farmland birds in the UK? *RSPB Conservation Review*, **9**: 32–40.

EVANS, A.D., SMITH, K.W., BUCKINGHAM, D.L. & EVANS, J. (in press) Seasonal variation in breeding performance and nestling diet of cirl buntings *Emberiza cirlus* in England. *Bird Study*.

EVANS, J., WILSON, J.D. & BROWNE, S. (1995) Habitat selection and breeding success of skylarks *Alauda arvensis* on organic and conventional farmland. In *Part III British Trust for Ornithology Research Report 154. The Effect of of Organic Farming Regimes on Breeding and Winter Bird Populations*, pp. 1–34. Thetford.

Financial Times (1995) Britain stands alone on farm policy reform. 1 August.

FULLER, R.J., GREGORY, R.D., GIBBONS, D.W., MARCHANT, J.H., WILSON, J.D., BAILLIE, S.R. & CARTER, N. (1995) Population declines and range contractions among farmland birds in Britain. *Conservation Biology*, **9**: 1425–1442.

GIBBONS, D.W., REID, J.B. & CHAPMAN, R.A. (eds) (1993) *The New Atlas of Breeding Birds in Britain and Ireland: 1988–1991*. London: T. and A.D. Poyser.

HARTLEY, I.R., SHEPHARD, M., ROBSON, T. & BURKE, T. (1993) Reproductive success of plygynous male corn buntings (*Milaria calandra*) as confirmed by DNA fingerprinting. *Behavioural Ecology*, **4**: 310—313.

JOSLING, T. & TANGERMANN, S. (1995) *Towards a Common Agricultural Policy for the Next Century*. London: European Policy Forum.

MARCHANT, J.H., HUDSON, R. CARTER, S.P. & WHITTINGTON., P. (1990) *Population Trends in British Breeding Birds*. Tring: British Trust for Ornithology and Nature Conservancy Council.

McGREGOR, P.K. & THOMPSON, D.G.A. (1988) Constancy and change in local dialect of the corn bunting. *Ornis Scandinavica*, **19**: 153–159.

MAFF (Ministry for Agriculture Food and Fisheries) (1995) *European Agriculture: The case for radical reform. Conclusions from the Ministry for Agriculture Food and Fisheries Review Group*. London: Ministry for Agriculture Food and Fisheries.

O'CONNOR, R.J. & SHRUBB, M. (1986) *Farming and Birds*. Cambridge: Cambridge University Press.

PORTER, R., BIBBY, C., ELLIOT, G., HOUSDEN, S., THOMAS, G. & WILLIAMS, G. (1990) Species Action Plans for Birds. *RSPB Conservation Review*, **4**: 10–14.

RAYMENT, M. (1995) *A Review of the 1992 Common Agricultural Policy Arable Reforms*. Sandy: The Royal Society for the Protection of Birds.

RSPB (1991) Species Action Plan 1858 Cirl Bunting *Emberiza cirlus* . A Red Data Bird. Prepared by the Royal Society for the Protection of Birds in association with the Joint Nature Conservation Committee and Country Conservation Agencies. 30 p. Sandy.

RSPB (1994) Species Action Plan 1858 Cirl Bunting *Emberiza cirlus* . Prepared by the Royal Society for the Protection of Birds in association with the Joint Nature Conservation Committee and Country Conservation Agencies. 30 p. Sandy.

RSPB (Royal Society for the Protection of Birds) (1995) Environmental Land Management Schemes in England. Unpublished Report.

SHARROCK, J.T.R. (1976) *The Atlas of Breeding Birds in Britain and Ireland.* Berkhamstead: Poyser.

SITTERS, H.P. (1982) The decline of the cirl bunting in Britain, 1968–80. *British Birds*, 75: 105–108.

SITTERS, H.P. (1985) Cirl buntings in Britain in 1982. *Bird Study*, 32: 1–10.

SITTERS, H.P. (1991) A study of foraging behaviour and parental care in the cirl bunting *Emberiza cirlus*. MSc Thesis, University of Aberdeen.

TUCKER, G.M. & HEATH, M.F. (1994) *Birds in Europe: their Conservation Status*, BirdLife Conservation Series no. 3. Cambridge: BirdLife International.

WARD, R.S. & AEBISCHER, N.J. (1994) *Changes in Corn Bunting Distribution on the South Downs in Relation to Agricultural Land Use and Cereal Invertebrates.* English Nature Research Report No 134.

WILSON, J.D., EVANS, A.D., POULSEN, J.G. & EVANS, J. (1995) Wasteland or Oasis? The use of set-aside by wintering and breeding birds. *British Wildlife*, 6: 214–223.

VAN WINGERDEN, W.K.R.E., MUSTERS, J.C.M., KLEUKERS, R.M.J.C., BONGERS, W. & VAN BIEZEN, J.B. (1991) The influence of cattle grazing intensity on grasshopper abundance (*orthoptera: Acrididae*). *Proceedings of Experimental and Applied Entomology, NEV, Amsterdam*, 2: 28–34.

VAN WINGERDEN, W.K.R.E., VAN KREVELD, A.R. & BONGERS, W. (1992) Analysis of species composition and abundance of grasshoppers (*orthoptera: Acrididae*) in natural and fertilized grasslands. *Journal of Applied Entomology*, 113: 138–152.

13

Conclusions: a future for farming and birds?

DEBORAH J. PAIN & MICHAEL W. PIENKOWSKI

SUMMARY

In this chapter we draw on those preceding to synthesize common themes, and look at any divergence from these. We outline the importance of farmland for birds and biodiversity conservation, and the reasons why, and how, this diversity is being lost, as well as discussing future research needs. We also consider the extent to which measures under the Common Agricultural Policy (e.g. set-aside), including its Accompanying Measures (e.g. the Agri-environment Regulation), have benefited, and could potentially benefit birds, along with the type and scale of environmentally sensitive management needed to conserve biodiversity in the future. We finish with an overview of farming and birds, stressing the necessity of flexible policies in order to maintain a diverse agricultural landscape, for the environment in general, for birds and other wildlife, and for people. General policy conclusions resulting from previous chapters are outlined. The final chapter (Dixon, Chapter 14) considers the potential for achieving conservation management in the countryside through changes to policy and discusses the likely opportunities to do this.

INTRODUCTION

Chapters 4–12 show, quite clearly and emphatically, that conservation value is found not only in predominantly natural areas, but that farmed land can, and often does, support an abundance and diversity of wildlife. However, floral and

Copyright © 1997 Academic Press Ltd
All rights of reproduction in any form reserved

faunal diversity has been shown, through the numerous examples presented in this book and elsewhere (e.g. Beaufoy *et al.*, 1994; Bignal *et al.*, 1988, 1994; Goriup *et al.*, 1991; Tucker & Heath, 1994) to be more threatened on farmland than on almost any other habitat in Europe. This is well illustrated by the fact that, of the bird species associated with farmland in Europe, almost half are of conservation concern (Tucker, Chapter 4).

Farmland birds are declining not just in Europe but in many places subject to a high level of intensification. For example, Peterjohn & Sauer (1995) have shown that grassland birds in the USA exhibit steeper and more consistent declines than any other group of birds monitored by the North American Breeding Bird Survey since 1966 (see also Peterjohn & Sauer, 1993). In the USA, agricultural intensification has proceeded over a similar time scale to that in Europe – many parallels exist between the situations on the two continents.

The underlying reasons for this conservation crisis are the changes in agriculture, especially intensification. This has been enabled by technological developments and their widespread adoption, although government intervention (largely through the CAP) has certainly fuelled the process (Potter, Chapter 2). It should be remembered that, during the last 40 years of rapid change in farming, it has not been the decisions that individual farmers have taken to increase production that should be condemned or questioned, but rather the nature of the policy framework within which they made those decisions.

Working towards solutions for the farmland conservation crisis must not be delayed, and the increasingly widespread recognition of the impacts of modern farming methods on wildlife, and the changing imperatives for farming, provide an opportunity not to be missed.

Public perceptions of farmers as environmental managers

The public's perception of the part that farmers play as environmental managers, rather than just food producers, varies throughout Europe. This is not surprising considering the diversity of goods produced, production techniques used, and levels of intensification on an EU scale. In those areas of Europe where traditional low-intensity farming systems remain (such as the dehesas and pseudosteppes of Spain, see Díaz *et al.*, Chapter 7; Suárez *et al.*, Chapter 11; and other areas, Bignal *et al.*, 1994), nature conservation value also remains, although it is often under threat. Such areas represent an important but declining part of the farmed landscape of the EU. Elsewhere, where agricultural intensification has been rapid, farmers have moved from a position of either creating or maintaining an attractive and diverse landscape to one of destroying it in many cases. The public's perception of farmers as custodians of the countryside has changed along with this, as illustrated by the following UK example.

The Scott Report (1944) states that 'The landscape of England and Wales is a striking example of the interdependence between the satisfaction of man's material wants and the creation of beauty. [and] . . . the beauty and pattern of the countryside are the direct result of the cultivation of the soil and there is no antagonism between use and beauty' (Scott Report in Blunden & Curry, 1985). However, in 1959, Bracey stated that 'From 1920 onwards, country people and lovers of the countryside gradually became aware that throughout wide areas the tranquillity of the countryside was being destroyed, traditional landscapes were disappearing . . . and in many places natural flora and fauna were suffering drastic modifications and often destruction' (in Blunden & Curry, 1985). Thus, although predominant thinking in the 1940s still viewed agriculture as playing a custodian role in the countryside (see Chapter 1), changes to this were already taking place in some areas.

Our hope is that the increasing recognition of the importance of a structurally and biologically diverse farmed environment will result in policies which assist farmers in returning to the position of custodians of the countryside – not just of small pockets of still traditionally managed farmland, but of whole landscapes.

It is important to note that the best land in conservation terms is usually that which has not been intensified, but farmers there tend to get little or no support (although they need it most). This is because payments are usually made to change something, rather than to keep doing what is good (even when that would otherwise change, as it is tending to). Payments for environmental benefit could overcome this (see Robson, Chapter 3). We must move towards policies that both incorporate the environment as a central feature, and provide sufficient financial security for farmers to encourage the continuation of the industry at an approximately similar level to present.

The remainder of this chapter summarizes the information presented in this book and related work on the problem, i.e. the effects of agricultural intensification, and its solutions, including the type and scale of action needed to maintain farmland biodiversity.

THE ENVIRONMENTAL EFFECTS OF AGRICULTURAL INTENSIFICATION – DECLINING FARMLAND BIRDS

Farmland habitats across Europe support what might seem a surprisingly rich avifauna. However, as illustrated by Tucker in Chapter 4, more birds are threatened on farmland than in other habitats.

Tucker illustrated that, in terms of absolute numbers, arable and agriculturally improved grasslands have more Species of European Conservation Concern (SPECs) associated with them than do other farmed habitats. However, a higher proportion of birds associated with cereals managed in a low-intensity way and with dry grasslands are SPECs than is the case in other habitats (see also Donázar et al., Chapter 5). In addition, many bird species associated with low intensity cereals and dry grasslands have their populations concentrated in this

Figure 1 Pesticide spraying of a cereal monoculture. The indirect effects of pesticides threaten a wide range of declining agricultural species. (Photo by M.W. Richards/RSPB)

habitat. This is an apt illustration of the importance of conserving the low input, often traditionally managed and marginally economic farming systems, as well as improving the conservation value of some of the more intensively managed land – both strategies are essential to conserve farmland biodiversity.

In *Birds in Europe*, Tucker & Heath (1994) summarized the major threats to all SPECs with substantially declining European populations. Their analysis showed that agricultural intensification (excluding pesticide effects) affects more species than any other threat (42% of all SPECs). Other factors associated with agricultural change, including the indirect effects of pesticides, and agricultural abandonment, each affected over 20% of species.

In Chapter 4, Tucker takes this analysis one step further and analyses the direct agricultural threats (splitting intensification into its component parts) to agricultural birds. This points to grassland conversion, the indirect effects of pesticides, abandonment, cropping changes (e.g. fertilizer additions), loss of non-cropped habitat (such as field margins), high stocking rates, drainage and irrigation, as affecting the highest proportions of declining agricultural species (see Figure 6, Chapter 4). Other factors, such as changes in crop timing and farming operations affect a smaller number of species (but may be integrally linked to some of the other changes mentioned above).

These aspects of intensification affect birds through: (1) habitat destruction or loss (e.g. grassland conversion to arable, abandonment) which often results in species loss; (2) changes in the structural quality of habitat (e.g. loss of hedgerows and other non-cropped habitats); (3) loss of the biological quality of habitats (e.g. food shortage resulting from the indirect effects of pesticides).

Below, we review briefly examples of the effects of some of these factors on agricultural species, as illustrated throughout Chapters 5–12. These factors are all inter-related, but have been divided into broad categories.

Irrigation

Although in recent years supply control measures have been aimed at reducing arable production, there are still many large areas of fairly low-intensity arable production where further intensification is certain to take place (see Potter, Chapter 2; Beaufoy *et al.*, 1994). A large proportion is in the low-intensity dryland arable areas of Spain, such as the pseudosteppes. To illustrate the scale of this process, 1 million ha of land were brought under new irrigation between 1970 and 1989 in Spain alone (Egdell, 1993) and a further 600 000 ha are to be irrigated according to the National Hydrological Plan (Suárez *et al.*, Chapter 11). It is only in the areas with poorest soil that intensification is not likely to take place, and here abandonment (see below) is a real possibility.

Irrigation *per se* affects birds and other wildlife through the disturbance it creates (which may result in desertion of areas by shy species like the globally endangered great bustard *Otis tarda*). The infrastructure associated with irrigation can also affect birds, and great bustards have been killed through flying into overhead cables supplying electricity to pumping stations (MOPT, 1992; Martín-Novella *et al.*, 1993; MOPTMA, 1994; Tucker, Chapter 4).

However, the greatest threats to wildlife usually result from the further intensification that irrigation makes possible, with high applications of fertilizers, modern fast-growing crops, loss of marginal habitats and frequent pesticide applications. The decrease in the area of dehesa in Extremadura and Andalucia in Spain has been partly attributed to increased irrigation and cultivation (see Díaz *et al.*, Chapter 7).

Irrigation usually results in significantly increased production levels, and increases in revenue and profits. However, this is not always the case. The investment made by farmers to increase production has resulted in increased debt. For example, in Spain this grew by 50% from 1987 to 1991 (Egdell, 1993) and in some cases farmers have not been able to pay for the costs of the distribution network of the irrigation system, or have questioned its economic profitability. In such cases the irrigation infrastructure may remain unused (San Agustín, 1993).

Drainage

As with irrigation, intensification almost invariably follows drainage. Grassland drainage may result in habitat loss through conversion to cereals, or deterior-

Figure 2 Cutting drainage channels in lowland wet grassland in the UK. Agricultural intensification almost invariably follows drainage. (Photo by C.H. Gomersall/RSPB.)

ation in habitat quality through intensification. Although grassland drainage, particularly in the uplands, is now much reduced, grassland conversion is a threat to a large number of agricultural birds as described above (see Tucker, Chapter 4).

Intensification of rough grass through drainage, re-seeding and fertilizer applications is thought to be responsible for declines in a number of waders, including curlew *Numenius arquata*, black-tailed godwit *Limosa limosa* and redshank *Tringa totanus*, as described in Chapter 10 (Beintema *et al.*). Invertebrate prey composition changes with increasing levels of fertilizer application, and this may be to the detriment of wader chicks (Siepel, 1990; Beintema, 1991). The accessibility of soil invertebrates to waders is reduced through drainage, and lower water levels and increased fertilizer applications can result in more rapid vegetation growth in spring, making grasslands unsuitable for nesting (Green & Cadbury, 1987; O'Brien & Self, 1994; Beintema *et al.*, Chapter 10) or feeding (Bignal *et al.*, in press).

In addition, grassland drainage reduces the likelihood of winter flooding and consequently feeding opportunities for a variety of wildfowl. Breeding sites such as marshes and ponds, formerly of considerable importance for garganey *Anas querquedula* and pintail *A. acuta* (Rutschke, 1989), have also been lost.

Figure 3 Bullocks. Increases in livestock densities have frequently resulted from agricultural intensification. In lowland wet grasslands this has often led to increased destruction of wader nests through trampling. (Photo by A. Hay/RSPB.)

Livestock densities

Several chapters refer to the effects, or potential effects, of changes in livestock densities upon birds and biodiversity. Changes have often been increases in density. In many places this has been made possible through other aspects of intensification, such as improved drainage, re-seeding and increased fertilizer applications (e.g. in the Netherlands, Beintema *et al.*, Chapter 10). Agricultural payments per head of livestock have further accelerated this process.

In the Netherlands, the increased stocking densities that follow intensification often result in increased trampling of nests, a common cause of breeding failure for many wader species (see Beintema *et al.*, Chapter 10).

Overall, in southern Europe, livestock levels increased considerably following accession, in 1986, to the EC and thereby access to subsidies per head of livestock. In the Less Favoured Area pseudosteppe regions of Spain, evidence suggests that local increases in livestock densities and consequent over-grazing could reduce grass cover and pasture quality, and result in lower food densities for species like the globally threatened lesser kestrel *Falco naumanni* (Parr *et al.*, in press; Naveso & Fernández, 1993; Donázar *et al.*, Chapter 5).

Although livestock densities have generally increased, there have also been cases of reductions in stocking densities, especially on marginally economic land with low production potential, and also of complete abandonment (see Lefranc,

Chapter 9, Díaz *et al.*, Chapter 7, Donázar *et al.*, Chapter 5; Suárez *et al.*, Chapter 11; EFNCP, 1996). Achieving the appropriate intensity of grazing is crucial to sustain the conservation value of pastureland.

Díaz *et al.* (Chapter 7) discuss how both intensification and abandonment can affect the dehesa system of Spain. Accelerated tree loss would result from an increased intensity of livestock and arable farming – and scrub invasion from decreases in stocking density or a reduction in ploughing and periodic cropping (Diario Oficial de Extremadura, 1986).

Loss of non-cropped habitats

Lefranc (Chapter 9) describes the close association of shrikes *Lanius* spp. with a particular type of farmland which is less well defined than many others. Shrikes require an 'untidy', or rather 'structurally diverse', landscape, with infrequently managed field margins, overgrown hedgerows, trees and areas of scrub interspersed with open land. They also require low chemical inputs, with consequent abundant invertebrate fauna. Such landscapes have declined for about 40 years throughout large parts of Europe. This is partly the result of the replacement of farm jobs by capital-intensive machinery and the energy inputs to operate this (see Chapter 2). It is likely that a combination of intensification-related factors have resulted in the decline of shrikes, and it is difficult to identify a single most important factor for any individual species. However, the weight of circumstantial evidence linking the decline of shrike species with agricultural intensification and the loss of structural habitat diversity is overwhelming. The need for a heterogeneous landscape (and the consequent varied opportunities for foraging and shelter) is common to many species (e.g. Bignal *et al.*, 1988; Stowe *et al.*, 1993). The public needs to recognize the importance of such 'untidy', but wildlife-rich, landscapes (Gummer, 1993).

Chemical inputs – pesticides and fertilizers

There have been substantial increases in chemical inputs since the 1950s, as described by Potter (Chapter 2). Within the EU, applications of nitrogen fertilizer have increased by well over 400%, and increases in the scale and quantities of pesticides used have also been significant. In France, for example, total annual pesticide use increased from 25 000 to 100 000 tonnes between 1971 and 1981 (Potter, Chapter 2).

The effects of fertilizer applications have included increases in grass sward and crop growth rates, which has allowed for changes in the timing and frequency of cropping. On grassland, this has enabled increased stocking rates (as described above), and the production of silage rather than hay in many areas. The effects of such changes upon some birds are quite well documented. A classic example is the globally endangered corncrake *Crex crex*. Changes in

Figure 4 The corncrake is a globally threatened species, declining throughout much of Europe. Changes in grassland management are thought to be partly responsible for the declines in many areas. (Photo by C.H. Gomersall/RSPB.)

grassland management are thought to have contributed to the decline of this species, and nests and chicks are destroyed through early mechanized harvesting of silage or hay (e.g. see Stowe & Hudson, 1988; Williams *et al.*, 1991; Stowe *et al.*, 1993; Green, 1995). The corncrake was once a common and widespread species in Britain, and as a result of agricultural intensification is now restricted to a few small pockets on the west coast of Scotland. It is declining in much of Europe.

There are many indirect effects of pesticides upon birds, through reducing numbers and diversity of both wild plants and invertebrates. Fertilizer applications may be associated with food reduction for some bird species. Grasshoppers and crickets (orthopterans) are important food items for the chicks of many species (such as cirl buntings *Emberiza cirlus*, see Evans, Chapter 12; little bustards *Tetrax tetrax*, Pain (1994); and shrikes *Lanius* spp., see Lefranc, Chapter 9). Whilst there are no quantitative data on historical trends in grasshopper populations on farmland, application of nitrogen-based fertilizers is known to lead to uniform, species-poor swards which are poor habitat for orthopterans (van Wingerden *et al.*, 1992).

Potts (Chapter 6), presents the results of possibly the most detailed long-term study into the population dynamics of a declining species – in this case the grey partridge *Perdix perdix*. The decline of this species was shown to have been driven by an increase in chick mortality through starvation, brought about by the use of herbicides. As well as pesticide applications, changes in cropping methods have influenced food availability. Sawfly larvae are an important chick food item and they depend upon undersowing (i.e. the use of cereals as a nurse for grass) which declined rapidly from the 1960s onwards.

Reduced food supply is also considered to have played a part in the declines of many other species (such as shrikes, see Lefranc, Chapter 9), although evidence is often less direct than for the grey partridge.

We note elsewhere the problem that the environmental and other costs of the use of chemicals are not charged to the user, thereby distorting the economic comparison between low-input and intensive systems.

Abandonment and afforestation

In addition to specialization (see below) and intensification, EU policies have also encouraged abandonment, particularly in areas where farming is marginally economic under current policies. For example, in both the dehesas and cereal steppes of Spain, there has been a trend towards intensification of cultivation on land with the highest production potential, and abandonment or afforestation of the less productive areas (Díaz et al., Chapter 7; Suárez et al., Chapter 11). Although this may appear superficially to be a rational use of farmland resources, it fails to consider the wildlife and social implications, and its sustainability must be questioned. Lefranc (Chapter 9) also stresses the part that abandonment of marginal pastoral areas, such as the Causse of the Massif Central in France, has played in transforming the landscape. Abandoned areas on the Causse have become forests, either through subsidized reforestation schemes or secondary succession. This represents total habitat loss for many of the species associated with open pastureland. Similar trends occur in the north and west uplands of Europe such as Ireland, Scotland and Wales, with the sale of hill land for afforestation liberating funds for the intensification of agriculture the 'in-bye' land (Bignal et al., 1988; Pienkowski, 1989). The economics of afforestation schemes is outside the scope of this book but has itself been subject to serious questioning (National Audit Office, 1986; Tompkins, 1986; Stroud et al., 1987). In many cases, the intensification of land-use or abandonment are effectively irreversible in wildlife terms, in that many species will not be able to recolonize on human timescales.

Regional specialization and loss of diversity in the farmed landscape

At a more general level, the loss of diversity at scales from regional to individual farm has played an important part in the declines in population and changes in distribution of many species (e.g. Potts, Chapter 6; Bignal et al., 1989; Hudson *et al.*, 1994; Stowe *et al.*, 1993; Green & Robins, 1993; Bignal & McCracken, in press).

European agriculture is still diverse on a continental scale due to the immovable factors of climate, latitude, altitude and topography. However, habitat diversity on a national, regional and farm scale has undoubtedly been lost in many areas, and has remained high only in areas still extensively managed (Bignal *et al.*, 1988; Donázar *et al.*, Chapter 5; Díaz *et al.*, Chapter 7). In much of Europe, farming systems have become polarized, and farmed landscapes locally homogeneous. The rice fields of northern Italy, and the east to west separation of cereal and pastoral farming in the UK provide good examples of this (Fasola & Ruíz, Chapter 8; Evans, Chapter 12).

The specialization of farming, and loss of crop and structural diversity (and mixed farming), is at least partly responsible for declines of the grey partridge (Potts, Chapter 6), the cirl bunting (Evans, Chapter 12), lapwing *Vanellus vanellus* (Hudson *et al.*, 1994), chough *Pyrrhocorax pyrrhocorax* (Bignal & Curtis, 1989) and other species (Tucker, Chapter 4). The cirl bunting, for example, requires pasture where little artificial fertilizer or pesticide is used, close to arable land managed to leave weedy stubble fields over winter (Evans, Chapter 12). Similar farm-scale mosaics are required for chough (Bignal *et al.*, in press) and a variety of raptors as illustrated by Donázar *et al.* (Chapter 5).

Human health and the farmed environment

Although marginal to the remit of this book, the general environmental effects of agricultural intensification merit a brief mention, as they concern many components of the environment of importance to humans, both directly and through wildlife.

The intensification of farming, including, for example, increased water extraction and the increased use of fertilizers and pesticides, has resulted in considerable environmental degradation both within, and outside farmed areas. Effects include a decrease in water quality (with increased levels of nitrates, etc.) and wetland eutrophication. Examples of such effects outside farmed areas are described by Tucker (Chapter 4). Many similar cases can be cited. For example, the National Rivers Authority (NRA) in the UK launched its first 'Pesticides and the Environment' report at the end of 1995. The levels of certain pesticides in ground waters frequently exceeded EU limits for drinking water (pesticide removal facilities are generally not employed for ground waters). Triazon and uron herbicides breached the limits most. Levels of bentazone, a herbicide used on peas, beans and potatoes, were found to exceed drinking water limits in both surface and ground water (*The Advisor*, 1996).

In many areas continuous cropping has resulted in a degradation of soil structure and significant soil erosion. An extreme example is given by the great plains of the USA, where many soil conservation measures (such as the

Conservation Reserves Programme) are now underway in an attempt to alleviate this problem (see Vickery *et al.*, 1995) and similar effects can be seen in parts of the EU.

Intensive farming methods and the chemicals employed to help ensure high yields have had direct effects upon human health. During the 1950s and 1960s there were numerous incidents of pesticide poisoning, often involving hundreds of people. These mainly resulted from unsafe carriage or handling of pesticides, and frequently involved farm workers (for example, see Graham, 1970). More recently, strict control of the transport and use of pesticides has certainly reduced cases of direct human mortality, although debate continues over the sublethal effects of many substances.

Over the last few decades, intensive animal production methods have come under considerable scrutiny. In the UK, there has been considerable publicity concerning bovine spongiform encepalopathy (BSE), a fatal disease in cattle. It is believed that cattle became infected after eating feed containing sheep-meat contaminated with a similar disease, scrapie. Dr John Wilesmith, who leads government research into BSE, stated that 'All the evidence indicates that cattle got it from sheep scrapie in the feed. The disease developed because in the early 1980s the rendering industry changed its methods of processing sheep meat to make money' (*The Times*, 28 November 1994).

Public fears over the possibility of cross-contamination have had an economic impact upon the cattle industry. Similarly, a scare over *Salmonella* toxin in battery-farmed chicken eggs in the UK damaged the poultry industry in 1988.

Such problems can result from the intensification of agricultural systems and economic pressures to increase profit margins. These have pushed animal production systems farther and farther away from the 'more natural' extensive agriculture. Although not all such problems would disappear as a result of more extensive and environmentally sensitive farming practices, many of them would be alleviated.

Other aspects

Many other factors associated with intensification have influenced birds in a variety of ways. These include changes in field size, resulting from farm restructuring, increased mechanization, and changes in cultivation techniques and timing. These are all closely related to other aspects of intensification, as described above, and examples of these are given throughout this volume. Bignal *et al.* (in press) provide a good example of the interaction of farming operations with the food density and availability of food for choughs.

In conclusion, this book has shown how farmland birds, many of which are still common, could easily become the rare birds of tomorrow if action is not taken soon. Nine species that regularly use agricultural habitats in Europe are already on their way to global extinction (Tucker, Chapter 4). Their existence is important for biodiversity conservation throughout Europe. Maintenance of the habitats occupied by such species is crucial also for many other wildlife populations (e.g. Bignal *et al.*, 1994).

The most significant threats to farmed areas and the conservation of the diversity that they support are intensification (encompassing many factors), abandonment and inappropriate afforestation. These are also, for economic reasons, more of a threat in the low-intensity areas, where farming is often a marginal activity (Suárez *et al.*, Chapter 11; Donázar *et al.*, Chapter 5; McCracken *et al.*, 1995). It is also in such areas, often semi-natural, where such changes would do the most damage.

THE NEED FOR RESEARCH AND ACTION

An understanding of the distributions and requirements of any species or group of species is essential before developing prescriptive measures for their conservation. This makes birds very appropriate subjects of investigation, as they are probably the best-known taxa (see Tucker, Chapter 4; Moser *et al.*, 1995), and can act as appropriate barometers of environmental change, as discussed by Potts (Chapter 6). Throughout Europe, bird populations are better monitored than other taxa, and the continuation of such monitoring is essential, both at a continent-wide scale, and at a small scale, to enable the evaluation of beneficial or detrimental effects of changes in land-use and management.

There are many examples of ways in which either individual, or a combination of factors associated with agricultural intensification can affect birds, as illustrated in the previous section. In spite of this, there is still a considerable amount that we do not know about the interactions of many species with their environments, especially as agricultural habitats have been in a constant state of flux over recent decades. In only a few cases have detailed long-term studies been carried out that allow for the modelling of population responses to agricultural change. The study of the grey partridge by the Game Conservancy Council in the UK provides one of the few examples (Potts, Chapter 6). However, it is not possible to contemplate such detailed long-term studies for all of the 84 declining agricultural bird species in Europe. There are neither the financial resources available to conduct such work, nor the time. Given the rate at which many birds have declined in response to agricultural change, it is essential to act on the information currently available if we are to avoid further declines in farmland biodiversity. Indeed, in many northern European countries, some agricultural habitats have been changed to such an extent that certain species have become locally (e.g. the corncrake in most of north-west Europe), or even nationally (e.g. the great bustard in the UK) extinct.

Fortunately, although undoubtedly desirable, it is not always necessary to tackle (or even identify) the main factor responsible for a species' decline in order to stabilize the population or reverse the decline (Green, 1994). For example, if reduced chick survival has driven a population decline, the decline may, hypothetically, be reversed through finding ways of increasing adult survival, thus reducing the number of chicks that need to survive to maintain stability.

For many farmland birds, we do not know which factors have had the most influence upon their population dynamics – or at which part of the life cycle they have been acting. What seems likely, however, is that for many species, declines have been influenced by the interplay of a wide range of factors in combination (e.g. loss of habitat quality, seasonal availability of food). Consequently, it may be possible to stem the declines of at least some species through adopting a general extensification of some of the more intensively managed farmland, as this could benefit some parts of the life cycle of a range of species. Extensification should incorporate many of the features that we know could benefit birds (e.g. reduced chemical inputs, later cutting dates of hay/silage, leaving weedy over-winter stubbles or fallow, increased habitat diversity – see Chapters 5–12).

Should such an approach be adopted, monitoring the outcome would be essential – both in terms of measuring its success, and adapting different components of the extensification process to allow for more targeted conservation action through extensification in the future.

Integrated research

Both Díaz *et al.* (Chapter 7) and Suárez *et al.* (Chapter 11) illustrate the need for integrated studies which provide a good understanding of the relationships between wildlife and farming systems, and also evaluate the benefits of specific production techniques both in terms of the commercial products of farming, and the non-commercial environmental benefits. This is developed further by the European Forum on Nature Conservation and Pastoralism (EFNCP, 1996).

Integrated studies enable a prediction of the likely effects of habitat change, owing to changes in production techniques, upon wildlife (see also Hötker 1991; Bignal *et al.*, in press). They also allow for practical suggestions to be made (in economic or policy terms) as to how to maintain environmentally beneficial production techniques.

An example is given by Díaz *et al.* (Chapter 7). The wildlife of the dehesas requires a mosaic habitat created through management incorporating livestock grazing, ploughing and periodic cropping, in the right equilibrium. An increase in the intensity of livestock and arable uses of dehesa would undermine their long-term future by accelerating tree loss and inhibiting regeneration. At present, trees are not regenerating sufficiently. This problem could be tackled through, for example, making livestock payments conditional upon specified grazing regimes that allow for tree regeneration. The needs of a multi-use,

Figure 5 Common cranes flying over dehesa in Extremadura, Spain. Dehesa wildlife requires a habitat mosaic, maintained through an appropriate balance of livestock grazing, ploughing and cropping. (Photo by D.J. Pain.)

sustainable system (such as dehesa) are not assisted by EU policies that tend to address product sectors, rather than farming systems. This may be appropriate for intensive monocultures, but in a sustainable, multi-product system, several different EU commodity regimes may potentially apply and may often be incompatible; in dehesa systems, EU policies for various livestock, cereals and woodland may conflict (EFNCP, 1996).

Future needs

What is urgently needed is a combination of carefully targeted and integrated research, action based on the evidence already available, monitoring of the results of such action, and suggestions for practical ways to reverse the trends in agriculture that have undoubtedly led to many species' declines (see also Moser *et al.*, 1995).

Such research and monitoring should be adequately funded through EU and other sources. The importance of monitoring the biological effects of all schemes that result in significant land-use changes should be stressed, whether they have environmental objectives (such as ESAs), or simply have incidental conservation spin-offs (such as set-aside – see below).

It is also essential to monitor trends in bird populations, as indicators of biodiversity, across the whole of Europe. This is a major way in which we will be able to gauge the success of changes to farming policy and other conservation actions, both in the EU today, and the expanded EU of the future.

SET-ASIDE AND THE AGRI-ENVIRONMENT REGULATION – ARE THE ENVIRONMENTAL BENEFITS ENOUGH TO CONSERVE FARMLAND BIODIVERSITY?

Set-aside

Since 1988, the introduction of set-aside, as a supply control measure aimed at reducing surplus grain production, has resulted in substantial changes to the farmed landscape of the EU (see Robson, Chapter 3). In 1988, set-aside was voluntary, but it effectively became compulsory in 1992, with Arable Area payments made conditional upon entering the scheme (see Robson, Chapter 3). Set-aside regulations have changed considerably over time and differ between Member States, but have included rotational and non-rotational five-year set-aside (with 20-year set-aside options available under the Agri-environment Regulation).

Changes in land-use following the introduction in set-aside differed significantly between Member States. In the UK, the area under annual set-aside increased from comparatively little in 1988 to 662 000 ha, or 10% of the arable area in 1994/95 (Robson, Chapter 3). In Spain, traditional farming methods already incorporated over 4 million ha of winter fallow, constituting 50% of the cereal growing area or 20% of all cultivated land (Suárez et al., Chapter 11). The distribution of obligatory set-aside within the EU is very uneven, from less than 1% to 12% of utilized agricultural area across the EU (Robson, Chapter 3), partly because the actual area set aside is dependent on the proportion of holdings exceeding the lower limit (approximately 92 tonnes of production) at which set-aside becomes compulsory. In the UK, for example, this is most farms; in Portugal it is very few (see Robson, Chapter 3). Consequently, the potential effects of set-aside also vary between countries.

The UK experienced one of the largest changes in land-use of all Member States. At first compulsory set-aside was unpopular (Evans, Chapter 12) and initial rules for set-aside management in the UK were harmful to birds (with early cutting of green cover destroying many nests). However, rules have subsequently changed, and several farmland bird species, especially seed-eaters, appear to have benefited as a consequence. One-year set-aside, allowed to regenerate naturally, provides weedy winter stubble fields that are preferred feeding areas for a range of wintering birds in the UK, including skylark *Alauda arvensis*, linnet *Acanthis cannabina*, reed bunting *Emberiza schoeniclus* and cirl bunting (Wilson *et al.*, 1995), and fallow can also provide nest sites for several species, including the skylark (Evans, Chapter 12).

However, while some species appear to have benefited, so far others do not. The benefits to individual species are largely dependent upon the type of set-aside introduced and regulations governing its management (see Potts, Chapter 6).

There appears to be agreement that set-aside has substantial conservation potential, which is increasingly being realized for species in some situations, but not for others (Evans, Chapter 12; Potts, Chapter 6). However, set-aside is not a land-use policy, but a supply control measure, and conservation objectives were not among its primary objectives.

Set-aside cannot be viewed as a long-term, or sustainable conservation option – it is a supply control measure, and as such its future is uncertain (see Dixon, Chapter 14). Nevertheless, it is important not to under-estimate the potential conservation 'spin-offs' of such measures, and to ensure that they are realized, while working towards long-term sustainable solutions.

The Agri-environment Regulation

Unlike set-aside, certain voluntary measures are available (and have been for some years) within the CAP that support farming in an environmentally friendly way, e.g. Environmentally Sensitive Areas (ESAs – see Robson, Chapter 3). ESAs cannot be said to have universally benefited all declining bird species (as illustrated by Potts, Chapter 6 – although they probably could not be expected to). However, they have generally benefited a wide range of wildlife, and were certainly a step in the right direction in terms of bird conservation – through helping maintain those more traditional farming practices upon which many SPECs depend (see Tucker, Chapter 4). Such measures have been important in the conservation of globally threatened species like the great bustard (e.g. Naveso, 1993; Naveso & Groves-Reines, 1992). Initially, ESAs were effectively site-based, and consequently not sufficient to allow for the conservation of the many widely distributed declining farmland species. However, the Agri-environment Regulation (EC Reg. 2078/92) has extended the concept of ESAs, and there now exists the opportunity for farmers to adopt alternative land management practices across whole regions. For example, within the Agri-environment Regulation, premiums are paid for more extensive farming for a period of at least five years, and there are payments for environmental set-aside, which must be undertaken for at least 20 years (Robson, Chapter 3).

At present, the Agri-environment Regulation probably offers the best opportunity for the management of farmland in a way that is compatible with environmental conservation. Within the regulation, there is real potential for both the maintenance of traditional farming systems that currently support high diversity, and for the more sensitive management or extensification of the more heavily managed areas. However, ESAs cover less than 4% of the Utilized Agricultural Area (UAA) of the EU12, and uptake varies considerably between countries, from practically nothing to over 20% of the UAA in Germany (see Robson, Chapter 3). This is largely because they are under-funded, and their uptake by Member States is voluntary, and consequently dependent upon the financial incentives attached to them. In order for a high level of uptake to be achieved, the financial benefits accrued by the farmer need to at least balance, if not exceed, the financial benefits from alternative choices; this is often not the case (BirdLife International, 1994; EFNCP, 1996).

In addition, the Agri-environment Regulation is an Accompanying Measure. The importance of making environmental protection a central objective of the CAP has been noted by the European Parliament, the European Commission and conservation organizations alike. However, the necessary change is slow in coming, and covers a pitifully small percentage of the rural areas in danger of losing some of their environmental value (see Robson, Chapter 3). As has been illustrated and stressed throughout this volume, environmental concerns must be an integral and even central part of agricultural policy covering all farmed land, and not just a spin-off, if we are to maintain biological diversity on European farmland. Robson (Chapter 3) outlined a series of different 'models' that can be developed for the future of agricultural policy, and its integration with environmental and other policies in the future. The last chapter of this book (Dixon, Chapter 14) expands upon some of these options for the agricultural policy of the future.

THE TYPE AND SCALE OF ENVIRONMENTALLY SENSITIVE MANAGEMENT NEEDED TO CONSERVE BIODIVERSITY

That nature reserves and protected areas alone are insufficient to conserve widespread species like farmland birds is largely undisputed (see Pain & Dixon, Chapter 1). Reserves cover only a small proportion of the land surface in EU countries, whereas farmland covers over 40% of the EU15 (58% of the EU12). For example, in the UK in January 1995, agricultural land occupied more than 70% of the land surface, and nature reserves just over 2.8% (RSPB, 1995). Similarly, as discussed above, ESAs currently cover a very small proportion of agricultural land.

One suggested approach to biodiversity conservation has been the setting-aside of large amounts of land across Europe as reserves. Such ideas may have resulted partly from the recently (1980s to 1992) reduced drive for food production in the EU, and the removal of a percentage of land from production in an attempt to reduce surpluses. However, future trends are by no means certain (see Dixon, Chapter 14). Partly, this approach may result from the concept that substantially increased areas of nature reserves side by side with substantially decreased areas of agricultural land could provide both food and wildlife benefits. However, were this realized, it would probably result in more intensive management of the remaining agricultural land. Indeed, it has even been proposed that such intensification should be encouraged so that less land is needed for farming and more can be released for nature conservation (*Agra Europe*, 1996). In any situation where agricultural intensification is pushed to its extreme, simplification to a uniform habitat and decreases in floral and faunal diversity are likely to occur (as has happened in the Netherlands, see Beintema *et al.*, Chapter 10).

As discussed by Tucker (Chapter 4), the intensification of substantial amounts of farmland to release more land for nature conservation and other purposes could be deleterious for bird conservation for a variety of reasons. Not only would the quality of remaining farmland for birds and biodiversity in general be reduced, but the increase in areas of scrub and eventually some forest habitats may be of low quality and so low conservation value (see Tucker, Chapter 4). Also, if large areas of land were taken out of farming, it is unlikely that the majority would be used for conservation, which would be in competition with economic uses, such as forestry and development. Even if large areas were released for reserve creation, it is debatable whether there would ever be sufficient funding to manage such areas positively. However, we do not wish to under-estimate the potential conservation benefits of diverting a small amount (of the scale of a few per cent) of land away from agricultural production for habitat re-creation (see Dixon, Chapter 14). At such a scale, habitat re-creation could benefit rare, endangered or localized species, and would be unlikely to have a negative impact upon the management of remaining agricultural land.

We do suggest, however, that given constraints mentioned above, taking significant blocks of land out of agricultural production is not an appropriate option for biodiversity conservation on a large (EU wide) scale, as long as we have as an objective to maintain and improve the wildlife communities that we have, or have had in the not too distant past. Although in some areas, reserves are all that it has been possible to retain, elsewhere the creation of a landscape composed of networks of reserves within an intensively managed farmland would result in significantly different species' compositions, distributions and community structures, and it would be very difficult to predict what these might be.

Throughout most of the EU and Europe, sustainable management of all farmland is the keystone of the maintenance and enhancement of a major proportion of existing European biodiversity. Even if a reduced drive for food production (currently hypothetical) means that small amounts of land are taken out of production for reserve creation and a range of other purposes, the impact of such actions should be carefully assessed beforehand. The temptation to farmers must always be to take the least economically viable, i.e. least productive areas, out of production. However, this can also be the land of highest conservation value – if appropriate agricultural management continues. Reserves undoubtedly play an essential part in biodiversity conservation, but this should be in complement to, and not as a replacement for, positively managed farmland. Such positive management implies lack of abandonment, and sustainable management with food production, social and environmental objectives.

An example of an attempt at conservation through reserves in conjunction with more environmentally sensitive farming is given by Beintema *et al.* (Chapter 10). In the Netherlands, two-thirds of the country is covered by the most intensively managed lowland wet grassland in the EU, with highly manipulated water tables, and a much altered fauna as a result of high fertilizer inputs. Although this habitat in the Netherlands supports over 80% of the European breeding population of black-tailed godwit, populations of this and other wading species are declining owing to the high level of intensification. Site protection alone, through a network of reserves, has so far proved insufficient to conserve these widespread 'wet grassland' birds. The introduction of 'Relatie-nota' has provided some hope for the conservation of these species. This is a voluntary scheme, under which farmers in designated areas can be paid for more environmentally sensitive management of all of their farmed land, along with another part of their land being managed as a reserve. However, for this scheme to work, it is essential to have sufficient uptake (which, for a voluntary scheme, implies large enough incentives) and appropriate management requirements attached to the payments.

Taking some land out of agricultural production is certainly not a bad thing *per se*, and can, have obvious conservation benefits. Relevant considerations are the scale of land diverted, the type of land taken out of production, the long-term financial commitment to the management of such land, and the type of management that takes place on the remaining agricultural land.

Site-protection and wider countryside approaches to conservation are entirely complementary; neither, alone, is sufficient to conserve biodiversity, especially when species that have widespread distributions, sometimes large territory sizes, and migratory habits are concerned. Indeed, when considering the maintenance of wildlife populations over wide areas, it may be sensible to consider such biodiversity as a measure of the sustainability of land-use practices.

AN OVERVIEW OF FARMING AND BIRDS: HARMONIOUS PAST, FAILED PRESENT, SUSTAINABLE FUTURE?

Heritage, farmers, policies and history

We have noted that the value of many farmed landscapes to wildlife and cultural heritage is often not realized. Indeed, the fact is frequently overlooked that some of the landscapes most treasured as part of our natural heritage and for recreation, especially in the uplands, are farmed land (Bignal *et al.*, 1994; Bignal & McCracken, 1993, in press). It is not surprising that such traditional landscapes are viewed as 'normal countryside', as human usage and wildlife developed in association over most of the period since the glaciations in north-west Europe. Indeed, this is probably one of the best examples in the world of humans as an integral part of the biodiversity and practising something like sustainable use – until recently (Pienkowski & Bignal, 1993). This interaction of natural processes, opportunities and constraints, with human agricultural and other land-use activities, has given rise to the characteristic regional diversity of landscapes, wildlife, farming practices and food products that we value so highly (e.g. Rackham, 1986).

Wildlife has been able to adjust and exploit these agricultural situations because modifications to the environment have been gradual. However, in the last century and particularly in recent decades, this has changed. Modern machinery and chemicals allow rapid changes to the farmed environment over huge areas, to impose a standard, factory landscape over the previous character-istic regional features.

This is why the argument that farming will necessarily protect the environ-ment in the future, because it always has done so in the past, is invalid. One has only to look at the present to see the evidence of this, as preceding chapters demonstrate. It is interesting that, as governments at last recognize and call for sustainable use of the environment, one of the largest sustainable human activities, farming, continues to move away from its environmentally sensitive traditions. For centuries, farming was sustainable. Why is this changing?

It is not correct to attribute this to some supposed wickedness on the part of individual farmers. Farmers need to make a living in what are often difficult conditions. Although farmers may claim to be independent people making their own decisions as to how to operate, for many years these decisions have been made in a climate of very strong interventionist economic policies set by governments, albeit influenced by the farming lobby, itself dominated by intensive farmers. Governments acted initially individually, but increasingly jointly in the European Union, whose policies also affect those of other European countries. Farmers have shown themselves very capable in responding well to policy directions. These policies are set by governments in response to their perception of public needs. However, these policies can be slow to respond to changing circumstances, especially where powerful interests, such as the agro-chemical industry, benefit from their continuance. Furthermore, changing technical capabilities may be incorporated owing to their effects on one aspect of the objective (e.g. increasing local food production; reducing food imports) without analysis of other aspects (e.g. pollution of water supplies; increasing chemical and fuel imports; impact on wildlife, jobs).

Why are governments – in the name of us, the public – promoting these policies of intensifying food production (despite surpluses, pollution and en-vironmental effects), and thereby abandoning the multiple use of the country-side, the sustainable use of which its other policies promote? The answer lies in history. The people of almost all the countries of Europe suffered great hardship in World War II, a war which for the first time took the fighting and other hardships far from any conventional battle-front to the civilian populations of most nations involved. The scarcity and even absence of many foods, and blockades to international transport (with the loss of many sailors and ships), were integral to this process, and the general food shortage was frequently felt by individual people. Shortages and rationing continued in many countries for several years after the war, a time when many senior policy-makers of today's Europe were children. The production of as much as possible of each nation's food supply from within its own boundaries was an obvious reaction to these problems, and the trauma of the wartime experience meant that the policy and its implementation were rarely questioned for many years (see Evans, Chapter 12). It is not totally unreasoned to comment that, at least until recently, agricultural policies were still fighting the last world war. Even after questions were being raised both by environmentalists and farming associations, a British Government policy paper published in 1975 was entitled 'Food from our own resources'.

This accounts for the drive, noted in our Introduction, to grow two ears of corn where previously there had been one. The unquestioning acceptance of this has led to value-laden words becoming part of normal language. For example, heavily fertilized and drained grassland is often referred to as 'improved' – which it may be in terms of production per unit area, but it may well be 'damaged' in terms of wildlife and could be 'damaging' in terms of pollution of waters. As editors, we have tried to use more neutral terms such as 'intensified grassland' but, such is the pervasiveness of common practice, we suspect that a few terminological failures have crept through.

From people to machinery: efficiency in farming?

As this book has tried to make clear, much of Europe's wildlife depends on continued farming – but the nature of farming has been changing, to the detriment of wildlife and other human interests. The relentless intensification of agriculture has been manifest in many forms, as reviewed earlier in this chapter.

A general trend running alongside the increasing industrial nature of farming activity is the reduction in numbers of agricultural workers, with consequent falling employment and decline of rural communities (Beintema et al., Chapter 10; Suárez et al., Chapter 11). This is exacerbated by young people increasingly considering that the rewards of farming are inadequate compensation for the hardships of the lifestyle. We return to this important issue later.

One of the continuing justifications of the greater support which is given to intensive, rather than extensive, agriculture is that the latter is in some way 'inefficient'. Extensive agriculture may involve more people than intensive and may produce less food per hectare, but that does not mean it is inefficient – because intensive systems depend on so much input of externally supplied energy and chemicals (see Evans, Chapter 12). It is something of an irony that the delivery of the outdated wartime concept of self-sustainability in food supply is in fact sustained by massive chemical imports and the use of huge quantities of energy – goods which themselves would be strategic in an international conflict.

It will come as a surprise to many that energetic efficiency (output per unit input) has been sacrificed by modern agriculture to the extent that it takes more additional energy input to grow some of the produce than is released through its consumption (Johnson, 1993). In addition to the energetic costs of external fuel and energy to produce the food, have to be added the energetic costs of increased transport and distribution now that supply areas are specialized in preference to mixed farming near its markets (Potter, Chapter 2; Potts, Chapter 6; Evans, Chapter 12).

The huge increases in the uses of chemicals and energy are not without major additional costs – but these costs are not charged to the industry – nor, therefore, are the costs of food production by intensive methods. The costs of consequent pollution/eutrophication, as well as social and environmental changes are met by others or the public.

The dominance of intensive food production has meant, for example, that most support for disadvantaged rural areas on ostensibly social grounds is paid via limited aspects of farming, neglecting other parts of rural society. Subsidized agricultural production has raised land prices and encouraged the adoption of afforestation policies aimed at 'marginal' agricultural land, so threatening semi-natural habitats and the farming communities associated with them (Potter, Chapter 2).

Some of the anomalies of current agricultural policies are at last being recognized – but only in part. Recognition tends to be limited to the problems of over-production, the costs of the policy in terms of subsidy of production and, to some extent, the pollution damage. However, the value of lower input systems has not been widely recognized. In the words of a German ecologist, the need for a 'green' agriculture has been recognized, but not yet the need for a 'brown' countryside. In other words, lush, green fields are usually more a sign of high inputs than health; patchy brown fields are more likely to be environmentally sustainable and retain the nature value.

Central and eastern Europe

The messages outlined will be as, if not more, significant as the EU enlarges to encompass many central and eastern European countries (CEECs). The potential for agricultural intensification in the near future in these countries in enormous, and if agricultural, structural and other types of financial support are granted or applied in inappropriate ways, the results could be disastrous, both ecologically and socially (Anon., 1995). Much biological diversity is maintained on farmed land in the CEECs, and many bird species do not have an unfavourable conservation status in Europe simply because of large CEEC populations. Tucker (Chapter 4) notes that 33 such species have declined by more than 33% in western Europe but not in the CEECs.

Figure 6 Afforestation in 'marginal' agricultural land has often threatened semi-natural agricultural habitats. (Photo by C.H. Gomersall/RSPB.)

There are many examples of low-input farming systems supporting abundant and diverse wildlife in the CEECs. Beintema *et al.* (Chapter 10) made reference to the situation in eastern Europe (Biebzra marshes of Poland), where traditional, very labour-intensive farming manages an area that supports large numbers of breeding waterfowl. The continuation of such management, in a rapidly modernizing country, is highly uncertain, unless sufficient financial aid can be found to allow for the continuation of traditional management on a large scale.

The CEECs need to avoid repeating the mistakes of the 'West' in losing the existing sustainable aspects of farming (Pienkowski, 1995). There could be tremendous opportunities to be grasped. For example, for economic reasons the chemical inputs to many areas have fallen drastically in recent years. This allows the way for re-establishing low-input, high-quality products. The impediment to this in some other countries is the difficulty in passing the transition stage; circumstances in some CEEC areas have forced the systems past this stage.

The need for regional and other flexibility in policies

Flexibility within policies is essential if the landscape, biological and cultural diversity that exists in Europe is to be maintained. At a continental scale, the farmed landscape will always present considerable diversity. Even if economics and politics can, and often do, supersede traditional and cultural considerations, technology is never likely to overcome completely the barriers to production resulting from different latitudes, climates and soil types. Indeed, the landscapes, wildlife and culture resulting from these constraints and the history of human interactions with them are some of the main aspects of value (Rackham, 1986).

Partly because of this, and partly because of the comparatively recent dates of accession of many southern European countries to the European Community (now European Union), rates of farm restructuring and the intensity and rates of intensification of farming methods also vary considerable across the EU.

This is well illustrated in Chapters 5–12, which cover farming systems as intensively managed as the lowland wet grasslands of the Netherlands, where no semi-natural vegetation remains (Beintema *et al.*, Chapter 10), to the dry grasslands and cereal pseudosteppe of Spain, where there is no clear distinction between natural vegetation and agricultural areas (Suárez *et al.*, Chapter 11). A further apt comparison is given by the average nitrogen fertilizer application rates, being 39 kg ha^{-1} in Spain compared with 552 kg ha^{-1} in the Netherlands (Díaz *et al.*, 1994). This diversity will increase as the EU enlarges to encompass many central and eastern European countries (CEECs) – see above.

Chapters 6 and 8 identify the inflexibility of policy-making as a major problem. Essentially, policy-makers tend to look for blanket solutions, rather than designing measures which would allow application in a regional sense to maintain the valuable regional diversity. Attempting to find a system which allows policies to be applied at a large enough scale to be acceptable to policy-makers while still small enough to avoid too gross a distortion in environmental terms is challenging (Pienkowski *et al.*, 1995). Potts (Chapter 6) notes the muddled policy thinking, even when policy changes are initiated, partly because of politicians' wish for instant solutions. The full range of consequences of a policy change are rarely thought out, rather than assuming that the intended target will be the only outcome (see Potter, Chapter 2; McCracken *et al.*, 1995). It is also important to note that changes in one zone can have consequences well outside of it. For example, a sudden favouring of sheep rearing over cereal growing in the lowlands could drastically affect the viability of sheep rearing (and hence farming) in the uplands.

Governments have increasingly recognized the importance of environmental sustainability, multiple use of the countryside, and the taking account of conservation throughout the countryside, at least as a general concept, even if they have some difficulty relating these to practice. As long ago as 1971, the first global nature conservation convention, the 'Ramsar' Convention on Wetlands of International Importance, spoke of 'wise use' of wetland areas. The EC Directive on the Conservation of Wild Birds in 1979 required that special conservation measures be taken both within and outside special sites. The concept was developed most fully to date in the Convention on Biological Diversity. This requires contracting parties (essentially governments) not only to develop plans for the conservation of biological diversity, but also to ensure that the conservation of biological diversity is incorporated in all other policies for other activities (see Hill *et al.*, 1996).

The conservation of biological diversity is not just about protecting rare species but is about using the countryside in a way which prevents currently common species from becoming rare (Pienkowski, 1993; Hill *et al.*, 1996). There is also the potential of using wildlife species as a measurable indicator of sustainable use. In these situations, the interests of wildlife, rural communities and the public interest in the heritage of wildlife and landscape largely run in parallel. Nature conservation is not just another land-use, but an approach to the wise use of all land. To do this we need to maintain agriculture traditions, rather than separating conservation and farming in different areas (Díaz *et al.*, Chapter 7).

People and the land

Overall, this means that we must create conditions in which young people want to come into, or stay in, farming and farm in a sustainable way while earning a fair standard of living (see Potter, Chapter 2; Díaz *et al.*, Chapter 7; Bignal *et al.*, 1994; McCracken *et al.*, 1995). A key element may also be to find ways of supporting more people working in farming. This is apparent from Díaz *et al.* and Suárez *et al.* (Chapters 7 and 11) and studies in Highland Scotland (Allen, 1995). These could include payments for providing environmental benefits, as well as support for establishing 'high-quality' products including regional foods, eco-tourism business, etc.

In order to inform the development of such policies, and their appropriate implementation at regional and local scales, studies need to be of whole farming systems and embrace ecology, economics etc. (as discussed earlier in this chapter). The study of whole systems at farm scale should elucidate what determines people's decisions and therefore the outcome for wildlife (Diaz *et al.*, Chapter 7). We need to study mechanisms linking nature requirements to farming practice and the latter to national/EU policies (Diaz *et al.*, Chapter 7; Pienkowski *et al.*, 1995).

If policies are to be successful, they need clear objectives. It is essential that local and national biodiversity priorities be set, both in terms of individual species, and groups of species or ecosystems. Once set, conservation measures based upon these priorities must be co-ordinated at local, regional, national and international scales. This should enable appropriate implementation of both present and future 'agri-environmental' schemes (see EFNCP, 1996). Not only must conservation priorities be co-ordinated to avoid conflict, but policies influencing land-use (in addition to the CAP) must be integrated with environmental policies, again at a range of levels from local to international.

It is clear from the preceding chapters (e.g. Potts, Chapter 6) that the general objectives for nature conservation should be to maintain existing extensive farming systems and to extensify those previously damaged by intensification. Within these, many more precise objectives need developing for particular systems.

One reason why governments are not keen on this is allegedly because they see policing difficulties, i.e. how does one know that a farmer is de-intensifying? This falls into the danger of trying to measure the means, rather than the ends. The maintenance or restoration of target birds (or other conspicuous target wildlife) is a possible means of measurement (Tucker, Chapter 4). There are pilot examples of this approach (Beintema *et al.*, Chapter 10).

Although the public subsidy of food production is increasingly dubious, it is appropriate for public money to be spent on environmental benefits as these have no market. Given that the environmentally most useful farms tend to be small enterprises, it would also be appropriate to support the development of marketing mechanisms for unique regional products (Díaz *et al.*, Chapter 7).

Overall, the maintenance of any system will depend on the income generated by it being greater than that achievable through alternative options. It is somewhat surprising that this rather simple concept does not seem to have featured at the forefront of thinking in past policy-making.

It is not difficult to develop a vision for the sorts of European countryside which would sustain wildlife and rural communities (e.g. Donázar *et al.*, Chapter 5; Potts, Chapter 6; Bignal *et al.*, 1994). This is not just a matter of turning back the clock but of keeping the good aspects of current farming methods that we know about, assisted by appropriate new technology (Bignal & McCracken, 1993, in press). While our prescriptions for achieving this will always be enhanced by further research, it is not lack of knowledge, but the will to achieve this, that is the limiting factor. As Sir Crispin Tickell (1996) has noted: 'We do not have to exhaust top soils, watch them erode into the sea, rely upon artificial aids to nature, eliminate the forests with their natural wealth of species, poison the waters, fresh and salt, or destroy the life support of the planet.' Politicians need to perceive and act on a public will to maintain their environmental heritage.

What do people want for their public money? We believe that, especially with a fuller picture, they will want to move the balance of support towards the extensive end of the range of farming systems, and will be concerned about the previously hidden costs of the more intensive approaches. How are existing policies to be modified in this direction? This is the subject of the following, final chapter. The contents of this suggest that sustained public enthusiasm may be necessary to shepherd through the gradual changes that will be necessary in this already complex package.

REFERENCES

The Advisor (1996) Winter 1995/1996: p. 13.

Agra Europe (1996) High-yield farming 'key to increased food demand'. 16 February: 4.

ALLEN, S. (1995) Scottish Natural Heritage NW Region; agriculture demonstration projects. In D.I.M. McCracken, E.M. Bignal & S.E. Wenlock (eds) *Farming on the Edge: the nature of traditional farmland in Europe.* Proceedings of the Fourth European Forum on Nature Conservation and Pastoralism. 2–4 November 1994, Trujillo, Spain, p. 189.

ANON. (1995) *Action Plan to 2010 for Central and Eastern europe.* Report on a conference held at Gödöllö Agricultural University, Hungary, 14–15 September 1995. Sandy: Royal Society for the Protection of Birds.

BEAUFOY, G., BALDOCK, D. & CLARK, J. (1994) *The Nature of Farming. Low intensity farming systems in nine European countries.* London: Institute for European Environmental Policy.

BEINTEMA, A. (1991) Insect fauna and grassland birds. In D.J. Curtis, E.M. Bignal & M.A. Curtis (eds) *Birds and pastoral agriculture in Europe,* Proceedings of the second European Forum on Birds and Pastoralism. Port Erin, Isle of Man, 26–30 October 1990, pp. 97–101.

BIGNAL, E. & CURTIS, D.J. (eds) (1989) *Choughs and Land-use in Europe.* Clachan: Scottish Chough Study Group.

BIGNAL, E. & McCRACKEN, D. (1993) Nature conservation and pastoral farming in the British uplands. *British Wildlife,* **4**: 367–376.

BIGNAL, E.M. & McCRACKEN, D.I. (in press) Low-intensity farming systems in the conservation of the countryside. *Journal of Applied Ecology,* **33**.

BIGNAL, E.M., CURTIS, D.J. & MATTEWS, J.L. (1988) Islay: land-types, bird habitats and nature conservation. Part 1: land use and birds on Islay. Peterborough: Chief Scientist Directorate Report No. 809, Nature Conservancy Council.

BIGNAL, E., BIGNAL, S. & CURTIS, D.J. (1989) Functional unit systems and support ground for Choughs – the nature conservation requirements. In E. Bignal and D.J. Curtis (eds) *Choughs and land-use in Europe,* pp. 102–109. Clachan: Scottish Chough Study Group.

BIGNAL, E., McCRACKEN, D., PIENKOWSKI, M. & BRANSON, A. (1994) *The Nature of Farming: traditional low intensity farming and its importance for wildlife.* Brussels: WWF.

BIGNAL, E.M., McCRACKEN, D.I., STILLMAN, R.A. & OVENDEN, G.N. (in press) Feeding behavior of nesting choughs in the Scottish Hebrides. *Journal of Field Ornithology.*

BIRDLIFE INTERNATIONAL (1994) Implementation of the agri-environment regulation (EEC 2078/92). Sandy: BirdLife International, c/o Royal Society for the Protection of Birds.

BLUNDEN, J. & CURRY, N. (1985) *The Changing Countryside.* London: Croom Helm.

DIARIO OFICIAL DE EXTREMADURA (1986) *Ley 1/1986, de 2 de mayo, sobre la Dehesa en Extremadura.* Department of the Environment, **40**: 503–528.

EGDELL, J.M. (1993) Impact of agricultural policy on Spain and its steppe regions. Sandy: Royal Society for the Protection of Birds.

DÍAZ, M.C., GARRIDO, S. & GARCÍA, R.A. (1994) Contaminación agraria difusa. *El Campo,* **131**: 93–107.

EFNCP (European Forum on Nature Conservation and Pastoralism) (1996) *The Common Agricultural Policy and Environmental Practices.* Proceedings of a seminar held in Brussels on 29 January 1996. European Forum on Nature Conservation and Pastoralism.

GORIUP, P.D., BATTEN, L.A. & NORTON, J.A. (eds) (1991) *The Conservation of Lowland Dry Grassland Birds in Europe,* Proceedings of an international seminar held at the University of Reading, 20–22 March 1991. Peterborough, UK: Joint Nature Conservation Committee.

GRAHAM, F. Jr. (1970) *Since Silent Spring.* London: Hamish Hamilton Ltd.

GREEN, R.E. (1994) Diagnosing causes of bird population declines. *Ibis,* **137**: 47–55.

GREEN, R.E. (1995) The decline of the corncrake *Crex crex* in Britain continues. *Bird Study*, 42: 66–75.

GREEN, R.E. & CADBURY, C.J. (1987) Breeding waders of lowland wet grassland. *RSPB Conservation Review*, 1: 10–13.

GREEN, R.E. & ROBINS, M. (1993) The decline of the ornithological importance of the Somerset Levels and Moors, England and changes in the management of water levels. *Biological Conservation*, 66: 95–106.

GUMMER, J. (1993) Keynote address: environmentally sensitive farming. In J.B. Dixon, A.J. Stones & I.R. Hepburn (eds) *A Future for Europe's Farmed Countryside: proceedings of an international conference*, No. 1, pp. 1–8. Sandy: Royal Society for the Protection of Birds (Studies in European Agricultural and Environmental Policy No. 1).

HILL, D., TREWEEK, J., YATES, T. & PIENKOWSKI, M. (eds) (1996) *Actions for Biodiversity in the UK: approaches in UK to implementing the Convention on Biological Diversity*. Ecological Issues No. 5. British Ecological Society/ Field Studies Council.

HÖTKER, H., (ed.) (1991) Waders breeding on wet grasslands. *Wader Study Group Bulletin*, 61(Supplement).

HUDSON, R., TUCKER, G.M. & FULLER, R.J. (1994). Lapwing *Vanellus vanellus* populations in relation to agricultural changes: a review. In G.M. Tucker, S.M. Davies & R.J. Fuller (eds) *The Ecology and Conservation of Lapwings* Vanellus vanellus, pp. 1–33. Peterborough: Joint Nature Conservation Committee (UK Nature Conservation Series 9).

JOHNSON, N. (1993) *Cleaner Farming*. London: Centre for the Exploitation of Science and Technology.

MARTÍN-NOVELLA, C., CRIADO, J. & NAVESO, M.A. (1993) [The mark of the new Common Agricultural Policy: nature conservation and water management]. *Ecosistemas*, 5: 24–27. (In Spanish.)

McCRACKEN, D.I.M., BIGNAL, E.M. & WENLOCK, S.E. (1995) Farming on the edge: the nature of traditional farmland in Europe. In *Proceedings of the Fourth European Forum on Nature Conservation and Pastoralism*, 2–4 November 1994, Trujillo, Spain.

MOPT (Ministerio de Obras Públicas y Transportes) (1992). [*Project Guidelines of Hydrological Catchment Plans*]. Madrid: Ministerio de Obras Públicas y Transportes. (In Spanish.)

MOPTMA (Ministerio de Obras Públicas, Transportes y Medio Ambiente) (1994) [*Natural Hydrological Plan: analysis of scenarios*]. Madrid: Dirección General de Obras Hidráulicas, Ministerio de Obras Públicas, Transportes y Medio Ambiente. (In Spanish.)

MOSER, M., BIBBY, C., NEWTON, I., PIENKOWSKI, M., SUTHERLAND, W.J., ULFSTRAND, S. & WYNNE, G. (1995) Bird conservation: the science and the action: conclusions and recommendations. *Ibis*, 137: S3–S7.

NATIONAL AUDIT OFFICE (1986) *Review of Forestry Commission objectives and achievements*. London: HMSO.

NAVESO, M. (1993) *Estepar, aves y agricultura*. Madrid: La Garcilla, Sociedad Española de Ornitología/BirdLife International.

NAVESO, M.A. & FERNÁNDEZ, J. (1993) Propuesta de programa de zona para el área de La Serena en aplicación del reglamento CEE 2078/92. Madrid: Sociedad Española de Ornitología (unpublished).

NAVESO, M.A. & GROVES-REINES, S. (1992) Propuesta de declaración de la zona de Tierra de Campos como Area Ambientalmente Sensible. Madrid: Sociedad Española de Ornitoloia-BirdLife (unpublished).

O'BRIEN, M. & SELF, M. (1994) Changes in the numbers of breeding waders on lowland wet grasslands in the UK. *RSPB Conservation Review*, 8: 38–44.

PAIN, D. J. (1994) Case studies of farming and birds in Europe: Arable farming in France. Sandy: Royal Society for the Protection of Birds Unpublished Research Report.

PARR, S., NAVESO, M.A. & YARAR, M. (in press) Habitat and food surrounding lesser kestrel *Falco naumanni* colonies in Central Turkey. *Biological Conservation*.

PETERJOHN, B.G. & SAUER, J.R. (1993) North American Breeding Bird survey Annual Summary 1990–1991. *Bird Populations*, 1: 1–15.

PETERJOHN, B.G. & SAUER, J.R. (1995) Population status of North American Grassland Birds. p 26. of *Aabstracts from the International Conference and Training Workshop on Conservation and Ecology of Grassland Birds*, 26–28 October 1995, Tulsa, Oklahoma, USA.

PIENKOWSKI, M.W. (1989) Introduction, overview and discussion. In Bignal, E.M. & Curtis, D.J. (eds) *Choughs and Land-Use in Europe*, pp. 1–3. Argyll: Scottish Chough Study Group.

PIENKOWSKI, M.W. ed. (1993). A contribution to the development of a system to assess nature conservation quality and to set targets for the national action plan required by the Convention on Biological Diversity. Peterborough: JNCC Report No. 163.

PIENKOWSKI, M. (1995). International conference on land-use changes and nature conservation in central and eastern Europe, Palanga, Lithuania, June 1995. *La Cañada*, 4: 3.

PIENKOWSKI, M. & BIGNAL, E. (1993) Objectives for nature conservation in European agriculture. In J.B. Dixon, A.J. Stones & I.R. Hepburn, (eds) *A Future for Europe's Farmed Countryside: proceedings of an international conference*, No.1, pp. 21–43. Sandy: Royal Society for the Protection of Birds (Studies in European Agricultural and Environmental Policy No. 1).

PIENKOWSKI, M.W., BIGNAL, E.M., GALBRAITH, C.A., McCRACKEN, D.I., BOOBYER, M.G., STILLMAN, R.A. & CURTIS, D.J. (1995) A simplified classification of broad land-type zones to assist the integration of biodiversity objectives in the development of land-use policies. *Biological Conservation*, 75: 11–25.

RACKHAM, O. (1986) *The History of the Countryside*. London: J. M. Dent and Sons.

RSPB (Royal Society for the Protection of Birds) (1995) *Rural White Paper – Comments from the RSPB*. Royal Society for the Protection of Birds.

RUTSCHKE, E. (1989) *Die wildenten Europas [Ducks of Europe]*. Berlin: VEB Deutscher Landwirtschaftsverlag.

SAN AGUSTÍN, M. (1993) Los planes de regadío: su encaje en la nueva Política Agraria Común. *El Boletín*, pp. 33–39. Madrid: M.A.P.A.

SIEPEL, H. (1990). The influence of management on food size in the menu of insectiverous animals. In M.J. Someijer and J. van der Blom (eds) *Experimental and Applied Entomology*. Amsterdam: Nederlandse Entomologische Vereniging.

STOWE, T.J. & HUDSON, A.V. (1988) Corncrake studies in the Western Isles. *RSPB Conservation Review*, 2: 38–42.

STOWE, T.J., NEWTON, A.V., GREEN, R.E. & MAYES, E. (1993) The decline of the Corncrake *Crex crex* in Britain and Ireland in relation to habitat. *Journal of Applied Ecology*, 30: 53–62.

STROUD, D.A., REED, T.M., PIENKOWSKI, M.W. & LINDSAY, R.A. (1987) *Birds, Bogs and Forestry: the peatlands of Caithness and Sutherland*. Peterborough: Nature Conservancy Council.

TICKELL, C. (1996) Economical with the environment: a question of values. *Journal of Applied Ecology* (in press).

TOMPKINS, S.C. (1986) *The Theft of the Hills: afforestation in Scotland*. Ramblers' Association and World Wildlife Fund.

TUCKER, G.M. & HEATH, M.F. (eds.) (1994) *Birds in Europe. Their Conservation Status*. Cambridge: BirdLife Conservation Series no 3.

VAN WINGERDEN, W.K.R.E., MUSTERS, J.C.M., KLEUKERS, R.M.J.C., BONGERS, W. & VAN BIEZEN, J.B. (1992) The influence of cattle grazing intensity on grasshopper abundance (orthoptera: Acrididae). *Proceedings of Experimental and Applied Entomology, NEV, Amsterdam*, 2: 28–34.

VICKERY, P., HERKERT, J. & REINKING, D. (Scientific Committee) (1995) *Abstracts from the*

International Conference and Training Workshop on Conservation and Ecology of Grassland Birds, 26–28 October 1995, Tulsa, Oklahoma, USA.

WILLIAMS, G., STOWE, T. & NEWTON, A. (1991) Action for Corncrakes. *RSPB Conservation Review*, 5: 47–53.

WILSON, J.D., EVANS, A.D., POULSEN, J.G. & EVANS, J. (1995) Wasteland or Oasis? The use of set-aside by wintering and breeding birds. *British Wildlife*, 6: 214–223.

CHAPTER

14

European agriculture: threats and opportunities

JAMES DIXON

SUMMARY

European agriculture has been influenced as much by policy as by market forces. Despite massive criticism and the many good reasons for radical reform of the Common Agricultural Policy (such as its high costs, poor economic efficiency, distorting effect on trade and the need to address rural needs beyond agriculture) it is unlikely to be removed entirely. Acting against reform are some significant constraints: the need for secure food supplies, the complexity of farming and rural economic situations in Europe, and short-term political concerns. Not surprisingly, reforms to date have been incremental and limited in effect.

However, the changing demands of international trade, worries about the costs and inequalities of the CAP and future enlargement of the EU all mean that the CAP will be further reformed. For the environment, a CAP is needed which encourages ecologically sustainable farming, particularly farming systems that support high biodiversity and other natural values. EU enlargement offers an opportunity for reforms which avoid the mistakes of the past, and build on the lessons; namely, to minimize the environmental harm caused by production subsidies and to develop agri-environmental policies to support high natural values.

This chapter reviews the factors causing change, forces for the status quo, and the likely timetable of future reforms to the CAP.

FARMING AND BIRDS IN EUROPE
ISBN 0-12-544280-7
Copyright © 1997 Academic Press Ltd
All rights of reproduction in any form reserved

LESSONS FROM THE PAST

The future of Europe's land-use and wildlife depends largely on agriculture policies (Tucker & Heath, 1994) which are themselves complex, politically-charged and influenced by changing global markets for agricultural products (RSPB, 1995). In order to predict what that future may hold it is necessary to understand the past, although the ability to predict agriculture policy accurately will always be questionable. The preceding case studies and context chapters by Potter (Chapter 2), Robson (Chapter 3) and Tucker (Chapter 4) provide a strong basis from which to develop some broad conclusions. This chapter draws on some lessons from the past, considers the forces at work prompting or constraining change and attempts to describe the likely future for both the European countryside and its land-use policies.

Necessarily, the validity of such predictions will be limited and largely personal and so any error of interpretation, emphasis or judgement lies with the author rather than other authors in this book or elsewhere.

European agriculture

European agriculture is strongly influenced by climatic gradients (Boreal north to Mediterranean south and Continental east to Atlantic west); by cultural and national preferences for food and landscapes; and by national or regional land-use and economic policies. It will, therefore, continue to be highly diverse. However, the increasingly powerful 'Single Market', and the collapse of centrally-planned economies in central and east Europe and northern Asia, mean that market forces (and whatever financial policy framework is in place) will become more influential than ever – favouring some places for some products, and so encouraging specialization and intensification (Marsh & Tangermann, 1992). For example, Mediterranean areas have a climatic advantage for field vegetable production, while north-west Europe has advantages for meat and dairy production (Egdell, 1993).

Specialization across Europe as a whole, rather than simply within countries, is now being encouraged by such factors as economies of scale, national policies to support 'export' industries and improved (and subsidized) Trans-European transport networks. This mirrors the United States, where the pattern of agricultural production is determined across the whole of North America, rather than within states.

Of course, production patterns may occasionally be 'frozen' by specific policy interventions such as production quotas, but the general trends towards regional specialization will continue largely unaffected by such factors. Moreover, rapidly fluctuating market forces, even if modified to some extent by intervention measures, are likely to cause rapid 'opening' and 'closing' of trading opportunities, and of supplies 'flooding' or replacing local or long-established markets (Tracy, 1993). The earlier policies which served to 'buffer' European agriculture from these factors will play little part: the role of the CAP in 'buffering' against world prices is likely to continue declining. Nor will any 'new economics' (under which the costs of resource use are made part of market prices) be sufficiently developed to be anything other than a relatively small check on the effects of 'classical' market economics on European agriculture.

The effects, for European farmers, will be greatly increased volatility, working against the continuity of traditional, stable forms of agriculture which are of high natural value (Beaufoy et al., 1994). To survive in this new climate farmers will require an entrepreneurial spirit and business management acumen concentrating on the economic 'bottom-line' and long-term financial viability. History shows that these can act as potent forces for incidental environmental damage (Woods et al., 1988). New markets could, however, support some specialized, environmentally compatible products, such as those of dehesas in Iberia (see Díaz et al., Chapter 7) or integrated crop management, although such opportunities are likely to be limited.

The farmland area of Europe has been relatively stable, with much the same area in cultivation today as 25 years ago (Eurostat, 1995). Overall, this is unlikely to change very dramatically, apart from local exceptions including small losses to forestry, built development and abandonment (see Robson, Chapter 3). Despite the theoretical question-mark over how much land is actually needed for production (Netherlands Scientific Council, 1992), the overall area of Europe's farmland has been largely unresponsive to such factors as high and growing population density, changing land values and varying taxpayer support. Instead, the response has largely been of rapid change in the structure and type of farm, cropping patterns (such as the shift from wheat to sunflowers in Spain), the distribution of livestock (concentrating production in fewer units), and yield increases. Until recently the pace of change in southern parts of the EU was comparatively slow, though this is no longer so. The availability of markets, capital and technology make these trends likely to continue, rapidly in the south but at a less pronounced rate in the north (see Robson, Chapter 3; Eurostat, 1995).

Social change in rural areas will continue, again with differences between parts of Europe. In areas where farming is still undergoing rapid change the consequences may be further rural unemployment and demands for rural development, especially infrastructure and alternatives to the traditional economic sectors. In northern and central Europe, assimilation of urban people into rural areas, together with their needs, values and wealth, is already a major factor in rural policies, with recreation, sport, environmental management and transport assuming greater prominence and agriculture becoming relatively less important (Lake, 1995).

Such changes make the retention of long-established, extensive and high natural value farming systems more difficult (Beaufoy et al., 1994). With so many social, technological and market trends working against them, such farming systems will increasingly rely on EU and state intervention, requiring in

Figure 1 Corncockle *Agrostemma githago* in a traditionally managed barley field in the Massif Central, central France. The small-scale farms in this area, with low inputs, support a diverse array of wild plants, many of which have been lost from more intensive systems. (Photo by D.J. Pain.)

turn a shift in the emphasis and distribution of the benefits of agriculture policy, from production towards social and environmental purposes. For these reasons, understanding the relationship between agriculture and the environment will be central to future rural policy (CEC, 1995a; MAFF, 1995; RSPB, 1995).

Agriculture and the environment

Their power to cause change means that agricultural markets, technology and policies need to be treated as central concerns by those seeking rural policies which support biodiversity (Woods *et al.*, 1988; Taylor & Dixon, 1990; Beaufoy *et al.*, 1994). However, these influences, powerful though they are, are erratic and unpredictable. Conservation will rarely, if ever, be their prime objective and will continue to need a legislative system of species and site protection to complement new agriculture policies (Wynne *et al.*, 1995). Nature conservation policies have, in the past, given insufficient weight to the protection, management and promotion of biodiversity across the whole of the countryside. The reasons for this are explained in Chapters 1–3, and the consequences are illustrated in Chapters 4–12.

Instead of being of secondary importance (after 'sites' and 'species' protection), sustainable management of the whole countryside is of at least equal importance. Farmed, 'semi-natural' (and sometimes intensively-managed) habitats within 'cultural landscapes' are of interest for both the degree of biodiversity they hold (see Tucker, Chapter 4) and because that biodiversity is inextricably linked to human activities. Cultural landscapes are, therefore, a blueprint for the sustainable development of future agriculture, illustrating that it is possible to protect and steward wildlife and other resources, while growing food and sustaining a rural economy (Beaufoy *et al.*, 1994).

So far, it has proved difficult to convince farmers, policy-makers and 'agri-business' to integrate environmental requirements into the core of agriculture policy and businesses. Rather, the environment has been treated as a 'bolt-on' to activities and policies mainly aimed at increasing production (Wildlife Link, 1992). Even efforts based on free advice, coercion and voluntary payment schemes have sometimes failed to achieve much of significance. In some cases, resistance to conservation ideas led to over-concentration on conservation 'at the margin' of farming, giving undue priority and resources to low priority concerns (such as planting of hedgerow trees) at the expense of more urgent and damaging matters (such as proper management of wetlands for wildlife). In addition, voluntary incentives (such as the Environmentally Sensitive Areas in the UK) have been undermined by the much greater forces of the CAP and markets, partly because the latter do not reflect real environmental costs (of pollution, for example) (RSPB, 1991; Whitby, 1994; BirdLife International, 1994).

However, in the last ten years the threat to public spending on farming has meant that the industry has cast its net widely for a clearer role and justification for its privileges. This search will continue, providing opportunities for dialogue and progress (CEC, 1995a).

A major objective must be to construct policies so that they fully 'internalize' the environmental costs and benefits of agriculture into practices, markets and policies. That is, when farmers, agri-business or policy-makers make decisions, positive rewards for environmental benefits and penalties for environmental damage should be built-in so that the environment features as part of all such decisions. 'Greening' the CAP would be a step towards such internalization, particularly if accompanied by better environmental assessment of policies, and identification, protection and maintenance of sustainable 'extensive' farming systems of high natural value.

European agriculture policies

Whilst not the only influence over farmers, the CAP operates alongside national agriculture and other land-use policies, and is likely to continue to provide the main policy framework for European farming (Marsh & Tangermann, 1992;

Tracy, 1993; Robson, Chapter 3). Many constraints act against there being 'radical' reform of the CAP – the existence of subsidies, supply controls and other CAP policy instruments is likely to be very nearly permanent – but the CAP has not been a static policy and will evolve in response to political, market, technological and social factors, which are discussed further below.

Structural changes in farming in the next five to ten years, especially in southern Europe, will cause pressures for CAP reform (Eurostat, 1995). In northern Europe, new technologies and the shift of political focus on to 'wider' issues of rural policy, such as rural development, social change and the environment, will be important stimuli for change. Growing concerns over equity (of who receives subsidies), transparency (to the public of the levels of subsidy paid) and value for money in public and EU spending will add to periodic budgetary crises, and cause further questioning of the basis for agricultural support (MAFF, 1995; Tracy, 1995). This may serve to add weight to the existing trend away from production support and towards environmental and social payments to farmers.

In the longer term (into the next century), the EU's role as a trading bloc under the General Agreement on Tariffs and Trade (GATT), and its relations with potential new members (especially countries in central and eastern Europe) will exert a growing influence over the CAP (MAFF, 1995; CEC, 1995a). The influence of these forces may be matched, in rhetoric if not practice, by the global environment agenda, following governments' commitment at the Earth Summit in Rio de Janeiro in 1992 (UNEP, 1992).

Integrating agriculture and environment policies, one of the aims of Rio's Agenda 21, requires the complexities of international agriculture and the factors influencing it to be understood. However, to bring about benefits for the species for which farmland is their main habitat it is necessary to reduce this exceptionally complicated 'machine' to its constituent 'parts'. The remainder of this chapter attempts to overview these 'parts'. History shows that progress in integrating agriculture and environment 'on the ground' is made best when the broad direction of policy enables and supports it (Robson, Chapter 3). Therefore, this chapter also attempts to identify future opportunities for such progress.

FORCES FOR CHANGE: OR WHY THE CAP SHOULD BE REFORMED

In agricultural production terms, the CAP has been remarkably successful although it is increasingly criticized on economic efficiency, natural resource use, equity, rural development and environmental grounds (NFU, 1994; CLA, 1994; Buckwell *et al.*, 1995; MAFF, 1995). It has failed to balance production and demand.

Figure 2 View of set-aside farmland in the UK. Set-aside was introduced to reduce arable crop production. (Photo by C.H. Gomersall/RSPB.)

Short-term pressure for change

As the EU has grown from the original six to the current 15 countries, the CAP has expanded and developed, with objectives and policy instruments being amended in a process of incremental reform (Robson, Chapter 3). Reforms made in the late 1980s reduced the support prices and introduced means of reducing supply, such as quotas on production (e.g. for milk) and on land (e.g. for cereals). A number of concurrent crises, particularly over international trade, forced the Council of Agriculture Ministers to adopt more substantial reforms in May 1992 (CEC, 1992a). Further controls on the area of cultivation were introduced for cereals, oil-seeds and proteins, with semi-compulsory set-aside being introduced in concert with a 29% reduction in cereal prices (CEC, 1992b).

Accompanying these reforms, a package of measures was introduced promoting early retirement (CEC, 1992c), forestry (CEC, 1992d) and protection of the environment – the so-called Agri-environment Accompanying Measures (CEC, 1992e).

The 1992 reforms left a legacy of new measures which are now being implemented (Rayment, 1995). Some commodities remain unreformed, such as wine, rice, fruit and vegetables and dairy products (though the latter underwent radical change in 1984 with the introduction of dairy quotas). Further reforms are likely in the wine, fruit and vegetable and livestock sectors; to the Agri-environment Regulation (EC 2078/92); and to the system introduced in 1992 for Set-aside and Arable Area Aids.

While not as radical as proposed by some (e.g. House of Lords, 1991), these reforms signalled new objectives for farm policy and were important in considering the nature of support to farmers, not just its level. A key feature of the 1992 reforms was that new types of payments (particularly Arable Area and Set-aside Payments) were introduced which were (and remain) difficult to justify on the 'traditional' grounds of efficiency, food security or the need to redress some disadvantage suffered by farmers. The justification for making large transfers of money overtly from tax-payers to farmers had been questioned for some time (Tracy, 1995). A number of critics of the CAP had argued that the only justification for payments such as these would be if they were used to promote better countryside management, through the attachment of environmental conditions (Taylor & Dixon, 1990; Baldock & Mitchell, 1995). The 1992 reforms began to shift CAP payments and their purpose towards this approach.

Many commentators question the effectiveness of the 1992 reforms in meeting their objectives of reducing production levels (e.g. NFU, 1994; CLA, 1994; Ockenden & Franklin, 1994).

The 1992 reform will reduce the level of subsidized prices for cereals by only 20% in a fixed period up until 2001, when the Uruguay round agreement of the international trade agreements under the GATT runs out. The extent to which subsidies will need to be paid on cereal exports depends greatly on world market conditions. Currently, these markets are buoyant and there is little need for the EU to subsidize prices (although the 'compensatory' payments are still being made automatically). Whether further toughening of supply controls (such as set-aside) or increased subsidizing of prices will be required is largely an arithmetical decision, based on the need to balance production, consumption and exports (CEC, 1993; Rayment, 1995).

Other sectors, particularly livestock, are likely to need changes to policies to 'adjust' production to meet GATT requirements to the end of the century with beef a likely priority (Egdell et al., 1993; SNH et al., unpublished data).

It is very unlikely (because of buoyant world markets and political unwillingness), that we will see changes to the CAP so soon after 1992. The EU will resist attempts to change cereals policy, save for minor adjustments to (for example) reference yields, prices and set-aside percentages (Rayment, 1995). Reform would then be delayed until the longer term (1998 at the very earliest) when other forces for change become more pressing.

Long-term pressures for change

It is widely accepted that the continuation of the CAP in its current form is unlikely (e.g. MAFF, 1995; Ockenden & Franklin, 1994; CEC, 1995a). Some of the factors which will cause further change are outlined only briefly here (each is considered in more detail elsewhere) before considering the most pressing of these, the enlargement of the EU.

Factors influencing the long-term future of the CAP, and which in combination are likely to prompt reform, are as follows:

Compatibility with the GATT Uruguay Round agriculture agreement and the next World Trade round on agriculture

The influence of the Uruguay Round in constraining the CAP was a major factor in the 1992 reforms. Its effects are quantifiable and certain (e.g. CEC, 1993; NFU, 1994; Rayment, 1995) but operate only until the year 2001, after which the future is unclear, at least until the next trade round agenda is set and negotiated. Predicting the outcome is very difficult, but limits on subsidized exports and tariffs are likely to be tightened further and the extent to which area payments (including those for environmental reasons) will continue to be permissible will be discussed.

Budget and other economic costs

The CAP has been fairly resilient to criticism of its costs to tax-payers, the EU budget, consumers and the food industry (Buckwell *et al.*, 1995; Robson, Chapter 3). Whilst some still argue (and it remains true) that the CAP misallocates resources, is economically inefficient and damages the interests of (poor) consumers (MAFF, 1995; Ministry of Agriculture for Sweden, 1995) this is unlikely to force reform. The CAP is a declining (if still at 50%) proportion of an expanding EU budget (Tracy, 1995). Economic difficulties (in Germany, for example) may cause more overt pressure on budgets, but the main result for CAP decision-making is likely to be the political difficulty of public scepticism about the cost of 'supporting' farmers.

A changing rural society

Shifting demographic patterns, with farmers ageing and leaving the land, and people moving into the countryside for recreation and non-agricultural jobs, is causing a shift in policy (CEC, 1988). In some areas this will force the pace for rural development and in many areas it will raise demand for high environmental standards (Lake, 1995). Both factors question the traditional objectives and emphasis of the CAP in supporting a limited range of crops and farmers. While these will add to the political difficulty referred to above, in themselves such pressures are unlikely to bring about substantial reform.

Enlargement of the EU to include Central and Eastern Europe

The simple extension 'eastwards' of the current CAP to embrace the agricultural industries of central and east European countries (CEECs: Poland, Hungary, Czech and Slovak Republics, Bulgaria, Romania and possibly Slovenia and the Baltic States) is highly unlikely. Farming in those countries is already undergoing massive change following the collapse of the former communist systems, but to assume that all east European farming was under the collectivist model of huge State-run holdings, with centrally-set plans and output quotas is very wrong. There are such holdings – they are now being split into 'family' farm units. But there are also many small and medium sized farm holdings with every conceivable sort of European farming situation well represented, from the most traditional, to some modern agri-business concerns. The range and volume of output of those farms in aggregate is huge, and could arise rapidly as new technology and land reform take effect. The impact of their inclusion in the CAP would be a major cause for reform, even if simply to allow their assimilation into something approximating to the existing regime. In fact, it is difficult to imagine that a high cost CAP consisting of an administrative jungle of subsidies, market regulation and other measures will survive intact in a Union of 20 or more Member States, and there is a substantial debate developing as to how the EU might address an apparent incompatibility between the CAP and enlargement policies (Tracy, 1995).

This is likely to be the factor which most influences the future of the CAP and so is discussed later. However, the notion that the CAP will be somehow abolished and agriculture policy 'renationalized' is not realistic, whatever its merits (RSPB, 1995). The pressure will be for reform, not abolition, but there will always be considerable constraints on the pace and direction of reform and so these are examined below.

BRAKES ON REFORM: OR WHY THE CAP WILL NEVER BE ABOLISHED

Debate on CAP reform is such that it may appear that there is universal acceptance of the need for its abolition, and that this is imminent (e.g. CLA, 1994; MAFF, 1995). In fact, the CAP has survived continuous onslaughts of criticism from economists, environmentalists, consumers and now, increasingly so, from farmers. Across much of Europe there are many powerful influences ready to defend the CAP (and criticize those wishing to change it), calling on political, economic and practical reasons to oppose reform. These forces, as much as forces for change, will dictate the pace and direction of future reform.

Central to the future of the CAP is the degree to which EU farming is seen as part of a global 'free' market, or as a separate 'closed' market (Buckwell *et al.*, 1995; CEC, 1995a). Whether the major EU countries and international agencies (especially the OECD and G7) are 'pro-free trade' or 'protectionist' dictates the extent to which such policies as GATT impact on the CAP. During the 1980s, the political philosophies driving international policy were distinctly 'free' trade, but this is now perhaps less so (e.g. Hines & Lang, 1994).

Whatever the theoretical economic or environmental benefits (or costs) of 'free trade', it is being challenged by sections of industry, by commerce and political groups in Europe, partly in response to concerns about competition from the emergent economies, especially in central and eastern Europe, the former Soviet Union, China and the Pacific Rim. Such economies 'threaten' developed countries with cheaper labour, lower employment and environmental standards and other 'unfair' competition. This new attitude is beginning to impinge on the CAP debate and may act as a brake on the trend to liberalized trade in farm products. The political 'climate' for the next international trade round (which begins negotiations in 1999) may be very different from that which surrounded the 1980s–90s Uruguay Round.

Of course, the economic development of emergent economies may also have the effect of stimulating world agricultural markets, as developing economies import more food, and more open markets may actually advance the cause for CAP liberalization (e.g. MAFF, 1995).

At national level in Europe, there are many views on the CAP, but rarely is there serious debate on its costs, or its future, and vested interests (such as export-orientated farmers or traders) often dominate discussion. There is a need for more informed action, debate and pressure for CAP reform at Member State level. In particular, there is a need for a well informed debate on the environmental options and implications of reform in France and Germany to match the discussion in the UK and the Netherlands (see for example NABU, 1995). Discontent with the 1992 reforms and changing rural society in France, and the debate on EU enlargement in Germany may be fertile ground for CAP reform discussions.

There are widely differing national perspectives and objectives for rural policy among EU countries. Rural development is a high priority in Ireland, Portugal, Greece and Spain. Many regions face real difficulties in balancing sustainable development (including environmental protection) with employment generation (Egdell, 1993; Lake, 1995). Maintaining family farms is a priority in Austria, Sweden, Germany and some countries of the UK (Wales, Scotland and Northern Ireland), while promoting an 'efficient' (although questionable in environmental terms) export-driven and competitive agri-industry is the priority in the Netherlands, Denmark, France and the UK. There are also widely different environmental problems to further complicate CAP decision-making.

Decision-making in the Council of Agriculture Ministers has often been criticized for its secretiveness and complexity. Critics have described the CAP as a 'Secret Garden' where only those who understand the complexity benefit from its policies (LUFPIG, 1995). Decision-making may be even more problematic

Figure 3 Milk is collected from family farms in Lower Austria. Maintaining family farms is a priority in Austria. (Photo by J. Dixon.)

with more countries involved. Member States, chairing the Council in their rotating, six-monthly term as Presidents, often seek to achieve positive outcomes from their term of office. Laudable though this seems, it may contribute to short-termism, and unworkable or expensive compromises. Nor do other European institutions, such as the Parliament, have good track-records of influencing the CAP. In any case, many decisions are taken by technocratic and secret committees (Gardner, 1994).

At a very practical level, governments and the Commission need to manage the CAP day-to-day, including implementing any new measures such as those introduced in 1992. Monitoring and reviewing the operation of the CAP is itself enormously difficult. Set-aside and the new arable policy are examples of new measures whose impact is difficult to assess and which continue to evolve (Rayment, 1995). New ways of paying subsidies such as Arable Area Aids required an entirely new system of bureaucracy to be installed at massive disruption and cost to the EU, governments and farmers (i.e. the Integrated Administration and Control System (IACS)) (CEC, 1992a). There is, perhaps rightly, a growing reluctance to create further bureaucracy both among governments (who fear the cost, scope for corruption, and the gradual transfer of power to Brussels) and the Commission (who fear that governments will use it as a rod with which to beat them!).

Since the Single European Act and the Maastricht Agreement, managing the 'internal economic market' to promote 'fair' competition has been a clear priority for the EU. Harmonization of the economic 'playing field' has become a key factor in the CAP debate, constraining national government initiatives (including environmental initiatives) and limiting the development of environment policies, particularly those which attempt to modify substantial programmes such as agriculture subsidies, compensatory payments, trade policy and infrastructure development.

This list of constraints on reform is not exhaustive. It illustrates that CAP reform is likely to be incremental and erratic (Robson, Chapter 3). 'Radical' change or abolition of the CAP are unlikely and talk of such is often unhelpful in achieving significant, if less dramatic, real changes to the CAP (Tracy, 1995). However, all eventualities should be considered as possible in the distant future.

It is possible that a complex mix of farmer, consumer and tax-payer dissatisfaction with the CAP, adverse international trade relations and EU enlargement, may generate a sufficient 'head of political steam' to prompt 'radical' reform of the CAP. At present, however, this seems unlikely. Many ambitious plans to abolish the CAP languish unheeded in libraries across Europe.

From the perspective of nature conservation, it is clear that there will have to be further reform of the CAP (Beaufoy et al., 1994; RSPB, 1995). Before considering what those changes should be, we need to be clear why and for what purpose reform is necessary. We need a vision of a future countryside.

A NEW DIRECTION FOR EUROPEAN AGRICULTURE

From a nature conservation perspective it is clear that land-use policies in Europe, particularly the CAP, will need to change despite the very great difficulties and limitations. Before outlining how that might happen, it is worth taking a forward look at what sort of countryside would sustain the farming systems on which wild birds and other biodiversity depends. In this section, I have tried to 'paint' a somewhat idealized picture of a future countryside and, naturally, this includes more emphasis on those things that contribute to conservation objectives than other, legitimate, needs (although these need not conflict with such other needs). However, it is hoped that this vision of a countryside is one that could be shared by farmers, decision-makers, conservationists and the public. Quite rightly, readers will ask how this vision might be accomplished, what would it cost and who pays? The vision is complemented by a set of 'targets' for changing policies in the future, and the remainder of this chapter is devoted to evaluating specific policy options that could make this vision a reality.

The countryside of the future

The rural economy should be prosperous, producing sufficient quantities of high quality food for the nutritional needs of Europe. It should also contribute to an equitable trading system, based on a diversity of integrated commercial and internationally competitive land-uses: farming, forestry, recreation and tourism, rural industry, housing and protection and enhancement of nature. A principal 'commercial' product of the countryside will be its management and protection as a service to society at large (Taylor & Dixon, 1990).

The countryside should consist of diverse, peopled and wildlife-rich landscapes, with regionally sensitive policies that recognize natural and human characteristics in a viable and sustainable way (Lake, 1995). Farming is the basis of the economy and the social and cultural heritage of many regions throughout the EU (illustrated, e.g., by Bignal *et al.*, 1994). However, pursuing single objective policies, whether for food production or nature conservation, would repeat the mistakes of past policy. Rural areas should be allowed to optimize human and natural resources to develop sustainably, respecting the environment whilst contributing to overall economic development and allowing for social changes in rural areas.

Agriculture should be sustainable, internalizing the 'external' environmental and social costs and benefits of production, trade and consumption, and applying the polluter pays principle (Baldock, 1992). Subsidies should only be for achieving wider social and environmental objectives, rather than to promote or limit food production *per se*. Production, trade and consumption should be appropriate to soils and climate, and should not rely on technologies that are harmful to biodiversity, such as inappropriate irrigation, or be wasteful of energy and other natural resources. They should lead to a more 'extensive' agriculture which minimizes inputs, especially fertilizers and pesticides but also land. A more generally 'extensive' agriculture, which does not cause destruction of other habitats by encroachment and uses fewer chemical inputs need not prevent many farms continuing to 'rationalize' and farm at an appropriate level to supply for market needs.

Definitions of sustainable agriculture must include conservation of biodiversity, whether as part of agricultural systems or as habitats and species currently threatened by farming practices (Wynne *et al.*, 1995; UNEP, 1995). Agricultural land, particularly that which is extensively managed but also much that is fairly intensively managed, is important for nature conservation. Up to 30% of farmland is currently of special conservation value – extensive, high natural value farming – and so particular attention should be given to retaining this whilst also enhancing the value of the whole of the remainder (Beaufoy *et al.*, 1994; RSPB, 1995; Tucker, Chapter 4; Pain & Pienkowski, Chapter 13). A small amount of land could come out of agriculture to expand nature reserves and to create habitats (up to perhaps 5% of the EU's farmland area by the year 2020) which will much enhance European landscapes and biodiversity, but this must be done in a way which protects the most valuable farmland for biodiversity.

Agriculture and the rural economy should, once again, be respected, so that the public has confidence in the health of the rural environment as well as the supply, quality and quantity of food. This vision has to be translated into

Figure 4 Cattle grazing with a southern marsh orchid *Dactylorhiza praetermissa* in the foreground in Suffolk, UK, a sight infrequently seen today as many traditional grazing meadows have been subject to agricultural intensification. (Photo by C.H. Gomersall/ RSPB.)

objectives for reform and then into specific negotiating targets for policy-makers (RSPB, 1995).

A way forward: how should policy change?

There should be a gradual reduction in the level of subsidies for farm products to remove the damaging distortions in land-use, farming practices and the economy. The scale of EU subsidies is such that nearly half of the total economic activity of farming is currently represented by subsidy (OECD, 1995; Buckwell *et al.*, 1995). High subsidy to some products puts others (often those from low input farming) at a disadvantage, 'sucks' capital and other inputs into farming and inflates the value of land (further fuelling the tendency to maximize production) (Rayment, 1995). These trends should be reversed by paying subsidies only for costs incurred in stewardship of the countryside or for defined social reasons (e.g. MAFF, 1995).

Removing subsidies will not automatically lead to conservation benefits.

'Marginal' farms, especially in southern Europe, would need to be sheltered from this change (see e.g. Suárez *et al.*, Chapter 11; Díaz *et al.*, Chapter 7). Such farming areas are generally of high nature conservation value (see Chapters 4–11) and therefore, any reduction of subsidies may need to be differentiated between regions and farming types. Indeed, in some circumstances, an enhanced subsidy should be paid to support the continuation of high conservation value systems (RSPB, 1995).

Economic instruments (taxes and incentive payments) could be used much more vigorously to sustain certain farming practices for conservation reasons. In particular, management agreements, such as payments to farmers under the EU's Agri-Environment Regulation (CEC, 1992e), need to become a central part of CAP spending, focused clearly on conservation objectives. At least the 30% of the land surface which is of high natural value, or traditionally-managed, should be eligible for payments by the year 2000 (CEC, 1992f). A system of economic measures, including tighter regulations, should be applied to ensure that inputs of chemical fertilizers and pesticides form part of a more sustainable food chain, and the prices of energy and water should be set to ensure that they are not used excessively (Baldock, 1992).

Policy should move from one of being interventionist, dictating what crops are grown for what market and when, to one of giving strategic guidance based on targets for social, economic and especially environmental standards. These targets should be more clearly articulated in EU, national and farm scale plans (Tucker, unpublished data). There should be greater coherence between agriculture, rural development, forestry, natural resource and environmental protection policies and programmes. Too often at present, forestry policies 'cut across' the objectives of agri-environment programmes and agricultural subsidies undermine forestry, environment and rural development programmes (BirdLife International, 1994).

There should be better environmental appraisal of all strategic policy decisions (such as future options for the CAP) and specific policy instruments and decisions (such as amending set-aside or milk quotas) (Therivel, 1992). The European Commission is currently required to make a statement on the costs of all proposed legislation, and this should be extended to consider the environmental costs. Rarely in EU agriculture are the environmental consequences of programme and policy-level decisions considered, contrasting with EU legislation on environmental assessment of built developments such as bridges and airports (which cover a far smaller land area). Moreover, when considering the budgetary costs (e.g. to UK and EU tax-payers) or the economic efficiency of the CAP, ways of including environmental costs are needed so that a more complete understanding of 'economic' costs, as opposed to merely 'financial' costs, can inform decisions (House of Lords, 1991).

Such a future CAP may appear 'theoretical' or abstract. In fact, it represents little more than the full development and extension of many existing policy instruments, and relatively few new ones. I now go on to consider these instruments.

BUILDING THE NEW EUROPEAN AGRICULTURE

Choosing the building blocks: evaluating policy options

Clearly, conservation of farmland birds (and other wildlife) depends on factors that have wide-scale influence, rather than site protection measures. Few European farmland birds have significant populations within Important Bird Areas (IBAs) (Grimmett & Jones, 1989), and for those species that do (such as great bustard *Otis tarda*) few IBAs are protected. The habitat remains vulnerable to changes in agricultural policy. Thus, a strategy for influencing land-use in selected farmed areas or generally across farmland needs to consider local, regional, national and international policies for influencing these factors (Tucker, Chapter 4). What is needed is a mix of policies integrated by common and clear objectives.

Policies fall into three categories:

(1) large-scale global, political, economic or social policies, which conservationists should understand but cannot expect to influence to a major extent (such as multilateral policies to reduce subsidies);
(2) large-scale international or regional policies, which have wide effects on conservation and can be influenced, but cannot be expected to have conservation as their sole objective (such as CAP reform and land privatization);
(3) national or regional policies with specific conservation objectives, (such as the EU Agri-environment Regulation).

Within these categories the following policy areas are the most important for achieving nature conservation on farmland.

Choosing the options

Information, education and extension services

Several countries have voluntary or state-supported extension services which provide applied research, training and advice in new environmental management for farmers. In some countries, such as the Netherlands, Germany and UK, habitat management is taught in agricultural colleges.

Quality ecological and practical advice needs to be available for farmers to adjust to requirements of conservation management. Nature conservation organizations can contribute advice on certain aspects, advising other farm management or conservation advisors, agricultural colleges, etc. They also have a role in promoting the provision of advisory services where none exist, and ensuring that advisors are re-trained and supplemented by conservation scientists (Winter, 1995). Conservation organizations cannot substitute for government and industry funded research and development, training and extension services, however. The scale of the task far exceeds their ability to fulfil it, and, in any case, what is needed is an enormous effort to redirect Europe's agriculture towards new forms of management, and approaches to land-use. Education, training and advice have a role to play, but can be effective only if allied to something more forceful – EU and international legal and economic stimuli will be the main 'driving force' for change, just as they have been in former agricultural changes.

Changing the fundamental objectives of rural policies

The amended Treaty of Rome, Single European Act (Article 130r) and Maastricht Treaty require environmental protection to be a component of all EU policies (CEC, 1957, 1987, 1992g). However, the objectives of the CAP as outlined in the Treaty of Rome (Article 39) remain unchanged, resulting in confusion about the objectives of agriculture policies and the marginalization of environmental considerations in most policies, such as set-aside (BirdLife International, 1993). This contrasts with some countries, such as Norway, where the objectives of rural policy have been brought up to date to include sustainable use of inputs and protection of biodiversity (Beaufoy *et al.*, 1994).

EU rural land-use policies need to reflect directly the objectives of EU and international environmental legislation. Opportunities to move towards this, by redefining the objectives of EU rural policy to encompass protection of farmland biodiversity and promote sustainable resource use, will arise through CAP reform, EU enlargement negotiations and the 1996 Intergovernmental Conference (Dixon, 1994a).

Overall levels and forms of subsidy

Border controls and tariffs, price supports and direct subsidies work together in the CAP to create an overall level of subsidy which has a powerful influence on land-use, input use and farm incomes. Subsidies account for approximately 50% of the turnover of agriculture in the EU (Buckwell *et al.*, 1995). In central and eastern European countries the 'effective' subsidy level is much lower (*c*. 8% in Hungary, for example), although EU accession would probably raise this (CEC, 1995b).

Subsidy to agriculture is probably the single most important area of policy needing reform if conservation objectives on farmland are to be achieved (Woods *et al.*, 1988). Many advocate that overall levels of subsidies should be reduced (Buckwell *et al.*, 1995; MAFF, 1995). Reductions are likely to be incremental with small reductions in the next ten years, and subsidies shifting from the former largely indirect price support systems to more direct payments.

Policies to restrict farm production (such as milk quotas and set-aside) act to support product prices and allow reduced direct subsidy levels. They can take various forms, including limits on saleable outputs (quotas), limits on inputs such as land (set-aside), or pesticides and fertilizers (extensification, taxes or bans). Various combinations of such instruments are already in use in the EU. For example, in 1995, 7.2 million ha of arable land was set aside under an annual scheme, and limited livestock extensification measures including quota and premia for reduced stocking exist (CEC, 1992a). Prior to EU accession Austria and Sweden operated nitrogen taxes, though they had only limited effects on nitrogen use and the environment, and have been abandoned.

Input restrictions are new, rarely evaluated, often limited and sometimes multi-objective policies (Beaufoy *et al.*, 1994). There is considerable scope for using them for both specific conservation purposes, and for achieving wider changes in farmland use, by adding conservation conditions to subsidies, for example (Baldock & Mitchell, 1995; Tracy, 1995).

Schemes to promote environmentally 'friendly' products exist in most countries, operating by enhancing market prices through premia (for organic products, for example) (CEC, 1991b).

The response of farmers and land-use to falling support prices needs further study. It is likely that falling supported prices will have some beneficial effects, such as reduced incentives to overstock or apply fertilizers, but some low intensity farm systems may be abandoned or change in nature, unless direct payments are able to maintain them (Beaufoy *et al.*, 1994). EU prices and the transitional supports in former communist countries adjusting to western-style policies need to be monitored carefully. For example, in Hungary prices have collapsed and increased input costs have led to a 55% fall in production but only a 5% reduction in farmed area (CEC, 1995b). Perhaps this is extensification in practice.

Where it is clear that subsidy reductions or changes to area payments (for example) will bring benefits, this should be encouraged as part of future reforms. Where direct subsidies replace indirect price supports, environmental conditions (or cross compliance) could be attached to these (Baldock & Mitchell, 1995).

Trading arrangements

As well as being influenced by subsidies, market prices are also affected by trading patterns, over which the major trading blocs have considerable control. For example, the EU encourages trade within the 'Single Market' which has contributed to specialization and intensification of production in some regions,

Figure 5 Traditionally managed meadow rich in wild flowers in the Jura, eastern France. Some low intensity farming systems may be abandoned or changed in nature unless policies can maintain them. (Photo by D.J. Pain.).

and abandonment in others (Dixon, 1994b). Trade agreements exist with European Economic Area (EEA) countries (Norway and Switzerland) and former communist countries under bilateral agreements (Association or Europe Agreements) (Tracy, 1994).

Environmental considerations are gradually being brought into trade debates (Cameron, 1994). At the time of writing (February 1996) the European Commission was considering whether to propose an amendment to GATT (Article 20) to allow closer integration of global trade and environment policy. Payments to farmers in the form of management agreements have less distortionary effects on trade than production subsidies: trade agreements could therefore reinforce a shift towards such forms of subsidy. Restricting exports may help to restrain intensification in the EU. Restricted access to markets through the erection of barriers, for example, can harm sectors of agriculture such as beef raising that are important for the management of some important farmland habitats. Incorporating countries with extensive farming systems into a large single market exposes such systems to increased competition (Egdell, 1993).

These issues are little understood and more analysis is necessary (Dixon, 1994b). The relationship between farming systems and trading arrangements across the whole of Europe needs to be analysed and monitored so that policy can be guided and changed if necessary.

Economic instruments

Farmers can be 'compensated' or 'penalized' by a variety of economic measures such as their treatment in general tax systems, application of specific environmental taxes or payments made under environmental incentive schemes. All of these can be broadly described as economic instruments.

Numerous forms of taxes and exemptions could be applied to encourage farmers to support environmental objectives. Examples include taxes on fertilizers or exemption from land taxes for specific purposes in France and the UK. Specific reductions in pesticide use could come from taxing them, and taxes could be used alongside regulations to control toxic substances. Taxes might be appropriate for limitations on fertilizer use, although for locally specific reductions to improve water quality, this is unlikely to be effective.

Payments can be made for capital items or revenue, and can be environmental or have mainly agricultural production or social objectives. Capital grants for agricultural development have been harmful (Baldock, 1990) and in some countries, such as Denmark and the UK, have largely been withdrawn.

In areas subject to depopulation, or unintensive agriculture, capital support for land drainage, irrigation and other damaging works continues (Beaufoy *et al.*, 1994). Support for infrastructure development in objective 1 and 5b regions of the EU, and through aid programmes in central and east Europe, should be subject to strategic environmental assessment. Capital grants to farmers could be made conditional on not harming sites of conservation value or could be withdrawn altogether.

Management contracts paid to farmers annually can be made as compensation for the 'foregone' potential higher earnings from higher output, or as direct rewards for managing habitats or crop systems of value to wildlife. Such schemes have existed in the EU for over ten years, particularly in the Netherlands, Denmark, UK, France and Germany (BirdLife International, 1993). Under the 1992 'agri-environment' regulation, plans for such schemes now apply in all EU countries. Spending on them will exceed ECU 6.6 bn between 1993 and 1997 (CEC, 1992e). Outside the EU, similar proposals based on pilot areas have been made for Poland, Hungary and the Czech Republic.

The benefits of such schemes for wildlife have not been fully evaluated. Funding is often limited, and objectives are often unclear (BirdLife International, 1994). However, the approach of treating environmental benefits as products deserving financial support and capable of making income for farmers offers farmland birds more immediate prospects of benefit than other, less focused policies (Tucker, Chapter 4). The potential to develop such schemes as

Environmentally Sensitive Areas and similar specific, targeted, management agreement forms of farm support is now considered in detail.

A SIGNPOST TO THE FUTURE: THE AGRI-ENVIRONMENT REGULATION

In addition to the mainstream reforms to the commodity regimes, the 1992 reforms incorporated three accompanying measures, on environmental incentives (EC Regulation 2078/92), early retirement (EC Regulation 2079/92) and forestry (EC Regulation 2080/92) (CEC, 1995c–e). Each of these will have an impact on the environment but the most exciting in terms of its potential to bring about change that benefits farmland wildife is the Agri-environment Regulation.

Schemes of this kind are not new. One objective for designation of Less Favoured Areas (LFAs) under the original EC Directive was the maintenance of the environment. In reality, few Member States used the measure in that way, preferring LFAs to prevent rural depopulation and using livestock production subsidies as the main means of support. The result, perversely, was that doing so contributed to further environmental degradation (RSPB, 1984).

There were some exceptions to this. The Dutch government used LFA designation in a way much more akin to Environmentally Sensitive Areas, for which they could probably claim to have been the pioneers.

National schemes to pay farmers for specific environmental management have been in existence in the UK, Germany and the Netherlands for many years. In 1985 the EC became formally involved by beginning to 'co-finance' such schemes under Article 19 of EC Structures Regulation 797/85 (later 2328/91) (CEC, 1991a).

The 1992 regulation (see Table 1) expanded the scope, funding and the coverage across EU countries of such schemes. It also requires that payments should be made subject to positive effects on the environment and the countryside (Article 2, 1), and that zonal programmes should include an indication of the Community environment legislation the objectives of which the programme seeks to fulfil. Thus, for the first time there is a specific requirement for environmental monitoring and evaluation of schemes that give environmental incentives to farmers.

Since the agri-environment measures were introduced Member States have submitted for co-financing approval nearly 200 separate programmes of schemes which apply voluntary schemes to all farmland. The Commission has allocated an 'illustrative' budget of up to ECU 7000m by 1997 (CEC, pers. comm.).

Examples of schemes submitted include:

(1) Measures to reduce nitrate pollution to protect water supply aquifers across the EU (a so-called horizontal measure);

Table 1 Extract from Council Regulation (EEC) No 2078/92. On agricultural production methods compatible with the requirements of the protection of the environment and maintenance of the countryside

---

Article 1: Purpose of the aid scheme

This Community aid scheme is intended to promote:
a) the use of farming practices which reduce the polluting effects of agriculture, a fact which also contributes, by reducing production, to an improved market balance;
b) an environmentally favourable extensification of crop farming, and sheep and cattle farming, including the conversion of arable land into extensive grassland;
c) ways of using agricultural land which are compatible with protection and improvement of the environment, the countryside, the landscape, natural resources, the soil and genetic diversity;
d) the upkeep of abandoned farmland and woodlands where this is necessary for environmental reasons or because of natural hazards and fire risks, and thereby avert the dangers associated with the depopulation of agricultural areas;
e) long-term set-aside of agricultural land for reasons connected with the environment;
f) land management for public access and leisure activities;
g) education and training for farmers in types of farming compatible with the requirements of environmental protection and upkeep of the countryside.

Article 3: Aid Programmes

1. Member States shall implement, throughout their territories, and in accordance with their specific needs, the aid scheme ... by means of multiannual zonal programmes covering the objectives referred to in Article 1. The programmes shall reflect the diversity of environmental situations, natural conditions and agricultural structures and the main types of farming practised, and Community environment priorities.
2. Each zonal programme shall cover an area which is homogeneous in terms of the environment and the countryside and shall include, in principle, all of the aids provided for in Article 2. However, where there is sufficient justification, programmes may be restricted to aids which are in line with the specific characteristics of an area.
4. By way of derogation ... Member States may establish a general regulatory framework providing for the horizontal application throughout their territory of one or more of the aids ... That framework must be defined and, where appropriate, supplemented by the zonal programmes.

Article 8: Rate of Community Financing

The rate of Community part-financing shall be 75% in regions covered by the objective defined in point 1 of Article 1 of Regulation (EEC) No 2052/88 and 50% in the other regions.

Source: CEC (1992e).

(2) measures to extensify arable farming by reducing inputs, and livestock farming by extensifying pasture across the EU;

(3) conversion payments for organic farmers;

(4) schemes to encourage conversion of arable land to grassland, wetland, coastal marsh and river margins;

(5) Environmentally Sensitive Areas for landscape and nature conservation in the UK, Netherlands, Denmark and France;

(6) the Marktentlastungs- und Kulturlandschaftsausgleich (MEKA) programme of Baden Würtemburg and Kulturlandschaftsprogramm from Bayern, Germany for promoting extensive farming;

(7) plans for maintaining and improving cereal steppelands in Spain (e.g. in Castilla y León and Extremadura), Portugal (e.g. Castro Verde) and France (e.g. Le Crau);

(8) measures to protect perennial crops of cultural, landscape and wildlife conservation value such as olive groves in Greece, Portugal and Spain.

However, the Agri-environment Regulation has its limitations, and the following examples illustrate some of these.

The effect of extensification measures on livestock numbers

It seems likely that the livestock extensification measures will have only a small and local effect on livestock numbers, and hence on overall production levels. EU funds allocated to the regulation may seem large (by the standards of spending on the environment) but are very small compared with overall CAP spending (Egdell, 1993). Livestock extensification is only one, limited element of the regulation, which means the funds available for it are extremely limited, certainly when compared with the main subsidies available to livestock production.

The regulation relies on voluntary uptake by farmers choosing to forgo increased intensification, market returns, subsidy and in some cases quota, in favour of compensations under the regulation. Farmers can sometimes reduce variable costs, such as veterinary costs, by pursuing extensification measures, but fixed costs such as labour and buildings remain high. The incentive to join a scheme needs to be set higher than the theoretical loss of income or costs incurred in following the prescriptions (Whitby, 1994).

Full take-up of the sheep and cattle extensification scheme in France will mean only a 0.45% reduction in numbers, whilst the Moorland Scheme in the UK could reduce sheep numbers by 1.6% (BirdLife International, 1994; BirdLife International, unpublished data). Such figures are the most optimistic estimates to be achieved by these schemes by 1997. In fact, some countries have no intention of introducing livestock extensification (e.g. Denmark) and others will only be introducing schemes in some regions (e.g. Italy and Spain) or restricted sub-zones such as ESAs (in the Netherlands, for example).

For many horizontal measures, such as those in Germany, Portugal and Ireland, rates of compensation are such that only a small proportion of farmers will be tempted to take payments. These are likely to be farmers whose production levels are not high (BirdLife International, 1994).

Uncertain effects on the environment

Recent reviews of implementation in Portugal, Greece, Germany, Ireland, UK and Spain, show that schemes are often of limited geographical coverage, limiting their effectiveness (BirdLife International, 1994). An additional problem is that programmes often have multiple objectives, such as protection of flora, fauna, groundwater and landscape (for example) together with farm income and social objectives.

Confusion of objectives often leads to confusion in operation, and to situations where environmentalists consider scheme conditions too 'light' (i.e. undemanding or unlikely to secure any benefit), while farmers think them too 'heavy'.

Poor integration with other policies

Agri-environment incentive schemes offer an effective means of achieving targeted, localized or other specific environmental objectives in agriculture. However, unless linked to mainstream policies their effect will be limited or even undermined. A key test of agri-environment schemes ought to be how well they are integrated with other policies. Generally, this is poor, even within the range of agricultural policies.

Poor policy integration means for example, that the UK Moorland scheme will pay up to £7m per annum to reduce upland sheep numbers which are maintained at artificially high levels by over £200m paid under the sheepmeat regime and HLCAs. In Portugal, afforestation incentives (under regulation 2080/92) will be four times greater per hectare than proposed agri-environment incentives. In many areas re-introduction of grazing to abandoned lands will be restricted by quotas (BirdLife International, 1994).

Despite these problems the Agri-environment Regulation marks a new era in European farming, offering tremendous opportunities for farmers, governments and conservationists. For the first time, significant financial incentives are available for governments to pay farmers for hitherto unrewarded environmental services. Amended funding, particularly enhanced EU reimbursement rates (75% for Objective 1 countries such as Portugal, Spain, Ireland and Greece) make such schemes viable for the first time. This is welcome and overdue.

Whilst imperfect, the Agri-environment Regulation provides a blueprint for the sort of farm policies that could address many conservation problems in the future.

THE CHALLENGE OF AN ENLARGED EUROPEAN UNION

A Union for the whole of Europe?

The collapse of the Berlin Wall was symbolic of the economic collapse of both the former Soviet Union and the countries in central and eastern Europe: probably the most important factor influencing the future of the CAP (MAFF, 1995; RSPB, 1995). Land-use and farming practices in central and eastern European Countries have changed dramatically in response to a collapsed agricultural market.

Discussions have begun on how at least some of the countries can join the EU, possibly as soon as 2000 (Strak & Black, 1996). There is, however, no 'strategy' for agriculture and enlargement. Instead there is a complicated debate restricted by poor data, inadequate analysis and limited evaluation of existing aid, trade and CEEC agriculture policies (Tracy, 1995; Strak & Black, 1996).

Agriculture is recognized as an exceptionally difficult aspect of enlargement negotiations (CEC, 1995a,b). It is proportionately more important to the economies of most CEECs than the EU, despite the low market prices and state of development of agriculture (Tracy, 1995). The 'gaps' in living standards and state of development between CEECs and the EU are much greater than for earlier countries joining the Union (Vonthron, 1995).

The political, agricultural and land-use consequences of accession are difficult to predict and more analysis is needed (Strak & Black, 1996). Several analyses have described CEEC agriculture during transition to market orientation (e.g. Buckwell *et al.*, 1995; CEC, 1995a,b). Studies of the accession of Spain to the EU indicate that opening markets had a marked effect on land-use, farming and the environment (Egdell, 1993).

The most comprehensive analyses so far have been undertaken by the EC Directorates for External Affairs (DGI), Economics and Finance (DGII) and Agriculture (DGVI) (see Strak & Black, 1996 for an overview). The third is the most significant, because of the pragmatism of its analysis and because it formed a precursor to a 'White Paper' on agriculture and enlargement agreed at the Madrid summit of Heads of State (December 1995). This sets strategy for a five- to ten-year period (CEC, 1995a).

Agriculture and environment: key issues for enlargement

Environmental issues in the enlargement debate include the environmental legacy of former CEEC policies, the consequences of recent agricultural 'crises', and environmental aspects of future policies of both the EU and CEECs (BirdLife International *et al.*, 1995).

In much of Central and East Europe under former regimes there was a trend to increase fertilizer, pesticide and machinery use in arable cropping, and to concentrate livestock production in intensive units. Across much of the region, the landscape has been considerably altered and simplified by collective farms. These changes resemble those achieved by entrepreneurial farmers in the EU (IUCN, 1991, 1992, 1993).

Collectivized and state land ownership led to distinctive land-use patterns and consequent environmental problems. It also led to the ordered management of land in ecological units (such as catchments) in a way in which private landownership in the west often hampers.

A range of serious environmental problems exist in the CEECs, often on a scale greater than in the west. Soil erosion, salinization and contamination, groundwater pollution, mismanagement of water resources, pollution from vast, intensive livestock units and contamination through pesticides and nuclear radiation have been widespread (OECD, 1994). The scale of degradation is such that, in many areas, farmlands' productive capacity has been irreversibly affected and human health harmed. Solving environmental problems will be a prerequisite to agricultural development in some regions.

The habitat destruction resulting from landscape change has been documented in several reports (IUCN, 1991, 1992, 1993). Examples include the ploughing of steppe grassland across the plains of Eastern Europe, drainage of wetlands, destruction of forests and 'simplification' of agricultural landscapes. Vast state-funded agricultural developments were widespread in Eastern countries. For example, 2 million ha of steppe grassland were ploughed in Kazakhstan during two years in the 1970s. One million hectares of wetlands were drained in Lithuania between 1979 and 1978.

Nevertheless, the CEECs retain a significant proportion of Europe's biodiversity, much of which depends on farmland (Tucker, Chapter 4). This is partly because production outside the collective or state systems was not encouraged. Unlike family farms subject to the market and EU policies farming in many regions has remained economically under-developed, retaining high natural values and biodiversity. Overall, the income inefficiency and limited development of much of CEEC farming led to less environmental damage than farming in much of western Europe.

There has been a recent collapse of markets and domestic consumption, with increased imports. The collapse of central planning has led to higher costs for such items as chemical inputs. Together, these factors have caused agricultural output to fall, by as much as a half in real terms from 1989–94 (CEC, 1995b).

The environmental effects of this have been profound. For example, arable farming output has fallen to nearly half previous levels, although roughly the same area has remained in cultivation. This may have allowed the populations of some farmland birds which are declining in the EU to increase. Less capital is available for damaging land developments than under the former regimes.

Conversely, abandonment of many formerly grazed areas, such as the Biebrza National Park in Poland, is a threat to semi-natural grasslands. The process of privatization has caused large areas to be abandoned. There is a danger that some large-scale patterns of land-use important for wetland catchments or extensive grasslands will be broken up. Similarly, attempts to 'rationalize' farm structures where small-scale and long-established farming still exists may damage farming systems of high conservation value (IUCN, 1994).

Future prospects for an enlarged EU

When speaking of the difficulties their Hungarian counterparts face, Austrian farmers say 'to make fish soup from an aquarium is easy; reversing the process is more difficult'.

Uncertain policies and land tenure, fluctuating and depressed markets, and lack of capital will limit agricultural development in the CEECs (CEC, 1995b). However, for political, food security and economic reasons, an agricultural renaissance will undoubtedly happen, triggered in large measure by EU accession, prior to which the EU (and other international agencies and governments) will provide substantial aid, for agricultural development.

Some estimate that existing EU spending on the CAP, Structural funds and Cohesion Fund will largely need to be switched to the CEECs (House of Lords, 1994). At whatever level this occurs, the environmental consequences will need to be assessed and monitored, guidelines for environmental protection be introduced, and resources be 'ear-marked' for sustainable and environmentally-sensitive farming (BirdLife International *et al.*, 1995). In the medium term, it will be necessary to ensure at the very least that EU environment policies are 'carried over' to the CEECs, otherwise the prospects for much of the biodiversity for which those regions have acted as Europe's main reservoir will be gloomy indeed.

A TIMETABLE FOR REFORM

Table 2 outlines the possible timetable that European policy-makers will be working to for CAP reforms. These reforms will both have consequences for the environment and also create opportunities for integrating environmental objectives. Unlike the United States, which has a definite cycle of farm policy-making leading to the compendium 'Farm Bills' every five years, the EU has no formal timetable (CEC, 1995b). Rather, reforms happen in relation to market demands, political crises or opportunities. This haphazard approach leads to confusion, speculation and little possibility of environmental interests making a full input into policy reviews. It is therefore necessary to track very carefully the political, market and budgetary situation in the CAP, spotting opportunities for change as they arise.

Table 2 Opportunities for reform of the CAP until 2010

Medium term (1996–1997)
1. The EU Council is likely to be considering a review of CAP (arable, livestock and Regulation 2078/92) but the timetable and priorities are very uncertain. There will be a probable follow-over of discussions on enlargement, fruit and vegetables as part of the 96/97 price package. There will also be environmental opportunities for cross-compliance and linkages with Regulation 2078/92.
2. The European Commission will be continuing to review the 1992 arable and livestock Regulations, Regulation 2078 and probably enlargement in detail. Inter-Governmental Conference 1996/7 will review the basic EU treaty.
3. There is likely to be an expansion in aid and 'restructuring' programmes to the CEECs as part of a long, aid-dominated accession process. There will probably be political rancour about slow accession. There will be serious opportunities to promote pilot agri-environment measures, to assess the environmental consequences of new policies and to promote more sustainable agriculture in the CEECs.

Long term (1997–2010)
1. Likely changes to the CAP regimes so as to be compatible with GATT requirements. These could include price cuts, changes to quotas and a likely shift to area payments. This is likely to be driven by internal pressures and changes to GATT and the enlargement of the EU.
2. The next round of world trade negotiations will begin in 1999. Theoretically this should lead to an agreement between 2001 and 2006. Reductions in agricultural tariffs and subsidies are likely, along with further opportunities to promote environmentally-based, area payments.
3. Long-term restructuring of Mediterranean agriculture will lead to increased specialization, competitive pressures and probably increased pressures on CAP budgets leading to reform.
4. Enlargement of the EU to include countries of central and eastern Europe will lead to substantial changes to the CAP, subsidy levels, decision-making, Structural Fund distribution and environmental issues in agriculture.
5. Increasing globalization of food markets is likely to drive EU policies, but it is difficult to predict how and when.
6. There are likely to be revisions to EU Structural Funds policies as they 'run their course', as priorities are shifted, as budgets are squeezed or expanded and as the environment features increasingly.

CONCLUSIONS

Agricultural policies will continue to evolve and change in response to circumstances, only some of which are predictable. Society, in the shape of governments, academics, conservationists and (the ultimate arbiters, of course) consumers will go on asking farmers to change their long-established habits and use land in new, unfamiliar ways.

We cannot say whether the significance of the first attempts to cultivate crops and raise livestock was clear to our ancestors at the dawn of the age of farming. We know that it must have been exciting to have been part of the successive agricultural 'revolutions', not least the most recent technological change in European farming. But we also know the price paid by the environment, and therefore by us all, for an approach to farming which puts technology and production at the forefront, and relegates stewardship and the 'un-marketable' products of farming to the rear.

Future reforms of the CAP provide the opportunity to learn from the mistakes of the past, and set about creating a new kind of farming.

Birds are great 'indicators' of the sort of farming that not only allows them to survive on farmland, but which may also benefit other wildlife and perhaps too farming communities. What then of the excitement of being at the dawn of another new era, with the prospect of a countryside rich in the beauty and interest of birds and other wildlife. We must all grasp these opportunities before it is too late.

ACKNOWLEDGEMENTS

I wish to thank my fellow professionals in the RSPB and within the BirdLife International partnership who have assisted in the development of my ideas. In particular I wish to thank Dr John Taylor, Matthew Rayment, Dr Deborah Pain and Hannah Bartram for commenting on the text.

REFERENCES

BALDOCK, D. (1990) Agriculture and habitat loss under the CAP. WWF CAP Discussion Papers.
BALDOCK, D. (1992) *The Polluter Pays Principle*. London: Institute for European Environmental Policy.
BALDOCK, D. & MITCHELL, K. (1995) *Cross Compliance*. Netherlands Ministry of Agriculture/ UK Department of the Environment, London. London: Institute of European Environmental Policy.
BEAUFOY, G., BALDOCK, D. & CLARK, J. (1994) *The Nature of Farming*. Joint Nature Conservancy Council, World Wide Fund for Nature, Institute of European Environmental Policy, c/o IEEP London.
BIGNAL, E., McCRACKEN, D., PIENKOWSKI, M. & BRANSON, A. (1994) *The Nature of Farming: traditional low intensity farming and its importance for wildlife*. Brussels: World Wide Fund for Nature.
BIRDLIFE INTERNATIONAL (1993) Comments on: CEC (1993) Possible developments in the policy of arable land set aside. Reflection paper of the Commission COM (93) 266 final. Sandy: BirdLife International, c/o Royal Society for Protection of Birds.
BIRDLIFE INTERNATIONAL (1994) Implementation of the Agri-environment Regulation (EEC 2078/92). Sandy: BirdLife International, c/o Royal Society for Protection of Birds.
BIRDLIFE INTERNATIONAL, World Wide Fund for Nature and World Conservation Union

(IUCN). (1995). Action plan to 2010: integrating agriculture and the environment. Sandy: BirdLife International, c/o Royal Society for Protection of Birds.

BUCKWELL, A., HAYNES, J., DANIDOVA, S. & KWIECINSKI, A. (1995). *Feasibility of an Agricultural Strategy to Prepare the Countries of Central and Eastern Europe for EU Accession.* DGI, Luxembourg: Commission of the European Communities, DGI, Luxembourg.

CAMERON, J. (1994). *International Trade and Environment.* Cameron May Associates.

CEC (Commission of the European Communities) (1957) The Treaty of Rome. Luxembourg: Official Journal of the EC.

CEC (Commission of the European Communities) (1987) The Single European Act. Luxembourg: Official Journal of the EC.

CEC (Commission of the European Communities) (1988) The future of the rural world. Luxembourg: Official Journal of the EC.

CEC (Commission of the European Communities) (1991a) Council Regulation 2328/91. Luxembourg: Official Journal of the EC.

CEC (Commission of the European Communities) (1991b) Organic farming regulation. Luxembourg: Official Journal of the EC.

CEC (Commission of the European Communities) (1992a) Various regulations on CAP Reform. Luxembourg: Official Journal of the EC.

CEC (Commission of the European Communities) (1992b) Arable reforms, Council Regulation 1765/92. Luxembourg: Official Journal of the EC.

CEC (Commission of the European Communities) (1992c) Council Regulation 2079/92. Luxembourg: Official Journal of the EC.

CEC (Commission of the European Communities) (1992d) Council Regulation 2080/92. Luxembourg: Official Journal of the EC.

CEC (Commission of the European Communities) (1992e) Council Regulation 2078/92. Luxembourg: Official Journal of the EC.

CEC (Commission of the European Communities) (1992f) Towards sustainability: vth action programme on the environment. Luxembourg: Official Journal of the EC.

CEC (Commission of the European Communities) (1992g) The Maastricht Treaty. Luxembourg: Official Journal of the EC.

CEC (Commission of the European Communities) (1993) Compatibility between the 1992 CAP reforms and the Uruguay round agreement of the GATT. Belgium: CEC DGVI.

CEC (Commission of the European Communities) (1995a) Study on alternative strategies for the development of relations in the field of agriculture between the EU and the associated countries with a view to future accession of these countries Draft for discussion by EU Heads of Government. Brussels: CEC.

CEC (Commission of the European Communities) (1995b) Agricultural situation and prospects in the Central and Eastern European Countries. Brussels: Summary report European Commission, Directorate for Agriculture.

CLA (Country Landowners Association) (1994) *Focus on the CAP.* London: CLA.

DIXON, J.B. (1994a) Changing the objectives and institutions of the CAP. Internal RSPB working paper. Sandy: RSPB.

DIXON, J.B. (1994b) Agriculture and environment in Europe: paper presented to international conference on trade and environment, Minneapolis, 13–15 November 1994.

EGDELL, J. (1993). The impact of agricultural policy on Spain and its Steppe regions. Studies in European agriculture and environment policy. Sandy: RSPB.

EGDELL, J., DIXON, J.B., TAYLOR, J.P. & APPLEBY, M.J. (1993) *Proposals for the Reform of EC Livestock Policies.* Studies in European agriculture and environment policy. Sandy: RSPB.

EUROSTAT (1995) *Statistics in Focus Agriculture, Forestry and Fisheries.* Luxembourg: Eurostat, ISSN 1024–4263.

GARDNER, B. (1994). Decision-making in the Common Agricultural Policy, paper presented to the

European Parliament Environment Committee conference on agriculture and the food chain. Brussels: European Parliament.

GRIMMETT, R.F.A. & JONES, T.A. (1989). *Important Bird Areas in Europe*. Cambridge: BirdLife International.

HINES, C. & LANG, T. (1994) *The GATT*. London: Earthscan.

HOUSE OF LORDS (1991). *The Development and Future of the Common Agricultural Policy*. European Communities Committee 8th report. London: HMSO.

HOUSE OF LORDS (1994) *The Implications for Agriculture of the Europe Agreements*. European Communities Committee 10th report. London: HMSO.

IUCN (International Union for the Conservation of Nature) (1991) *Country Study Integrating Agriculture and the Environment – Poland*, Cambridge: IUCN.

IUCN (International Union for the Conservation of Nature) (1992) *Country Study Integrating Agriculture and the Environment – Hungary*. Cambridge: IUCN.

IUCN (International Union for the Conservation of Nature) (1993) *Country Study Integrating Agriculture and the Environment – Czeck and Slovak Republics*. Cambridge: IUCN.

IUCN (International Union for the Conservation of Nature) (1994). *Land Re-privatization in Central and Eastern Europe*. Cambridge: IUCN.

LAKE, R. (1995) *The Structural Funds and Biodiversity*. Sandy: BirdLife International, c/o RSPB.

LUFPIG (Land Use and Food Policy Intergroup) (1995) *The Secret Garden*. Brussels: LUFPIG, European parliament.

MAFF (Ministry of Africulture Food and Fisheries) (1995) *European Agriculture: the case for radical reform*. London: MAFF.

MARSH, J. & TANGERMANN, S. (1992) *The Changing Role of the Common Agricultural Policy*. London: Belhaven Press.

MINISTRY OF AGRICULTURE FOR SWEDEN (1995) *Statement on the Common Agricultural Policy*. Stockholm: Ministry of Agriculture.

NFU (National Farmers Union) (1994) *Real Choices II*. London: NFU.

NABU (Naturschutsbund Deutschland) (1995) *Proceedings of an International Conference on the Common Agricultural Policy*. Bonn: NABU.

NETHERLANDS SCIENTIFIC COUNCIL (1992) *Grounds for Choice: four perspectives for the rural areas in the European Community*. The Hague: Netherlands Scientific Council.

OCKENDEN, J. & FRANKLIN, M. (1994) *European Agricultural Policies*. London: Royal Institution for International Affairs.

OECD (Organization for Economic Coordination and Development) (1994). *Agriculture and the Environment in the Transitional Economies*. Paris: OECD.

OECD (Organization for Economic Coordination and Development) (1995) *Agricultural Policies, Markets and Trade in the Central and Eastern Countries, Selected New Independent States, Mongolia and China: monitoring and outlook 1995*. Paris: OECD.

RAYMENT, M. (1995). *A Review of the 1992 CAP Reforms*. Sandy: Royal Society for the Protection of Birds.

RSPB (Royal Society for the Protection of Birds) (1984) *Hill Farming and Birds*. Sandy: Royal Society for the Protection of Birds.

RSPB (Royal Society for the Protection of Birds) (1991) *A Future for Environmentally Sensitive Farming*. Sandy: Royal Society for the Protection of Birds.

RSPB (Royal Society for the Protection of Birds) (1995) *The Future of the Common Agricultural Policy*. Sandy: Royal Society for the Protection of Birds.

STRAK, J. & BLACK, L. (1996) EU trade policy and its impacts on land use in Eastern Europe. Paper prepared for the BirdLife International European Programme, c/o Sandy: Royal Society for the Protection of Birds.

TAYLOR, J.P. & DIXON, J.B. (1990) *Agriculture and the Environment: towards integration*. Sandy: Royal Society for the Protection of Birds.

THERIVAL, R. (ed.) (1992) *Strategic Environmental Assessment*. London: Earthscan.

TRACY, M. (1993) *Food and Agriculture in a Market Economy: an introduction to theory, practice and policy*. Belgium: Agriculture Policy Studies (APS), La Hutte, Genappe.

TRACY, M. (1994) *The Association Agreements of the European Union*. Belgium: Agriculture Policy Studies (APS), La Hutte, Genappe.

TRACY, M. (1995) Strategies for Agriculture in an Enlarged European Union. Paper presented at an international conference: Integrating Agriculture and the Environment, Gödöllö Agricultural University, Hungary, 14–15 September 1995.

TUCKER, G.M. & HEATH, M. (1994) *Birds in Europe: their conservation status*. Cambridge: BirdLife International.

UNEP (United Nations Environment Programme) (1992). Nairobi: Convention on Biological Diversity United Nations Environment Programme.

UNEP (United Nations Environment Programme) (1995). Cambridge: Global Biodiversity Assessment Cambridge University Press.

VONTHRON, J. (1995) Future EU policies for CAP and enlargement. Paper presented at an international conference: Integrating Agriculture and the Environment, Gödöllö Agricultural University, Hungary 14–15 September 1995.

WHITBY, M. (ed.) (1994) *Incentives for Countryside Management: the case of environmentally sensitive areas*. Wallingford: CAB International.

WILDLIFE LINK (1992) *Environment at the Heart of the CAP*. London: Wildlife Link.

WINTER, M. (1995) *Networks of Knowledge*. Godalming: World Wide Fund for Nature.

WOODS, A., TAYLOR, J.P., HOUSDEN, S.D., HARLEY, D.C. & LANCE, A.N. (1988) *The Reform of the Common Agricultural Policy*. Sandy: Royal Society for the Protection of Birds.

WYNNE, G.R., AVERY, M.I., CAMPBELL, L., GUBBAY, S., HAWKSWELL, S., JUNIPER, A., KING, M., NEWBERRY, P., SMART, J., STEEL, C., STONES, A., STUBBS, A., TAYLOR, J.P., TYDEMAN, C. & WYNDE, R. (1995) *Biodiversity Challenge*. Sandy: Biodiversity Challenge Group, c/o Royal Society for the Protection of Birds.

Index

Page numbers in *italic* refer to illustrations and tables; **bold** page numbers indicate a main discussion.